Ch-E. Jeanneret ~ architecte

ARCHITECTE-
CONSEIL POUR TOUTES
QUESTIONS DE DECORATION
INTÉRIEURE, DE TRANSFORMATIONS,
D'AMENAGEMENTS MOBILIERS,
D'ARRANGEMENTS DE
JARDINS, ETC.

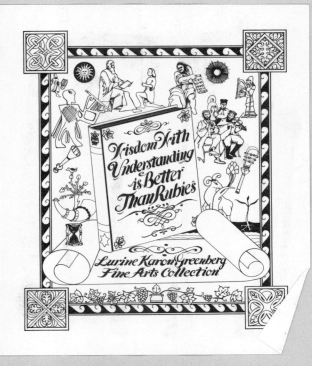

LE CORBUSIER BEFORE LE CORBUSIER

LE CORBUSIER

APPLIED ARTS · ARCHITECTURE

BEFORE LE CORBUSIER

PAINTING · PHOTOGRAPHY · 1907–1922

Edited by Stanislaus von Moos and Arthur Rüegg

Published for The Bard Graduate Center
for Studies in the Decorative Arts, Design, and Culture, New York,
with the Langmatt Museum, Baden, Switzerland,
by Yale University Press, New Haven and London

This catalogue is published in conjunction with the exhibition *Le Corbusier Before Le Corbusier: Applied Arts, Architecture, Painting, and Photography, 1907–1922* held at the Langmatt Museum, Baden, Switzerland, with the title, *Der junge Le Corbusier* (March 30 – June 30, 2002), and at The Bard Graduate Center for Studies in the Decorative Arts, Design, and Culture, New York (November 22, 2002 – February 23, 2003)

Project directors and exhibition curators: Stanislaus von Moos and Arthur Rüegg
Project assistant in Switzerland: Klaus Spechtenhauser
Project coordinator at the Bard Graduate Center: Olga Valle Tetkowski
Project assistant in New York City: Ronald Labaco

Director of exhibitions: Nina Stritzler-Levine

Editor: Martina D'Alton
Designer: Sally Salvesen
Translators: French language manuscripts: Caroline Beamish, Diane Roth, and Richard Wittman. Italian-language manuscripts: Fabio Barry, Rachel Bindman. German-language manuscripts: the late David Britt, Fiona Elliott

Printed in Italy by Conti Tipocolor

Endpapers: Letterheads designed by Charles-Edouard Jeanneret in 1912 (left) and still in use in 1917 (right)
Frontispiece: Le Corbusier, Villa Berque, perspective for the new terrace and the projected salon, 1921, FLC; see fig. 363

A catalogue record for this book is available from the Library of Congress
720'.92—DC21   2002006945
ISBN 0-300-09357-8

"Le Corbusier Before Le Corbusier: Applied Arts, Architecture, Interiors, Painting, and Photography, 1907–1922" has been funded in part by generous grants from the Graham Foundation for Advanced Studies in the Fine Arts and Bank Julius Baer & Co. Ltd.

Additional funding has been provided by Pro Helvetia, Arts Council of Switzerland, and Furthermore grants in publishing, a program of the J.M. Kaplan Fund.

This exhibition has been organized in collaboration with the Langmatt Museum, Baden, Switzerland.

NOTE TO THE READER

Charles-Edouard Jeanneret (1887–1965) adopted his famous pseudonym "Le Corbusier" around 1920, using it in the premiere issue of *L'Esprit nouveau*. He and cofounder Amédée Ozenfant contributed multiple articles to each issue of the journal under a variety of pseudonyms—De Fayet, Saugnier, and Paul Boulard, among others—which can confuse modern scholarship. In some cases they coauthored articles under a single pseudonym, adding to this confusion. In endnote citations, we have simply used "[pseud.]" to indicate these names. The authors of the essays that follow have variously used Jeanneret, Le Corbusier, and Jeanneret/Le Corbusier, as deemed appropriate to the context of their essays.

Jeanneret's six-month journey in 1911, with stops in the Balkans, Turkey, Greece, and Italy, is known as the Voyage d'Orient, and this is how we refer to this important event throughout the text. Jeanneret published his observances in installments in his hometown newspaper, *Feuille d'Avis de La Chaux-de-Fonds,* and eventually gathered these together for subsequent publication, which occurred posthumously as *Le Voyage d'orient* (1966); italics indicate this publication. Similarly, his sojourn in Germany has been called the Voyages d'Allemagne. Several of his sketchbooks, notebooks, and other archival material from these and other trips have been published in facsimile editions (see the Bibliography) or have formed the basis of exhibitions.

Most of the contributors to this catalogue cite Le Corbusier's first major publication, *Vers une architecture* (1923). This book has appeared in several editions, including one in English, and we have left the authors' citations as submitted rather than attempt to standardize them. In addition, some of the authors have retranslated quotations from this work for greater clarity. Archival material, primarily correspondence, has similarly been translated by some of the authors or by the translators credited on the copyright page. And in some cases, quotations from other publications by Jeanneret/Le Corbusier have been newly translated for this catalogue.

In the captions references in brackets at the end of each item relate to the exhibition checklist which starts on p. 303.

ABBREVIATIONS	CEJ	Charles-Edouard Jeanneret
	LC	Le Corbusier
	BN	Bibliothèque Nationale, Paris
	BV	Bibliothèque de la Ville, La Chaux-de-Fonds
	FLC	Fondation Le Corbusier, Paris

CONTENTS

FOREWORD

Le Corbusier Before Le Corbusier: Applied Arts, Architecture, Painting, and Photography, 1907–1922 examines the early years of one of the greatest architect-designers of the twentieth century. In the United States, where Le Corbusier received only one major commission — The Carpenter Center at Harvard University — his reputation is largely based on the extensive bibliography associated with his name. The prolific writings helped draw international attention to the remarkable architectural and design work of the interwar years, and it is this so-called heroic period that we generally associate with Le Corbusier. Indeed, the Villa Savoye in Poissy, and the tubular steel furniture of the late 1920s, which he designed in collaboration with Charlotte Perriand and Pierre Jeanneret, have become icons of modern architecture and design.

The exhibition history of Le Corbusier has not accurately demonstrated the extent of his unique contribution to the arts of the twentieth century. The Museum of Modern Art, a leading proponent of Le Corbusier featured him in no less than five exhibitions. Yet it has been more than fifteen years since Le Corbusier has been the focus of a major exhibition. In 1987 the centenary year of his birth, there were exhibitions held in various locations throughout the world; to date, however, no museum in the United States has organized a comprehensive Le Corbusier retrospective. Thus despite his remarkable achievements and international fame — and even though we may think we know his work well — important aspects of his life and career remain elusive. Le Corbusier himself was a master at constructing his own image, emphasizing in his writings only those segments of his life that appeared most flattering to his achievements and to his self-made identity as a modern architect. This is especially true of the early years about which Le Corbusier remained circumspect. Toward the end of the twentieth century a few scholars began to research this period. H. Allen Brooks, for example, in his groundbreaking study, *Le Corbusier's Formative Years*, reconstructed the narrative of Le Corbusier's life in his birthplace of La Chaux-de-Fonds, Switzerland. Yet while Brooks has served as a catalyst for interest in the young Le Corbusier among academics, the exploration of this period has largely remained outside the public purview of exhibitions.

Le Corbusier Before Le Corbusier is intended to further illuminate the diverse and rich cultural explorations and artistic achievements of Le Corbusier's life prior to the 1920s and the central Parisian years of his career. The magnificent drawings and sketches, penetrating photography, and surprising selection of decorative arts objects in both the exhibition and its accompanying catalogue shed light on the fledgling years of one of the most influential and innovative individuals of the twentieth century. The exhibition considers how the young and highly ambitious Charles-Edouard Jeanneret (his name prior to adopting "Le Corbusier" in 1920) satisfied his thirst for knowledge about architecture, design, and culture, and his deep yearning to become an artist, specifically a painter, not an architect. It reveals his artistic successes, struggles, and failures. By studying this period of his life, we discover a remarkable landscape filled with unexpected sources of inspiration for Le Corbusier's ideas extending from Gothic architecture in France to the art and culture of the age of Louis XIV, from the ancient world to the Italian Renaissance and the cultures of Eastern Europe, Central Europe, and the Middle East. We also learn of Le Corbusier's varied educational experiences and business exploits, of his studies of the decorative arts and ornamental design, his travels, and his experiments with photography, painting, and drawing.

This contribution to the study of Le Corbusier is certain to stimulate the imagination of our readers and visitors to the exhibition. I know it will reveal some surprises and will serve as an affirmation of the belief that to innovate one must maintain a persistent creative dialogue, as did Le Corbusier, with past, present, and future.

* * *

The Bard Graduate Center is honored to have been invited to participate in this project by Eva-Maria Preiswerk-Lösel, curator of the Langmatt Museum, Baden, Switzerland, where the exhibition was inaugurated in March 2002. I am grateful to Kurt Forster for suggesting this collaboration. Stanislaus von Moos and Arthur Rüegg first proposed the idea of an exhibition examining the early work of Le Corbusier. They have served admirably as project directors, curators, and editors of this volume. Klaus Spechtenhauser played a major role in the realization of the exhibition and was tireless as the project assistant in Zurich. Silvio Schmed has contributed creatively to the exhibition plans and to their implementation in New York and in Baden. I appreciate the diligent work of Brigitt Schär-Wettstein who was the liaison between the Langmatt Museum and the Bard Graduate Center.

I am also grateful for the generous contributions to this volume from the Graham Foundation for Advanced Studies in the Fine Arts; and Furthermore grants in publishing, a program of the J. M. Kaplan Fund. Additional support was provided by Pro Helvetia, Arts Council of Switzerland.

The Fondation Le Corbusier is the principal lender to the exhibition and has been helpful in numerous ways with this project. Early on, the exhibition received the support of Evelyn Tréhin, director of the Fondation Le Corbusier, who deserves a special word of thanks. I am grateful to the institutions and individuals who loaned work to this exhibition, and whose generosity has provided a rare view of Le Corbusier's remarkable artistic pursuits: the Bibliothèque de la Ville, La Chaux-de-Fonds, Switzerland; Madame de Freudenreich-Jornod; Langmatt Museum, Baden, Switzerland; Musée des Beaux-Arts, La Chaux-de-Fonds, Switzerland; Musée de L'Air et de L'Espace, Paris-Le Bourget; Musée Léon Perrin, Môtiers, Switzerland; Museum of Modern Art, New York; Nationalmuseum, Stockholm; Marie-Françoise Robert; Schweizerische Theatersammlung, Bern, Switzerland; Marc Stähli, and an anonymous lender.

Our knowledge of Le Corbusier's early career has increased substantially due to the fine essays contributed to this volume by Antonio Brucculeri, Françoise Ducros, Stanislaus von Moos, Francesco Passanti, Arthur Rüegg, Leo Schubert, and Pierre Vaisse. In addition, dozens of catalogue entries, based on new research, were prepared by H. Allen Brooks, Antonio Brucculeri, Corinne Charles, Marie-Eve Celio, Françoise Ducros, Giuliano Gresleri, Stanislaus von Moos, Francesco Passanti, Arthur Rüegg, and Klaus Spechtenhauser. Franz Xaver Jaggy has provided wonderful new photography of work that Le Corbusier designed in Switzerland. The difficult task of translating many of the catalogue texts has been skillfully accomplished by: Caroline Beamish, Francesco Passanti, Diane Roth, Stanislaus von Moos, Nina Stritzler-Levine and Richard Wittman (French-language texts); Fabio Barry and Rachel Bindman (Italian-language texts); and the late David Britt and Fiona Elliott (German-language texts). Martina D'Alton has done a splendid job as copyeditor, and Sally Salvesen has produced a stunning design that evokes the wonder of Le Corbusier's work. I also want to thank Jean-Louis Cohen and Barry Bergdoll for their assistance and recognition of the scholarly importance of this project.

Many individuals at the Bard Graduate Center contributed to the realization of this exhibition and catalogue. I want to thank Nina Stritzler-Levine for her work on this project. She was assisted by the staff of the exhibition department, including Edina Deme, Ronald Labaco, Susan Loftin, Jennie McCahey, Linda Stubbs, Olga Valle Tetkowski, and Han Vu. Additional exhibition assistance was provided by two students in the Bard Graduate Center masters program: Lisa Skogh and Brandy Culp. A marvelous array of public program events was created by Lisa Podos with Jill Gustafson and Sonia Gallant. Susan Wall and Tara D'Andrea of the development office skillfully found the necessary funding for this important exhibition. Tim Mulligan assisted by David Tucker organized a successful press campaign. Sandra Fell provides assistance with many related matters in my office. I appreciate the work of Lorraine Bacalles who, assisted by Dianora Watson, gave important administrative support to this project. The library staff under the direction of Greta Ernest answered numerous calls for assistance. The gallery facility is managed by John Donovan and his able staff. Finally, my thanks go to Chandler Small and the Bard Graduate Center security staff for looking after the galleries with great professionalism.

Susan Weber Soros
DIRECTOR
THE BARD GRADUATE CENTER

PREFACE

The early work of Le Corbusier in its various aspects has never before been exhibited outside La Chaux-de-Fonds, Switzerland, where he was born Charles-Edouard Jeanneret in 1887. Between 1907 and 1923, with no formal training, he learned his trade, and defined his position as architect and artist, and in 1920 he adopted the name Le Corbusier. While his architecture and ideas on urban design from 1920 to 1960 profoundly influenced the concepts of construction and city planning for decades, he was always strangely reticent about his background and early career. Nonetheless, before moving to Paris in 1917 he had built six private houses and a cinema, and designed furnishings and interiors.

Photographs and sketches record Le Corbusier's travels, studying and immersing himself in Europe's cultural heritage. This was the premise for his revolutionary later work. Watercolors and early pictures — some not previously exhibited — indicate an interest in the aesthetic preoccupation of the avant-garde at that time: not only Matisse, Munch, and Signac, but also Cézanne and Braque. His early career as architect and interior designer in the tradition of neoclassicism is illustrated by drawings, sketches, architect's models, photographs, and rare wood furniture together with a digital model specially prepared for this exhibition.

We are pleased that this exhibition has engendered international interest, and in a slightly enlarged form will transfer from the Langmatt Museum in Baden, Switzerland, to the renowned Bard Graduate Center for Studies in the Decorative Arts, Design, and Culture, New York. Located in distinguished houses from around 1900, both establishments are able to present the exhibition in the comforting ambience of former homes; an elegant New York town house, and the Villa Langmatt set in a large garden in rural Baden. We wish to thank the staff at Bard Graduate Center, which has pursued in exemplary fashion the study and presentation of applied art, for their trust and close collaboration, especially founder and director Susan Weber Soros. Our particular thanks go to exhibition director Nina Stritzler-Levine and her team for coordinating the exhibition and tending to the creation of this catalogue. Everyone engaged on this complex project has shown extraordinary commitment to its success.

For the preparation and selection of the early work we extend thanks to Stanislaus von Moos, professor of modern and contemporary art at Zurich University, and to Arthur Rüegg, architect and professor of architecture at the Swiss

Amédée Ozenfant, Albert Jeanneret and Charles-Edouard Jeanneret, photographed in the studio at the Jeanneret-Perret house in August, 1919, FLC (see fig. 409)

Federal Institute of Technology (ETH), Zurich. With many publications and a number of exhibitions, including *L'Esprit Nouveau: Le Corbusier und die Industrie, 1920–1925* (1987), these two curators have long made their mark internationally as Le Corbusier scholars.

Our thanks are equally due to our patrons and sponsors. The exhibition in Baden has been aided by the Friends of the Langmatt Museum, Baden; UBS AG, Aargau; Boner Stiftung für Kunst und Kultur, Davos; Axpo Holding, Zurich; Artephila Stiftung; Vontobel-Stiftung, Zurich; Andersen / Arthur Andersen, The Global Professional Services Firm; Möbel-Transport AG, Zürich.

The museum housed in the Villa Langmatt in Baden was inaugurated in 1990. In the setting of the original domestic interior, with French furniture of the eighteenth and nineteenth centuries, it houses a permanent collection of exquisite French Impressionists accumulated from 1908 onward by industrialist Sidney Brown-Sulzer and his wife Jenny. The museum's additional annual exhibitions have hitherto been held with partners in French-speaking Switzerland and in Germany. This is the first transatlantic coproduction. It is our hope that this glimpse into the origins of the "Architect of the Twentieth Century," as Le Corbusier was called in a 1987 exhibition at the Hayward Gallery in London, will generate new interest both in Europe and the United States.

Eva-Maria Preiswerk-Lösel
CURATOR
THE LANGMATT MUSEUM

INTRODUCTION

The idea for an exhibition on the early work of Le Corbusier originated in the context of the remodeling of some formerly private rooms of the Villa Langmatt, a country house built by Karl Moser around 1900 in Baden, Switzerland, and now home to the Langmatt Museum. Given the mutual respect that Moser and Le Corbusier had for each other an informal display of some of the furniture designed by Le Corbusier between 1915 and 1922 seemed to be an attractive prospect for display in the Lagmatt's "new wing." Our combined scholarly interests and the remarkable work to date by other scholars motivated us to expand the scope of the exhibition. The result is a survey of Le Corbusier's production from 1907 to 1922, including a fresh look at his early travels.

The present book is conceived as a companion to the exhibition. It does not attempt to follow a consistently biographical, contextual or theoretical line of thought. Nor does it pretend to give a survey of its deceptively vast subject. Rather, like our *Esprit Nouveau* catalogue of 1987 (*L'Esprit Nouveau. Le Corbusier und die Industrie, 1920–1925*, Zürich and Berlin, Museum für Gestaltung and Ernst & Sohn), it adopts the format of a collage, combining a series of in-depth chapters with a catalogue that assembles thematic groupings. The chapters purposefully vary in style from the speculative essay to the monographic study. The introductory essay, "Voyages en Zigzag," discusses the eclecticism of Jeanneret/Le Corbusier's early work in its cultural and biographical context. More specific theoretical and thematic aspects of the work are addressed in the succeeding two essays concerning the Gothic and the role of the Classical tradition in Le Corbusier's early concerns and work. His understanding and use of photography around 1911–12 is the subject of another essay (the latter two studies stem from recent doctoral work at the Istituto Universitario d'Architettura dell'Università di Venezia, IUAV, where Stanislaus von Moos was invited to teach a seminar in 1999/2000).

The main focus however is architecture, furniture design and interior decoration in the context of La Chaux-de-Fonds, Jeanneret's home town, between 1912 and 1923. For the first time, Jeanneret's early buildings in Switzerland are studied in terms of their implicit approach to proportion and classicism. With respect to furniture design and interior decoration, rather than surveying the entire field there is an in-depth analysis of Le Corbusier's year-long collaboration with Marcel Levaillant.

Finally, the selection of works documented in the catalogue section reflects both the contingencies of the exhibition and the wish to situate the chosen works in their cultural context. We are proud that some of the most experienced Le Corbusier scholars in Europe and the United States have agreed to be part of the project as contributors to this catalogue.

LA CHAUX-DE-FONDS: AN INDUSTRIAL CAPITAL?

A brochure published in 1898 speaks of La Chaux-de-Fonds as a "capitale industrielle et commerciale." In fact, only the considerable boom of the Swiss watch industry accounts for the fact that La Chaux-de-Fonds, despite its relatively modest size and remote location in Western Switzerland, near the French border, was able to become the only true center of design reform in Switzerland in the years 1900 to 1915.[1] The rapid expansion of wristwatch manufacture in the late nineteenth century had attracted numerous energetic spirits to La Chaux-de-Fonds; many of them of Jewish origin who had found refuge in the Canton Neuchâtel after the German annexation of Alsace in 1878. Thanks largely to its enterpreneurial spirit, the Swiss watchmaking industry at one time manufactured about 90% of world watch production. The boom lasted at least until 1914, when the Collectivité des fabricants d'horlogerie de La Chaux-de-Fonds announced that it controled $3/5$ of the value of Swiss watch exports—which means that at this time approximately 55% of the world's watches were either manufactured from A to Z, or at least assembled in La Chaux-de-Fonds.[2]

For a long time, real factory work had played only a subordinate role; most of the workforce comprised pieceworkers occupied at home. In their workshops they assembled the individual parts of watch meachnisms supplied by the factory, enameled or labeled the faces and decorated the cases. In 1867, Karl Marx coined the term "heterogeneous manufacture" for this type of work.[3] La Chaux-de-Fonds seemed to him, "[A] perfect model for these production methods; the whole city could be designated as one giant watch factory." Engravers and chasers played a decisive role in the design of these products. In order to ensure that a professionally educated workforce was available to the watchmaking industry, the Ecole d'Art was officially founded in La Chaux-de-Fonds as early as 1877.

TOWARDS A CENTER OF DESIGN REFORM

In the late nineteenth century the industrially finished wristwatch began to replace the traditional watchmaker's art, leading to crisis and unemployment for thousands of pieceworkers. Considerable effort was needed to help the "pocketwatch" regain market competitiveness. Only with the help of richly decorated Art nouveau cases, it was thought, was the slow but relentless decline of the pocketwatch to be halted (see fig. 309).[4] The painter Charles L'Eplattenier, appointed director of the Ecole d'Art in 1903, played a major role in this project. Several of the cases created under his aegis achieved international success, winning, among other things, prizes at the International Exhibition in Milan in 1906. But even so, pocketwatch production continued to wane, and consequently, the watch industry's need for enamelers, engravers and chasers steadily decreased, giving the Ecole d'Art no choice but to wait for its certain end or to redefine its curriculum so as to include architecture, interior decoration and furniture design. L'Eplattenier applied all his considerable energies to the project, initiating a post-graduate course approximating to the model of a full-grown design school ("Cours Supérieur d'Art et de Décoration," founded in 1905 and rebaptized as "Nouvelle Section de l'Ecole d'Art" in 1911). Yet the goal of building a local counterpart to the "Wiener Werkstätte," proved too ambitious. La Chaux-de-Fonds neither wanted nor could afford a "Bauhaus" and in 1914 the experiment came to an end.

JEANNERET: FROM REGIONALISM TO NEOCLASSICISM

This is the context in which Charles Edouard Jeanneret evolved a career as an architect and furniture designer. At first this son of a watchface enameler had been educated as an engraver. Louis Fallet, who as a jeweler was still intimately involved in the craft's "rearguard action" against the triumphant wristwatch, decided to ask the young Jeanneret to help his architect Chapallaz with the design and in particular with the decoration of his own small villa—a kind of journeyman's piece, emblematic of the "Cours supérieur" (see cat. 17). Only five years later, in 1912, with a large house for his parents on Rue de la Montagne, Jeanneret turned his back on his Regionalist and Art nouveau beginnings; after a five-month stay in Berlin, he had become an advocate of neoclassicism, cultivating an architectural style comparable to that practiced by his contemporary Ludwig Mies van der Rohe (see cat. 19).[5]

The manufacturing elite of La Chaux-de-Fonds and its neighbouring town Le Locle recognized the young architect's seriousness and talent. And it knew how to utilize his skills for its representational needs, now growing by leaps and bounds. As to Jeanneret, torn between his ambitions as a great architect and the more down-to-earth goals of his not always enlightened patrons, he found it so difficult to survive in Switzerland that in 1917, during World War I, he moved permanently to Paris and there adopted his pseudonym in 1920. Later, in his numerous books and catalogues, Le Corbusier for the most part covered up his early work. Foregrounding these Swiss projects inevitably contradicts—or at least questions—the image of a "Modern Architect" that Le Corbusier was so eager to promote. To those who may be at odds with such a proposition, the editors would answer that "the Project of Modernity" can, in the end, only be understood in the light of its origins. The care with which Le Corbusier documented every trace of his early work (even if he was eager to keep it under lock and key) adds to the legitimacy of this point of view.

ACKNOWLEDGMENTS

Scholarly interest in early Le Corbusier is not a recent phenomenon. It has been extremely lively ever since Paul Venable Turner submitted his PhD thesis on *Le Corbusier's Education* in 1970 and Patricia May Sekler hers on *The Early Drawings of Charles-Edouard Jeanneret (Le Corbusier) 1902–1908* in 1977.[6] Imposing books by H. Allen Brooks, Giuliano Gresleri, Luisa Martina Colli, Geoffrey Baker, Mario de Simone, Nancy Troy and more recently Adolf Max Vogt have followed, not to mention the important contributions by Jacques Gubler, Edmond Charrière, Marc Emery and many others, including a whole wealth of PhD dissertations from the four corners of the world. This list alone may indicate that, apart from some fresh material and, so we hope, some pertinent insights, our project and more particularly this book draws on the research done by many others.

Both exhibition and book would have been impossible without the support of the Fondation Le Corbusier, in Paris, which owns the majority of the works exhibited, as well as the Musée des Beaux-Arts at La Chaux-de-Fonds, the owner of most of the furniture now included in the exhibition. Our thanks therefore go first to the Fondation Le Corbusier and its director, Evelyne Tréhin, as well as to her assistant Isabelle Godineau, for her indefatigable understanding, support, and skill. Edouard Charrière, director of the Musée d'Art, La Chaux-de-Fonds, as well as

Sylvie Béguelin, librarian, Bibliothèque de la Ville de La Chaux-de-Fonds offered their help, advise and expertise from the beginning. The same goes for Marie-Eve Celio-Scheurer from the Fondation Léon Perrin in Môtiers, Switzerland, as well as the Museum of Modern Art, New York, the Oeffentliche Kunstsammlung Basel, the Philadelphia Museum of Art, and also various private lenders. Special thanks go to Kurt W. Foster who suggested that we contact the Bard Graduate Center for the realization of this project. Among the scholars who gave us advise and support during its preparation we would like to single out H. Allen Brooks, Giuliano Gresleri, Francesco Passanti, Marie-Eve Celio-Scheurer and Leo Schubert. Among the staff and students at the Kunsthistorisches Institut of the University of Zurich as well as of the Federal Institute of Technology, ETH Zürich whose help has been particularly important we would like to single out Karin Gimmi, Robin Rehm and Bruno Maurer.

Needless to say that without the enthusiasm and the professionalism of many people at the Langmatt Museum, the Bard Graduate Center, as well as at Yale University Press, nothing at all would have been possible. Until now, the Langmatt Museum in Baden has organized exhibitions principally in the field of late nineteenth- and early twentieth-century painting. As a result, the present project represented an unusual technical and organizational challenge for this small organization. We therefore wish to thank Eva-Maria Preiswerk-Lösel for the kindness and professionalism with which she has supported our initiative from its beginning. At the Bard Graduate Center for the Decorative Arts, New York, Nina Stritzler-Levine has played a crucial role throughout the project; her inspiring partnership has ensured its realization. In addition, our thanks go to Olga Valle Tetkowski as well as, especially with respect to the catalogue, to Martina D'Alton. And finally, Sally Salvesen from Yale University Press made what might otherwise have remained a mere catalogue into a beautiful book.

In the last stages of the project, the help of Brigitt Schär-Wettstein, Langmatt, proved invaluable, while Klaus Spechtenhauser, art historian, Zurich, made sure that the project flourished despite the cultural and technical complexities involving three institutions situated on either side of the Atlantic, three working languages (not to mention Italian), and almost as many differing computer programs. As in our earlier "career" as exhibition curators, design and mounting of the exhibition in Baden as well as in New York was supervised by Silvio Schmed, interior architect, Zurich.

Stanislaus von Moos AND Arthur Rüegg
APRIL 2002

CHRONOLOGY

compiled by Klaus Spechtenhauser

1887 October 6: Charles-Edouard Jeanneret is born at 38 rue de la Serre, La Chaux-de-Fonds. His parents are Georges Edouard Jeanneret-Gris (1855–1926) and Marie Jeanneret-Perret (née Marie-Charlotte-Amelie Perret; 1860–1960). He has an older brother, Jacques-Henri Albert Jeanneret (called Albert; 1886–1973).

1898 Charles L'Eplattenier is appointed to teach at the École d'Art, La Chaux-de-Fonds. He will found and direct its Cours Supérieur in 1905–12 and head its Nouvelle Section in 1912–14.

1902 April: Jeanneret enrolls at the École d'Art in La Chaux-de-Fonds, first as a student in the regular program, then after 1905 in the Cours Supérieur.

1906 Winter–spring: L'Eplattenier arranges for Jeanneret to meet Louis Fallet, a local designer and producer of jewelry, who becomes Jeanneret's first client. Spring–summer: L'Eplattenier's students at the Cours Supérieur design a music room in the Villa Matthey-Doret in La Chaux-de-Fonds (demolished in 1963).

1907 September–October: Makes his first trip to Italy, with his friend and classmate, the sculptor Léon Perrin: Pisa, Florence (including visits to the Certosa at Galluzzo in Val d'Ema, which Jeanneret henceforward calls "Certosa d'Ema"), Siena, Ravenna, Padova, Ferrara, Verona, Venice. November: Arrives in Vienna. Designs the Villa Fallet, La Chaux-de-Fonds, 1906–7, with the architect René Chapallaz.

1908 In Vienna. Designs the Stotzer and Jaquemet Houses, La Chaux-de-Fonds, 1907–8, with architect René Chapallaz. March: travels to Paris from Vienna via Nuremburg, Munich, Strasbourg, and Nancy. Works part-time in the architectural firm of Auguste and Gustave Perret, 25 bis rue Franklin, Paris; spends the rest of his time in the city's museums and libraries. Visits Rouen and Le Havre.

1909 Fall: Returns to La Chaux-de-Fonds and settles in a farmhouse at Mont-Cornu.

1910 January: Project for a building for Les Ateliers d'Art réunis at La Chaux-de-Fonds. March 15: Founding of Les Ateliers d'Art réunis at La Chaux-de-Fonds. April–May: Sojourn in Munich; tries, without success, to find employment in the office of Theodor Fischer. Begins work on the manuscript of "La Construction des villes." May: Makes the aquaintance of William Ritter (1867–1955), a Swiss writer and literary, art, and music critic living in Munich. Ritter becomes one of Jeanneret's mentors. In June travels to Berlin and visits the exhibitions *Ton-Kalk-Zement* and *Allgemeine Städtebau*. June 28: Meets August Klipstein (1885–1951), a student in art history, at the Staatsbibliothek in Munich. A close friendship will develop between the two. July–September: Returns to La Chaux-de-Fonds. September– October: Back in Munich. October 1910–March 1911: Five-month stay in Berlin where he works in the office of Peter Behrens. Spends Christmas 1910 at Dresden-Hellerau with his brother Albert who is a student at the Institute Jacques-Dalcroze.

1911 April–May: Travels in Germany, a period known as the Voyage d'Allemagne, to study the German Arts and Crafts Movement. May: Embarks on his Voyage d'Orient, a six-month journey, with August Klipstein to Prague, Vienna, Budapest, Serbia, Rumania, Bulgaria, Turkey (Istanbul), Greece (Athos, Athens) and Italy (Naples, Pompeii, Rome, Florence, Pisa). Between July and November, Jeanneret's impressions during the Voyage d'Orient are published in installments in *La Feuille d'Avis de La Chaux-de-Fonds*. November 1: Returns to La Chaux-de-Fonds; settles at Ferme du Couvent.

1912 Opens his first office as architect, in La Chaux-de-Fonds. Designs the Villa Jeanneret-Perret, La Chaux-de-Fonds, and the Villa Favre-Jacot, Le Locle. Competition design for the Town Hall, Le Locle. Exhibits a selection of Voyage d'Orient drawings under the title *Le Langage des pierres* in Neuchâtel (April–May) and Paris (Salon d'automne, October 1–November 8). December: Makes a trip to Paris. Publishes *Etude sur le mouvement d'art décoratif en Allemagne* (La Chaux-de-Fonds: Editions Haefeli).

1913 April–May: Shows *Le Langage des pierres* at Kunsthaus Zürich. June–July: Journeys to Germany, visiting the Internationale Baufach-Ausstellung in Leipzig. Architectural project for Paul Ditisheim Department Store, La Chaux-de-Fonds. Designs interiors for Jules Ditisheim apartment, La Chaux-de-Fonds, and for Anatole and Salomon Schwob apartments, La Chaux-de-Fonds.

1914 June–July: Journey to Colmar, Strasbourg, Nancy, Cologne (visiting the Werkbund-Kongress and -Ausstellung), and Lyon for the Exposition internationale urbaine: "La Cité moderne." December: Begins to work on Dom-ino concepts with Max Du Bois. Architectural work includes competition design for the Banque Cantonale de Neuchâtel, project for a garden city estate, aux Crêtets, La Chaux-de-Fonds, and project for Villa Klipstein, Laubach, Germany. Designs interior of Marcel Levaillant studio, La Chaux-de-Fonds (completed in 1917).

1915 July–September: Sojourn in Paris where he studies prints and books at the Bibliothèque Nationale in preparation for "La Construction des villes." Competition design for the Pont Butin in Geneva (together with Max Du Bois). Sketches for Dom-ino and for Villa Zbinden, Erlach, Switzerland. Designs interior of the Hermann and Ernest-Albert Ditisheim apartments, La Chaux-de-Fonds.

1916 Project for apartment building "Projet F," La Chaux-de-Fonds; designs the Villa Schwob, La Chaux-de-Fonds (1916–17), and Cinema Scala, La Chaux-de-Fonds. Designs interior (library) for Mme Raphy Schwob, La Chaux-de-Fonds, 1915–16.

1917 Leaves La Chaux-de-Fonds for Paris and rents an apartment at 20 rue Jacob, where he remains until 1934. December: forms association, as businessman and factory owner, with the Société d'entreprises industrielles et d'études (SEIE) and the Briqueterie d'Alfortville (ends in 1921). Designs projects for slaughterhouses at Challuy and Garchizy, France; for Workers Settlement, Saint-Nicolas-d'Aliermont, France; for power station and dam, L'Isle Jourdain, France. Designs Water Tank, Podensac, France.

1918 January: Meets Amédée Ozenfant, who will become his close associate in matters of art and cultural criticism. November: completes *La Cheminée* (The Mantelpiece), Jeanneret's "first painting." December: Exhibition of paintings, with Ozenfant, at Galerie Thomas in Paris. Publishes *Après le cubisme*, written with Amédée Ozenfant.

1919 Designs projects for Monol housing and for Workers Settlement (for the J. Jourdain and Company, Troyes, France).

1920 October 15: Publishes first issue of *L'Esprit nouveau* and begins to use his pseudonym "Le Corbusier." Projects for Workers Settlement at Thourotte (Oise) and another at Grand-Couronne (Seine-Maritime), France.

1921 January–February: Shows his paintings, with Ozenfant's, in the second Purist exhibition, at Galerie Druet, Paris. August: Travels to Rome with Amédée Ozenfant and Mme Bongard, owner of the Galerie Thomas. Project Maison "Citrohan." Villa Berque, Paris (1921–22).

1922 Opens his office at 35 rue de Sèvres, Paris (with his cousin Pierre Jeanneret). September: Trip to Venice and Vicenza with Raoul La Roche. Project " Immeuble villas" and *Ville contemporaine pour 3 millions d'habitants*.

1923 Designs the Villa Besnus, Vaucresson; the Villa La Roche/Jeanneret, Paris (1923–24); and the Atelier Ozenfant, Paris, 1922–23. Designs interior (library) for Madeleine Schwob, La Chaux-de-Fonds, 1922–23. Designs interior of Marcel Levaillant apartment, La Chaux-de-Fonds. Publishes *Vers une architecture*.

1965 August 27: Dies at Roquebrune-Cap-Martin, France.

I

VOYAGES EN ZIGZAG

Stanislaus von Moos

We feel the thirst of a Montaigne or a Rousseau setting out on their journeys, to seek answers from "naked man" (Nous avons la soif de Montaigne ou de Rousseau entreprenant un voyage pour aller questionner "l'homme nu.")

Le Corbusier, *Précisions*, 1930

1. ARCHITECTURE AND GRAND TOURISM

MODERN HOUSES LOOK AS IF they are "ready to go," like "boxes on mobile stilts," if not like boats. They have "a flat deck, portholes, a gangway, a deckrail, they have a white and southern glow, like ships they have a mind to disappear."[1] In this oft-quoted passage from *Das Prinzip Hoffnung* (The principle of hope), the philosopher Ernst Bloch, writing around 1940, borrowed the imagery of travel to characterize modern architecture. It is tempting to believe that Bloch's assessment may have been inspired by *Vers une architecture* (1923), where Le Corbusier had used pictures of ocean liners, automobiles, and airplanes clipped from advertisements as emblematic of the "new spirit" in architecture. (fig.2). Be that as it may, there is no doubt that he found this kind of machine imagery to be synonymous with both a radical rejection of historic reference and a tragic failure to produce "home." He wrote:

> That is why for over a generation, this phenomenon of steel furniture, concrete cubes, and flat roofs has stood there ahistorically, ultra-modern and boring, ostensibly bold and really trivial, full of hatred towards the alleged flourish of every ornamentation and yet more schematically entrenched than any stylistic copy in the nasty nineteenth century ever was.[2]

Since these lines were written, Le Corbusier's architecture has frequently been analyzed in terms of nautical and machine metaphors, as well as, perhaps paradoxically, its intense and multilayered dialogue with history. In the light of these analyses, perhaps Bloch's diatribe against the "flat decks, bull's eyes, metal stairs, deck rails" in modern architecture, reveals a dimension of Le Corbusier's work that had by no means been on the philosopher's mind. For Le Corbusier's complicity with tourism, may be suspected to go far beyond stylistic references to cars, ocean liners, and airplanes; it appears to be a leitmotif in his entire life and work. In fact, while it is true that the ocean liners in *Vers une architecture*, combined with the invocation "Des yeux

1. Title page from Rodolphe Töpffer, *Voyages en zigzag ou excursions d'un pensionnat en vacances dans les cantons suisses et sur le revers italien des Alpes*, Paris, 1846 [1844]

2. "Compagnie Générale Translatantique". Advertisement, designed by Le Corbusier or Amédée Ozenfant published in *L'Esprit Nouveau*, no. 8, 1921

3. Le Corbusier, *Quand les cathédrales étaient blanches. Voyage au pays des timides*, Paris 1936, book jacket designed by Le Corbusier

4. Cover of Le Corbusier, *Le Voyage d'Orient*, designed by Jean Petit, Paris, 1966

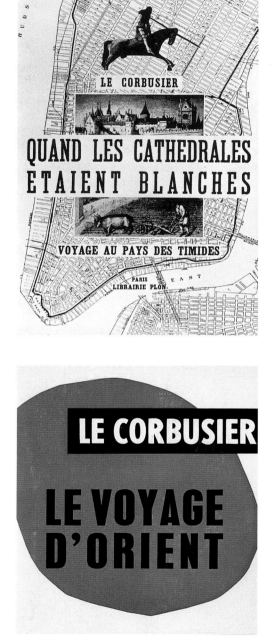

qui ne voient pas" (eyes that do not see), are an intriguing metaphor of the globalized commodity that tourism has since become, the architect's prolific activity as an author (he wrote more than forty books) owes more to the genre of the travel memoir and thus to the cultural legacy of the Grand Tour than has hitherto been acknowledged.

AUTHENTICITY AND ADVENTURE

Throughout his career, Le Corbusier kept romanticizing his life and work as a sequence of explorations and adventures tributary to his "Patient Search" ("recherche patiente"). It is worth remembering, in this context, that his *carte d'identité*, which was issued around 1940 under the name "Le Corbusier" (he had become naturalized as a French citizen in 1930), identified him as *homme de lettres* (writer), at a time when even a customs officer might have recognized him as an internationally known architect.[3] Despite this piece of evidence, he has not been seriously studied as a literary figure, nor have his postures as a writer been systematically unentangled. Oscillating between the roles of storyteller and theoretician, moralist and technician, exploiting a multitude of voices from intimate raconteur to forensic preacher, he has in fact frequently used his travels as a springboard for didactic and doctrinal discourse.[4] The presence in his knapsack of books by John Ruskin (*Mornings in Florence*) and Hippolyte Taine (*Voyage en Italie*), as well as the usual Baedeker guides, underlines the importance of travel writing to the student Charles-Edouard Jeanneret as he left La Chaux-de-Fonds for his first trip to Italy in 1907. Later, in 1911, he used William Ritter, his personal mentor (cat. no. 42), as a guide to the discovery of the "Orient." Apart from Taine's *Voyage en Italie*, Ritter's *L'Entêtement slovaque*, itself based on a journey undertaken to the Balkans, is the most immediate among the models for Jeanneret's travel accounts, which were first published as a series of articles in his local newspaper, *Feuille d'Avis de La Chaux-de-Fonds,* and much later — posthumously — as *Voyage d'orient* (1966; fig. 4).[5] The genre of travel account, as explored by Jeanneret/Le Corbusier in articles written for the Swiss newspaper and then in a book prepared in the last months of his life, thus bracketed his entire writing career.[6] It also left its mark on most of the books that appeared in between, either in subtitles such as "Voyage au pays des timides" (*Quand les cathédrales étaient blanches*, 1937; fig. 3) or in the titles themselves, as in *Sur les quatre routes* (1940). The theme of "traveling" is insistently present, either as a token of authenticity or as a suggestion of adventure, and so is of course, as with his mentors, an often puzzling mix of admiration and colonialist prejudice with respect to "primitive" peoples.

Throughout his writings, the narrative relies heavily on impressions and materials collected along the way. *Vers une architecture* (1923) was largely constructed around thoughts and reflections on buildings that Jeanneret had seen in Rome, Athens, Pompeii, and elsewhere (see cat. nos. 12–14), although the illustrations — based on the best architectural photography then to be found in Paris — somewhat obscure the autobiographic nature of the discourse. In *Urbanisme* (1925) an entire section consists of Le Corbusier's travel notes and sketches, and in *L'Art décoratif d'aujourd'hui* (1925) the concluding chapter ("Confession") gives a lively picture of hikes by Jeanneret and friends through the Jura mountains in the early years. Some of his most vivid travel accounts however are found somewhat later in *Précisions* (1930), a collection of ten lectures delivered in Argentina and Brazil. The introduction ("prologue américain") and visionary postscript ("corollaire brésilien") are considerably more powerful than the declamatory and repetitive rhetoric of the lectures themselves. The opening statement emphasizes the immediacy of the experience:

December 10, 1929
On board the *Lutetia*
Along the coast of Bahia

The South Atlantic Company has kindly put at my disposal a luxury apartment, and thus, far from the noise of the engine and in the quietest spot on the ship, I can tackle the final editing of my ten lectures. . . .

We are in the midst of tropical summer; the sun is magnificent; during the entire preceding week there has appeared before my eyes the unforgettable, incredible magic of Rio de Janeiro . . . .[7]

The ocean liner is of course part of the spectacle described in the book, as is the airplane that took the architect for the inaugural trip of the South American Navigation Company from Buenos Aires to Asunciòn de Paraguay. In *Précisions* Le Corbusier deciphers the earth from the vantage point of an airplane, describing it as a "poached egg," and philosophizing on air travel, calling it the future "nervous system" of America.[8] The climax is reached, however, on the concluding pages of the book, when the topography of Rio, seen from above (or rather clipped from a travel brochure), generates the vision of a freeway viaduct meandering along the coast, becoming a horizontal skyscraper of sorts that potentially contains Rio's entire housing infrastructure. In this phantasmagoria of a many-miles-long housing project, the demands of mobility and those of sedentary life merge. Tourism and urbanism become one (fig. 5).

5. Le Corbusier, Proposal for the Urbanization of Rio de Janeiro (illustration from *Précisions sur un état présent de l'architecture et de l'urbanisme*, Paris 1930)

"VOYAGES EN ZIGZAG"

Seen against this background of intra-cultural "flânerie" across the world and across cultures, some seemingly marginal aspects of Jeanneret's early biography take on new meaning. Albert Jeanneret recalled, for example, that his younger brother Charles-Edouard made his earliest drawings as copies after Rodolphe Töpffer's *Voyages en zigzag* (fig. 1).[9] The book's many charming illustrations of the Alps, its humor and edifying morals, had earned it a place of honor on bookshelves of many middle-class households in French-speaking Switzerland by 1900 (cf. fig. 7). The subtitle promised an account of the "excursions of a boarding school on vacation in the Swiss cantons as well as on the Italian slopes of the Alps," and the illustrations by Töpffer (as well as fifteen drawings of Alpine sceneries by Alexandre Calame) are a Romantic celebration of the Alps, mixed with genre scenes observed with a Hogarthian eye for the popular everyday.

As an illustrator, Töpffer was a contemporary of Gustave Doré and Grandville,[10] and at the same time, as head of a private boarding school in Geneva, he could be considered part of an enlightened triumvirate of men engaged in the reform of education, the other two being Jean-Jacques Rousseau (whom he admired) and Heinrich Pestalozzi. *Voyages en zigzag* is a rare document in the early history of tourism; it eloquently represents educational reform on the one hand and the commodification of the picturesque landscape on the other. In this way it refers, albeit with some irony, to the eighteenth century tradition of the Grand Tour, which had itself originated, at least in part, as an attempt to compensate for the shortcomings of the English university system. The Grand Tour, whereby the aristocracy sent its young out into the world to become fit for life, finds a reflection in Töpffer's "Petit Tour" (the itinerary only occasionally reaches beyond the confines of Switzerland), as well as a confirmation of its nature as a distinctly educational enterprise.[11]

Charles-Edouard Jeanneret once confided to a friend that he "would be delighted to write a doctoral thesis" on Töpffer.[12] This enthusiasm survived into the 1920s, as confirmed by a seven-page "strip" by Töpffer published in *L'Esprit nouveau*, the journal founded by Le Corbusier and Amédée Ozenfant. The "strip" was made of sections taken from *L'Histoire du Dr. Festus* and *L'Histoire de Mr.Pencil*, two of Töpffer's illustrated stories that had been published before *Voyages en zigzag*. Accompanied by a short article signed "de Fayet," a pseudonym used by both editors.[13] Töpffer's stories were told through small illustrations arranged in sequence and accompanied by short captions in the style of a comic strip.[14] *L'Histoire de Mr.Pencil* describes with some irony the mores of an English tourist on his way to discover Switzerland (as well as himself) with the help of "pencil" studies made en route. On the first page of the book, Mr. Pencil, "qui est artiste," is seen in his role as an observer of nature and then as a connoisseur of art, contemplating the artistic quality of his work from various angles — including upside down (fig. 6).

True, when Töpffer surfaced in *L'Esprit nouveau*, it was not in his capacity as a traveler but as a forerunner of cinema (see pp. 36f.). Le Corbusier was no filmmaker, however, and while he owned a copy of Töpffer's *L'Histoire du Dr. Festus*[15] apart from the article in *L'Esprit nouveau* (and an indirect allusion to the *Voyages en zigzag* in the opening statement of *Urbanisme*, 1925), the architect may not have explicitly referred to Töpffer in his innumerable writings. Nor did he share Töpffer's addiction to the Alps (which in turn must have made the book precious to Le Corbusier's father, a passionate mountain climber).[16]

"MENU," OR THE LOGIC OF BRANDING

The closest Le Corbusier perhaps ever came to Töpffer's archetypal version of the comic strip was a curious "menu" he devised for *L'Esprit nouveau,* in which he presented a choice of emblematic cityscapes. The drawing, a summary of Jeanneret's intermittent Grand Tour of 1907–11 covers topical issues of the architect's dialogue both with the history of urbanism and with the visual arts (fig. 8). It provides an inventory of traditional city-types, or so it appears, especially in light of the somewhat grandiloquent title of the article it illustrates—"Classement et choix" (Ordering and choice). The term *menu* and the allusion to gastronomy are made perfectly explicit in the accompanying text: "As the palate can experience the diversity of a well-composed menu, our eyes are ready for organized pleasures."[17] The image itself includes a drawing of Pera (a suburb of Istanbul) and another drawing, immediately below, of Istanbul itself as seen from the Bosporus. Then follows a catalogue of geometric forms (cube, cylinder, pyramid) symbolizing the monumental works of the architecture of Rome, and finally, at the bottom, a drawing made after a seventeenth-century print that shows the "skyline" of Siena. (It is probably no coincidence — in the context of Le Corbusier's interests — that this skyline is also reminiscent of New York). To make the graphic "menu" look like a systematic demonstration, notes in the margins postulate a correspondence between the images and the "character" of the places they represent:

> Pera: the sawteeth of the city of merchants, pirates, gold seekers.
> Istanbul: the fervor of the minarets, the calm of the low domes. Allah vigilant but, in an oriental fashion, immobile.
> Rome: geometry, implacable order, war, organization, civilization.
> Siena: the anguished tumult of the Middle Ages. Hell, and paradise.[18]

In this way, urban form is explained in terms of culture, and culture in terms of urban form. Yet what sense is to be made of that "cinematographic" demonstration? The

6. Mr. Pencil examining his work, Rodolphe Töpffer, *Histoire de Mr. Pencil*, Paris, c. 1923 [1840], p. 2

7. Childhood photograph of Ch. E. Jeanneret (right), with his brother Albert (second from left) and their cousins. Before 1900, photograph

diversity of the "menu" is not really about urban typologies. Rather the "menu" deals with the various ways of representing cityscapes in graphic terms. First (at the top of the page) there is the rapid "impression" of the urban skyline integrated in the landscape; then (in the middle), the typological inventory of the monumental architecture of Rome; and finally (at the bottom), the quotation of an historic *veduta*. Why should "impression" be associated with Pera or Istanbul, typological inventory with Rome, and antiquarian *veduta* with Siena? Why should not Istanbul instead of Rome be seen as the theater of bold architectural geometries, and why should Rome not be represented as a classical landscape in the tradition of Corot or Ingres, and so on? — The answer is simple. More often than not Le Corbusier's theorizing resembles the advertiser's job: the "menu" at hand serves as an example. The focus of interest lies not so much in the urban configurations as such, but in the mechanism of their perception. As with "Mr. Pencil" in Töpffer's "strip," it is the drawing that matters, not the landscape it represents (fig. 6). And as with branding a tourist destination, what counts is the emotion a place generates, not the nature of that place as such.

2.   THE LURE OF ART

It is difficult not to be confused by the eclecticism — the "zigzag" quality — of the innumerable sketches Jeanneret/Le Corbusier brought home from his intermittent Grand Tour through Italy, Austria, France, Germany, Turkey and Greece, quite apart from the zigzag nature of the itineraries themselves (see cat. nos. 1–16).[19] Yet while the eclecticism of these works reflects the vision of the Grand Tour, it also corresponds with a deliberately chosen method of self-education. If grudgingly, Jeanneret understood that self-education in a variety of disciplines simultaneously was the price to be paid by those who wanted to be architects. By the time of his first trip to Italy, he appeared not only to have been fully aware of this predicament, but also to have decided to accept it as inevitable. Unlike his travel companion Léon Perrin, a sculptor, who "concentrates on sculpture and somewhat on fresco," as Jeanneret wrote to his parents, he himself felt "compelled to be interested in all things. . . . ."[20] The exigencies of architecture (as defined by Charles L'Eplattenier, his teacher) had thus first of all an eye- and mind-opening function. Architecture, with respect to the other arts, was meant to widen the scope and to take on the outlook of an educated universalist.

27

Sienne : le tumulte angoissé
du moyen âge.
Enfer et Paradis.

Rome : la géométrie, l'ordre implacable, guerre, organisation, civilisation.

Stamboul : la ferveur des minarets,
le calme des dômes aplatis, Allah vigilant mais orientalement immuable.

Péra : la dent de scie de la ville
des marchands, des pirates, des
chercheurs d'or.

Jeanneret's sketchbooks filled with notes and drawings, and the innumerable letters sent home, are a patchwork of explorations based on an eclectic mix of interests, played out side by side.[21] The general effect is that of a kaleidoscope. The artwork alone represents a true "voyage en zigzag" through the labyrinth of graphic techniques as mediated by the traditions of the "École." According to the challenges of the moment, the roles attributed and emphasis given to the diversified genres practiced together rapidly and violently shifted over time.[22] During his first trip to Italy (1907), it was primarily by way of "copying" and producing "annotated sketches" that Jeanneret did what was required of him as a student at the École d'Art in La Chaux-de-Fonds; among the more than seventy studies made by him during this part of the Grand Tour there are practically no "plans" (figs. 11–14; cat. nos. 1, 2). Even though, with the English Arts and Crafts movement, direct imitation of historic forms had become compromised as a design strategy, copying was still considered indispensable for the training of both the eye and the hand. Choosing an object of inquiry, then drawing it carefully, was not only a way of avoiding the mere distraction caused by the overabundance of things, but also, as William Morris had explained, a way to avoid being cheated by those who produce fakery by mere imitation. Thus learning a craft or an art around 1900 also meant learning by looking carefully and producing a copy.[23]

The models for these copying exercises were provided by John Ruskin (primarily for architecture) and by L'Eplattenier (for sculpture and painting, fig. 9). That Jeanneret and Perrin were usually working side by side is documented by many drawings (see cat. nos. 1, 3). At times they competed in their efforts to be precise, and at other times they focused on qualities of the work that were relevant to their own differing interests.[24] In the church of Santa Croce in Florence, for example, they both worked from the same vantage point in the nave, trying to reproduce the effect of light and space at the intersection of volumes and surfaces. While Jeanneret used a

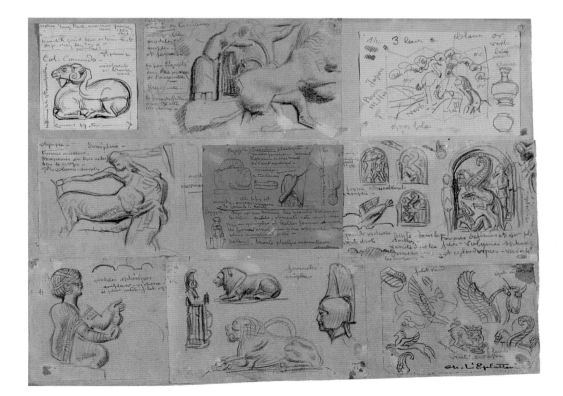

8. "Classement et choix," illustration from an article by Le Corbusier in *L'Esprit nouveau*, no. 21, 19, a comparison of types of urban agglomerations, Le Corbusier, *Urbanisme*, Paris, 1925, p. 57

9. Charles L'Eplattenier, Monumental sculptures from various museums (including the Louvre?), pencil and ink on 9 sheets of notepaper, pasted on wrapping paper, BV [277]

10. Léon Perrin, Interior View of S. Croce, Florence, 1907, pencil on paper, Musée Léon Perrin, Môtiers [282]

11. Charles-Edouard Jeanneret, Interior Study of S. Croce, Florence, 1907, pencil and watercolor on ivory paper, FLC [149]

combination of watercolor and notes in pencil, Perrin used pencil alone. While Jeanneret analyzed the architectural and spatial makeup, Perrin studied the effect of light (figs.10, 11). — After surveying the spatial organization of the nave, including the structure of the roof,[25] Jeanneret may have gone on to "copy" frescoes by Giotto in the Bardi and Peruzzi chapels (fig. 14).

"SYMBOLIC" COLORS

The term "copy" however is hardly appropriate here. Jeanneret's study of Giotto's *Ascension of Saint John* in the Peruzzi chapel reveals an impatience with the rules of the genre that results in a use of color that might be called expressionist.[26] When compared to the often more "correct" studies by L'Eplattenier and Perrin, Jeanneret's sketches suggest that he found it difficult to contain the color within the straitjacket of the graphic structure. Not long afterward, in Siena, the light effect in the aftermath of a thunderstorm appears to have been all he needed to set free his coloristic drive. The subject at hand was architectural: a medieval town hall, the Palazzo Pubblico. In Florence, studying the Palazzo Vecchio, he had produced a pedantic graphic inventory of the building as seen from his room (cat. no. 1), yet in Siena the Palazzo Pubblico, although stylistically analogous to its Florentine counterpart, was reinvented as an outburst of color (fig. 12). The green cloud against the red facade of the town hall, the purple patch of sky answering the yellow top of the campanile — these are colors not copied from nature.[27] The play of contrasts serves to call forth rather than to reproduce the scene. As Jeanneret later wrote (in another context): "Color . . . is not of a descriptive, but of an evocative character; always symbolic. It is the end and not the means."[28]

What are the premises in art history for such an assessment? In 1908 Jeanneret sent this watercolor, entitled *Après l'orage* to L'Eplattenier from Paris. Considering that the master had recently advised his student to be content with being an architect ("Dessine, ça suffit"), there may be a double meaning to the gift. In his letter,

Jeanneret apologized for the "impressionistic" extravagance of the work by attributing it to stormy weather:

> Please don't come down too hard on this small impression of the Pallio [*sic*] Square in Siena. You know that Siena is the city of colors. It takes little—a storm comes, it lights up all the hues like a fresh watercolor, it leaves behind some big black clouds strewn on a raw green evening sky, while the quenched earth exhales its bliss in marvelous pink vapors, which come to lap the walls of the formidable Palazzo Comunale [Pubblico], tapestried with Persian shawls—it takes little and you will understand that, presented with such symphony, one may have let oneself be carried away and give in to such resonant harmonies.

Not content, Jeanneret decided to go even further and let his teacher benefit from a small lesson on contemporary art:

> But maybe, in fact, you will not understand at all that a kid like me would presume to put down his impressions in a lousy painting, badly drawn, wrong in perspective, wrong in tonality. . . .
>
> When I think back to that evening I get excited again because really it was thrilling. . . .[29]

Après l'orage remained an isolated episode. Perhaps after this excursion into the forbidden land of "free art," Jeanneret returned to a more "professional" mode of render-

12. Charles-Edouard Jeanneret, Study of the Palazzo Pubblico, Siena, with the Torre del Mangia, 1907, pencil and watercolor on paper, FLC [154]

13. Charles-Edouard Jeanneret, Facade and details of the Baptistery, Siena, 1907, pencil, ink and watercolor on paper with numerous anotations, FLC [153]

14. Charles-Edouard Jeanneret, Study after Giotto's Ascension of St. John, Bardi Chapel, S. Croce, Florence, 1907, pencil and watercolor on paper, FLC

ing and produced an industriously compiled study of the baptistery facade a short distance away (fig. 13). While the Palazzo Pubblico is seen with the eyes of the Nabis,[30] the baptistery is an exercise à la Ruskin. While on the Piazza del Campo Jeanneret tried to capture a momentary sensation that might otherwise be lost, at the foot of the baptistery he produced an inventory of the work at hand. In such a way, this traveler changed identities according to weather, time, and circumstance.

LOOKING BY WRITING

Jeanneret's letters to his parents, friends, and teacher L'Eplattenier reveal, that the visual culture invested in the various stages of the Grand Tour was anything but naive. Paintings seen in museums and churches were described and judged with a precision and wit that display considerable literary ambition. Again, shifting roles and perceptual modes were part of the game. Quality may be assessed with Owen Jones in mind in terms of the organization of decorative surfaces, and then again it may be considered as a question of the massing of volumes in space. Canonized treasures of art either emerged through the aura that had been handed down by narratives of art history or through the aesthetic preoccupations of contemporary art as enacted by the Impressionists, Nabis, or even fauves.

In architecture, quality is most often a question of principle, such as when, with Ruskin in mind, international Gothic is praised at the expense of Giotto and Brunelleschi. Yet buildings can also be understood through, for example, the chromatic effects produced by the reflection of a sunset on a facade. In a letter to L'Eplattenier, dated September 19, 1907, Jeanneret described his first visit to Pisa:

> At six o'clock in the evening, the Duomo is a magic play of colors, a distillation of yellows in all hues and intensities, of ivory white and black patina, all that against an ultramarine so intense that, it you stare at it long enough, you see black. The part where the baptistery casts its shadow is all gentle vibration of rich, yellows, of red inlaid marbles lighting up, of blue marble turning darker: it is the triumph of flat surfaces, vibrant and in gentle conversation —7 in the evening, this Duomo is even more beautiful than ever; what tones! It's some sort of brown, some sort of blue, such quiet! Behind me the sky is orange and mauve, the green in the doors is dead, yellow marbles come out, they are natural sienna, while the columns are a white pink, like the petal of a wild rose. Under the small arches of the vaults, you would think that you see the frescoes next door [in the camposanto], the beautiful frescoes in gold and red; the diffuse shadow projected by the colonnettes is emerald green, and the black marble is gray like the neck of some birds. In this andante burst out the 3 mosaics, their gold shimmering with the most beautiful sunset, while the virgin's green dress vibrates gently. The crimsons have disappeared.

Then there is a reference to complementary color contrast (a topical theme in avant-garde art): "Some *bambini* play in front, a little one with a scarlet red dress against one of the green bronze doors." And finally Jeanneret made a fairly paradoxical attempt to justify to L'Eplattenier his choice of architecture as a profession (in fact L'Eplattenier had never placed much confidence in Jeanneret's talents as a painter):

> What do we need painters for? Give me rather the emotion of the stones! You see, I was so moved that I said to myself: to hell with painters, to hell with their lousy works, a corner of the Duomo is worth more than all the bunglers in the world.[31]

That it had taken painters to make Jeanneret see this kind of sight is another story. A

15. Charles-Edouard Jeanneret, View of the Orangerie at Schloss Sanssouci, Potsdam, 1910, pencil and water-color on paper, pasted on cardboard, FLC [171]

16. Edvard Munch, *Young women on a bridge*, 1905, oil on canvas. Wallraf-Richartz-Museum, Cologne

few days later, in Siena, Jeanneret resumed the artist's trade that he had just sent to hell, in an attempt to capture *as a painter* the rich chromatic effects he had so far been content to describe in words (see fig. 12).[32]

MUNCH AND SIGNAC

In 1907 Jeanneret had visited Tuscany as a student in a school of Arts and Crafts, but by 1910, in Potsdam, at Schloss Sanssouci, he was pursuing painting in the context of international modern art (figs. 15, 16). Although a professional architect (he was working with Peter Behrens in nearby Neubabelsberg), he appears to have been more fascinated by the abstractions of trees and buildings reflected in the pool than by the architecture of Sans-Souci. His watercolor also suggests a knowledge of Edvard Munch, but if so, the Norwegian artist was visited only in passing during the zigzag voyage through contemporary art that increasingly interfered with the actual Grand Tour. At Istanbul, the "free" study of the urban landscape reigned supreme; Jeanneret's views of the Golden Horn and of Pera and Istanbul across the Bosporus presented the city as a neo-Impressionist seascape, a reference to Paul Signac. In a let-ter to William Ritter, sent from Munich in 1911, a few days before departing for Istanbul, Jeanneret had written: "Constantinople! I shall probably not see this city in a more enchanting light than this one magic painting by Signac at the Munich exhibi-tion."[33] Upon arrival in Turkey he wrote more precisely about the subject (this time to L'Eplattenier):

I believe that there is an hour of the day when everything begins to "orientalize" itself or, if you want, when everything acquires a bit of the magic that launched our entire dream. That is to say around 3 or 4 in the morning when the sun rises and Istanbul is clothed in fog. That is when imagination can begin to work. For . . . I had constructed my idea of Constantinople with the help of Signac.[34]

Signac, too, made only a brief appearance on Jeanneret's horizon (fig. 17). His magic as an ideal evaporated almost as soon as Istanbul was left behind. The Acropolis in Athens, the next stage of the journey, could not really be conceptualized with an Impressionist's eye. A distinctly "heroic" vision instead was required for the appropriation of the Parthenon and its site.[35] In fact, as the Voyage d'Orient approached its climax, architecture was increasingly treated thematically as the unfolding of sculptural bodies in space. The Hagia Sofia and the Suleiman mosque in Istanbul had already been evoked in such a way, both in words ("an elementary geometry disciplines the masses: the square, the cube, the sphere"[36]) and with the help of sketches (see cat. no. 10). Is Behrens to be regarded as the driving force behind this emerging "cubist" sensibility?

Seen in this context, the "plastic" force of the Parthenon studies confirms a trend that had originated earlier (figs. 19, 20), even though the means employed — strong strokes of pencil (or watercolor) indicating volume against the open sky — differ from the more equipoised pencil studies made in Istanbul (fig. 18). In any case, when, a few weeks later, Jeanneret passed through Pisa again, on his way home from Athens, Naples, and Rome, he no longer had time for a detailed study of the cathedral facade

and its sculptural decoration, nor did he indulge in lengthy comments on the chromatic effects at sunset. Rather, he practiced "the heroic landscape." Architecture was elevated — or reduced — to a play of volumes in light, almost suggesting the proverbial definition in *Vers une architecture* "L'architecture est le jeu savant, correct et magnifique des volumes assemblés sous la lumière" (Architecture is the masterly, correct and magnificent play of volumes arranged under the light). [37] Photography in the meantime had provided more and more visual raw material for Jeanneret's "heroic" shorthand, as did the picture postcards purchased in 1911 and probably in later travels (cat. nos. 12–15).

ART AND THE MAGNETISM OF FRANCE

As a rule Jeanneret's studies of buildings reflect architectural preoccupations, while his landscape studies refer more immediately to the world of art. As to an intermediary group of works that one may describe as urban landscapes — Siena, Istanbul, Athens, Pisa – they play with both frames of reference. Predictably, upon returning to Switzerland, Jeanneret did a series of studies of the Jura landscape. He knew that it was like stumbling into a minefield; L'Eplattenier himself had set the standard in this genre. It was impossible for a former student to ignore his teacher's large, carefully calibrated winter landscapes. L'Eplattenier's overpowering presence as artistic super-ego, however, appears to have triggered off his former pupil's wish to be more "modern" than the teacher, by taking liberties with painterly execution and thus displaying an absence of formality. This is no mere speculation. In a letter from Germany, written in 1911, Jeanneret blamed L'Eplattenier for not having understood a single thing about the revolution in contemporary art since Courbet, Manet, and Rodin.[38] Clearly, Jeanneret's urge to demarcate his position with respect to that of his teacher had become imperative; he now seemed ready even to side with the once-criticized painter Cuno Amiet, whose loose and flaky landscapes, only slightly earlier than Jeanneret's, represent what Jeanneret himself was exploring (figs.21, 22; cat. no. 43).[39]

In short, in the years just after 1911, Jeanneret began to cast himself as a "great artist," and his increasing animosity toward L'Eplattenier may have been a driving force. In the larger context of European cultural politics, this transition implied the increasingly fervent wish to dissociate himself from Germany and become part of

21. Charles-Edouard Jeanneret, *Paysage du Jura* (Jura Landscape), 1914–15, charcoal and watercolor on paper, FLC

22. Cuno Amiet, *Verschneite Obstbäume* (Snow-laden fruit-trees), 1906, oil on canvas, private collection, Switzerland

23. Sonja Delaunay and Blaise Cendrars: "Prose du Transsibérien et de la Petite Jehanne de France". Leporello, Paris (1913). The left strip shows S. Delaunay's colour composition alone; the right strip as it was printed in combination with the text. MNAM, Paris (left), Musée Rath, Geneva (right)

24. Poster advertising the Trans-Siberian railway at the Exposition Universelle, Paris (1900). Schweizerische Landesbibliothek, Bern

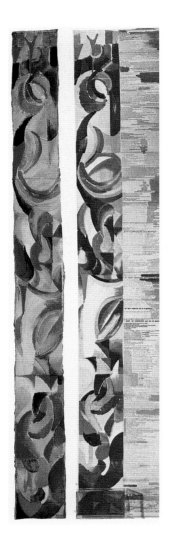

the cultural system of France, where the liberal arts had long been agents of cultural progress. The message of his first published book, *Etude sur le mouvement d'art décoratif en Allemagne* (1912) is clear in that respect.[40] For Jeanneret it was Germany versus France, the applied arts versus liberal arts (including to some extent music and literature). And what was important in modern art was based on the accomplishments of such men as Delacroix, Courbet, Manet, Daumier, Cézanne, and Van Gogh, rather than on the ideas of Ruskin or William Morris on the applied arts. Jeanneret may not yet have become a painter himself, but he was determined to do so.[41]

3. RAILWAY, PHOTOGRAPHY, AND THE CINEMATIC VIEW

In its early days, the rite of the Grand Tour required considerable amounts of time, money, and stamina. By 1900 modernization had significantly altered the predicaments of time and space that were characteristic of the structure of the voyage. The railway and photography not only were the premise for an avalanche of travel literature, both erudite and popular, but also resulted in the rapid transformation of the bourgeois educational trip into mass tourism. While new means of transport simplified access to wonders of nature and to famous monuments of history, the relatively new technology of photography and cinema also made these "attractions" widely available to nontravelers and at low cost. The World's Fair translated such attractions into colossal stage sets that offered its visitors a synthetic view of the world as reflected in its accumulated architectural curiosities (fig. 24).

These innovations had a profound impact on the everyday life of urbanized society. Around 1910, as Jeanneret prepared for his Voyage d'Orient, new configurations of time and space also emerged as a major theme in avant-garde poetry and art, starting with Symbolism, unanimism, and futurism. With Guillaume Apollinaire, Blaise Cendrars, Robert and Sonja Delaunay, as well as Fernand Léger, among others, this new sensibility gained a strong foothold in Paris.[42] Cendrars, like Le Corbusier, had been born in La Chaux-de-Fonds in 1887 (they eventually became friends). Cendrars can be said to have inaugurated a specifically avant-garde tradition of the travel account. In 1912–13, together with the painter Sonja Delaunay he collaborated on *Prose du Transsibérien et de la Petite Jehanne de France* (1913), a "poème simultané" (simultaneous poem) made of words and imagery. In it they programmatically exploited the structure of traveling as a model for the modernist experience, using "free verse" in ways that anticipate Balla's or Marinetti's "parole in libertà" (1914ff.). The base of the visual narrative is a map showing the Russian railway line from Saint Petersburg to Wladiwostock. The experience of travel was brought to life through words, images, and clouds of color, establishing links between the places seen along the way and those remembered from an earlier time (fig. 23).[43] Meanwhile Sonja's husband, the painter Robert Delaunay, had already made the deconstructed image of the Eiffel Tower into an icon of the modernist conception of space-time.

Jeanneret, like the Swiss art historian Jacob Burckhardt a generation before him, wore trousers and used the railway. Furthermore — unlike Burckhardt, as well as Ruskin — Jeanneret practiced photography. Yet even so, his culture appears only marginally preoccupied by poetic conceptualizations of modernity as those concocted by Cendrars or Delaunay. True, in Paris, while working part-time at Perret's office, he had visited the Galerie des machines of 1889, a few months before it was demolished (fig. 26). And while it is also true that en route to Turkey he photographed one or two iron bridges over the Danube, his interest (as measured by the number of photographs taken) in industrial or technological achievements at that time was minor compared to his interest in "folklore" and "culture"(see cat. no. 8). The more specifically modernist preoccupations were to surface only later, in his first articles for *L'Esprit nouveau*, in which the Eiffel-Tower, "Grande Roue," airplane, and blimp, i.e. the tourist iconography of the Delaunays, were also recycled as part of the promotion of a new architecture.

So in short, from 1907 to 1911, while the artistic and literary avant garde began to plant the seeds of modernism, Jeanneret, Baedeker in hand, was discovering a world that looked much as it had to Ruskin, Taine, Sitte, and Schultze-Naumburg. Against this background, Jeanneret's interest in Töpffer's "cinematographic" narrative seems a curious anticipation of later interests. We do not know what triggered off this interest, but there are hints in some early landscape studies, in which mountains are shown from different perspectives as if in temporal succession (c. 1905; fig. 27).[44] Similarly, using the "modern" medium of photography, Jeanneret took some pictures in Biel/Bienne, Murten and Neuchâtel and "mounted" them in such a way as to give a synthetic view of different aspects of the buildings he photographed (c. 1914; fig. 25; see also cat. no. 16). With such montages Jeanneret appeared to explore techniques

25. Charles-Edouard Jeanneret, Murten/Morat, Switzerland. Close-up view of the City Hall and a general view of the city from the medieval wall, photograph, inscribed on verso: "Murailles de Morat 1916 / Morat 1916." FLC [91]

26. Paris, interior of the Galerie des Machines, built 1889, photograph by Charles-Edouard Jeanneret, 1908. BV

27. Charles-Edouard Jeanneret: Studies of a mountain seen at intervals of time, pencil on sketch paper, (1905–07), FLC

28. "Sur la plastique," montage illustrating the "Purist" position on modern art, from *L'Esprit Nouveau*, no. 1, 1920, p. 45

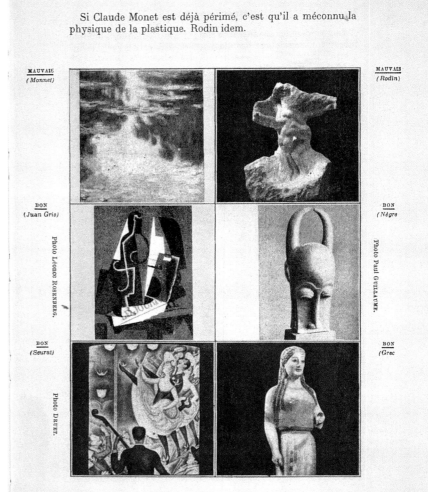

that bridge Töpffer's "strip" and the cinema. No wonder his work later served as a pretext for writing about the miracles possible in the new medium of cinema.

EDITING AS MONTAGE

In an article already referred to, De Fayet (in fact probably Jeanneret) wrote in 1921:

> Cinema can be anything, Gargantua just as well as Ali Baba. But it can do much more. Beyond making use of people, landscapes, the air and the sea, it can also, by animation, show the most unexpected creations; it can use sequential geometric constructions to organize impressive virtual realities inconceivable until now.[45]

Since the nineteenth century, industrialization had slowly revolutionized the ways by which images could be manipulated and books illustrated, and the cinema — especially in the way it is described above — can well be seen as a metaphor for what Ozenfant and Jeranneret themselves were exploring as writers, journalists, and editors engaged in developing new techniques of constructing an argument with the help of imagery. That Töpffer should surface with new force at the time of *L'Esprit Nouveau*, therefore, comes as no surprise. By then, the magazine itself could be said to have become a theater of "virtual realities" based on "successive geometric constructions (organized) in hitherto unthinkable ways," and this cinematic approach, perhaps formalized by cubism, did not fail to leave its mark on Le Corbusier's practice as an architect (see fig. 28).[46]

The "Retour à l'ordre," as promoted by Ozenfant and Jeanneret in the years after World War I, implied Purism as an aesthetic religion. Yet Purism did not sweep from the architect's mind the experiences gathered from 1907 onward — even if the Symbolist and Impressionist imagery was formally banned from Purism's official pictorial canon (fig. 28). In fact, the structure of the illustrated magazine or book rather worked in the opposite direction. Purism may have become the trademark for Ozenfant's and Jeanneret's production as artists, but that did not prevent the *L'Esprit nouveau* from displaying an aesthetic that was playfully combinative and eclectic. After all, journalism had its own logic, its secret based on intelligently manipulated variety, as in the key-image of the "menu" (fig. 8). The logic of journalism corresponds seamlessly with that of tourism: As Le Corbusier was an expert in both areas, his attempts to abandon his own early career as a decorative artist and would-be-painter did not prevent him from filling the pages of his magazine — and subsequently of his books — with entire collections of early travel studies and photographs (cat. nos. 12–14). But even his practice as an architect in a narrower sense turned out to provide for a multitude of niches where older genres were cultivated freely: from the annotated sketch to the heroic landscape, academic figure study, still life, and classical allegory. Apart from the "art" quality of many of Le Corbusier's Purist floor plans, the art of architectural rendering alone was thus turned into an abbreviated handbook of the history of art from Nicolas Poussin to Juan Gris.

While Le Corbusier the architect was eager to remain in touch with the horizons of art, Le Corbusier the artist took the risk of being trapped by his own past. Much of his later work may in fact be linked to this kind of autobiographical rumination. It is a process that reverberates with the work of other artists as well as his own. In a rapid sketch of a sunset, made in 1955, from an airplane above Manila, for example, there is an echo of Ferdinand Hodler's *Vues du Léman*; or in the series of drawings dated October 6, 1957, of Le Corbusier's dying wife, Yvonne — rare documents of privacy — there are hints of the monumental paintings by Hodler of his mistress Valentine Godet-Darel on her deathbed in 1915.

4. TOWARDS "PROMENADE ARCHITECTURALE"

Ultimately, Töpffer's zigzag theme is derived from the switchbacks along the roads climbing up and down the slopes of the Alps. These meanderings make it easier to traverse the mountains (figs. 29, 30). Le Corbusier associated this kind of road design to what he called the "donkey's path":

> We shall not forget the demonstration that a little donkey pulling a big load gave us one rainy day. We were standing at the window of a building that blocked the top of a straight sloping street leading up toward it. Fresh rain had turned the pavement into a uniform carpet on which the wheels of the cart, pulled by our friend, drew two bright lines. At the beginning of the slope the tracks started parallel to the sidewalk; but soon after, they drifted to one side, then to the other, then again to the first and so on for some hundred meters. Then the serpentine straightened out; the inflections became less marked, the line recuperated its parallelism to the sidewalks. Then the donkey stopped; but under the whip he started off again in a marked serpentine that became more and more emphatic until he reached the top of the street and disappeared from view. . . . The lesson of the donkey must be retained.[47]

celle-ci contraste d'autant plus avec le milieu naturel que son but est plus près de la pensée et plus éloigné, plus détaché du corps. On peut dire que plus les œuvres humaines s'éloignent de la préhension directe, plus elles tendent à la pure géométrie : un violon, une chaise qui touchent notre corps sont d'une géométrie amoindrie, mais la ville est de pure géométrie. Libre, l'homme tend à la pure géométrie. Il fait alors ce qu'on appelle de l'ordre.
L'ordre lui est indispensable, sinon ses actes seraient sans cohésion, sans suite possible. Il y ajoute, y apporte, l'idée d'excellence. Plus l'ordre est parfait, plus il est à l'aise, en sécurité. Il échafaude dans son esprit des constructions basées sur cet ordre qui lui est imposé par son corps, et il crée. L'œuvre humaine e

30. "La loi du méandre," Le Corbusier, *Précisions sur un état présent de l'architecture et de l'urbanisme*, Paris, 1930, p. 142

31. Le Corbusier, Selfportrait as a raven carrying a donkey, and as donkey carrying a raven (undated; 1960s?)

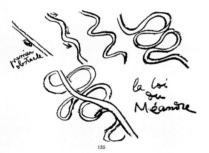

Around 1910–11, when these lines were written, Jeanneret may have been convinced that the point of view coincided with that expressed by Camillo Sitte in *Der Städtebau nach seinen künstlerischen Grundsätzen* (1889). Sitte associated the charm of medieval cityscapes with the principle of irregularly winding streets.[48] As Jeanneret traveled through Germany to collect material for "La Construction des villes," what interested him was the variety of spatial configurations and picturesque views to be experienced as one walked through the towns. These sites were "read" and documented mostly with Sitte (but also with Schultze-Naumburg) in mind. Jeanneret took the same approach, at least to some degree, in the *Voyage d'orient*. From 1910 onward, however, and parallel to these Sittean interests, Jeanneret was increasingly attracted to Baroque and neoclassical compositions (see cat. no. 16). By 1925, monumental axial compositions reigned supreme, so that the "donkey's path" survived but as an example of what to avoid, and in the opening pages of *Urbanisme*, Le Corbusier wrote:

> Man walks in a straight line because he has a goal; he knows where he is going . . . .The donkey zigzags, hesitates a bit, scatterbrained and distracted, zigzags to avoid big stones, to avoid the slope, to gain some shade; he doesn't care . . . .[49]

The "zigzagging" donkey may be Le Corbusier's only published reference to Töpffer. And Le Corbusier laconically described Sitte, the alleged romanticizer of the "donkey's" way, as "an intelligent and sensitive Viennese who simply stated the problem badly."[50]

SELF-PORTRAIT?

It is tempting to read the opening passage of *Urbanisme* as an encoded self-portrait.[51] On the first page of the book, the architect's two selves as "l'homme qui marche droit" and as "donkey" are displayed side by side: two identities among many, both directly linked to his biography, and both rather evocative of the atavistic opposition between intellect and instinct, reason and emotion (cf. fig. 31). Salient aspects of Jeanneret's career as a student and young architect can more easily be associated with the "donkey's path" than with "l'homme qui marche droit," but this lies in the nature of the Grand Tour and needs no further discussion. More troubling is Le Corbusier's spectacular about-face with regard to the once adored Sitte, for it is symptomatic of a more deeply rooted zigzag-strategy — a "structural" more than simply sentimental sympathy with the "donkey" and his "cervelle brûlée."

Much of Le Corbusier's Purist theory is clearly about "l'homme qui marche droit" and his desire to suppress his more irrational alter ego. More generally Purism and its fascination with business, geometry, and engineering is about "male" interests.[52] Yet the alter ego, documented with other issues in the eclectic harvest of the Grand Tour, did not altogether disappear from the agenda. Soon enough, the "donkey's path" reemerged, naturalized, and was presented almost as a cosmic law that dictates life on earth:

I draw a river. The goal is clear: to get from one point to the next: river or idea. A tiny hitch develops— the incidents of the spirit: a minimal little nudge, barely noticeable. The water is thrown to the left, it cuts into the bank; from there, by reaction, it is thrown back to the right. With that, the straight line is gone. Left, right, always deeper, the water bites, hollows, cuts away — wider and wider, the idea explores the field. The straight line has become wavy; the idea has been enriched by circumstances. The waviness takes on a characteristic shape, the meander appears; the idea has branched out . . . .

The loops of the meander have come to look like figure eights, and that's idiotic. Suddenly, at the most exasperating moment, there they go, the loops touch at the outer bulge of their curves! Miracle! The river runs straight! Thus, the idea has burst forth in its purity, the solution has emerged. A new phase begins [fig. 30]. . . [53]

In such a way, the "donkey's" domain — *la culture du méandre* — has been sublimated as a geological law. A few years previously, it had already been transferred from urbanism to architectural design. And as a result, the "Voyage en zigzag" has begun a second life-cycle under the aegis of *promenade architecturale*. The term first was introduced almost casually in connection with Le Corbusier's Villa La Roche-Jeanneret: "This second [of the two adjacent houses — in fact the Villa La Roche] then will be a bit like a *promenade architecturale*. You enter: the architectural spectacle unfolds in succession before your eyes: you follow an itinerary and the perspectives develop with great variety [etc.]."[54]

At first the "picturesque" implications of the *promenade* seemed to have been the object of a certain embarrassment on Le Corbusier's part, but by 1942 this feature had been transformed into an axiom: "Architecture can be classified as dead or living by the degree to which the rule of *sequential movement* has been ignored or, instead, brilliantly observed."[55]

The roots of the idea lay in the tradition of the English garden, with William Burgh, among others, who had defined "variety" and the "path" as the topical component of the "picturesque principle."[56] In two chapters of *Vers une architecture* — "Rappels à MM.les architectes" (part 3, "Le plan") and "Architecture" (part 2, "L'illusion des plans") — Le Corbusier illustrated his claim that throughout history, the organization of sequential movement through space had been the essence of great architecture. Not by coincidence, the first of the two chapters used an illustration from Choisy's *Histoire de l'architecture* showing the Periclean Acropolis (fig. 32). In fact, while Sitte may have initiated Jeanneret in the study of urban design, Choisy provided a basis for Le Corbusier's concept of the *promenade*:

ACROPOLIS OF ATHENS. View of the Parthenon, the Erechtheion, and the statue of Athena Promachos seen from the Propylaia. Lets not forget that the ground of the Acropolis is very uneven, with considerable differences of level that were used to create imposing bases for the buildings. The whole thing being out of square makes for vistas that are rich as well as subtle: the asymmetrical masses of the buildings produce an intense rhythm. The scene is massive, elastic, nervous, terribly sharp, dominating.[57]

Le Corbusier cites other examples studied during his Grand Tour, including buildings organized as organisms conceived for a sequential discovery in space and time, such as the Green Mosque in Bursa, whose spatial organization is such that "you are enthralled by a sensorial rhythm"; the "Casa delle Nozze d'argento" (Le Corbusier remembered it as the "Casa del Noce") and the House of the Tragic Poet at Pompeii,

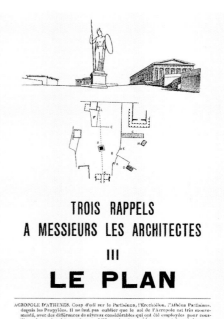

32. "Trois rapelles à Méssieurs les architects. III. Le plan An illustration from Auguste Choisy's "Histoire de l'architecture" showing the Acropolis as reproduced in Le Corbusier, *Vers une architecture*, 1923

33. Le Corbusier, Villa La Roche-Jeanneret, Paris, 1923–25, view of the entrance hall as envisioned in July (?) 1923, FLC

34. Le Corbusier, Villa La Roche-Jeanneret, Paris, 1923–25, the hall as built; photograph by Fred Boissonas, 1926

where "you . . . note clever distortions of the axis which give intensity to the volumes." [58]

PROMENADE AND INITIATION

Like the Periclean Acropolis, the La Roche house is difficult to grasp in a single view because it is approached laterally via the Impasse du Docteur Blanche. [59] It is conceived as a spatial experience to be gained in an organized temporal succession. Unlike the Acropolis, however, but very much like a Pompeian house, [60] the program is domestic, albeit combined with that of a private picture gallery or museum.

As has often been described, the variety of spaces not only relates to the different functions of a small house (with hall, living area, dining room, sleeping area, servants quarters and study), but also is "themed" to serve as a frame for the presentation of post-cubist painting in its evolution from analytical cubism through "crystal" cubism to Purism. After the house was completed, Le Corbusier himself planned the arrangement and hanging of the pictures. In this way linked to the course of art history, the promenade through the La Roche house assumes the character of an initiatory rite. On the other hand, as a built invitation to a walk through space and time the villa may also be seen as a tribute to its owner, the banker Raoul La Roche — and perhaps even to Le Corbusier's "voyages en zigzag," in which La Roche had at one point taken part, inviting the architect in 1922 to join him for a trip to Venice (incidentally the only important non-Swiss destination in Töpffer's *Voyages en zigzag*). [61]

In many respects, yet not in all, the final design is based on a project submitted to La Roche in July 1923. What made Le Corbusier change his mind so radically in view of the final concept of the entrance hall submitted only a few months later, in November of the same year? Evidently, this pristine space, three stories high, all in white, with a cubical balcony projecting from the wall and openings that suggest rather than establish apertures to the adjacent parts of the house, is among the elements of the design that depart most clearly from the earlier proposal (figs. 33, 34)? That Le Corbusier had been impressed by the De Stijl exhibition shown at Léonce Rosenberg's *Galerie de l'Effort moderne* is only part of the story. [62] In what respect did the formal language proposed there by van Doesburg and van Eesteren (in their "artist's studio"; fig. 36) offer a solution that his own earlier proposal did not? The answer is not merely architectural, let alone functional. Rather it has to do with preoccupations in the visual arts at large, including cinema, cubism, the mythology of space–time, and the urge to create a single space within the house where the narrative of the promenade could be experienced all at once. In his description of Cendrars' *Prose du Transsibérien et de la Petite Jehanne de France*, Guillaume Apollinaire succinctly characterized the aesthetic strategy at hand:

> Blaise Cendrars and Mme Delaunay-Terck [*sic*] have made a FIRST ATTEMPT AT A WRITTEN SIMULTANEITY, where color contrasts served to accustom the eye to read the whole poem AT A SINGLE GLANCE, like the conductor of an orchestra who reads the superimposed notes in his score in a single moment, like the words and pictures of a poster that one sees at a single glance. [63]

Logically, the stylistically most advanced part of the house, the part that transcends the pack-donkey-romanticism of the promenade with its sweeping ramps, and that crystallizes the house into a single sculptural form, became the envelope of the most advanced art in La Roche's collection: "crystal" cubism.

In Le Corbusier's eyes, the hall appears not to have been strong enough as a counterweight to the spatial events attached to it. In a diagram entitled "The Four

Compositions," the Villas La Roche-Jeanneret, were described as pertaining to a "rather simple, picturesque, animated genre" ("genre plutôt facile, pittorresque, mouvementé"), less "serious," in short, than Le Corbusier's Purist "cubes" of the other three houses shown: the Villa Stein in Garches, Villa Baizeau in Carthage, and Villa Savoye in Poissy. Held against the ideal of classical perfection (the "absolute", as required by "l'homme qui marche droit"), the complicated cluster of the La Roche-Jeanneret houses must have appeared to show too much indulgence for "variety."[64] The opposite strategy, tending toward the ideal (that is, the perfectly calibrated "box") and thus representing a "very difficult" genre ("très difficile [satisfaction de l'esprit]"), is emblematically represented by the subsequent Villa Stein at Garches (1927). As to the Villa Savoye at Poissy (1928–31), it represents a "very generous" type, whereby on the exterior an "architectural will" is affirmed, and "all the functional needs (sunlight, contiguity, circulation)" are satisfied in the interior (fig. 35).[65]

Yet even at Poissy, the quest for the absolute in no way precludes variety, nor does it avoid another reference to the donkey's path. In fact, even this archetype of modernist "concrete cubes and flat-roofs" turns out to celebrate, albeit with the help of "a flat deck, . . . a gangway, a deckrail," the colonial dream of the Grand Tour as well as *L'Esprit nouveau*'s proud defense of Western art. The visitor is guided through the house with the help of ramps that culminate in front of the Claude Lorraine view of the Seine valley, arranged as a rectangular opening in the solarium wall. Radicalized and simplified, the "promenade" along the doubly broken, explicitly zigzag ramp, is once again the key idea. Le Corbusier himself established the link to his "Oriental" memories: "Arab architecture teaches an invaluable lesson. It is appreciated by walking, by one's feet; it is by walking, by moving, that one sees the order of the architecture unfold."[66]

ux esprits
pposent : la
dition de
nce, Notre-
me, Plan
oisin » (les
tte-ciel
rizontaux»)
a ligne amé-
aine (tu-
lte, hérisse-
nt, premier
explosif
n nouveau
oyen âge.)

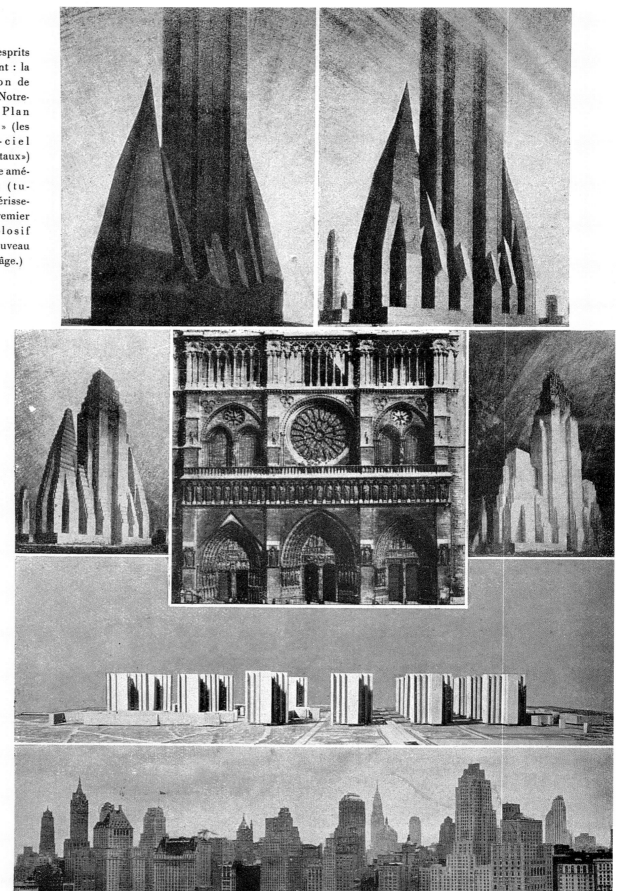

44

2

LE CORBUSIER AND THE GOTHIC

Pierre Vaisse

HOWEVER NEW IT MIGHT HAVE claimed to be, the architecture of the Modern Movement nevertheless had its roots in the architecture of the past, particularly the Gothic. As early as 1932, Henry-Russell Hitchcock and Philip Johnson had commented:

> In the handling of the problems of structure it [modern architecture] is related to the Gothic, in the handling of the problems of design it is more akin to the Classical. In the preëminence given to the handling of function it is distinguished from both.... As late as 1904 it was possible to conceive of modern architecture chiefly as a sort of renaissance of the Gothic. Yet it should be stressed that the relation of the modern style to the Gothic is ideological rather than visual, a matter of principle rather than a matter of practice. In design, indeed, the leading modern architects aim at Greek serenity rather than Gothic aspiration.[1]

Subsequent authors have further analyzed the role of the Gothic in the genesis of modern architecture,[2] but the definitions of "modern" that underpin such analyses are often imprecise. In one broad interpretation, for example, the modern style is shown to extend from the Eiffel Tower in the late 1880s to the works of Buckminster Fuller in the 1970s.[3] Johnson and Hitchcock, however, were speaking of a phenomenon far more restricted in time and of great formal unity, although they shared with other scholars the same conception of Gothic as a rational system of construction. This view has provided modern architecture with a historical justification for its rationality. Modernism has not been the only movement to refer to Gothic in this way; in France, for example, these ideas can be traced to Viollet-le-Duc and before him to origins in the eighteenth century. This current of thinking, however, was not the source of the ideas on Gothic held by Le Corbusier, who played a dominant role in the genesis of the International Style, and in whose work the close connection between ideas and practice is well known (fig. 37).[4]

VIOLLET-LE-DUC: THE CONVERSION TO RATIONALISM

In spite of its diversity, Jeanneret/Le Corbusier's architecture in no way recalls the Gothic, with one exception—an early project for a building in the form of a church, drawn when he was eighteen years old for the Union chrétienne de jeunes gens (Christian Youth Union) in La Chaux-de-Fonds.[5] A few years later, in 1908, Jeanneret

37. Notre-Dame, the American Setback-Skyscraper and Le Corbusier's *Ville Contemporaine* compared. Le Corbusier, *La ville radieuse*, 1935

38. Paris, Notre-Dame, Gargoyles, 1910 (?), postcard, FLC [124]

39. Paris, Notre-Dame, postcard with geometric inscription indicating proportions and cropping lines for publication, c. 1910, added notes c. 1921, FLC

felt he had made the discovery that architecture was a matter of construction, not plastic values; this conversion to rationalism was accompanied by a new enthusiasm for Gothic architecture, spurred on when he acquired a copy of Viollet-le-Duc's *Dictionnaire raisonné de l'architecture française*.[6] In a letter that year to Charles L'Eplattenier, his teacher, Jeanneret wrote as a convert to the interpretation of Gothic put forth by Viollet-le-Duc and his disciples:

> And I went to Notre-Dame, and I attended the end of Magne's Gothic course—at the École des Beaux-Arts. . . and I understood. . . . [Boeswillwald] taught his course on Romanesque and Gothic architecture, and there you could see what architecture really is.[7]

Sixteen years later, Le Corbusier wrote again of this period, in even more explicit terms:

> I was possessed by the fervor for "construction." I would pass entire afternoons in Notre-Dame in Paris, armed with an enormous bunch of keys from the Ministère des Beaux-Arts. I knew every corner of the cathedral, down to the tips of its towers, pinnacles, and flying-buttresses. This was for me the Gothic period.[8]

By then, however, this period in Le Corbusier's development had virtually come to an end, as he made clear in the same article in *L'Esprit nouveau*:

> But that admiration for Gothic form and poetry which I would so eagerly have expressed was bound up with the structure. Nowadays I am ravished by the primary beauty of a cathedral plan, and stupefied by the weakness, in plastic terms, of the work itself. The Gothic plan and section are magnificent, sparkling with ingeniousness. But none of this is evident to the eyes of one examining the actual building. Amazing apogee of the engineer, defeat of plastic art.[9]

A few years earlier, he had formulated the same critique more precisely in one of the articles that would eventually comprise *Vers une architecture* (1923; translated into English in 1927 as *Towards a New Architecture*):

> Gothic architecture is not, fundamentally, based on spheres, cones and cylinders. Only the nave is an expression of a simple form, but of a complex geometry of the second order (intersecting arches). It is for that reason that a cathedral is not very beautiful and that we search in it for compensations of a subjective kind outside plastic art. A cathedral interests us as the ingenious solution of a difficult problem, but a problem of which the postulates have been badly stated because they do not proceed from the great primary forms. *The cathedral is not a plastic work; it is a drama; a fight against the force of gravity, which is a sensation of a sentimental nature.* [emphasis by Le Corbusier][10]

There is nothing surprising in this judgment, because what Le Corbusier defended in *Vers une architecture* is in fact an aesthetic that is foreign to cathedrals, instead finding its inspiration in Roman antiquity. His attitude thus seems to confirm the opinion of Hitchcock and Johnson concerning the International Style and would do so even more strongly if Le Corbusier had at this point still shown the slightest interest in the structure of the Gothic cathedral. The only positive aspect he conceded, however, also concerned form ("only the nave is an expression of a simple form"). He conceived the struggle against heaviness not as a problem of construction, the solution of which would depend upon calculation, but rather as a "drama." The two terms of the opposition underlined by Hitchcock and Johnson, therefore, do not constitute—in Le

40. Charles-Edouard Jeanneret, Paris, Notre-Dame, gallery below south rose window, 1908 (?), pencil, ink and watercolor on paper, private collection, Switzerland

Corbusier's thought, at any rate—two aspects of his work beginning around 1920, but instead represent two phases of an evolution that led him from admiration for Gothic structure in 1908 (figs. 38, 40) to a dislike of Gothic form some ten years later.

This admiration for Gothic structure was hardly original in 1908. Jeanneret even mentions courses taught by Lucien Magne and Paul-Louis Boeswillwald—to which could be added those taught by Anatole de Baudot at the Musée de Trocadéro starting

41. Charles-Edouard Jeanneret, the façade of Palazzo Grottanelli, Siena, 1907, pen and tempera on paper, FLC

42. Charles-Edouard Jeanneret, Study of Chartres Cathedral, 1917 (?), black ink on paper, FLC

in 1887 and published in 1916.[11] In these, de Baudot referred again and again to the theories of Viollet-le-Duc, which had nourished the whole of rationalist thought in French architecture. These ideas became so commonplace that it seems surprising for them to be a revelation when encountered by the young architect:

> . . . judging from Jeanneret's unusual response to these new concepts, he seems never to have been exposed to them before. This last point is odd since these concepts were nothing new in France, and indeed in many ways were part of the architectural "establishment," through the writings of Viollet-le-Duc, Hippolyte Taine, the courses taught by Anatole de Baudot, and those taught at the École des Beaux-Arts by Julien Guadet—Perret's teacher.[12]

RUSKIN, CHOISY, AND THE REJECTION OF GERMANY

Regardless of the great diffusion of Viollet-le-Duc's thought abroad, especially in French Switzerland, where Viollet-le-Duc died, at least at La Chaux-de-Fonds it was nonetheless eclipsed totally by the work of another theoretician of the Gothic who defended a vision that was anything but rationalist: John Ruskin.[13] For the young Jeanneret, Ruskin's *Mornings in Florence*, which he owned in a French translation of 1906, was an important influence.[14] Jeanneret's mentor L'Eplattenier may have studied in Paris, but L'Eplattenier's teaching was rooted in the principles of the Arts and Crafts movement. While L'Eplattenier does not seem to have been especially open to the ideas of Viollet-le-Duc, he admired Ruskin profoundly and passed that enthusiasm on to his student.[15] Thus the young Jeanneret was educated in a milieu dominated by the English vision of the Middle Ages, particularly the Gothic, making his 1908 discovery of the French tradition such a revelation.

Despite the fervor of his 1908 letter to L'Eplattenier, it is far from certain that Jeanneret fully converted to French rationalism. The appeal to truth and honesty, the accusation of dishonesty leveled against certain representatives of Art Nouveau, in short, that confusion of architecture and morality which would characterize Jeanneret/Le Corbusier's thinking throughout his career, all this derives directly from Ruskin's *Seven Lamps of Architecture*. He was also to remain faithful to Ruskin over Viollet-le-Duc in his abhorrence for the restoration of architectural monuments, a hatred that he would articulate again in *Quand les cathédrales étaient blanches*, in which he speaks of Périgueux Cathedral in terms that recall the sixth of Ruskin's "lamps," the "Lamp of Memory."[16]

Ruskin's influence is also evident in drawings Jeanneret made during his trip to Italy in 1907 (fig. 41). Nothing in them reveals any interest in the structure of medieval buildings. His interest lay rather with the sculpted decoration, polychromy, and skin of the stone. Later, in 1917, he viewed the cathedral of Chartres with the eyes of a painter (fig. 42).[17] Another example, however, seemed to point in a different direction: the geometric scheme superimposed on a photograph of the facade of Notre-Dame in Paris, published in *Vers une architecture* to illustrate the concept of regulating lines (see fig. 39).[18] Clearly the issue here was proportion, not construction. The immediate source for this illustration was not Viollet-le-Duc but Auguste Choisy, whose *Histoire de l'architecture* Jeanneret had acquired in 1913.[19] Choisy, who was among Viollet-le-Duc's admirers, promoted architectural rationalism, and it was supposedly from him that Le Corbusier had taken the idea of regulating lines, at least according to what he admitted in 1924.[20]

Le Corbusier actually owed far less to Choisy than he claimed. Only a portion of the pages of Le Corbusier's copy of Choisy's book were even cut.[21] Although in *Vers une architecture* Le Corbusier borrowed one of Choisy's illustrations, showing the proportions of an Achaemenian temple, Choisy himself had borrowed this picture from a book by Marcel Dieulafoy on ancient Persian art.[22] Neither Dieulafoy's geometric outline nor Choisy's for Notre-Dame, however, have any connection with the regulating lines that Le Corbusier used for his own works, which depended upon a very different system. According to what he wrote later in *Le Modulor* (1951), the revelation upon which his system depended occurred while he was studying the facade of the Senators' Palace on the Roman Capitoline.[23] It was a system that had been used by Heinrich Wölfflin in 1889, and before him by August Thiersch in his famous *Handbuch der Architektur* (1883).[24]

In fact, Le Corbusier seems to have claimed Choisy's influence just to obscure his debt to German theorists. After World War I, Le Corbusier was forced to eliminate all memory of or reference to what he owed to Germany,[25] and he vigorously attacked German architecture. This same hostility explains the vision of Gothic he forged around 1920, which owed nothing to the rationalist tradition associated with Viollet-le-Duc and in which the picturesque qualities admired by Ruskin took on a negative value. Nowhere is this view more forcefully stated than in *Urbanisme* (1925; figs. 43, 44) and in his Sorbonne lecture entitled "L'Esprit nouveau en architecture":

> And there is the cathedral, with its pointed forms, its jagged silhouette, with a clear desire for order, but totally lacking in that calm and equilibrium that are the mark of fully developed civilizations (Rouen Cathedral).[26]

In the lecture he compared Romanesque and Gothic towns, though he refrained from using "Gothic." According to him, the Romanesque was characterized by simple and pure geometric forms inherited from ancient architecture and by the domination of the horizontal, while the Gothic town, which he referred to simply as the town of the Middle Ages, presented "a totally different aesthetic."[27] This difference in aesthetics expressed a cultural difference. As the mind and spirit of a society were expressed in geometry, the irregularity of medieval forms (Gothic forms) betrayed a residue of barbarism that remained until the inauguration of a new "intellectual clarity" during the Renaissance.

43. Rouen Cathedral as illustrated in Le Corbusier, *Urbanisme*, Paris, 1925, p. 32

44. Reims Cathedral and Perrault's facade of the Louvre compared, Le Corbusier, *Urbanisme*, Paris, 1925

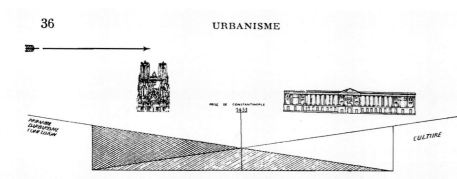

45. Charles-Edouard Jeanneret, Study of the "Markt" at Nürnberg, with the "Schöner Brunnen" and Marienkirche (background), 1910 (?), pencil and watercolor on paper, FLC [172]

"BARBARISM"

The idea of the Middle Ages as a somber parenthetical period of barbarism, bracketed by antiquity at one end and its rebirth at the other, derived from a centuries-old view of history, which by 1925 might well have seemed totally outmoded. Although the official historiography of the French Republic condemned feudalism and the domination of the medieval Church over mind and spirit, this judgment in no way concerned Gothic architecture. In fact it was thought of in a totally different manner, derived from the theory of Viollet-le-Duc, as a reflection of the emancipation of the medieval communes, which was itself seen as a first step in that long evolution toward the eventual triumph of free thinking and Republican government. The return of barbarism was instead dated nearly a millennium earlier, with the demise of antiquity after the invasion of the Roman empire by the barbarians—that is, by the Germanic peoples. Le Corbusier took up this idea, which originated in the Renaissance, but to salvage Romanesque architecture he did not hesitate to reposition the great invasions "between the year 1000 and the year 1200."[28]

This crude manipulation of history had its own special logic. The term *Gothic* derived from the name of Alaric's Goths, those barbarians from the north who sacked Rome in A.D. 410 and who were considered to have brought with them an architecture that the Italians of the Renaissance called either "maniera gotica" or "maniera tedesca." Much later, during the Romantic period, when a more precise use of the term *Gothic* came to designate the architecture that today is known by that name, the idea that its origins were Germanic allowed it to be taken up in Germany as the national style. Even though the progress of medieval archaeology quickly established that the Gothic system of construction had in fact been invented in north central France, the idea that the Gothic style constituted the purest expression of the Germanic soul persisted in Germany and even enjoyed a resurgence at the beginning of the twentieth century. In explaining the passage from the Romanesque to the Gothic through the trick of moving by some six to eight centuries what the Germans call the "Völkerwanderungen" (migration) and what the French at the time called "les invasions barbares," Le Corbusier managed to give a historical basis to the German conception of the Gothic, while at the same time confirming the negative value the term had possessed from the Renaissance to the Romantic period.

PSYCHOLOGICAL AESTHETICS

The need to justify what are ultimately existential convictions via rational, functional, or factual arguments must be considered one of the fundamental features of Le Corbusier's mind. This recourse to history—albeit an extremely manipulated history—is one example, but he also based his critique of Gothic architecture on another discipline, so-called psychological aesthetics, which at the time claimed a scientific status, having enjoyed a considerable success in Germany during the second half of the nineteenth century.[29] Wölfflin referred to psychological aesthetics in his doctoral thesis on the psychology of architecture, in which he mentions the agreeable or disagreeable effects produced on the human eye by different lines.[30] Echoing this theory, Le Corbusier argued that broken lines creating irregular forms (those of the Gothic, needless to say) provoked an unpleasant sensation in the viewer.[31] Expounding such a theory, Le Corbusier again shows his debt to Germanic culture (figs. 45–47).[32]

Lines are not simply straight or curved, sinuous or broken; they are also horizontal or vertical. For a long time, this opposition held great importance in the historiography of architecture. By 1920 it was already a commonplace, which in both France and Germany encompassed the opposition between classicism and the Gothic. Gothic verticality was thus held in Germany to be the natural expression of the Germanic soul, as Wölfflin wrote in his doctoral thesis: "One could almost say that the opposition of southern and northern ways of life is expressed in the opposition between horizontal and vertical proportions."[33]

Such a view is difficult to reconcile with the existence and chronological primacy of the cathedrals of north central France. German writers such as Wilhelm Uhde responded that the system of rib vault construction was but a marginal aspect of the Gothic, that it must not be confused with its more profound essence, and that in its essence the Gothic was never fully adopted in France because of the character of the populace, who were, they said, too tinged with Gaulish or Latin elements. This was why, as Uhde wrote in 1928, "the Gothic style invented by that genius who had created Gallo-Roman forms slowly freed itself from the Gothic mentality, to which it was foreign, and then developed according to the spirit of its race, which is to say that it became Romanesque and horizontal."[34]

However absurd such ideas may seem today, they are identical to those found in Le Corbusier's writings of the same period. He too thought that verticality characterized German architecture, as he wrote in 1920 in *L'Esprit nouveau*: "The systematic use of the vertical in Germany is a mysticism, a mysticism of physical things, the poison of German architecture."[35]

As for French architecture, including that of the Gothic cathedrals, horizontality was the key principle, as Le Corbusier claimed to have demonstrated in an illustration accompanying an article on American and French cities of the future (see fig. 37).[36] The image was a photomontage in which a perspective view of the *Plan Voisin* for Paris and the facade of Notre-Dame were surrounded by several drawings of skyscrapers rising in a pyramid and a photograph of the skyline of Manhattan, accompanied by a caption that read: "Two opposing spirits: the French tradition, Notre-Dame, *Plan Voisin* (horizontal skyscrapers), and the American line (tumult, bristling, first explosive stage of a new Middle Ages)."[37]

By the terms used, Le Corbusier clearly likened the architecture of Manhattan to German architecture (that is, to the Gothic), while the perspective of the *Plan Voisin* shows skyscrapers of equal height whose flat roofs are horizontally aligned. The image of Notre-Dame is cropped to exclude its towers, thereby emphasizing the horizontality of its facade.

Le Corbusier always had a marked preference for horizontality. The account of his *Voyage d'Orient* revealed him even then to be particularly sensitive to the horizontality of the dominant lines of the landscape. Just as, according to him, pure geometric forms reflected the profound laws of the universe, so the horizon provided us with "the most humanly perceptible measure of the universe."[38] Consequently, it was in architecture that the meaning of this line affirmed itself. The Romanesque city was horizontal, like the succession of skyscraper roofs in the *Plan Voisin*. There is perhaps no more revealing text in this connection than a short article of 1925 on the traditional houses of Brittany (fig. 48).[39] For Le Corbusier, the value of these lay in the horizontal crowning of the gable, "the only horizontal against the sky, like the meeting of sea and sky," because "without this horizontal crown above the gable, the Breton lands would no longer exist for our eyes as they do at present."[40] But the replacement of traditional thatch by modern slates or tiles would have entailed a modification of these gables; they would have lost their character as a result. It would not have been surprising for Le Corbusier to approve a new form resulting from the use

46. The "Markt", Nürnberg, with the "Schöner Brunnen" and Marienkirche, c. 1900, postcard. BV

47. Charles-Edouard Jeanneret, Study of the "Markt", Nürnberg, after engravings in the Bibliothèque Nationale, Paris, 1915, ink on paper, FLC

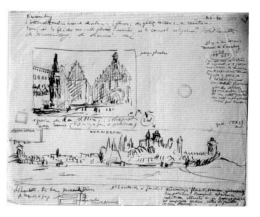

of a new material, but this was not the case, for the loss of the rectilinear gable also entailed the loss of that cosmic harmony between the line of the roofs and the line traced by the meeting of sky and sea. Fortunately, he added, an Italian immigrant was able to construct an inn in concrete with a roof terrace, thereby re-creating this harmony (drawing on a Mediterranean architectural tradition).

Le Corbusier was drawn to Mediterranean culture,[41] while repelled by the Germanic. The two responses were inseparable, like two complementary aspects of the same vision. The opposition between north and south, between the Germanic world and the Latin world, dominated his mind just as it had dominated European thought for generations. Confronted with it at the start of the twentieth century, however, the Swiss architect found himself in a special situation. The Helvetic Confederation of cantons—that is, Switzerland—as shaped and defined by the Constitution of 1848 was still a young country in search of a national identity. In French Switzerland, in the first years of the century, this led to the adoption of an architectural style, later baptized *Heimatstil* (homeland style). It was strongly influenced by the traditional architecture of the old cities of Alemannian Switzerland — an aspect of the international regionalism to which Le Corbusier made concessions in the villas he constructed at La Chaux-de-Fonds between 1906 and 1908.

Around the same time, French Switzerland reacted against Germanic culture, which was also that of Alemannian Switzerland, and began to favor the Mediterranean world, the cradle of Latin culture. In a book entitled *Les Entretiens de la Villa du Rouet*, published in 1908, Alexandre Cingria-Vaneyre (the painter Alexandre Cingria) postulated fictive dialogues set in a villa in Florence during which the tenets of this intellectual movement were debated.[42] Le Corbusier read the book during his stay in Berlin,[43] and several of its ideas later flowed from his own pen, including an admiration for bridges, dams, railways, and other engineering works. The definition of southern architecture offered by Constance, one of the interlocutors in the book, comes very close to his own ideal, which was the development of constructions in terms of width, in the horizontal sense, and a "horizontal or at least flattened termination of roofs and their ridges."[44]

It seems logical to attribute the classical orientation assumed by Le Corbusier's architecture in 1912 in the Villa Favre-Jacot and the Villa Jeanneret to his reading of *Les Entretiens*,[45] but more likely what he found there was an ideological justification for this new orientation. The return to classicism was actually very widespread in Europe beginning around 1910, as evidenced in, for example, the Théâtre des Champs-Elysées by Perret in Paris, the Nouvelle Comédie by Henry Baudin in Geneva, or the Villa Primavesi by Hoffmann in Vienna. It was particularly noticeable in Berlin, in the town halls of Schöneberg and Spandau, or the Reichsmarineamt, not to mention the works of Peter Behrens, especially the Villa Wiegand. Le Corbusier must have been using Mediterranean classicism as a pretext, when in fact he was making use of developments occurring in Germany.[46]

As for Cingria's book, it was not only a manifesto in favor of classicism, but also, through the device of a conversation among friends, a protest against "the false direction our national life is taking," and a call for "again taking up the Latin cause, right to the frontiers of the empire, and for giving French Switzerland the right to live as a culture and as a nation amongst the peoples of Europe." [47] In short it urged an end to German domination. In architecture, this meant a break not only with the Gothic—"a sort of sickness of our European spirit"—but also with the medievalizing picturesque, the "colored roofs" such as those one saw "in the old Swiss towns" whose "Germanic silhouettes affirmed that in the twentieth century Helvetia had definitively

conquered this beautiful and classical corner of the earth."[48] This description is reminiscent of the medieval, or Gothic, town that Le Corbusier attacked sixteen years later in his "L'Esprit nouveau en architecture" (1924).

Jeanneret not only read Cingria's book, but also made the acquaintance of the author, participating in 1916 in a reunion of colleagues from the journal *Cahiers vaudois*.[49] These contacts confirm a recent hypothesis that Cingria's book influenced Jeanneret to return to La Chaux-de-Fonds in 1911, where he would remain for several years.[50] His ultimate disillusionment with his homeland, however, where he found little work, was profound, and when he left in 1917 he was in despair and with scant hope for the future.[51] This departure does not mean that Le Corbusier had made a break with Switzerland, despite the bitterness he later harbored toward his country.[52] His attitude concerning Gothic in the years after World War I, the corollary to his attachment to Latin culture, showed that he was still influenced by ideas he had absorbed within the intellectual milieu of French Switzerland.

His change in attitude came only after 1930, just as a parallel change occurred—quite abruptly—in his architecture, from which the long horizontals of uninterrupted windows disappeared.[53] The Gothic ceased at that time to be either explicitly or implicitly opposed in his mind to the pure forms of Mediterranean classicism. At the time, he even referred to the relationship that Viollet-le-Duc had theorized between materials and construction techniques (though he neglected to cite its source).[54] The essential point for him, however, lay neither in construction nor in form, but in the meaning of the cathedral, understood as an incarnation of the unity of the French people and of their vitality. When in 1937 he entitled a book *Quand les cathédrales étaient blanches*, it was because he saw in these buildings "an act of optimism, a gesture of courage, a sign of pride, a proof of mastery," which he compared to their present condition, covered with the "blackness of soot and corroded by wear."[55] In the fall of 1939, while writing *Sur les quatre routes*, Le Corbusier saw the cathedrals as a symbol of the renewal that France needed.[56] After World War II, in 1946, in his *Manière de penser l'urbanisme* (translated as *Looking at City Planning*), he depicted the cathedral in its glory, fully isolated on all sides, as the center and heart of the city—as it had been seen by German architects from Karl Friedrich Schinkel to Bruno Taut.[57] For Le Corbusier then, as after World War I, the Gothic—whether rejected or exalted—embodied both his loathings and his longings. But since the Romantic era had it ever really been anything else, whether for historians and archaeologists or for artists and poets?

3

JEANNERET, THE CITY, AND PHOTOGRAPHY

Leo Schubert

> I bought myself one of the little Kodak cameras that Kodak was selling at six francs so they could sell film to all the idiots who use it (I was one of them), and I noticed that by entrusting my emotions to a lens I was forgetting to have them pass through me—which was serious. So I abandoned the Kodak and picked up my pencil, and ever since then I have always drawn everything, wherever I am.[1]

THERE ARE SOME 550-PLUS PRINTS from glass plates and negatives in the Fond Le Corbusier-Jeanneret at the Bibliothèque de la Ville de La Chaux-de-Fonds, and other prints are now at the Fondation Le Corbusier in Paris. To look through them all is to realize that Charles-Edouard Jeanneret used his camera regularly, as a work-ing tool, for only a very brief time. More than half of the photographs taken by Jeanneret himself date from his travels in Germany, the Balkans, Turkey, and Italy in 1910–11. In addition a number of pictures were made at later dates, in connection with trips to Russia and Italy, as well as—time and again—in Switzerland. By com-parison, very few date from his first visit to Italy in 1907 (fig. 50). Again, his visits to Vienna and Paris in 1908–9 are recorded by only a few, albeit highly interesting, photographs (see cat. nos. 4, 5). As for the photographic record of his own build-ings, there exists a series of ninety or so pictures taken by him of the Villa Jeanneret-Perret, the house he built for his parents in La Chaux-de-Fonds in 1912 (see figs. 70, 71, 73; cat. no. 19), but his later works were all recorded by professional photographers.[2]

For the photographs that he took between 1907 and the end of 1910, Jeanneret used the Kodak he mentioned above, but the results must have been unsatisfactory to him.[3] As soon as this inexpensive camera is tipped out of horizontal alignment, the square images taken with it (printed from square, roll-film negatives) display the converging lines that are unavoidable with this kind of equipment—a visual defect that reveals that the photographer lacked the proper equipment for architectural work. Early in 1911, to remedy this defect, Jeanneret bought an elaborate (and expensive) camera called a Cupido 80, which he used to make glass or film negatives in roughly $3 \frac{5}{8} \times 4 \frac{3}{4}$ inch (9×12 cm) and $2 \frac{3}{8} \times 3 \frac{5}{8}$ inch (6×9 cm) formats. This camera works to a high standard. The larger format permits a good resolution; the level built into the viewfinder and the "rising front" lens permit perfectly orthogo-nal images to be obtained.[4]

49. Charles-Edouard Jeanneret, Pompeii, Via die Sepolcri, 1911, photograph, BV [7]

50. Charles-Edouard Jeanneret, Venice, the Ca d'Oro from the Canal Grande, 1907, photograph, BV [74]

51. Students of Charles L'Eplattenier's "Cours supérieur d'art et décoration", Villa Matthey-Doret, La Chaux-de-Fonds. Music room (demolished), 1906

"OH THE MIRACLE OF PHOTOGRAPHY!"

Jeanneret's acquisition of the Cupido, shortly before his departure for the Voyage d'Orient—as he called his tour of the Balkans and Turkey—thus flatly contradicts his later assertion that after using the Kodak for a while he abandoned photography for good. The cheap Kodak was indeed laid aside, but it was not really "replaced" by the drawing pencil. It is well known that Jeanneret took photographs assiduously, especially in 1910 and 1911.[5] From Istanbul he wrote in 1911:

> Oh the miracle of photography! Bold lens: what a valuable extra eye! I have treated myself to a terrific camera. It's quite difficult to work with, but the results are perfect, and since April I haven't spoiled a single negative.[6]

Working with this new and complex piece of equipment was indeed time consuming. Obtaining a precise focus on the ground-glass screen demanded practice and patience, as did changing the plates.

Jeanneret's euphoric evocation of the "miracle" of photography had been preceded by some skeptical remarks on the value of the new medium. In a letter from Vienna in 1908 to his mentor, Charles L'Eplattenier, for example, Jeanneret took the view that architecture could not be adequately illustrated solely by photographic means.[7] Here he was referring to the photographs that he had been asked to take of the music room at Villa Mathey-Doret (this room was a collective work by the students of the École d'Art in La Chaux-de-Fonds). His photographs, so he argued, failed to convey the effect of the elaborately contrived wooden decoration, which was based on conscientious study of, and abstraction from, the local countryside (fig. 51). The photographs that L'Eplattenier had given him of interiors in Vienna and Darmstadt by Josef Hoffmann and Joseph Maria Olbrich, respectively, also came in for criticism on the grounds that their superb quality as images glossed over the total absence of structural and aesthetic qualities in the spaces they represented. As a result, Jeanneret's visits to Hoffmann's and Olbrich's buildings had been a "disappointment even more acute because we had before us the stunning reproductions of Hoffmann's interiors that you sent us."[8]

"LA CONSTRUCTION DES VILLES"

From 1910 onward, Jeanneret's career as a photographer was largely inseparable from his intended book on urban planning, a collaboration with L'Eplattenier, which began at that time. The book's working title ("La construction des villes") and the views contained in it, clearly echo Camillo Sitte's work, *Der Städtebau nach seinen künstlerischen Grundsätzen* (1899), which Jeanneret read in the translation by Camille Martin (1902), containing an added chapter on curving street-lines.[9] In June 1910, on his way back from Berlin to Munich, Jeanneret made a four-day detour through some of the most famous and picturesque medieval cities in Germany to collect illustrations for "La Construction des villes." He visited, notably, Halle, Naumburg, Weimar, Jena, Coburg, Lichtenfels, Würzburg, and Rothenburg. Postcards bought en route were used to supplement his photographs. On the backs of these, and in his sketchbooks, he drew plans of the buildings concerned, each with an indication of the camera position. His main interests were streets and squares, fountains and monuments, garden walls and gateways, terraces and monumental flights of steps.[10] The importance that Jeanneret attached to this undertaking is evident from his complaint over the delay in the arrival of eighty or so photographic prints: "You can imagine how disastrous this loss would be to me.

The whole point of my visits to eleven German cities last summer was to take photographs for my book."[11]

And yet, while searching for suitable illustrative material, Jeanneret had written to L'Eplattenier as late as April 1910: "I find that photography doesn't adequately illustrate what we are trying to bring out."[12] How had photography suddenly acquired such importance as to be considered indispensable for the completion of "La construction des villes"?

In discussions of Jeanneret's early studies in urban planning, much is made of the influence of Sitte's writings on L'Eplattenier and his student.[13] This is to undervalue the fact that Jeanneret's reading of Sitte—impeded as it was by the impossibility of locating a copy of the Martin translation in Germany—served merely as the point of departure for his consideration of planning.[14] Among the books that he consulted while impatiently awaiting the arrival of the French edition of Sitte was one work that required no special knowledge of the language. Its layout and the expressive force of its photography influenced a whole generation of artists. This was *Kulturarbeiten*, by Paul Schultze-Naumburg. Published in nine volumes (plus one supernumerary volume) between 1901 and 1917, it constituted a virtual guidebook to architecture, garden design, landscape design, and urban planning.[15] Countless images illustrate the transformation and impoverishment of the urban and rural environment by modern industrial society—and, by contrast, the visual wealth and variety of historic cities.

SCHULTZE-NAUMBURG'S "KULTURARBEITEN"

Schultze-Naumburg's purpose was to open the reader's eyes to the truth that the criteria of conscious visual judgment must extend beyond beautiful/ugly to good/bad, in both senses—both practically usable/unusable and morally good/bad—and that the eye need not be bound by the verbal reasoning that is customarily regarded as the only "logical" form of thought. The eye can draw logical conclusions of its own.[16] Schultze-Naumburg agreed with Sitte that, however true it may be that traditional architecture cannot meet modern requirements, at least the beauty of old buildings must underlie the principles of design which are formulated for purposes of architecture and planning. Where he went beyond Sitte was in his effective use of juxtaposition and contrast to convey his ideas through images. In volume 4, which deals with urban planning, Schultze-Naumburg supplemented Sitte's teaching by exemplifying additional categories of street and square design, both good and bad (see figs. 56, 57); he also discussed individual architectural elements and the ways in which these lend character to the public space.

The result was a morphological vocabulary of elements necessary for construction in traditional cities. With more than 250 photographs per volume, Schultze-Naumburg illustrated street doors and shop windows, garden walls and retaining walls, terracing and flights of steps, arbors and pedestrian passageways, bridges and pedestrian overpasses. At the same time, his "counterexamples" revealed the extent to which these rules of good design and construction had been undermined by modern speculative development and insensitive street design. Jeanneret's intensive engagement with Schultze-Naumburg's *Kulturarbeiten* is confirmed by the quotations in "La construction des villes" and by the illustrations that he traced from volume 4 of the work.[17] Rightly, he identified Schultze-Naumburg as one of the most influential exponents of "neo-Biedermeier," an architect whose designs sprang from the concerns addressed by Paul Mebes in his book *Um 1800*. Wrote Jeanneret: "Schulze-Naumburg [*sic*] has capitulated altogether and copies Louis XVI *word for word*, down

52. The disadvantages of orthogonal street layout from Paul Schultze-Naumburg, *Kulturarbeiten*, vol. 4: *Städtebau*, Munich, 1906, p. 65

53. Charles-Edouard Jeanneret, the disadvantages of orthogonal street layout (after Schultze-Naumburg, *Kulturarbeiten*), ink and pencil on paper, FLC

54. Charles-Edouard Jeanneret, Sketch of the Market Square at Lichtenfels, 1910/11

55. Charles-Edouard Jeanneret, Lichtenfels, Market Square, 1910–11, photograph, BV

56. Example of good street alignment terminating with a view, from Schultze-Naumburg, *Kulturarbeiten*, vol.4

57. Example of bad street alignment, from Schultze-Naumburg, *Kulturarbeiten*, vol.4

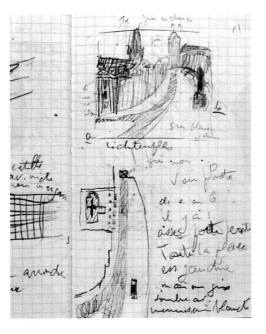

BEISPIEL — 44 —

Abbildung 10

Strasse in Lobeda. Beispiel für gute
Kurvenführung in einer Strassen-
flucht. Durch die Abwickelung
werden alle Hausfronten sichtbar

— 45 — GEGENBEISPIEL

Abbildung 11

Ungünstige Strassenanlage. Die
Strasse führt auf kein sichtbares
Ziel hin. Der Knick wirkt hart.

to the smallest details. His influence is enormous" [emphasis by Jeanneret].[18]

One of the illustrations copied by Jeanneret shows a grid street plan with rectangular blocks, which Schultze-Naumburg used to illustrate the drawbacks of orthogonal traffic flows (see figs. 52, 53). The other shows the consequences of infelicitous street layouts that ignored existing building patterns and it also illustrates by way of comparison a well-contrived layout on sloping ground, created with the aid of terracing.[19] In a caption for a pair of diagrammatic cross sections through different forms of development on an incline, Schultze-Naumburg wrote: "Skillful use of the existing lay of the land for street layouts with terracing," and (the counterexample in this case) "Streets and hillside layout without reference to the lay of the land." In a marginal note, Jeanneret specifically referred to illustrations of outdoor flights of steps in volume 4 of *Kulturarbeiten*.[20]

"PICTURESQUE" TOWNSCAPES IN GERMANY

Jeanneret's reading of *Kulturarbeiten* not only forms the background to his sketches and brief commentaries on the photographs taken in Germany in June 1910 and on the picture postcards bought at the same time, but also explains most of the selected subjects. The intention behind his photograph of the marketplace at Lichtenfels in Upper Franconia, for example, is better understood by studying a sketch of the subject (see figs. 54, 55).[21] In Schultze-Naumburg's terminology

58. Charles-Edouard Jeanneret, Würzburg. St. Burkhard Church, 1910, photograph, BV

59. Pedestrian passage, the Clementinum, Prague, fromSchultze-Naumburg, *Kulturarbeiten*, vol.4

60. Row of houses fronted by a masonry wall, from Schultze-Naumburg, *Kulturarbeiten*, vol.4

61. Charles-Edouard Jeanneret, Würzburg. Theater Street, June 1910, photograph, BV

(figs. 56, 57), this is an "example of good street alignment terminating with a view," combined with a "laterally placed square that forms an island of calm amid the traffic."[22]

The fountain, set to one side of the traffic axis, and the ascending slope of the curved street, are further elements of picturesque urban form. The photograph in this case, however, shows only the gently curved, elongated marketplace itself, with the city gate at the end of it. It does not do justice to the fountain or the square tucked away to one side in front of the church, which are correspondingly emphasized in the sketch. An example of a self-sufficient photographic image is Jeanneret's view of the Prell house in Bamberg, in which—like Schultze-Naumburg in Prague—he illustrated a "front terrace on a corner."[23] Again, Jeanneret's photograph of the church of Saint Burkhard in Würzburg (fig. 58) is matched by a corresponding sketch in his sketchbook, with an arrow to indicate the passageway beneath the apse, also clearly visible in the image. As an "example of a pedestrian connection to ease communication and relieve traffic on the main streets," Jeanneret's photograph is actually more telling than Schultze-Naumburg's view of the Clementinum in Prague (fig. 59).[24]

VOYAGE D'ORIENT

Countless photographs confirm that Jeanneret went on collecting similar examples during the Voyage d'Orient. The visually satisfying motif of a "row of houses fronted by a masonry wall" is illustrated not only by an image of Baroque buildings in Würzburg, but also by an example of village architecture in Bulgaria (figs. 60, 61).[25] There, Jeanneret also found countless variations on the boundary and garden walls described by Schultze-Naumburg, who wrote:

The masonry wall contributes these mood values not only for the interior of the

62. Charles-Edouard Jeanneret, Serbia, Farmhouse with loggia and internal courtyard, June 1911, photograph, BV

63. Goethe's garden house at Weimar, from Schultze-Naumburg, *Kulturarbeiten*, vol.4

site but also for the view from outside.... It is the noblest and most beautiful form of enclosure that exists.... The feelings that a wall arouses in us are so many and various that only the utmost coarsening of our visual sensibilities can explain the emergence of this mass anti-wall campaign.[26]

In the chapter on enclosure walls in "La Construction des villes," Jeanneret wrote:

A wall is beautiful, not only in a physical sense, but also in the thoughts that it can awaken in us. It speaks to us of comfort; it speaks of delicacy; it speaks of power and brutality; it is forbidding or it is welcoming; sometimes it conceals a mystery. A wall always evokes feeling.[27]

Contradicting his own remarks made in 1908, Jeanneret here seemed to assume that photography is quite capable of adequately conveying the principles that underlie good architecture—or, more often, the absence of those principles. His new-found reliance on its ability to reproduce reality was revealed, for instance, by his comment on several photographs (now lost) of La Chaux-de-Fonds: "... the published views of La Chaux-de-Fonds correspond to reality; and it is precisely *that reality* that is defective, and not the lens of our Kodak" [emphasis by Jeanneret].[28]

In the Balkans, far removed from their west European small-town counterparts, Schultze-Naumburg's *Kulturarbeiten* continued to provide a highly effective key to the identification, simplification, and recording of the architectural character of the villages that Jeanneret visited on the advice of his friend William Ritter. A kind of work that had previously been undertaken to illustrate "La construction des villes," now became a tool to enable him to register and understand the experience of architecture. Sketches served the same purpose and followed the same thematic trail as photography. Jeanneret's eye was now schooled to the point where he could recognize in a Serb farmhouse the simple beauty of Goethe's garden house (figs. 62, 63), made up of a wall and a cuboidal structure.[29]

64. Charles-Edouard Jeanneret, Istanbul. Remains of the Beyazit and Ak-Serail quarters after the great fire of August 22, 1911, photograph. BV

MOVING ON FROM SCHULTZE-NAUMBURG: ISTANBUL

Not until Jeanneret reached Istanbul (Constantinople) did his photographs break free from the Schultze-Naumburg model. This was not a city that could be understood in terms of aesthetic categories drawn from *Kulturarbeiten*, which may explain the initial difficulty that the youthful Jeanneret experienced with Istanbul before enthusiasm set in: "It is not at all easy to love Constantinople. You have to work damn hard at it."[30]

It was indeed difficult to discover a formal principle amid the city's chaotic jumble of wooden houses. Ultimately, it was the mosques, with their geometric masses, that defined the city's profile. The photographs of neighborhoods ravaged by fire illustrate this with stark urgency (fig. 64). The townscape had been reduced to the sculptural effect of the mosques and of the house chimneys that were all that remained standing.[31] Accordingly, in photographing buttresses—which in Prague had lent sculptural enrichment to the terraced layout—Jeanneret monumentalized those of Hagia Sofia as abstract, geometric volumes.[32] Was this a logical consequence of a growing disagreement with Sitte's principles and Schultze-Naumburg's aesthetics? Had Jeanneret begun to tire of photographing an endless succession of arbors, garden walls, fountains, courtyards, oriels, and gateways? At least the numerous sketches of such subjects made in Istanbul demonstrate that drawing can present them equally effectively and more economically.

In Athens, the next stop on Jeanneret's Grand Tour, the townscape itself vanished entirely from his photographs. Here, he concentrated on the architecture of the Acropolis (see cat. no. 11). After this, it comes as no surprise that, on his homeward journey through Italy, he photographed almost nothing but large monuments, including the Coliseum, Saint Peter's, and the Basilica of Maxentius, all in Rome, and the Campo Santo in Pisa.

Pompeii was an exception. In the ruins of its villas and gardens, Jeanneret discovered an architecture that formed a far more rewarding study than the cities previously visited (see cat. no. 12). Using his well-tried combination of sketching and photography, he set about recording observations that went far beyond the theories of Sitte and Martin and would have found no place in Schultze-Naumburg's listing of architectural elements.

POMPEII, OR THE DISCOVERY OF THE PROMENADE ARCHITECTURALE

At Pompeii, variety and richness are achieved not through enclosed squares, effective shifts of scale, or curved street lines, but through the axial ordering and sequence of buildings and wall surfaces, the rhythm of light and shade, the dimensions of the individual forms, and their proportions.[33]

Jeanneret photographed these elements in accordance with their architectural significance. The freestanding votive column on the Forum was deliberately isolated and placed on the central axis of the image (fig. 65); the columns lining the courtyard of the gladiatorial barracks and the monuments along Via dei Sepolcri formed a rhythmic accompaniment to the visitor's walk (see fig. 49).[34] By contrast, the prosceniumlike windows in the great walls of the rooms around the atria were an invitation to rest, framing the view of the gardens beyond ("and in the distance the blaze of the garden").[35]

In the villa known as the House of Sallustius, Jeanneret found the happiest architectural application of these combined "principles" of motion and repose. Two photographs and a number of sketches reflect the architectural riches that this building concentrates into the smallest compass. The photograph taken from the atrium, looking out, shows a large room in shadow, on the far wall of which a window 16 feet, 4 ¾ inches wide (5 meters) and 13 feet, 1 ⅛ inches high (4 meters) affords a view of the garden beyond. The window symmetrically frames two columns, intersecting their shafts exactly halfway up (fig. 66).[36] The reverse view holds a surprise that could hardly be greater. Jeanneret photographed the full length of the elegant garden (fig. 67). The columns are revealed as part of a pergola at right

65. Charles-Edouard Jeanneret, Pompeii. Forum with the Temples of Venus and Apollo, 1911, photograph, BV

66. Charles-Edouard Jeanneret, Pompeii. Portico of the Gladiators' Barracks, 1911, photograph, BV

67. Charles-Edouard Jeanneret, Pompeii. House of Sallustius, Atrium, 1911, photograph, BV

66. Charles-Edouard Jeanneret, Pompeii. Portico of the Gladiators' Barracks, 1911, photograph, BV

67. Charles-Edouard Jeanneret, Pompeii. House of Sallustius, Atrium, 1911, photograph, BV

angles to the window axis, with a small fountain at the end. The perspective is accelerated by converging walls, making the walk appear longer than it is (see figs. 68, 69).[37]

Numerous photographs and sketches of the ruins of Pompeii testify to the same eagerness with which, in Germany the year before, Jeanneret had taken pictures to illustrate "La Construction des villes." Here at Pompeii, however, all interiors had been turned into exteriors. The remaining walls stand at a height of around 9 feet, 10 inches (3 meters), and only the ceilings and roofs are lacking. The atria, with their

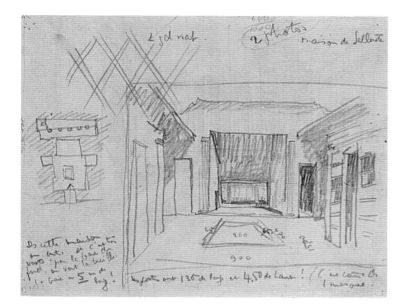

fountains and colonnades, became little plazas, and rooms became patios.[38] The Pompeian villas, with their gardens and sequences of rooms, are miniature cities within a city. Understandably, therefore, in his sketches Jeanneret presented ground plans of houses not as systems of walls but as simplified urban plans. Complexes of rooms became complexes of plazas, and everything that lies behind these was hatched as if it were a solid mass.

In Jeanneret's photographs, strong light and deep shadow define simple geometric forms: the bases of the monuments are simple cubes, the columns cylinders. Like stage flats, the large wall surfaces of the buildings block the view, or free it, or frame it. Jeanneret's observations at Pompeii of wall surfaces, light and volume, vista and axis, interior and exterior space, and the hierarchy and rhythm of architectural elements were recorded in an article on "the illusion of ground plans" in *L'Esprit nouveau* in 1922.[39]

EPILOGUE 1: VILLA JEANNERET-PERRET

Against the background of the photographic strategies just described, it makes sense to consider the ninety or so photographs that Jeanneret took between 1911 and 1919 of the Villa Jeanneret-Perret, the house that he built for his parents (see cat. no. 19). He started work on the design in 1911, a few weeks after his return from the Voyage d'Orient.[40] These photographs were probably the last that he took with his Cupido 80.

The Villa Jeanneret-Perret stands on the sunward slope of Mont Pouillerel, above the city of La Chaux-de-Fonds. Jeanneret had by now learned Schultze-Naumburg's lesson on good and bad hillside development. While the neighboring Fallet, Jaquemet, and Stotzer villas, which he had designed in association with René Chapallaz in 1906–8, had been placed on the slope without terracing, here the difficulties of the terrain were used to enrich both the building and the gardens with the elements of landscape architecture that he had since learned. On the east side, buttresses take the load, as it were, of the hillside, which is steep at this point. On the west side, a massive retaining wall is crowned by a garden terrace and a summerhouse of the kind seen in many photographs of bourgeois villas in Schultze-Naumburg's *Kulturarbeiten*—and also in the hanging gardens that Jeanneret had

68. Charles-Edouard Jeanneret, Pompeii, House of Sallustius, floorplan and view of the atrium, 1911, pencil on squared paper, FLC

69. Charles-Edouard Jeanneret, Pompeii, House of Sallustius, the portico and garden, 1911, pencil on squared paper, FLC

LEO SCHUBERT

70. Charles-Edouard Jeanneret, Villa Jeanneret-Perret, La Chaux-de-Fonds, the pergola and garden, c. 1915–16, photograph, BV [71]

71. Villa Jeanneret-Perret, patio with pergola: Jeanneret's parents, in the background Jeanneret and his brother Albert, c. 1915–16, photograph, FLC

72 . Charles-Edouard Jeanneret, Rome, the choir of St. Peter's, Oct. 1911, photograph, BV

73. Charles-Edouard Jeanneret, Villa Jeanneret-Perret, side view of west façade, 1912 (?), photograph, BV [86]

photographed and sketched in Istanbul (fig. 70).[41] Another frequent feature of his photographs and sketches, the garden wall, was used here as the northern termination of the terrace. On the garden side, it supports a pergola, which Jeanneret photographs from the same angle as the one at the House of Sallustius at Pompeii (fig. 71). Inside the villa, the ground-floor back room is duly dominated by a huge prosceniumlike window. Hung with heavy drapes, this originally framed a view of forest and valley (now obscured by trees). The truth is, however, that the large window seen in Jeanneret's photograph looks less like the House of Sallustius than like the well-known photograph of the music room at Villa Mathey-Doret (see fig. 51). A comparison of two photographs by Jeanneret, one of the exterior of Villa Jeanneret-Perret and another of the right-hand transept of Saint Peter's in Rome (figs. 72, 73), reveals his desire to emphasize in his own building the interplay, observed in Rome, between the prefixed wall and the main structure behind. Another photograph shows the garden with the pillar of the pergola in the foreground on the central axis of the image, just as in the photograph of the votive column at Pompeii. Since the pavilion in the background was not exactly the Temple of Jupiter, nor was its garden terrace the Forum, the image could be said to reveal the limitations imposed on the photographer by the relative inexperience of the architect (fig. 70 and see fig. 65).

On the whole, the photographs of Villa Jeanneret-Perret strongly suggest that in the architecture the intended fulfillment of a wealth of artistic goals has been smothered by the sheer mass of formal references to the architecture, old and new, seen by Jeanneret in Germany and on the Voyage d'Orient. Not until he came to design a second house for his parents—Le Lac, at Corseaux—did Jeanneret succeed in realizing those intentions through a new architectural language.[42]

EPILOGUE 2: "UNE PETITE MAISON"

The "little house" on Lake Geneva—designed while Le Corbusier worked on the 1922 article for *L'Esprit nouveau*, mentioned above—is markedly more modest than the grand Villa Jeanneret-Perret in La Chaux-de-Fonds. By restricting the design to the ascetic formal repertoire of industrial architecture, the architect gave free rein to the unfolding of his formal ideas. The garden-wall theme returns, as does the picture window of the *chambre d'été*, the spacious terrace (this time on the roof, but with a similar concealed flight of steps), and the retaining wall (here facing the lake). Even the isolated column reappears, except that the ponderous support of the pergola has been replaced by a slender iron pole (fig. 74).[43]

All the elements of the design are bound up with a *promenade architecturale*. Through its wealth of planes and volumes, and its unexpected vistas of garden and landscape, this house, with a footprint of only 646 square feet (60 square meters), aims to inspire the emotions that Jeanneret had experienced at Pompeii and sought to recapture at Villa Jeanneret-Perret. Photography was once again involved when, thirty years later, the sixty-year-old Le Corbusier prepared his little book *Une petite maison*, in which thirty-six photographs afford the reader a guided tour of house and garden.[44] The choice and framing of subjects is noticeably similar to his own photographs of the first villa for his parents. By comparison, the twenty-four sketches that accompany the didactic text serve a purely ancillary function.

In view of Le Corbusier's increasing dislike of the photographic medium, it comes as no surprise to find that in his later years he published his own youthful drawings but very few of his own photographs (but see pp. 182, 191). On the other

Une colonne

La maison, ici, a quatre mètres de façade. La porte sur le jardin, trois marches, l'abri.

32

hand, the photographs that he commissioned under the name of Le Corbusier in order to publicize his later buildings—images that made a notable contribution to his success as an architect—show just how much he had learned from his personal experience of photography. If in the case of *Une petite maison*, photography is an indispensable aid to conveying just what Le Corbusier meant by his own important term, *promenade architecturale*, then the same is true for his careful use of photographs from other books and periodicals to reinforce his arguments in his many publications, which had already or were shortly to appear. Time and again he made use of the rhetorical device of example and counterexample, which he had learned from Schultze-Naumburg. He also had no compunction against retouching photographs whenever this suited the argument, and this all the more clearly reveals the true extent of his confidence in the effectiveness of the medium.[45]

4

ARCHITECTURE: PROPORTION, CLASSICISM AND OTHER ISSUES

Francesco Passanti

LE CORBUSIER'S CAREER AS A modernist architect took off in Paris in 1922 with the much-noted diorama of the *Ville contemporaine* at the Salon d'Automne, leading in short order to a book contract for *Vers une architecture* and to four residential commissions, among them the Villas La Roche–Jeanneret (fig. 75). Le Corbusier was thirty-five years old, and a great deal is known about his education and professional life during that first part of his life.[1] Yet we still feel a special thrill, tinged with disbelief, when standing in front of the Villa Favre-Jacot (1912), for example, near Le Corbusier's hometown La Chaux-de-Fonds (figs. 76, 79–81): could the architect of a revolutionary work like the Villas La Roche–Jeanneret possibly have done something as traditional as this, just ten years earlier? If we did not know its author, we might pass this house by as a routine neo-Biedermeier house of the prewar years, like many others from Neuchâtel to Berlin. In fact, even the title of this publication, *Le Corbusier Before Le Corbusier*, plays on such feelings of surprise.

How should one look at such early work by Le Corbusier, or for that matter at the early work—always derivative—of any innovative architect (Frank Lloyd Wright, Mies van der Rohe, and so on)? On the one hand, just seeking early signs of later achievements would be teleological and of limited use, given the gulf separating the early and later work. On the other hand, taking the work on its own terms and not asking what it leads to would lack relevance: after all, the Villa Favre-Jacot is of interest because it is by Le Corbusier. This essay focuses on the process by which the young Le Corbusier constructed his own architectural concept, layering borrowed ideas and personal insights, whether casually encountered or consciously pursued, in a long open-ended process. An early house by Le Corbusier is then seen as the working out of his architectural concerns of that moment, as a way to take stock of those concerns, as an organic whole belonging in that moment, and, at the same time, as a step in the long process of constructing a modernist architectural concept.

In the case of Le Corbusier, attention to the dialogue between concept and design is particularly relevant: throughout his life, he consciously operated at two parallel levels, practice and theory, and this is true also in the early years that interest us here. Aside from his voracious reading, one can document a steady self-reflexive and synthetic effort during his early years, not only in his sketchbooks, notes, and letters, but also in formal texts: the unpublished manuscript, "La Construction des villes" (1910); the booklet *Etude sur le mouvement d'art décoratif en Allemagne* (1912); the articles "La Maison Suisse" (1913) and "Le Renouveau dans l'architecture" (1914); the text for *Le*

75. Le Corbusier and Pierre Jeanneret, Villa La Roche–Jeanneret, Paris, 1923–25. View from the Square du Docteur Blanche

76. Charles-Edouard Jeanneret, Villa Favre-Jacot, Le Locle, 1912, library pavilion (Chambre de Monsieur)

77. Raphael, Villa Madama, Rome, begun 1516

78 . Peter Behrens, Villa Obenauer, Saarbrücken, 1905–6

Voyage d'Orient (finished 1914, but not published until 1966); the booklet *Après le Cubisme* (1918) with Amédée Ozenfant, and articles in *L'Esprit nouveau* beginning in 1920, leading to *Vers une achitecture* in 1923 and beyond.

This essay, then, examines some of Le Corbusier's early work against the concerns that occupied him at that time. It focuses primarily on two works, the Villa Favre-Jacot (1912) and the Villa Schwob (1916), a selection that is not meant to represent the range of designs tackled by Le Corbusier in those years, but to enable a rich discussion of the issues.

VILLA FAVRE-JACOT

The Villa Favre-Jacot (figs. 76, 79–81) was built for the wealthy owner of the Zenith Watch Company in the town of Le Locle near La Chaux-de-Fonds.[2] Le Corbusier designed it in February–April 1912, immediately after the Villa Jeanneret for his parents. He was fresh from four years of study abroad, which left a strong imprint in his design (see chap. 1). These years had consisted of a long exposure to modern practice (notably in the offices of Auguste Perret in Paris and Peter Behrens in Berlin), followed by a half-year visit to classic paradigms in Turkey, Greece, and Italy (the study trip that he called the Voyage d'Orient).[3]

The villa is built on a spectacular site where an earlier chalet had been, on a preexisting artificial podium, halfway up a promontory where two faces of the mountain meet, with a view wider than 180 degrees. The podium, on which the villa and its garden sit, is on one side of the promontory and parallel to one face of the mountain. The sloping access road is on the other face of the mountain, hence it meets the house on a diagonal. The site is difficult, narrow and long, but the house mocks the constraints, multiplies its parts, and spreads on its platform with apparent ease, as if the steep slope were no problem at all.

The public front, however, gives no inkling of the playfulness beyond. It is a facade of unpretentious symmetry and bourgeois comfort, specifically recalling the architecture of the early nineteenth century—its vernacular examples, its great architect Karl Friedrich Schinkel, and recent elaborations by Behrens.[4] Reference to this architecture was fashionable in the cultural sphere of early twentieth-century Germany, and it was meant to bring up a time, *um 1800* (c. 1800), that was modern yet still free from the dislocations of industrialization: it evoked a harmonious modernity and implied a public debate about the kind of modernity present society may strive for.[5]

The road approaches the house from the right, on a slight diagonal, protected on the mountain side by a low retaining wall. In front of the house, the wall spirals to a stop after forming two wings around a forecourt, with an arrangement recalling French *hôtels particuliers* and that paradigmatic house on a slope, the Villa Madama by Raphael (fig. 77). The spiral winds itself around a circle which is marked on the pavement, and the center of the circle is displaced to the right from the axis of the door; the facade responds, in turn, with an echo of its own profile sliding out on the right. Thus, a silent dialogue takes place between diagonal road and sliding facade. And through this dialogue Le Corbusier articulates not only their relationship, but also that between horizontal platform and sloping mountain, between two faces of the mountain meeting at the promontory, and ultimately between the human ideal of symmetry and the varied circumstances of nature.

To the sober symmetry of the facade corresponds, inside, a formal axial procession—entry, vestibule, hall, and salon or living room (see fig. 80)—based on the plan of Behrens's Cuno house (1909), itself inspired by Schinkel and, through him, by antiquity. Like that of the Cuno house, the procession here is checked by the transverse

79. Charles-Edouard Jeanneret, Villa Favre-Jacot, Le Locle, 1912, entry court, photograph

80. Charles-Edouard Jeanneret, Villa Favre-Jacot, Le Locle, 1912, plan of the ground floor

81. Charles-Edouard Jeanneret, Villa Favre-Jacot, Le Locle, 1912, view from the garden (the dormers were altered later), photograph

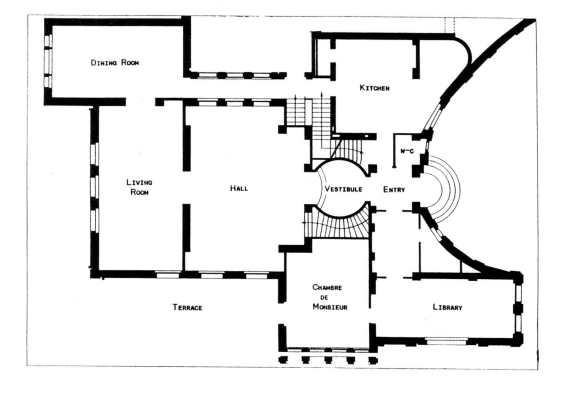

82. Athens, the Erechtheion, plan

83. Charles-Edouard Jeanneret, Pompeii, sketch plan of the House of the Tragic Poet, 1911

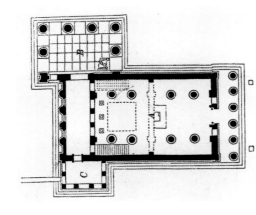

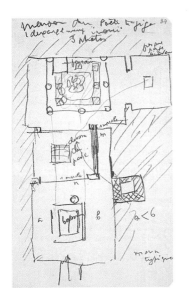

orientation of the spaces and by the unexpected quality of each space. After a compressed entry, the top-lit cylinder of the vestibule rises through the second floor. Then the hall arrests the visitor by its vast expanse, hesitating between square and transversal rectangle, and by the bright light streaming in from right and left. The transversal salon follows, with windows, relatively narrow and far apart, overlooking an intimate, sunken rose garden but affording no access to it. Rather than providing a Baroque escape into deep vistas, this situation throws one back to the central hall, which acts like a Roman atrium or tablinum, the psychological center of inward-looking houses that Le Corbusier had often sketched in Pompeii during his trip.

Around the axial sequence and its center, the house develops centrifugally into a variety of asymmetric situations. To the left and back from the hall is the private business suite of the owner, acknowledged on the outside as a separate block, and overlooking the valley through an emphatic colonnade. To the right and forward from the salon is the dining room, housed in a pedimented tempietto jutting out of the main block of the house. Just as the central axial sequence was indebted to Behrens's Cuno house, so its centrifugal counterpoint, juxtaposing a large symmetrical block with smaller appendages pinwheeling out asymmetrically, was probably suggested by Behrens's Obenauer house, which may also have inspired some formal plays on the entry facade (fig. 78).

If, on the entry side, Le Corbusier articulated the topographic tensions of the site, inside and toward garden and valley, he articulated its luxuries: the surprise, the freedom, the delight of being perched high and narrow yet being free to stretch like a cat in the sun, the delight of possessing an unlimited view yet cozying in contained security. In conceptualizing an architectural expression for these luxuries, Le Corbusier was helped not only by Behrens's example, but also by several older and paradigmatic models which mediated, so to speak, between site and architecture, and which further extended the timeless resonance already present in Behrens's modern precedent.

The most obvious model is the Erechtheion, the "happy" temple on the Acropolis, where Le Corbusier affectionately sought respite from the crushing power of the Parthenon. Like the villa, the Erechtheion is placed on a cliff overlooking the landscape and shows a different face in each direction. And, like the villa, it comprises a main and relatively closed rectangular block with a formal facade at one end, and two attached pavilions on the sides, pointing in different directions (fig. 82).[6] The Erechtheion helped Le Corbusier to articulate a poetic expression for the circular sweep of situations that the site offered, from access slope to wide view to intimate garden.

Another model is the House of the Tragic Poet in Pompeii (fig. 83). During Le Corbusier's visit there, this house had struck him by its mix of axiality, centrality, and asymmetry.[7] Here, it helped Le Corbusier to articulate a sense of playful containment and respite from the power of the landscape; at the same time, it helped reconcile the axiality of the Cuno house with the centrifugal sweep of the Erechtheion. In the House of the Tragic Poet, the axial procession moves through the fauces, atrium, tablinum, and peristyle; to the right of the peristyle is the triclinium. In Le Corbusier's villa, after a narrow door (the fauces), the procession moves through a stairhall lit from above and up a step through the hall (a free combination of atrium and tablinum) and through the transversal salon in contact with the garden (the peristyle); to the right, after a zigzag, one reaches the dining room (the triclinium).

A further "antique" model, which helped Le Corbusier in conceptualizing the villa as a collection of separate and ambiguously related parts, is the so-called gardener's house ("Gärtnerhaus") at Charlottenhof near Potsdam, by Schinkel, a complex

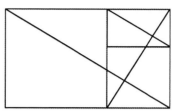

repeatedly visited and photographed by Le Corbusier when he worked nearby in Behrens's office (fig. 84). Behind the house but not directly accessible from its rooms, Schinkel placed a square parterre with flower patterns and central fountain, paralleled by Le Corbusier's square rose garden. To the side, Schinkel had a freestanding tempietto opening to a terrace separated from the parterre by a parapet: Le Corbusier echoed this with the dining room pavilion and its raised parapeted terrace.

All three of these models pushed the design in the direction of a rich assembly of parts, thus raising, at the same time, the issue of control—of each part and of their mutual relationships. In this, Le Corbusier relied on the lessons of Behrens and, through him, of Schinkel. From Schinkel's Altes Museum, for example, he borrowed the giant order that pulls together the main block at its corners, with the characteristic separation of corner pier and adjoining wall.[8] From both Schinkel and Behrens, Le Corbusier learned to control the tension of symmetry and asymmetry: the relationship of parterre, tempietto, and house in Schinkel's gardner's house, and the relationship of projecting pavilion and main block in Behrens's Obenauer house, can be compared with the sliding symmetry of the entry facade in Le Corbusier's villa.[9] Finally, in Behrens's office, Le Corbusier refined his use of proportions, a theme exemplified in the plan and entry facade of the villa.[10]

The Villa Favre-Jacot is an early example of Le Corbusier's lifelong use of the golden section (the ratio $\Phi = 1.618\ldots$)[11] While, in his later book *Le Modulor* (1950), Le Corbusier spoke of this ratio mathematically, as the proportional subdivision or multiplication of linear segments on a measuring tape, in his early work he seems to have operated geometrically in terms of golden rectangles, that is, rectangles in which the ratio of long versus short side equals the golden one. A key property of such rectangles is that, if you start from a golden rectangle and remove from it the inscribed square, you are left with a smaller golden rectangle at 90 degrees from the first (fig. 85); and vice versa, if you add, side-by-side, a square and a vertical golden rectangle of equal height, their sum is a horizontal golden rectangle. The square, then, is an inherent component of golden rectangles; and it is from this property that a system of golden rectangles derives its remarkable combinative richness and visual legibility.[12]

In the plan of the Villa Favre-Jacot (figs. 80, 86), the block containing the main spaces of the axial procession is a golden rectangle divided in three parallel transversal bands roughly corresponding to stairwell, main hall, and salon. At the center of the block, the transversal rectangle of the main hall is then extended into a square of such

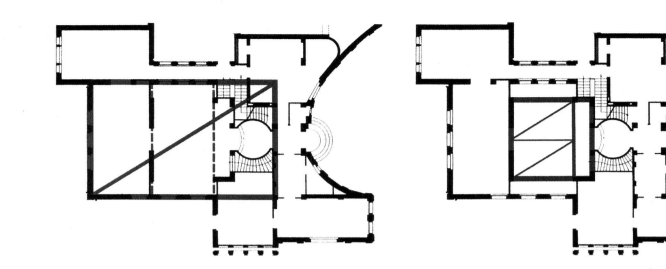

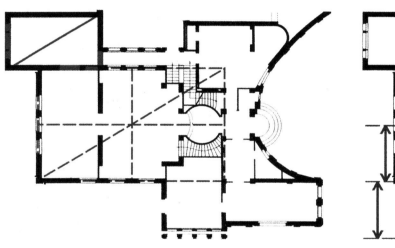

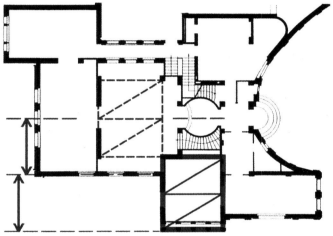

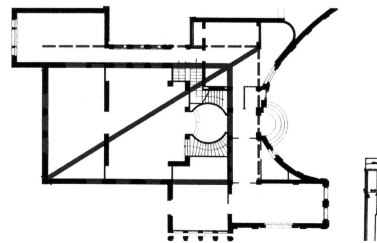

86 . Charles-Edouard Jeanneret, Villa Favre-Jacot, Le Locle, 1912, plans with proportional diagrams

87. Charles-Edouard Jeanneret, Villa Favre-Jacot, Le Locle, 1912, elevations with proportional diagrams

dimensions that the overlap of the two figures is a double golden rectangle (two golden rectangles sharing a long side). At the periphery of the block, the dining room is a golden rectangle echoing that of the block and one quarter its area, while the owner's room is a double golden rectangle identical to that at the center of the house. The dimensions of the main rooms having thus been set, the principal block is extended along its diagonal to achieve the L-shaped layer of service circulation radiating from the kitchen, and this extension is then acknowledged on the entry side by the "sliding" facade.[13] Finally, the smaller subsidiary spaces (including the owner's library) are given proportions based on golden rectangles.

In the entry facade (figs. 79, 87), the pivot of the whole composition is the monumental square window at the center—or better, a system of two framing squares, one inside the other and with dimensions related through the golden ratio (that is, the ratio of their sides is $S/s = O$).[14] This figure has an important property: if the bottom side of the smaller square is prolonged in both directions, the portion of the bigger square located above this line is a double golden rectangle, composed of two golden rectangles side-by-side. Thus, the same figure that we have encountered at the center of the plan (square with inscribed double golden rectangle) is already announced at the center of the facade, setting a note that the visitor will encounter throughout the house. This figure, with its implied proportional extensions through squares and golden rectangles, reverberates throughout the facade.[15]

For the viewer these proportional figures of the elevation achieve unity and control by establishing rhythmic correspondences: between facade and plan, as already mentioned; between the entry facade and the other ones; and, within the entry facade, between its various parts. At a more poetic level, the proportional figures on the facade articulate the tensions of both plan and facade, and, through them, those of the site. They set up plays between center and periphery by calling attention to the center and then echoing it in the periphery, for example by repeating the central square in the termination of the left wing. It is in the very structure of the proportional system, however, that the tensions of the site find their most poetic embodiment. Just as the front of the house interprets them through the lateral sliding of one facade behind the other, so the system of proportional figures on the facade is pervaded by this "sliding" theme too. After a first impression of square clarity, any attempt to make sense of the proportions of the facade immerses the visitor in the ambiguities of overlapping figures, as if the whole facade were a deck of cards spread out to create the various fields of the elevation.

All in all, the Villa Favre-Jacot is a work of considerable erudition and richness of meaning, and it announces aspects of Le Corbusier's later work, from ambiguous plays of symmetry and asymmetry (as in the villas La Roche–Jeanneret and Stein) to the use of golden proportions. Still, it is a derivative work heavily influenced by Behrens and fitting easily within the current fashion of *um 1800* classicism. What makes this work, and others of the same period, part of an itinerary that we can reconstruct retrospectively, lieading to Le Corbusier's modernist architecture?

The next sections of this essay will analyze specific concerns of Le Corbusier, beginning with some that obviously affected the design of the villas Jeanneret and Favre-Jacot (proportion, classicism, volume), and continuing with others that came into focus later (type, *Sachlichkeit*). In all this Le Corbusier's concerns will be seen as durable and evolving over time, while his designs will be seen as discrete events where those concerns come together at a particular moment and are modified by their interaction, to then continue and enter into later designs. The Villa Schwob (1916) will be discussed as one of those discrete events.

Our understanding of Le Corbusier's attitude to architectural proportions has been heavily influenced by his book *Le Modulor*, published late in his life (1950). On the one hand, the book encourages a Platonic understanding of architectural proportions, both because it posits a direct correspondence between the human body and the golden section and because its date of publication suggests comparison with the Platonic argument of Rudolf Wittkower's *Architectural Principles in the Age of Humanism* (1949). On the other hand, a short autobiographical section early in the book describes a young man spontaneously rediscovering some ancient forgotten knowledge, not a student routinely learning current practice.[16] Thus framed—as Platonic absolutes and ancient expertise—architectural proportions have been seen as the academic, classical, or transcendent counterpart to his modernism.[17]

But how did Le Corbusier see architectural proportions in 1912, when he designed the Villa Favre-Jacot? He was then focused more on artistic will and visual effect than on transcendent truth. His most recent mentor, Peter Behrens, attributed no metaphysical value to architectural proportions. And far from discovering proportions by happenstance and spontaneously, one can fairly say that Le Corbusier could not not have learned methodically about proportions, so pervasive was their presence, both in his education and in the practice of contemporary architects, from his teachers Perret and Behrens to Hendrik Petrus Berlage, Theodor Fischer, Edwin Lutyens, and others.[18]

Indeed, as early as elementary school Le Corbusier was taught proportional geometric constructions, such as one used to draw spirals.[19] This early teaching of geometric drawing, widespread in Europe since the educational reforms sparked by the Great Exhibition of 1851 in London, was meant to develop, early on, the visual abilities useful for future decorators and skilled workers. This ability was then further developed by Le Corbusier's training in art school, initially meant to make a watch engraver of him. By the time he left school, Le Corbusier was an expert at geometric manipulation.

His first built work, the Villa Fallet of 1906–7, was based on a proportional system inspired by Viollet-le-Duc, who had analyzed Gothic buildings in terms of diagonals in plan and triangles in elevation (fig. 88).[20] We cannot tell whether this use of *tracés générateurs* (generating lines) was Le Corbusier's initiative—he could have read Viollet-le-Duc in the library of the École d'Art—or whether it came from René Chapallaz, a more experienced local architect who supervised the design. In any case, what matters is that Le Corbusier was exposed to these concepts. Soon after, he read Charles Blanc's *Grammaire des arts du dessin* (1867), where he could find the classical view that architectural proportions set the harmonious and anthropomorphic relationship of the parts and the whole.[21] This view was certainly echoed in classes that he attended at the École des Beaux-Arts and in conversations with Auguste Perret, who had a Beaux-Arts education.[22]

Equally important, in Perret's office Le Corbusier was exposed not only to ideas, but also to the practice of architectural proportions taught at the École des Beaux-Arts. An analysis of Perret's work, since his student days and well into the 1920s, shows that virtually every one of his designs made use of some geometric scheme to set the overall outline of the composition: this includes a facade that Le Corbusier worked on during his employment in the office.[23] Perret's schemes tend to be simple, based on squares, on so-called Egyptian triangles, and on their combination in a famous diagram by Auguste Choisy, who had extended Viollet-le-Duc's geometric

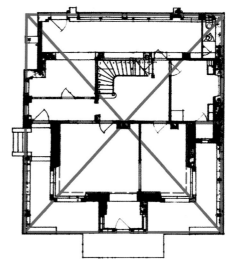

88 . Charles-Edouard Jeanneret, René Chapallaz, Villa Fallet, La Chaux-de-Fonds, 1906–07, south elevation and plan of the ground floor with proportional diagrams. BV

89. Peter Behrens, Bootshaus Elektra, Berlin-Oberschöneweide, 1910–12. Plan with diagrams

90. Peter Behrens, Villa Obenauer, Saarbrücken, 1905–6, plan with diagrams

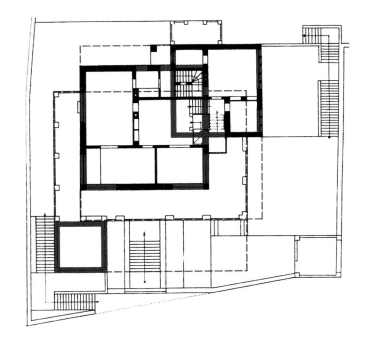

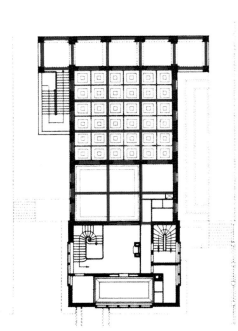

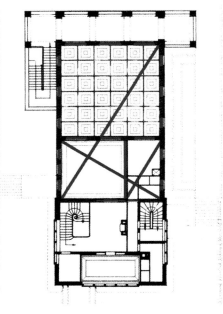

approach to the study of Greek architecture.[24] By the time Le Corbusier left Perret, then, he was familiar with Viollet-le-Duc's notion of *tracé générateur de proportions* and with its recasting by Choisy, the *tracés régulateurs* (regulating lines): geometric constructions, often hidden, used by the architect as a practical design aid and inherently capable of generating mysterious mathematical harmonies. It is this French intellectual tradition that Le Corbusier invoked in 1921 when he published his first essay on proportions and called it "Les Tracés régulateurs."[25]

Next, in Behrens's office, Le Corbusier layered a different outlook upon these many approaches—an outlook focused on expression rather than on inherent harmony. Behrens's views were part of the German aesthetic discourse focused on form and the psychology of visual perception (Konrad Fiedler, Heinrich Wölfflin, and others).[26] Within this discourse, the standard statement about architectural proportions was August Thiersch's *Proportionen in der Architektur* (1883). Building on the classic aesthetic category of "unity in variety," Thiersch drew a startlingly simple rule: what matters is not this or that proportion, but the repetition of the same proportion throughout a work, creating a visual analogy of the parts with each other and with the whole—hence the most characteristic visual feature of his illustrations, the presence of parallel diagonals drawn over plans and elevations to indicate the similar proportion of their rectangular components.[27] Despite (or maybe thanks to) its overly simplistic quality, Thiersch's book durably focused the German practice of architectural proportions on what the eye can see, rather than on some mysterious underlying order.[28] This was also the slant of Fritz Hoeber in his doctoral thesis of 1906, a systematic survey of proportional theories in architecture from antiquity to the present, based on the premise that "the meaning of proportions is not intrinsic but only a matter of their effect" (*Wirkung*).[29] While working within the same intellectual categories of Thiersch, Hoeber overcame his simplistic conclusions, and ended up advocating complex systems, particularly those based on the golden section.

Much like Hoeber, who in 1913 would publish a monumental monograph on him, Behrens was singlemindedly interested in *Wirkung*, the visual effect on the viewer, and had eclectically integrated into that concern techniques taken from Viollet-le-Duc's Dutch followers J. L. M. Lauweriks and Berlage, as well as from Thiersch, and others.[30] Two points must be stressed here.

First, from a technical point of view, proportions were clearly a routine practice in Behrens's office, since Behrens designed not only buildings but also a continuous stream of graphics for the Allgemeine Eliktrizitäts Gesellschaft (AEG), and all of them—buildings and graphics—clearly entailed proportional systems and rhythmic visual patterns: plays of squares, modular grids, $\sqrt{2}$ rectangles, golden rectangles, circles, and so on. Also, while Le Corbusier was working in Behrens's office in 1910–11, Hoeber was probably there as well, gathering material for the monograph that he would publish in 1913. Hoeber's thesis was certainly well known in the office as was Thiersch's book.[31] In short, Le Corbusier had probable access not only to a practice, but also to a resident expert and to textbooks as well. Added to the practical expertise that Le Corbusier already possessed from his years in school and in Paris, this explains his remarkable virtuosity in the use of proportions after his return to La Chaux-de-Fonds.[32]

Second, from an artistic point of view, Behrens used proportional systems expressively, or one might say musically, to set a theme and then play on its variations, to set a rule and then willfully break it, to set up several clashing rules and then willfully reconcile them.[33] The expressiveness of Behrens's proportions lies in the *structure* of the proportional system, not in any intrinsic quality of a particular proportion. To name just two examples relevant to Le Corbusier, first in the Obenauer house of 1905, both plan and elevation draw their emotive power from the sliding overlaps of squares and golden rectangles (fig. 90)[34]: Le Corbusier used a similar "sliding" quality in the Villa Favre-Jacot. Second, in the AEG recreational club Bootshaus Elektra of 1910, a project on which Le Corbusier worked while in the office, the front part of the plan is of interest (fig. 89). Behrens set up a modular (additive) system of squares that combine to form a large square hall, a smaller square meeting room, and a rectangular service space; he then forced this modular arrangement to fit the more organic and well-known figure of three spiraling golden rectangles. Since golden ratios are irrational numbers, they are theoretically incompatible with modular subdivisions and can only be approximated by them: hence, some fudging is necessary, and this is why the squares are slightly compressed in their longitudinal direction.[35] One can read the whole thing as the forcing together of two incompatible systems; as the approximation of a golden scheme through an additive modular grid (numerically, the approximation of the golden ratio $\varnothing = 1.618\ldots$ by the ratio of whole numbers $5/3$); or finally as the striving of an additive system toward an organic form, imposed by the artist's will. This latter reading is probably how Le Corbusier saw it; he used the same device later, in his *Ville contemporaine*.

In Behrens's office Le Corbusier had seen how one may think about architectural proportions in a modernist key, in which proportions do not stand for the authority of tradition or for a metaphysical harmony, but are expressive means in the architect's hands, like a language or a musical scale, which may be used to signify any number of contents.[36] Thus Le Corbusier's knowledge of proportions, acquired gradually since his school years, could be aligned with the broad aesthetic approach that he was developing at this time, influenced by symbolist painting and poetry.

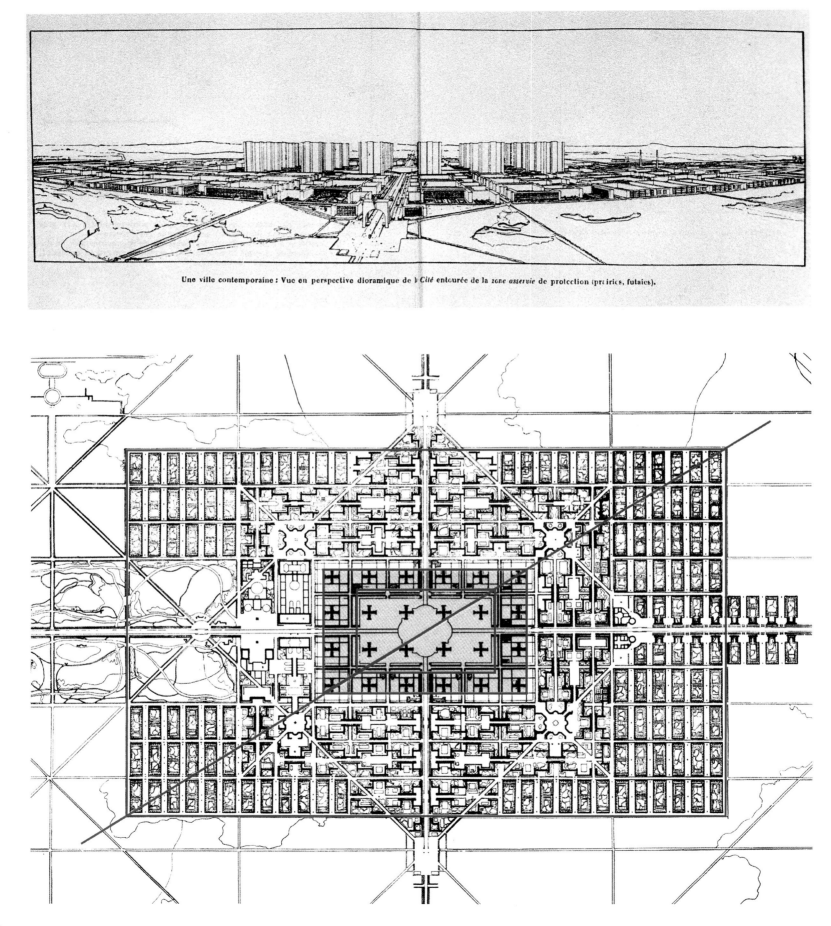

Une ville contemporaine : Vue en perspective dioramique de la *Cité* entourée de la *zone asservie* de protection (prairies, futaies).

In Le Corbusier's work, proportions will serve a variety of purposes. Some recur throughout his oeuvre—for example, the achievement of an identity and a unity of intent in each design, as he explained in "Les tracés régulateurs" when describing the effect of "regulating lines" in Michelangelo's Campidoglio: "The work...pulls inward, centers itself, unifies itself, expresses the same law throughout its mass, becomes massive."[37] Other purposes are specific to each case, for example the poetic articulation of the site in the Villa Favre-Jacot. One more example is discussed below.[38]

In the *Ville contemporaine* of 1922, the basic pattern throughout the plan is a modular grid of squares, established by the twenty-four skyscrapers downtown (figs. 91, 92). At the center of the city Le Corbusier placed a public square of sorts; a continuous building, four stories high and terraced down toward the center with cafés and shops, encloses a rectangular space of very large dimensions, a sort of giant Place des Invalides containing the central station and an airport (today we would say heliport) and the inner eight skyscrapers. But while the skyscrapers, inside and outside this ribbon building, are on a regular square grid, the "urban square" has a rectangular form that does not fit that grid. It is a golden rectangle, and in order to achieve golden proportions it must violate the square grid of streets; hence it must run outside the grid on two sides, and inside the grid on two other sides. We recognize the tension of proportional systems learned from Behrens. Looking down from an approaching airplane or from a café on one of the terraces, the visitor is meant to experience both the utilitarian practical reality of the grid (which, in itself, is formless) and the ideal goal that it is meant to strive for. The proportions of the "square" are the DNA, the guiding intent that is meant to govern the growth of the city. And indeed, around it, the masses of the skyscrapers form a composite block with proportions close to the golden ratio,[39] while farther out, as new rings of housing are added, the edge of the city is approximating a golden rectangle again.

CLASSICISM

What did classicism mean for Le Corbusier at the time of his Villa Favre-Jacot? At one level, of course, it meant joining the dominant architectural trend in Germany and France.[40] Yet his espousal of classicism had involved a difficult conversion, reluctant both in terms of artistic beliefs and personal allegiances and driven by motives deeper than professional opportunism.

In tune with the Ruskinian education that he had received from his teacher Charles L'Eplattenier, Le Corbusier had been intensely opposed to classicism at first. Attention went to nature and its growth process, to the artist's process of invention and making, and to medieval precedents. When Le Corbusier visited Tuscany, fresh out of school in 1907, he looked almost exclusively at things medieval. But, even then this medievalism coexisted in Le Corbusier with a mythicized and ultimately classicist view of the south, "that land where lemon trees blossom," in Goethe's wonderful words. Like Goethe more than a century earlier, Le Corbusier entered Italy by boat (on the lake of Lugano); during the trip he spent two days on a steamer sailing up and down Lake Garda, with its cypresses, olive trees, and terraced winter shelters for lemon trees (fig. 93); and he exited Italy by boat from Venice—as if Italy were a dream land set in a mythical sea.[41]

The same tension continued in 1908 in Paris. He insistently visited the cathedral of Notre-Dame and, while studying architectural history, he derided the Renaissance ("by its contrary...I learn what architecture is") and praised the Romanesque and Gothic ("there it becomes evident what architecture is").[42] In the following spring, he resisted for months Perret's suggestion that he visit Versailles, because he considered

91. Le Corbusier, Ville contemporaine pour 3 millions d'habitants, perspective view, 1922, from: Le Corbusier, *Urbanisme*

92. Le Corbusier, Ville contemporaine pour 3 millions d'habitants, plan with diagrams, 1922

93. Lake Garda near the town of Limone, with wooden shelters for lemon trees, postcard acquired by Le Corbusier in 1907, BV

classicism "decadent."[43] That visit turned out to be a revelation; in Le Corbusier's later words, "classical clarity revealed itself."[44] And yet, a full year later, in April–May 1910, Le Corbusier still admired the medieval charm of old Stuttgart and several medievalizing buildings by Carl Moser and Theodor Fischer, and he advocated picturesque curved streets in his manuscript on urban planning, "La Construction des villes."[45]

Le Corbusier's ambivalence was suddenly resolved in June 1910, during a short visit in Berlin to see several exhibitions. By the end of the visit he was admiring Louis XV interiors at the palace of Sans-Souci and had decided to seek work with Peter Behrens or Bruno Paul, both of them classicists.[46] On the way back from Berlin, he rejected the picturesque medieval fabric of Augsburg because "modern life cannot fit in there any more."[47] Back in Munich he completed his chapter on streets for "La Construction des villes," with an emotional paean to the straight street that totally upended his previous advocacy of the curved one.[48] By September 30 he was planning the ultimate apostasy for a Ruskinian Gothicist, a stay in Rome to study Bramante's architecture.[49] And on January 16, 1911, he finally dared to declare his new beliefs to L'Eplattenier: "So, all my enthusiasm goes now to Greece and Italy, and I have a merely eclectic interest for those arts that give me discomfort, northern Gothic, Russian barbarisms, German torments."[50]

What happened in Berlin in June 1910 to so radically resolve his conflicting feelings? Meetings and visits organized by the Deutsche Werkbund, which he attended, certainly confirmed what he could see in architectural magazines, the dominance of classicism among the top German architects. More important, a visit to Sans-Souci brought back his memories of Versailles and his nostalgia for the south. Still, there were no really new factors in any of this for Le Corbusier. The decisive new developments probably had to do more with modern life than with architecture or personal attachments.

On the first day in Berlin, fresh off the night train, Le Corbusier toured the AEG factories with a group from the Deutsche Werkbund, devoting most of his notes not to Behrens's buildings but to the industrial production process inside:

> My absolute admiration for the genial engineers and managers of this colossal operation is balanced by dismay and pain, as I see these thousands of men and women at the service of machines and less skillful than they are. Soon, human arms will be totally useless. I saw several machines watched over by just one man. The most varied operations are done automatically.[51]

Then, on the third day, Le Corbusier visited the Ton-Kalk-Zement exhibition devoted to the new artificial building materials, such as asbestos cement, artificial limestone, linoleum, and paneling, eventually commenting: "There is enough there to seriously shake our principles about true and false. Anyhow, those materials are very beautiful."[52]

Thus, in just a few days, two pillars of his earlier Ruskinian aesthetic were demolished: the emphasis on individual invention and making (hence the belief that the meaning of an artifact resides in the traces of the human labor that produced it), and the importance of truth. They were demolished not by an argument, but by a reality—industry—at once impersonal and normative, too big to be ignored, and superior in the quality of its products.[53] With this the emphasis shifted from creativity in detail to organization of the whole, and the hierarchical, normative, and artificial aesthetic of classicism, so long avoided by Le Corbusier, acquired a purpose and could now fill a void. At the same time, Le Corbusier's professional self-image underwent a shift of scale from small to large, from details to systems, from decorator to architect; and classicism provided the means for conceptualizing and controlling the new scale. In Le Corbusier's own words a few months later:

> Ah, but I do owe them a candle, to those Germans, for wrenching me from my medievalizing morass, by showing me those admirable styles . . .Versailles . . . classical clarity. But it sure took a long time before I managed to rid myself of so many small petty things that made me see architecture very small [emphasis added].[54]

Le Corbusier's conversion aligned him with the mainstream in German architecture, which had collectively undergone a similar shift, ultimately driven by the same reasons, during the previous decade. After the Berlin visit, his new receptivity to classicism was formalized by reading Albert E. Brinckmann's *Platz und Monument*, which praised the uniformity of detail and the large formal gestures of Renaissance, Baroque, and eighteenth-century urbanism and its classical architecture. Brinckmann asserted, like many others at that moment, that the eighteenth-century was closest to modern sensibility, and that modern planners and designers should reconnect to the classicism of that time.[55] Since the fall of 1910 Le Corbusier worked in Behrens's office, where he learned the formal rules of classicism.

Le Corbusier's personal itinerary, then, directly connected classicism and modernity and thus put him in line with the views of Brinckmann, Behrens, and others. For them and Le Corbusier, in those years, classicism was not about the past, but about an appropriate expression of the present.[56] It was part of a broader pursuit of cultural unity, seeking to convey unity through not only classicism, but also traditional building types, or the new building types and products of industry and commerce—all solutions perfected anonymously and collectively, and for that very reason representative of society as a whole, in opposition to the individualist excesses of Art Nouveau.[57] Within such a perspective, which was articulated by the discourse on *Sachlichkeit* (factualness), it would be possible to substitute classicism with the artifacts of modern life as signifiers of modernity—moving from a Villa Favre-Jacot to a Villa Savoye, for example, with its vocabulary partly borrowed from transatlantic liners and ordinary use objects.

VOLUME

A new sensitivity to architectural volume is immediately apparent if we compare the villas Jeanneret and Favre-Jacot (both designed soon after Le Corbusier's return from his study abroad) with the earlier villas Fallet, Jaquemet, and Stotzer. The Villa Jeanneret is treated as a cubic mass bound by walls and held together by a molding at the corners, in a conscious pursuit of volumetric control: in fact, the row of colonnettes at bedroom level, which was initially dark, was repainted white "to help the cube," as Le Corbusier wrote in a letter.[58] In the Villa Favre-Jacot, a large central block is bound by clear stretches of wall on the garden side and by a network of moldings on the entry facade; it is pulled together at the corners by a giant order and consciously juxtaposed to smaller blocks, some more open than others, but each clearly bound as a unit. All this contrasts with the earlier works: the Villa Fallet was very much an open structure, a fragmented assembly of masonry protected by the wide overhang of a thin roof; villas Jaquemet and Stotzer exhibited massive buttresslike walls, but the overall envelope of the building was fragmented and open.

A fundamental change, then, occurred during the years spent abroad (1908–11), and Le Corbusier acquired a new permanent category. What did this change and the new category of architectural volume mean for Le Corbusier at this point? On one level, like classicism, it meant a change of scale, a shift from decorator to architect. On another level, it meant a change in aesthetic outlook.

Le Corbusier's new awareness of architectural volume marked a new attention to form—a change from his early Ruskinian interest in nature, material, and process, and from his Parisian interest in structure and distribution. Early indications that Le Corbusier had acquired new formal concepts are found in his manuscript "La Construction des villes," in a chapter on urban squares, probably written in Munich in July 1910. Significantly, his comments go beyond architecture to encompass the broader field of the visual arts. Urban squares, he wrote, must be concrete and visually comprehensible, just like any other work in the visual arts, hence they must have *corporalité* (corporeality) and have "the character of volume, of a room." Monuments within the squares are ornaments: as such, they are something objective, a pure matter of color, line, and volume; they cause pleasure without meaning anything, "formes jouant en de beaux volumes sous les caresses de la lumière" (forms playing in beautiful volumes caressed by the light).[59]

These statements are interesting here not for their specific concern with urban planning, but for the broad aesthetic outlook that they reveal.[60] Understanding the latter requires a longish detour into the sources upon which Le Corbusier, an avid reader, had built that outlook, before returning to Le Corbusier's statements, which so closely anticipate his famous definition of architecture. One may think of Le Corbusier's sources as an old foundation on which he placed two new discourses.

The foundation had been laid by Le Corbusier's earlier reading of such works as Charles Blanc's *Grammaire des arts du dessin*, an eclectic mid-nineteenth-century synthesis of aesthetic theories ranging from ancient Greek philosophy to French and English eighteenth-century theories and German idealism.[61] Through this and similar works, Le Corbusier was familiar with Hegel's observation that architecture and sculpture work through forms made visible by external light, as well as with such generic conceptualizations of architecture as "combinations of lines and surfaces, solids and voids," "rational combination of those volumes," "sculptural drama…under the beneficial activity of the light."[62] But that earlier foundation had remained latent in Le Corbusier until it was activated by two contemporary discourses: the German discourse on form, and the French one on symbolist painting.

The German discourse went back to Kant's notion of the *Zweckmässigkeit* (purposiveness) of form, according to which aesthetic delight occurs when a form displays an internal necessity or purposiveness, free of outside constraints.[63] Building upon this, figures such as Herbart, Fiedler, Wölfflin, Göller, Schmarsow, and Riegl had articulated a theoretical edifice focused on form—on its autonomy and its *Wirkung*—its impact on the viewer—without regard to meaning. Their aesthetic categories, in turn, informed the critical discourse that Le Corbusier encountered in Germany by 1910. To name but two examples, the book that Le Corbusier was reading in July 1910, Brinckmann's *Platz und Monument*, had chapters titled "Plastic dimensional relationships in urban form" and "Spatial rhythm" and ended by advocating a new "Gefühl für Körperlichkeit" (feel for corporeality); and in an important essay published just before Le Corbusier's visit to Berlin, Behrens designated "the plainly rhythmical" and "Körperlichkeit" as essential qualities of architecture.[64] The discourse on form was available to Le Corbusier through these readings, and more directly through his acquaintance with August Klipstein, a German student in art history who later accompanied him on his Voyage d'Orient.[65] The fresh impact of this discourse on Le Corbusier is betrayed by his concoction of neologisms based on German, for example by his use of the word *corporalité*, or by the comment that, in a performance of

Hamlet, the actors "étaient trop faiblement vêtus et ne 'Wirktaient' pas" (the design of their clothing was weak, and they did not work on the public).[66] But the impact of this discourse was durable and, throughout his life, attention to the *Wirkung* of form provided a focus amid the complexity of factors impinging on architecture.

The French discourse on symbolist painting had developed around 1890 as critics tried to account for the work of Gauguin, van Gogh, and their circle.[67] One of the critics, Maurice Denis, asserted that "a painting, before being a representation of anything, is a flat surface covered with colors arranged in a particular order and for the pleasure of the eyes," and that Gauguin and his followers "believed that for each emotion, each human thought, there exists a plastic decorative equivalent."[68] Here, Denis was grafting the recent language about form, mentioned above, onto a view of art that ultimately went back to Goethe's concept of "symbol": expressing emotions or ideas through a formal equivalent which has its own coherence and justification (the "pleasure of the eyes" for Denis) independent of that content, and which can act directly and not just narratively.[69] To this coupling of form and symbol, by 1900 Denis had also added classicism in a timely response to French conservative politics and then had used the triad—form, symbol, classicism—to promote Paul Cézanne and Aristide Maillol during the first decade of the century.[70] In the same conservative vein, in 1909 Denis had restated his earlier theory of symbolism in terms of equilibrium between subjective and objective, arguing that the "subjective deformation" of the depicted objects (necessary to express individual emotion) must be balanced by the "objective deformation" of the same objects (necessary to achieve the "pleasure of the eyes," that is, beauty): objective decorative composition balances subjective expression.[71] Le Corbusier certainly knew this recent essay, and he drew from it the equation "objective = decorative = pure form" that he used in his tirade about monuments in squares. More in general, Denis was important to Le Corbusier's maturation around 1910 because he functioned, for him, as an intellectual intermediary. On the one hand, Le Corbusier had easy access to Denis's thinking through language and circumstances, and this facilitated his access to the German discourse on form that Denis had incorporated.[72] On the other hand, the very hybridity of Denis's position helped Le Corbusier move fluidly from one to another of its component categories (form, symbol, classicism).[73]

Le Corbusier repeated his view of urban monuments as "forms playing in beautiful volumes caressed by the light" a few months later, in early 1911, when he described Maillol's sculpture as "volumes qui jouent sous la lumière en rythmes à base géométrique, joie de la forme enfin retrouvée pour le régal des yeux" (volumes playing under the light in rhythms of geometrical order, joy of form found again at last for the feast of the eyes).[74] The words of both statements are tantalizing, since they so closely anticipate his famous definition in *Vers une architecture* ten years later: "L'architecture est le jeu savant, correct et magnifique des volumes assemblés sous la lumière" (Architecture is the masterly, correct and magnificent play of volumes arranged under the light).[75] It is thus surprising to realize that, at this point in 1910–11, Le Corbusier was referring to sculpture only: it would take him a long time to transpose the concept of "jeu des volumes" to architecture.

In fact, his first explicit comments about (convex) volume in actual buildings came in April 1911, when he was preparing to leave Germany. He described a villa by Bernhard Pankok in Stuttgart as having "volume in the manner of a Stuck or a Behrens" and Josef Olbrich's work in Darmstadt as poor because "the block is missing," although Olbrich had made substantial progress to which Behrens had much contributed.[76] The date and the recurrent reference to Behrens, in these comments,

94. Charles-Edouard Jeanneret, Pompeii, sketch of the Forum and a street, 1911

suggest that it was Behrens's tightly controlled architecture that opened Le Corbusier's eyes to the experience of architectural volume a considerable time *after* he had acquired the theoretical concepts. Having been educated first by L'Eplattenier in terms of Ruskinian categories (nature and the process of making), and then by Perret in terms of structural frame and cladding, it was not an easy step to conceptualize architecture in terms of volume. And this is confirmed by his sketches of buildings that he visited at that time; while not insensitive to architectural volume, the sketches are in no way focused on this aspect.[77]

It took even longer for Le Corbusier to focus on the *mutual interaction* of architectural volumes. He was well into his Voyage d'Orient when he wrote about the exterior of Hagia Sophia in Istanbul—"It is the cubes that operate here"—and about the interior of the Green Mosque in Bursa—"admirable concordance between the volumes."[78] These comments are still somewhat generic, and the corresponding sketches do not highlight the issue. But soon after, in Athens, Pompeii, and Rome, Le Corbusier's sketches suddenly show a singleminded, even obsessive, focus on the interaction of architectural volumes, both convex and concave, and more in general on the formal relationships of volumes, surfaces, light, and shadow (fig. 94). The reason is suggested in a letter written at the end of the trip: "But Rome has the old Romans of baked brick, and our good Lord has allowed all marble revetments to be stolen. Now, that's magnificent, unique, enthralling. That's an architect's real museum!"[79] It took ruins—naked, their use and distributional logic often illegible or, in short, abstract—for Le Corbusier to really *see* the abstract form of architecture, the architectural volumes and their play, and to turn intellectual concepts, absorbed over the previous two years, into emotional experience.

The sketches and his letter to Klipstein clearly show that it was this play, seen in the ruins, that captured the essence of architecture for Le Corbusier at that point, and this would remain his belief and the focus of his ambition, evident in his later definition of architecture in *Vers une architecture*.

But when he came back to reality, so to speak, and set out to design his two villas in La Chaux-de-Fonds for actual uses and a specific cultural setting, that experience born of abstract ruins was not easily applicable, and Le Corbusier had to fall back on more conventional schemes and language. This is why the intense awareness of "jeu des volumes" that one can see in his travel sketches is missing in the villas Jeanneret and Favre-Jacot; the ambition was there, but the tools were not.

To translate that awareness of "jeu des volumes" into actual designs, Le Corbusier still needed to develop several more frameworks, two of which can be designated by the shorthand "type" and *Sachlichkeit*.

TYPE

The interest in typicality first arose during the Voyage d'Orient in 1911. As Le Corbusier tried to define and explain his reactions during and after the trip, he used, in turn, designations such as "type," "symbol," "word." It is the whole cluster of these that matters here.

During the trip, moving from one place to another in the "East" (Hungary, Serbia, Bulgaria, Turkey, Greece), Le Corbusier was deeply struck by the typological unity within each culture, and he lamented the lack of such unity in the "West" once he came back.[80] This experience was still very much on his mind in September 1913, when he wrote an article about Swiss vernacular architecture that begins, based on notes from the trip, "Towards the East, where everything boils down to extreme simplification, we could transparently talk of Greek, Turkish, Czech or Serbian architecture; *type* reigned strong and serene, symbol of a monolithic race, of monolithic institutions, of a uniform nature" (emphasis by Le Corbusier).[81] In viewing types—temples, mosques, houses, pottery, music, and so on—as the embodiment of culture and place, Le Corbusier was simply repeating a well-established discourse, whose best-known spokesman for fifteen years had been the German Paul Schultze-Naumburg. Le Corbusier had absorbed the discourse from reading Schultze-Naumburg and other writers and, even more sharply, from his friend William Ritter in Munich.[82]

More than the cultural content of types, however, what mattered to Le Corbusier was their aesthetic potential as symbols, and this considerably broadens the architectural implications.[83] There are early inklings in notes made in Italy, at the end of the Voyage d'Orient in 1911. In Naples he wrote: "I had lived those four months of fantastic simplicity…. Turkey with the mosques and the wooden houses and the cemeteries, Greece with the Byzantine churches of Athos, with the Temple and hut. The Temple is always columns and an entablature."[84] In other words, proffer a simple grouping of columns and entablature, and Greece comes up. In Rome, soon after, he tried to distill his architectural experience of the city and to extract a few simple visual logos that would capture the essence of Bramante's Belvedere complex, of the Torre delle Milizie, temples, and other sites (fig. 95).[85] A few months later, the little pavilions jutting out from the Villa Favre-Jacot, each so clearly diagrammatic and different from the other, may well reflect those attempts.

But the full meaning of those Italian notes became explicit only by the spring of 1914, when Le Corbusier wrote a retrospective essay about his visit to Mount Athos, as a chapter for his book *Le Voyage d'orient*. He began the narrative with an amazing passage about his arrival by boat, after three days on the flat sea:

> I believe that the horizontality of an unchanging horizon, and especially, at noon, the awesome uniformity of the materials we see, set up in each of us a measure of the absolute, as humanly perceptible as can be. In the glow of the afternoon, suddenly appeared the pyramid of Athos! … Some pilgrims … keep among themselves a radiant or anxious silence, and this, at the moment when the propellers stop working, confers upon the short orders coming down from the bridge the solemnity of a halt and a decree. Grinding of chains, sinking anchors, immobility … I am obsessed, deep inside me, with the notion of symbol, with a type-expression of language limited to the value of a few words. Vocation is the origin of this: the system of masonry and scaffolding, of volumes, of solids and voids, gave me an understanding, perhaps too comprehensive, of the vertical and the horizontal, of the meaning of length, depth, height. And it led me to see these elements, even these words, as holders of infinite meanings that should not be diluted, since the word in itself, in its absolute and strong unity, expresses them all. … I will let my training waste away, with its scruple for detail that a teacher instilled in me. The thought of the Parthenon, block, columns and architraves, will satisfy my desires, like the sea in itself, and nothing but for this word. … The whole Orient seemed to me forged by great blows, each one a symbol. … And I would love relations of geometry, the square, the circle, and proportions that are simple and characterized.[86]

The central insight in this passage is the notion of visual words (*mots*), valued for the meaning (*signification*) that they carry, and composing a language (*langage*). The notion of visual "words" will be incorporated by Le Corbusier and Amédée Ozenfant into their Purist theory of painting, as in this definition of Purist elements, the stylized bottles, guitars, and so on, with which they composed their pictures: "The Purist element is like a plastic word fully formed, complete, leading to specific and universal

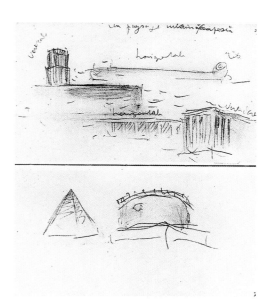

95. Charles-Edouard Jeanneret, "Un paysage urbain à composer," Rome, sketches of Torre delle Milizie, Vatican Walls, two types of collonades, the Pyramid of Caius Cestius and Hadrian's Mausoleum, 1911

96 ."Tout est sphères et cylindres," illustration to Jeanneret's and Ozenfant's article "Sur la plastique I. Examen des conditions primordiales," *L'Esprit nouveau*, no. 1, 1920

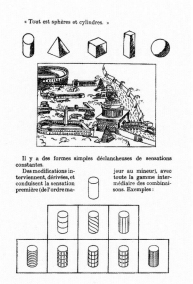

reactions."[87] More important, the notion of "words" will play an essential role in Le Corbusier's architecture of the 1920s. Not only will his buildings include typical distilled figures such as the ribbon window, studio window, and ramp, and even larger paradigmatic ones such as the transatlantic liner (the Villa Savoye in its landscape), but also the very fabric of his interiors will be conceptualized in terms of spatial "words" juxtaposed, discrete spaces open to each other yet individually characterized: for example, in the Jeanneret living floor of the Villas La Roche–Jeanneret or in the living area of the Villa Cook.[88]

This linguistic approach to the visual arts, in Le Corbusier's passage from *Le Voyage d'orient*, is a recurrent theme in his correspondence of this period, and it ultimately goes back to symbolist ideas of the 1880s.[89] In fact, Le Corbusier's passage was probably inspired by his reading of the symbolist poet Stéphane Mallarmé.[90] Particularly relevant are a few lines from "Crise de vers" (1886), Mallarmé's theoretical statement about the new symbolist poetry:

> One of the undeniable ideals of our time is to divide words into two different categories: first, for vulgar or immediate, second, for essential purposes. . . . Why should we perform the miracle by which a natural object is almost made to disappear beneath the magic waving wand of the written word, if not to divorce that object from the direct and the palpable, and so conjure up its *essence* in all purity? When I say: "a flower!" then from that forgetfulness to which my voice consigns all floral form, something different from the usual calyces arises, something all music, essence, and softness: the flower which is absent from all bouquets.[91]

Like Le Corbusier a few years later, Mallarmé sought a poetic language different from that of everyday transactions—an essential use of the language, which evokes dense notions, a use in which the word *flower*, for example, evokes not this or that flower but the essence of all flowers.

Le Corbusier's text and its connection to Mallarmé, the poet, clarify the meaning of Le Corbusier's reductive aesthetics of the 1920s. He was not trying to achieve abstract form devoid of content; to the contrary, he sought intensified meaning by reducing the form and number of "words" to bare essentials. Nor was his pursuit Platonist. True, he wrote of square and circle in his text of 1914, and, together with Ozenfant, he would call for the use of Phileban solids in 1920 (cylinder, pyramid, cube, sphere; fig. 96), but his initial impulse was to seek density of meaning, not ideal truth or beauty.[92]

SACHLICHKEIT

During his years abroad, in 1908–11, Le Corbusier had already been exposed to ideas about the architectural relevance of industrial materials and artifacts. In France the discourse about steel and concrete was concerned with rationality and progress; and in Germany, that on *Sachlichkeit* was concerned with the search for a new cultural unity.[93] But Le Corbusier had paid little attention to these issues. His focus, in those years, had been on the fundamentals of architecture, and when the new industrial realities affirmed their presence, during that first Berlin visit, it was through classicism that they were accommodated.

Only in 1913–14, a full two years after his return home, did Le Corbusier turn his attention to the new realities and the discourses that tried to conceptualize them. In this he was certainly encouraged by a sharp economic downturn in La Chaux-de-Fonds, which had left him without work and had led him to question the role of architects in society. First, in the summer and fall of 1913, he read several important essays by Walter Gropius and Adolf Loos and renewed his dialogue with Perret. Then, in the summer of 1914, he participated in the congress of the Deutsche Werkbund in Cologne and witnessed the famous debate about industrial types.

Gropius's essay about industrial buildings had just been published in the *Jahrbuch des Deutschen Werkbundes 1913*, and Le Corbusier probably read it in July 1913 (fig. 97).[94] Gropius argued that *Grundform,* (basic overall form), not the added ornament, is what counts in architecture, and that American factories and silos have a majesty and monumental power worthy of ancient Egypt, more so than the industrial buildings by European architects (Behrens included) because, in American engineers, "the natural sense for large, tightly bound form seems to have remained self-sustaining, healthy and pure."[95] Le Corbusier, who wrote at this time: "I am trying to leave for America…I need big work," certainly listened.[96]

Loos's two essays, "Architecture" and "Ornament and Crime," had recently appeared in French, and Perret had lent them to Le Corbusier in the early fall of 1913.[97] In them Loos dismissed ornament as superfluous, wasteful, and primitive. He argued that modernity is characterized by the absence of ornament and that ornament cannot represent our culture any more; that architects, focused on ornament, are superfluous; and that the house put up by a simple farmer is automatically appropriate and superior to that of the architect, precisely because the farmer acts un-self-consciously.

Le Corbusier discussed these essays with Perret, an enthusiastic admirer of things American, during several trips to Paris in the fall of 1913. Perret certainly added a further dimension, introducing the French debate between architects and engineers, specifically the juxtaposition of bold engineer versus timid architect, progressive science versus retrospective art, which had been crystallized twenty-five years earlier during the polemics about the Eiffel Tower and the Galerie des Machines.[98] If Gropius and Loos framed their discussion in terms of authenticity, Perret framed his in terms of progress. Taken together, Gropius, Loos, and Perret amounted to a double-barreled message for Le Corbusier.

First, there was an issue of meaning. Engineering works, bold and monumental, embodying progress and representative of modern society, commanded a new respect; and together with this came a view of the engineer as "noble savage," who had kept ("erhalten," as Gropius said) a natural, healthy, and pure sense of form just as Loos's farmer had, while the architect was lost in futile ornament and architectural styles.[99] For Le Corbusier, at this point, classicism began to lose its role as a signifier of modernity and to be replaced in that role by the "facts" of modern life, such as factories, ships, and reinforced concrete.

Second, there was an issue of form. On the one hand, the new technologies and building programs raised the question of what is an appropriate architectural form for them, and of what formal possibilities are opened by them. This issue continued to occupy Le Corbusier from his Dom-ino project of 1914–15 to his "Five Points of a New Architecture" in 1927 and beyond. On the other hand, Loos's moral condemnation of ornament and Le Corbusier's aesthetic interest in architectural volume and bare "words" formed a powerful argument when put together—that the right thing is also the beautiful one. And this argument opened Le Corbusier to the quality of nakedness, which would help him to achieve, in his architecture, a focus on "jeu des volumes" and a distilled language like those that he had so powerfully experienced among the ruins of the Mediterranean region.

All this was pulled together by Le Corbusier, soon after reading the essays, in a letter to Perret and in an essay, "Le Renouveau dans l'architecture." The core of the

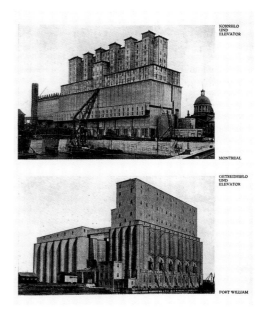

97. Two American granaries, illustration from Walter Gropius's article "Die Entwicklung moderner Industriebaukunst," *Jahrbuch des Deutschen Werkbundes 1913*

98 . Charles-Edouard Jeanneret, Villa Schwob, La Chaux-de-Fonds, 1916–17, the street facade, photograph

99. Auguste Perret, Charles-Edouard Jeanneret, Project for "Maison Bouteille", 1909, view of the front façade, from *L'Esprit nouveau*, no. 6, 1921

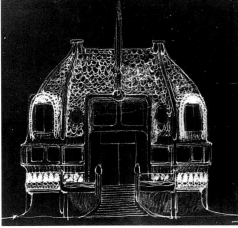

essay, framed by two polemics against regionalism aimed at his Swiss audience, was a paean to nakedness in architecture: architects are stuck in ornament, in maquillage; scraping off that maquillage, as time did with the Parthenon and Pompeian houses, reveals good architecture by "the rhythm, the cadence of volumes, the development of masses, the proportion" of the remaining naked building.[100] The letter made the same argument but connected it to the engineer: "when the architect will have put into houses the same honest expression of the ship builder…the *art* aspect of architecture will suddenly shine;…one will find an emotional note *in plastic terms*" (emphasis by Le Corbusier), to which Le Corbusier added the wish that he were an engineer, maker of bridges, tunnels, dams, and railroads, free from the slavery of timeworn habits.[101] The argument of Le Corbusier's opening chapters in *Vers une architecture* is essentially set here.

The effects of this thinking are obvious in Le Corbusier's designs for the Dom-ino housing system (1914–15) and for the Villa Schwob (1916), in both of which Le Corbusier explored the formal and typological possibilities of an architecture of reinforced concrete. They are also evident in his designs for the slaughterhouse at Challuy (1917) and for a *Ville contemporaine* (1922), where Le Corbusier uses raw facts of modern life, factory and skyscraper blocks at their most functional, as building material to achieve both meaning and form, to emphatically signify "modernity," and at the same time to achieve monumental "jeux des volumes."

A second phase of Le Corbusier's exposure to *Sachlichkeit* began a year after he read Gropius and Loos, when he participated in the congress of the Deutsche Werkbund in Cologne in July 1914.[102] There, he witnessed the famous debate sparked by Muthesius, who had advocated *Typisierung* and called on German designers to rally around a few standardized designs, so that German products would both foster a uniform cultural tone within Germany and have enhanced recognition abroad.[103] By skillfully playing on the ambiguities of the German root word *Typ*, which covers industrial standardization, marketing brands, and vernacular types alike, Muthesius suggested that industrial mass products have the same ability to embody organic culture that vernacular types have—solutions perfected anonymously and collectively, representative of their society precisely because of the anonymity of the process that had embedded the collective identity into the form. In other words, he presented industrial mass products as modern vernacular.[104]

Le Corbusier had come to Cologne with a longstanding interest in typicality—an interest that went beyond vernacular types (valued as expressions of their culture) to include any characteristic form or arrangement (valued as recognizable "words" within a visual language). Given Le Corbusier's double interest, the Cologne debate left two marks. First, it helped turn his interest in typicality into a search for a modern vernacular—hence, the particular quality of his involvement with housing types to which he would attribute a cultural role, as representations of modern society, that goes beyond their dwelling function.[105] Second, at a broader level, the Cologne debate broadened his palette of visual "words" to include standard consumer products of modern industry, turning them into *objets-types* as he and Ozenfant later called them in Purist manifestoes—like the industrial ramp, standard washbasin, and industrial glazing with which Le Corbusier composed the entry hall of the Villa Savoye.

VILLA SCHWOB

The Villa Schwob (1916) provided the first concrete occasion to integrate Le Corbusier's new thinking about type and *Sachlichkeit* with his earlier concerns (figs. 98, 100, 101).[106] The villa marks several transitions in Le Corbusier's approach to archi-

100. Charles-Edouard Jeanneret, Villa Schwob, La Chaux-de-Fonds, 1916–17, view from the garden, photograph, BV

101. Charles-Edouard Jeanneret, Villa Schwob, La Chaux-de-Fonds, 1916–17, plan of the ground floor, from *L'Esprit nouveau*, no. 6, 1921

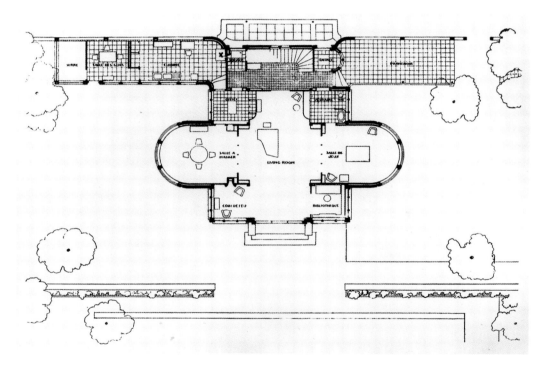

tecture. On the one hand, it marks a shift from a German to a French allegiance— from the classicism of Schinkel at Potsdam to that of Gabriel at the Trianon, so to speak—and also from Behrens to Perret and to his preoccupation with concrete.[107] On the other hand, under the continuity of classicism, it reveals the gradual coalescence of a different paradigm. In fact, it is the last overtly classicist building that he built, and it can be said to close a period.[108]

The history of the villa's design has been recently established by H. Allen Brooks. As he shows, the point of departure was an older design that had caught the client's attention (fig. 99): the "Maison Bouteille." Probably a villa prototype, it had been drawn by Le Corbusier during his Paris years 1908–9 (with unspecified input by

102. Peter Behrens. Wiegand House, Berlin-Dahlem, 1911–12, view of the street facade

103. Charles-Edouard Jeanneret, Pompeii, sketches of the Villa of Diomedes, 1911

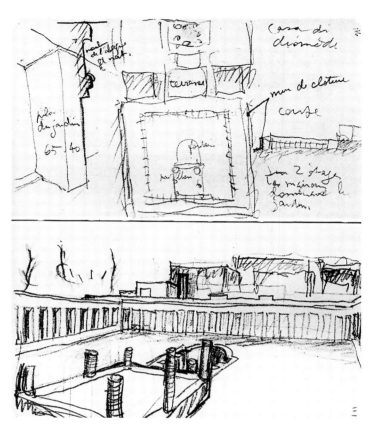

Perret): it entailed a two-storied central hall with full studio window at one end and staircase with internal balcony at the other end, with lower lateral rooms opened onto the hall at ground level.[109] Starting from this, the Villa Schwob design evolved in two successive phases. In a first phase, a master block was set, encasing the Maison Bouteille scheme within a cubic mass with absidal projections and capped by a cornice.[110] In a second phase, the core block was left essentially intact, and growing program demands were accommodated by adding an L-shaped and "piggybacked" extension on the street side and over the roof of the master block. As this addition grew to meet client demands, the street facade was not only widened, but also acquired curved protrusions on the sides.[111] Brooks also shows that the internal logic of these schemes entailed, on the street facade, both a set of paired doors (instead of a central one) and a "blind" decorated panel.

Notable elements of the design include the contrast between master and service block, the blind panel along the street, the two-storied central hall, the cornice, and the brick cladding.[112]

The contrast of cubic block and piggybacked addition is a key source of this building's enigmatic power, because it introduces a multilayered tension between "ideal–fixed-first" (the master block) and "circumstantial–growing-later" (the service addition)—a tension that the naked brick cladding sharpens by bringing everything to bear on the volumetric play, particularly on the sides of the service block. Far from being a circumstantial product of the client's growing demands, this tension derives from a deliberate aesthetic strategy that exploits those demands, a strategy probably inspired by Behrens's Wiegand house where a service block is jammed laterally into a symmetrical master block (fig. 102).[113] Le Corbusier had already used such strategy in the Villa Favre-Jacot, where the addition of an L-shaped service circulation in plan had occasioned the "sliding" facade. Behrens's tension is a purely formal game, how-

ever, and Le Corbusier's "sliding facade" remains just that, a facade. The tension in the Villa Schwob instead arises from the *sachlich* "naked" acknowledgment of a fact, the growth process of the house, and from the sharp individual characterization of the two large components, the master block with symmetry and cornice and the service block treated in an ad-hoc manner. Le Corbusier was learning to use the expressive potential of *Sachlichkeit* and type.

The blind panel facing the street raises similar points.[114] The relevant issue here goes beyond the panel itself to the broader tension between blind street wall and open garden view.[115] This tension suggests an ancient Roman precedent: the Villa of Diomedes admired by Le Corbusier in Pompeii (fig. 103).[116] The location of Villa Schwob at the edge of the city would have naturally suggested this memory to Le Corbusier. Coming from the center of Pompeii, one encounters the Villa of Diomedes at the edge of the city, where the orthogonal grid of streets breaks into country roads, left of the road and on terrain sloping down gently to the left, just as with the Villa Schwob. Like all Pompeian houses, the Villa of Diomedes presents a continuous closed wall to the street. Through a door one enters into the open atrium which acts as the hub of the whole house, and then, after a sequence of grand rooms, one emerges on a terrace overlooking a sunken garden and, beyond, the landscape and the sea. The corresponding sequence at Villa Schwob entails crossing a blind wall along the street, expanding into an open "hub," and eventually emerging on a terrace overlooking a lower garden and the landscape beyond.[117] Le Corbusier used the Pompeian memory as a mediating key in interpreting this site, just as he had used the Erechtheion to interpret that of the Villa Favre-Jacot. But whereas, there, the precedent simply inflects a traditional Biedermeier villa, in Villa Schwob the Roman precedent is turned into a driving concept of the design (closed to the street and open to the landscape), nakedly displayed and sharply characterized as such.[118]

The central hall of the Villa Schwob marks a nodal point in the development of Le Corbusier's spatial typology, thanks to the intersection, in its design, of present circumstance, memories from ancient Rome, and the concepts of "words" and "play of volumes." The hall was inspired by a modern precedent, the Maison Bouteille with its two-storied space. Once placed within the Pompeian siting concept for Villa Schwob, the Maison Bouteille could not have failed to suggest ancient Roman echoes: a luminous central space rising above one's head (the atrium) with lower rooms abutting it on the ground floor through full-wall openings.[119] The central space and the lower adjoining ones must then have reminded Le Corbusier of a note he had made at Hadrian's Villa near Rome in 1911: "Remember that in each Roman room there are always three full walls. The other wall opens generously and lets the room participate in the ensemble."[120] This note about a paradigmatic spatial arrangement was part of his emerging interest in "type" and "words." Starting with the Villa Schwob, that arrangement acquired, for Le Corbusier, the quality of a type—both in the elementary version of one tall room with big window and rear balcony (the Maison "Citrohan"), and in the combined version of one tall room with lower abutting ones (the villas Meyer and Cook of 1925–26; fig. 104). This spatial type must have appealed to Le Corbusier on three counts. First, a space closed on three sides and fully open on the fourth has the simplicity and the force of a sharply characterized visual "word." Second, alone or with abutting lower spaces, the big hall provided spatial focus for the house, just as the atrium did for ancient Roman houses. Third, and most important, the Schwob arrangement allows spatial play to happen: if one imagines how one may extend Le Corbusier's concept of "jeu des volumes" to the interior spaces of a house, a precondition is that the visitor be able to see several spaces at once, and this is precisely what the type of ancient Roman rooms made possible, because in each of them "the other wall opens generously."[121]

The cornice over the master block warrants discussion because it shows the complex transition, from classicism to *sachlich* concerns with function and type, that Le Corbusier was undergoing at the time. On the one hand, the cornice was consistent with the villa's construction in reinforced concrete, and it was justified in terms of use. This was not a cornice from the Greek orders, inseparable from the entablature (with the implied presence of a roof above and supporting columns or pilasters below), but instead it was a flower planter clearly resting *above* the flat roof slab.[122] On the other hand, typological considerations had been central to the design: this kind of cornice had been developed a year earlier, in 1915, as an optional component for the Maison Dom-ino, a housing system with standardized concrete frame, meant for the reconstruction of villages destroyed in World War I.[123] The process of design, part of a broad research in housing types and architectural language, took place more at the library (the Bibliothèque Nationale in Paris) than at the drafting table, and it was concerned with type both in the sense of producing a repeatable design—a type as understood by Muthesius—and in the sense of developing a typical language appropriate for reinforced concrete—a longstanding concern of Perret, with whom Le Corbusier was in constant dialogue at this time; precedents ranged from Henri Sauvage to Louis Sullivan to the ancient Assyrians.[124] In summary, while the cornice of the Villa Schwob achieves a classical effect (and is obviously intended to do so), behind that effect one can see Le Corbusier working out new concerns that are separate from classicism and reflect his new involvement with *Sachlichkeit* in its French and German versions.

The brick cladding is interesting because it demonstrates new synergies among old and new concepts that preoccupied Le Corbusier at the time: *Sachlichkeit*, type, and volume. The choice of brick for the cladding, unusual in La Chaux-de-Fonds, was probably triggered by the Pompeian interpretation of the site. But more interesting is the way in which the brick is used, and on this aspect three points stand out. First, the smooth skinlike continuity of the cladding, which hides the concrete posts (see, for example, the corners of the cubic master block), not only is consistent with the construction in reinforced concrete, but also is explicitly expressive of it. Since the turn of the century, the French discourse about reinforced concrete saw the architectural problem of concrete precisely as one of defining the cladding, not as one of displaying the frame. Perret's Théâtre des Champs Elysées, recently inaugurated, stood as a loud proclamation of this view.[125] Second, the naked uniform brick cladding, which "turns the corner" at the edges and in which the upper windows act as cutouts, serves to emphasize the architectural volumes throughout the building; here, Frank Lloyd Wright's use of brick was probably the catalyst.[126] The focusing power of this naked uniformity at the Villa Schwob is extraordinary. The absidal projections appear as pure cylinders, making one think of the volumetric power admired by Gropius in the American silos, and despite the fact that openings take up two-thirds of the garden facade, the master block is still seen as a sharply cut cube. Clearly, Le Corbusier had learned to use Loosian nakedness to pursue artistic effect, "jeu des volumes." Third, in pursuing that effect, he showed a new clarity of purpose, which derived from his having formulated the concept of visual "word." When composing a "jeu des volumes" Le Corbusier did not just seek a multiplication of the contour but began with the sharp characterization of individual volumes: intact cylinder, sharp cube, and so on. Because of this characterization, the meeting of individual volumes at the Villa Schwob acquired the tension of a clash of personalities, like that Le Corbusier had admired at the Pantheon in Rome: "The marble cube of the portico penetrates arbitrarily into the cylinder of the nave."[127]

The Villa Schwob is a transitional building, maybe his most forcefully classicist design, but also his last one. Under the cover of a classicist continuity with the earlier work, Le Corbusier was layering old and new concerns—history, volume and proportion, type, "words," *Sachlichkeit*—and was developing new synergies among them. Thus, thanks to a *sachlich* willingness to let naked facts be, circumstances and memories acquired the poetic power to structure a design, as in the tension between block and extension and in the blind panel. Memories of ancient Roman architecture not only helped Le Corbusier to conceptualize a particular site, but also assisted the process of distilling a typical spatial "word" later seen in the Maison Citrohan. History, Muthesius's notion of type, and Mallarmé's "words" became mutually reinforcing. Also, the moral argument about nakedness learned from Loos helped to sharpen the structural expression of reinforced concrete through its cladding, to characterize the individual "words," and to focus the "jeu des volumes"; Loos, "words", and volume became mutually reinforcing. Under the cover of classicism, a wide range of concerns that are independent from it began to coalesce into a new package, a new architectural concept, which would eventually stand alone.

* * *

Looking ahead to Le Corbusier's work of the 1920s, what enabled him to move from the Villa Schwob to such work as the Villas La Roche–Jeanneret? Proportion, volume, type and *Sachlichkeit* may account for works like the slaughterhouse at Challuy or the *Ville contemporaine*, in which a symmetrical diagram provides the point of departure for both design and interpretation, as it does in the Villa Schwob. But the Villas La Roche–Jeanneret and later work operate on a different principle. They are marked

105. Le Corbusier, Pierre Jeanneret, Villa La Roche/Jeanneret, Paris, 1923–25, Jeanneret living room

precisely by the *absence* of any "suggested reading," and they owe this quality to Le Corbusier's Purist experience of 1918–21.[128] Two new notions were absorbed by Le Corbusier in those years.

One, already discussed by Yve-Alain Bois and Bruno Reichlin, is the cubist reliance on the arbitrariness of the sign, hence the cubist refusal of referentialism.[129] These qualities of cubism were incorporated in the Purist painting of Ozenfant and Le Corbusier (Jeanneret), resulting, for example, in the well-known device of "marriage of contours," which associates objects (say, a glass and a pot) that have nothing in common except the line that unites them. They enter the "whole" of the painting solely by virtue of formal relations that suspend referentiality (thus not, for example, as the logical situation of a glass and a pot on the table). In architecture, the refusal of referentialism appears in "the overflow of one space into another or, again, the breaking of the congruence between functional space and structural space."[130]

The other notion that Le Corbusier absorbed during his Purist years came from the poet Reverdy, a friend of cubist painters and a collaborator in *L'Esprit nouveau*. In 1918 Reverdy had argued that the poetic image is born "from the bringing together of two more or less remote realities," restating in simple language a central concept of Mallarmé: that, in poetry, something new arises from the tension between two images or words.[131] Having absorbed this concept through Reverdy, in 1921, Le Corbusier could now think of architecture starting from individual "words" (for example, from individual spaces), instead of starting from an overall *parti*. Thus, while in Villa Schwob the various internal volumes opening onto the central hall seem to be generated from a Lorraine cross (a cross with two transversal bars of different length; see fig. 101), in the Villas La Roche–Jeanneret the various volumes of the Jeanneret living floor have, each, an autonomous presence and character (fig. 105); they "play" with each other, whereas in the Villa Schwob they obediently line up.[132] Thus, volume and type ("words") move up in rank; from being qualifiers of architecture, they are now the generators of it.

A similar comparison can be made between two descriptions of the Green Mosque in Bursa, which Le Corbusier had visited during the Voyage d'Orient (fig. 106). In 1910, in his notebook, Le Corbusier described the interior relationships as "admirable concordance between the volumes." In 1922 in his article "Architecture II: l'illusion des plans," beside a sketch from the notebook he wrote:

> You are in a large space of marble white, flooded with light. Beyond, a second space opens, similar and of equal dimensions, full of shade and raised up by some steps (repetition in minor); on each side, two spaces in shade, still smaller; you turn around, two dark spaces, very small. From full light to dark, a rhythm. Minuscule doors and very large bays. You are taken, you have lost the sense of normal scale. You have been subjugated by a sensory rhythm (light and volume) and by clever dimensions, to a world in itself which tells you whatever it has chosen to tell you.[133]

Veüe et perspectue du Château et Jardin de Versailles, comme il est a present.

5

THE CHALLENGE OF THE "GRAND SIÈCLE"

Antonio Brucculeri

BEGINNING IN 1920 LE CORBUSIER consistently criticized, at times harshly, French architecture of the classical period. At the same time, however, he continued to draw practical lessons—in terms of conceptual method and principles of composition—from the documents he had studied at the Bibliothèque Nationale in the summer of 1915. To understand his approach to these materials,[1] it is particularly valuable to examine the many drawings he completed after consulting two influential books: Gabriel Pérelle's *Topographie de France* (published by Jombert in 1753 and 1766) and Pierre Patte's *Monumens érigés en France à la gloire de Louis XV* (published in 1765), both of which had engravings.[2]

FRENCH CLASSICISM BETWEEN HISTORY AND CRITICISM

Jeanneret's interest in early modern France was conditioned by the self-education that led him to demand precise answers from the study of history. At the same time he compared his results with the documentary analyses that French scholars and art historians had begun to produce in the last decade of the nineteenth century. In 1915, for example, Jeanneret consulted the volumes of the *Procès-verbaux* of the Académie royale d'architecture, which had begun to be published in 1911 by Henry Lemonnier, the first professor of early modern art history at the Sorbonne (1893).[3] Beginning around 1910, Jeanneret's curiosity led him to examine the Empire-style interiors of Versailles, Compiègne, and Fontainebleau, images of which he collected in postcard form.[4] Lemonnier's student Louis Hautecoeur also wrote about the genesis of this style, a point of no return as far as the stylistic eclecticism of the nineteenth century was concerned, reaffirming the early studies in French art, between the Revolution and the Empire, published by François Benoît, another student of Lemonnier, in 1897.[5] From 1909 onward, Jeanneret's curiosity about Versailles was matched by a powerful turn of conscience over the cultural role that the palace had played in history, a role emphasized in the monographs and courses that had been taught since 1892 by Pierre de Nolhac, curator at the museum of Versailles.[6] Above all, however, it was the work of Marcel Poëte, and his interest in the French context of urban historiography, that galvanized Jeanneret.

In the 1910s Poëte had initiated the systematic revision of Parisian history, from its origins through to the grand transformations of the late nineteenth century[7]. This work became an essential source for Jeanneret, and the two men were in steady contact during the early 1920s.[8] Poëte's history of seventeenth- and eighteenth-cen-

107. Charles-Edouard Jeanneret, Bassins de Latone, Bassin d'Apollon, sketches after engravings by Gabriel Pérelle, 1915, pencil on tracing paper, FLC

108. Gabriel Pérelle, "Vue et perspective du Château et Jardin de Versailles" engraving, Bibliothèque Nationale, Paris

tury Paris, based on period plans and views sparked Jeanneret's own researches in 1915. The Bibliothèque des Travaux historiques de la ville de Paris, where Poëte was chief curator, mounted an exhibition in 1911 entitled *Paris durant la Grande Epoque classique*.[9] Although far removed from any explicit monarchical pretensions, the Third Republic nevertheless invoked the history of ancien régime France, especially Versailles, as a token of cultural identity.[10] In any case, the quest for a national, cultural continuity also included architectural culture.

In the early 1920s several important exhibitions of French architecture of the seventeenth through nineteenth centuries proposed philological research as an efficient weapon against both stylish eclecticism and the programmatic denial of any reference to past architecture. These exhibitions were held within a year of each other; one was organized by Robert Danis, director of the new École régionale d'architecture, in Strasbourg (May 1922), and the other, by Louis Hautecoeur, in Paris (January 1923).[11] Although critic Léandre Vaillat had few words of praise for the projected *cité future* (*Ville contemporaine*) that Le Corbusier presented at the Salon d'Automne in 1922,[12] when assessing Hautecoeur's Paris exhibition of 1923 he focused on the continuity of a classical ideal capable of connecting the history of French architecture to the present: "The way of the world, we have to remember, is that those who proudly call themselves modern today, will become ridiculous and old-fashioned faster than the teachers of yesteryear."[13] Vaillat was clearly alluding to the brand of poetics that would become a recurrent theme in Auguste Perret's theoretical analysis of his own architecture. It is equally clear exactly whom he meant when he referred to a "new architecture" (*architecture nouvelle*) that would be innovative in obliterating the historical context.

THE PROBLEM WITH PERRET

It was in the spring of 1922 that relations between Perret and Le Corbusier finally deteriorated, after events surrounding the design of the *hôtel particulier* Gaut.[14] They disagreed over two themes essential to classical architecture: the capping cornice and the vertical window.[15] Ten years later Le Corbusier still referred to Perret as a "continuateur – pas du tout révolutionnaire" (continuator – not at all a revolutionary) when he recalled Perret's insistent invitations to visit the Palais de Versailles together (during Le Corbusier's first Paris sojourn, 1908–9). Le Corbusier's words unequivocally expressed his own distancing from a modernity that still traced its lineage to French classicism.[16] It hardly mattered that Perret criticized at Versailles the lack of structural clarity that he vaunted in his own architectural poetics.[17] Even so, it was by comparing the structural organisms of the Dôme des Invalides and the Théâtre des Champs-Elysées that Jeanneret, on the eve of World War I, grasped the capacity of contemporary architecture for change.[18] When he presented his plans for a *Ville contemporaine* in 1922, however, it was the editorial of the journal of the Société Centrale des Architectes, *L'Architecture*, that championed his proposal.[19] In an article for the journal, Raymond Cogniat emphasized the legacy of French classicism in Le Corbusier's designs, despite the criticisms the design had received:

> undoubtedly, one may object to the monotony of these rectilinear avenues. Do not our rectilinear perspectives—rue de Rivoli, les Champs-Elysées, la place Vendôme, la place des Vosges, la rue Royale—attract foreigners, surely they will increase admiration.[20]

In effect, from the late 1920s onward, Le Corbusier distanced himself from the most radical wing of architects (such as Hans Schmidt), who had participated in the creation of the CIAM. This distancing, as well as the academicism identified in his project for the Mundaneum,[21] only demonstrated the importance that Le Corbusier attached to French "classical architecture" in his approach to design.

VERSAILLES AND THE ENGRAVINGS OF GABRIEL PÉRELLE

Pérelle's engravings are essential to documenting the architecture of Paris and the Île-de-France in the latter half of the seventeenth century. Nevertheless, Jeanneret during his studies at the Bibliothèque Nationale, did not focus primarily on their architectural details. Instead, these views apparently led him to understand the buildings as emergent architectural objects on an urban or, better still, an environmental scale.[22] In this light, the sketch that he made after Pérelle's engraving of Saint-Adjuteur du Vernon is a representative example: the settlement had become the subject of the illustration and a hierarchy was adduced from the system of elements that unite the village of Vernon with the suburb of Vernonnet (figs. 109, 110).[23] But it was the complex of palace and gardens of Versailles that truly fascinated Jeanneret. His 1915 sketches after Pérelle's engravings are critical reconsiderations of the palace's spatial construction—not only the architecture, but also the landscape; this is demonstrated by his repeated studies of the fountains in the park of Versailles. In the case of the *bassin de Flore*, for example, Jeanneret emphasized the architectural character of the gardens, which evoked an "admirable image of clipped groves with deep fountains, fences, paths etc. (*very sculptural*)" [emphasis added].[24] He reduced Pérelle's regular and patterned drawing of the water jets to such an extent that the putti, embracing the vases from which the water flows on the central fountain, disappear and all the surrounding figures are either omitted or sketched as abstract marks. Jeanneret was mainly impressed by the scale of the groves, those constructed masses that seemed to him to define urban and architectural space (figs. 111, 112). In a contemporary notation he alluded to the difficulty

109. Charles-Edouard Jeanneret, Saint-Adjuteur du Vernon, sketch after an engraving by Gabriel Pérelle, 1915, pencil on tracing paper, FLC

110. Gabriel Pérelle, "Saint-Adjuteur du Vernon", engraving, Bibliothèque Nationale, Paris

111. Gabriel Pérelle, "Le Bassin de Flore," engraving, Bibliothèque Nationale, Paris

112. Charles-Edouard Jeanneret, Sketches after engravings by Gabriel Pérelle (*Bassin de Flore*, Gardens of Versailles), 1915, purple pencil on tracing paper, FLC

that a lay person would have in reading the "engraved bird's-eye views of the gardens of Lenôtre [*sic*]"; in effect what was required was a spatial perception of the garden as architectural object:

> entering the house, here are the billowy volumes, that move in rhythm, that lighten or darken, that are intensely, violently or delicately colored. It is the same when one penetrates the gardens of Lenôtre.[25]

THE GARDENS

The study of seventeenth-century French gardens had a profound impact on Jeanneret's approach to early modern, architectural classicism precisely because of its prerogative as planned space.[26] This aspect began to dominate the notes he drew from Antoine Dézallier d'Argenville's *Théorie et la pratique du jardinage* (1747 edition). He was interested not only in the design of the *boulingrins* ("bowling greens") and parterres, but also in the garden's other three-dimensional and tectonic elements, its *cabinets, salles, pièces, cloîtres* (figs. 113–15).[27] It is no coincidence that one undated study, which examined the gardens of the Orangerie de Versailles, emphasized the counterpoint inherent in the "pointillisme cubique" of the flower boxes of oranges and dwarf oranges "that play with the adjacent flower beds."[28] His drawings of the fountains of Latone and Apollo go on to underscore the mass and volume of the adjacent woods (fig. 107).[29] His notation on the drawing of the fountain of Latone also suggests the wide gap between his concerns and those of contemporary art historians: "the prestige of Louis XIV is great because of today's Versailles, and not because of some bygone marvel where the colorful stories might just as well be the gossip of courtesans."[30]

This idea of grandeur was born from his reading of a geometry of space that dissolved only at the horizon. In the margin of the same drawing, Jeanneret also wrote: "The large avenues—today, grand cathedral naves, consist of countless small bands of chestnut trees at the end of a row— . . . in Clagny, in Sceaux just as in Versailles

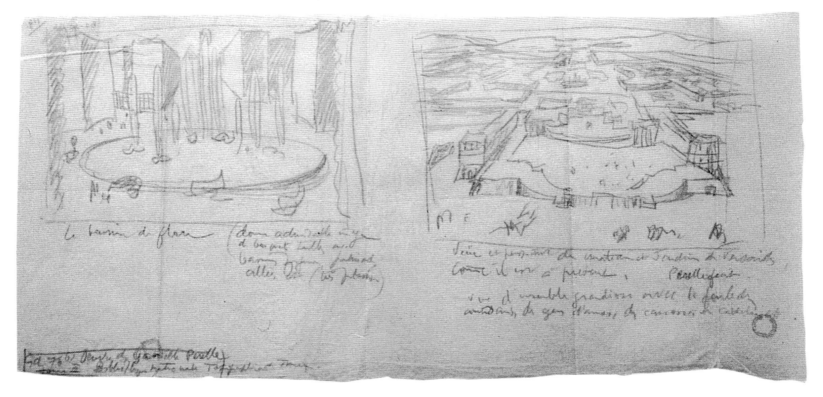

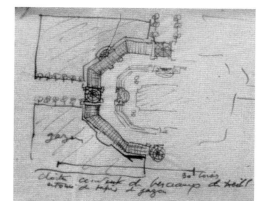
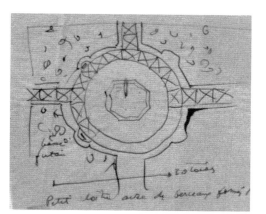

113–15. Charles-Edouard Jeanneret, Sketches after
A. Dézallier d'Argenville, *La théorie et la pratique du
jardinage*, Paris 1747, 1915, ink on tracing paper, FLC

one thought large and for the future."[31] Hence Jeanneret used line to stress the progression of the avenues toward the horizon, almost as though they were a system of ascending ramps. In his sketch the horizontal plane seems to rise up to meet the viewer.

Jeanneret's interpretation of the engraving of the fountain of Apollo appears all the more significant: He elevates and, more importantly, shifts the perspective from the axis of Pérelle's representation. This deliberate rotation departs from the axiality of the geometric system around the basin, but does not negate it. Instead it focuses attention on a system of axes at the scale of the landscape and one readily recalls the bird's-eye perspectives that Le Corbusier later adopted to represent space on the grand scale, like those of the "centre de Paris" in the *Plan Voisin*.

"LOUIS XIV S'EST TROMPÉ"

Two sketches are particularly evocative of the relationship between the Palais de Versailles and the surrounding areas: once again they depart from Pérelle's engravings depicting Versailles from opposite sides of the palace courtyard. In the first instance (fig. 112),[32] Jeanneret concentrates on the plastic elements that characterize its spatial disposition, in particular the two curvilinear ramps that lead from the entrance and bridge the difference in level between the courtyard and the two terraces stretched along the palace wings. These ramps become still more evident in the second sketch (fig. 117), which emphasizes their correspondence with the system of *parterres* and *allées* that branch off from the entrance and bypass the stables in a star-shaped arrangement. The other feature that Jeanneret emphasizes is the staggered profile of the main palace block surrounding the courtyard, which Pérelle

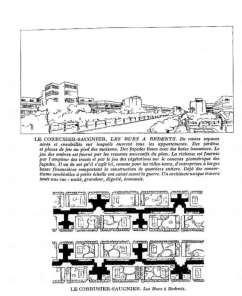

116. "Les rues à redents," Le Corbusier-Saugnier, "Trois rappels à MM. les architectes. III. Le plan", in L'Esprit nouveau, no. 4, 1921

had illustrated in the first engraving (fig. 108). The sketch that Le Corbusier traced from this engraving reappeared in *Vers un architecture* in 1923. By that time Le Corbusier had chosen a polemical tone, denying the project's star shaped planning:

> a man has only two eyes, at a height of 1 meter 70 [centimeters], which can only fix upon one point at a time. You can only see the arms of the stars one at a time-and they are like a right-angle masked by foliage. A right-angle is not a star; stars disappear. And so on; the large fountain, the embroidered flower beds that are not part of a total vision, the buildings that can be seen in fragments and by moving around. This is the snare and illusion. Louis XIV deceived himself by his own volition. He violated the architectural truths because he did not proceed with the objective elements of architecture.[33]

Despite this critique, Le Corbusier still included the staggered plan of the Versailles *cour d'honneur* in one of his earliest projects to integrate the scales of landscape and architecture—the *rues à redents* (fig. 116).[34] Moreover, the similarities between his studies for the palace of the League of Nations in Geneva and the scheme of the Palais de Versailles still resonate in 1926.[35] Although he chose to denounce the *vanité immense* of Louis XIV by 1923, in the summer of 1915 the lesson of Versailles was still a prime motivating force for him, because it was the Sun King whom he credited for active innovation outside the boundaries of the medieval city. As Jeanneret observed:

> examining the prints of Pérelle, one finds a Paris so poorly organized, so picturesque and so dirty, that one imagines the desire to clean, and even almost a helplessness to create an ensemble, because everything must be redone —quays, houses, etc. Palace, pinnacles, gables, spires, lanterns, etc. One understands why Louis XIV left for Versailles, a new place.[36]

Not surprisingly, therefore, Jeanneret's interest in Pérelle's engraved representations of urban buildings was limited to reading the interludes—the Observatoire, the Invalides, even the Jardins des Plantes (fig. 117)—that, like Versailles, challenged the city's compact fabric.[37]

PIERRE PATTE AND THE EXAMPLE OF THE "EMBELLISSEMENTS"

Jeanneret consulted the four volumes of Jacques-François Blondel's *Architecture française* (1752–56), which together with Blondel's theoretical works were essential to understanding the overall context of French classical architecture.[38] The most conspicuous collection of Jeanneret's sketches and notes from 1915, however, are actually based on Patte's publication of the projects for the *places royales* commissioned by Louis XV. During his research for "La Construction des villes" (already completed),[39] Jeanneret may have made his first contacts with the French eighteenth-century theory of *embellissements,* while he was in Germany, via the work of Werner Hegemann and Albert Erich Brinckmann.[40] This initiation was enriched in 1915 when Jeanneret began systematically combing through the original documents in the Bibliothèque Nationale. Jeanneret's interest stretched well beyond historical analysis; his aim was to establish a repertoire of models through his own reexamination of Patte's engraved plates.[41]

The organization of plates in the *Monumens érigés en France à la gloire de Louis XV* (1765) became Jeanneret's authentic guide to understanding urban design in France during the mid-eighteenth century, from the scale of the building to that of the city. It was an understanding that Jeanneret acquired both in the spirit of analysis and of

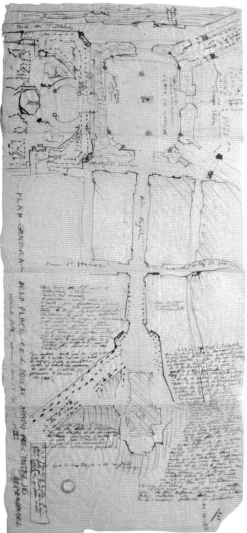

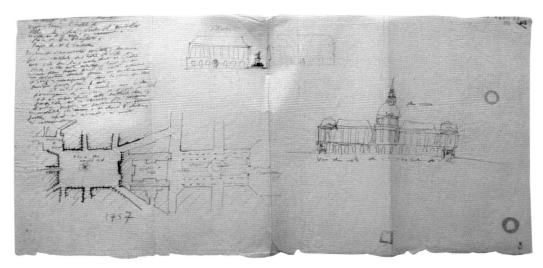

reformulation,[42] one in which his interest in the consistency of scale predominated. The case of Rouen serves as an example. Patte had devoted several plates to Carpentier's project for the new *hôtel de ville*. Jeanneret rapidly distilled its elevations while concentrating on Rouen's overall urban layout, duplicating Patte's pertinent comments about the "chain of remarkable buildings, where the Place du Roi could be considered as the city center" (fig. 118).[43] In the same spirit, Jeanneret interpreted the linkage of open spaces in Nancy – where the volume of the Place Louis XV (onto which the town hall faced) was connected to that of the Place de la Carrière. Moreover, at Nancy, the Place de la Carrière was circumscribed by "uniformly decorated buildings erected at the King's expense,"[44] including the double exedrae that the Hôtel de l'Intendance faced. Jeanneret noted on the page: "Nothing is so beautiful and nothing declares itself so majestically as that building. The ground floor is open and leads to a public garden."[45]

On many later occasions Jeanneret would return to the concatenations of Nancy, especially the manner in which its gardens complemented the architecture.[46] Yet, in this regard, it was the Place de Louis XV in Paris that interested him most and

117. Charles-Edouard Jeanneret, Observatoire, the Invalides, the Jardin des Plantes, the Tuileries, the Château at Versailles, Studies after engravings by Gabriel Pérelle, 1915, ink and pencil on tracing paper, FLC [264]

118. Charles-Edouard Jeanneret, Buildings and Squares of Rouen, Place Louis XV, Studies after engravings by Pierre Patte 1915, pencil on tracing paper, FLC

119. Charles-Edouard Jeanneret, The Tuileries, Rue Royale, Place Louis XV, Studies after engravings by Pierre Patte, 1915, ink on paper, FLC [268]

120. Le Corbusier, study after an engraving by Pierre Patte (Tuileries Gardens; 1915), from *Urbanisme*, Paris, 1925, p. 251,

121. Pierre Patte, View of the Tuileries Gardens, from Pierre Patte, *Monuments érigés en France à la gloire de Louis XV*, Paris, 1765

would become part of his intellectual journey to understanding the city's growth. His drawings only confirm the importance he attached to the relationship between urban space and natural context, whether exemplified by the River Seine or the Jardin des Tuileries. The 90-degree rotation of Patte's engraving of the overall plan emphasizes the relationship between the river and the axis connecting the *place* to the church of the Madeleine by way of the rue Royale (fig. 119).[47]

SHAPING THE RIVERFRONT

Jeanneret's focus on the transformations of Paris along the Seine was constant, as is evident from his choice of Pérelle's engraving of the Porte de la Conférence. Jeanneret's interest recalls the emphasis that Poëte had placed on this aspect in his reading of the urban development of Paris between the seventeenth and eighteenth centuries.[48] Jeanneret noted the dimensions and catalogued the elements that made up the Place Louis XV, but his drawings reveal his interest in the relationship between the jardins des Tuileries and the space of the *place*.[49] He stressed the "terrasses promenoirs pour jouir de la place" (promenades for enjoyment of the place) and redesigned Patte's view of the Tuileries, framing the octagonal fountain with two semielliptical ramps that lead toward the same terraces (figs. 120, 121).[50] The theme of the ramp reappears here, as at Versailles, as a *promenade* between nature and architecture, the conceptual origin of the *promenade architectural* that would become part of Le Corbusier's architecture during the 1920s, as for example in the curvilinear ramp in the gallery of the Villa La Roche.

THE COALITION AGAINST "PASTICHE"

Jeanneret, therefore, used his historical reading of the city as a way of understanding the present. The objective of his critique was that same language of eclectic pastiche that academic and professional circles also attacked during the early postwar period.

> The feeling of volume so powerfully expressed in previous eras disappeared in the 19th century. The "Classicism" of that period wished to retain from that past only the outlines with which it had expressed itself; it had lost its spirit. Hypnotized by the magnificent mementos of Louis XIV and Louis XV, our builders have studded our towns with star- and square-shaped *places* with monuments situated in the geometric center, on the pretext that they are no different from the splendid forms that the seventeenth and eighteenth centuries have handed down to us. By applying this dry and arid formula, they forget art, which is to say, they do not trouble themselves with volume, contrasts, nor "human scale;" in a word, they ignore *corporality*.[51]

The interest that the projects recorded by Patte assumed in Jeanneret's eyes is exemplified by the attention he devoted to Patte's *plan d'extension de la cité*, placed in the margins of a plate that once again joined several projects for embellishing the map of Paris.[52] Jeanneret highlighted the focal points – the "mushroom" of water at the point of the island, the obelisks, the statue of Louis XV, and the connecting bridges (figs. 122, 123). In particular he examined the western knot of these interlinked isles, marking the key elements of urban composition with annotations: a "new, colossal cathedral at the place dauphine," "the large flight of stairs [that leads] directly to the Point Neuf," the space fronting the eastern facade of the Louvre, its counterpart on the Left Bank, and the twin churches that had caused the destruction of Saint-Germain-l'Auxerrois.[53] Jeanneret's decision to note down the few

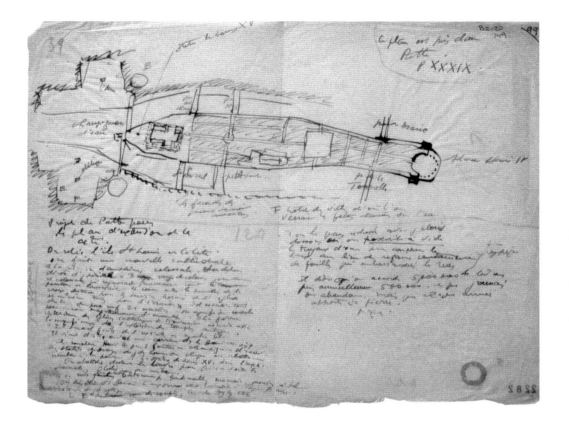

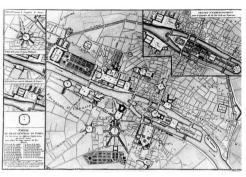

122. Charles-Edouard Jeanneret, sketch after the project by Pierre Patte for the Ile de la Cité in Paris, 1915, ink on paper, FLC

123. Pierre Patte, Plan for the *embellissements* for Paris, from *Monuments érigés en France à la gloire de Louis XV*, Paris 1765

technical details that Patte announced, like the "redesigned quays, with galleries below, where one could place the empty water hoses" is equally significant. It is also quite evident that in Jeanneret's eyes this project was an unprecedented example of forceful intervention in an urban center. The conclusions he reached when faced with these projects translated into a warning against contemporary planning culture. One of his notations reads:

> It is an interesting idea: during the time of Louis XV, one can see what [Patte] foresaw. Everything opened, breathed and acquired breadth. Today such an approach would be unfeasible because to live, those squares must have narrow road openings, etc. Today one needs enormity, an abundance of other factors: let us therefore *create accordingly, with equal audacity!* [emphasis added].[54]

Patte's proposals represented important stimuli for the experimental, citywide designs that Le Corbusier would propose for Paris. They suggested the real design solutions with which he planned "to liberate" the center of the city with the *Plan Voisin*, exhibited at the Pavillon de l'Esprit Nouveau in 1925. Beyond its formal content, his method of looking at urban space was nourished by the experiments of the eighteenth century.

6

MARCEL LEVAILLANT AND
"LA QUESTION DU MOBILIER"

Arthur Rüegg

THE EXTENT OF LE CORBUSIER'S involvement in furniture design was long assumed to be just four seating forms from the 1920s which were brought back into production around 1959 and have since taken their place among the most widely distributed icons of modernism: the famous chaise longue, two different "Grand Confort" armchairs, and the *fauteuil à dossier basculant*.[1] It was as if no other designs by Le Corbusier had existed, either before or after these pieces. One hypothesis attributed Le Corbusier's brief interest in furniture to his collaboration with the young interior designer Charlotte Perriand, who worked on projects that went through the office of Le Corbusier and Pierre Jeanneret beginning in the fall of 1927; some even assumed that she might have been solely responsible for the pieces in question, which were celebrated at the time within a circle of initiates.[2] In any case, it appeared as though Le Corbusier's interest in furniture design had been short-lived. For his own part, he continued to surround himself with chance finds, casually arranged, that seemed to typify the bohemian world.[3]

This misunderstanding about Le Corbusier as a furniture designer was compounded by the obvious lack of interest shown by Le Corbusier's team in the reinvention of seat furniture—a theme of considerable importance to such designers as Marcel Breuer and Mart Stam.[4] In addition, the four classic Le Corbusier pieces, first shown to the public at the Salon d'Automne in Paris in 1929, had little in common in structural details. They were welded *and* bolted; bent *and* miter-jointed; painted *and* chrome-plated. The frame of the "Grand Confort" armchair was assembled like plumbing pipes from standard lengths of straight and curved tubing; the L-profiles of the seat frame were so crudely welded to the pipes as to look like an amateur's do-it-yourself project. The cushions, made from expensive glove leather and sewn with *Kedernaht* (piping), were supported by a network of wire cables. Despite this simplicity of construction, the "Grand Confort" armchair was so expensive to make that it never went into quantity production during the 1930s. The collector and patron Raoul La Roche complained in 1930 about a price of 4,230 francs asked for a slightly damaged exhibition model; a few years earlier, he had paid just under half that sum for English club armchairs with the finest "maroquin" upholstery.[5]

This glimpse of Le Corbusier's work in furniture is revealing in itself but leads nowhere. Something more is required: an additional (and possibly antithetical)

124. Charles-Edouard Jeanneret, Sketch of an armchair from the Musée des Arts Décoratifs (Pavillon Marsan), Paris, (Carnet bleu, p.35), c. 1912–14, pencil on paper, FLC

125. Letterhead used by Levaillant & Bloch (1917), FLC

126. La Chaux-de-Fonds, aerial view, c. 1930, photograph by Walter Mittelholzer

FABRIQUE DE MONTRES

LEVAILLANT & BLOCH

LA CHAUX-DE-FONDS
(SUISSE)
FONDÉE EN 1874

Marques de Fabrique déposées:

ASTRONOME
PAON
CELSIUS
NOVELTY

„SENSATION"   „LA VAILLANTE"
ADRESSE TÉLÉGRAPHIQUE:
LEVAILLANT CHAUX-DE-FONDS
TÉLÉPHONE 186

reading that brings out not only the specificity of the work (as against other significant modernist designs), but also the developmental process within the designer's output as a whole. In this connection, his design philosophy is of interest. On several occasions, he explicitly posed "la question du mobilier" (the furniture question) and sought to position himself within his own context. Countless notes, sketches, photographs, and postcards on the subject are now stored in archives at La Chaux-de-Fonds and in Paris. At the same time, a pilgrimage to the works of his youth as well as of his old age, a quest for artifacts, will lead not only to the icons of modernist architecture, but also to previously overlooked modifications, to furniture dealers and private collectors, to museums and flea markets. The developmental process that began as early as 1906–7, under the influence of Art Nouveau, continued after 1912 in a different spirit and with unprecedented intensity.[6] Space does not allow a panoramic survey,[7] but by concentrating on a few clues and one specific case study, some new light may be shed on Le Corbusier's role as a furniture designer. In the process, Marcel Levaillant, a faithful friend of Le Corbusier's—the correspondence between the two extends from 1914 until 1965—and an important patron and collector of his furniture, will be rescued from oblivion and, for once, given center stage.[8]

MARCEL LEVAILLANT, SON OF A SWISS WATCHMAKERS DYNASTY

The trail begins within the urbane social milieu of the clock and watch magnates of La Chaux-de-Fonds, who in the years before World War I controlled more than half of the world market for timepieces.[9] Jeanneret's early clientele was composed of a few interrelated families from among these industrialists, most of whom had originally come from Alsace: the Ditisheim, Levaillant, and Schwob dynasties. One of Charles-Edouard Jeanneret's first interior design clients, in the fall of 1913, was Salomon Schwob, who had just returned, with his wife and a daughter born abroad, from several years spent as a company representative in Kobe, Japan. As in other cases, the cosmopolitan background did nothing to ease dealings with an architect whose reputation was purely local. The situation was often difficult, especially when

the client was expected to accept radical design ideas, without question, on matters connected with the intimate sphere of the family home.

All these families lived very close together, near their factories, which stood on the western edge of the rectangular grid plan of the city. Some lived in detached villas, but most occupied the row and apartment houses that make up the urban fabric of La Chaux-de-Fonds.[10] The Jewish community, to which these families belonged, was a major stimulus to cultural life in the watch metropolis and patronized the work of talented artists. For Jeanneret, who was just setting up as an architect and designer after concluding his studies in the Cours Supérieur at the École d'Art, and who was now himself an instructor in the Nouvelle Section of the school (1911–14),[11] these were the ideal, if discerning clients and patrons.

An early client, Yvonne Schwob, wife to Raphaël Schwob (of Schwob Frères), seems to have kept open house for talented artists,[12] and in 1916, Jeanneret was given the opportunity to design a library, which was decorated by his painter friend Charles Humbert, in Yvonne and Raphaël's villa.[13] A number of major interior remodeling projects were carried out for various branches of the Ditisheim family (of the Vulcain and Paul Ditisheim companies); these included some very fine groups of furniture, such as the pieces made for the *fumoir* (smoking room or den) of Hermann Ditisheim (now in the Musée des Beaux-Arts, La Chaux-de-Fonds; see pp. 230–33). Moïse Schwob (also of Schwob Frères) commissioned Jeanneret to design a veranda, with furniture that is also still extant. In 1913 Moïse's brother Anatole employed Jeanneret to remodel a salon in his apartment at 73 rue Léopold-Robert (in the same building as Salomon Schwob) and was later to take his furniture

127. The Levaillant family, c. 1929, photographed in Marcel Levaillant's apartment, A. Adolphe Levaillant (father), B. Marcel Levaillant, C. Anatole Schwob, D. Camille Schwob-Levaillant, E. Madeleine Schwob, private collection, Switzerland

128. Charles-Edouard Jeanneret, Study of a desk-book-case-music cabinet for Marcel Levaillant, 1914, pencil and ink on drawing paper, BV

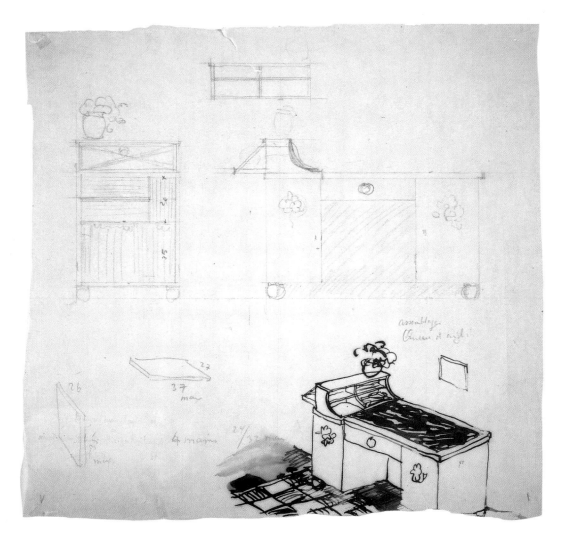

with him on moving into his own new house, the Villa Schwob (1916–17; also known as the Villa Turque), one of Jeanneret's most important early commissions.[14] In all, Jeanneret received around two dozen commissions, comparatively few of which—notably the interior for his own parents and the remodeling of a house in Zurich for his cousin, Marguerite Hauser-Jeanneret-Gris—originated outside the circle of Jewish families already mentioned.

Jeanneret's formal relationships with clients other than his own family were often marked by bruising exchanges of correspondence. Only one such connection developed into a lifelong friendship: that with Marcel Levaillant (1890–1972). Marcel was the youngest of the eight children of Adolphe and Sarah (née Bloch) Levaillant. He was sensitive, rather introverted, and small in stature. As a bachelor, he continued to live with his parents in their palatial apartment in the southwestern part of town. It was not until he was forty-eight that he moved to a place of his own, on the rue du Nord. In 1956 he acquired and decorated an additional apartment, in Geneva. He had retired early from his managerial position in the family watch and clock firm, Levaillant and Bloch, which changed its name to Fabrique Novelti, Levaillant and Company in the 1920s, and later again to Novelty Watch. Julien Levaillant, the second-youngest of the eight siblings, took sole charge of the company, while Marcel devoted himself to his favorite pursuits, primarily music. He was an enthusiastic amateur pianist; his concert grand piano occupied a dominant position in the plans that were drawn for all of his homes.[15]

In 1905 Marcel Levaillant's older sister Camille (1882–1944) married Anatole Schwob (1874–1932). A temperamental character, with a lightning-fast intelligence, Camille probably first encountered Jeanneret in 1913 when he remodelled her apartment at 73 rue Léopold-Robert; later, she sided with him in a disagreement with her husband over the building of Villa Schwob. Madeleine, the daughter of yet another of Marcel's sisters, Hélène (1881–1972), would later become an important client, too.

MARCEL LEVAILLANT MEETS CHARLES-EDOUARD JEANNERET: FURNITURE FOR THE 1914 STUDIO

Marcel Levaillant first encountered Jeanneret, who was only three years older than himself, at the time of the work projected for Camille and Anatole Schwob, if not earlier (yet in the earliest letters between the two men, they still address each other formally as "vous"). Around the beginning of 1914, Levaillant engaged Jeanneret to provide him with a *chambre d'étude* (study), which was completed in May of that year,[16] earlier, that is, than the two six-room Schwob apartments in the neo-Baroque building at 73 rue Léopold-Robert.[17] Salomon Schwob's apartment in that building was furnished mostly with pieces bought in Paris[18]; and the group of seat furniture designed for Anatole Schwob's apartment was not made until slightly later, by which time Levaillant's study already contained a piece wholly conceived and designed by Jeanneret. This was a light, faintly exotic-looking desk, which serves as early proof of his skill as a furniture designer.[19]

Described as a *pupitre-bibliothèque-casier à musique* (desk-bookcase-music cabinet), it is straight-edged in outline. The drawer and side compartments on the front are supplemented by shelves for books and musical scores in the back and on right-hand side. On the right, above the desktop, is a curved superstructure designed to contain writing implements and hold sculptures or vases. Directly over the side elevation, this superstructure opens to reveal a compartment with a hinged door, containing on its back wall a painting by the designer's friend Charles Humbert. The whole piece stands on six ball feet. Its outer surfaces are painted ivory color; all the recesses or niches are red.

For seat furniture, Jeanneret still turned to France, using selected Directoire, Empire, and Restauration (equivalent to early Biedermeier) pieces; but for case furniture he tried his hand at designs of his own, drawing on a variety of influences garnered on his extensive travels. At the time, he thus seems to have regarded seats and tables as "types" (standardized forms) hardly open to further development. Functional problems of storage and display, on the other hand, could be solved anew each time by means of an "architectural design." It comes as no surprise to find that the compositional rules in his furniture and architecture were similar. In many cabinets the architectural themes are immediately obvious (see p. 234); the writing desks (and bookcases) are to be interpreted as a kind of *capriccio*, in which classical architectural and furnishing motifs interlock with the simple, cubic forms of modernism. In this sense the Levaillant writing desk recalls kindred designs by the early-nineteenth-century Prussian architect Karl Friedrich Schinkel, notably the Crown Princess's desk at Charlottenhof, Potsdam (1828), which also has a superstructure, for which Schinkel had used acanthus motifs.[20] Jeanneret, when later designing a desk for his mother, abruptly juxtaposed classical arches with a pure cubic form (see p. 236). In the desk for Levaillant, the specific element of "invention" is to be discovered in the compartment that contains the painting by Humbert (only visible when the compartment is opened); in this, with a rhetorical gesture,

129. Charles-Edouard Jeanneret, Desk-bookcase-music cabinet, 1914, painted wood, decoration by Charles Humbert, location unknown

function and form unite with art. In the 1950s Le Corbusier was to revert to the same idea in his reflections on the "architecturalization" of picture frames.[21]

Stylistically, this desk also documents the disparate worlds that Jeanneret was trying to synthesize after 1912. His internship with Peter Behrens and his study of the German Arts and Crafts reform movement, which he made in 1910–11 in preparation for his *Etude sur le mouvement d'art décoratif en Allemagne* (1912),[22] undoubtedly left a mark. He also demonstrably made direct use of items from his German sketchbooks (see p. 234). At the same time, he was now seeking to align himself with French culture (Latin and Mediterranean), which was closest to his own heart and was also influencing German interior designers such as Bruno Paul. A whirlwind visit to Paris in December 1912 opened his eyes to the great interiors of Versailles, Compiègne, and Fontainebleau, and to the classical art of furniture that he encountered at the Musée des arts décoratifs.[23] He took advantage of further visits in 1913, occasioned by his work for Salomon Schwob, to discover contemporary French furniture and explore the important showrooms of international firms such as Kohn and Innovation.[24]

Finally, French-speaking Switzerland itself possessed an independent and sophisticated bourgeois tradition of uniting art and technology. Pressed plywood furniture, for example, was made at Yverdon from the 1830s onward in the workshops of Jean-Pierre-Moïse Guichard and Edouard Wanner.[25] There was also the elegantly simple, often floral-patterned porcelain from Nyon, fabricated between 1781 and 1813.[26] As a founding member of L'Oeuvre, the "association suisse romande de l'art et de l'industrie" (a sister organization to the Schweizerischer Werkbund that originated somewhat earlier in Zurich), Jeanneret was himself a prominent representative of the modernist awakening in French-speaking Switzerland.[27] The program of the Nouvelle Section at the École d'Art of La Chaux-de-Fonds was undoubtedly the most ambitious within that movement. This was the context of his work with Humbert, who had added painted decoration to Levaillant's ivory-colored desk.

"CONSULTANT ARCHITECT FOR ALL QUESTIONS OF INTERIOR DECORATION"

Jeanneret's earliest experiences in furniture and interior design from 1906–7 onward were dominated by the idea of a "synthesis of the arts" (the total work of art or *Gesamtkunstwerk*), as promoted by Art Nouveau.[28] After his studies in Germany and during his Voyage d'Orient, he made an apparently clean break with the regionalist concerns of his youth, which he had pursued under the tutelage of his gifted teacher at the École d'Art, Charles L'Eplattenier.

The interiors Jeanneret designed beginning in 1912 reflect a neoclassical spirit influenced by a French group of designers known as the Coloristes.[29] He now took a decidedly more relaxed approach that could absorb a range of chance finds. At the same time, Jeanneret had by no means abandoned his goal of asserting complete control of space. The contents of a dossier (now lost), concerning a lawsuit between Jeanneret and Anatole Schwob in 1918–20, gave some interesting information on the nature of these early interiors, including "the installation of electric lighting, the purchase of furniture, wallpaper, curtains, and light fittings, forming a harmonious whole."[30] Jeanneret himself went on record as stating that it was his practice to insist on "the demolition of decorated ceilings, of paintwork encrusted with gold, of imitation marble and imitation wood, the elimination of over ornamented wooden paneling, so that he could replace these superfluous elements by extreme simplicity."[31] He always aimed at "a simplicity

130. Charles-Edouard Jeanneret, Piano lesson. Hand-drawn postcard sent to William Ritter, December 18, 1915: Marie Charlotte Amélie Jeanneret-Perret teaches Marcel Levaillant in his study. The desk-bookcase-music cabinet is visible in the foreground, Schweizerische Landesbibliothek Bern, Archiv William Ritter

131. Château de Versailles, the library of Marie-Antoinette, postcard acquired by Jeanneret, probably 1913, FLC [120]

131 VERSAILLES. — Le Château. — Bibliothèque de Marie-Antoinette.

132. Jacob frères, "Directoire" armchair from the collection of Raphaël Schwob, photograph from an auction catalogue, Geneva 1982

133. Charles-Edouard Jeanneret, Armchair for Moïse Schwob, 1916, wood with original velvet upholstery, MBA [11]

of forms, a simplicity in the use of materials, and these were real innovations in that locality."[32]

This radically simplifying approach was bound to meet with a certain amount of resistance, especially from the building tradesmen, who were not used to it at all. As one master builder stated: "It was simple, but all the same it was expensive. I had problems with the client."[33] No doubt those problems were mainly financial. Jeanneret's insouciance (and inexperience) in such matters probably served to deter his early clients from giving him major projects, even though he seems to have appealed very successfully to the *taste* of those same clients.

The study that Jeanneret designed for Levaillant is recorded in a postcard sketch sent to the Swiss artist and art critic William Ritter on December 18, 1915 (fig. 130).[34] In the background, the twenty-five-year-old Levaillant is seated at a grand piano with Charlotte Amélie Jeanneret-Gris, Jeanneret's mother; no doubt a music lesson is in progress. In the foreground, the writing desk holds an inkwell, some literature on Rembrandt, and a brandy bottle. The pictorial conception, with its Old Master echoes, is clearly intended as a humorous characterization of Jeanneret's young friend's mental cosmos, which also includes the Neuchâtel pendulum clock on the right. Estimates and invoices from 1914 provide additional information on the interior: coconut-fiber matting with a check pattern in blue and beige, an antique couch covered in blue toile de Jouy,[35] a matching throw on the piano, red drapes, newly installed electric light (50-watt) with a cloth lampshade favored by the architect.[36] Jeanneret advised Levaillant to keep the Viennese chairs and had the walls painted in a plain color to match the paneled dado. He also took responsibility for the pictures on the walls: engravings after Raphael and Rembrandt, a portrait of Erasmus, an engraving of Pompeii, and a Japanese print, which were purchased and put into old frames.[37]

The invoices also record the meticulous nature of the accounting process—which reveals that the desk made by the firm of Richard cost 150 rather than the 120 Swiss francs of Jeanneret's estimation, even without allowing for the late addition of the painting by Humbert.[38] The almost obsessive manipulation of financial details—always involving his own fees or discounts from suppliers—is evident not only in Jeanneret's interior design projects but in all of his undertakings. In general, he gave the closest attention to every detail even of this small project: "I repeat that I am interested in this interior installation in order to derive publicity from it. But I would ask you not to reveal the price to anyone whatever. This price could not be maintained for a second undertaking."[39]

In subsequent years, a number of pieces were added to the interior, including in 1916 a floor lamp, the invoice for which constitutes one of the few authentic records of the activities of Société Lumière, the lamp manufacturing firm set up at Jeanneret's prompting (see p. 238). As late as August 1917, after Jeanneret's move to Paris, he designed his celebrated divan couch, displayed on a platform and backed on two sides with an L-shaped balustrade that ended in a swan-neck motif (see p. 240). The drawing for this unique piece in dark gray painted wood also shows a night table in the Louis XVI style and a "period" candlestick on the dresser. In the fall of the same year, Levaillant took an interest in an even more eccentric object, a three-legged aquarium by the Société Lumière that also served as a lamp. After a traveling exhibition organized by L'Oeuvre in 1916, the aquarium was offered for sale, in need of some repair, for 365 francs.[40] Clearly, Levaillant was not far from becoming a collector of unique items by Jeanneret/Le Corbusier.

Levaillant did, however, pass up the chance to acquire one of the suites of seat furniture that Jeanneret began to design on commission around 1914 or 1915. It remains a moot point whether Jeanneret, in his preference for neoclassical furniture types, was pushing at a half-open door or conforming, at least partly, to the milieu that already existed among his clients. Yvonne and Raphaël Schwob, for example—owners of a villa built by Léon Boillot in the French manner in 1913—in which Jeanneret installed a library in 1916, owned valuable pieces of Directoire furniture, some of which bore the mark of Jacob Frères, one of the esteemed French furniture makers at the turn of the eighteenth-century (fig. 132).[41] (The *ébéniste* Georges Jacob seems always to have been important to Jeanneret.[42]) Not surprisingly, Jeanneret, who started by buying period furniture or having it reproduced with slight modifications,[43] soon carried out an *exercice de style* that, while using identical motifs within a suite of furniture, sought to achieve an even greater purity and simplicity, a still stronger "sobriety" (fig. 133). With time, his selective use of historic furniture pieces gave him a range of types to fill different functions, all marked by a rigorous structural logic and an elegant precision of form. This empirical approach, based on a selection process, is a precursor of his later classification of seating categories (1920–27), in which each function was represented by an extant furniture type; the period pieces were then progressively replaced by a range of *objets-types* (type-objects): anonymous, industrially fabricated pieces that were, so to speak, emblematic of their own function.[44]

The furniture groups designed by Jeanneret in 1915–16 owe far more to a formal and structural analysis of types than to the exploitation of decoration. Even so, unlike later assemblages of *objets-types* (or serial ready-mades), they still imply the idea—then current in Switzerland—of *Raumkunst* or spatial art[45]: a homogeneous design subordinated to the architectural idea of interior space. Writing to Salomon Schwob in 1913, Jeanneret had gone so far as to define the apartment as "a whole that is moved in a single direction."[46] The interiors for Levaillant, however, only partly reflect this ideal. One at a time, the pieces of furniture designed by Jeanneret for Levaillant came together as precisely datable items that traced the client's life in a kind of "construction of a biography." This anticipated the modernist principles, already mentioned, that aimed at heterogeneous objects within a homogeneous ideology.

134. Le Corbusier, perspective study of Madeleine Schwob's library, March 3, 1922, heliograph on paper, watercolor, FLC [247]

135. Le Corbusier, Madeleine Schwob's bookcase, made by Jean Egger, detail, 1922, MBA [13]

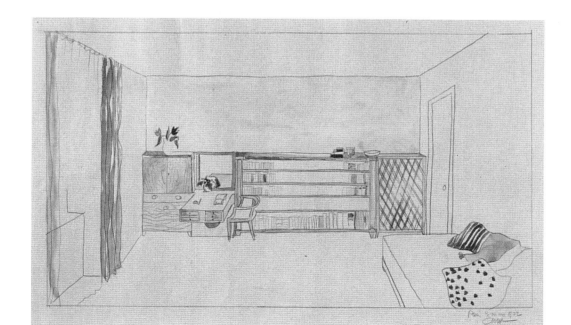

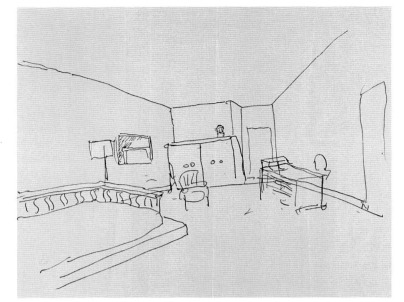

136. Le Corbusier, perspective sketch of Marcel Levaillant's bedroom, 1923, ink on paper, private collection, Switzerland

137. Le Corbusier, perspective sketch of Marcel Levaillant's library and music room, 1923, ink on paper, private collection, Switzerland

"TOWARD PURISM": THE INTERIORS OF 1922–23

In 1921 Levaillant's niece Madeleine (1901–2000), married René Schwob (1885–1937), a scion of the Schwob Frères dynasty. Writing from Besançon in January of 1922, she (or her mother, Marcel's sister Hélene Floesheim-Levaillant) asked Jeanneret/Le Corbusier if he would design a library and bedroom for her.[47] He accepted and in the early months of that year designed an interior in which, once more, he specified the minutest details, down to the pale blue and pink wallpapers and classical wall fixtures (fig. 134). In the bedroom, he filled in a rectangular window and replaced it with a semicircular arch in plasterwork, into which he built a set of shelves;[48] this was shortly before the publication of his manifesto *Vers une architecture* (1923) and at a time when Purist painting was at its height. A floor lamp consisted of an automobile headlight on a hand-crafted wrought-iron stand (see p. 244). The four-part bookstand in wild-cherry (*mérisier*) is vintage Jeanneret/Le Corbusier (see p. 246), but here, too, the use of concave pilasters with capitals in direct proximity to a cantilevered desktop comes as a surprise at first sight (fig. 135). On the way to definitive new formulations, he once again explored stylistic contrasts to the full. His superb working drawings (now at the Fondation Le Corbusier) conclusively disprove the allegation that he knew nothing of the technical refinements of furniture making (see p. 247).

As Le Corbusier embarked on the planning stage of Madeleine Schwob's commission, he enlisted Levaillant as an ally, appealing to their old friendship (and at the same time urging him to subscribe to *L'Esprit nouveau*). In December 1923, when Madeleine Schwob brusquely rejected some long-sought armchairs, Le Corbusier resigned, observing that he had had quite enough of "payment on the La Chaux-de-Fonds system"; whereupon the loyal Marcel Levaillant intervened, appealed on behalf of his niece, and simultaneously reproached Le Corbusier for trying to settle an old La Chaux-de-Fonds debt cheaply with the help of Levaillant "under the Paris system."[49]

By then one of the best-documented and most elaborate interior design commissions that Le Corbusier ever received was well in hand: the remodeling and interior design of a library and bedroom for Levaillant himself (figs. 136, 137). On November

10, 1922, Le Corbusier had accepted the commission, requested photographs of the space, and stipulated that work could not possibly be concluded by the end of December.[50] By January 1923 a lively correspondence was in progress between the two men, conducted with the aid of plans, perspective renderings, and material samples. At the end of 1923 Le Corbusier counted "fifty-seven letters between you, me, and Egger."[51] Jean Egger was a Paris-trained cabinetmaker, who worked in La Chaux-de-Fonds making furniture of high artistic quality until 1943. Jeanneret considered this gifted *ébéniste*, whom he had discovered in the 1910s, able to give perfect practical expression to his ideas.[52] Theirs was a relationship that was entirely analogous to that between Adolf Loos and his favorite joiner, Josef Veillich.

The two rooms involved were on the ground floor of the Villa les Eglantines, one of the most luxurious apartment buildings on the west side of La Chaux-de-Fonds, which suggests something of the lifestyle of the town's watch and clock magnates in the years before World War I. Designed by Jeanneret's former rival Léon Boillot in 1909, the building consisted of four floors, each with a ten-room apartment comprising kitchen, dining room, *fumoir* with veranda, large and small drawing rooms, billiard room, three bedrooms, and guest room, plus servant quarters, bathroom, and separate toilet. The ground floor was the home of Levaillant's parents, with direct access to a richly planted garden by way of a terrace and an outside flight of steps. The billiard room—which opened onto the terrace—and the nursery were to be converted into a suite of rooms for Marcel Levaillant (figs. 138–40).

Le Corbusier blocked the superfluous openings—boarding over the sliding door to the large drawing room with plywood panels—and created a new opening between the two rooms. The paneling of the billiard room was dismantled and put into storage. In the bedroom, the centerpiece was the 1917 bed designed by Jeanneret, with its balustrades and pedestal adapted for the new setting. It is not entirely clear whether the 1914 desk was now placed in the bedroom or—as shown in the first sketch—in the library.[53] To these two characteristic pieces, Le Corbusier added a third: a large but low wardrobe. This featured in his first sketch, as well as in the correspondence. Le Corbusier forbore to mention that in this case he was recycling a design (possibly unexecuted) that he had done in 1922 when remodeling Jean Berque's house at Villa Montmorency in the 16th Arrondissement of Paris (see pp. 228).[54] The designs were practically a direct tracing of the originals, but in the end

138. Le Corbusier, project for Marcel Levaillant's apartment at Villa Les Eglantines, 1923, pencil on paper, FLC

139. Léon Boillot, Villa Les Eglantines, La Chaux-de-Fonds, 1909, ground floor plan, heliograph, Service d'Urbanisme, La Chaux-de-Fonds

140. Marcel Levaillant apartment, 1923, reconstruction of plan, Arthur Rüegg and Barbara Thommen, 2001

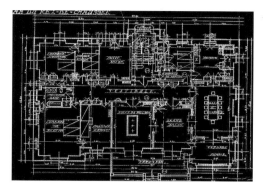

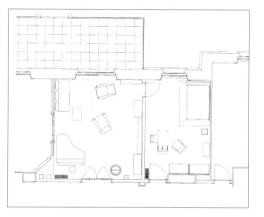

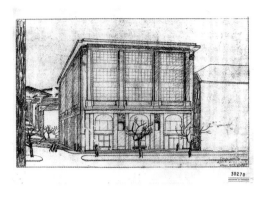

141. Le Corbusier, color sample for the bedroom wardrobe for Marcel Levaillant, ink on yellow paper, private collection, Switzerland

142. Charles-Edouard Jeanneret, project for the Paul Ditisheim Building to be located at 120, Avenue Léopold Robert, La Chaux-de-Fonds, 1913, charcoal on paper, FLC [222]

143. Le Corbusier, wardrobe for Marcel Levaillant's bedroom, with a detail, private collection, Switzerland

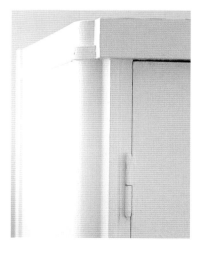

the piece was divided in two, one section for hanging garments and one for folded items, with drawers based on the Innovation models. It was originally to have been white, but ultimately the solid timber carcass was painted gray (to match the bed) on the outside and yellow on the inside, a color that Le Corbusier defined on a scrap of paper (fig. 141).[55]

The design is of interest, among other things, as a model for the formal interiors of Villa Berque, a neoclassical townhouse with an elongated, triangular garden that was an early Paris commission of Le Corbusier's, the exact scope of which has never been traced. For this, in 1921–22, as with the design for Madeleine Schwob, Le Corbusier reverted to his La Chaux-de-Fonds repertoire and revived architectural motifs from his early projects there. The neat and elegant solution for the corner of the wardrobe, for example, is reminiscent of the concrete palazzo-type watch factory designed for Paul Ditisheim in 1913 (figs. 142–43).[56] In the Ditisheim building, the transition between the side elevation and the slightly projecting facade toward rue Léopold-Robert was made with a small-diameter curve. The house and the wardrobe share these rounded corners and horizontal transoms that are above and below the door or window openings. The wardrobe design forms a direct link between the beginning and end of Jeanneret/Le Corbusier's neoclassical period. Although it was 1923, Le Corbusier clearly still accepted the validity of his early formulation. It does not seem likely that he would have tried to integrate this new piece into the context of the earlier furniture if he had considered its formal grammar to be outdated.

In contrast to this use of a "stock" idea in the bedroom, the interior design of the former billiard room was developed from scratch (fig. 144). A three-bay bookcase, stood against the wall between library and bedroom, and a cabinet for musical scores, against the window wall. In contrast to the painted furniture in the bedroom, Le Corbusier had recourse to the tradition of more lavish, formal furnishings in costly natural wood. In numerous letters, with the aid of sketches and renderings, countless details were discussed, right down to the concealed hinges. In the left section of the bookcase, which was a *casier à estampes* (print cabinet), the ultimate solution was to use a simple shelf-rack. On the right (referred to as the *meuble de droite*), Le Corbusier had originally planned for a writing desk with an ingenious hinged mechanism that would allow the owner's typewriter to be stowed away, but this became a writing desk with an open storage compartment and slide-out working surfaces half-way up, a lockable compartment with shelf-rack and retractable doors, and a set of shelves below. The separate music cabinet contains compartments for flat storage below and vertical storage above, both with shutterlike doors that retract vertically into the cabinet.

What is new in this interior is the incorporation of all these custom-built fittings within pieces of furniture that were essentially cubes and rectangles of equal height, which could thus be combined in any way. Le Corbusier designed not only bronze knobs for the drawers and other pull-out components (fig. 145), but also adjustable, sharp-edged bronze feet that lift the chestlike pieces off the floor and make them seem to float in midair. These two innovations mark a decisive advance in relation to the library for Madeleine Schwob, made less than a year earlier, in which individually styled elements were conceived with a specific overall composition in view. Just one year later Le Corbusier completed the *casiers standard*, which were to be the centerpiece of the exhibit in the Pavillon de l'Esprit Nouveau in Paris at the Exposition des Arts décoratifs et industriels modernes in 1925 (see p.248). These stackable containers in the form of half-cubes could be added to and combined ad infinitum to form whole walls, thus providing the architect with a single structural element that would eliminate all the chests, dressers, sideboards, wardrobes, and so on that had previously been in use.[57]

This was the moment for Le Corbusier—for the first time since the *Etude sur le mouvement d'art décoratif*—to pose the rhetorical "question du mobilier" in public and to provide his own answer: death to traditional "furniture"—long live the *équipement de l'habitation*! The interior design formula that he had hinted at before 1925 was now a mature, comprehensive program, supplemented by a select repertoire of objects:

> The program: to negate Decorative Art . . . A new term replaces the term *furniture*. . . . The new word is *the equipment of the house*. To equip the house is, by analyzing the problem, to classify the various elements necessary for domestic operation. Shelving . . . and seats alone remain, along with tables.[58]

With this radical statement, Le Corbusier finally turned his back on the mere modernization and variation of stylistic formulas which had typified the traditional approach of L'Oeuvre (or of the French *ensembliers*) and culminated in the Art Déco style of 1925.

144. Le Corbusier, Marcel Levaillant's apartment at Villa Les Eglantines, 1923. Perspective of library and music room, pencil on drawing paper, private collection, Switzerland

145. Le Corbusier, Bookcase for Marcel Levaillant, plan for bronze support, detail of working drawing, 1923, pencil and colored pencil on drawing paper, private collection, Switzerland

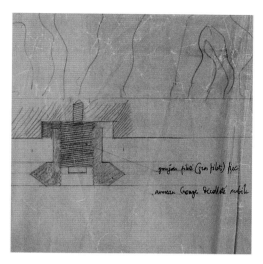

146. Armchair called "Franklin," Maple & Co. London and Paris. Bought by Marcel Levaillant in 1923, leather and velvet, private collection, Switzerland [21]

147. Armchair called "Bernard," Maple & Co. London and Paris. Bought by Marcel Levaillant in 1923, leather and velvet, private collection, Switzerland

148. Le Corbusier, sketches of Maple & Co. armchairs and recommendation to buy for Marcel Levaillant, 1923, ink on green paper, private collection, Switzerland [254]

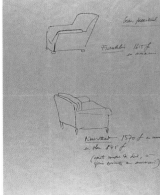

The Levaillant bookcase thus marked an important step in the virtually unbroken developmental process that culminated in Le Corbusier's case furniture of 1925, 1929, and 1931. It even anticipated case furniture's grammar of components: the *casiers standard* of 1925 were painted yellow ocher on the outside, but with mahogany veneer door and drawer fronts (see p. 249). This distinction between carcass and container is anticipated in the Levaillant furniture of 1923, where it is established not by the paint finish but by the use of different veneers. The frames are in plain pearwood, and the drawers and doors in burr elm outside and dark bubinga veneer inside (this last jointed diagonally). By the beginning of February, Le Corbusier had visited Chossonnerie, a firm of timber merchants, in Paris to select and finally order his veneers in person; it was impossible to reserve these expensive items in advance, because the pattern of the wood varied from tree to tree.[59]

SEAT FURNITURE FOR LEVAILLANT, 1923–26: "OBJETS-TYPES"

In 1915 and 1916, while planning groups of high-quality neoclassical seat furniture, Jeanneret was scouring the antique shops of Lausanne or Geneva for "farm furniture"[60] for his parents' house in La Chaux-de-Fonds, among others (see p. 252). Sketchbook A1 records a variety of discoveries of this kind, with notes on shape, dimensions, price, and condition (such as "good straw").[61] His perspective drawings in 1922 of interiors for the "Immeuble-villas" project still illustrate traditional pieces of this kind,[62] and his own Paris apartment at 20 rue Jacob was also furnished with them. They document Jeanneret's early interest not so much in the decorative features as in the generalized characteristics of *production normale*.[63]

In 1923, however, Le Corbusier advised Levaillant to purchase bulky English club chairs (figs. 146–48). Evidently, both men had already visited the Paris branch of the famous English furniture emporium, Maple and Company. Levaillant agreed at once to order two armchairs in high-quality undyed "maroquin" leather, with brown velvet cushions: one "Franklin" and one very deep "Bernard"—"very agreeable for long-legged individuals (such as myself)!"[64] Writing in *L'Esprit nouveau* for June 1921, Le Corbusier had included these chairs in a first list of seats that qualified as *objets-types*:

> There exist straw-bottomed church chairs, price 5 francs; Maple's armchairs, price 1,000 francs; and Morris chairs with adjustable inclination, movable reading-stand, tray for coffee cup, extendable foot-rest, adjustable back, with crank-handle to adopt the perfect angle, from taking a nap to working, hygienically, comfortably, correctly. Your *bergères*, your Louis XVI *causeuses* with their Aubusson or Salon d'Automne [tapestries of] pumpkin motifs: are those machines for sitting on?[65]

Le Corbusier's later classification of seat furniture is already implicit in this early list. It eventually was developed, at first simply by replacing one example with another. Traditional *bergères à paille* gave way to Thonet (especially the writing chair, No. 6009; see p. 254). In place of the Morris chair mentioned in 1921, Le Corbusier discovered another "machine for sitting on," this time devised by a French physician named Pascaud: the "Surrepos" chair, which was based on the technology of dentists', barbers', and invalid chairs.[66] In 1925 the only item from Le Corbusier's initial list that found its way into the model interior of the Pavillon de l'Esprit Nouveau was Maple's club chair. The criteria for the admission of any specific model into the "repertoire" were evidently formal quality plus conformity to the criteria of *production normale*, as established for the *objets-types* of Purist painting. Dr. Pascaud's armchair, with its heavy cast-iron base, had obviously failed to pass muster, along with the antiquated-looking Morris chair. The English club chair, however, was the very embodiment of being comfortable and relaxed while seated: an *objet-type* that Le Corbusier long continued to favor (as, for example, in 1925 for the interior designed for Raoul La Roche)[67] It was an object of such perfection that it required no design input from him. Such objects that were, so to speak, extensions of the human limbs ("objets-membres humains" [68]) derived their formal perfection from an ongoing process of adaptation, and their legitimacy from a long period of use. In this way—again in accordance with Purist ideology—the *objets-types* acquired the emblematic quality proper to "the object in itself":

> . . . perfect in their legibility, and recognized without effort, they obviate the dispersal, the diversion of our attention, which would be distracted from its contemplation by any singularities, or by the unknown, or by the poorly known.[69]

Le Corbusier's way of matching a specific function to an emblematic, visually effective *objet-type* and assembling a repertoire of such objects with which to furnish interiors is of immense importance for his later development. The four pieces of seat furniture that he designed jointly with Charlotte Perriand in 1928–29 were actually a further development of the *objets-types*, retaining their individual characteristics, as well as their specific structural details. These classic pieces have no common design features, formal or structural, that would constitute a "furniture suite" of the kind represented by Jeanneret's own neoclassical seat furniture of 1915–16 (see p. 230)—or, for that matter, by the avant-garde German and Dutch tubular steel furniture of the later 1920s.[70] The kinship that unites the four is both less obvious and more fundamental than this, because it resides in a programmatic idea.

Levaillant's two light-colored club chairs from Maple's are undoubtedly the finest surviving examples of this type from the Purist period. They differ in distinctive ways: not only in their proportions, but also in the configuration of the arms and back, and in the feet—balls in one case, tapering cones in the other. The constituent elements, however, are the same: three upright masses of upholstery on wooden frames enclosing springs that support a velvet-covered down cushion. This was exactly the design formula adopted in 1928 for Le Corbusier's "Grand Confort" armchair. In this, too, springs rested on a rigid base and supported a down-filled cushion. However, the upholstered sides and back were held in an iron frame fabricated by architectural hardware techniques. The analogous balcony railing used at Villa Besnus in 1923 illustrates the technique employed in this new piece of furniture, which marks a conceptual step forward in the separation of supporting from supported members.[71]

It may be assumed that Levaillant followed new developments closely, and that he visited the Pavillon de l'Esprit Nouveau in Paris in 1925. At the end of that year, he made an unsuccesful attempt to clear up the financial mess left by the fiasco of the Scala movie theater in La Chaux-de-Fonds, built by Le Corbusier in 1916–17, a gesture that greatly strengthened the friendship between the two men.[72] On January 5, 1926, after Levaillant had visited the Villas La Roche–Jeanneret,[73] Pierre Jeanneret recorded a further order from Levaillant, related to the *équipement de l'habitation* exhibited at the Pavillon de l'Esprit Nouveau. The order consisted of one *table juxtaposable,* with two interchangeable mahogany tabletops of different sizes, as a dining table (Le Corbusier's first piece of modernist "type" furniture, in a previously unexecuted variant), plus four dark gray, painted Thonet armchairs. For his bedroom Levaillant wanted just one *casier standard*, and for his library, the

149. Le Corbusier, Globe for Marcel Levaillant, 1926, nickeled tubes and brass ring, globe, private collection, Switzerland

150. Rodolphe Töpffer, *Histoire de Mr. Pencil*, Paris, 1840, extract published in *L'Esprit nouveau*, no. 11/12, 1921, p. 1339: "Les vignettes se succèdent comme les feuillets de petits cinés en carnet..."

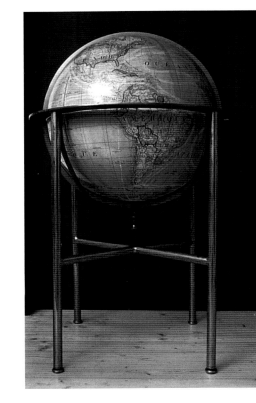

huge, metal-framed globe that harked back to magnificent examples made for monastic and private libraries in the post-Renaissance period (fig. 149). In July 1926, Levaillant added to his list a small metal table by the firm of Schmittheissler to replace an antique occasional table that stood next to the green-upholstered couch. Le Corbusier recorded the look of the *casier* and globe on spare photo proofs from the *Almanach de l'architecture moderne,* a monograph on the Pavillon de l'Esprit Nouveau.[74]

While this order from a new, commercial furnishing range might seem straightforward, it involved Le Corbusier in lengthy correspondence and much effort, since he still took personal charge of all business connected with Levaillant—although the correspondence was now shared with his office, represented by Pierre Jeanneret. On June 12, 1926, Le Corbusier recorded the dispatch of the small *casier standard*, expressing regret, however, that the finish was so poor that Jean Egger would have to touch up some parts of it in La Chaux-de-Fonds.[75] Unlike the pieces in the Pavillon de l'Esprit Nouveau, this one had not been painted, with mahogany inserts, but was made entirely of mahogany, varnished *à l'antique*. This gave it a monotonous and rather ponderous appearance.

On February 26, 1927, Le Corbusier reported that he had been to Schmittheissler's to inspect the completed metal table. Here, too, he was unsatisfied with the gray paint job, which would have to be redone. He felt compelled to make his excuses: "Until January 25, I was incommunicado, locked into forced labor with a dozen draftsmen for the League of Nations competition."[76] Work on the globe, a somewhat purified variant of the one shown at the Pavillon de l'Esprit Nouveau, took even longer, as it was broken in transit and had to be replaced. Ultimately, the commission was not completed until May 1927.

ICONOGRAPHIC REFERENCES: THE "TECHNIQUE DES GROUPEMENTS"

At this point, Levaillant possessed an unbroken run of examples to illustrate the development of Jeanneret/Le Corbusier's work in interior design. The chronological range extended from January 1914 to 1927, the year that Charlotte Perriand

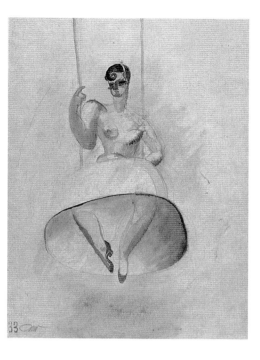

joined the office. It included some of the architect's rarest and/or most eccentric pieces: writing desk, bed, bookcase, terrestrial globe. These form part of a vast body of evidence that records the gradual formation of Le Corbusier's *équipement de l'habitation*—and of his architectural and artistic thinking as a whole—out of the initial neoclassicism that was conditioned by his travels and early practical experience. In January 1926 Le Corbusier sent Levaillant the newly published theoretical foundation of his position—the four volumes of the *Collection de L'Esprit nouveau*—with revealing hand-written inscriptions on the flyleaves. In *La Peinture moderne*, for example, he made this ambiguous statement: "A leap into modern painting—it's hard, maybe?"[77] This can be interpreted either as a rueful comment from a member of the avant-garde bruised by his frontal assault on convention, or as a reference to the impossibility of simply severing all links with tradition in favor of a "leap" into an abstract future.

Levaillant's papers contain further references to Le Corbusier's stubborn endeavor to reconcile tradition and a utopian ideal. Even before the summer vacation season of 1926, Le Corbusier had started work on a series of figurative paintings, commissioned by Levaillant, on the theme of the music hall (figs. 152–53).[78] These are steeped in the romanticism of his early work. On November 5, he reported that he had completed fifty watercolors, "cutting no corners," because "I have no desire to have garbage appearing under my name."[79] He asked to keep the watercolors for a while longer, in order to show them to friends. It was only after a number of reminders from Levaillant that, on September 19, 1927, Le Corbusier at last notified him that the watercolors were at Villa Le Lac, Corseaux, awaiting the next opportunity for delivery:

> I have been told that it is a crime on my part to sell them. Well may you feel flattered, happy owner.—I am enclosing with the bundle some instructions for use. No kidding! These daubs are not to be framed. It only works when seen rapidly, cinematically [see fig. 150]. I rely on you.

His so-called instructions were for the viewer to "Hurry up, hurry on by, take a

151–53. Le Corbusier, *50 aquarelles de Music-Hall ou le "QUAND-MEME" des Illusions*, title page and plates 24 and 33, pencil and watercolor on paper

154. Le Corbusier, sketch for the support of the plaster cast of the head of Prince Gudea from the Louvre, 1923, ink on paper, FLC

155. Le Corbusier, sketch for positioning the plaster casts from the Louvre in Marcel Levaillant's apartment, 1923, ink on paper, FLC [257]

156. Head of the Chaldean Prince, Gudea, Lagash, 2130 B.C. found 1881, Louvre Museum, Paris, modern plaster cast, private collection, Switzerland [137]

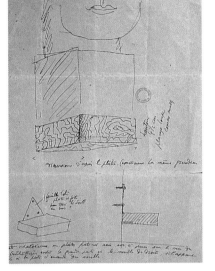

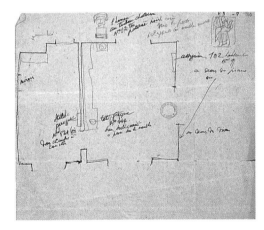

quick look. That's enough. Music-hall is a fast and momentary thing. It sets up a certain dazzle that emerges from the din and the ladies' legs."

The subtitle of the suite, "Le 'Quand-même' des illusions" (Illusions, even so), precisely illustrates the status of this early attempt by a prominent Purist to reengage with mood and atmosphere—and with the human figure, which only later became a central theme of his sketches and paintings.[80] Le Corbusier situated the experience of these watercolors—which he self-deprecatingly described to his friend as "daubs"—in an avant-garde, cinematic context that almost automatically recalls the floor lamp for Madeleine Schwob, with its trial marriage between a traditionally made wrought-iron stand and an automobile headlight (see p. 244).

Studies of this kind engineered confrontations between disparate worlds, sharpening the perceptions and enabling Le Corbusier to annex an iconographic vocabulary that would serve the further development of his artistic ideas. This, of course, was also the function of the notes made on his travels with camera and sketchbook—some of which have been meticulously edited for publication in recent years—and of his still underrated private collection, which contained an enormous variety of artifacts as testament to an uninterrupted visual quest.[81]

Early in his life, Jeanneret found another way to expand his own visual repertoire, one that has hitherto escaped analytical attention. He asked most of his interior design clients to set up a line of credit that would oblige (and also, in his own and others' eyes, authorize) him to spend his time systematically picking over the contents of galleries, antique shops, and furnishing stores. For his earliest commissions, he had plunged into the exhilarating atmosphere of Paris in connection with the Salomon Schwob project (1913); and for the first interior design for Levaillant's study (1914) he came up with engravings and Japanese prints in tune with his own current taste. Thereafter, he regularly assumed the dual roles of buying agent and mentor for his clients. In September 1919 he offered his services to the purchaser of his parents' house in La Chaux-de-Fonds, Fritz Ernst Jeker:

> One question quite rightly concerns you: that of the minor objects, vases, paintings, drawings, prints, bibelots, etc. . . . Have no anxieties on this score. Above all, be in no hurry to purchase: you will find nothing where you are, whereas here I can add your name to the list of those friends and clients who have mandated me to make purchases on their behalf. This is easy for me to do in a city like PARIS, where anything can be found if one knows where to look, and at some astounding prices, too. . . . In this matter, if this were to suit you, I would ask you simply to open a line of credit for me, and I would account for my expenditure as purchasing proceeded.[82]

In May 1923 Le Corbusier ordered four plaster casts from the cast workshop of the Musée du Louvre, to be sent to Levaillant's apartment. He supplied Levaillant with sketches to show their exact positioning in the apartment: in the drawing room, a turbaned head was to be attached to the wall on a base veneered with the same burr veneer as the bookcase; a relief from Mesopotamia was to be installed elsewhere in the room; a Greek sculpture was to stand on the print cabinet; and a Greek stele in the bedroom (figs. 154–56).[83] This is the only transaction for which the correspondence contains no comment from Levaillant, but a few years later, he expressed the desire to possess an ancient Greek vase. Le Corbusier's response in February 1926 was brief and to the point: "Couldn't find a Greek vase. There are none left. On the other hand, for 10,000 francs, or for 4,000, or for 3,000, Paul Guillaume has some magnificent Negro woodcarvings (heads), as in the *E[sprit] N[ouveau]* number (*sculptures nègres*)."[84]

Levaillant bought 7,750-francs' worth, and was happy with his purchase: "The Negro woodcarvings are very good and look well on the bookcase. Against all expectations, they have many admirers. Humbert came by the other evening and touched them all over."[85] In a Levaillant family group photograph, a female figure and a white-painted mask can be seen in Marcel's library—the only surviving trace of these purchases on Le Corbusier's part (fig. 157).

In mid-1926, finally, Levaillant sought to acquire a small painting by Picasso. In September he received a report that a good Braque of 1911 or so ("looking very like the Picasso you showed me") had come up for sale at a price of 30–35,000 francs, but Le Corbusier seems to have dissuaded him from buying by reporting that pieces like it could still have been acquired for just 800 francs in 1922.[86] The matter presumably went no further. Interestingly, Le Corbusier had been involved in the sale of the collection of art dealer Daniel-Henry Kahnweiler, which ran from 1921 to 1923. On Le Corbusier's urgent recommendation, Raoul La Roche sent Amédée Ozenfant and Oscar Miestschaninoff to attend the various auctions as La Roche's representative, thus laying the foundation of one of the greatest collections of cubist and Purist art.[87]

Le Corbusier's activities on his clients' behalf reflect the changing interests, as well as the complex and at times contradictory character, of his quest. He had the ability to recognize trends intuitively and process them in his own way. He always kept for himself those pieces that seemed to him essential, so that in time his apartment became almost the private museum of an urbane eccentric—an impression also conveyed by the odd assortment of objects displayed at the Pavillon de l'Esprit Nouveau in 1925.[88] The impact of all these objects was defined most of all by the worlds of experience that they evoke and by the relevance of those worlds to the idea of a "new" architecture.

157. Afrcian sculptures bought by Marcel Levaillant at Galerie Paul Guillaume, Paris, 1926, c. 1930, detail of family photograph (fig. 127), private collection, Switzerland

"Culture," "Folklore," and "Industry"—such were the categories under which Le Corbusier retrospectively classified his experiences, most notably those garnered on his Voyage d'Orient and processed later. The programmatic collection of "finds" shown at the Pavillon de l'Esprit Nouveau can be organized under the same three headings. That those objects were a conceptual model of a natural relationship between society and its artifacts, and that vernacular form was the archetype of the anonymous industrial culture of the age, were the central lessons of Jeanneret/Le Corbusier's collecting activity. [89]

To analyze and organize his discoveries, and ultimately to reuse them in a different context, was a true passion. In 1935 Le Corbusier's *technique des groupements* (grouping technique) gave rise to an exhibition at his then-new apartment on rue Nungesser-et-Coli in Paris, in which he deliberately juxtaposed ancient and modern cultural materials. Its aim was "to recognize 'series,' to create 'unities' that transcend time and space, to bring to palpitating life the sight of those things on which man has inscribed his presence."[90]

In pursuit of these ends Le Corbusier cut across temporal sequences, thematic connections, and spatial separations. He simply synthesized the things that he found into a new whole and in the process, cast himself in a somewhat strange light as the propagandist and prophet of a new age and a progressive architecture. But in this way he succeeded in resolving the fundamental antithesis between tradition and innovation—unlike the exponents of a modernist movement that found its sole justification in the idea of progress.

COHERENCE THROUGH COLOR—AND THE "SYNTHESIS OF THE ARTS"

Unlike others, such as the Swiss architect Hannes Meyer (who in his famous Coop Interior of 1926 used a number of standard products to make a forceful presentation of the "New Man's" "collective demand" for "satisfaction of the same needs by the same means"[91]) Le Corbusier always went beyond purely ideological premises in his assemblages. While on the one hand, by means of his *objets-types*, he developed the categories of requisite furniture types, on the other, he deliberately selected—increasingly often from a remote context—those sculpturally interesting objects that enabled him to achieve a "composition" in his interiors, just as he did in his painting.[92] This means that, despite—or because of—the heterogeneous assemblages in his interiors, Le Corbusier aspired to a new kind of unity in interior design, an alternative to the "spatial art" of art moderne that was the acknowledged enemy of "l'esprit nouveau."

An essential feature of this method of composition was "architectural polychromy." Earlier, Jeanneret had given color designations for Levaillant's study (1914), which conformed to the precedent laid down by the Coloristes, and also had chosen pink and pale blue wallpapers for Madeleine Schwob (1922), which followed tradition by covering all the walls uniformly, while conferring a Purist tonality on the rooms as a whole (see pp. 117, 118). In Levaillant's apartment (1923), the chests in the bedroom were not painted white as originally planned but the same gray as the 1917 bed. This use of color enabled the two very different pieces of furniture to relate to each other. Again, the Thonet chairs that Le Corbusier ordered in 1926 were also painted gray and thus cut off from their original context; they were "annexed" and incorporated into the interior (see p. 123). In 1923 to accompany this gray tone and the natural wood color of the bookcase suite, Le Corbusier planned a textile floor covering that would not be black but a dark, gray-tinged shade of ocher. In a letter he repeated almost verbatim the arguments that he had used previously, for example, to Jeker, the purchaser of his parents' house. For the colors, which had to be precise, he specified "*tête de nègre*," "*cachou*," and "dark blackish gray" and wrote, "I particularly insist on this issue, which is vital: a discordant background tone would jeopardize the whole ensemble."[93] After a certain amount of deliberation, Le Corbusier visited the Printemps department store early in March 1923 to buy the lengths of material required for Levaillant's apartment in a slightly lighter tonality ("suede brown, paler than *tête de nègre,* very pretty"), plus four geometric patchwork hide rugs ("these rugs are a real bargain and will lend a very special cachet to your interior"). [94]

The wallpapers were also shipped from Paris by the architect. In January Levaillant agreed to a pinkish white paper, and at the beginning of April Le Corbusier specified that the strips should be hung without borders at top or bottom. To set off the light-colored walls, white drapes were planned from the start. For the bedroom, materials arrived—again from Paris—for a red bedspread (slightly darker than the wallpaper) and for red and dark blue cushions. For the library, a blue-gray silk and a green material were used, presumably for the piano and couch, and blue-green, green, and red material for cushions. "I am certain," said the architect at the end of a letter written in early March, "that the harmony of the chosen colors will be entirely agreeable and very strong."[95]

All this laborious accumulation of detail conveys something of the fresh and welcoming mood of the rooms as they were installed in 1923. This description also helps confirm Le Corbusier's early use of color to join the elements of his interiors. The "architectural polychromy" of Purism is the outcome of an ongoing developmental process that can be traced, via the early designs under French and German influence, at least as far back as the impressions gained during his travels in 1910–11. Initially, this approach to color extended even to strongly patterned wallpapers (see p. 242). Gradually, Jeanneret/Le Corbusier developed a color palette that helped to pull together the varied objects in an interior and set them off advantageously in relation to the surfaces that enclosed the space.

Although Le Corbusier himself alleged in the *Oeuvre complète* that his first experiments with color in interior design dated as late as 1925,[96] his efforts obviously began earlier. It is certainly untrue that his 1925 interest merely represented a reaction to the experiments of the Dutch group De Stijl.[97] Instead, between 1923 and 1925—and via a complex synthesis of largely discrete developments in painting, architecture, and interior design—Le Corbusier achieved the decisive reorientation that he organized into a coherent program at the Pavillon de l'Esprit Nouveau (fig. 158).

Levaillant never treated himself to a modern house in which the space-changing effects of Purist polychromy could have taken full effect. However, the letters and drawings among his papers faithfully trace the subsequent changes in Le Corbusier's color palette. On February 26, 1933, the architect wrote to him from Algiers in response to a query:

> This is my seventh foreign trip since Christmas. On one of my stopovers in Paris, I found your letter. Here is what you can do: ask your wallpaper dealer for the Salubra Le Corbusier Collection. In this, there are all the plain colors you need to act with perfect safety.[98]

Here, Le Corbusier was able to fall back on a color range that he had put together in 1930–31 for the Basel wallpaper firm Salubra. [99] The key to this collection of forty-three hues (plus some patterns), which may be regarded as the legacy of Purist color theory, resides in twelve sample cards, on each of which three wider strips provide

158. Le Corbusier and Pierre Jeanneret, Pavillon de l'Esprit nouveau, Paris 1925. Living room (detail), reconstructed by Arthur Rüegg and Silvio Schmed (1987).

159. Le Corbusier, Matroil coulour samples for Marcel Levaillant's Geneva apartment, 1956, colored paper on heliograph, pencil and color pencils, private collection, Switzerland

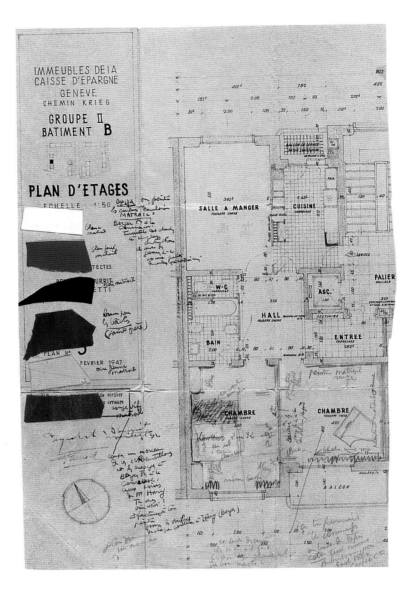

room colors and two narrower strips show contrasting tones. A slide enables the user to find appropriate, or at least compatible, color combinations for any desired mood.

At that time, paint colors were often mixed on-site or applied as painted wallpapers; they were based on a number of traditional powder pigments that were in international use. After World War II, this practice changed radically. Paint manufacturers began to market ready-to-apply colors in tones that varied from one maker to the next. Initially, Le Corbusier dealt with this situation by working with the French subsidiary of the British paint manufacturer Berger, which brought out a "Gamme Le Corbusier" for him. Thus, in 1956, when Levaillant decided to retire to an apartment in Geneva, Le Corbusier used drawings of the apartment, on which he added color indications, with samples (fig. 159), together with a categorical statement of his opinion on the current state of affairs:

> The essential point of my letter is to tell you that, if you want to be in an acceptable color environment, you cannot and must not use any paints other than the Matroil range from Peintures Berger.... There is no other paint to compare with it; and, if your painter objects, fire him.[100]

These colors, far more intense than those of the Purist period, were brought out shortly afterward in a second Salubra range, again marketed as a "color keyboard."[101] With this, for the second time, Le Corbusier had achieved something with color that he had long attempted in a wide variety of fields (including that of furniture): the establishment of harmonious relationships among precisely selected elements that would satisfy typical needs and provide consistent stimuli. The knowledge of these rules would, he believed, give him everything he needed "to act with perfect safety."

Le Corbusier and Levaillant were to exchange many more tokens of friendship. But Levaillant had just one more opportunity to integrate a sensational piece of furniture by his friend into his living quarters. In 1954 Levaillant requested a copy of the table in Le Corbusier's Paris apartment at 24 rue Nungesser-et-Coli.[102] This table was a slice from a tree trunk, which Le Corbusier had had mounted on a three-legged wrought-iron base (fig. 160)—a typical manifestation of the architect's interest in organic forms, beginning in the 1930s, as well as in rustic materials like those used in the monastic simplicity of his vacation cabin at Roquebrune (1952). Once again, Le Corbusier showed little interest in Levaillant's request, until Levaillant sent a young mosaic artist, François Petermann (who made mosaic tables, among other things), to visit the master in Paris with the idea of redesigning one of his own models on the model of the "tree trunk table."[103] Le Corbusier rose to the challenge and sent a drawing by return mail. At the same time, through his photographer, Lucien Hervé, he sent Levaillant a detail from one of his own paintings, which was to be reproduced on the tabletop in the largest possible colored marble pieces.[104]

The contour of this wonderful, unique piece, resembles what may be the shape of a pebble from Roquebrune beach (or perhaps another cross section of a tree). The table top is supported by an iron ring and three legs in wrought iron. This piece encapsulates *pars pro toto* the "synthesis of the arts,"[105] a concept that went a long way beyond simple color configurations. This synthesis fascinated Le Corbusier more and more during the 1950s, when it also found expression in designs for furniture and for liturgical vessels.[106]

By the late 1950s, the array of Le Corbusier's work in Levaillant's homes embraced objects and color schemes derived from all the major creative periods in the architect's career.[107] Over the years, Le Corbusier seems to have come to regard Levaillant's interiors as a kind of repository of his contributions to the art of interior design, and despite logistical difficulties and time constraints he showed an unexpected dedication to meeting his friend's wishes. Levaillant rewarded this effort with a touching devotion and by returning many little favors. With advancing age, Le Corbusier referred with increasing frequency to the uniqueness of their relationship. For example, on January 27, 1959, he wrote:

> My dear Marcel, you are the best of fellows! Your [gift of] chocolates tell[s] me so. I very much appreciate your friendship, which has held firm for all these years. You are the only one from La Chaux (along with Georges Aubert, who moved abroad) who was kind.[108]

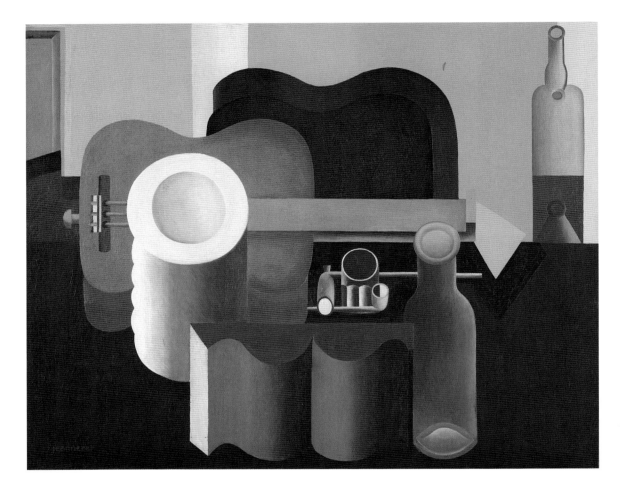

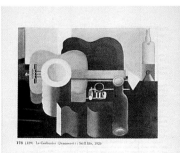

178 (129) Le Corbusier (Jeanneret): Still life, 1920

179 (317) Le Corbusier: Chair

180 (299) Le Corbusier: Model of Savoye house, Poissy-sur-Seine, 1929-30; cf. Le Corbusier, fig. 178.

181 (304) Le Corbusier: de Beistegui penthouse, Paris, 1931

7

FROM ART NOUVEAU TO PURISM: LE CORBUSIER AND PAINTING

Françoise Ducros

LE CORBUSIER WAS AS MUCH an artist as he was an architect. His famous thesis of the 1950s concerning the integration of the arts shows that his work as a painter was essential to him. Around the same time he let it be believed that *La Cheminée* (The Mantelpiece; figs. 168, 454), painted in 1918, the year that Purism was launched, was his first oil painting. Le Corbusier's activity as a painter began precociously in 1902, at the start of his training at the École d'Art in La Chaux-de-Fonds, a school oriented toward the applied arts, architecture, and Art Nouveau. He attempted watercolor and tried oil painting, even though Charles l'Eplattenier, the director of the school and himself an academically trained painter, offered no instruction in this area. The practice of drawing and the study of geometry and ornament, however, were fundamental elements of L'Eplattenier's teaching, but they were intended for a decorative approach to style and its different practical applications.

BEFORE PURISM: THE CHALLENGE OF THE AVANT-GARDE

Even though L'Eplattenier discouraged his pupil's vocation as a painter, encouraging him instead to practice architecture, Le Corbusier continued to execute watercolors and drawings in the form of sketches, studies, and travel impressions. These works can be characterized in two ways. Many of them show the architect-in-training setting down his observations in the purest Ruskinian manner, while others reveal the emergence of a painter in close touch with avant-garde developments. The watercolors presented in group exhibitions of 1912 and 1913 under the poetic title, *Le Langage de pierres* (The language of stones) must be considered true creative efforts independent of his architectural studies.[1] Le Corbusier's emergence as a painter shows the notable influence of Art Nouveau, and also contains references to German Expressionism and French fauvism.

While he pursued his architectural training in the offices of Auguste Perret in Paris and Peter Behrens in Berlin, Le Corbusier continued to be interested in painting.[2] His preferences for "French" art range from Maurice Denis to Van Gogh, and from Kees van Dongen to Matisse, though the possibility that Le Corbusier could also have been influenced by the German artists cannot be ruled out.[3] His *Vue fantastique de la cathédrale de Chartres* (1907) rather recalls the compositions of Ernst Ludwig Kirchner or Franz Marc. Whatever the case, in expressing architecture in a fantastic and theatrical form, for instance through a dissonant use

161. Charles-Edouard Jeanneret, *Nature morte à la pile d'assiettes et au livre* (Still life with a pile of plates and a book), 1920, oil on canvas, Museum of Modern Art, New York [49]

162. Alfred H. Barr, *Cubism and Abstract Art*, exhibition catalogue, Museum of Modern Art, New York 1936, pp. 164–65

133

163. Charles-Edouard Jeanneret, *Pietà* (after Rogier van der Weyden), 1917, oil on canvas, FLC

164. Charles-Edouard Jeanneret, *The Roofs of Paris*, 1914–15, oil on canvas, FLC [46]

of color, and in presenting an occasionally extreme vision of the female body, as in *Scène de genre, avec femmes* (1907), his youthful painted work can be situated within the avant-garde circle.

The early artistic endeavors parallel his architectural studies and do not prepare the way for the Purist period. The roots of Purism, however, can be found in Le Corbusier's writings. The theoretical and poetic character of some of his comments draws upon his power of observation, but his visual evocations reveal above all the hallucinatory vision of a language he had begun to intuit. There are several examples from his 1911 Voyage d'Orient of this other aspect of his work, of his literary contribution to his approach to painting. On the Athenian Acropolis, for example, he viewed the Parthenon as a "cube" situated in space (see fig. 260).[4] In the same year, during his second visit to Pisa, he sent his friend William Ritter a rapturous interpretation of the buildings of the Campo Santo (see fig. 296):

> I experiment clumsily with elementary geometry eager to understand it and eventually master it. In their mad race, the blue and yellow have become white. I'm crazy about the color white, the cube, the sphere, the cylinder, and the pyramid, and the undecorated disk, and the wide open space. Prisms stand up, balance themselves, gain rhythm, and start moving.[5]

These remarks, which spring directly from his literary and philosophical foundation, are not without reference to the pictorial experiments connected with cubism. But Le Corbusier did not discover cubism before 1913, at which time he denied its artistic interest. Only later, in 1918, after his meeting with Ozenfant and after he had taken up an industrial conception of architecture, did he recognize the plastic qualities of cubism.

LE CORBUSIER BEFORE LE CORBUSIER

The present exhibition establishes for the first time that the architect-painter had

165. Charles-Edouard Jeanneret, *Still life: Flowers and Books,* 1916, oil on canvas, FLC [45]

166. Charles-Edouard Jeanneret (Le Corbusier), *Study for a still life with carafe and pitcher,* 1921 (?), pencil on paper, FLC [261]

executed his first oil paintings before 1918. Contrary to the official history, which makes *La Cheminée* his first painting, there are four earlier small-format oil paintings, all with different subjects, at the Fondation Le Corbusier in Paris: a Pietà (fig. 163); a still life composed of flowers and books (fig. 165); a landscape entitled *Les Toits de Paris* (Rooftops of Paris; fig. 164); and a Symbolist composition, *Femme et coquillage* (Woman and shell; fig. 445). These four paintings, which appear to have been done in 1917, have critical relevance. The *Toits de Paris* has references not found in his watercolors, particularly to the influence of Cézanne and of cubism, which had begun to stimulate his work. At the same time, he continued in his romantic or fauvist mode, finding inspiration in Matisse as well as in the more transgressive work of Rupert Carabin. The subject of *Femme et coquillage* remains hermetic, but it also shows that he might have looked at the work of Cézanne for his blue tonalities and approach to space. The Pietà, copied after Rogier van der Weyden, recalls Rouault. In these paintings Le Corbusier used a thin wash, sometimes leaving the bare canvas exposed. These stylistic characteristics disappeared in the course of the next year, while his artistic development led him to convert to an interpretation of painting that was rooted in the critical aftermath of cubism.

OZENFANT AND THE LAUNCHING OF PURISM

In 1917, a year after settling in Paris, Le Corbusier became acquainted with the painter and theoretician Amédée Ozenfant.[6] By January 1918 Le Corbusier began to show enthusiasm for Ozenfant's painting, as well as for cubism.[7] This was to lead in the fall of 1918 to the creation of Purism, which sprang from their joint publication, *Après le Cubisme*. Le Corbusier's own development was also to be marked by the public appearance of a new aspect of his artistic production: the oil paintings that he exhibited with Ozenfant at their first joint exhibition.

167. Charles-Edouard Jeanneret, *Le bol rouge* (The red Bowl), 1919, oil on canvas, FLC

Ozenfant had played an active role in the Parisian artistic avant-garde since 1915, and he provided Le Corbusier with the opportunity to enrich his understanding of it at a critical moment in its history at the end of World War I. Le Corbusier appreciated not only the plastic qualities of Ozenfant's paintings, but also the artist's intellect. Even so, despite allusions to Ozenfant in his correspondence with William Ritter, Le Corbusier left little information about their collaboration and the depth of their relationship. As a result Ozenfant's influence on Le Corbusier has been underestimated.[8]

From 1915 to 1916 Ozenfant had edited *L'Elan,* a review that published the work of poets and artists close to cubism, including two of its major figures, Apollinaire and Picasso. Ozenfant was a habitué of the artistic community and had organized exhibitions with Germaine Bongard, Paul Poiret's sister. He was also associated with the architect August Perret and was interested in industrial technique and, more importantly, in artistic theory. Since Le Corbusier was also interested in theory, it is likely that he learned much from reading *L'Elan.* At the instigation of Léonce Rosenberg,[9] Ozenfant published an excerpt from Plato's *Philebus,* concerning the beauty of geometric forms, and Le Corbusier must have seen this as a reflection of his own poetic interest in the subject, relating directly to his vision of the Parthenon or the buildings of Pisa. The "Notes on Cubism" published by Ozenfant also represented an original interpretation of cubism, insisting on the visual autonomy of the plastic arts while rejecting ornamental abstraction.[10] In Ozenfant's interpretation of cubism as "a movement of purism," Le Corbusier may have recognized his own preoccupations with the universal memory of artistic forms. Ozenfant initiated a theoretical discussion of painting that also revealed, in the context of the end of World War I, the renewal of avant-garde thinking and the search for precepts that would constitute the "organic laws" of painting. Ozenfant's *Composition avec polyèdre flottant* (Composition with floating polyhedron) attests to his belief in a pictorial experience that goes beyond cubism, while he was trying to disseminate his interpretation of painting.

REVISIONS

Confronted by Ozenfant's artistic theory and practice, Le Corbusier realized that his critical position—one characterized by passion—was no longer relevant. The recent theories of Ozenfant completely rejected the credo of spontaneity, in favor of an intellectualized conception of painting. Le Corbusier began to adopt Ozenfant's working methods, doing pencil drawings of Médoc wine bottles, coffeepots, and pipes—the everyday objects of cubism, which Purism sought to conceptualize through the notion of *thème-objet.* The clarity, polish, neatness, and volume that Le Corbusier sought are in opposition with his earlier work. They may suggest a return to classicism, but Le Corbusier had described Ozenfant's painting by referring to aesthetic values that could evoke an industrial aesthetic.[11] Even as he gave evidence of how he had been influenced by Ozenfant's personality, Le Corbusier suffered a personal crisis over his dissatisfaction with his industrial work and yearned to be a painter.[12] Ozenfant strongly advised him to work toward this goal and taught him techniques for obtaining smooth surfaces and modeled volumes.

Le Corbusier identified himself with the values of Purism more closely still by participating in the theoretical development of its founding program. In this complex operation of synthesis and the articulation of the constituent ideas of Purism, the search for plastic laws was the decisive issue for the two artists. But it is possible that Le Corbusier included this formalism as a doctrinaire and symbolic study.

168. Charles-Edouard Jeanneret, *La cheminée* (The Mantelpiece), 1918, oil on canvas, FLC [47]

169. Amédée Ozenfant, *Bouteille, pipe et livres* (Bottle, Pipe and Books), 1918, oil on canvas, Musée de Grenoble, Grenoble

This interpretation can be offered at least for some of his paintings. *La Cheminée* (fig. 168), while not the first oil painting by Le Corbusier, is nonetheless the first to reflect his interpretation of the rules of Purism. In arranging a cube next to books on a mantelpiece, Le Corbusier affirmed his personal interpretation of constants, one of the concepts of *Après le cubisme*. Ozenfant, in his own painting *Bouteille, pipe et livres* (Bottle, pipe, and books; fig. 169), showed that he could reconcile the search for pure form with the visual study of objects in a structured composition. If in *La Cheminée* Le Corbusier gives the cube a stable, poetic, and spatial presence, in *Le Bol rouge* (The red bowl; fig. 167) he created the opposite effect by placing the bowl in a precarious position. This composition evokes a traditional genre laden with symbolism; in this case the attribute of the cube is associate with the values of virtue, truth, and science.[13] This interpretation is corroborated by the fact that the two squares and the roll of paper in *Le Bol rouge* symbolize architecture. The open book in Le Corbusier's *Nature Morte avec livre ouvert, pipe, verre et boite d'allumettes* (Still life with open book, pipe, glass and matchbox; fig. 453) has been compared with the sculpted representation of the Bible on the facade of the Temple de l'Oratoire in Paris.[14]

AUSTERITY AS A CREATIVE METHOD

By choosing to develop his art within the French avant-garde, Le Corbusier curtailed the romantic side of his nature and began to pursue a rigorous purity of form. This severity coincided with a period of profound "austerity," accompanying the new aesthetic values to which the two artists subscribed. They were to explore its doctrinal aspect in two theoretical texts published in their journal, *L'Esprit nouveau*, which presented the Purist grammar, its physical and psychological attributes, its constructive

170. Auguste Choisy, *Histoire de l'architecture*, Paris, 1899, vol. I, pp. 358–59

and chromatic principles, as well as its theory of the *objet-type*.[15]

The early days of *L'Esprit nouveau*—from the end of 1919 until around 1921—was a period of close collaboration between Ozenfant and Le Corbusier, to such a degree that their respective personalities seemed almost to merge. Together they sought a more ascetic lifestyle. In reality, however, their lifestyle reflected the aesthetic values of their pure conception of modernity during the postwar period. In his memoirs Ozenfant included a reference to Daniel-Henry Kahnweiler commenting on their asceticism,[16] a characterization that is confirmed by Jean Epstein, an avant-garde filmmaker, who wrote, after visiting Fernand Léger:

> I had one last visit to make, to the journal *L'Esprit Nouveau*, edited by Amédée Ozenfant and Jeanneret, two painters, the masters and moreover the only representatives of the purist school. Jeanneret was already beginning to be better known as an innovator of architecture under the name of Le Corbusier. Their pictorial purism was a sort of austere Cubism, traced in a straight line, on a single projection plane. The reverent purist brothers, as they were sometimes known, both equally serious and dressed all in black, in an office where every chair, every board, and every sheet of paper had its strictly determined use, intimidated me terribly.[17]

Epstein described with a certain humor the atmosphere of the "editorial board" of *L'Esprit nouveau*, dominated by a geometric order that commanded the placement of every object. His remarks also suggest a reading of that phase of Purism that can be connected to the paintings Jeanneret and Ozenfant exhibited at the Druet gallery. This pictorial Purism "traced in a straight line," in Epstein's words, establishing a direct link with architecture. The comparison between a picture and a single projection plane alludes also to film, an art form that was important to the editors of *L'Esprit nouveau*.[18] The synthesis between the canvas, blueprint, and cinema screen, enabled a new interpretation of the object around a cinematic vision grounded in pure form.

358 ARCHITECTURE GRECQUE.

Le chapiteau fig. 20 provient du portique septentrional de l'Érechtheion.

Ce chapiteau rappelle par plus d'un trait ceux des colonnes archaïques de Délos ou de l'Acropole.

Pour se représenter le tailloir et les volutes, on peut imaginer un double bandeau de matière flexible qui s'amincit progressivement et dont les extrémités s'enroulent sur elles-mêmes : on dirait un ressort élastique qui transmet au fût le poids de l'architrave.

Entre l'échine et cette sorte de ressort s'interpose, à la manière d'un coussin, un membre intermédiaire profilé en tore ; et, au-dessous de l'échine, se place le collier archaïque.

Sur les faces latérales, le balustre se dessine d'un trait ferme et simple ; le balustre se resserre vers le milieu, et l'allure tournante de son profil est accentuée par des cannelures analogues à celles du vieux chapiteau d'Éphèse. Mais ici les têtes des balustres sont exactement verticales, et la variation de largeur des canaux paraît provenir (pag. 356, fig. 19 E) d'une simple division du profil E par parties égales a, a...

Les détails sont d'une richesse tout asiatique :
Le collier est orné de palmettes. Des oves décorent l'échine ; des entrelacs tapissent le bourrelet sur lequel s'appuie le tailloir et, en rappelant l'aspect d'un lacis de rubans, précisent l'idée d'un coussin déjà indiqué par le profil.
Avant les mutilations que le monument a subies, des rosettes

ORDRE IONIQUE. 329

de métal doré s'enchâssaient dans le marbre et formaient l'œil de chaque volute, et des émaux colorés marquaient sur le bourrelet les points de croisement de la tresse.

Le chapiteau de l'Érechtheion fut très probablement exécuté dans la seconde moitié du 5e siècle.

Plus ancien par sa date, mais plus dégagé des influences de l'archaïsme, le chapiteau de l'ordre intérieur des Propylées n'emprunte à la tradition que la silhouette d'ensemble : les détails se simplifient. L'Érechtheion était un petit édifice où l'on ne pouvait chercher que la grâce ; ici il s'agit d'un édifice de grande dimension : l'architecte s'attache à cette sobriété d'ornement qui éveille l'impression de la grandeur.

La fig. 21 montre l'aspect du chapiteau des Propylées.

Comparé avec celui de l'Érechtheion, il se distingue par les caractères suivants :
Tailloir exactement carré ;
Absence du bourrelet qui, à l'Érechtheion, séparait l'échine du tailloir ;
Absence du collier qui terminait le fût ;
Réduction du nombre des lignes spirales à deux ;
Balustres lisses, présentant à la gorge trois cannelures seulement et un profil en doucine qui s'accentuera aux derniers temps de l'art grec : Poursuivant l'idée si évidente à l'Érechtheion d'emprunter l'idée à la décoration aux formes d'une matière souple et flexible, on a donné au balustre l'aspect d'une nappe enroulée serrée en son milieu par une quadruple ligature ; cette

AXONOMETRY AND SPATIO-TEMPORAL CINETISM

The rules of codification for axonometry were one of the sources of this plastic approach to the object. Ozenfant and Le Corbusier sought to define a new perspective:

> Perspective means creation of virtual space. Purism admits as a constructive means of the first order the sensation of depth, which generates the sensation of space, without which volume is a useless word.[19]

Contrary to the linear perspective used by artists of the Renaissance, which presumes a vanishing point where parallel lines converge, an axonometric construction gives an account of the spatial arrangement of objects according to three planes perpendicular to one another. The architectural historian Auguste Choisy assigned it a particular role in his writing; his *Histoire de l'architecture* (1899; fig. 170) is integral to understanding Le Corbusier's sources. Underscoring the importance of this book to him, Le Corbusier represented it in *Nature morte avec livre ouvert, pipe, verre et boîte d'allumettes* (Still life with open book, pipe, glass and matchbox; fig. 453) and reproduced several of its plates in his articles in *L'Esprit nouveau*. According to Choisy, the advantages of axonometry were that:

> In this system, a single image, animated and dynamic like the building itself, takes the place of an abstract figuration through plan, section, and elevation. The reader has before his eyes, at the same time, the plan, the exterior of the building, its section, and its interior disposition.[20]

The objects in paintings by Le Corbusier such as *Nature morte à la pile d'assiettes et au livre* (Still life with pile of dishes and book; figs. 161 and 457) can be seen from multiple perspectives "at the same time," in Choisy's words. In this painting, the ordinary objects that comprise the iconography of Purism are grouped according to a median axis identified by the gutter of the open, vertically placed book. The lower part of the picture where the objects are arranged is viewed from above. This perspective in the tightly woven composition emphasized volume and its relation to space. The upper part of the painting offers a more frontal view. A rhythm of forms results from the depiction, on the right and in the background, of the undulating surface and profile of the guitar and its case, flattened into the picture plane. Le Corbusier situates these objects in a space composed of juxtaposed colored planes.

Ozenfant, in his paintings from the same group, such as *Maroc* (fig. 171), arranged objects in an architectonic space. Le Corbusier chose the same viewpoint, but a vertical line on the left establishes the ground plane that recedes into the background via a sort of passage. The balance of these architectural compositions depends on rotations of planes that allow the viewer to grasp the nature of the objects, which can all be recognized for what they are—guitar, book, bottles, and so on—and also as geometric abstractions of pure form. This interpretation of space—with changing places and perspectives—was a decisive experience for Le Corbusier. As a painter, he was compelling the viewer to shift the gaze from foreground to background within the frame, which evokes his rhythmic approach as an architect to architectural space.

As Epstein pointed out, Ozenfant and Le Corbusier were the only artists in France to paint pictures with this conception of space, which would continue to develop. Purism would eventually present a spatial equivalent, both French and Swiss, to experiments in geometrical abstraction, as seen in *La Nature morte au siphon* (Still life with siphon; fig. 462), painted in 1921. By that date, Le Corbusier had become a creative force whose work was identified with the international avant-garde. He was recognized simultaneously as painter and architect (see fig. 162), although it was as an architect that he was to make his mark.

CATALOGUE

EDITORS' NOTE

The catalogue is divided into four sections, in keeping with the essay part of the book:

1. Itinerant Education
2. Architecture
3. Toward "L'Equipement de la Maison"
4. Paintings, Drawings, Sketches, Watercolors

Within each section there are separate thematic groupings or "catalogue entries" that comprise an explanatory text, and illustrations, and each section is arranged in chronological order. Works included in the exhibition either at the Langmatt Museum, or the Bard Graduate Center, have a checklist reference number in brackets at the end of their captions, and the checklist is to be found on p. 303. Those illustrations that do not have checklist numbers are included in the catalogue entries for comparative purposes. Rather than being a complete catalogue of the exhibition, these sections act as an additional exploration of the themes around which the exhibition is organized—for a more detailed explanation of these, see the introduction to the checklist.

CONTRIBUTORS

A.B.	Antonio Brucculeri
A.R.	Arthur Rüegg
C.C.	Corinne Charles
F.D.	Françoise Ducros
F.P.	Francesco Passanti
G.G.	Giuliano Gresleri
H.A.B.	H. Allen Brooks
K.S.	Klaus Spechtenhauser
M.-E.C.	Marie-Eve Celio
S.v.M.	Stanislaus von Moos

Part I · Itinerant Education

I. FLORENCE AND SIENA

PALAZZO VECCHIO

The Villa Fallet had been barely finished (see pp. 202–5) when Jeanneret left La Chaux-de-Fonds for Italy on September 3, 1907, with his first architect's fee in his pocket. He arrived in Florence a week later, where he and Léon Perrin, his closest school friend, who had preceded him to Italy, rented a room at the corner of Via dei Calzaioli and Piazza della Signoria, opposite the Loggia dei Lanzi.[1] From here Jeanneret made the impressive study of Arnolfo di Cambio's Palazzo Vecchio (fig. 172). He began his sketch too high on the page to accommodate the tower in its entirety, and so the crenellated, two-story machico-lated-gallery and pavilion, supported by four "superb" columns (as described by Jeanneret), had to be sketched below. Notes in the margin comment on aspects of the palace's design, proportion, and ornamentation, as well as the sculpture arranged around its main entrance:

> Undecorated wall; entry completely to one side aligned with the next to last window, symmetrically in front of the door to each side of two very ugly statues, Adam and Eve. Further forward still atop great cubic plinths are colossal statues, the very ugly *vainqueur* and Michelangelo's David (at the time the David had been taken off its plinth).[2]

172. Charles-Edouard Jeanneret, View of the Palazzo Vecchio, Florence, from his room at Via dei Calzaioli, 1907, pencil and black and blue ink on gray paper, FLC [145]

173. Charles-Edouard Jeanneret, Ideal view of S. Maria del Fiore and Palazzo Vecchio in Florence, with surrounding landscape, 1907, pencil and watercolor on paper, FLC [157]

les coupoles de Toscane

Michelangelo's *David*, which in fact was not in place at the time of drawing (the statue had been removed in 1905 and was not replaced until the 1920s) is indicated by a rough scribble made from memory. The "Vainqueur" (in fact Hercules and Cacus by Baccio Bandinelli), however, is almost recognizable in Jeanneret's sketch. The two figures Jeanneret identified as Adam and Eve, of which only one can be discerned in the sketch, are in fact the *termini* ("chain holders"), whose purpose was to mark the boundary of the palace.

In a letter to L'Eplattenier, Jeanneret wrote at length about the negative aspects of architectural draftsmanship, a medium he practiced primarily because his teacher had wanted him to be an architect: "Why draw the Palazzo Vecchio. One doesn't know from which side one might be able to wrest its mystery. It takes your breath away; it has such beautiful finesses on its brutal face, so much strength in its watch tower, its color is so warm and so full;

and then to say that the Palais Fédéral is in the Florentine style!"[3]

By Palais Fédéral Jeanneret meant the Swiss Houses of Parliament in Berne, a neo-Renaissance building of the 1890s that he evidently enjoyed criticizing.

"THE DOMES OF TUSCANY"

The volumetric study of the Palazzo della Signoria, with its many notations, and the idealized view of Santa Maria del Fiore and the Palazzo Vecchio echoing the surrounding hills of Fiesole and San Miniato (annotated "Les coupoles de Toscane"), suggest the range of visual languages practiced by Jeanneret in his Tuscan sketches (see fig. 173). The view is as unreal as its association with the Middle Ages, a claim made by Jeanneret in a letter to L'Eplattenier, in which, apparently referring to this sketch, he described the view as one that ". . . was seen by medieval foreigners when they arrived at the summit of a hill and all at once, through the blue mist of morning, this monster of stone reared up, this hill that, because it was ordered, was larger than those surrounding it."[4] Unlike the study of Palazzo Vecchio, the airy sketch, reminiscent of Turner, pursues deliberately "artistic" ends, revealing Jeanneret's desire to be a painter.

BAPTISTERY OF SANTA MARIA DEL FIORE

Painting and the decorative arts, not architecture, were the prime objectives of Jeanneret's curiosity during his first visit to Tuscany. With only a few exceptions, the Renaissance was sacrificed to a search of the origins of art, which led to a preference for the Middle Ages and more specifically for the Baptistery of Santa Maria del Fiore, "the central building of Etrurian Christianity—of European Christianity" as Ruskin had described it in *Mornings in Florence*. This study of the pavement in the baptistery (twelfth-century and later, figs. 174, 175) exemplifies Jeanneret's Ruskinian interest in decoration as the essence of architecture.

WALL-TOMBS AT SANTA MARIA NOVELLA

Once again, John Ruskin appears to be the raison d'être behind the choice of the Gothic wall-tombs as the subject matter of one of Jeanneret's most carefully finished Florentine watercolors (fig. 176). In *Mornings in Florence*, Ruskin wrote that he "would fair have painted, them, stone by stone," except for the street urchins who threw pebbles at him. Jeanneret's own persistence was rewarded with a severe sunburn.[5] A photograph taken by Jeanneret shows the position of the wall-tombs in relation to Leon Battista Alberti's facade of Santa Maria Novella (fig. 177). While one of Léon Perrin's watercolors shows the tombs from a slightly different angle, suggesting that the two friends worked side by side, a pencil drawing by Perrin demonstrates his interest in sculptural detail (fig. 178).

174. Charles-Edouard Jeanneret, detail of the Pavement in the Baptistery, Florence, 1907, pencil and watercolor on paper, pasted on cardboard, FLC [148]

175. Florence. Baptistery, postcard with marginal notes by Jeanneret, c. 1900, FLC

176. Charles-Edouard Jeanneret, Florence. S. Maria Novella. Study of the exterior wall-tombs, Oct. 1907, watercolor, gouache and black ink on paper, FLC [158]

177. Charles-Edouard Jeanneret, Florence. S. Maria Novella. Detail of facade (with tombs at far left), Sept. 1907, photograph, FLC

178. Léon Perrin, Florence. S. Maria Novella, detail of exterior molding, 1907, pencil on paper, Musée Léon Perrin, Môtiers [283]

179. Léon Perrin, Florence. Study of the Cantoria (choir gallery) in the church of S. Lorenzo (school of Donatello), with annotations, 1907, pencil and colored pencil on paper, Musée Léon Perrin, Môtiers [284]

180. Florence. Museo dell'Opera del Duomo, Cantoria (choir gallery, by Donatello) from the Duomo, with notes on verso, postcard, c. 1900, FLC

181. Verso of fig. 180

182. Florence. Museo dell'Opera del Duomo, Cantoria (choir gallery, by Luca della Robbia) from the Duomo, postcard, c. 1900, FLC

183. Verso of fig. 182

CANTORIA IN THE CHURCH OF SAN LORENZO

Sculpture was the only domain in which Jeanneret preferred Renaissance to Gothic forms.[6] Perhaps guided by Perrin, Jeanneret drew Cellini's *Perseus* as well as Donatello's *Judith and Holofernes*, in the Loggia dei Lanzi (later installed directly in front of the Palazzo Vecchio).[7] No Renaissance work received more attention than the Cantoria (choir gallery) in Brunelleschi's church of San Lorenzo. Significantly, the decorative detail of the richly carved console and mullion held Jeanneret's interest more than the gallery as a whole (fig. 184). The same holds true for Perrin's subtly colored drawing of the same motif, although, paradoxically, Jeanneret's study with its strong shadow-effect is more "sculptural" than Perrin's (fig. 179). The interest in Donatello is further underscored by two postcards illustrating the choir galleries in the Museo dell'opera del Duomo (one by Donatello, the other by Luca della Robbia), with the back entirely filled with comments on the decorative work (figs. 180–83).

184. Charles-Edouard Jeanneret, Florence. Study of the Cantoria (choir gallery) in the church of S. Lorenzo (school of Donatello), with annotations, 1907, pencil and charcoal on paper, FLC [147]

SIENA AND THE PALAZZO PUBBLICO: AMBROGIO LORENZETTI'S "BUON GOVERNO"

Much time was devoted in Tuscany to the study of medieval wall decorations and frescoes in the churches of Santa Croce and Santa Maria Novella (Florence), in the camposanto in Pisa, as well as in the Palazzo Pubblico in Siena (see pp. 30f.; fig. 186, 188). The sketches were usually done in the standard way taught by L'Eplattenier—in pencil with a watercolor wash through which the drawing could be seen. Jeanneret's visit to Siena (September 29 to October 5) produced a particularly rich harvest of studies, although no works by Perrin have survived. The importance of color suggests that the studies of frescoes were generally done in situ; the black-and-white postcards (such as fig. 185) probably served primarily for reference.

S.v.M.

185. Siena. Palazzo Pubblico, Allegory of Good Government (by Ambrogio Lorenzetti), postcard, c. 1900, FLC

186. Charles-Edouard Jeanneret, Study of the Allegory of Good Government (by Ambrogio Lorenzetti), Palazzo Pubblico, Siena, 1907, gouache and pencil on paper, FLC [156]

187. Siena. Church of S. Domenico. Complimentary postcard of the Pensione "La Scala," postcard, c. 1900, FLC

188. Charles-Edouard Jeanneret, View of the Church of S. Domenico in Siena, 1907, pen and watercolor on paper, FLC [152]

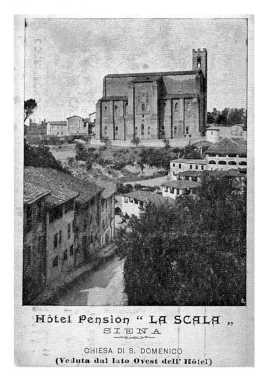

189. Charles-Edouard Jeanneret, Facade and details of the Baptistery, Siena, 1907, pencil, ink and watercolor on paper, FLC [153]

190. Siena. Facade of the Baptistery, annotated by Ch. E. Jeanneret, c. 1900, postcard, FLC

2. VENICE

191. Charles-Edouard Jeanneret, Venice. Doges' Palace, detail of gallery, 1907, pencil and ink on paper, FLC

192. Léon Perrin, Venice, Doges' Palace, a capital, 1907, pencil and black ink on paper, Musée Léon Perrin, Môtiers

193. Charles-Edouard Jeanneret, Venice, S. Marco (?), capital, 1907, photograph, BV

SAN MARCO AND THE PALAZZO DUCALE

In the scenario of the Grand Tour as conceived in the seventeenth and eighteenth centuries—and as presented in abbreviated form in Rodolphe Töpffer's *Voyages en zigzag* (1846), a book Jeanneret read as a child (see pp. 25–27)—Venice was considered the climax to an educated traveler's visit to Italy. For Jeanneret/Le Corbusier, four encounters with the city appear to have shaped his vision of it. The first, in November 1907, brought his first trip to Italy to an end. The second, and probably not the least important, was through his studies of prints in the Cabinet des Estampes at the Bibliothèque Nationale in Paris in 1915. The third was in 1922, when he visited Venice with his friend and patron Raoul La Roche, and the fourth took place in 1934, in the context of "Arts contemporains et la réalité, l'Art et l'Etat," an international conference on art organized by the League of Nations.

During the two-week visit to Venice in 1907, "plagued by bad weather and flagging interest," Jeanneret appears to have made only two drawings; in fact, as he explained: "the pencils are no longer used, and the paper remains white." [8] All the more interesting are the few surviving photographs, which are here published for the first time (figs. 193–96). Their subject matter ("the noble and fine harmony of the ample surfaces of the Doges palace, or the hot cadence of the vaults and turrets of San Marco") is very Ruskinian in its Gothic focus. [9] Jeanneret was particularly interested in decorative detail, such as the tracery (fig. 191) or the capitals of the doges' palace (which Perrin sketched, figs. 192, 193). Although the snapshots show the typical defects of photographs taken with an ordinary "kodak"—architecture is inevitably shown from below with converging verticals—Jeanneret was pleased when he saw the prints but subsequently never used them for publication. [10]

194. Charles-Edouard Jeanneret, Venice, corner view of the Doges' Palace, 1907, photograph, FLC

195. Charles-Edouard Jeanneret, Venice, Palazzo Marcello, 1907, photograph, FLC

196. Charles-Edouard Jeanneret, Venice, S. Marco, 1907, photograph, FLC

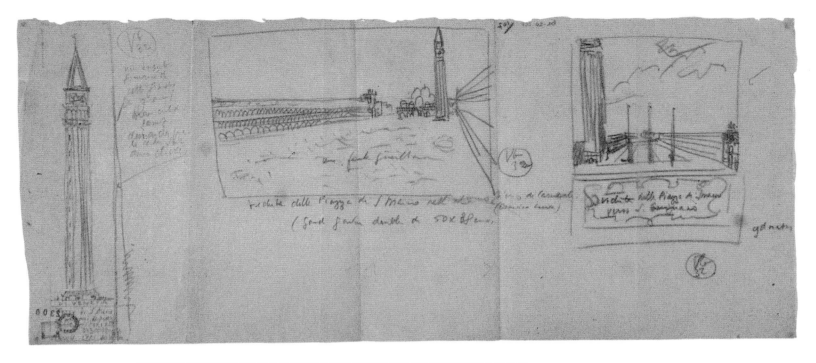

197. Charles-Edouard Jeanneret, Venice, Piazza S. Marco: Campanile and two sketches of the Square, 1915 (?), pencil on paper, FLC

198. Domenico Lovisa, View of the Piazza S. Marco on the final day of Carnival, eighteenth-century engraving, Bibliothèque Nationale, Paris

URBAN SPACE

When in 1915 Jeanneret consulted the Bibliothèque Nationale to gather material on historic European townscapes for "La construction des villes" (see pp. 98–107) Venice turned out to be a particularly rich laboratory of interesting spatial configurations. As a result, the eighteenth-century Venetian prints by Marieschi, Carlevarijs, and others were among the most intensely studied subjects at the Cabinet des Estampes. In myriad sketches he tried to memorize the often complex sites depicted in these prints. As the focus shifted from ornamental detail to the organization of public space, Ruskin as a reference began to be replaced by Camillo Sitte; the *Stones of*

Venice gave way to *Der Städtebau nach seinen künstlerischen Grundsätzen*. Figures of people are in general eliminated from these views, or at best hurriedly suggested by a few scribbles, as in a well-known sketch of the Piazza San Marco after a print by Lovisa (figs. 197, 198). Such drawings were often reused by Le Corbusier in later publications, such as *Propos d'urbanisme* (1946; fig. 199).

The next step in Jeanneret's exploration of Venice was taken in September 1922, when his friend and patron Raoul La Roche took him on a journey to the lagoon and the environs of Venice. Le Corbusier had just published an article entitled "La Leçon de Rome" in *L'Esprit nouveau* (see pp.192–93) and presumably was planning to write an analogous essay on Venice, although it never appeared. His eclectic interests in Venetian art and architecture [in 1922]—including not only the churches of Palladio, but also the paintings of Bellini, Tintoretto, and Tiepolo—remained virtually unknown until the recent facsimile publication of the *Album La Roche*.[11]

199. A page from Le Corbusier, *Propos d'urbanisme*, Paris, 1946, showing the Piazza S. Marco

200. "Je prends Venise à témoin", a page from Le Corbusier, *La ville radieuse*, 1935

201. "Venice est un brillant encouragement à nos études d'organisation des villes de la civilisation machiniste," an illustration from Le Corbusier, *La ville radieuse*, 1935

VENICE AS MODEL

In later years, Le Corbusier referred to Venice as a model for the solution of the widest range of architectural and urban problems: repetition used to organize the surfaces of large buildings (the Procurazie Vecchie); separation of traffic lines to organize circulation (the canals, fig. 200); and acceptance of tension and contrast of forms and styles within an urban whole, as opposed to superficial "harmony" (Piazza San Marco). In the 1930s, while often proposing wholesale urban demolition, Le Corbusier also discovered the advantages of the opposite strategy, meaning the integral preservation of historic urban areas, and Venice was once again the key reference (fig. 201).[12] In view of Le Corbusier's special attachment to Venice it is noteworthy that his last project was for that city (the unbuilt Venice hospital, 1964–65).

S.v.M.

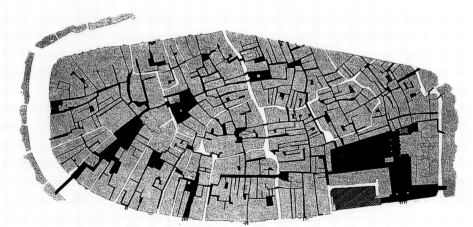

3. PARIS AND ROUEN

202. Charles-Edouard Jeanneret, Paris, Notre-Dame, one of three pinnacles at the southeast of the ambulatory chapels, 1908, ink wash and watercolor on paper, private collection

203. Charles-Edouard Jeanneret, Paris, Notre-Dame, view of the tower seen from the roof, 1908, photograph, FLC

204. Paris. Ch. E. Jeanneret photographed in front of the window at 9, Rue des Ecoles, 1908, photograph, BV

DISCOVERING PARIS

Around March 25, 1908, after spending the winter in Vienna, Jeanneret and Perrin arrived in Paris. Jeanneret would not return to La Chaux-de-Fonds until Christmas 1909. The works on paper that survive from this period fall into two categories: studies of architecture, primarily Notre-Dame, and studies of decorative arts made in the Paris museums, mostly from casts. His first Paris address was 9 rue des Écoles (fig. 204), from which he moved to a mansard directly opposite Notre-Dame, at 3 quai St. Michel. His part-time employment with Auguste and Gustave Perret gave him enough free time not only to explore Notre-Dame, but also to pay extended visits to the museums, to take classes at the École des Beaux-Arts and the Musée de la Sculpture Comparée, and to read.[13]

NOTRE-DAME

On August 1, 1908, with his first paycheck from the Perrets, Jeanneret purchased Viollet-le-Duc's ten-volume *Dictionnaire raisonné de l'architecture française du XIe au XVIe siècle* (1854–68). A few days later he wrote L'Eplattenier: "I have Viollet-le-Duc and I have Notre-Dame which serves as my laboratory." Jeanneret's 1908 studies of Notre-Dame resulted in a sketchbook devoted entirely to this building (fig. 202; see also pp. 45–48).[14] Paradoxically, these studies reveal a more lively interest in decoration than in structure, a fact already noted by H. Allen Brooks (see fig. 203). Even as Jeanneret began to think of himself as a "structural rationalist" following in the footsteps of Viollet-le-Duc, Ruskin still appears to have been very much on his mind.[15] At the same time, Notre-Dame was also the subject of a series of explicitly pictorial watercolors, some of them to be counted among his best (fig. 205). The church, in particular the main facade with its two rectangular towers and "classical" proportions, remained a reference for Le Corbusier's later theoretical work (fig. 206; see also p. 44).

205. Charles-Edouard Jeanneret, View of Notre-Dame de Paris, 1908, pencil and watercolor on paper, FLC [161]

206. Paris, Notre-Dame, postcard with geometry added to indicate proportions, and cropping lines for reproduction, c. 1900; added notes c. 1921, FLC

PARIS – Le Canal et Notre Dame
The Canal and Notre Dame

ROUEN

Chartres and Rouen were the only major Gothic cathedrals other than Notre-Dame that were studied in any depth by Jeanneret.[16] The city of Rouen appears to have been rather randomly picked for a visit by Jeanneret and three other L'Eplattenier students (Perrin, Perruchot, and Aubert) in July 1908.[17] Using his Kodak camera, Jeanneret was unable to show the cathedral towers without exaggerated foreshortening ("converging verticals"). In some pictures, however, this "defect" became an expressive device, as in the detail of the base of one of the pillars flanking the Portail de la Calende (fig. 209). As if to compensate for the shortcomings of photography, Perrin has given an "undistorted" view of the same detail in a drawing (fig. 210).[18]

Why did Jeanneret choose Rouen, as opposed to other French cathedrals, such as Amiens, Reims, Laon? It might have been because Monet had made it a key subject of modern art, but a more likely explanation is the city's convenient location between Paris and Le Havre, the primary holiday destination of the group of friends. Some of the numerous postcards purchased at the time or perhaps later suggest that what interested Jeanneret almost as much as the cathedral itself was the bold post–Viollet-le-Duc ironwork of the turret on top of the crossing ("today we want a lyricism of steel," Jeanneret noted on one of these cards; fig. 209). Nevertheless, in his studies at the Bibliothèque Nationale (1915), Jeanneret was especially drawn to Rouen Cathedral (fig. 207).[19] As a result, it appears again and again in Le Corbusier's books, and in various guises, depending upon his polemical agenda. It is either the focus of an exemplary urban composition that merges a regular (Roman) plan with the meandering "donkey's path," or it is a demonstration of the "pointed forms, resulting in a broken skyline, with an obvious wish for order, but completely devoid of the calm and equilibrium characteristic of civilizations that have reached maturity."[20] In 1915, while copying an eighteenth-century print at the Cabinet des Estampes, Jeanneret became fascinated by the charm of the Portail de la Calende as it emerges from the low houses that surround it. But by 1945, after the bombings suffered by a number of French cities during World War II, the beauty of the cathedral was more often evoked as it emerged independent from its surroundings as in some paintings by Karl Friedrich Schinkel—or in Bruno Taut's concept of the "Stadtkrone."[21]

S.v.M.

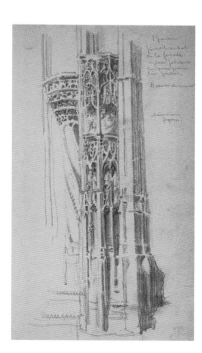

207. Charles-Edouard Jeanneret, Rouen Cathedral, studies after engravings in the Bibliothèque Nationale, Paris, 1915 (?), ink on paper, FLC

208. Charles-Edouard Jeanneret, Rouen Cathedral, Portail de la Calende, 1908–09, photograph, FLC

209. Rouen Cathedral, facade, with the "Tour de Beurre" on the right, c. 1900, postcard, FLC [121]

210. Léon Perrin, Rouen Cathedral, study of the pillar flanking the Portail de la Calende, 1908, pencil on paper, Musée Léon Perrin, Môtiers

MUSÉE DU TROCADÉRO

In 1924 Le Corbusier explained why he found museums more rewarding than libraries in his search for truth:

> Museums have given me seamless, untreacherous certitudes. The works are there as wholes, and conversation carries no burden, the encounter is shaped by the questioner; the work always responds to the questions one asks of it. I have only perused those works that are not part of what we call Great Art. I would go on Sundays to see the Cimabues, the Breughels, the Raphaels, the Tintorettos, etc. But to work, to draw, to understand how much richness to give to one's work, the degree of concentration, of transposition, invention, re-creation, I went to those places where at the time no one set up his easel — well away from the Grande Galerie. I was always alone . . . with the museum guards.[22]

He then offered a list of the Paris museums in which he had studied the decorative arts: Musée de Cluny, Musée Guimet, Pavillon de

Marsan, and Musée Ethnographique du Trocadéro, among others. He also included a list of the museums in Florence, London, Belgrade, Athens, and Naples which had served as mines during his Grand Tour.[23]

He did not explicitly mention, however, the part of the Musée du Trocadéro where these hitherto unpublished photographs of Khmer and Cambodian shrines were taken (figs. 212–15).[24] The Palais de Trocadéro, built for the of 1878 Exposition Universelle, is best known for the Musée de Sculpture Comparée,

211. Charles-Edouard Jeanneret, Study of Wall Mosaic (Procession of the Virgins) in Sant'Apollinare Nuovo, Ravenna, Oct. 1907, pencil and tempera on paper FLC

212. Charles-Edouard Jeanneret, Paris, Trocadéro Museum, detail from Khmer Shrine (?), 1909, photograph, FLC

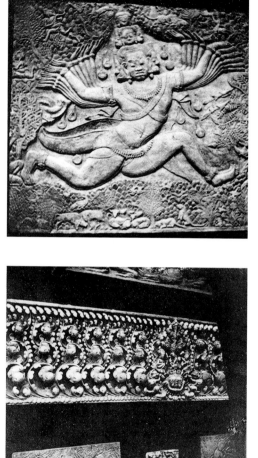

founded by Viollet-le-Duc. Located in the east wing, it consisted mainly of plaster casts of French medieval cathedral sculpture and architectural details, which together formed a "museographic version of Viollet-le-Duc's writings."[25] The west wing housed the Musée Ethnographique with its important holdings of African art (later reorganized as the Musée de l'Homme),[26] as well as the Musée Indochinois du Trocadéro dedicated to East Asian architecture and decorative art (mostly reconstructions, with some authentic works).

When, for the 1937 Exposition Internationale des Arts et Techniques, the Palais du Trocadéro practically disappeared behind the massive envelope of the Palais de Chaillot, the Musée Indochinois and its painted plaster reconstructions were dismantled, while the pieces of authentic sculpture and decoration, such as the lion figure in figure 213, were transferred to the Musée Guimet.[27] As a result, Jeanneret's photographs are among the few surviving visual records of the original museum installations in the east wing. Also in 1937 the east wing and its Musée de Sculpture Comparée became the Musée National des Monuments Français.[28]

Because the Perret studio at 21 rue Franklin, where Jeanneret worked as a draftsman, was located immediately behind the Musée du Trocadéro, Jeanneret may have been a frequent visitor to these collections. There are, however, no known written comments by him on the Khmer and Cambodian shrines. It is tempting to relate these works to the theories espoused by Eugène Grasset in *Méthode de composition ornamentale* (1905; see cat. no. 41), as well as to the decorative work produced under L'Eplattenier in the Cours supérieur d'art et de décoration at the École d'Art at La Chaux-de-Fonds. An interest in "all-over" surface decoration is also evident in Jeanneret's studies of the mosaics of Ravenna, such as at San Vitale, and especially of San Apollinare in Classe, done in 1907 (fig. 211).[29]

213–15. Charles-Edouard Jeanneret, Paris, Trocadéro Museum, details from Khmer Shrines (?), 1909, photographs, FLC

216. Charles-Edouard Jeanneret, Study of a terracotta relief in the Louvre Museum, Paris, 1908–09 (?), pencil on paper, FLC [164]

217. Charles L'Eplattenier, Studies of monumental sculptures from various museums (including the Louvre?), pencil and ink on 9 sheets of notepaper, pasted on wrapping paper, BV [278]

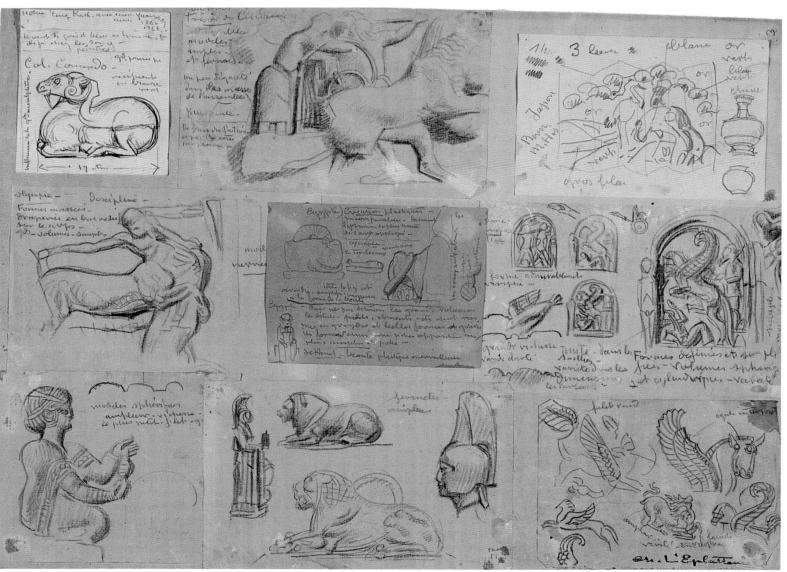

EGYPTIAN AND PERUVIAN DECORATIVE ART

For Le Corbusier's generation, copying historical works of art was still an integral part of their training, even if a direct application of such studies in "modern" designs was by no means intended. The situation was slightly different with L'Eplattenier, who as late as 1923–26 would decorate the Musée des Beaux-Arts at La Chaux-de-Fonds in a style based directly on Egyptian models made in museums.[30] In fact Jeanneret's interest in Egyptian art was inspired by L'Eplattenier (see cat. no. 41). At the École d'Art, L'Eplattenier used to mount his studies or sketches as groups on large sheets of wrapping paper so that his students could easily study them (fig. 217).[31] Many of Jeanneret's most beautiful museum studies appear to follow L'Eplattenier's style closely (fig. 216). Like L'Eplattenier, Jeanneret added notes to indicate the formal qualities of the works that he considered outstanding.[32] His studies after Peruvian vases in the Musée Ethnographique du Trocadéro, whose sculptural wit appears to have exerted a special charm, were also annotated (figs. 218, 219).[33] The memory of this pottery from South America may have influenced some of Jeanneret's purchases during his travels in the Balkans in 1911.

S.v.M.

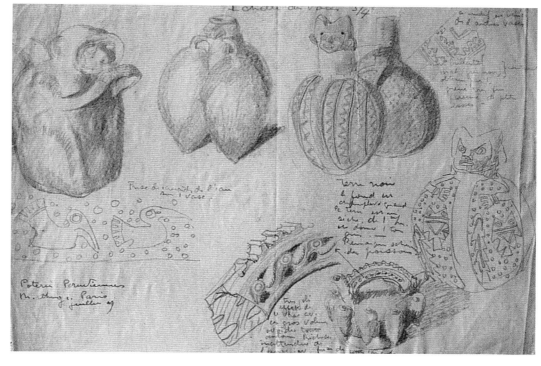

218. Charles-Edouard Jeanneret, Paris, Trocadéro Museum, study of Peruvian vases, July 1909, pencil, ink and watercolor on yellowish paper, FLC [166]

219. Charles-Edouard Jeanneret, Paris, Trocadéro Museum, study of Peruvian vases, 1909, pencil and gouache on paper, FLC [167]

5. VERSAILLES

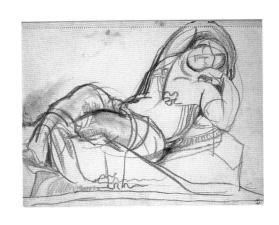

THE PALACE

When in 1932 Le Corbusier reminisced about his first visit to Versailles (May 1909), he described how he had come to confront the palace long before his 1915 studies of Gabriel Pérelle's engravings: "it is not *architecture* for me, far from that, but rather it is an exquisite chapter on proportion, charm and human scale [emphasis by LC]."[34]

The postcards he had collected and, to a greater extent, the photographs that he took from 1909 onward attest to his interest in the composition and spatial arrangement of Versailles. Taken from different angles, his photographs illustrate the way in which the palace facade advances and retreats in correspondence with the garden's north and south parterres:[35] they are studies in the principle of setbacks (*à redent*), which would become an underlying theme in *Urbanisme* (1925; figs 222, 223; see also pp. 98–107). Above all, however, it was the building's means of reconciling differences in level that preoccupied Jeanneret. In 1932—perhaps with the additional reference to one of the postcards in his possession—he recalled: "I fell into the flower beds of the Château de la Belle au Bois Dormant; and I found myself nose-to-nose with the Orangerie, at the foot of the Escalier des Cent-Marches."[36] The view of the Staircase of the Hundred Steps, the parterres, and the facade of the Orangerie, behind which the palace silhouette emerges, were often drawn and photographed from the same viewpoint.[37]

"Proportion" and "human scale" continued to animate Jeanneret's reading of the Petit Trianon. *Vers un architecture* would later disseminate his study of the *tracés régulateurs* superimposed on one of its facades to legitimize his composition of the facade of the Villa Schwob,[38] but his considerations extended to the building's entire conception. Jeanneret was interested in the Trianon's vertical connections—he acquired two postcards of the main staircase—and, above all, the way it was distributed and organized on two different access levels. One of these, facing the garden parterres along an axis rotated about 90 degrees, seems to have underpinned the planning of the music pavilion (1927) for the Villa Church in Ville d'Avray that he designed to overlay the ruins of an eighteenth-century pavilion.[39]

By Jeanneret's own admission, the memory of the "spectacle colossal et inattendu de Versailles" (colossal and unexpected spectacle of Versailles) in 1911 already signaled the preeminence of "clarté classique" (classical clarity) over its predecessor of "mythologie enténébrée" (obscure mythology).[40] In January 1913, he wrote to William Ritter: "I believe that seeing Versailles from time to time places one back on the stairway to beauty. I will work that year, and the bubbling of creative desires will act upon me and force me to make decisions."[41]

His recollection, several months later, of the statue of the "sleeping Ariane in the gardens of Versailles, . . . undressed [and] . . . painted like a large opulent strawberry, against a background of intense green" would become almost a metaphor of this creative will (fig. 220).[42] A watercolor entitled *Le Versailles du grand turc* is clearly related to these studies (1914; fig. 221).

A.B.

220. Charles-Edouard Jeanneret, Sketch of the "Sleeping Ariane" in the gardens of Versailles, 1912–14, black pencil on paper, FLC (Carnet bleu)

221. Charles-Edouard Jeanneret, Sketch of the "Sleeping Ariane" in the gardens of Versailles, 1912–14, black pencil on paper, FLC (Carnet bleu) [207]

222. Charles-Edouard Jeanneret, Versailles, Château, 1908–09, photograph, FLC

223. Charles-Edouard Jeanneret, Versailles, Château, 1908–09, photograph, FLC

Jeanneret's involvement in urbanism was "purely a matter of chance,"[43] yet chance in this case had a lot to do with being Swiss. L'Eplattenier, director of the École d'Art, had been invited to present a paper entitled "L'Esthétique des villes" at a national assembly of architects and urban planners in September 1910 in La Chaux-de-Fonds ("Schweizerischer Städtetag").[44] L'Eplattenier, although a layman in matters of urban design, was already familiar with the French translation of Camillo Sitte's book *L'Art de bâtir des villes* (1902) when he asked for Jeanneret's assistance. Work on the project started swiftly. In late June 1910 Jeanneret told his parents that "this study will be published as a book, the importance of which surpasses my expectations…. It will be signed by L'Eplattenier and by me."[45]

By then Jeanneret had already been touring for several months in Germany, speaking to architects (Theodor Fischer, among others), analyzing medieval and more recent townscapes in the light of Sitte's principles, and putting together a collection of photographs and postcards that would constitute the raw material for the book (see pp. 55–60).[46]

MONUMENTS AND PEDESTRAIN TRAFFIC FLOW

Sitte's ideas on public sculpture and its relationship to circulation of traffic and urban space must have been particularly relevant to L'Eplattenier. The subject of monumental sculpture in Swiss towns—often showing armor-clad figures standing on fountains—had played a considerable role in his teaching for years (figs. 224, 225, and an early sketch by Jeanneret made in Fribourg in 1907 appears to relate to these drawing exercises).[47] For Alexandre Cingria-Vaneyre, a man who was shortly to enter Jeanneret's orbit, armored fig-

ures were typical of "the eccentricity" of the old days in Switzerland:

> All the people who are on their way toward death and always laughing in some corner, make one think of the most extravagant orchids, of insects from the Americas and of those colorful and quarrelsome birds that one brings back from the islands.[48]

While L'Eplattenier was working on an impressive statue, *Monument de la République*, unveiled in La Chaux-de-Fonds in the summer of 1910,[49] the "Sittean" preoccupation with the monument and its placement within the town's traffic pattern had moved toward the top of the agenda. Because L'Eplattenier's job in connection with the Schweizerischer Städtetag was to address an audience of Swiss architects and city officials on the state of urban design, he needed readily available examples of public monuments. After having been dissatisfied by the quality of the postcards sent from twenty or so Swiss municipalities, L'Eplattenier seems to have asked Jeanneret to photograph historic townscapes in Swiss cities such as Solothurn, Fribourg, Zurich, or Saint Gallen (figs. 226–29).

Only a few of these photographs relate to L'Eplattenier's preoccupation with Swiss patriotic iconography, but many connect to Jeanneret's research in Germany. The impres-

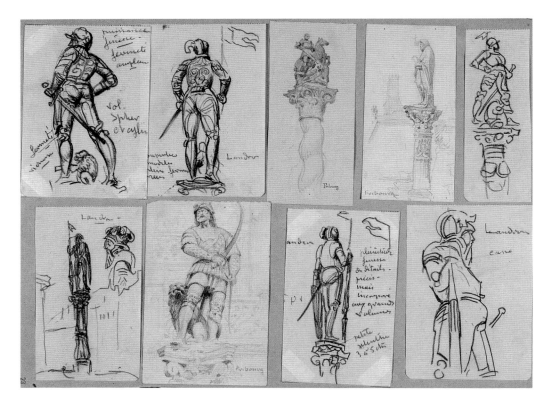

224. Charles L'Eplattenier, Studies of fountain sculptures from Bern, Fribourg, and Le Landeron, pencil and ink on 9 sheets of notepaper, pasted on wrapping paper, BV [279]

225. Charles-Edouard Jeanneret, Fribourg, lower town with fountain, 1911, photograph, BV

sive "tunnel" view across the arcades of a sixteenth-century guild hall in Zurich (fig. 227),
for example, corresponds to analogous views
and postcard images illustrating pedestrian
walks that functionally serve and spatially cir-
cumvent or even "subvert" the extant fabric
of old cities (see p. 59). Some of these photographs were apparently considered as illustrations for "La Construction des villes."[50]

S.v.M.

226. Charles-Edouard Jeanneret, Solothurn, apse of the
Jesuit Church, 1910, Photograph, FLC

227. Charles-Edouard Jeanneret, Zürich, Zunfthaus zur
Zimmerleuten, 1910, photograph, FLC

228. Charles-Edouard Jeanneret, Solothurn, view of St.
Mauritius Fountain, 1910, photograph, FLC

229. Charles-Edouard Jeanneret, St. Gallen, traditional
working-class houses, Sept. 1910, photograph, FLC

7. MUNICH

MEETING RITTER

Munich was an important destination in Charles-Edouard Jeanneret's extensive tours of Germany in 1910 and 1911.[51] He had visited the city earlier, for four days in March 1908, on the way from Vienna to Paris, but had been rather disappointed. From mid-April through mid-October of 1910, however, he used Munich as the base from which he undertook a number of research expeditions across Germany. During this period, he made the acquaintance of two men who were to remain friends for many years: William Ritter and August Klipstein. In April 1911, he visited Munich again, devoting himself to his work on the "Etude sur le mouvement d'art décoratif en Allemagne." He and Klipstein left Germany shortly after, en route to southeastern Europe.

In common with his time in Germany as a whole, the visits to Munich are extremely well documented: drawings, photographs, picture postcards, notes in the *carnets*, and an extensive correspondence make it possible to reconstruct his interests at the time.

THE URBAN FABRIC

First and foremost, there was the quest for materials for Jeanneret's projected book, "La Construction des villes." As with other German cities, the urban fabric of Munich offered a number of features that attracted Jeanneret's attention. On an accurately drawn plan, he recorded the route of Neuhauserstrasse and Kaufingerstrasse, together with adjacent church buildings, and defined two opposite lines of sight that unmistakably conformed to the definition of good urban space given by Paul Schultze-Naumburg in the fourth volume (on urban planning) of *Kulturarbeiten*.[52] A similar townscape, similarly marked by variety and tension, was found in the area around Odeonsplatz, with the impressive vitality of its cluster of historic buildings (such as Feldherrnhalle, Theatinerkirche St. Kajetan, and Residenz). Here, Jeanneret showed his appreciation by buying a picture postcard that recorded the view.[53] However, a sketch, probably made during his extended stay in Munich in 1910, does not show the square as a whole but leads the eye from one of the approaching streets, Theatinerstrasse, along a building line partly

230. William Ritter, Munich, view of Hofgarten, Bazar-Gebäude, Theatinerkirche and the twin towers of the Frauenkirche in the background, April 13, 1908, watercolor on paper, BV [288]

disrupted by the end arches of the Feldherrnhalle loggia, to the wide expanse of the square
in the background (fig. 231). This refreshingly
unfamiliar perspective emphasizes the function of the loggia as an element in the urban
fabric, linking the buildings with the open
space of the square. Friedrich von Gärtner,
the architect of the Feldherrnhalle (built
1841–44), had recognized the Loggia dei
Lanzi in Florence as a perfect model for such
a composition, and Camillo Sitte agreed that it
was the finest example of the loggia type. It is
no surprise, therefore, to discover the analogy
between Jeanneret's drawing and the illustration of the Loggia dei Lanzi in Sitte's work on
urban planning, *Der Städtebau nach seinen künstlerischen Grundsätzen* (fig. 232). [54]

231. Charles-Edouard Jeanneret, Munich, view from
Theatinerstrasse along Feldherrnhalle (right) towards
Odeonsplatz, 1910–11, pencil on paper, FLC [173]

232. The Loggia dei Lanzi in Florence, from Camillo
Sitte, *Der Städtebau nach seinen künstlerischen
Grundsätzen*, Vienna, 1889

233. Charles-Edouard Jeanneret, Study of Theatinerkirche St. Kajetan, Munich, 1911, pencil on paper, FLC

234. William Ritter, View of the Frauenkirche, Munich, 1911, pencil on paper, BV [175]

of varied masses.[55] The church seems to grow organically from the subordinate buildings around it.

Jeanneret was offered an unusual view of one of the distinctive sights of Munich, the Frauenkirche (fig. 235), because of a temporarily vacant lot. In 1911 work started on replacing the demolished Augustinerstock, a monastery between Augustinerstrasse and Ettstrasse, with the new police headquarters for the city (the Polizeipräsidium, designed by Theodor Fischer). For a short time, there was thus a completely unobstructed view of the facade of the Frauenkirche. Jeanneret's water-color must have been done at this time. His aim, evidently, was not to create an architectural record but to capture the immediate effect of the church, which he reduced to a silhouette. The towers and nave merge into a vague overall form that looms above a scene that appears almost to be a stage set.

K.S.

MONUMENTAL STRUCTURES IN A NEW LIGHT

While with the Feldherrnhalle Jeanneret was primarily interested in the urban context, he treated the imposing Baroque Theatinerkirche St. Kajetan as a building in its own right (fig. 233). Jeanneret visited the Theatinerkirche on Ritter's recommendation in April 1911, and in a letter to Ritter, he described it as "one of the most beautiful things that I know." What he drew, however, was not the main facade facing Odeonsplatz (visible in a postcard purchased by Jeanneret), but the rear elevation, which he shows from a viewpoint to one side of the main longitudinal axis as a tense combination

235. Charles-Edouard Jeanneret, View of the
Frauenkirche, Munich, 1911, waterolor, pencil and black
ink on paper, Institut für Geschichte und Theorie der
Architektur ETH Zürich

8. PRAGUE

The first destination on Jeanneret and Klipstein's journey to southeastern Europe was Prague, then the capital city of Bohemia. They arrived from Dresden on or around May 24, 1911, stayed in the city for "three wonderful days," as Jeanneret reported to his parents, and departed on Saturday, May 27, for Vienna, where they arrived via Tábor toward evening.[56] Seventeen years later, Le Corbusier seems to have had a precise memory of his impressions, which he described in an interview with Karel Teige:

> There is no need to talk about the old Prague. Believe me, I genuinely like it. Not Saint Vitus Cathedral, but those old houses of beautiful proportions, the local civic buildings, even though modest, are always dignified and noble; it is the architecture of the Southern spirit.[57]

Although most of Le Corbusier's remarks to Teige are in his customary polemical vein, these descriptions of Prague reflect, with considerable accuracy, the way in which he saw the city in 1911. Then, it was Baroque Prague—with its winding alleyways, impressive town houses, and picturesque street lines—that interested him. In his *carnets* he noted: "Baroque: Prague the most marvelous of European cities."[58]

Jeanneret made no mention—not even a negative one—of the buildings of Prague's Art Nouveau period, such as the almost-completed Municipal House (Obecní dům) on what is now Republic Square (Náměstí republiky), or buildings by Osvald Polívka or Bedřich Ohmann in the historic town center. Nor did he register such important early modernist buildings (viewed in the context of his experiences in Germany) as the Urbánek House by Jan Kotěra (a pupil of Otto Wagner) or the Štenc House by Otakar Novotný. For this, either his time in Prague was too short, or he knew nothing of the contemporary architectural scene in Prague and was not interested.

PICTURESQUE PRAGUE

Jeanneret's specific view of Prague is not surprising. His choice of motifs was determined by the project of collecting materials for the planned publication "La Construction des villes." There exist a number of photographs, a few noted in the carnets, and four watercolor drawings, which Jeanneret gave to his friend Ritter (Jeanneret might well never have stopped in Prague on the way to Vienna, had Ritter not suggested it).[59] The subjects are almost all situated along the Královská cesta (Royal Way), a route that leads from Republic Square through the old city and across Karlův most (Charles Bridge) to the Malá strana ("Little Quarter") and on to Pražský hrad (Prague Castle). In some cases, he showed exactly the same views and motifs that are presented as "good examples" in Schultze-Naumburg's Kulturarbeiten (a book that Jeanneret knew well).[60] He also photographed the intersection of Melantrichova and Staroměstské náměstí (Old Town Square), with the striking little arch between the houses that flank the street entrance. He documented urban contexts that set dissimilar buildings in a conflicting relationship with each other: Křížovnické náměstí (Knights of the Cross Square) with the Old Town Bridge Tower (fig. 236); Charles Bridge with the impressive skyline of Malá Strana and Prague Castle; Fürstenberg Palace with Prague Castle as "viewstopper."

Four watercolors present the four access routes to Prague Castle hill. Two of them capture perspectives that directly follow each other, opening up the view of Prague Castle very much in the spirit of a "promenade." One of them shows (from a somewhat greater distance) the same view of the steps linking Nerudova and Loretánská Streets that is given by Schultze-Naumburg (figs. 238–39).[61] The fourth and probably finest drawing was made from the monumental Castle Steps (Zámecké schody) and leads the eye along the gently curving boundary wall of the Castle Garden and up to the south front of the castle (fig. 237).

236. Charles-Edouard Jeanneret, Prague, Knights of the Cross Square with Monastery and Church of the Knights of the Cross, Saint Kliment Church, Old Town Bridge Tower and Charles Bridge, 1911, photograph, BV

237. Charles-Edouard Jeanneret, Prague, view of Prague Castle from Castle stairs, 1911, pencil and watercolor on tracing paper, BV [177]

238. Prague, view of stairs between Nerudova and Loretánská Street, as seen from Ke Hradu Street, from Paul Schultze-Naumburg, *Kulturarbeiten*, vol.4: *Städtebau*, Munich, 1906, p. 184

239. Charles-Edouard Jeanneret, Prague, view of stairs between Nerudova and Loretánská Street, as seen from Ke Hradu Street, 1911, pencil and watercolor on tracing paper, BV [176]

— 184 —

Abbildung 106

Treppenanlage in Prag

RETURN TO CENTRAL EUROPE

Although the visual documents of Jeanneret's visit to Prague in 1911 seem subsequently to have vanished from his memory,[62] he concerned himself with Prague and/or Czechoslovakia in different ways on three subsequent occasions.[63] In 1925 he and Amédée Ozenfant lectured in Prague and Brno; in 1928 he stopped in Prague on his way to Moscow; and early in 1935 he went to Zlín, in southern Moravia, to work on a project for the Bat'a footwear company. The negative outcome of this undertaking, which would have involved the expansion of Zlín itself in the spirit of Le Corbusier's *Ville radieuse* (1935), marked the end of his contacts with Prague and Czechoslovakia.

K.S.

9. THE BALKANS

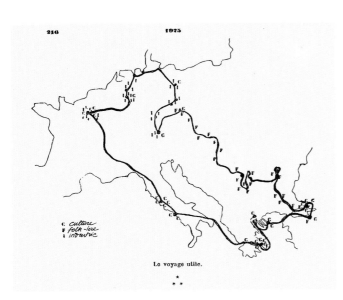

240. Charles-Edouard Jeanneret, "Le voyage utile" (Itinerary for Voyage d'orient), Note Jeanneret's markings for Culture (C), Folklore (F) and Industry (I), 1911, from: Le Corbusier, *L'Art décoratif d'aujourd'hui*, Paris, 1925

A NOTE ON THE VOYAGE D'ORIENT

Jeanneret was twenty years old when he completed his first exploratory trip beyond the borders of the "Swiss universe," the Grand Tour of Tuscany which would galvanize his early calling as an architect (cat. nos. 1, 2). He was twenty-four when, along with his friend August Klipstein (1885–1951), a graduate student in art history and a student of Wilhelm Worringer, he journeyed east, following the Danube from Berlin to Prague, crossing the Balkans to Istanbul and Athens, and visiting Florence, Rome, Naples and Pompeii.

During the trip, the two companions stopped at the most famous sites and visited the most acclaimed monuments (from the great mosques of Edirne and Istanbul to the Parthenon, Pantheon, and Hadrian's Villa). With similar confidence they ventured to regions that were off the usual tourist itineraries of the period: the terrains of Campina and Passarea in Romania; the city of Kazanlak in Bulgaria, Eyüp on the Golden Horn and the cemeteries of Ok-Meydany in Istanbul, Mount Athos in Greece, and so on. Often these places were "inaccessible" or unknown to Westerners, but Jeanneret and Klipstein visited them at the suggestion of William Ritter (see cat. no. 7).

In 1919 Le Corbusier, who had met Ritter in 1910, spent time with him in Munich, gaining access to his extensive private library, filled with texts on Near Eastern and Asian subjects. It was here that Jeanneret discovered the works of Jules Renan, Pierre Loti, Claude Farrère, Montesquieu, Gerard de Nerval, and Alexandre Cingria-Vaneyre. Ritter's extraordinary collection expanded the interests and culture that Jeanneret had developed during his years at the École d'Art in La Chaux-de-Fonds. Thanks to Ritter and his library, Jeanneret learned of "unimaginable" places and monuments to visit, which his sketches would make part of his formal and typological—in short, his architectural—world from then on. During a six-month journey (May to November; fig. 240)—which he would call his

Voyage d'Orient—by train and horseback, but mainly on foot, Le Corbusier executed approximately three-hundred drawings, annotated six *carnets*, sent dozens of reports to his hometown newspaper, *La Feuille d'Avis de La Chaux-de-Fonds*, wrote hundreds of letters to friends and relatives, and took over 400 photographs with his Cupido 80 camera.

There are often surprising analogies between this material and Le Corbusier's later work, as well as a close "structural" and linguistic relationship between the two. It is almost impossible to fully comprehend the significance of Le Corbusier's work without delving deeply into the fertile moment of his cultural formation during the Voyage d'Orient, as well as his travels in Europe in general. It was a context that Le Corbusier, despite his relative experience at the youthful age of twenty-four, proved able to manage remarkably well.[64]

RAILWAY BRIDGE OVER THE DANUBE

On June 6 or 7 Jeanneret photographed a bridge over the Danube (probably somewhere between Baja and Novi Sad; fig. 241). Although he usually emphasized images in his *carnets* that he intended to develop more fully, the original manuscript of *Le Voyage d'orient* makes no mention of this subject. In fact, in the 1966 edition, there is a note by Le Corbusier that perhaps dates from 1965: "Some railway bridges boldly jut out onto the water. Each time there is the same type: a long rigid beam and entirely openwork structure, a masterpiece of lightness and technology."[65] Le Corbusier added another note with the clear intention of explaining the later comment: "One of these bridges is the work of Eiffel."[66]

Jeanneret took the photo of the bridge from a boat. Its exact location cannot be determined from the photographic plate, which was damaged when an early contact print was made; moreover, this region has since been devastated. The extremely steep bank on the right might be that of Fruška Gora on the outskirts of Novi Sad. According to Jean Petit, the editor of *Voyage*, Le Corbusier, speaking of the bridge, referred to a recollection that he had not originally recorded in his notebooks. The comments of a casual interlocutor, an "étudiant architecte de Prague rencontré la veille" (student architect from Prague I met the day before) was the pretext for him, so he said, to develop his point of view on the aesthetics of engineering and to reflect on the formal autonomy of the

"modern," forcibly inserted into a poetic landscape. These remarks thus come to represent Jeanneret's interest in this type of "object," which he will later count among the "icons of modernity."[67]

NEGOTIN

South of Belgrade (which Jeanneret and Klipstein had reached on June 8), passing by the landing point at Turnu Severin, but before Knjazevac, the duo decided to disembark at Negotin. As Jeanneret later recalled: "Yesterday morning, we saw twenty-six square towers flanking a large, severe wall on the edge of a river."[68] His photograph, of surprising beauty, shows the towers on the distant banks of the river, upstream from a place called "Trajan's gates" (or the "Iron gates"; fig. 242). The architecture, reduced to a line of blocks, stands on the horizon, which almost exactly bisects the picture, evoking the famous image of the plan for Buenos Aires shown on the cover of *Précisions sur un état présent de l'architecture et de l'urbanisme* (1930; fig. 243). In fact, the "horizontal dimension" is a spatial constant of the lands along the Danube. Jeanneret contrasted this horizontality with the apparition of architectural blocks emerging from the water, just as Italian architect Adalberto Libera would later do in his project to systemize the shoreline of Castelfusano near Ostia (1933–34).[69]

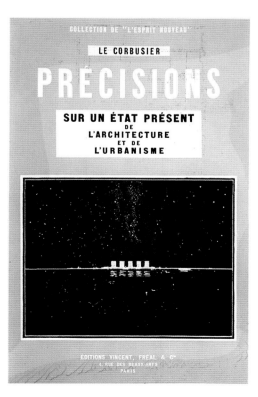

241. Charles-Edouard Jeanneret, Danube with Railway Bridge (probably between Baja and Novi Sad), 1911, photograph, FLC

242. Charles-Edouard Jeanneret, Danube beyond Beograd, Fortress near Negotin, 1911, photograph, FLC

243. Cover of Le Corbusier, *Précisions, sur un etat présent de l'architecture et de l'urbanisme*, Paris, 1930

GABROVO

En route from Ruse in Bulgaria to Stara Zagora (where Jeanneret and Klipstein arrived on 29 June), the two travelers stopped in Tarnovo (today Veliko Tarnovo) and Gabrovo. Jeanneret found these places, which had been part of the kingdom of the tsars of Bulgaria from 1187 to 1396, still intact at the time of his journey. At Tarnovo Jeanneret wrote some of his most vivid journal entries in the *Voyage*; they are rich in descriptions of the typological details and chromatic qualities of the buildings. During his stay in Gabrovo he was particularly fascinated by the antiquity of the surroundings. The camera focused on three objects: the bridge over the Jantra River, the square with the civic tower, and the base of this tower with its adjacent fountain. Whereas the bridge is the typical sort of land-scape study that Jeanneret "learned to see" during the trip, the photos of the civic tower demonstrate the techniques the author employed in his "portraits of buildings" (fig. 245). Just as with the photos of Germany, Jeanneret "selected" the architectural detail that interested him, extracting it from an over-all view framing the area for study. The the full height of the tower becomes invisible in the photograph; in fact the tower ceases to be a tower. It is transformed into an architectural incident involving a series of secondary events that are individually insignificant but whose collective interaction is extraordinarily evocative. In this picture Jeanneret reveals the high level of refinement that his "regard photographique" had reached.

244. Charles-Edouard Jeanneret, Gabrovo. Square with Tower and Fountain, 1911, photograph, FLC [64]

THE CHURCH

In April 1912, Jeanneret participated in the *Exposition de la Section Sculpteurs, peintres et architectes* in Neuchâtel with a series of watercolors entitled *Langage de pierres* (Language of stones). The exhibits, twelve in all, were either earlier studies that had been reworked or sketches that had been culled from the *carnets*. Some dated to his 1907 trip to Italy (Fiesole and Siena); two derived from his German travels of 1910 (Potsdam) and 1911 (Frankfurt); and eight were of Eastern subjects (Istanbul); Greece (Parthenon), and Italy (Pompeii; cat. no. 12). The watercolor of the famous monastery church of Gabrovo, which was actually fourth in the series, is authenticated by the inscription "Gabrovo Ch. E. Jt" and (on the cardboard mounting) "Fait à Gabrovo, Bulgarie" (fig. 246). The foreshortened view of the subject, seen from the foot of the stairs, is typical of Jeanneret's other photographic and painting efforts, as, for example, in views of Prague Castle from the ramp of the Malá Strana, or photographs of the Escalier des Cent-Marches at Versailles made in 1908 (see cat. nos. 00, 00). Ritter had recommended that the young Le Corbusier visit the church in Gabrovo, and the architect's watercolor is reminiscent of similar ones made by Ritter many years earlier. The image also bears visual similarities to several photographs taken by Lucien Hervé for Ronchamp, which the painting seems to have distantly but surprisingly anticipated.

G.G.

245. Charles-Edouard Jeanneret, Gabrovo, Bulgaria,
Church exterior, 1911, pencil and watercolor, FLC
[179]

10. ISTANBUL

246. Charles-Edouard Jeanneret, Panorama of Istanbul with the Golden Horn in foreground and the Marmara Sea beyond, July 1911, watercolor on paper, FLC [193]

247. Charles-Edouard Jeanneret, Istanbul. The great fire of July 23, 1911, photograph, BV [67]

THE FIRE

Jeanneret took this remarkable photograph (fig. 247) on the night of July 23, 1911, from the terrace of his lodgings in Ainali Passage near the church of Saint Anthony, located in the then-European quarter of Pera. Today the panorama from the upper floors of the building is still superb: it ranges from the promontory of the Serraglio to the Sultan Selim Camii and beyond. These landmarks also mark the boundaries of that intricate labyrinth in which, day after day, Jeanneret isolated the subjects of architectural exploration "on sight" (fig. 248). This particular scene was evidently photographed by hurriedly placing the camera on the windowsill in the aftershock of a nocturnal fire that destroyed the entire quarter of the Laleli Camii, including the residential area around the university. The fire may be remarkable because it coincided with Le Corbusier's presence in Istanbul, but otherwise this kind of calamity was fairly common in the city's millenial history. The event gave Jeanneret cause to reflect on buildings that fire had reduced to a bare essence, and he discussed this in *Voyage* ("Le desastre de Stamboul") and in *Une Maison, un palais*. After visiting the site of the disaster the next morning, Jeanneret began to write a report for *Le Feuille d'Avis de La Chaux-de-Fonds*. In revised form, this would become the chapter in *Voyage* devoted to describing events and places in a literary, picturesque and dramatic language that was modeled on Claude Farrère and Pierre Loti.

PANORAMA

This extraordinary panorama (fig. 246), similar to the famous "skylines" of Istanbul that Le Corbusier published in his *Oeuvre complète*,[70] was probably one of the last drawings made from the window of the house where Jeanneret and Klipstein had stayed after the fire of 1923.[71] Even today it is possible to gain a similarly broad view of the great mosques (the Fatih, Sultan Selim Camii, Süleymaniye) from the tall houses of Pera above Ainali Passage. Jeanneret kept the roofs of Pera below him in shadow, made the lights reflected in the Golden Horn only just visible, and managed to focus the observer's attention on the "unyielding horizon of the sea," tracing the silhouettes of the two mosques. It is clear that in this sketch the architect resumed a theme that was important to the *Voyage*: the ecstatic *contemplation* of a unique panorama, which the gray monochrome of the fire's ashes had rendered still more dramatic.[72]

248. Charles-Edouard Jeanneret, View on Pera, probably from Taxim, towards the Golden Horn, with Süleymaniye Mosque, Istanbul, in the background, 1911, watercolor on paper, FLC [184]

CARAVANSARY

Jeanneret stopped at Edirne between June 29 and 30. This drawing, of extraordinary beauty and precision (and never published by Le Corbusier; fig. 249), shows how he had refined his surveying method to select the part of a scene that would best represent the whole. The brown and purple pigment, smeared on with a finger, give remarkable depth to the portico vaults, and in this way Jeanneret was able "to record" the special effect of a "weightless" covering, one that has been reduced simply to shadow. He used the same method on several later occasions. The miniscule plan on the side allowed him to record the architectural device of two symmetrical staircases leading to the upper floor. The inscription reads: "Entrée du grand / caravanserrail / solution des escaliers / Constantinople / ou Adrianople / 1911" (Entrance of the large / caravansary /

249. Charles-Edouard Jeanneret, View into the Caravansaray of Edirne, with plan and notes, 1911, pencil on paper, FLC [180]

250. Charles-Edouard Jeanneret, Istanbul, Rüstem Paša Mosque in the Egyptian Bazar, 1911, photograph, FLC [65]

solution for the stairs / Constantinople / or Adrinopolis / 1911).

Using an essentially pictorial technique, Jeanneret grasped with extreme precision the "dramatic" passage from a shaded space, filled with architectural elements, to the "sheer light" of the *avlu*, or inner courtyard.

RÜSTEM PAŠA

Jeanneret was especially impressed by this small and unusual mosque. One of the masterpieces by Sinan, Turkey's most celebrated architect, the building was constructed beginning in 1561 and is located near the Egyptian Bazaar. It must have captured Jeanneret's attention because its plan easily conformed to the golden section. Rising high up from the street, the mosque faces a large terrace that is almost entirely covered by a deep loggia and connected to the street by a remarkable system of stairs placed within a square tower. Jeanneret completed several overall and detail sketches of the mosque that same day, but this may be the only photograph (fig. 250).[73] The view is somewhat difficult to explain. In fact, Jeanneret seems more interested in complex network of metal rods that cover the terrace than the space of the porticoed *avlu*. He was probably deceived by the distance, thinking that he could capture the grandiose panorama of Galata bridge through the loggia arches, but in the final result the bridge is barely visible.

SÜLEYMANIYE MOSQUE

Le Corbusier used several sketches of this subject to illustrate the chapter entitled "Les Mosquées" in his *Almanach d'architecture moderne*.[74] He studied Sinan's great work (1550) with a specific criterion in mind, leading him to walk around the complex and represent it from outside the great court (figs. 251, 252). Only later did he explore the interior of the *avlu* and observe the heavy mass of the mosque in very foreshortened perspectival views, first on the western side and then of the eastern one facing Pera. Most remarkable is the "axonometric" view he made of the same building, which was probably copied from a postcard or drawn from a "high place" that can no longer be identified.[75]

Nonetheless, even now, a person arriving from the ridge of Stambul or the Egyptian Bazaar would see the large construction frontally, just as it appeared to Jeanneret in July 1911. It is significant in that he chose not to use a camera to document the building (as he did the Erski Selimiye Mosque at Edirne), instead concentrating on drawing an analytical study of the building and its parts.

Having walked around the enclosing wall, Jeanneret entered the large courtyard from the southeast gate, of which he made an exact study (FLC 6103), and proceeded to the western gate. From this vantage point, the architectural block appears in a perspective converging on the northern entrance, also depicted with unusual skill (FLC 6087). Jeanneret was thus able to grasp the complexity of the architectural masses in their mutual counterpoint and cohesion: the exterior of the *avlu* with its minarets, the main facade with the large porticoed wall; the minor cupolas, and finally the straight, low, cemetery wall that bounds the sacred Türbe of the founders. The studies that Jeanneret completed at the Süleymaniye mosque show how carefully he investigated the compositional logic of this organism, which was considered Sinan's mas-

terpiece and one of the greatest monuments of Ottoman architecture. The scale of this spectacular structure must have made an enormous impression on the young Le Corbusier. He acquired some "ambience" photographs by the famous Joaillier, including one of the mosque taken from the same viewpoint that Jeanneret had chosen for his drawing.[76] One finds echoes of such thinking in the *Voyage*, in the chapter entitled "Les Mosquées," in which Jeanneret strives to describe the details of a built space that, to his mind, was disconcertingly novel and essential.[77]

251. Charles-Edouard Jeanneret, Study of the Süleymaniye Mosque, Istanbul, 1911, black pencil on paper, FLC [182]

252. Charles-Edouard Jeanneret, View of the northwest façade of the Süleymaniye Mosque, Istanbul, 1911, pencil on paper, FLC [181]

STREET SCENE

During his first days in Istanbul, Jeanneret was unusually taken by the exaggerated perspective of its streets. In the old city, whether at Stambul or Scutari (Üsküdar), it is easy to find oneself in spatial situations exactly like those drawn by Le Corbusier. A long wall seen at the end of an uphill street seems compact and closed, rigorously circumscribing the space of the "mysterious" interiors (fig. 253). It is not difficult to understand the architect's interest in what can be seen above this, namely the upper part of the Mosque with its strongly projecting, brown, wooden eaves of the roof. On the left, the entrance gate to the *avlu* (inner courtyard) opens under a barrel-vaulted passageway sheathed in lead. There are dozens of drawings of similar subjects in both the notebooks and loose album pages whose margins have been trimmed at a later date. Many observers have commented on the remarkable analogies between the sketches of the streets of Istanbul and the early designs for the Dom-ino project and Citrohan quarters that were published in 1923 in *Vers un architecture* and subsequently in the *Oeuvre complete*.[78]

ISTANBUL: STUDY OF A FOUNTAIN WITH A HANGING GARDEN

There are two versions of this drawing, practically identical except for a slight exaggeration of the perspective in the fountain niche in one of them (fig. 254).[79] The inscription at the bottom reads: "mauvais / c-a-d [c'est à dire] dessiné / en mauvaise / proportion" (bad / [that is to say] drawn / in poor / perspective). The other drawing, evidently drawn immediately after the first, is annotated: "inscription / peinte rouge" (inscription / painted red). This minimal correction allowed Jeanneret to insert the simple calligraphic dedication in the border of the niche, leaving the rest surprisingly unaltered. Otherwise, the resemblance between the two drawings is so close that they could almost be superimposed. They bear further testimony to Jeanneret's working method, obsessed with problems of detail and "moldings." Although the fountain and its colored inscription are what caught Jeanneret's attention again, no less surprising is the carefully drawn suspended pergola, which protrudes from an upper garden. There are readily apparent similarities between this light wooden trellis and the pergola in the garden in the Villa Jeanneret at La Chaux-de Fonds (1912), which was completed immediately after Jeanneret's return from the Voyage d'Orient (see p. 209).

253. Charles-Edouard Jeanneret, View of a Mosque wall with wooden houses in Istanbul, 1911, watercolor, pen and pencil on paper, FLC [188]

254. Charles-Edouard Jeanneret, Study of a fountain and garden with pergola in Istanbul, 1911, pencil and colored pencil on paper, FLC

WOODEN HOUSE

Jeanneret carefully studied the functional "mechanism" of the Turkish house. He observed in particular the relationship between the building and the space around it. In Istanbul, given the obvious difficulties of entering private homes, he studied only the exteriors (fig. 255). The Turkish house, especially during the period in which Jeanneret visited Istanbul was still a closed "world," open to visitors only in exceptional circumstances. In *Le Voyage d'orient*, the architect recorded this sensation of exclusion in an obsessive, almost "painful," way. Jeanneret strolled the streets of Istanbul, attracted by the beauty of the wooden houses, with roofs that jutted out over high plastered, rose-colored walls, beyond which one could cast only furtive glances.[80] In the Mahmut Pasa Camii quarter and around the Aivan Serai near the western walls (where this photo was probably taken) there existed a multitude of such wooden houses at the time of Jeanneret's visit, and several very interesting examples are still to be found around the Kilissé Camii (Church of the Pantocrator).

CEMETERY WALL

Eÿup is located at the farthest point of the Golden Horn. It is one of the holiest of places for Muslims, an obligatory pilgrimage destination thanks to the the great mosque housing the tomb of Mehmet the Conqueror (1458). In literary tradition, Eÿup was the theater for the accounts of Pierre Loti, the indispensable starting point for anyone wishing to understand the essence and exoticism of Constantinople (Istanbul) at the beginning of the century.[81] Jeanneret completed a far greater number of drawings of Eÿup than has previously been thought. Surrounded by large cemeteries, Eyüp is unusual for the walls that line its streets and allow one to glimpse serried graves under cypresses beyond. In this sketch (fig. 256), Jeanneret noted the particular architectural feature of windows with grilles that allow passersby to view the diversity of sacred spaces that the wall encloses. The areas on either side of the wall are joined by these filters; they are true *fenètres tableaux* (picture-windows), participating in an iconography that Le Corbusier would later discover to be a formidable design option. The marginal notation states: "a, b bleu caeruleum / av[ec] lettres vert retouches / en or / le grillage est exquise" (a, b blue *caeruleum* / w[ith] repainted green letters / in gold / the grillwork is exquisite).

G.G.

255. Charles-Edouard Jeanneret, Istanbul, traditional wooden houses, 1911, photograph, FLC [68]

256. Charles-Edouard Jeanneret, View of Eyüp Cemetery enclosure wall, Istanbul, 1911, pencil on paper, FLC [185]

II. ATHENS

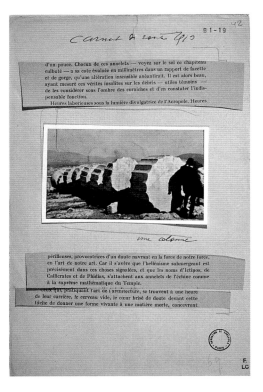

THROUGH THE BACK DOOR

Jeanneret and Klipstein arrived in Athens on September 12, 1911 (fig. 257), six weeks behind schedule. The goal, and in many respects the raison d'être, of their "reverse Grand Tour" was of course not the Acropolis but Istanbul where they had spent seven weeks.[82] In a way, they entered Greece through the back door, but this was only logical—or, at least, the art historian Wilhelm Worringer would have thought so. In his view, Byzantium, as the realm of "abstraction," definitely ranked higher than Hellas, with its leaning toward naturalistic "empathy."[83]

There are no direct, written records of this visit to Athens.[84] The chapter "Le Parthénon" in *Le Voyage d'orient* (1966) was not written until 1914 and was thus entirely retrospective. Le Corbusier himself first published it in *Almanach d'architecture moderne* in 1926 (figs. 258, 261). In both conceptual content and rhetoric, this essay reveals the influence of Ernest Renan's brief, twelve-page pamphlet,

Prière sur l'Acropole, which Jeanneret had presumably bought and read while in Athens. Renan wrote:

> The impression that Athens made on me is by far the most powerful that I have ever received. There is one place where perfection exists; there are not two: … I had not imagined anything like this. What made itself manifest to me was the Ideal, crystallized in Pentelic marble.[85]

There is an unmistakable echo of Renan's Attic imperative in Jeanneret's words:

> I do not really know why this hill enshrines the essence of artistic thought … I have long since accepted that this is, as it were, the repository of the standard measure, the basis of all measurement in art. … But why … must I the designer acknowledge this, the Parthenon, as the indisputable Master, as it rises above its rocky base; why bow, albeit in anger, to its supreme authority?[86]

257. Athens. Jeanneret next to a column of the Parthenon, Sept. 1911, photograph, FLC [110]

258. Layout by Le Corbusier for the article "Sur l'Acropole" in Le Corbusier, *Almanach d'architcture moderne*, Paris, 1926 using the photograph of Jeanneret next to a column of the Parthenon (fig. 259), collage, 1925–26, FLC

259. Charles-Edouard Jeanneret, Athens, the Acropolis, Parthenon, 1911, photograph, FLC

THE PARTHENON

On the day of their arrival, having resolved to keep up with the literary tradition of the Hellenic traveler, Jeanneret and Klipstein waited until the romantic hour of sunset before climbing the Acropolis. The effect must have surpassed all expectations, because the days that followed were almost exclusively dominated by the Acropolis (figs. 259, 262, 263). At the same time, the collection of sketches and drawings by Jeanneret is more modest than one would have expected for a stay of two weeks.[87] The two watercolors reproduced here—among his most impressive—blend the real scene with reminiscences of stage designs by Adolphe Appia (figs. 260, 264) and could be characterized as "heroic landscapes." The same goes for the drawings in the sketchbooks, which are mostly dashed down in soft pencil, with no indication of detail: the panoramic views from a distance emphasize the harmony between temple and topography, and those done on the Acropolis itself focus on the relationships of the temples to each other.[88]

260. Charles-Edouard Jeanneret, Athens, view from the Parthenon, 1911 (or 1914?), watercolor on paper, FLC

RECYCLING

Characteristically, Le Corbusier later "recycled" his response to the Parthenon, as documented here, in the pages of *L'Esprit nouveau*. However, by that time he was illustrating his "case" not with his own photographs and drawings but with plates from archaeological works.[89] The Parthenon was, as it were, subpoenaed to testify in support of the aesthetic position of *L'Esprit nouveau*, a gambit that must have seemed promising in the wake of the *retour à l'ordre*.[90] By referring to the Parthenon, Le Corbusier's aim was to establish "ultimate" rules of architecture: the supremacy of the ground plan; the necessity of standards; the nature of the architectural artwork as a "pure creation of the mind"; "austerity" (which in practice leads to a kind of modernist recycling of the eighteenth-century "ruin" aesthetic); and architecture as an "abstract" art. When he came to publish his theses in book form (*Vers une architecture*, 1923), he filled no fewer than twenty-nine pages with magnificent illustrations related to this theme (figs. 11.5, 11.9).

S.v.M.

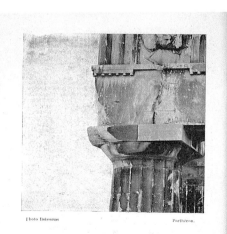

261. Title page of Le Corbusier's article "Sur l'Acropole", *Almanach d'architecture moderne*, Paris, 1926, p. 62

262. Charles-Edouard Jeanneret, Athens, the Acropolis, with Klipstein next to one of the capitals of the Parthenon, 1911, photograph, FLC

263. Charles-Edouard Jeanneret, Athens, north side of the Erechtheum, 1911, photograph, FLC [70]

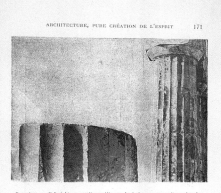

264. Charles-Edouard Jeanneret, Athens, view from the Acropolis, 1911 (or 1914?), watercolor on paper, pasted on cardboard, FLC [187]

265. Athens, The Parthenon, from Le Corbusier and Saugnier, *Vers une architecture*, Paris, 1923

266. Athens, The Parthenon, from Le Corbusier and Saugnier, *Vers une architecture*, Paris, 1923

12. POMPEII

1937

THE FORUM

Ever since the first excavations of Pompeii in the eighteenth century, studying its ruins was an erudite pastime in architectural academia, especially at the École des Beaux-Arts in Paris.[91] Jeanneret, who had studied at the École in 1908/09, appears to have had a clear idea of what to expect when he arrived in Pompeii on October 8, 1911. Marks in his copy of the Baedeker guide (*Italie des Alpes à Naples*, 1909) indicate precisely what he wanted to see, had seen, or wanted to see again.[92]

During his five-day stay he was most interested in the Forum with Jupiter's temple and the spatial organization of the Pompeian houses. The theatre and amphitheatre were all but overlooked. In one drawing he highlighted the "cubism" of Jupiter's temple as it domi-

nates the Forum, with the two monumental archways on either side (fig. 267). Below this he sketched the same view as it would look in reconstruction.[93] The source for these hastily sketched reconstructions was provided by a book Jeanneret had probably acquired on the spot, *Pompei com'era, Pompei com'è*, by Luigi Fischetti (Naples, 1903). His interest in such reconstructions, however, was more for their spatial effects than for archaeology. The oft-published watercolor from his "Langage de Pierres" series, in fact, which shows a reconstructed view from the temple onto the Forum, is based not so much on archaeology as on a sketch and written comments made on-site, exploring the rhythmic play of the ring of columns of the temple and Forum, and of the mountains in the background.[94]

STREETS AND HOUSES

The many photographs of the Via dell' Abbondanza, the Via dei Sepolcri, and the Forum illustrate the public spaces as they unfold along straight axes and open onto rectangular squares, making the best of the autumn sunshine and its dramatic play of light and shadow (figs. 268–73). As is argued elsewhere in this book (see pp. 63–67), this sustained experience of rectangularity and the play of brightly lit volumes and voids in space also revealed the limits of an urban aesthetic too exclusively grounded in the picturesque tradition. The most profound insights, however, were gained from Jeanneret's detailed inspection of a series of Pompeian houses, such as the House of the Silver Wedding ("Nozze d'argento" — repeatedly referred to by Le Corbusier as "Casa del Noce"), the House of Sallustius, the House of the Tragic Poet, the House of Diomedes as well as the House of M. Lucretius.

In Pompeian houses (as well as at Hadrian's Villa) Jeanneret noted that "in each Roman room there are always three full walls. The other wall opens generously and lets the room participate in the ensemble."[95] What interested Jeanneret was the paradigmatic simplicity of such arrangement, the visual impact of the three full walls, and the "participation in the ensemble" provided by the fourth open side—a participation that is physically understandable and goes far beyond the functional connection provided by a door. These analyses served as an immediate background for the design of Maison Blanche in La Chaux-de-Fonds as well as of the Villa Favre-Jacot in Le Locle. Ultimately, however, this could engender complex and ambiguous arrangements, in which space is continuous and yet additive, the result of smaller spaces juxtaposed and playing with each other, both hierarchically and not.[96] Whether in the Maison Citrohan or the hall of the La Roche house, in the living rooms of the villas Cook and Stein, or in the Unité d'Habitation and Ronchamp, this combinatory and ambiguous internal "play of volumes" will be a defining quality of Le Corbusier's architectural space.[97]

S.v.M. / F.P.

268. Charles-Edouard Jeanneret, Pompeii. View of the Temple of Jupiter, with sketched reconstruction below, 1911, photograph, FLC [201]

268–73. Charles-Edouard Jeanneret, Pompeii: the Forum, as seen from the Temple of Jupiter; Via dell'Abbondanza; Via die Sepolcri, and other views, 1911, photographs, FLC [73–78]

13. ROME

TOWARDS A "HEROIC" VIEW OF ARCHITECTURE

Rome can mean different things at different times. For Jeanneret in 1910 it meant classicism—the order of classical architecture and the dream of a mythical harmony. His first idea for what became the Voyage d'Orient was focused on Rome alone, where he wanted to visit Bramante's architecture and walk in the gardens. He was "obsessed by a vision: nice straight lines, but elegant and classical proportions . . . clear harmonies . . . a dry and naked plain, but blue Appennines. And then cypresses. Rome!" [98]

Jeanneret's first Italian trip, in 1907, had not reached further south than Siena (see cat. no. 1). By the time he actually visited Rome in 1911, the preoccupation with classicism appears to have diminished somewhat. Now architecture was the issue, not classicism: not even classical architecture, with its canonical orders and its symmetries. Instead it was architecture reduced to the raw play of horizontals, verticals, volumes. This "heroic" view of architecture had exploded in his sketchbooks, so to speak, when he had visited the Athenian Acropolis the previous month, his

first encounter with ancient ruins (cat. no. 11). In Pompeii, in Rome, and at Hadrian's Villa, he reveled in this approach, applying it in passionate and lucid sketches (and photographs) that are focused on the essentials. Ancient ruins, which by nature are divested of many original meanings and thus are "abstract," held pride of place. The same was to be true when, in 1915, Jeanneret "revisited" these sites at the Bibliothèque Nationale in Paris, establishing an inventory of the monuments of Rome as documented in eighteenth-century prints at the Cabinet des Estampes (fig. 275).

274. Charles-Edouard Jeanneret, Rome, the Colosseum, 1911, photograph, FLC

275. Charles-Edouard Jeanneret, Sketches of famous monuments in Rome and elsewhere including the Pyramid of Cestius, the Pantheon, St. Peter's Square, after Piranesi, *Vedute di Roma*, in the Bibliothèque Nationale, Paris, 1915, ink on paper, FLC [272]

276. Charles-Edouard Jeanneret, Rome, the Forum, Basilica of Maxentius, as seen from the Temple of the Dioscures, Oct. 1911, photograph, FLC [79]

277. Charles-Edouard Jeanneret, Rome. Piazza Colonna, Column of Marcus Aurelius, Oct. 1911, photograph, FLC

278. Charles-Edouard Jeanneret, Rome, the Baths of Caracalla, Oct. 1911, photograph, FLC [80]

MODERN ROME

Yet at the same time, "modern" Rome held much to interest the expert in "la construction des villes," much that was relevant to the teachings of Sitte, Schultze-Naumburg, Ritter, and Cingria-Vaneyre. There was, for example, the spectacle of a public space that, while being enclosed on three sides, also served as a belvedere overlooking an entire city (Piazza del Campidoglio; fig. 280, in which note the

279. Charles-Edouard Jeanneret, Rome, the gardens of the Villa Medici, 1911, photograph, FLC [83]

280. Charles-Edouard Jeanneret, Rome, Piazza del Campidoglio, 1911, photograph, FLC [82]

281. Charles-Edouard Jeanneret, Rome, apse of S. Maria Maggiore, 1911, photograph, FLC

282. Charles-Edouard Jeanneret, View of the Villa Lante (by Giulio Romano), Rome, 1911, black pencil and green pastel on paper, FLC [203]

"old" pavement of the piazza as it existed prior to the reconstruction of Michelangelo's design in the 1940s). There were stairs used to "dynamize" urban space (at S.Maria Maggiore; fig. 281), as in Prague, Gabrovo, or Pisa, and seigneurial villas emerging from elaborately planted gardens (Villa Medici and Villa Lante; figs. 279, 282), perhaps suggesting erudite conversations about architecture to the former reader of Cingria-Vaneyre's *Entretiens à la villa du Rouet*. Interestingly, the center of the elaborately composed picture of the gardens of Villa Medici is marked by a sphere, and the watercolor of Giulio Romano's Villa Lante makes the volume resemble a perfect cube.[99]

283. Charles-Edouard Jeanneret, Rome, the Pantheon, Oct. 1911, photograph, FLC

284. "Le sentiment déborde", Le Corbusier, *Urbanisme*, Paris, 1925, p. 29

culminates in an eloquent text praising S. Maria in Cosmedin: "This altogether tiny church of S. Maria, a church for poor people, set in the midst of noisy and luxurious Rome, proclaims the noble pomp of mathematics, the unassailable power of proportion, the sovereign eloquence of relationship."[103]

A series of photographs of drum, dome, and apse suggest that Michelangelo's Saint Peter's was the phenomenon studied most carefully in situ (figs. 285–88). Some of the more curious photographs, however, do not imply the "Divino" (fig. 289), and in *L'Esprit nouveau* only professional photographs were considered good enough to represent Saint Peter's, and the snapshots were set aside. This was an Olympian prelude to the architecture of the new age: "Michelangelo is the man of the last thousand years as Phidias was the man of the thousand years before."[104] And who will be the man of the next millennium? Le Corbusier continued: "The work of Michelangelo is a *creation*, not a Renaissance, and overshadows the classical epochs. . . . He had seen the Colosseum and retained its fine proportions."[105]

In general Roman architecture is seen as a combination of abstract forms (fig. 290) representing order, articulation (*modénature*), and scale, whether in the Colosseum, in a medieval church, or in Saint Peter's. Rome is seen as the ultimate case study for a notion of architecture in which emotion is conveyed through the direct impact of form, without the mediation of narrative.

F.P. / S.v.M.

"LA LEÇON DE ROME"

When Le Corbusier returned to Rome in 1921, with Ozenfant, he wanted once again to "breathe the big air of the ruins and see the Sistine" chapel.[100] By then, the architecture of Rome had already become a reference in *L'Esprit nouveau*.[101] Both he and Ozenfant must already have been thinking of writing an article on the city. Their retrospective analysis of the experience resulted in three essays written soon after the trip: "La Leçon de Rome," "La Sixtine de Michel-Ange," and "L'Illusion des plans" (the first and third articles are signed "Le Corbusier-Saugnier" and the second, "De Fayet").[102]

"La Leçon de Rome" has four sections: "Rome antique," "Rome byzantine," "Michel-Ange," and "Rome et nous." While the first section basically repeats the common notion that the ancient Romans were mere organizers, who contributed infrastructures and simple order (Le Corbusier's personal feelings about ancient Roman architecture are found more in "L'Illusion des plans"), the second

285. Amédée Ozenfant (?), Rome. Ch. E. Jeanneret on the roof of St. Peter's, 1921, photograph, FLC [95]

286. Amédée Ozenfant (?), Rome, drum of St. Peter's, 1921, photograph, FLC [96]

287. Amédée Ozenfant (?), Rome, view of St. Peter's and the Vatican City, 1921, photograph, FLC [101]

288. Amédée Ozenfant (?), Rome, apse of St. Peter's, 1921, photograph, FLC [102]

289. Amédée Ozenfant (?), Rome, the roof of St. Peter's, Le Corbusier's silhouette (with pipe) is visible in the background, 1921, photograph, FLC [108]

290. Amédée Ozenfant (?), Rome, Sant'Ivo della Sapienza (by Borromini) 1921, photograph, FLC [104]

14. PISA

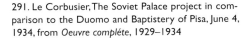

THE HEROIC URBAN LANDSCAPE

Pisa had been Jeanneret's first stop in Tuscany in the fall of 1907 (see cat. no. 1). At that time, he saw the city through Ruskin's eyes, at least in terms of architecture, with a marked interest in decorative detail.[106] When Jeanneret returned to Pisa in the fall of 1911, on his way back from the Voyage d'Orient, his focus was no longer ornamentation and rich chromatic surface decoration. The small format of his sketchbooks and the increasing importance of photography as a medium had encouraged a strategy of graphic abbreviation. During the Voyage d'Orient, while in Istanbul, Athens, Pompeii, and Rome, Jeanneret had perfected this new graphic style, capable of rendering complex spatial situations in terms of rough sketches that give the play of volumes in space.

Given the extraordinary urban configura-

291. Le Corbusier, The Soviet Palace project in comparison to the Duomo and Baptistery of Pisa, June 4, 1934, from *Oeuvre compléte*, 1929–1934

292. Title page of Le Corbusier's article "Classement et choix (Examen)", in *L'Esprit nouveau*, no. 21, March 1924

293. Pisa. Panorama of the city, 1900 (?), postcard, FLC

tion of cathedral, baptistery, campanile, and camposanto—a classic subject for *vedutisti* since the seventeenth century—the Pisa studies (figs. 295, 296), along with those from the Acropolis in Athens, have become emblematic of Le Corbusier's "heroic" urban landscape study. One cannot tell exactly which of these studies were done in situ and which were done looking at photographs or illustrated postcards (fig. 293). A similar ambiguity is raised at a later date by the famous sketch from *Oeuvre compléte* in which the skyline of Pisa was compared to the project of the Soviet Palace in Moscow (1931), thus incorporating the most boldly constructivist among Le Corbusier's projects into the tradition of Western architecture (fig. 291).[107]

With Pisa, so it appears, photography and drawing enter a dialogue that remained crucial in Le Corbusier's career as an architectural propagandist.[108]

S.v.M.

NEUCHÂTEL: HOTEL DE LA POSTE

294. Charles-Edouard Jeanneret, Pisa, the Duomo and Baptistery, 1911, retouched photograph, FLC

295. Charles-Edouard Jeanneret, Pisa, sketch of the Leaning Tower with the Duomo, 1911, pencil on paper, FLC

296. Charles-Edouard Jeanneret, Pisa, sketch of the Baptistery with the Duomo (left) and Camposanto (right), 1911, pencil on paper, FLC [204]

15. SWITZERLAND II

297. Charles-Edouard Jeanneret, Neuchâtel, the lake and the Alps, postcard sent to Auguste Perret, March 1914, FLC

298. Neuchâtel, Town Hall, postcard owned by Le Corbusier, c. 1910, FLC

299. Charles-Edouard Jeanneret, Competition design for the Banque Cantonale de Neuchâtel, Neuchâtel, view from the Avenue du Premier Mars, 1914, print on paper, Institut für Geschichte und Theorie der Architektur (gta) – ETH Zürich

Jeanneret's early career as an architect was closely entwined with issues of cultural identity, with respect to both the regional and the national context. No doubt the most interesting reference here is Alxandre Cingria-Vaneyre's book *Entretiens de la villa du Rouet* (1908), a treatise on architecture, art, and taste, written in the form of an erudite conversation among expatriate Swiss art lovers in a Florentine villa.[109] These conversations included commentary on a wide range of positions held by conservative Swiss intellectuals of the time on aesthetic theories and issues such as race, country, and language as premises of cultural identity. Somewhat paradoxically, Jeanneret had read this lengthy guide to a new visual hygiene, subservient to the cultural needs of French Switzerland while working for Peter Behrens in Neubabelsberg, in 1910. Cingria-Vaneyre's vision of an architecture that would express the Latin roots of French Switzerland became a major inspiration for Jeanneret's houses designed after 1911, such as the Villa Jeanneret-Perret in La Chaux-de-Fonds and the Villa Favre-Jacot in Le Locle (see pp. 70–77 and cat. no. 19, 23).

Around 1914 the Schweizerische Landesausstellung (National Fair) in Berne, but especially the outbreak of World War I, rekindled a certain patriotic sentimentality on Jeanneret's part with respect to Swiss architectural heritage as a whole, including German-speaking Switzerland. An essay entitled "La Maison Suisse," written in the form of a conversation among three *aficionados* of architecture, recalls Cingria-Vaneyre, as does its neoclassical bias (the gables of traditional Jura and Grisons houses are interpreted as reflections of the antique temple).[110] In more general terms, however, Jeanneret's praise of variety and multiculturalism as intrinsically Swiss values reflected the mainstream mythology of the "Village Suisse" shown at the 1896 Geneva Exposition Nationale (and at the 1900

Exposition Universelle in Paris).[111]

As to his own designs, such as the competition project for the Banque Cantonale in Neuchâtel (1914; unbuilt; fig. 299), they leaned toward a neoclassicism heavily influenced by Behrens and Tessenow.[112] Jeanneret appears to have been increasingly aware of the ambiguities involved in his stylistic preferences, especially as he wanted his Behrensian idiom to be understood as being expressive of Latin culture, characteristic of the French (as opposed to German) part of Switzerland. With the Villa Schwob, he overcame the dilemma by returning to the rationalism of Auguste Perret.

Perhaps the most interesting sources for Jeanneret's ambiguous feelings for his country are his many letters and postcards sent to Auguste Perret after 1914, with lyrical descriptions of certain landscapes and towns in Western Switzerland. A special favorite was

Solothurn and its seventeenth-century cathedral; fig. 300).[113]

300. Charles-Edouard Jeanneret, View of the Cathedral at Solothurn, Switzerland, 1915, pencil and watercolor on paper, FLC [208]

301. Charles-Edouard Jeanneret, Competition design for the Pont Butin, Geneva, Feb. 1915, charcoal on paper, FLC [223]

302. Bern, Halenbrücke, c. 1910, postcard, FLC

GENEVA: PONT BUTIN

In 1915 Jeanneret wrote to Perret: "I have posed an admirable problem: the competition for a gigantic bridge, 800m long over a deep gorge and in a landscape entirely worthy of the subject: stone was imposed, so the thing became quite naturally Roman."[114] In fact, the "Roman" typology of a massively arched bridge was rather elegantly combined with a more "rationalist" approach, as might be expected from an expert in reinforced concrete construction (figs. 301, 302). Although the structural solution belonged to Max Du Bois, Jeanneret/Le Corbusier was particularly proud of this design; it was even included in the first volume of the *Oeuvre complète* together with the Dom-ino studies of the previous year.[115]

BIENNE, MORAT: PHOTOGRAPHS

Sketches done around 1915–16 in the Val de Ruz (near La Chaux-de-Fonds), in the area of Biel/Bienne, in Avenches, or in Murten/Morat relate to a variety of interests Jeanneret cultivated in part according to the architectural commissions or proposals that happened to be on the drawing board, and relating also to his projected book on urbanism ("La Construction des villes"): a sixteenth-century church in the Val de Ruz; an eighteenth-century country estate at Concise, near Biel; and a Roman theater in Avenches (as extant as well as in a reconstructed form). Among the more intriguing sketches is the interior of an inn at Murten, the Croix Blanche, with a split-level arrangement and an "almost" *fenêtre en longueur*.[116] Photographs taken often relate to Jeanneret's taste for eighteenth-century or neoclassical *hôtels particuliers*; and country estates, such as the Hôtel de la Doûane near Murten/Morat (a neo-classical customs house on the border between two cantons; fig. 303). Several pictures from this series are mounted in a way that suggests a cinematographic approach (figs. 304, 305; see pp. 36–38).

S.v.M.

303. Charles-Edouard Jeanneret, At "La Croix Blanche", an Inn at Murten/Morat, (sheet from the "Landeron 1914" sketchbook, A1), 1914, pencil on paper, FLC

304. Charles-Edouard Jeanneret, Customs-house at Faoug, Lake Murten, Switzerland, 1916, photograph, FLC [92]

305. Charles-Edouard Jeanneret, Murten/Morat, Town Hall and walls, 1916, photograph, FLC [91]

16. PARISIAN URBANISM

L.C.B.N.15

When Jeanneret began studying Pierre Patte's plans for transforming the Île de la Cité, while doing research in the Cabinet des Estampes of the Bibliothèque Nationale in 1915, he set out to highlight the controversy that this project—among other eighteenth-century designs—had represented in the city's history (fig. 307).[117] The marginal notations that Jeanneret made while redrafting Jouvin de Rochefort's map of Paris (1676), emphasize the conceptual break that he saw between the medieval city and the interventions made during the reign of Louis XIV. The king, according to Jeanneret, was the first to show "that there is nothing to do in the good Paris of Henry IV and that one would have to go outside in order to do real work."[118]

On the one hand, consulting works such as Adolphe Berty's *Topographie historique du Vieux-Paris* (1866–68) demonstrated Jeanneret's desire to understand, via rigorous documentation, "le pourquoi du Paris tortueux (à travers l'histoire)" (the reasons for the contortions of Paris [through history]). On the other hand, the detailed study of documents such as the "plan general des différents projets d'embellissements" (general plan for various projects for improvements), which had been presented in 1769 by Pierre-Louis Moreau, an architect of the Académie royale d'architecture, allowed Jeanneret to appreciate the transformations of the urban core envisaged on the riverbanks. In fact, he emphatically underlined his notation: "l'ablation de 2 pavillons de l'institut (!!!) pour laisser le quai plus large" (the demolition of 2 pavilions of the institute [!!!] so that the quays could be widened).[119] In this respect, the plans for the Place Louis XV embodied the potential to renew the urban landscape. In a handwritten note, Jeanneret observed that "at that time, there was the Place des Vosges, Place Vendôme, [Place] des Victoires. The result was: Place Louis XV (Concorde)."[120]

Le Corbusier's *Plan Voisin* (1925; fig. 306) expressed that desire to take action—which he had long espoused—but which he now hoped

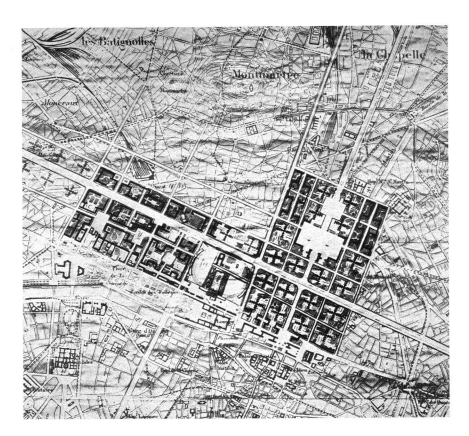

to put to modern purposes. The *Plan Voisin* is based on the designs he had originally presented at the Salon d'Automne of 1922 (*Ville contemporaine pour trois millions d'habitants*).[121] By now he had assimilated the lessons of history. The past only seemed to be obliterated; in reality, from his point of view, history constituted the intellectual baggage capable of generating new projects. Even in 1946, when Le Corbusier confronted the problems of postwar reconstruction in a cultural climate that had profoundly changed since the 1920s, he restated ideas first articulated in his much earlier studies of 1915, when he researched seventeenth- and eighteenth-century Paris. He wrote: "I admire here the aims of the architects of Louis XV, who drafted plans for improving Paris. The iconoclasts are not an invention of today."[122]

As he had in *Urbanisme* (1925), Le Corbusier once more declared his faith in the interventions that Patte and Boffrand had planned for the Île de la Cité, singling out architectural events such as the Hôtel des Invalides and École Militaire. He stressed their character as stereometric objects, "volumes in light (in relief)."[123] In this context, the Place Louis XV was exemplary: "A king has already lived . . . today's dream of suppressing the mud of the suburbs, seeing the wheat, the prairies and the orchards spring up all around the town. . . . So then why despair, my friends, in the hour when the world is at the height of its powers?"[124]

A.B.

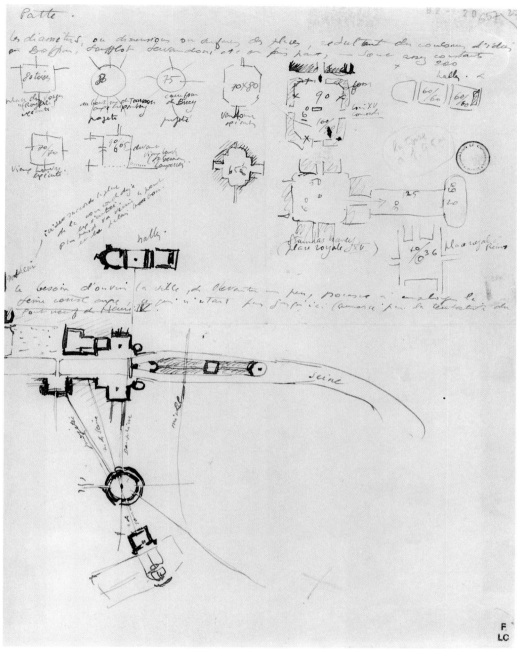

XVIIIᵉ siècle : aménagement de la Seine ; création du carrefour de Bucy, des Halles. Des droites au milieu de l'insupportable maquis.

Un véritable besoin de libération pousse à couper, à ouvrir : percées, perspectives, — en même temps qu'en esthétique architecturale croulent les encorbellements et les pignons pointus et qu'on veut s'attaquer même aux cathédrales (tant on est blessé par ce qui est hirsute et d'apparence confuse). Tout vient d'un coup, découle d'un système de l'esprit qui dans tous les domaines atteint aux expressions les plus hautes (Pascal, Voltaire, Rousseau, Blondel, Mansart, Gabriel, Soufflot). En vérité, sous ces rois absolus, s'exprimaient les puissances libres de la pensée et la Révolution était imminente : chirurgie.

Le passé, inépuisablement, nous donne des leçons de force. Prévoir et gouverner : médecine et chirurgie. En tout état de cause, de la clarté d'esprit et de la fermeté.

Paris aujourd'hui, n'a — en gros — plus de chevaux, mais 250.000 véhicules à vitesse décuple se précipitent dans ses rues. Merci à Colbert et merci aux Roys d'avoir, en leur temps calme, préparé ces avenues qui sont notre unique système artériel.

306. Le Corbusier, Paris, Plan Voisin, 1925

307. Charles-Edouard Jeanneret, Squares of Paris, studies after engravings by Pierre Patte in the Bibliothèque Nationale, Paris, 1915, ink on paper, FLC [266]

308. Le Corbusier, Proposed urban design for the area around the Pont Neuf in Paris (after Patte), from *Urbanisme*, Paris, 1925, p. 254

Part 2 · Architecture

17. EARLY HOUSES

VILLA FALLET (1906–7)

Jeanneret's first building designs make evident that his training was as a decorator and ornamentalist and that he was a devoted follower of John Ruskin and Owen Jones (figs. 312, 313). Unexpected, however, is the competence with which this nineteen-year-old, without schooling in the rudiments of architecture, could produce sophisticated and well-integrated designs. He actually disliked architecture at first (he wanted to be a painter) but reluctantly had entered the profession at the insistence of his teacher, Charles L'Eplattenier.[1] Fortunately, he possessed a good sense of proportions and scale, and this helped subsitute for his lack of professional training.

His earliest designs were refined by using the medium best known to sculptors—clay models (fig. 317). These helped him study massing, proportions, and detail. The architectural style of these buildings was the synthesis of various sources including certain medieval prototypes that derived from the Alsace region of France.

The Villa Fallet of 1906 (fig. 311) was his earliest executed work and also the most richly ornamented – moreso even than the original blueprints indicate.[2] Its decoration was entirely derived from local Jura motifs, the abstracted or conventionalized *sapin* (Swiss pine or fir tree) predominating (figs. 315, 316).

309. Charles-Edouard Jeanneret, Watchcase, gold, silver, copper and steel with diamonds, 1906, FLC [25]

310. Charles-Edouard Jeanneret, Villa Fallet, La Chaux-de-Fonds, study for the southeast facade, 1906–07, pencil and watercolor on tinted paper, private collection

311. Charles-Edouard Jeanneret (?), Villa Fallet, photograph, 1907, BV [63]

Figure 310 illustrates an early study for the principal facade, the dominant colors being pottery red and orange with some blue, black, and white. The pattern spreads outward from the bedroom window and conforms to the shape of the hipped gable roof. The executed decoration, however, is that of a regimented repeat pattern of identical stylized trees. The lower window mullions take the shape of leafless trees, the source of this idea being the Art Nouveau creations of architects from Nancy, France, and in the best tradition of the Arts and Crafts movement. Jeanneret and friends applied the sgraffito decoration to the exterior walls (fig. 314).

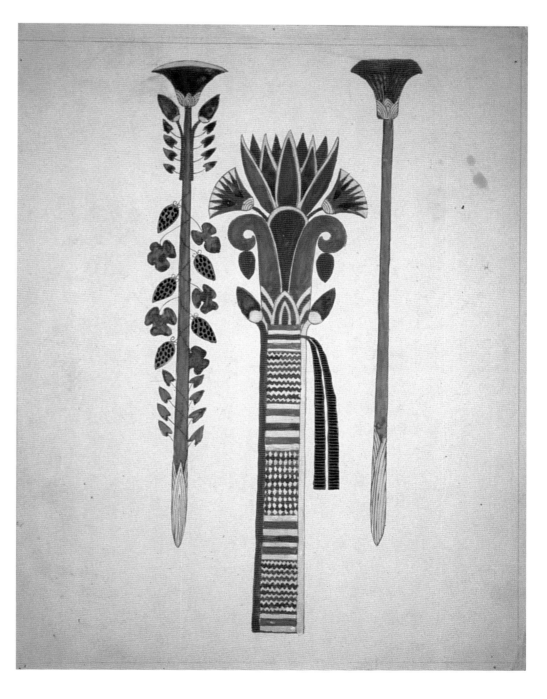

312. Owen Jones, *The Grammar of Ornament. Illustrated by examples from various styles of ornament*, London, 1856, pl. IV

313. Charles-Edouard Jeanneret, Lotus leaf and papyrus, after Owen Jones, *The Grammar of Ornament*, gouache on paper, FLC [137]

Although ornament covers every imaginable surface at the Villa Fallet—not just walls, but also exposed wood beams, iron railings on terraces, wrought iron on doors, window mullions, and even roof tiles—the total effect is one of unity, harmony, coherence, and pleasant proportions. And even though symmetry and balance rule throughout the design, thereby implying that Jeanneret is a classicist, he never used a single classical form.

VILLAS STOTZER AND JAQUEMET (1907–08)

While overwintering in Vienna during his European travels of 1907–8 Jeanneret designed two more houses for La Chaux-de-Fonds, the villas Stotzer and Jaquemet. Being away from home, however, he lacked the helpful advice of L'Eplattenier or wise council of René Chapallaz, who would later supervise construction, the result being that Jeanneret's fascination with ornament and sculptural decoration got out of hand. When he shipped his plans, elevations, and clay models home, they were rejected by clients and critics alike. Thereupon he reworked the designs, making the walls less plastic and gaining greater simplicity throughout—while endeavoring to bring construction costs in line. These houses proved to be his final executed works prior to 1912, by which time he had rejected color in favor of white and preferred rough-troweled exterior surfaces rather than more plastic, sculptural forms.

H.A.B.

314. Octave Matthey, Ch._E. Jeanneret and Louis Houriet working on the sgraffito decoration on the Villa Fallet, photograph, 1907, BV

315. Charles-Edouard Jeanneret, Study of pine trees, 1905–06 (?), black gouache and pencil on paper, FLC

[141]

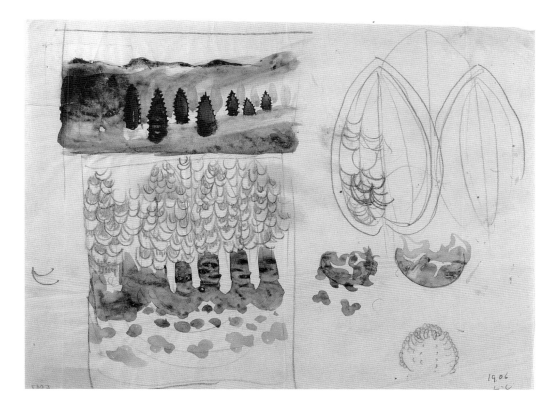

316. Charles-Edouard Jeanneret, Landscape study with pine trees and various close-up studies and ornamental derivations thereof, 1906, pencil and watercolor on paper, FLC [140]

317. Charles-Edouard Jeanneret, Three clay (?) models, probably for Villa Fallet, 1905–06, photograph, FLC

18. INHABITING THE VERNACULAR

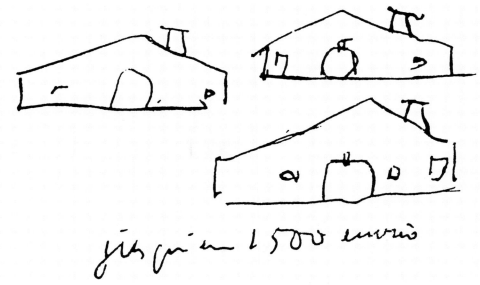

318. Farmhouse, Mont Cornu, near La Chaux-de-
Fonds, Jeanneret lived in this house Jan.–Apr. 1910,
photograph

319. Le Corbusier, Sketches of Jura farmhouses, Jan. 13,
1958, FLC

MONT CORNU (1910)

Jeanneret was profoundly influenced by a unique feature of the typical Jura farmhouse that had nothing to do with its exterior form or architectural details. Rather, it was a singular aspect of the interior space—the monumental central kitchen. Called *la chambre du tué*, this was essentially a room-sized pyramidal chimney supported on four head-height masonry walls and cut off diagonally above the roof.[3] One literally lived within the chimney! This interior space had a single door, no windows, and a fire against one wall. Meat and herbs (and the inhabitants) were gently smoked and dried in this dark environment, but they were nevertheless protected against the cold. The *tué* thus symbolized a place of family gatherings, of unity and solidarity in front of a comforting and light-providing fire.

Jeanneret, when twenty-two spent January through March 1910 living alone in such a farmhouse; it was located on the slopes of Mont Cornu around 2 miles (3 km) from town (fig. 318). The impact of this architectural experience remained with him for life. The form and symbolism of the *chambre du tué* found expression in his 1929 church project for Tremblay and again in his 1961 Firminy church (still unfinished at his death)—in each design the altar assumes the place of the *tué* fireplace. The *chambre du tué* also provided inspiration for the Assembly Chamber at Chandigarh in the 1950s (its footprint modified from square to round at the request of Nehru), and for the General Assembly chamber at the United Nations in New York.

LE COUVENT (1911–12)

Jeanneret again resided in a farmhouse in 1911–12, this time renting space in an old building known as Le Couvent (figs. 320–21) where he created a small apartment for himself and lived for almost a year. Numerous features of this design found expression in his 1914 project for Felix Klipstein.

H.A.B.

320. Jeanneret in front of "Le Couvent," La Chaux-de-Fonds, where he lived in Summer 1912, photograph, BV

321. Albert and Charles-Edouard Jeanneret and their parents in Jeanneret's apartment in "Le Couvent," 1912, photograph, BV

19. VILLA JEANNERET-PERRET

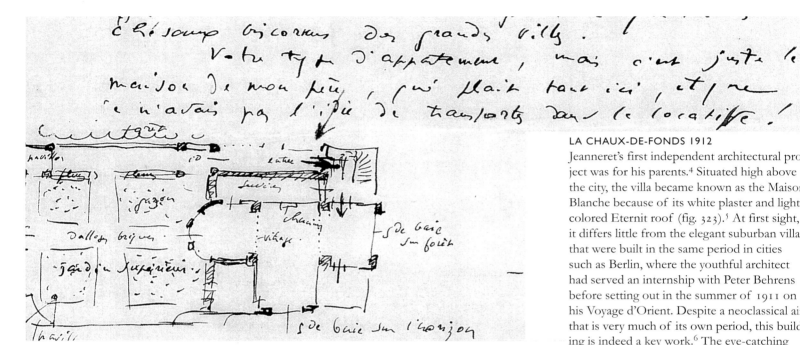

LA CHAUX-DE-FONDS 1912

Jeanneret's first independent architectural project was for his parents.[4] Situated high above the city, the villa became known as the Maison Blanche because of its white plaster and light-colored Eternit roof (fig. 323).[5] At first sight, it differs little from the elegant suburban villas that were built in the same period in cities such as Berlin, where the youthful architect had served an internship with Peter Behrens before setting out in the summer of 1911 on his Voyage d'Orient. Despite a neoclassical air that is very much of its own period, this building is indeed a key work.[6] The eye-catching strip windows on the bedroom floor have often been interpreted as a sign of things to come (fig. 323), and the villa marks Jeanneret's break with the regionalist Art Nouveau *style sapin* ("pine" style) to which his first three buildings belong (figs. 325, 326). It signals his commitment to rationalistic tradition in architecture (figs. 327, 329). Jeanneret described the villa as being built "at a moment when, having returned from a long journey through GREECE, ASIA, TURKEY and ITALY, I was still full of the great clear, formal architecture of the Mediterranean lands, the only architectures that I recognize."[7] The house also incorporates numerous experimental attempts to weld the acquired experience into his own work.

The T-shaped plan seems to have derived from the Stotzer and Jaquemet houses, built in

322. Charles-Edouard Jeanneret, Letter to Auguste Perret, June 20, 1916, detail with sketch of Maison Jeanneret-Perret, ink on paper, Institut français d'architecture, Paris, Fonds Perret

323. Charles-Edouard Jeanneret, Villa Jeanneret-Perret, view from west, 1911–12, photograph, BV [85]

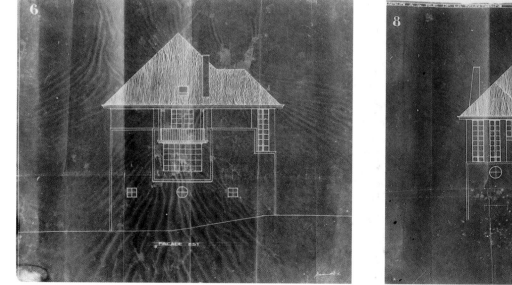

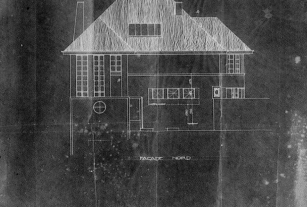

1908 in collaboration with René Chappalaz, but inside the house the plan evolved into a light and open sequence of rooms that corresponded to, or even anticipated, certain ideas of Auguste Perret's. "Your apartment type is just exactly my father's house, which is so well liked here," Jeanneret told Perret in a letter in

1916.[8] On the basement floor were his father's workrooms, while upstairs Charles-Edouard had a generous studio with a north light.

One enters the house at the end of a *promenade*, packed with spatial sensations and leading via the inclined garden to the *chambre d'été* (terrace; fig. 324) and through a pergola to the

324. Villa Jeanneret-Perret, pergola, in the background Charles-Edouard Jeanneret, his parents, and his brother Albert, c. 1915–16, photograph, BV

325. Charles-Edouard Jeanneret, Villa Jeanneret-Perret, east elevation, 1912, original blueprint, FLC [216]

326. Charles-Edouard Jeanneret, Villa Jeanneret-Perret, north elevation, 1912, original blueprint, FLC [217]

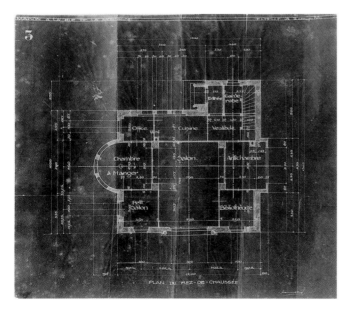

entrance (see p. 66). Another approach is via a cul-de-sac that runs along the slope. This sophisticated itinerary continues inside the house: from the narrow entry, one passes through the vestibule (fig. 329) to an anteroom with a *grande baie sur forêt* (large window with forest view) that frames the short-range view over the slope that falls away steeply to one side. The view in the opposite direction extends through folding glass doors and across the living room to the dining room and the garden beyond. The sequence continues with the large main room, which was also intended for concerts, and—after a change of direction—culminates in the distant view across the broad valley to the horizon. On the uphill side, a faïence fireplace designed and painted by Jeanneret faces the picture window, which consists of an outer skin with wooden frames and an inner skin with slender metal profiles. A small drawing room and library complete this multifunctional spatial design, and produce the compact, cuboidal form of the exterior (itself an echo of local tradition: "With us … all buildings always present a perfect rectangle and have light on four elevations"; fig. 328).[9]

The walls of the living room were hung with floral wallpaper and the floor covered by greenish linoleum (fig. 327).[10] The furnishing, which Jeanneret gradually supplemented from 1912 on, reflects his neoclassical leanings and personal dialogue with traditional architecture. He designed the couch as well as the six-legged grand piano case for his mother, a piano teacher. This was intended to blend well with the other furniture, such as the simple, probably early-nineteenth-century *bergères à paille* (see cat. 38): examples of the "type" furniture that Le Corbusier used throughout his life. By contrast, the writing desk is a unique piece, a sophisticated *étude* on Jeanneret's part, in which he negotiates between two concepts. In it, motifs of classical architecture and furniture engage with the simple, cuboidal forms of modernism (see cat. 30).

A.R.

327. Villa Jeanneret-Perret, living room looking towards dining room, c. 1915–16, photograph, FLC

328. Charles-Edouard Jeanneret, Villa Jeanneret-Perret, ground floor, 1912, original blueprint, FLC [219]

329. Villa Jeanneret-Perret, cloakroom with circular window and staircase to the upper floor, photograph, FLC

20. PROJECT FOR FELIX KLIPSTEIN

4019. - LES CHAUZES, près Sarliac (Dordogne)

NOV 1914

A COUNTRY HOUSE IN GERMANY, 1914
Felix Klipstein was the brother of Jeanneret's traveling companion during the five-month Voyage d'Orient in 1911; three years later he asked Jeanneret to design a country house for him near Laubach, Germany. The design process is most interesting and recalls that of designing the Maison Blanche two years earlier—first he reviewed what he particularly admired in both historic and contemporary architecture and then synthesized the chosen components into something unique and new. As part of this process Jeanneret sent Klipstein numerous sketches of buildings that he, Jeanneret, admired, thus hoping to learn what Klipstein most responded to.

Ultimately, however, Jeanneret chose his design ideas from those that had persisted since the Roman Empire in the Dordogne region of southwest France, a region from which he believed his own ancestors originated. Characteristic of this French farmhouse type was a two-story open loggia, several bays in width, that was flanked by projecting towerlike blocks at either side (figs. 331, 333). At Klipstein's house this loggia would overlook an orchard that sloped down to a gurgling brook. To one side was a private courtyard with rose garden and pool; a pergola opened toward the view. A separate entrance court, approached between two tall poplar trees, would lead down from the street above. The forms chosen were clean and sharp edged, totally lacking any embellishment, with horizontal and vertical lines emphasized throughout.

The house was entered by way of a well-lit, beamed-ceiling hallway that flanked a living room with a large fireplace (figs. 330, 332); all rooms were furnished with antiques. The ambience was that of an old house.

H.A.B.

330. Charles-Edouard Jeanneret, study for the hallway of Felix Klipstein's house (front entrance at the left, living room behind the wall at the right), 1914, ink on tracing paper, private collection

331. Farmhouse near Sarliac in the Dordogne, France, postcard from Jeanneret to his parents

332. Charles-Edouard Jeanneret, study of the living room of Felix Klipstein's house, ink on tracing paper, private collection

333. Charles-Edouard Jeanneret, perspective view of the project for Felix Klipstein's house (Carnet bleu p. 15) 1914 (?), pencil on paper, FLC

21. MAISON DOM-INO

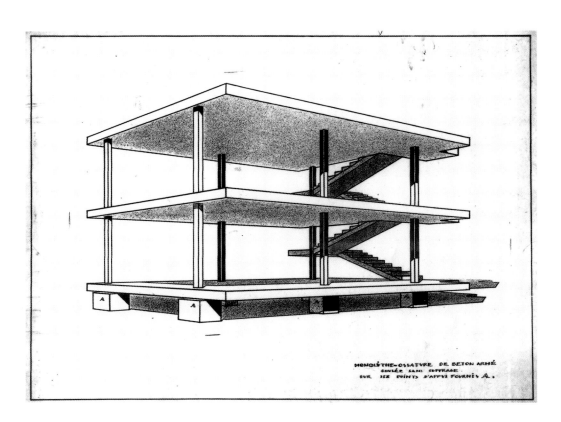

334. Charles-Edouard Jeanneret, perspective of a Dom-ino module, 1915, india ink, black and colored pencil on printing paper, FLC [224]

REINFORCED CONCRETE AND INDUSTRY

Dom-ino was conceived in 1914–16 as a patentable housing system and business enterprise to reconstruct areas destroyed during World War I.[11] In terms of the building process, Jeanneret proposed a sharp division of frame and infill: first, specialized traveling crews would erect modular frames of posts and slabs (smooth on both sides); then, on the blank rigid slabs, local manpower would install nonbearing walls, in layouts variable from house to house and from floor to floor (figs. 335, 336). In terms of style, Jeanneret proposed two kinds, plain and fancy. The fancy style, characterized by a flared planter acting as parapet and cornice, was used by him at the Villa Schwob soon afterward. The units were primarily envisioned as row houses combined in larger groups, though they could also be isolated.

Dom-ino represents the first conscious effort by Jeanneret to tackle, in a design, the issues of reinforced concrete and of industry, and to link them together. Reinforced concrete was conceptualized as a rigid post-and-slab frame with light infill walls, following the example of Perret and many others. Technically, then, the idea was not new. Architecturally, Jeanneret contributed a conceptual shift by focusing on the slabs alone. Indeed, the excitement of a revelation is palpable in the famous theoretical image of Dom-ino (fig. 334), an emotional celebration of "the magnificent play of floating slabs," to paraphrase his famous statement,[12] with the posts minimized as if Jeanneret wished them to disappear (and indeed, the two posts that should hold the stair landings have been omitted). If the theoretical image celebrated the slabs, however, it did not yet articulate the architectural implication of this new vision. Neither did the actual designs (figs. 336, 338, 339): plans and fenestration varied from floor to floor in a rationalist acknowledgment that the walls are nonbearing, but Jeanneret had few ideas for using the resulting freedom. A broader understanding of the slab's architectural implications—central among them the multiplication of the ground plane—would only emerge later, with *Five Points* in 1927 and *Obus Plan* for Algiers in 1930.

Industry was conceptualized, in Dom-ino, in terms of modular repetition, following two related German discourses that Jeanneret knew well. On the one hand, a discourse on urban planning advocated large city blocks made up of uniform components—a situation that was seen at once as determined by

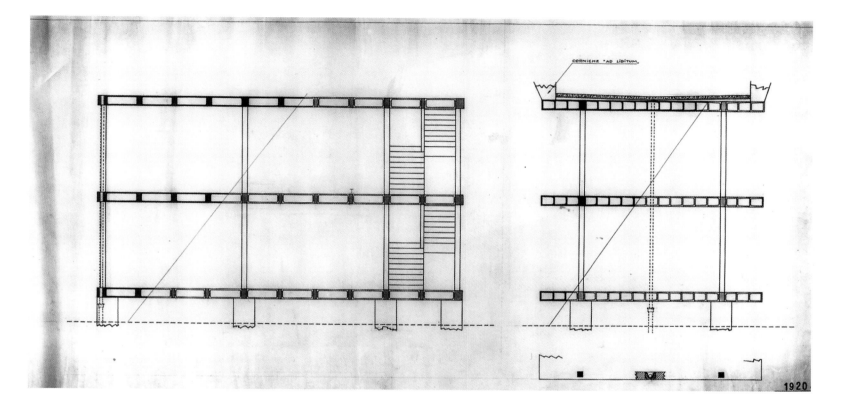

economic realities, representative of modern society, and aesthetically desirable.[13] On the other hand, a discourse about mass-produced consumer products saw their identical repetition as a way to promote and control a collective cultural identity.[14] From these discourses derives the modularity of Dom-ino, and Jeanneret proudly announced to Perret that "my streets would rise, all by themselves, with a palatial rhythm and a Pompeian tranquility."[15] Jeanneret's attempt to set up a production process, with patents and a company, was a corollary also derived from those German discourses: business control over the production process would translate into aesthetic control over uniformity and rhythm.

More than ten years later Le Corbusier placed the iconic image of Dom-ino slabs at the beginning of his *Oeuvre complète* with these words: "Intuition acts in sudden flashes. Here,

335. Charles-Edouard Jeanneret, cross-sections of a Dom-ino module, 1915, india ink and black pencil on thick paper, FLC

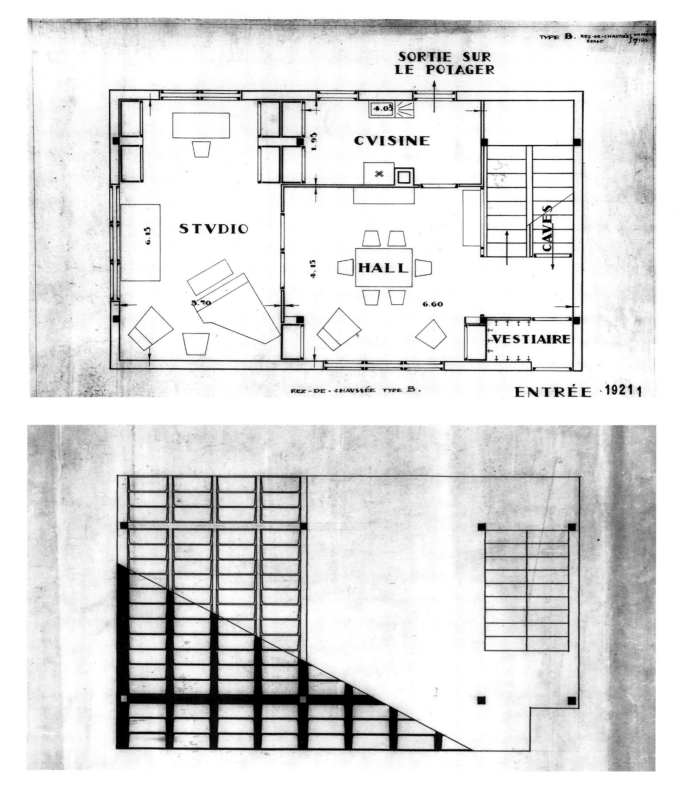

TYPE B . REZ-DE-CHAUSSÉE} un mère
ÉTAGE

SORTIE SUR
LE POTAGER

4.05

CVISINE

STVDIO

6.15

1.95

4.15

HALL

CAVES

3.70

6.60

VESTIAIRE

REZ-DE-CHAVSSÉE TYPE B .

ENTRÉE · 19211

336. Charles-Edouard Jeanneret, ground floor with
proposed layout for "Type B", 1915, gelatine print, FLC
[226]

337. Charles-Edouard Jeanneret, floor plan of a Dom-
ino module, 1915, india and colored ink and black pencil on transparent paper, FLC [225]

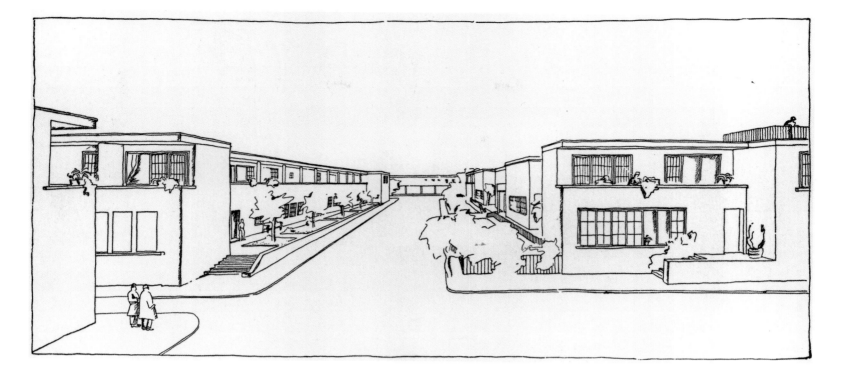

in 1914, we have the pure and total conception of a whole way of building, anticipating all the problems that will arise following the war."[16] Even discounting a "pure and total" birth of modern architecture from a flash of intuition, Dom-ino did mark a crucial step for Jeanneret/Le Corbusier—not as a solution, but as a formulation of the problem. First, he thought from the start in terms of concrete and industry, the technical and social aspects of modernity, together. Second, he formulated the issue of reinforced concrete in terms of rigid slabs, not frame. Third, he thought of all these aspects in terms of their *architectural* implications. Indeed, three days before submitting the patent application for Dom-ino, Jeanneret paid a compliment to Auguste Perret for his building in Rue Franklin, and in so doing betrayed his own ambition: "The new form could have been mere engineering. You did architecture."[17]

F.P.

338. Charles-Edouard Jeanneret, complex of several Dom-ino units, 1915, redrawn in 1921, from *L'Esprit nouveau*, no. 13, 1921, pp. 1528–29

339. Charles-Edouard Jeanneret, Individual Dom-ino house, 1915, from *L'Esprit nouveau*, no. 13, 1921, pp. 1534

22. "PROJET F"

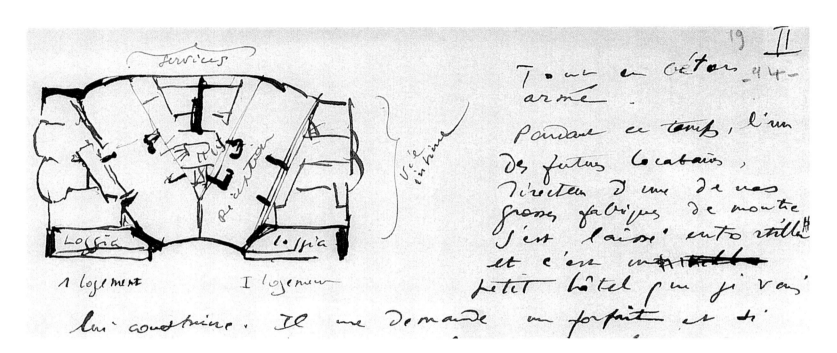

LUXURY MULTIUNIT HOUSE

The few documents that record this mysterious project consist of Jeanneret's sketch plans and perspective sketches for a luxury multiunit house that was proposed by a corporation (Société anonyme) in 1916.[18] Among the prospective tenants was Anatole Schwob, who soon changed his mind, however, and decided to build a villa. "One of the future tenants, the manager of one of our big watch factories, has taken the bait, and I shall be building him a little mansion," Jeanneret wrote to Auguste Perret on July 21 in the course of a consultation on "Projet F" (fig. 340). He continued: "The rental building has given rise to a plan that is bizarre but makes sense: a fan shape, and all the rooms absolutely and entirely regular and neat."[19]

In a brief analysis Brooks has likened this to a V-shaped plan by Germain Boffrand for the Palais de la Malgrange, Nancy (second project, 1712).[20] No other proposed building project by Jeanneret so strongly features the repertory of the architecture that he was later

to denounce as "academic." The "bizarre" ground plan is based on the principle of "backing" major spatial sequences with a hierarchy of subordinate spaces (in the terminology of the École des Beaux-Arts, this is known as *poché*). Access to the subordinate rooms is by way of lobbies or *dégagements* (another "academic" idea). For the interiors, the complete neoclassical vocabulary of surfaces and furnishings is deployed: floral wallpapers and moldings, guéridon tables and chests of drawers, sofas, and three-legged tables (fig. 341).

At the same time, Jeanneret made use of experience acquired while working on ground plans for apartments for the Perret brothers in 1908–9.[21] The apartment building that the Perrets constructed on rue Franklin in Paris in 1903–4 (fig. 343) was also based on the *poché* principle. The spatially transparent interlocking of the main spaces in that case arose from the use of a thin, concrete skeleton. In "Projet F" Jeanneret once more combined the *poché* layout with skeleton frame construction. He

used pairs of exposed supports to articulate the spatial sequences, and, as with Perret, the placing of the supports exclusively followed the logic of the plan (fig. 342). This is the complete antithesis of the Dom-ino system that Jeanneret was developing at precisely the same time (from 1914 onward); but the distinction between load-bearing and nonbearing elements was embodied in the construction and, to a degree, already expressed in aesthetic terms.

A.R.

340. Charles-Edouard Jeanneret, Letter to Auguste Perret, July 21, 1916, sketch of Projet F; "all in concrete", ink on paper, Institut français d'architecture, Paris, Fonds Perret

341. Charles-Edouard Jeanneret, "Projet F" Apartments, 1916, perspective view of living room, heliotype, FLC

342. Charles-Edouard Jeanneret, "Projet F" Apartments, 1916, plan of typical floor, July 4, 1916, ink on paper, FLC

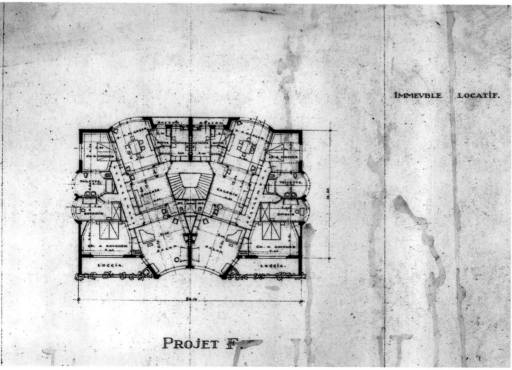

IMMEVBLE LOCATIF.

PROJET F.

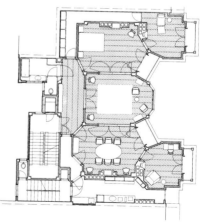

343. Gustave and Auguste Perret, apartment building
25 bis Rue Franklin, Paris, 1903–04, sixth floor, survey
plan with furnishings by Arthur Rüegg and Niklaus
Lohri (drawing), 1993

23. VILLA SCHWOB

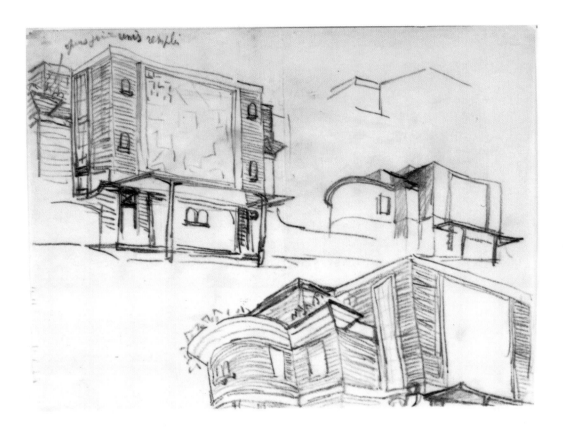

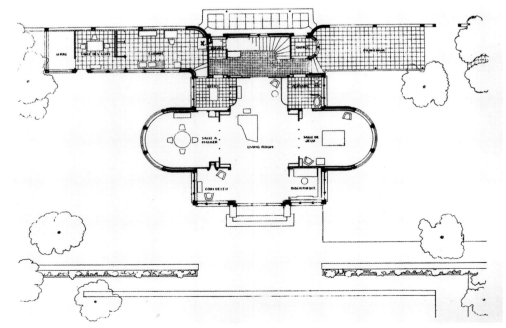

344. Charles-Edouard Jeanneret, Villa Schwob, studies of street façade, 1916, pencil on tracing paper, BV

345. Charles-Edouard Jeanneret, Villa Schwob, plan of the ground floor, from *L'Esprit nouveau*, no. 6, 1921, p. 689

MODERN INVENTION, ANCIENT TYPOLOGY

The Villa Schwob was designed in the middle of World War I, in the summer of 1916, for a wealthy watch manufacturer.[22] There had been four years of intellectual homework but no architectural commissions for Jeanneret, and the project is a major signpost in his development, the point of crystallization for an impressive amount of architectural thinking and for intense emotions.

Inside the villa, Jeanneret married a modern invention with an ancient typology (fig. 345).[23] On the one hand, he borrowed from the relatively recent "Maison Bouteille," a prototype of 1908–9 entailing a two-story central hall (fig. 99) with full studio window at one end, balcony at the other end, and lower rooms opening like alcoves along the sides—that is, a mix of English hall, Parisian artist's studio, and possibly Perret's Garage Ponthieu. On the other hand, he took from the ancient Roman House

type, in this case the house of Diomedes, which he had admired in Pompeii, and from which came a directional complex closed to the street, open to the garden and landscape, and organized around a central "hub," the atrium. Each model helped clarify the architectural implications of the other, and out of their interaction Jeanneret drew a new understanding of architectural space—as the play of discrete internal volumes—which is characteristic of his subsequent work, from the Villas La Roche–Jeanneret to the Villa Cook and beyond (figs. 348, 349).

Outside, Jeanneret turned the growing program demands of the client into a tense juxtaposition, in which the initial cube with apses (housing the big hall and its expansions; figs. 346, 347) is kept intact as an ideal master block marked by hard smooth surfaces and by sharp edges and cornice, while the growing service additions are piled up and piggybacked

346. Villa Schwob, view from the rooftop, 1917 (?), retouched photograph, FLC

347. Villa Schwob from the east, 1920, photograph, FLC

348. Charles-Edouard Jeanneret, Villa Schwob, view of the villa and garden from the south, 1916–17, india ink on tracing paper, FLC [234]

349. Charles-Edouard Jeanneret, Villa Schwob, perspective view of the kitchen forecourt, March 3, 1917, india ink on tracing paper, FLC [233]

350. Charles-Edouard Jeanneret, Villa Schwob, photograph taken during construction, 1916, FLC

351. Charles-Edouard Jeanneret, Villa Schwob, photograph taken during construction, 1916, FLC

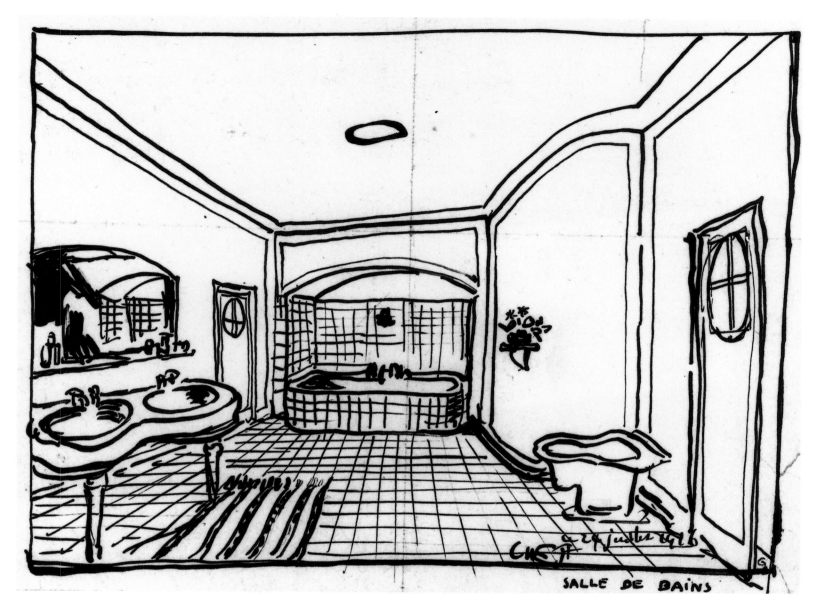

SALLE DE BAINS

toward the street, in broken profiles and layered moldings—thus contrasting the unchanging ideal with the dynamic struggle. All this is articulated through naked geometric volumes set off against each other, marking a new step in Jeanneret's architectural vocabulary (fig. 344).

Not long after the design, Jeanneret lost contact with the house, so to speak. He moved to Paris before the building was roofed; the relationship with the client soured over cost overruns and lawsuits; and his attention shifted to Purist painting and to writing. Only several years later, in the summer of 1919, did Le Corbusier see the completed house for the first time. It was a revelation to him, and his comments convey his intentions: "I want to paint serious, even learned works, i.e. paintings that are at least an extension of my Villa Schwob. . . . I am fixated on the Parthenon and Michelangelo. . . . An art without flinching. And choked passion. The aim, once more: the Parthenon, that drama."[24] Indeed, if we look back with this comment in mind, the tragic quality of Villa Schwob, its drama, and its passion, leap out: the Parthenon stands behind the master block toward the garden, with its ideal shape and impassive sharpness; and Michelangelo's architecture, with its emotional layering, also stands behind the multiple additions toward the street. Colin Rowe, the critic who called the street facade "Mannerist" (fig. 344 and even compared it with Michelangelo's apse of St. Peter's), certainly knew what he was saying (!), to paraphrase the title of his later book.[25]

F.P.

352. Charles-Edouard Jeanneret, Villa Schwob, interior perspective of the bathroom, July 24, 1916, india ink on tracing paper, FLC [230]

24. CHALLUY SLAUGHTERHOUSE

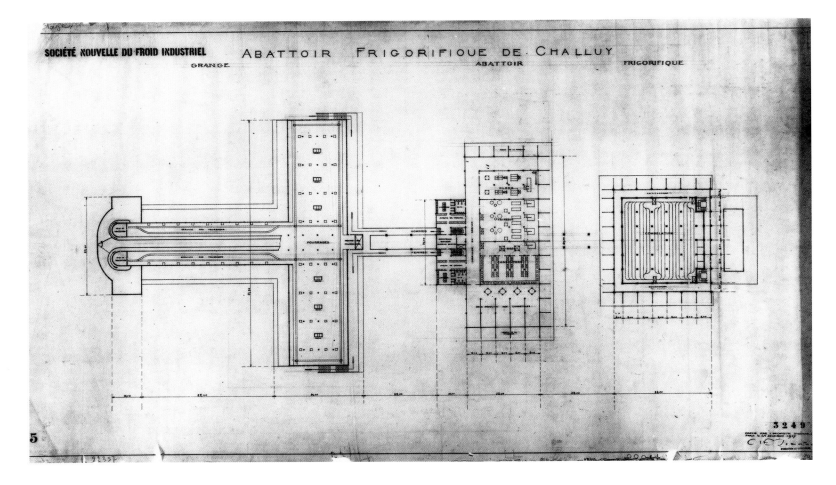

353. Charles-Edouard Jeanneret, Challuy Slaughter-house, plan of the assembly building, slaughterhouse and refrigerator building ("Grange-Abattoir-Frigorifique") Dec. 25, 1917, india ink on tracing paper, FLC

354. Charles-Edouard Jeanneret, Challuy Slaughterhouse, bird's eye view, Dec. 25, 1917, india ink on tracing paper, FLC [326]

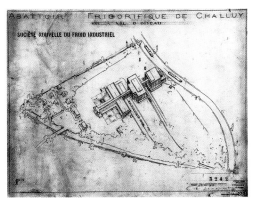

"MY FIRST IMPORTANT WORK"

In the winter of 1917–18 during the war, Le Corbusier participated in a competition for the design of a slaughterhouse at Challuy and another at Garchizy, near Nevers in the Loire valley.[26] Very pleased, he wrote in his journal of "the really good arrangement of [Challuy], its boldness, its grandeur, its harmonious modernism. . . . it is alive. . . . I feel that I have done real architecture. It is certainly my first important work. . . . it [is] a banner."[27] He was still proud enough in 1930 to include both designs in the opening pages of his *Oeuvre complète* (the first edition).

The design of Challuy involved close team-work with specialized engineers. It was based on the American model, entailing distinct

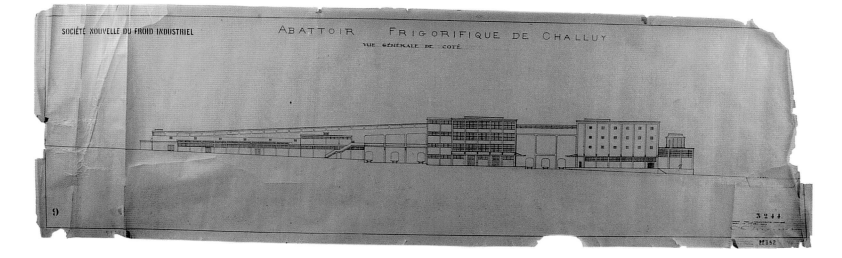

multistory factory blocks and a ramp to the top floor, so that the animals would walk up on their own power, and gravity could then be used to move the carcasses down, through various processing stages (fig. 353).[28]

Like his mentor Behrens at the AEG, Le Corbusier used these technical requirements to achieve a monumental composition. The ramp, which in America was often a wooden construction winding its way among buildings, became the formal spine of a symmetrical composition clearly inspired by ancient Egypt and Mesopotamia. By echoing the light slope of the land, the ramp even acquired a truly topographical scale, turning the buildings into so many platforms or giant altar blocks (fig. 355). The widths and intervals of the three blocks were chosen so that the blocks would hide behind each other when seen on axis from the entry gate and from across a nearby canal, and the elevations of the two tall blocks were given proportions based on the golden section (fig. 356). The alignments impress the unity of the whole on the viewer, while calling attention to the "play" of volumes emerging one behind the other as one moves sideways. Alignments, axiality, and proportions all affirm a higher intention beyond the mere utilitarian repetition of modular bays.

Le Corbusier was right in seeing Challuy as an important step forward. To begin with, Challuy was his first (and last) close collaboration with engineers. Its success, and the role model of Behrens, gave Le Corbusier the moral authority of an insider in redefining the relative roles of architect and engineer, art and industry. Second, having now fully absorbed the notion of *Sachlichkeit* (factualness), he used the facts of modern industrial life, plain fac-

tory blocks, as raw materials to set up an architectural "play of volumes." He would do the same, a few years later, with skyscrapers. Third, Challuy introduced him to the ramp as an architectural element and, more important, to its implications for the meaning of ground and upper floors. By echoing the sloping site and turning the top floor into the true point of entry, the ramp of Challuy introduced a sense of the "ambiguity of the ground," which would later be central to the concept of the *Five Points* and to the design of the Villa Savoye, the Millowner's Association building, and the Carpenter Center. Finally, the skewered layout of Challuy would be the obvious point of departure for that of the Palace of the Soviets.

While pleased with the design, Le Corbusier was not oblivious to the tragic overtones of Taylorized slaughter, especially in 1917. He wrote in his journal of being "sad and reticent" and of "Taylorism, the horrible and inevitable life of tomorrow;"[29] and his buildings are like giant sacrificial altar blocks in the landscape. The middle of World War I was not a time for regrets, however, and, like Behrens, Le Corbusier had reluctantly come to accept industry as an inevitable development to be marshaled to a purpose, not rejected out of hand.

F.P.

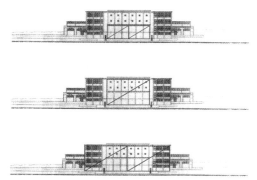

355. Charles-Edouard Jeanneret, Challuy Slaughterhouse, side elevation, Dec. 25, 1917, india ink and black pencil on tracing paper, FLC

356. Charles-Edouard Jeanneret, Challuy Slaughterhouse, elevations with proportional diagrams, and axonometric view showing alignments

25. "EVERITE"

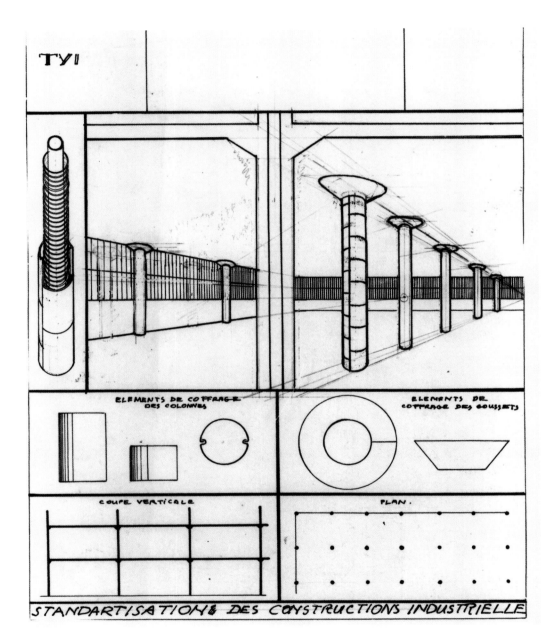

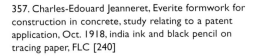

357. Charles-Edouard Jeanneret, Everite formwork for construction in concrete, study relating to a patent application, Oct. 1918, india ink and black pencil on tracing paper, FLC [240]

JEANNERET AS A BUISNESSMAN

The "Everite" file at the Fondation Le Corbusier has the raw material of a good novel. Everite was the French branch of Eternit, a world-wide brand of asbestos-cement products, such as flat and corrugated sheets.[30] The French branch had been started during the war by French investors, using a license from the Swiss Eternit. By the end of the war they had almost completed two factories for an intended workforce of about 500 people, but were deeply in debt and needed another 1–2 million francs to start production. In August 1918 Le Corbusier, who had already used Eternit products in La Chaux-de-Fonds, got involved through a Swiss banker with offices in Paris on the Place de l'Opéra, and over the next year he played high finance. First, he tried to set up an associated company that would buy plain sheets from Everite and mold them into special shapes, such as lost formwork for concrete aggregate (figs. 357–59), doors, and so on, for which he took out seven patents, some connected with his design for Monol housing (fig. 360), others with industrial refrigeration. Then he worked with the Swiss mother company, with a Swiss banker, and with a Belgian investor wishing to shift his investments from munitions to reconstruction. They engineered a takeover of Everite that included conditions about Le Corbusier's patents. When the Belgian investor tried to push him out of the deal, however, Le Corbusier found a new investor (who was also shifting funds from the war economy to new domains) and even traveled to Basel to meet Léopold Dubois, the head of the largest
Swiss bank, Schweizerische Bankverein. When this attempt also failed, the Everite venture evaporated.

Everite was one of Le Corbusier's many business involvements—from Dom-ino to the brick factory at Alfortville—during and immediately after World War I, when he was in close contact with Max Du Bois in Paris and his tight circle of Swiss businessmen and bankers. Among them was Le Corbusier's future patron Raoul La Roche, scion of one of the families that had founded the Schweizerische Bankverein.

There are several reasons why Le Corbusier, so committed to art, would involve himself so deeply in business. He wished to make money and thus gain artistic independence, and his association with Swiss investor friends frequently exposed him to potentially lucrative ventures. In addition, since witness-

ing the debate about *Type* at the congress of
the German Werkbund in 1914, he shared
Hermann Muthesius's belief that industrially
based types could further cultural unity—
hence his interest in technical solutions that
could anchor a type (the slabs in Dom-ino, the
Eternit formwork in Monol), in business and
licensing arrangements that could ensure control over it, and in catchy names that could
insure brand recognition (for example,
"Citrohan"). Finally, Le Corbusier clearly
saw these business and licensing arrangements
as ways to seize the initiative, to provoke and
control large-scale commisions, and to bypass
the dependent position vis-à-vis the client
that is inherent in the traditional role of the
architect.

All of these ventures failed, ultimately,
because Le Corbusier was not really interested
in business, and his actual activity as architect
took place, after all, within a traditional professional framework. Even so these attempts
at business were essential to his development.
Not only did they embed in personal experience a complex understanding of modern
types , but also and more importantly, Le
Corbusier drew from them a (somewhat illu-
sory) sense of legitimacy—the legitimacy of
the insider, with a special entitlement to
rearrange the boundary of engineer and architect, industry and art.

F.P.

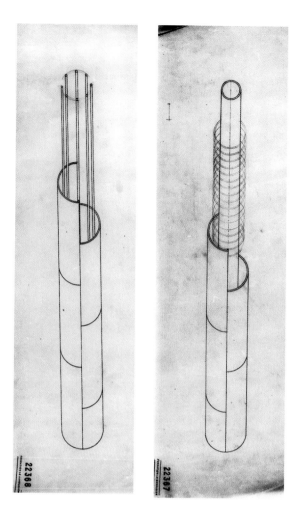

358. Charles-Edouard Jeanneret, Everite formwork for construction of concrete columns,
study relating to a patent application, Oct. 1918,
india ink and black pencil on transparent paper,
FLC [238]

359. Charles-Edouard Jeanneret, Everite formwork for construction of concrete columns,
study connected to a patent application, Oct.
1918, india ink and black pencil on transparent
paper, FLC [239]

360. Charles-Edouard Jeanneret, Project for
Maison Monol, perspective view of a group of
houses, 1919, heliograph, FLC [237]

26. VILLA BERQUE, PARIS

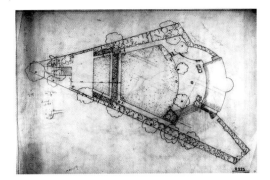

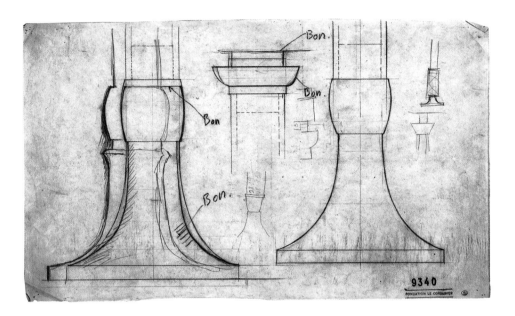

already look forward to the "picturesque" lay-out of the Villas La Roche–Jeanneret.[32] At the same time, the proposal fits in perfectly with the existing, conventionally neoclassical fabric of Villa Berque. It also confers on it a distinctive *Gestalt* that has been developed from the situation itself. With evident relish, Le Corbusier worked out the detail of the supports for the central balcony (reminiscent of those of Villa Schwob; fig. 361) and of the wrought-iron balustrade with its lattice and palisade patterns.

He was equally enthusiastic about the design of the interiors, which were to be articulated by color for the first time.[33] Here, however, the only detailed drawings that have survived are those for the closet complex on the upper floor, which were reused in 1923 for Marcel Levaillant's bedroom furniture, (see p. 120). One more folder of designs records Le Corbusier's response to the formalized perspectives of the *jardin à la française*. In these drawings the footprint of the (evidently unexecuted) drawing room extension is traced out in the plan of the terrace. These proposals all share a precise, virtuosic handling of the classical language of architecture[34]—as in the later projects for Henry Church at Ville-D'Avray—and a perfect grasp of the possibilities of the new view of classical interiors represented by such interior design contemporaries as Paul Follot and Jacques-Emile Ruhlmann.

A.R.

NEOCLASSICAL VILLA

No researcher has ever previously been able to report at first hand on this small neoclassical villa, for which, as early as 1921, Le Corbusier prepared a number of beautiful drawings (probably executed only in part) with a view to renovation and extension. The house stands within a completely self-contained residential development to which, in the early twentieth century, architects, sculptors, museum curators, physicians, and industrialists—among them Henri Bergson, Sarah Bernhardt, André Gide, and the brothers Goncourt—moved in search of peace and seclusion.[31]

In 1852 the Paris and Saint-Germain Railroad Company purchased the Château de Boufflers in order to complete its line, and the following year an architect named Charpentier drew up a development plan, duly notarized, for the surplus portion of the grounds. This area, which received the name of Villa Montmorency, occupies the steepest portions of the former park. The completed project resulted in a picturesque arrangement of houses on multiple levels, with more or less uninterrupted views for the residents.

Charpentier laid out curved avenues, like parkland rides. Two of these lie along the contours and are bisected at right angles by another avenue; they are terminated by a further pair of avenues that diverge, fanlike, as they descend the slope.

The lot on which Villa Berque stands is bounded on two sides by the horizontal avenue de Boufflers and the diagonal avenue des Tilleuls (fig. 362). The house itself is positioned approximately on the centerline of the block, so that it dominates the full depth of its triangular grounds. Access to the house is gained diagonally from behind, by way of a curiously shaped finger of land that leads to the central focus of the development, a traffic circle with garden plot and fountain. This arrangement prompted Le Corbusier to try a subtle variation on classical principles of composition. He proposed a grand access route, from a lateral flight of steps via a new terrace to the central axis of the villa; meanwhile, an extension to the existing drawing room, curved in plan, would echo the line of the lot boundary and mediate between the symmetry of the garden design and the asymmetry of the access (fig. 363). The sketches for this

361. Le Corbusier or Pierre Jeanneret, Villa Berque, sketches of the columns for the central balcony, 1921–22, pencil and charcoal on paper, FLC

362. Le Corbusier or Pierre Jeanneret, Villa Berque, site drawing with suggestions for the garden design, 1921–22, pencil and ink on tracing paper, FLC

363. Le Corbusier, Villa Berque, two perspectives for the new terrace and the projected salon, 1921, ink on tracing paper, FLC

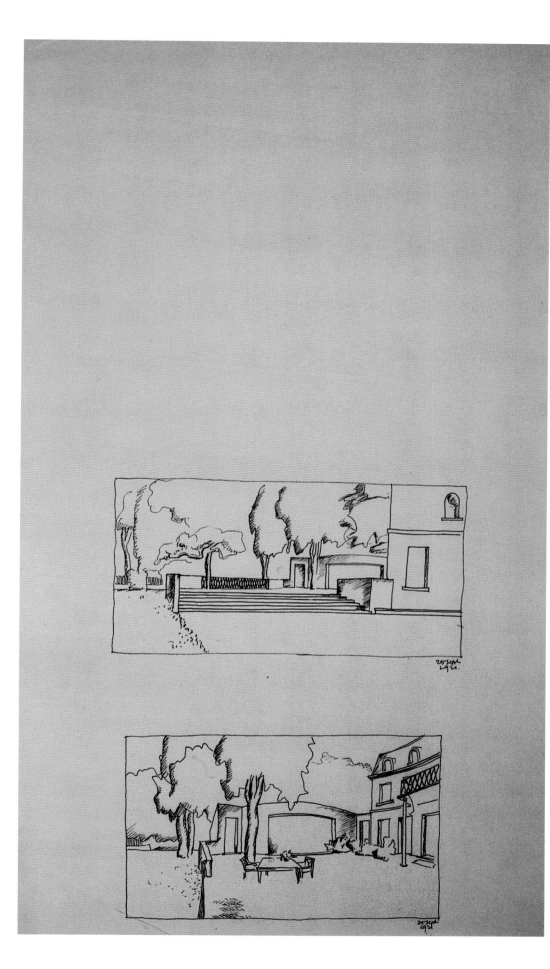

Part 3 · Toward L'Equipement de la Maison

27. ARMCHAIRS

FUMOIR FOR HERMANN DITISHEIM (1915)
The house built by Léon Boillot in 1914 for the brothers Ernest-Albert and Hermann Ditisheim (whose family owned the Vulcain company) is comparatively modest next to some of Boillot's other houses for the clock and watch magnates of La Chaux-de-Fonds. In December 1914 Charles-Edouard Jeanneret offered his services as consultant architect, "that is to say, your representative in all dealings with the suppliers involved in the decoration and furnishing of your villa."[1] His responsibilities included not only the two wrought-iron entrance doors, but also the stairwell to the upper apartment, the interior design of the rooms (fireplaces included), and the furniture. He worked on the project for a year and a half.

The interiors of Ernest-Albert's two-story family apartment are well documented (fig. 364), but there is little material available on the third-floor apartment in which Hermann—a widower since 1906—lived alone. His den or *fumoir*, however, for which a complete study (*étude approfondie*) had been completed by March 4, 1915, contained Jeanneret's most mature furniture suite of the period (fig. 365). It has been preserved intact in the Musée des Beaux-Arts of La Chaux-de-Fonds; the sofa and wooden armchairs even retain the original striped upholstery.

The seat furniture (fig. 366), with its curved backs and swordlike legs, bears an obvious resemblance to French prototypes of the Directoire or early Empire (fig. 367). Unlike some of Jeanneret's earlier seating groups, however, all the pieces combine harmoniously in a way that is strongly influenced by his idiosyncratic formal predilections. The attempt to give a homogeneous appearance to the furniture, which extends to a standardized ornamental treatment of the corners and joins on the wooden frames, is quite surprising, firstly in the context of Le Corbusier's later development and secondly in relation to Jeanneret's neoclassically minded French contemporaries.[2] The latter eschewed not

only total aesthetic control and homogenization of detail, but also the exaggeration of traditional French elegance in the work of those more conservative designers who still subscribed to the ideals of Art Nouveau.

A.R.

364. Charles-Edouard Jeanneret, decoration of the hall in Ernest-Albert Ditisheim's apartment, 1915

365. Smoking room in Hermann Ditisheim's apartment, 1915. The room, fireplace, and furniture were designed by Jeanneret, FLC

366. Charles-Edouard Jeanneret, armchair from Hermann Ditisheim's apartment, 1915, mahogany, original fabric, MBA

367. Private salon of de luxe-apartment on the SS. "France," 1912, ensemble of furniture in Directoire style (brochure of the Compagnie Générale Transatlantique, 1912, private collection, Switzerland)

368. Charles-Edouard Jeanneret, armchair with footrest from the smoking room in Hermann Ditisheim's apartment, 1915, mahogany, new fabric, MBA [2]

28. SIDEBOARD AND BOOKCASE

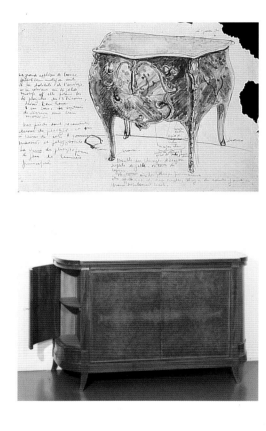

369. Charles-Edouard Jeanneret, drawing of an eighteenth-century commode from the Musée des Arts
Décoratifs, Paris, (1912), ink and watercolour, FLC
[206]

370. Charles-Edouard Jeanneret, sideboard from
Hermann Ditisheim's apartment, 1915, mahogany and
veneer, 99 x 141 x 49.5 cm. MBA [4]

371. Detail of fig. 370 with open side compartment

FUMOIR FOR HERMANN DITISHEIM (1915)

While Jeanneret evidently viewed seat furniture as akin to functional, anthropomorphic objects with formal characteristics that were hard to alter, he treated case furniture as design exercises. Their cuboidal outlines and the possibilities for integration into an interior scheme brought them within the purview of the architect (see p. 234); they tend to be more an "immovable" built structure (*immeuble*) than a "movable" item of furniture (*meuble*).

However, this relates only peripherally to the two pieces for Hermann Ditisheim's *fumoir*, they have curved legs to lift them off the floor (figs. 370, 372); this establishes a visual connection with the wooden frames of the seat furniture, and the object-nature of the piece is emphasized. Furthermore, the overall form of the sideboard is far more dynamic than in comparable pieces of the Directoire period; its curvature distantly recalls Jeanneret's 1912 watercolor of an eighteenth-century chest of drawers at the Musée des Arts Décoratifs in Paris (fig. 369) — a *meuble*, if ever there was one: "A piece with mahogany veneer, superbly curved. And such logic."[3]

The Hermann Ditisheim sideboard, however, is detailed in a very different spirit from the museum piece of 1748 (fig. 370). It has a flat front, framed by a base and architrave and two slender pilasters, with an artfully bookmatched burr veneer in the same grammar that is used for the bookcase. The framing members and curved sides are incorporated into a highly disciplined system, sparingly articulated at the intersections of horizontals and verticals (fig. 371). In its hard precision it recalls the late eighteenth-century taste for Egyptian forms. These frames — like those of all the seat furniture — are made of mahogany, another late-eighteenth-century favorite.

Jeanneret amused himself by treating the curved sides of the sideboard not only as a decorative idea, but also as functional features in their own right: each conceals a shelving compartment.[4] He tried this in a number of other pieces: compartments are often inserted above cabinet doors, into desk superstructures (see p. 112), or into substructures (see p. 237), always where they would be least expected. Form is—additionally—legitimized by function. And so the great themes of modernism are first heard in a scherzo.

A.R.

372. Charles-Edouard Jeanneret, Bookcase from Hermann Ditisheim's apartment, 1915, mahogany and veneer, glass, MBA [372]

29. CABINET

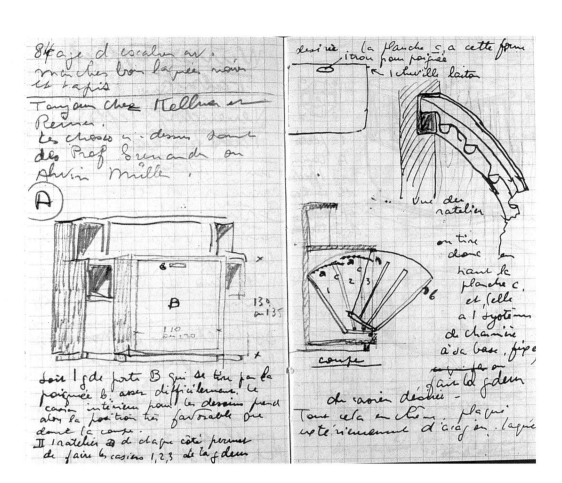

Compared to the sideboard for Hermann Ditisheim, this low, polychrome piece for the ground-floor apartment of Ditisheim's brother looks far more "architectural" (fig. 375). It is divided into four sections, each corresponding to a shelving compartment. Salmon-pink vertical spaces separate the frame-and-panel doors, which open on vertical hinges in such a way that no hardware is visible from the front to interfere with the pure forms. The panels are not made of glued boards but of Eternit, a material that neither warps nor shrinks as wood does. The Eternit trademark was used for asbestos cement products in Switzerland from 1903 onward; Jeanneret had already specified this "new" material for the roofing of his parents' house (see cat. no. 19). The salmon-pink paint finish on some parts of the structure matched a red linoleum floor covering, now lost.

This cabinet, which was long used as a toy chest, was made in 1915 as part of a well-documented interior design contract. Correspondence, invoices, and even time sheets for the planning work have survived, although the drawings have not. In many cases the makers of individual pieces can be identified. Some of the furniture for the nursery (including beds and night tables), for example, were made by the Geneva firm of L'Artisan, and bear its nameplate. Although the workmanship is good, these pieces are somewhat less elegant than the suite of furniture for Hermann Ditisheim (see pp. 230–33), which oral tradition has always associated with the master *ébéniste* Jean Egger. Although Egger never signed his work, the time sheets for Ernest-Albert's cabinets suggest that he was involved. On June 10, 1915, for example, there is a note, "surveillance Egger meuble fils" (supervision Egger, son's furniture).

This "meuble fils" (fig. 374) was intended for the books and drawings of Ernest-Albert's eighteen-year-old son, Robert, who was about to begin studying civil engineering at the Eidgenössische Technische Hochschule (Swiss Federal Institute of Technology). This extremely complex piece represents the first use of a hinged compartment for plans and drawings, which Jeanneret had discovered in Germany in 1910, taking copious notes on its design.[5] Above all, however, a comparison with the facade of Villa Schwob, designed one year later (fig. 377), reveals the decisive importance of the interior designs of the period for the development of Jeanneret's architectural themes. A.R.

373. Charles-Edouard Jeanneret, drawing of commode "pour ranger les dessins" exhibited by the firm of Keller und Reiner, Berlin, June 15, 1910, Carnet 1, p. 84/85

374. Charles-Edouard Jeanneret, Cabinet for Robert Ditisheim, son of Ernest-Albert, 1915, painted wood, with a compartment "pour ranger les dessins," private collection, Switzerland

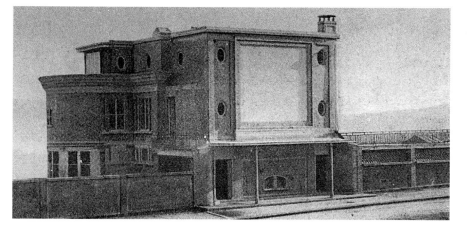

375. Charles-Edouard Jeanneret, Cabinet from Ernest-Albert Ditisheim's apartment, 1915, painted wood and Eternit panels, linoleum, MBA

376. Detail of fig. 375

377. Charles-Edouard Jeanneret, Villa Schwob, photograph of street facade, from *L'Esprit Nouveau* 6, 1921, p. 679

30. WRITING-DESK

FOR MARIE CHARLOTTE AMÉLIE JEANNERET-PERRET (c. 1915–16)

At every turn, the house that Jeanneret built for his parents in 1912 (see cat. 19) reveals itself as a sort of cornucopia. Like all the places that Jeanneret/Le Corbusier constructed for himself to live in, this house is steeped in his own complex and often contradictory dialogue with architectural forms, both ancient and modern. The furnishings, which he collected over a period of several years, carry many traces of this process of interaction.

The most spectacular piece Jeanneret designed for the villa is a writing-desk (*secrétaire*) for his mother (fig. 378). Photographs of the living room show it rather pointlessly placed in front of the drapes that cover the entrance to the *petit salon* (fig. 379). Even

when the desk was later moved to the Petite Maison in Vévey, it was positioned without any specific architectural relevance next to the long window on the guestroom side. It was, therefore, definitely a *meuble*—furniture in the sense of "movable" property, however laden with architectural themes.

As with the Levaillant desk (see fig. 129), the superstructure is most noticeable. Its base consists of a slightly projecting single tier of drawers. Above it, the left section is structured like a classical, arcaded portico, used for books and the display of small objects. Four arches support a thin, slightly overhanging platform. The two outer arches are narrower and separated from the wider, central pair by vertical moldings. This arrangement establishes a clear symmetry, although it breaks the classical rules by including a centrally placed

support. This idiosyncratic variant on a traditional architectural motif directly joins a somewhat taller, sharp-edged "prisme pur" of miniaturized drawers. With its inset niche, this geometrically defined element represents the antithesis of the arcade. The confrontation between the two worlds reflects the extremes — like fire and ice — to which Jeanneret was then deliberately exposing himself. The contrast provided the forward impulse for his design work of the early and middle 1910s.

In this piece, the morphological potential of the writing-desk as such is also explored to its utmost limits. A truncated pyramid, the shape of which stands emblematically for its function as a hinged compartment, replaces one of the slender, conical legs. Not only is the conical form legitimized, as it were, by a new use (see fig. 379), but through this use

the functionality of traditional forms is provocatively called in question. The piece thus reflects Jeanneret's interest in the relationship between ideal form and ostentatiously displayed function, as well as his simultaneous concern with the archetypal themes of furniture design and architecture.

A.R

378. Charles-Edouard Jeanneret, Desk for Mme Jeanneret-Perret, c. 1915/16 (?), detail, walnut and veneer, FLC (Villa Le Lac, Corseaux) [10]

379. Mme Jeanneret-Perret's desk in the Jeanneret-Perret house, photograph c. 1916–19, FLC [94]

380. Charles-Edouard Jeanneret, drawing of Mme Jeanneret-Perret's desk, pencil on paper, BV [242]

237

31. LUMIÈRE

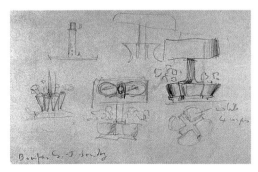

381. Charles-Edouard Jeanneret, table lamp, modeled in terracotta by Léon Perrin, painted by Jeanneret, c. 1915/16, location unknown

382. Charles-Edouard Jeanneret, sketches for table lamp c. 1915/16, from Carnet A1, p. 25

SOCIÉTÉ POUR LA FABRICATION DE LUSTRERIE D'ART (1914–17)

After resigning his post as instructor of the Nouvelle Section at the École d'Art in La Chaux-de-Fonds at the end of April 1914, Jeanneret stepped up his work as an interior designer, and in mid-year he plunged into the first of his adventures in manufacturing. Little is known about Lumière, the company that was set up to bring together skilled local craftsmen to produce contemporary electric light fittings. Fragments of correspondence, however, reveal Jeanneret's involvement. "My clients know very well that I design for Lumière," he wrote to his sculptor friend Léon Perrin, who was evidently also involved, and the name of Bonifas is also mentioned. In his letter, Jeanneret was concerned that a commission consisting of twenty-one sconces for the Nouveau Cercle club would be too much work for Perrin to undertake alone. He suggested, therefore, that Perrin leave the fabrication to the "skill of professional wood-carvers" and concentrate on artistically ambitious pieces such as the "Descoeudres lamp."[6]

A sketch for a table lamp is found in one of Jeanneret's sketchbooks.[7] Two pieces at least were executed (present whereabouts unknown).[8] These consisted of a terracotta base incorporating six removable cups—made by Perrin and decorated with blue motifs on one and red on the other by Jeanneret—and a lampshade covered with the loose fabric favored by Jeanneret (fig. 381).[9] A further sketch from Sketchbook A1 shows a still more fanciful piece (fig. 382), which Jeanneret described in a letter as a wooden "tripod bearing a jade basin filled with water, with live fish; the upper part of the basin being lit by a bulb submerged in a vase containing roses. The light illuminated, firstly the roses, which appeared translucent, and secondly the basin, in which the fishes glittered, yielding a truly rare effect."[10]

Shown in the touring L'Oeuvre exhibition of 1916 (fig. 386), this piece was offered to Marcel Levaillant, but, along with many others, it wound up unsold in Léon Perrin's workshop. By contrast, the Dr. Descoeudres lamp, which is still extant, is a comparatively traditional design. It bears a resemblance to Marcel Levaillant's floor lamp—known only from a perspective drawing and an invoice written on a form probably designed by Jeanneret (fig. 384)—and also to the piece illustrated here, which formerly belonged to Georges Schwob (fig. 383). This last was probably designed by the painter Charles Humbert, around 1922, in the Société Lumière tradition; the decorations on the fabric shade are by Humbert's wife, Madeleine Woog.

A.R.

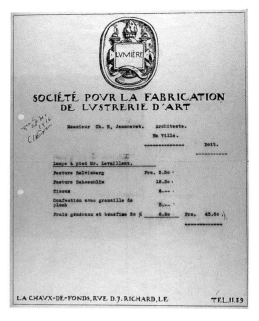

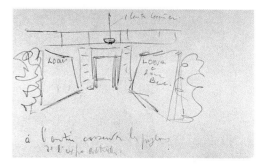

383. Charles Humbert, floor lamp for Georges Schwob, designed in 1922 to go with the armchairs designed in 1916 by Charles-Edouard Jeanneret, walnut (?), hexagonal lampshade with drawings by Madeleine Woog, MBA [17]

384. Invoice from the Société pour la fabrication de lustrerie d'Art for Marcel Levaillant, "reçu 28 déc. 1916 ChEJt," form probably designed by Jeanneret, private collection, Switzerland [41]

385. Charles-Edouard Jeanneret, sketch for "trépied" lamp, c. 1915/16, Carnet AI, p. 26

386. Charles-Edouard Jeanneret, sketch for the La Chaux-de-Fonds installation of the travelling exhibition "Les arts du feu," organized by "L'Oeuvre" in 1916, "1 lustre Lumière," Carnet AI, p. 30

32. DIVAN BED

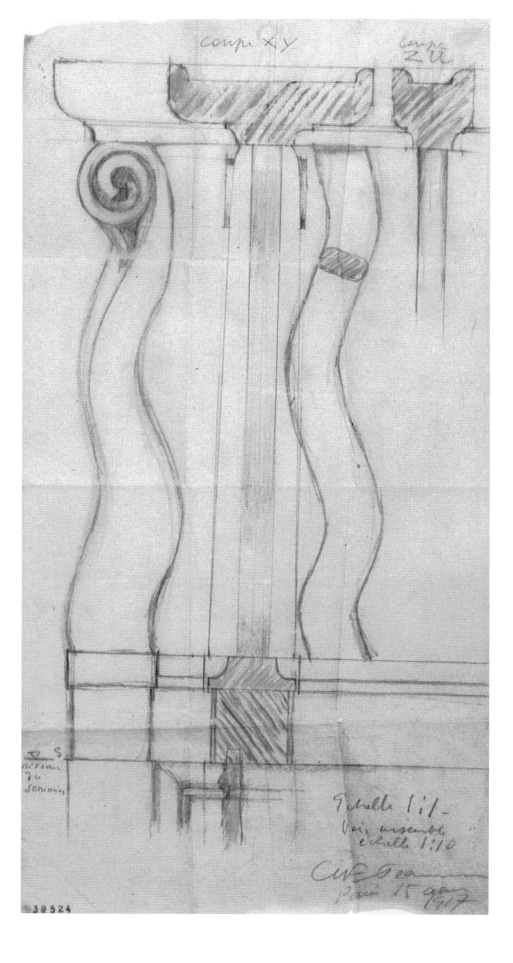

387. Charles-Edouard Janneret, divan for Marcel
Levaillant, 1917, detail

388. Charles-Edouard Jeanneret, divan for Marcel
Levaillant, 1917, working drawing, pencil and coloured
pencil on paper, FLC [244]

MARCEL LEVAILLANT APARTMENT (1917)

One of the most exotic pieces from the Levaillant collection (figs. 387, 390) is documented with two drawings (figs. 388, 389), but does not appear in the correspondence. Designed in 1917, after Jeanneret had moved to Paris, it was intended for the first interior created for Levaillant in 1914. The project drawing shows this asymmetrical piece in context (see fig. 137): it is freestanding against a wallpapered wall, next to an antique night table probably owned by Levaillant. A platform step at skirting height separates the piece from the floor and gives it a strangely solemn appearance. The mattress is at seat height; a striped bedspread covers one longitudinal and one transverse side. The key feature of the arrangement, however, is the wooden backrest (figs. 387, 388), painted gray with white trim, which runs along the two remaining sides and—as shown in the drawing—serves to support cushions. For use as a divan, this is essential, as the depth of the bed front to back is almost 47 inches (1.2 m). The second drawing is a masterful working sketch giving the precise detailing of the backrest with its wave-lined profiles, the front one being and forming part of the *ossature* (skeleton) of the bedstead, which here as elsewhere is carefully worked out. The form is emphasized here by a volute that suggests a swan-neck motif. Along the shorter side,

the top molding turns into a tray, on which decorative or "useful" objects can be placed—perhaps a candlestick, as suggested in the project drawing.

The source of inspiration for this design may have been the transparency of white-painted garden benches or balustrades, as illustrated in Paul Mebes's classic study *Um 1800*, but this is by no means certain.[11] Whenever Jeanneret was not setting out to perfect a "type," he tended to opt for complex programs, and—as in the writing-desk for his mother—the dynamism of asymmetry fascinated him. In this case, the price to be paid for asymmetry was the need for an additional contrivance to enable the bed to be set up the other way round. This was done by providing additional bedstock fitments on the *ossature* and supplying a second set of backrest components, so that the divan could be set up (as it probably was in 1923) with the open side to the right. Presumably there were also right- and left-handed platforms. The extant step has a cover made of the same dry brown carpet material that Jeanneret had proposed as a background for the 1923 interior (see pp. 128–29).

A.R.

389. Charles-Edouard Jeanneret, divan for Marcel Levaillant, 1917, plans 1:10, pencil on paper, private collection, Switzerland [243]

390. Charles-Edouard Jeanneret, divan for Marcel Levaillant, 1917, manufactured by Jean Egger, painted wood, MBA [12]

33. THE WALL-COVERING QUESTION

In 1931 and again in 1959 Le Corbusier designed wallpaper collections, which he described as "oil paint on rolls," by which he meant colors that could be ordered from the factory in a consistent range of tones. The same technique had been used for wallpapers for his early buildings—except that, then, the colors had not always been plain but very often patterned. And, indeed, both of his own wallpaper collections (issued by Salubra) also included a number of decorative motifs. In 1931 there were structured dot and diamond patterns; in 1959, imitation stone masonry and marble facing were offered. Le Corbusier wrote in 1931 of the danger of opening the door that led to the "garden of temptations" too wide,[12] and indeed any decorative wall covering is a violation of the modernist dogma that color is the surface quality of form.

As early as 1922, in *L'Esprit nouveau*, Le Corbusier denied having had any hand in the interior decoration of Villa Schwob. The wallpapers, he said, were due to the client's bad taste. The reality, however, was somewhat different. Documentary records of his early interior design commissions include references to wallpapers at least until 1923 (see p. 118). A yellow and green pattern in the Directoire style intended for the Ditisheims has survived, and scraps of wallpaper have been rescued from the Villa Schwob—including the lively red pattern from the boudoir illustrated in *L'Esprit nouveau* (figs. 393–95). These correspond fairly closely to the perspective drawings done by the young Jeanneret, who often favored the strongly colored and boldly patterned products of the factory at Jouy, near Versailles (fig. 391).[13]

A comparison between the Villa Jeanneret-Perret and Villa Schwob reveals a deliberate exploitation of color and decorative form. Whereas in the Jeanneret residence only the salon was decorated with a lively wallpaper pattern, in the Villa Schwob they were found in the bedrooms. In 1915 Jeanneret promised his painter friend Théophile Robert a wallpaper pattern at blossom time: "I'll bring my own [flowers], painted . . . on paper, or on canvas by others smarter than myself—people like Süe, Drésa, Carlègle. And we'll see what looks best between the columns of your dining room. And, finally, here is the bait that will stop you in your tracks: my numerous and weighty swatches of marvelous textiles and papers, old and new. It will be a rerun of the Epinal prints, with a difference."[14]

A.R.

391. Wallpaper sample from Le Corbusier's apartment at 20 rue Jacob in Paris (after 1917): "le papier peint qui tapisse mon antichambre," BV [35]

392. Paul-Théophile Robert, *Nature morte aux livres et au pot de tabac* (Still life with books and a tabacco jar), 1917, oil, private collection, Switzerland

393. Charles-Edouard Jeanneret, Villa Schwob, perspective of the boudoir, 1916, heliograph, FLC

394. Charles-Edouard Jeanneret, villa Schwob, photograph of the boudoir, c. 1920, from *L'Esprit Nouveau* 6, 1921, p. 699

395. Wallpaper sample from the boudoir of the villa Schwob, found in 1987 [33]

34. FLOOR LAMP

396. Le Corbusier, floor lamp for Madeleine Schwob, 1922/23, manufactured by La Boutique Verte, Paris, forged iron and etched glass, photographed in Madeleine Schwob's apartment, 1980 [14]

397. Le Corbusier, floor Lamp for Madeleine Schwob, detail

RENÉ AND MADELEINE SCHWOB APARTMENT (1922–23)

For Le Corbusier, 1922 was a decisive year. On the one hand, he was absorbed in theoretical studies of the Purist aesthetic as it applied to architecture, employing the grammar of anonymous workshop and factory buildings. In his article "L'Illusion des plans,"[15] he decisively separated himself from the formalism of historicist planning. On the other hand, he was shamelessly flirting with the language of neoclassicism, which had been familiar to him since La Chaux-de-Fonds days and remained the only idiom understood by an upper-middle-class clientele. This is most revealingly confirmed by his plans for an extension and for the remodeling of Villa Berque, a classical townhouse that nestles in a private residential park in the 16th Arrondissement of Paris.[16] There, of course, the context offers some mitigating circumstances, but in the interior designs for Madeleine Schwob, the daughter of Hélène Schwob-Floersheim (see p. 118), he must have been impelled purely by curiosity as to the possibilities of confrontations between different stylistic devices.

On May 3, 1922, Le Corbusier made a number of interior design suggestions to the newly married Madeleine, now Mme Schwob. He promised her wallpaper and carpet samples and, for the lighting, advised her to buy "little wall lights that are available very cheaply in the Paris department stores and look like the sketch that I am sending you by mail. These sconces are very pretty, although made with extreme simplicity, and cost almost nothing. They can be fitted up very nicely with candles and a shade."[17]

In addition to this choice, which lies somewhere between conventionality and frivolity, he suggested as the main light source either glass ceiling bowls or floor lamps, possibly for indirect lighting: "This device ... would be fitted with an automobile headlight inside the base and would cast an intense light on the ceiling, thus lighting the whole room."

Any expectations of a high-tech mounting

for this automobile headlight are instantly
dashed by the initial sketch enclosed with the
letter. This closely resembles the version eventually fabricated by La Boutique Verte (fig.
396), in rustic hammered wrought iron and
etched glass. From a metal ring with ornament
in shallow relief rise four rods, joined at top
and bottom (fig. 399), which conceal an electric cord and support a glass shade in the form
of a truncated pyramid. This one-of-a-kind
piece was finally delivered in the summer of
1923 (fig. 398). Its singularity lies in the blatant
mismatch between avant-garde lighting technology and traditional handcraftsmanship.[18]

A.R.

398. La Boutique Verte, invoice for Madeleine Schwob's
floor lamp, adressed to "Monsieur Jeanneret," with his
signature in upper left corner, FLC

399. Le Corbusier, floor lamp for Madeleine Schwob,
detail of forged iron foot

3 · TOWARD L'EQUIPEMENT DE LA MAISON

400. Le Corbusier, Bookcase for Madeleine Schwob, 1922, wild cherry and veneer, and bronze, MBA [13]

401. Le Corbusier, Bookcase for Madeleine Schwob, plan of installation, 1:20, ink on paper, private collection, Switzerland [245]

RENÉ AND MADELEINE SCHWOB APARTMENT (1922–23)

The design for René and Madeleine Schwob comprised a bedroom and library, and the area between the drawing room and dining room. In the bedroom, the existing antique bed was set off in front of a drape; the library, however, allowed for the design of a magnificent new piece of furniture—a bookcase that would occupy an entire wall. This was obviously Le Corbusier's main interest. A colored perspective drawing (see fig. 134) shows the arrangement of the four-bay bookcase (fig. 400), which stood opposite a large double door flanked by classical wall lights.

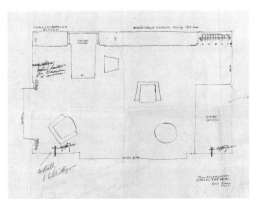

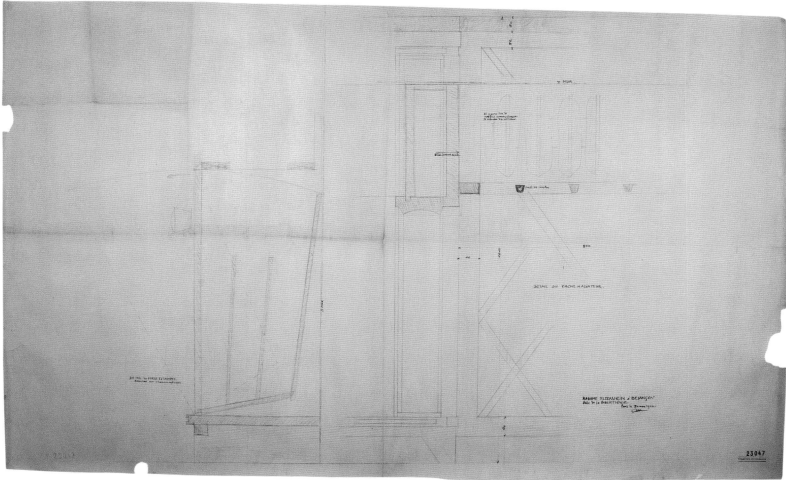

One of the narrow walls was broken by a window, and the other had a sofa against it. The room was also to contain two small arm-chairs; these led to a lengthy dispute that ended when Le Corbusier resigned the commission.

Once more, it is surprising how closely Le Corbusier's first sketch corresponds to the minutely detailed working drawings that he prepared a month or so later (fig. 402). It seems, in fact, that from the onset he had a grasp of the final scheme both as a whole and in detail. This may be partly explained by the exceptional continuity of Le Corbusier's exploration, in which every piece marks the point of departure for the next, although a throwback or cross-fertilization may occur at any time. Thus, the left-hand section (*meuble de gauche*) of the *casier* consists of a combination shelving unit, drawer, and drop-front print chest, which had already been tried out in 1915—albeit with different compositional intentions—in the *casier* for Robert Ditisheim

(see fig. 374). This chestlike section is topped by a gray marble slab, as is the bookcase proper, in which the slab crowns an elegant cornice supported by concave pilasters and is thus far more prominent. In the intervening gap, a framed mirror and a wheeled waste-paper compartment derive their raison d'être from the cantilevered desk surface that is, as it were, slotted in between the two unequal parts. The cantilever, that central feature of architectural modernism, causes the desktop to assert a world antithetical to that of the bookcase. In section this desk is rectilinear, but in plan it is shaped. It thus contributes to the blend of various approaches—as does the radiator housing that corresponds to the left section, with a neoclassical diamond trellis motif frequently used by the young Jeanneret.

A.R.

402. Le Corbusier, working drawing for Madeleine Schwob's library, 1922, ink and coloured pencils on paper, FLC [248]

36. CASIERS STANDARD

apart from the hardware, to two of the units shown in the "Boudoir" in the gallery of the Pavillon de l'Esprit Nouveau. Are they the same pieces? The firm of Tony Selmersheim and Monteil presented its invoice only in February 1926—after the close of the exhibition. It was addressed to the architect's office, as usual, but a note refers to "Meubles livrés chez Mme Jeanneret" (furniture delivered to Mme Jeanneret). Kerstin Rääf has recalled seeing them subsequently in use on the entrance floor of Villa Jeanneret. Their owner, Le Corbusier's sister-in-law Lotti Jeanneret-Rääf, later took them to Sweden, where they were eventually made part of the collection of the Nationalmuseum in Stockholm (fig. 405). These are racks of compartments painted in yellow ocher on the outside, with mahogany veneer doors and sliding flaps. This visual distinction between frame and panel was already present in the bookcases for Madeleine Schwob (1922) and Marcel Levaillant (1923), where it was established by using different woods and veneers. The Schwob and Levaillant bookcases also document the transition from the traditional chest, with individual formal features, to the "cubic" container (see pp. 121, 246). In 1922 there had still been wooden feet with a bevel on one side; by 1923 there were only adjustable bronze spacers.

A.R.

FOR LOTTI JEANNERET-RÄÄF (1925–26)
Jeanneret/Le Corbusier's consistent development of the theme of case furniture came to a temporary conclusion in 1925 with the "standard racks" or *casiers standard* that formed the backbone of the interior designed for the Pavillon de l'Esprit Nouveau at the *Exposition internationale des arts décoratifs industriels et modernes* in Paris (fig. 404).[19] The pavilion itself was a realistic model of a housing unit, which served to illustrate the project of the *immeuble-villas,* or villa block, a project that had been under development since 1922. The basic unit was a cubic element that could be combined and stacked to yield larger structural units. Similarly, the *casiers standard*, developed in 1924–25, could be combined and stacked to

form whole walls. For the architecture and *equipement* of dwellings, Le Corbusier had now abandoned individual form in favor of a system that permitted a free composition of pre-existing elements.

In both cases, only the inner organization reflects function. As in the furniture made for La Chaux-de-Fonds, function was rhetorically expressed and amplified by the way the elements worked, by the hinging open, swiveling, sliding out, and rolling back of compartments, drawers, and trays. At the same time, however, the dissimilarity to the earlier pieces is unmistakable: the form of the container was emancipated from that of its contents and now related to it via "dialectical" tension.

The *casiers* illustrated here correspond,

403. Le Corbusier, Cabinet from Madeleine Schwob's bookcase, 1922 (see p. 246)

404. Le Corbusier and Pierre Jeanneret, photograph of standard cabinets in the Pavillon de l'Esprit nouveau, 1925, FLC

405. Le Corbusier and Pierre Jeanneret, standard cabinets from Lotti Jeanneret-Rääf's estate, 1925/26, formerly in the Villa Jeanneret, Paris; Nationalmuseum, Stockholm[15]

READY MADES

37. FOLK ART: VASES

When Le Corbusier spoke jokingly about his "private collection" (*collection particulière*) he did not so much mean his paintings by André Bauchant or Fernand Léger, or his many drawings by Louis Soutter, or his *Sailor with Guitar* by Jacques Lipchitz,[20] as he did the assortment of meaningful objects that he had accumulated on his endless travels (fig. 406–08). He kept some of these close to him all his life; others were left with and used by his parents or his brother Albert. Undoubtedly, the most conspicuous items among the collection are the ceramics. He probably acquired the large, shallow dishes from Tafilalet, Morocco, on a trip to North Africa in 1931, and the off-white *botijos* from Agost, Spain, in the summer of 1930 while traveling with his brother Albert, his cousin Pierre, and Fernand Léger. By far the most numerous and valuable pieces, however, are those that he collected on his Voyage d'Orient of 1911. The sketchbooks record a number of purchases and arrangements for dispatch home.[21] Between Budapest and Belgrade, he began to discover, through vernacular ceramics, "folk art" as an alternative to "high" art. The second "letter" in his account of the trip—addressed to Léon Perrin and the "friends of the 'Ateliers d'Art' in La Chaux-de-Fonds"—is entirely devoted to this discovery:

I am here to tell you of vases, peasant vases, pottery of the people. . . . You know these delights: to touch the generous belly of a vase, to stroke its slender neck, and then to explore the subtleties of its curvature; with hands deep in pockets and eyes half-closed, to be gently transported by the fairytale glamour of enamels—blazing yellows, velvety blues—and to gaze raptly at the vigorous struggle between brutal masses of black and victorious elements of white. . . . Like an immutable warm caress, this art of the people enfolds the whole earth, covering it with the same flowers, uniting or confounding races, climates, and places. . . .

All along the Danube, and then later, at Adrianopolis [Edirne], we found precisely the same forms that the Mycenaean painters covered with their black arabesques.[22]

Sensuous and intellectual enjoyment were simultaneous. Jeanneret and his companion August Klipstein hurled themselves into a hunt for the best examples of the already endangered folk art: "You can be sure that ever since Budapest we have secured for ourselves an arsenal of bellies and spouts. . . . To unearth them, we have sifted through all the dismal, nameless, indistinguishable bric-a-brac that swamps the whole of Europe."[23]

A.R.

406–08. Pottery collected by Charles-Edouard Jeanneret during his trip to the Orient, 1911, between Budapest and Istanbul, FLC [27–29]

409. Le Corbusier with a Serbian vase, photographed at the Jeanneret-Perret house in August, 1919, FLC

410. Charles-Edouard Jeanneret, study of Spanish pottery, *Pitchers with Anemones*, 1914, pencil and gouache on drawing paper, FLC

411. Pottery collected by Charles-Edouard Jeanneret during his trip to the Orient, 1911, FLC [30]

38. ANTIQUES: BERGÈRES À PAILLE

412. Bergère à paille, bought by Charles-Edouard Jeanneret for the Jeanneret-Perret house, c. 1915/16. FLC (Villa Le Lac, Corseaux) [18]

413. Charles-Edouard Jeanneret, sketches of bergères à paille, drawn at Ruffy's antique shop, c. 1915/16, sketchbook A1, p. 24

414. Charles-Edouard Jeanneret, photograph of the living room in the Jeanneret-Perret house, showing three bergères à paille, BV [19, 20]

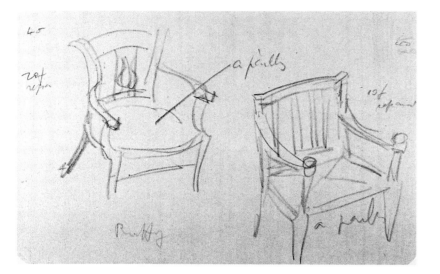

Le Corbusier's "private collection" encompassed an assortment of found furniture with which he surrounded himself all his life. Until he moved into the new apartment at 24 rue Nungesser-et-Coli in Paris in 1934, the pieces in question were nearly all antiques, and he continued to use most of them in the privacy of his studio. He mentioned one of them in a letter to the purchaser of his parents' house in 1919, Fritz Ernst Jeker:

> In a moment of confusion, my father listed among the furniture sold to you the oval table in my bedroom. I am attached to this table, which I have always owned; it is not in any case worth very much, and if the form pleases you, Egger, the cabinetmaker, could make you another very inexpensively. I hope you will not mind this posthumous claim.[24]

This was the simple table that later served both as a dining and a writing table at 20 rue Jacob and found its way into the new studio in 1934. A wood-framed sofa and armchairs, with carved backs and straw seats, belong to the same group, as seen in, for example, the portrait photograph taken by Brassaï on rue Jacob in the early 1930s.

Sketchbook A1 illustrates further examples of "farm furniture" discovered by Jeanneret in the antique shops of Lausanne and Geneva around 1916—pieces "that are always in perfect taste, very comfortable, and easy to handle" (fig. 413).[25] He carefully noted down the prices and the condition of the straw seats. One little sketch apparently records the dealer's attribution of a particular shape to the Louis XIII style. It is almost certain that a few of these chairs, which his drawings capture with such an assured line, were bought for the Villa Jeanneret-Perret, his parents' house in La Chaux-de-Fonds (fig. 414), now at Villa Le Lac in Vévey (figs. 412, 415), .

The importance of these pieces for Jeanneret's development is evident. Here, in the vernacular, he discovered the prototypical form of the anonymous industrial culture of the present. These were *objets-types*, legitimized to a degree by being made for centuries: with them, the style question did not arise. His first list of "type" furniture, published in *L'Esprit nouveau* in 1921, included "five-franc, straw-bottomed church chairs,"[26] simpler versions of the antiques he had found in 1916, but dis-

playing the same characteristics. The next step was to find contemporary industrial products with the same maturity and the same familiar image as the traditional *bergères de paille*.

A.R.

415. Bergères à paille from Jeanneret-Perret house, FLC (Villa Le Lac, Corseaux)

39. OBJETS-TYPES I: BENTWOOD CHAIRS

416. Le Corbusier and Pierre Jeanneret, Villa La Roche/Jeanneret, 1923–25, photograph of Jeanneret living room, c. 1925, bentwood furniture and a Mey armchair in the background, FLC

417. Robert Mey, invoice for "6 fauteuils 1224, siège et dossier canné," addressed to "Monsieur Jeanneret," 1925, FLC

Bentwood chairs were among the first factory-made items in the furniture trade.[27] By 1876 Michael Thonet and his sons were already employing around 4,500 workers in their factories and had a worldwide distribution system. Their famous Model No. 14, a chair that came onto the market in 1859 as a "cheap consumer model," was produced by the millions, not least by competitors who established themselves after Thonet's patent had elapsed.

In 1914 Jeanneret was already advising his client Marcel Levaillant to go on using his "Vienna chairs."[28] Amédée Ozenfant kept six beautiful Thonet chairs in the apartment that he emptied and painted white in 1918.[29] Despite these precedents, it was not until relatively late that Jeanneret/Le Corbusier discovered bentwood chairs for his own interior design repertoire, where they—as factory-made *objets-types*—supplanted the traditional style or rustic chairs. In the spring of 1925, for the Villa La Roche–Jeanneret, he ordered a variety of models, including the chairs and armchairs with "hairpin" backs (Model No.18). Photographs of the Pavillon de l'Esprit Nouveau of 1925 which was furnished not long afterward, show the writing chairs (Model No. 6009) that Le Corbusier was to use himself throughout his life.

As early as 1916 Jeanneret had designed a work chair with a semicircular, horizontal backrest (fig. 418). In 1919 he recommended it to a buyer of his parents' house as a dining chair: "Six demi-fauteuils accoudoirs sans dossiers tel que j'en ai exécuté un chez Hermann Ditisheim pour son bureau de travail; ces sièges sont extrémement confortables et donneront beaucoup de grandeur et d'espace à la pièce. . . ."[30] The Thonet "writing" chair No. 6009 can be described as a factory-made *objet-type* with similar features. It was generally painted gray for use in Purist interiors, so that it would contrast with the wooden table leaves and merge into the polychromatic interior. For the Pavillon de L'Esprit Nouveau, Le Corbusier also ordered similar

chairs from the Parisian firm of Robert Mey
(Model No. 1224; fig. 419), which have a
woven, oval medallion in the back. These rare
pieces can be seen in photographs of the
Villa Albert Jeanneret (where they were painted either white or ruby-red), and in Le
Corbusier's dining room in the rue
Nungesser-et-Coli in Paris. On the frame they
have the trademark "GLARIS," showing that
they were produced by the Swiss furniture
factory AG Horgen-Glarus, which made certain models exclusively for Mey at that time.[31]

A.R.

418. Charles-Edouard Jeanneret, desk chair for
Hermann Ditisheim, 1915, mahogany, original fabric,
MBA [6]

419. Desk chair 1224, marketed exclusively by the firm
of Robert Mey, fabricated by AG Möbelwerke Horgen-
Glarus, Glarus (Switzerland). From Villa Jeanneret,
Paris, bentwood, painted white, then red, private collection, Switzerland

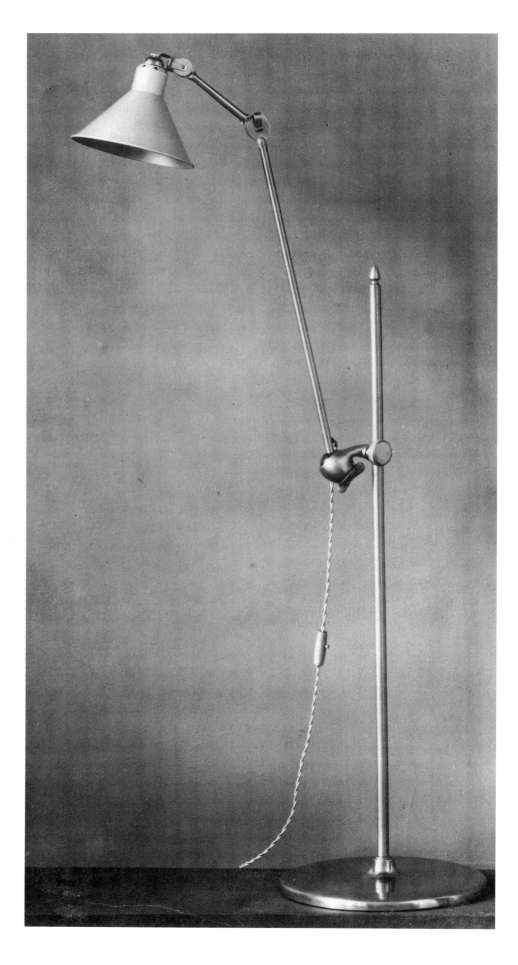

420. Table lamp, manufactured by Ilrin, Paris, as used in the Villa La Roche, Paris (after 1925), blue and white glass, brass, wood, private collection, Switzerland

421. Floor lamp "modèle Gras, type dessinateur," Didier des Gachons & Ravel, Paris, used in the interiors of Ozenfant, La Roche, Levaillant, etc., made of nickeled iron and cast-iron, brass, and aluminum, photograph from the Wohnbedarf archive, c. 1932, private collection, Germany [24]

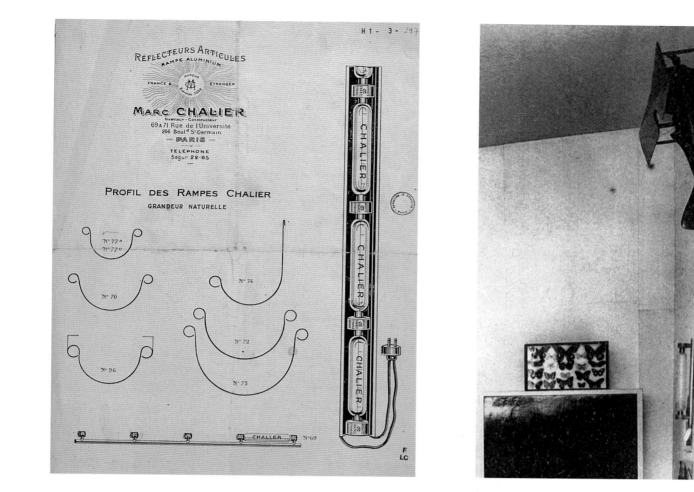

Another fascinating feature of Le Corbusier's output concerns the question of lighting.[32] His development took a significant step forward during the time he was working on plans for the Villa La Roche–Jeanneret, which—shortly before the Pavillon de l'Esprit Nouveau—was to become the first fully "modern" house by Le Corbusier. Particularly striking are the wall fixtures, which still exist today, consisting of a lighting tube and bracket (fig. 423). This minimalist light contrasts dramatically with the classical fabric and candle wall lights that Le Corbusier was still recommending in 1922 for an interior design for Madeleine Schwob. Nevertheless, the new model was not in fact a design produced by his office but part of a lighting system commonly used in window displays in Paris stores at the time—that is to say, a ready-made (fig. 422).[33]

In addition, Albert Jeanneret (like Le Corbusier himself) owned at least one watchmaker's lamp brought from La Chaux-de-Fonds with a horizontal arm that could be fixed, in any position with screws. Raoul La Roche, on the other hand, used two "Ilrin" daylight lamps: models derived from the design of the petroleum lamp with bluish glass shades and a wooden stem turned on a lathe, which was in turn mounted on a metal base (fig. 420). Both models bear witness to Le Corbusier's intense search for a readily available model with satisfactory formal attributes. In the summer of 1926, at the firm of L. Malabert and Company, Le Corbusier almost found such a piece for Marcel Levaillant—a metal standard lamp with an adjustable arm—but did not like the stepped base.[34] In September Le Corbusier had two "dessinateur" standard lamps sent to Levaillant instead, the same kind he had evidently already bought for La Roche (fig. 421). Made from metal tubes, sheet metal, and cast iron, and with aluminum shades, these factory-made lamps could be adjusted at the base by means of ball-and-socket joints; on the tubes there are two further disk joints that work by friction. It has been suggested that these lamps designed by a "Mr. Gras" did not "meet some formal ideal of their inventor," but had more to do with the "cheapest and most practical method of production".[35]

A.R.

422. "Rampes Chalier," leaflet of the firm of Marc Chalier, Paris, c. 1925, segments were used in Villa La Roche and Pavillon de l'Esprit nouveau, FLC

423. Le Corbusier and Pierre Jeanneret, Pavillon de l'Esprit nouveau, 1925, Chalier lamps in the library section, photograph from Les arts de la maison, Paris, 1925

Part 4 · Paintings, Drawings, Sketches, Watercolors

41. MASTERS: GRASSET AND L'EPLATTENIER

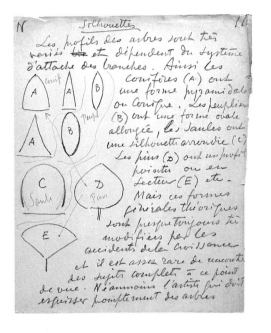

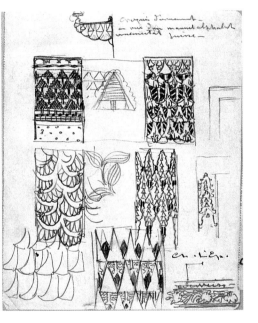

424. Eugène Grasset, Notes de cours d'Eugène Grasset, n.d. [1890–1905], pencil on paper, Orsay Museum, Paris

425. Charles L'Eplattenier, Ornamental motifs, pencil on notepaper, undated, pasted with six other drawings on wrapping paper, BV

Up until 1907, in my birthplace, I had the good fortune to have a teacher, L'Eplattenier, who was a captivating pedagogue; it was he who opened up the portals of art to me. We studied the masterpieces of all periods and places with him. I remember that modest library, in a simple armoire in our drawing studio, in which our teacher had gathered together everything he considered necessary for our spiritual nourishment.[1]

PIONEERS OF ART NOUVEAU

Among the works judged "necessary" was *Méthode de composition ornementale*[2] by Eugène Grasset (1845–1917), who had settled in Paris in 1871 but maintained close contact with friends and family in Switzerland. Grasset was among the first in France to develop the ideas of the Arts and Crafts movement and was considered a pioneer of Art Nouveau. His reputation derived from artistic activity, especially his teaching. The courses he taught became the bases for two treatises: *La Plante et ses applications ornementales* (1896) and *Méthode de composition ornementale* (1905; fig. 424).

By the time Charles L'Eplattenier (1874–1946) went to Paris to study, between 1894 and 1896, he probably already knew Grasset. While preparing for entry into the École des Beaux-Arts, he attended several courses, including those of Luc-Olivier Merson (1846–1920). Merson, like Grasset, taught at the École Guérin,[3] and was one of the chief designers for the master stained-glass artist Félix Gaudin (1851–1930).

L'Eplattenier's pedagogical program was modeled on that of Grasset and can be divided into three phases: first, instruction in techniques and in learning through observing nature; second, studies in which nature is simplified with reference to basic geometric forms — square, triangle, circle, and so on; and third, practical projects that responded to industrial needs.

Like Grasset, L'Eplattenier was an artist and teacher captivated by artists' techniques and intent on publishing a textbook, to judge by the inscription he put on one of his sketches: "Croquis d'ornement en vue d'un manuel alphabet[ique] ornemental-Suisse" (Ornament sketch for a Swiss alphabet[ical] ornament manual; fig. 425). The sketch itself, with its geometric simplification of natural forms, further suggests the connection between Grasset and L'Eplattenier.

This form of teaching, using both nature and geometry, is echoed in Jeanneret's writings. In 1908 he wrote to L'Eplattenier: "Where Parisians put a leaf modeled after nature, and the Germans a square polished like a mirror, we place a triangle with pine cones."[4] Or again in a letter to Léon Perrin, he stated: "our pine tree must be reduced to a geometric form."[5] This reduction of the pine to geometric forms is manifested in his sketches, timidly at first (see fig. 315), and then in such a way as to weave together a repetitive geometric network inspired directly by the *Méthode de composition ornementale* (figs. 426, 427).

In *L'Art décoratif d'aujourd'hui* Le Corbusier paid homage to Grasset and his geometric naturalist methodology by describing him as a "géomètre" and "algébriste des fleurs."[6] Evoking the influences of his artistic training, he added: "With him [Grasset] one has to admire all flowers, down even to the secret of their structure."[7] Grasset's name appeared several times in Jeanneret's writings about his training and upbringing at La Chaux-de-Fonds; he also wrote about his meetings with Grasset. On his arrival in Paris in 1908, it was to Grasset that Jeanneret went, and it was Grasset who advised Jeanneret to go and see the Perret brothers. Jeanneret had a lasting memory of that meeting and confided to his brother Albert: "he spoke to me with the prudence of a prophet."[8] In 1914 Jeanneret lamented that "France proved unable to understand or to support Grasset's work."[9] In 1917, after Grasset's death, he published an obituary in William Ritter's *Fillette slovaque*, a journal that once had been important reading for him.

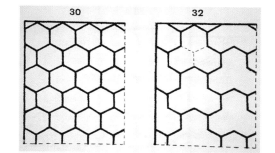

It was through L'Eplattenier that Jeanneret discovered Grasset, and both men were to be his mentors throughout his training:

There are in life benevolent men; and when circumstances have provided you with the extreme good fortune to encounter men like L'Eplattenier, first, as though by some miraculous and beneficial chance, and priests like Grasset, . . . to encounter these solid natures, these robust shepherds, . . .—meetings like that light a flame in your breast.[10]

M.E.C.

426. Charles-Edouard Jeanneret, *Pine Forest Ornament*, 1911, gouache on paper, FLC

427. Eugène Grasset, *Méthode de composition ornementale*, Paris, 1905, two illustrations from vol. I

42. THE MENTOR: WILLIAM RITTER

428. William Ritter with his friend Janko âádra in his appartment in Munich, c.1908, photograph, BV

429. William Ritter, Selfportrait, 1901–05, pastel and charcoal on paper, BV

I met a friend much older than myself in whom I could confide my doubts and incredulities because he welcomed them. William Ritter did not believe in Cézanne, and still less in Picasso, being "all for science"… Together we wandered across those wide regions of lakesides, uplands and Alps that are pregnant with historical significance. And little by little I gradually began to find myself, and to discover that all one can count on in life is one's own strength.[11]

DISCOVERING CENTRAL EUROPE

Although William Ritter (1867–1955)—writer, journalist, painter, and music and art critic— was one of the most dazzling personalities of his generation, today he is all but forgotten (figs. 428, 429).[12] While he was still a student in western Switzerland, his many talents were recognized and encouraged. Soon he was publishing his first concert reviews in the *Feuille d'Avis de Neuchâtel*, making music, and painting watercolors (fig. 430). He admired the music of Richard Wagner and in 1886 made his first visit to Bayreuth. In 1888 a lengthy stay in Paris brought him into contact with numerous artists, writers, and publishers. That same year he went to Vienna to continue his study of the history of music and art. From 1901 to 1914 he lived in Munich, where he was in regular contact with Anton Bruckner, Gustav Mahler, Arnold Böcklin, and Hans Sandreuter. He was particularly close to Giovanni Segantini and his sons, Gottardo and Mario.

In 1889 Ritter's first journey to Montenegro marked the start of an interest in the culture of central and southeast Europe that was to last until his death in 1955.[13] He made numerous journeys to Hungary, Bohemia, present-day Slovakia, Romania, and the southern Slavic countries. Residing for a considerable time in Bucharest and Prague, he delved deeply into the cultural life of those regions. Thus he became a committed champion of a culture that was largely unknown outside the region and even repressed by the Austro-Hungarian monarchy. Ritter's work for minorities, his enthusiasm for the "exotic" world of Central Europe had its roots not least in his own personal circumstances. His constant traveling, his unconventional views, which were often at variance with those of contemporary art and music criticism, and his homosexuality frequently gave Ritter the feeling of living his life outside the social norm. And the publication of an early autobiographical novels, *Aegyptiacque* (1891), provoked an immediate scandal.[14] In it Ritter openly criticized the mediocrity and fundamental conservatism of cultural life in Neuchâtel.

Ritter's multifaceted career as a critic reached a high point in 1906 with the publication of *Études d'art étranger*. In it he discussed the work of artists and musicians from Norway (Edvard Munch), Poland (Jósef Mehoffer), Russia (Nikolaj Rimskij-Korsakov), Romania (Nicolae Grigorescu), Austria (Gustav Mahler), Greece (Nikolas Gysis), and Switzerland (Albert Welti), as well as Arnold Böcklin, whose output and personality had an enduring fascination for him.

K.S.

430. William Ritter, View of Lake of Neuchâtel, 1886, watercolor, BV

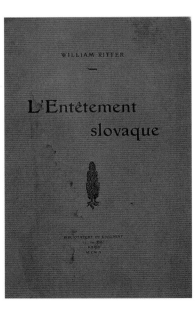

JEANNERET AND RITTER

The young Jeanneret first met William Ritter in late May of 1910 in Munich, having been given his address by Charles L'Eplattenier. They soon became close friends. Jeanneret regularly attended the Sunday salons Ritter held in his apartment and valued the experience and advice of the latter, who also put his extensive library at Jeanneret's disposal. The prolific correspondence between Ritter and Jeanneret, which continued into the 1940s, stands as a record of the intense intellectual exchange between the two men.[15]

Both Ritter's allegiance to the universal ideals of classicism and his openness to the culture of central and eastern Europe had a perceptible influence on Jeanneret's subsequent activities. Thus on Jeanneret's Voyage d' Orient he visited numerous locations that Ritter had seen years earlier. Without the latter's advice, recommendations, and contacts, Jeanneret would hardly have been likely to visit Prague and Belgrade, nor to make detours to Serbian villages or the regions around Budapest and Bucharest (figs. 431, 433, 444). Moreover, 1910 saw the publication of *L'Entêtement slovaque* (fig. 432), one of Ritter's typical ethnographic novels, in which the plot as such takes second place to detailed descriptions of the rural culture and landscape.[16]

The period of intense personal contact between Ritter and Jeanneret continued after 1914 when Ritter had to leave Germany and settled in Le Landeron, Switzerland. The two friends often spent time together painting watercolors of the landscape in the Neuchâtel Jura (figs. 431, 434), but despite their evident productivity during this time, it seemed that both were in fact waiting for the turmoil of World War I to come to an end before embarking on new creative projects. By 1917 Jeanneret already had left Switzerland for Paris, and in 1918 Ritter once again set out on extended travels through Europe.

K.S.

431. Charles-Edouard Jeanneret, Farmhouse in the surroundings of Budapest, June 1911, pencil on paper with traces of yellow pencil, FLC

432. William Ritter, *L'Entêtement slovaque*, Cover, Paris, 1910

433. William Ritter, Traditional farm house at Myjava,
Slovakia, 1906, watercolor, BV

43. LANDSCAPES

"ROOFTOPS OF PARIS"

The *Toits de Paris* (Rooftops of Paris; fig. 164), a nearly abstract landscape, figures among the small oil paintings that Le Corbusier executed before 1918. It shows a vertical approach to the view framed by the window. This view of trees and rooftops, painted with disconnected strokes, reveals a certain influence either from Cézanne or from cubism.[17] The picture takes artistic license, although the discovery of the passage between interior and exterior space might also have sprung from Le Corbusier's experience as an architect.

The Île de la Cité and the Île Saint-Louis were observed by Le Corbusier for their integration into an exceptional urban topography. Not content to be merely an observer attentively studying the birthplace of Paris, as *Pont Neuf with Île Saint-Louis* might lead one to suppose, Le Corbusier continued to demonstrate his taste for the fantastic by adding imaginary projections to the real urban elements (fig. 435). While all his studies show a relatively classic approach to spatial perspective, the mixture of techniques and the rapidity of execution here manifest a modernist *parti pris*. The quays of the Seine stimulated his imagination, perhaps surprisingly, although they had been a picturesque attraction since the nineteenth century. *Romantic River Landscape with Bridge* is an imaginary view from the Pont Neuf, as the tower in the upper part would seem to indicate (fig. 436). Saturated with black highlighted with red, this sheet indicates Le Corbusier's taste at the time for heavy, stormy atmospheres. Lively in color and more hastily executed—and full of incongruous details such as a gallows and a palm tree—his *Vue romantique de Paris* (Romantic view of Paris) conveys the feeling of the Seine quays (fig. 437).

JURA

Le Corbusier had a predilection for exterior views, which allowed him to express his sense of space. *Paysage du Jura* (Jura landscape), a wide vista, composed of plains, hills, and groves of trees, demonstrates his expressive approach to the landscape of the area around his birthplace, La Chaux-de-Fonds, where he still lived at this time. This quick sketch reveals the exceptional sense of place throughout his work (fig. 434).

434. Charles-Edouard Jeanneret, *Jura Landscape*, 1914–15, charcoal and watercolor on paper, FLC [139]

435. Charles-Edouard Jeanneret, *The Pont Neuf with the Ile Saint-Louis* (from Carnet 10), 1917, black ink and white gouache on paper, FLC

436. Charles-Edouard Jeanneret, *Romantic River Landscape with Bridge* (from Carnet 10), 1917, watercolor on paper, FLC

437. Charles-Edouard Jeanneret, *Romantic View of Paris*, 1917, pencil and watercolor on paper, FLC [209]

438. Charles-Edouard Jeanneret, *Study of Chartres Cathedral* (from Carnet 10), 1917, colored pencil and watercolor on paper, FLC

ARCHITECTURAL HISTORY

Le Corbusier appreciated the Gothic as one of the great achievements of architecture. *Chartres Cathedral* was the first in a series of studies of this subject, which reveal a rapid, skillful draftsmanship (fig. 438). This taste for Gothic just before the launch of the Purist movement shows the exceptional scope of Le Corbusier's references, as would soon become even more apparent in the photographs illustrating his writings during the period of *L'Esprit nouveau*. His receptivity to works of the past had as its corollary a nonconformity in the manner in which he reused them. *Nature morte avec coupe de fruits, lampe, bougier et boîte de cigarettes* (Still life with cup of fruit, lamp, candle, and cigarette box), one of the most surprising still lifes devoted to the theme of the table, owes its originality to the decorative scene on the lampshade (fig. 439). On it Le Corbusier showed the Pyramid of Caius Cestius, an ancient Roman monument that particularly interested him (he kept a postcard of it). The pyramid was at this time associated with light and was to be among the constants of the Purist grammar. In a sense it precedes the cube in *La Cheminée* (The Mantelpiece) while also indicating Le Corbusier's own cultural references.

EROTIC INTERLUDE

This same lamp and its motif (fig. 439)appear in a Le Corbusier drawing entitled *Deux nus féminins* (Two female nudes; fig. 442). Le Corbusier annotated this erotic lesbian scene: "the latest work by Rupert Carabin. It will be kept in a costly chest."[18] Ever since his arrival in Paris, Le Corbusier had frequented the studio of sculptor Carabin, who owned a collection of photographs.[19] This drawing depicts two views of an amorous scene sculpted by Carabin and reveals Le Corbusier's voyeurism. The sketch is based on a sculpture, which does not seem to be the case for other drawings, possibly from life, relating to this same theme,[20] even as it also shows the manner in which Le Corbusier's gaze sought a foothold, with sexuality one of the elements at stake. At this time, lesbianism was an accepted facet of the artistic and literary milieu of the Parisian scene in which Le Corbusier circulated. The writer Nathalie Clifford Barney, who hosted a literary salon, lived at the same address as Le Corbusier, and constructed for herself and Romaine Brooks a villa in the modern style at Beauvallon. It is appropriate to consider the possible sexualization of forms in Purist paintings.

Un Versailles du Grand Turc (A Versailles of the Great Turk; see fig. 221) and *Interior with Naked Woman dozing in a Chair* (fig. 440)can be related to one another by subject matter and by the indolent pose of the figure, which is given a fullness like that in the stems and petals of Le Corbusier's flowers. The simplified volumes also suggest that Matisse's sculp-

439. Charles-Edouard Jeanneret, *Still life with a Bowl of Fruit, a Lamp, a Candle and a Packet of Cigarettes* (from Carnet 10), 1917, watercolor on paper, FLC

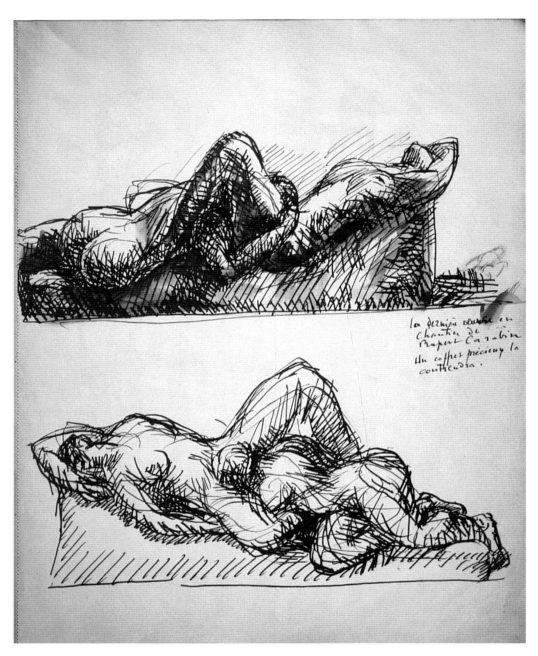

440. Charles-Edouard Jeanneret, *Interior with naked woman dozing in a chair*, 1919, pencil and gouache on paper, FLC

441. Henri Matisse, *Nu couché I*, 1907, bronze

442. Charles-Edouard Jeanneret, *Deux nus féminins* (Two Female Nudes, Study after a Sculpture by Rupert Carabin; from Carnet 10), 1917, pen on paper, FLC

tures might have been an inspiration. In fact Le Corbusier displayed a version of Matisse's *Nu couché* (Reclining nude; fig. 441) on a shelf in the Villa Stein perhaps as a statement: his architecture was in harmony with the body. The intimate and sculptural world of Matisse probably guided Le Corbusier in this search. Even as Matisse's art constituted an alternative to the dematerialized and fragmented of the cubists, it induced a perception of corporality and spirituality, as well as color, which might have influenced the later experience of the architect. Several works by Matisse were published in *La Peinture moderne*, written and published with Ozenfant.[21] It is also possible that the nude in *Un Versailles du Grand Turc* was inspired by the sculptures in the park at Versailles, given the enigmatic title that reveals a mix of references (see cat. no. 5).

VENUS AND THE SHELL

Le Corbusier was influenced by past and present artistic culture, from which he quoted in his own work. *La Naissance de Vénus* (The birth of Venus; fig. 444) is treated with and humor in a fauvist harmony of colors. At the same time he was working on *Eve s'enfuyant du Paradis terrestre* (Eve fleeing the earthly paradise; now in the Fondation Le Corbusier), a study after Masaccio of a very different subject.

These studies of nudes, which were invariably in small format, illuminate certain iconographic aspects of his still lifes. The scallop shell, an attribute of Venus that Le Corbusier depicted vertically like a crown, is found in other works, including *Femme et coquillage* (Woman and shell), an oil painting executed before 1918 (fig. 445). In *Nature morte au coquillage* (Still life with shell; fig. 443), the shell, placed beside a book, water glass, and some flowers, suggests feminine and sexual symbolism. It is found again in 1918 beside a bottle of Médoc in a pencil drawing (now in the Fondation Le Corbusier), that shows the change of style corresponding to the emergence of Purism, which nevertheless evokes another attitude. These were to change again, in 1928, becoming more imaginary than real, while the shell, associated with the natural world of the beach, will figure again, among objects eliciting a poetic reaction.

F.D.

443. Charles-Edouard Jeanneret, *Nature morte au coquillage (Still life with Shells)*, 1917, pencil and gouache on paper, FLC

444. Charles-Edouard Jeanneret, *The Birth of Venus*, after Botticelli (Carnet 10), 1917, pencil and watercolor on paper, FLC

445. Charles-Edouard Jeanneret, *Femme et coquillage sur fond bleu (Woman and Shells against a Blue Background)*, 1915–16, oil on canvas, FLC [44]

FLOWERS

Around 1917 Le Corbusier executed several still lifes that reveal his interest in floral motifs. *Study of Pinks* shows his ease with this genre, which he had begun to paint as a student (fig. 447). The perspective from above occurs again in the *Nature morte avec vase, fleurs et pommes* (Still life with vase, flowers, and apples), in which Le Corbusier intensifies the color contrasts and their expressivity (fig. 448). A similar perspective characterized *Deux nus féminins* (fig. 442), which invites the viewer to find a parallel between the treatment of the subjects, or at least to consider the feminine connotations of the floral motif.

Nature morte avec vase aux anémones (Still life with vase of anemones) reveals an important change, giving proof of a less spontaneous approach to reality (fig. 446). A frontal perspective seeks to coordinate the placement of the objects in space. The foreground, composed of various objects, is organized around the vertical axis established by the vase and anemones. A bowl of fruit is placed in the background and a mantelpiece closes the space with its "grooved" decorative motif, books, and footed bowl. The artist takes on reality with more naturalism, while his palette is brightened to offer tonalities of blue and ocher.

Nature morte aux toucans (Still life with toucans) is representative of still lifes in which Le Corbusier associated the decorative motif of the vase and flowers with more personal elements (fig. 449). The black-edged envelope, suggestive of mourning, placed to the side bears the address of the rue Jacob. The title was prompted by the illustration of two toucans, introducing an exotic note into the world of the artist. These colored birds harmonize with the overall composition while demonstrating the persistence of subtle ornamental effects and a certain pointilism in Le Corbusier's work at this time. Again capable of being linked to fauvism, *Nature morte aux toucans* reflects the diversity of Le Corbusier's sources of inspiration, such as his attachment to hidden messages as denoted by the fragment of the illustration in the upper right. The black border, again reminiscent of mourning, probably signals that Le Corbusier was about to change direction in his work.

F.D.

446. Charles-Edouard Jeanneret, *Nature morte avec vases aux anémones* (Still life with a Vase of Anemones), 1917, pencil and gouache on drawing paper, FLC

447. Charles-Edouard Jeanneret, *Study of Pinks* (from Carnet No. 10), 1917, watercolor on paper, FLC

448. Charles-Edouard Jeanneret, *Nature morte avec vase, fleurs et pommes* (Still life with Vase, Flowers, and Apples, from Carnet No. 10), 1917, gouache on paper, FLC

449. Charles-Edouard Jeanneret, *Nature morte aux toucans* (Still life with Toucans), c. 1917, pencil and watercolor on cardboard, FLC

45. A FRIEND: PAUL-THÉOPHILE ROBERT

450. Paul-Théophile Robert, *Nature morte à la cafetière et au journal* (Still life with a Coffee Pot and Newspaper), 1919, oil on canvas, private collection [62]

DIALOGUE WITH PURISM

P.-Théophile Robert and Charles-Edouard Jeanneret became acquainted as early as 1908–9. Robert, during his first trip to Paris, between 1900 and 1907, had met the architects Auguste and Claude Perret, with whom he was to enjoy a decades-long friendship. In 1908 he sent them a letter of introduction for Jeanneret[22] at a time when Jeanneret was already working in the Perret studio. Between 1909 and 1918, Jeanneret traveled several times to Saint-Blaise (Neuchâtel), to the house where Robert lived and worked. A few letters document his visits and tell of the friendship and mutual interests shared by these two artists from Neuchâtel. In March 1918 Jeanneret informed Robert that he was in close contact with Amédée Ozenfant, "a painter who is up to his eyes in *business* like me and . . . who, by lamplight at his desk in the evening, paints things of a remarkable force and strong modernism."[23] Beginning in November 1918 Jeanneret asked Robert to use his contacts in Switzerland to help distribute the first volume of *Commentaires*, which Jeanneret and Ozenfant had just completed.[24] At this time Jeanneret wrote that he deplored being more and more "absorbed by his *business*." He worked eighteen-hour days, but did "very little painting."[25]

Robert wished to settle in Paris immediately after World War I. To facilitate this move, Jeanneret wrote a letter hiring him as a decorator in his office, and on December 21, 1918, Robert was able to leave Switzerland for Paris where he was welcomed by Jeanneret and Ozenfant. Just prior to this, Robert felt himself to be at a turning point in his work: "I would have liked to send you photos of my latest paintings. I prefer to bring them to you; I think you will be surprised by the changes that have occurred in my work, or rather by the development in which my studies of these last years have culminated."[26] Impatient to join Jeanneret and Ozenfant in Paris, he wrote that he could not "wait to get to work 'with the machine operating at full pressure,'" anticipating the intensity of the discussions and exchange of ideas the three painters would have in Paris.[27]

In March 1919 the Galerie Thomas in Paris organized an exhibition of Purist paintings. In a letter to Louis Vauxelles on February 25, 1919, Ozenfant rejoiced that other painters, including Robert, were joining them. He wrote: "We shall have the pleasure, in about two weeks, of inviting you to the Galerie Thomas to see a few works by

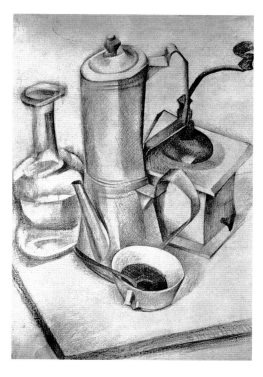

Robert, who has been won over to the Purist group."[28]

The mutual investigations that occurred in the studio in the rue Jacob were to last only until April 1919. Around April 10, Robert returned to Switzerland, but not before arranging to rent a studio of his own in Paris the following year.

Jeanneret and Ozenfant were understandably attracted to Robert's work. In their manifesto, *Après le cubisme*, they defined their objectives as aspiring to a new art that was "static, clear, lucid, organic, general, serious, controlled, concentrated, clearly conceived and clearly executed."[29]

In Robert's still lifes of 1918, his explorations were already leaning in that direction. Robert's *Nature morte à la cafetière et au journal* (Still life with coffeepot and newspaper; fig. 450) of 1919 was the culmination of this, with its balanced composition, precise execution, deep atmosphere, and rigor. The painter suceeded in creating a harmonious organization between symmetry and asymmetry by dividing the canvas into four unequal rectangles, shifting vertical and horizontal intersection in the lower right. This permitted Robert to plot diagonally the exact strategic center of the painting: the axis upon which he aligned the newspaper, jam jar, and cup on the napkin. This axis is reinforced by the chromatic palette. The objects placed on the diagonal, all white with various gray highlights, illuminate a group with muted colors—several shades of gray, blue, and dark green. As in the Purist language, Robert's painting allied tradition and modernity, even if only by the type of objects represented—classic objects, such as the jam jar and cup placed on the napkin, or modern ones such as the coffeepot, a motif also found in Jeanneret's *Nature morte avec cafetière, livres, pipe et verre* (Still life with coffeepot, books, pipe, and glass; fig. 452) and in Juan Gris's *Nature morte avec cafetière* (Still life with coffeepot; fig. 451).

In the same manner, the red cube on which Jeanneret places the bowl in *Le bol rouge* (The red bowl; see fig. 167) of 1919 recalls the parallelepiped in the background of Robert's *Nature morte*, which also functions as the support for a simple object, a box.

Sharing the studio in the rue Jacob during those first exciting months of 1919 certainly gave Robert's painting a new orientation. Nonetheless, Purist principles of harmony, order, and clarity were already the keywords in his art before that collaborative experience. In his still lifes of 1918–20, Robert added his personal touch, which was closer to nature than to the machine aesthetic, expressing the silent poetry of objects without removing them from their objective reality.

C.C.

451. Juan Gris, *Nature morte avec cafetière* (Still life with a Coffee Pot), 1915–16, pencil on paper, private collection

452. Charles-Edouard Jeanneret, *Nature morte avec cafetière, livres, pipe et verre* (Still life with Coffee Pot, Books, Pipe, and Glass), 1918 (?), pencil on paper, FLC

273

46. PURISM

453. Charles-Edouard Jeanneret, *Nature morte avec livre ouvert, pipe, verre et boîte d'allumettes* (Still life with an Open Book, Pipie, Glass, and Box of Matches), 1918 (?), pencil and watercolor on paper, FLC

OZENFANT'S LESSON: "LA CHEMINÉE"

In his *Nature morte avec livre ouvert, pipe, verre et boîte d'allumettes* (Still life with open book, pipe, glass, and matchbox; fig. 453), Le Corbusier took an approach to pencil drawing that simplified the object and brought into play Purist methodology. This development parallels the choice of an iconography composed of familiar objects evocative of cubist still lifes, such as the coffeepot in *Nature morte avec cafetière* (Still life with coffeepot; fig. 452), from 1915–16 which recalls a drawing by Juan Gris. Le Corbusier's drawing did not serve as a preliminary sketch for a painting, however, unlike his *Nature morte avec livre ouvert, pipe, verre et boîte d'allumettes*, the painted version of which (now in a private collection) must have been executed after *La Cheminée* (The mantelpiece; fig. 454). Brightened with watercolor, the drawing shows that Le Corbusier retained from the preceding composition the glass and pipe, to which he added a box of matches and a book, open to illustrations borrowed from Auguste Choisy's *Histoire de l'architecture*.[30] This direct citation of learned culture shows the role not only of this book, but also of architectural references and classical models in the formulation of Purism. A watercolor datable to 1917, *Nature morte au coquillage* (Still life with shell; fig. 443), includes another open book resting on a table, but it is shown in a stylistic context contrary to the values of Purism.

La Cheminée was painted by Le Corbusier in October 1918, while Ozenfant was teaching him how to paint smooth, flat surfaces and volumes, in a color range of brown, ocher, rose, and white shades. Both the painting and a preliminary drawing were reproduced in *Bulletin Thomas*, published on the occasion of Le Corbusier and Ozenfant's first Purist exhibition.[31] The choice of subject, however, is original, serving as a manifesto on the architectonic orientations of the "Corbusian" gaze. If Le Corbusier had been inspired by an actual location—his apartment—he framed the space at the bottom left, painting with a refined realism the upper part of a molding fragment. Thus he reveals his own attention to the formal game of architectural details, from which he would ultimately remove all ornamentation in order to elaborate one of the structural principles of his architecture. In his painting Jeanneret adopted a slightly skewed perspective, with a vanishing point off to the left. On the narrow horizontal plane, he arranges two books and a white cube. The presence of the books indicates the importance he and Ozenfant placed on intellectual reflection when they were putting together *Après le cubisme*. In this context, to paint a cube corresponded to a critique of cubist deconstruction, while affirming the existence of plastic constants that Le Corbusier postulated from the mathematical grammar of geometric solids. Le Corbusier here executed a conceptual picture, upon which he built his reputation as an architect-painter.

F.D.

454. Charles-Edouard Jeanneret, *La cheminée* (The Mantelpiece), 1918, oil on canvas, FLC [47]

NATURE MORTE À L'OEUF

The year 1919 was marked by the execution of still lifes showing Le Corbusier's engagement with the Purist program that he and Ozenfant were developing, according to a plastic method. The two artists intensified their approach to everyday objects, using a geometric grid that emphasized the architectonic dimension of their purpose as painters. In *Le Bol rouge* Purist principles were moving toward a more complex approach to space. Le Corbusier made several preparatory drawings for this painting, concentrating on its composition, particularly the placement of the roll of paper, which in the final composition is in the same oblique alignment as the pipe. In another version of this painting, *Le Bol blanc* (The white bowl; Kunstmuseum, Saint Gallen; see fig. 167) the paper sheet, placed flat, is replaced by two squares forming a lozenge. The pencil drawing (fig. 445) reproduced here signals by the absence of the central part that the artist had envisioned the possibility of variations within a fixed structure. The cube upon which the bowl is placed shows the importance Le Corbusier attached to this geometric form, which he had also included in *La Cheminée*. Here the cube is part of an exploration of the notion of balance, both philosophical and compositional. The bowl is poised on the edge of the cube, and the bowl's interior is divided by light and shadow. The abstract background is composed of a thin band across the bottom two flat areas, equally divided between volume and surface, figure and abstraction. A painting by Ozenfant, *Verre, bouteille, miroir et leurs ombres* (Glass, bottle, mirror, and their shadows; Kunstmuseum, Basel), from 1918 is based on an identical division of the surface.

Nature morte à l'oeuf (Still life with egg) takes up this same division of the composition, but in a larger format, a standard "40-franc" canvas as recommended in "Le Purisme" (fig. 456).[32] In this painting Le Corbusier develops the iconography of *objet-types*—glasses, bottles, a carafe, a stack of plates, a pitcher—which he multiplies through the projection of shadows even as he emphasizes the stylization of their forms. The open book and square create a continuity with the preceding compositions , and the envelope recalls the even earlier *Nature morte aux toucans* (fig. 449). The egg, however, is a new theme. A perfect shape and an almost mystical symbol, the egg joins other small forms, such as shells, that Le Corbusier chose to isolate in space. While working on the formal purity of figurative signs, Le Corbusier began to develop a mode of representation that stressed the geometric armature of objects and situated them in a perspective from above. If this was inspired by axonometric perspective, he also included references to industrial forms and played with color contrasts that permitted him to set the solidity of the browns against the unexpected lightness of the book, painted in clear blue and yellow tones.

F.D.

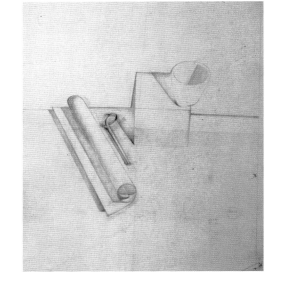

455. Charles-Edouard Jeanneret, *Study for "The Red Bowl,"* 1919 (?), pencil on tracing paper, pasted on white paper, FLC

276

456. Charles-Edouard Jeanneret, *Nature morte à l'œuf*
(Still Life with an Egg), 1919, oil on canvas, FLC [48]

NATURE MORTE À LA PILE D'ASSIETTES

During the 1920s, Le Corbusier completed a group of still lifes that are distinguished by the architectonic presence of objects in space. *Nature morte à la pile d'assiettes et au livre* (Still life with stack of plates and book) and a variation at the Kunstmuseum Basel constitute a synthesis of the studies Le Corbusier had made with Ozenfant since 1918 (fig. 458). This painting relates to the compositional development of two paintings in particular: *Nature morte avec livre, verre et pipe* and *Nature morte à l'oeuf*. Another picture, *Nature morte au violon rouge* (Still life with red violin; at the Fondation Le Corbusier) is also relevant; in it the same iconographic elements of the open book, stack of plates, and two pipes are in this case in a vertical format. The painting at the Museum of Modern Art, New York (Fig. 457), is distinguished by its geometric and chromatic arrangement, by the balance of its composition wherein a formal singularity parallels the definition of the theoretical program of Purism.

The iconography is relatively simple: guitar, stack of plates, book, carafe, glass, pipes, and bottles. Le Corbusier grouped the objects around the central axis of the painting, which coincides with the vertical spine of the open book. The neck of the guitar identifies the horizontal middle, and the objects are arranged in four planes: the book first, plates and carafe second, guitar, pipe, and glass third, and, finally, the bottle in the background and the profile of another guitar body. The three-dimensionality of the objects is indicated by shading and a raised viewpoint which allows the association according to an axonometric perspective of a view from above and an elevation. The picture ground is divided into a colored plane for the lower part and, in the upper part, several vertical planes that seem abstract on the right while on the left suggest a narrow passage between two rooms.

The point of view has a cinematographic character, bringing together several spatio-temporal sequences on the surface of the painting. A comparison of this painting with the version at the Kunstmuseum Basel reveals that the chromatic variations of the latter underscore the density of browns and greens and the modeling of the objects by light and shadow. The version in New York, which is dynamic and warmer, through its diversified harmony of the colors blue, red, pink, and ocher, and through its contrasts between somber and bright tones, concentrates more on surface effects and the arrangement of the planes in space.

Ozenfant and Le Corbusier codified the approach to painting that they had begun to explore in *Après le cubisme*. They drew on the logical and scholarly quest for a complex system that sought to form plastic elements from the characteristics and constants of objects. Affirming the architectural character of its forms, the open book placed on the plane of the table in *Nature morte avec livre ouvert, pipe, verre et boîte d'allumettes* (fig. 453) leans vertically to recall a molding, while the stack of plates evokes a column, perhaps, or plumbing pipes or a chimney. The play of the stem pipes reflected in the drinking glass also suggests the tools from a mechanic's toolbox. The curves of the guitar and case anticipate forms later to be found in Le Corbusier's architecture. While purifying his formal language, Le Corbusier was also formulating the plastic vocabulary that he would develop in his architecture and the decorative arts. Thus in 1936, on the occasion of the exhibition *Cubism and Abstract Art*, Alfred H. Barr made an inspired comparison between the forms of *Nature morte à la pile d'assiettes et au livre* and those of the Villa Savoye (1929–30), the *fauteuil à dossier basculant* (armchair with reclining back; 1928), and the terrace of the Beistegui apartment (1929–30).[33] This comparison (fig. 162) made it possible to confirm that painting preceded architecture and was the formal and semantic matrix of Purism. If painting set the tone for architecture by situating it within the development of modern painting since cubism (upon which Purism imposed a program of rationalization), it may always have been thus in the development of Le Corbusier's work. His earliest training leads one to consider the tangible character of this hypothesis, which cannot be reduced to a situation in which the painter redeploys his vocation in the realm of architecture. Le Corbusier relied heavily on the whole of artistic production in identifying plastic constants for the organization of technical elements in his new language.

F.D.

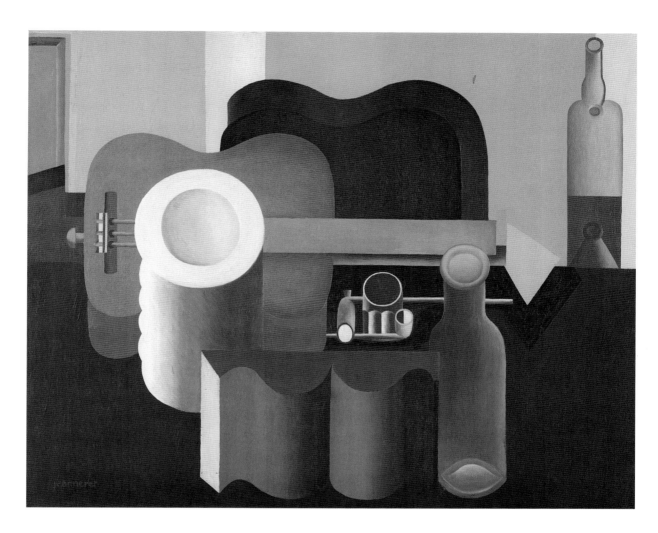

457. Charles-Edouard Jeanneret, *Nature morte à la pile d'assiettes et au livre* (Still life with a Pile of Plates and a Book), 1920, oil on canvas, Museum of Modern Art, New York [49]

458. Charles-Edouard Jeanneret, *Nature morte à la pile d'assiettes* (Still life with a Pile of Plates), 1920, oil on canvas, Kunstmuseum Basel

47. LE SIPHON

In 1921–22, the repertoire of *objet-types* did not change fundamentally, but there were new developments. In studies of formal groupings, objects became flatter and more abstract, affirming the planar quality of the painting. The axonometric construction of objects was abandoned in order to affirm the pure linear contours of the objects. Two drawings—*Study for a still life with carafe and pitcher* (fig 459) and *Nature morte avec verre, théière, pipe et bilboquet* (Still life with glass, teapot, pipe, and cup-and-ball game; fig. 460)—still present circular forms corresponding to the projection of the exterior surface of objects, for example a ball or glass, but the objects are almost two-dimensional, the exterior and interior forms nearly coincident. Using simple everyday objects, Le Corbusier succeeded in creating complex plastic effects, while also simplifying the surfaces and volume, and showing a deliberate attention to details. In the pastel (fig. 460), he also imparts a sensuality recalling his gouaches and watercolors. While affirming the richness of the expression of the drawing through different techniques, Le Corbusier explores and finalizes his compositions through preliminary pencil sketches. His *Three sketches with small pitcher, glass, pipe, and cards* drawn on a program from the Salle Bullier for an evening costume party in Montparnasse, could have been in accord with a more festive vision of life (fig. 461). The composition of *Nature morte au siphon* (Still life with siphon; fig. 462), one of the emblematic paintings for the period, was prepared through numerous studies.[34] A play of surfaces and lines forms a nearly abstract constellation, beginning with horizontal and vertical lines grounding a superimposed wine bottle–siphon. If the objects coordinate with one another through transparencies or linear connections that reinforce a flat-washed color, the composition owes its originality to the doubled and reversed form of the guitar. This form creates a play of curves and counter-curves that become more taut as the forms detach themselves positively and nega-

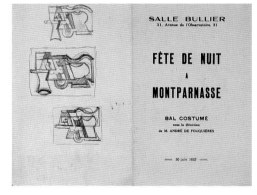

tively from the background through a contrast of alternating light and dark colors, reinforced on the right by a shadow. Pink and blue tones, which contrast to the whites, together underline the sweet, musical harmony of this painting, in which each form-color has found its precise place.

F.D.

459. Charles-Edouard Jeanneret, *Etude puriste* (Purist Study), c. 1921, pencil on paper, FLC [258]

460. Charles-Edouard Jeanneret (Le Corbusier), *Nature morte avec verre, théière, pipe et bilboquet* (Still life with a Glass, Teapot, Pipe, and Toy), 1921 (?), pastel on tracing paper, FLC [262]

461. Charles-Edouard Jeanneret (Le Corbusier), *Three sketches with small pitcher, glass, pipe and cards*, 1922, pencil on paper, FLC [263]

462. Charles-Edouard Jeanneret (Le Corbusier), *Nature morte au siphon* (Still life with a Siphon), 1921, oil on canvas, FLC [50]

NOTES

INTRODUCTION

1. Jacques Gubler, "De la montre au papillon," *Rassegna*, no. 3, 1980 ("I clienti di le Corbusier"), pp. 7–14. See also Jacques Gubler, "La Chaux-de-Fonds," *INSA* (Inventar der Neueren Schweizer Architektur), vol. 3, 1982, pp. 127–218.
2. Gubler, "De la montre au papillon," *op.cit.*
3. Karl Marx, *Das Kapital*, 1867, vol. II, chapter 12, § 3, note 32 (translated by the authors).
4. See Stanislaus von Moos, *Industrieästhetik*, Disentis: Desertina, 1992, pp. 37–41, for a summary of these developments.
5. See Terence Riley and Barry Bergdoll, eds. *Mies in Berlin*, New York: Museum of Modern Art, 2001.
6. See the list of sources cited, p.313.

CHAPTER I
VOYAGE EN ZIGZAG
Stanislaus von Moos

1. [. . . flaches Deck, Bullaugen, Fallreep, Reling, leuchten weiss und südlich, haben als Schiffe Lust, zu verschwinden], Ernst Bloch, *Das Prinzip Hoffnung* (Frankfurt: Suhrkamp, 1959): 858–59; in English, *The Principle of Hope*, vol. 2, trans. by Neville Plaice, Stephen Plaice, and Paul Knight (Cambridge, Mass. MIT Press, 1996): 733.
2. [Seit über einer Generation steht darum dieses Stahlmöbel-, Betonkuben-, Flachdach-Wesen geschichtslos da, hochmodern und langweilig, scheinbar kühn und echt trivial, voll Hass gegen die Floskel angeblich jedes Ornaments und doch mehr im Schema festgerannt als je eine Stilkopie im schlimmen neunzehnten Jahrhundert.], Bloch, *Prinzip Hoffnung* (1959): 860; *Principle of Hope* (1996): 735.
3. Jean Petit, *Le Corbusier lui-même* (Geneva: Editions Rousseau, 1970): 18.
4. Among the few studies on Le Corbusier as a literary figure see Jean-Louis Cohen, "De l'oral à l'écrit: 'Précisions' et les conférences latino-américaines de 1929," in *Le Corbusier: Ecritures*, ed. Claude Prélorenzo (Paris: Fondation Le Corbusier, 1993): 48–53, and Guillemette Morel-Journal, "Le Corbusier: Structure rhétorique et volonté littéraire," in: ibid., pp. 15–30. Morel-Journal singles out William Ritter, Paul Valéry, and Blaise Cendrars as authors who served to "temper" Le Corbusier's literary style.
5. That *Voyage d'orient* (1966) is written in a style similar to Taine's has already been noted Turner, *Education* (1977): 42f.; Turner also gives a complete list of the travel literature owned or consulted by Jeanneret in connection with his trip. Jeanneret was also familiar with works by Pierre Loti and Claude Farrère, although they are not included in the list; see Giuliano Gresleri, *Le Corbusier. Viaggio in Oriente. Gli inediti di Charles-Edouard Jeanneret fotografo e scrittore* (Venice: Marsilio, 1984): 43f.; and H. Allen Brooks, *Le Corbusier's Formative Years: Charles-Edouard Jeanneret at La Chaux-de-Fonds* (Chicago and London: University of Chicago Press, 1997): 256f.
   About half of the articles Jeanneret/Le Corbusier wrote while traveling on his "Voyage d'Orient" were published between 20 July and 25 November 1911 in *La Feuille d'Avis de La Chaux-de-Fonds*. He tried and failed to have them all published in the *Mercure de France* in 1914; ultimately they were published posthumously as *Voyage d'orient* (Paris: Forces vives, 1966).
6. This is also why the issue of orientalism and colonialism is of topical interest in connection with Le Corbusier; see Zeynep Celik, "Le Corbusier, Orientalism, Colonialism," *Assemblage* 17 (1992): 61–77.
7. [10 décembre 1929 / à bord du *Lutetia* / au large de Bahia./ La Compagnie Sud-Atlantique a mis aimablement à ma disposition un appartement de luxe et je puis ainsi, loin du bruit de la machine et au point le plus calme du bateau, entreprendre la rédaction de ces dix conférences. . . . / C'est le plein été tropical, le soleil est magnifique; ils ont, pendant la semaine précédente, créé devant mes yeux, l'inoubliable, l'enthousiasmante féerie de Rio de Janeiro. . . .], LC, *Précisions sur un état présent de l'architecture et de l'urbanisme* (Paris: Crès, 1930): 1.
8. Ibid., p. 3;. see also Stanislaus von Moos, "Les Femmes d'Alger," in *Le Corbusier et la Méditerannée*, exhib. cat., Vieille Charité (Marseille: Editions Parenthèses, 1987): 191–99; and Jean-Louis Cohen, "L'ombre de l'oiseau planeur / A Sambra de pássaro planador," in *Le Corbusier: Rio de Janeiro, 1929 1936*, ed. Y. Tsiomis (Rio de Janeiro: Secretaria Municipal de Urbanismo / Centro de Arquitetura e Urbanismo de Rio de Janeiro, 1998): 147–49 (French); 58–63 (Portuguese).
9. Albert Jeanneret, personal communication, Le Lac, Corseaux, ca. 1968; see Stanislaus von Moos, *Le Corbusier. Elemente einer Synthese* (Frauenfeld – Stuttgart: Huber, 1968): 13. The information appeared so anecdotal and Töpffer (1799–1846) seemed so random a reference that the detail was deleted from subsequent editions of the book, including the English translation, *Le Corbusier. Elements of a Synthesis* (Cambridge, Mass. and London: MIT Press, 1979). Rodolphe Töpffer, *Voyages en zigzag: Ou excursions d'un pensionnat en vacances dans les cantons suisses et sur le revers italien des Alpes* (1846; reprint, Geneva: Slatkine, 1998).
10. See Philippe Kaenel, *Le métier d'illustrateur, 1830–1880: Rodolphe Töpffer, Grandville, Gustave Doré* (Paris: Editions Messene, 1996).
11. Thanks to a 1997 exhibition, there has been renewed interest in the Grand Tour; see Andrew Wilton and Ilaria Bignamini, eds., *Grand Tour: The Lure of Italy in the Eighteenth Century*, exhib. cat., Tate Gallery, London - Palazzo delle Esposizioni, Roma (London: Tate Gallery, 1997). The essays include , e.g., Cesare de Seta,"Grand Tour: The Lure of Italy in the Eighteenth Century" (pp. 13–20). See also Yves Hersant, "'Grand Tour' et Illuminismo," in *Grand Tour: Viaggi narrati e dipinti*, ed. Cesare de Seta (Napoli: Electa, 2001): 20–27; and Attilio Brilli, *Quando viaggiare era un'arte: Il romanzo del Grand Tour* (Bologna: Il Mulino, 1995).
12. "A propos, faites venir ce livre-ci: les aventures de Monsieur Vieux-Bois (édité à Genève)... Vous pouvez voir là un Busch français, latin, et surtout un précurseur comme dessinateur. Je ferais volontiers une thèse de doctorat sur Töpffer" (That reminds me, please send the following book: the adventures of Monsieur Vieux-Bois [published in Geneva]. . . . In it you will find a French or Latin Busch, obviously a precursor as a draftsman. I should be delighted to write a doctoral thesis on Töpffer), CEJ to August Klipstein, n.d. [1911]; FLC E 26-145.
13. De Fayet [pseud.], "Toepffer précurseur du cinéma," in *L'Esprit nouveau*, no. 11–12 (1921): 1336–43. "De Fayet" is a pseudonym generally attributed to Amédée Ozenfant, but Ch.-E.Jeanneret also occasionally used it. Not by coincidence, given the magazine's anti-German stance, the spelling of Töpffer's name dropped the umlaut and became more correctly French. Le Corbusier's copy of *L'Histoire du DocteurFestus* is now in the FLC. Brooks indicates that Jeanneret used an illustration from the *Voyage en zigzag* in CEJ, "La Maison Suisse," in *Etrennes Helvétiques: Almanach Illustré* (Paris/Dijon/La Chaux-de-Fonds, 1914); see Brooks *Formative Years* (1997): 355 and 355, n. 42. I have been unable, however, to locate this illustration.
14. In fact, these picture books by Töpffer occupy a key role in the history of that genre. See David Kunzle, *The History of the Comic Strip. The 19th Century* (Berkeley / Los Angeles / Oxford: University of California Press, 1990) pp. 28–71; Thierry Groensteen and Benoît Peeters, *Töpffer: L'Invention de la bande dessinée* (Paris: Hermann, 1994); and Philippe Junod, "Actualité de Rodolphe Töpffer: Un précurseur de la sémiotique visuelle?", in: *Etudes de lettres* 4 (1983): 75–84.
15. See Turner, *Education* (1977): 237.
16. A rock crystal that his father had brought home from a trip in the Alps variously served as a motif in Le Corbusier's painting; for an interpretation of it as a symbolic self-portrait, see Mogens Krustrup, *Porte Email / Emaljeporten / la porte emaillée / the enamel door: Le Corbusier, Palais de l'Assemblée de Chandigarh* (Copenhagen: Arkitektens Forlag / Kunstakademiets Forlag, 1991): 45, 61.
17. [Ainsi que le palais goûte la diversité d'un menu bien fait, nos yeux sont prêts à des jouissances ordonnées.], LC, "Classement et choix," in *L'Esprit nouveau*, no. 21: n.p.; reprint, LC, *Urbanisme* (Paris: Crès, 1925): 56
18. [Péra: la dent de scie de la ville des marchands, des pirates, des chercheurs d'or. / Stamboul: la ferveur des minarets, le calme des dômes aplatis. Allah vigilant mais orientalement impérissable. / Rome: la géometrie, l'ordre implacable, guerre, civilisation, organisation. / Sienne: le tumulte angoissé du moyen-age. Enfer et Paradis.], Ibid.
19. For the most complete recent account of Jeanneret/Le Corbusier's early travels, see Giuliano Gresleri,ed., *Le Corbusier: Il viaggio in Toscana (1907)*, exhib. cat., Palazzo Pitti, Forence, (Venice: Marsilio, 1987); idem, *Viaggio in Oriente* (1984); and Brooks, *Formative Years* (1997): 95–306. Earlier accounts are not listed here. My own understanding of Le Corbusier's visual education has been enriched by German Hidalgo Hermosilla, "La Arquitectura del Croquis. Dibujos de Ch.E.Jeanneret en Italia, 1907, y en Oriente 1911: un estudio de sus antecedentes," Ph.D. diss., Escuela Tecnica Superior, Barcelona, 2000. Scholars have often reserved the term "Grand Tour" for Jeanneret's travels with August Klipstein, May to October 1911, from Berlin via the Balkans to Istanbul and from there via Rome and Florence to La Chaux-de-Fonds. I use the term to mean all travels undertaken by Jeanneret between 1907 and 1917: from his first trip, July 1907 to December 1909, from La Chaux-de-

Fonds to Florence, Venice, and Vienna and from there via Nuremberg and Strasbourg to Paris, finally returning to La Chaux-de-Fonds almost seventeen months after it began. I consider the excursions in 1910 and 1911 to Germany as much part of the "Grand Tour" as the various study sojourns in Paris after 1912, before Jeanneret finally decided to settle down in Paris (in 1917). For a similar view see Gérard Monnier, *Le Corbusier: Essai* (Tournai: La Renaissance du Livre, 1999): 14–22. Brooks ends the period he calls "Travels and Apprenticeships" in 1911, when what he calls the "Early Professional Career" began (1912–16); see Brooks, *Formative Years* (1997).

20. ". . . obligé de m'intéresser à tout, l'architecture embrassant absolument tout " (compelled to be interested in all things, since architecture embraces absolutely everything), CEJ to his parents, 8 October 1907, BV, quoted in English in Brooks, *Formative Years* (1997): 97; in Italian in Gresleri, *Viaggio in Toscana* (1987): 17.
21. Around seventy drawings and watercolors as well as a dozen or so photographs survive from the 1907 trip to Italy; and around three hundred drawings and watercolors, six sketchbooks (*carnets*) and more than four hundred photographs, from "Voyage d'Orient" (1911). For a facsimile of the *carnets* see: Giuliano Gresleri, ed., *Le Corbusier (Ch.-E.Jeanneret). Voyage d'Orient, Carnets* (Milan: Electa, 1987); see also idem, ed., *Le Corbusier (Ch.-E.Jeanneret): Les Voyages d'Allemagne, Carnets* (Milan: Electa, 1994).
22. An attempt to differentiate the "genres" or "representational modes" practiced by Jeanneret around 1907–12 would include at least six tentative categories: technical drawings that prefigure works of decorative art, such as furniture, carpets, or facade decoration ("industrial design"); drawings that prefigure architectural works ("architectural design"), such as plans, elevations, sections, facades, and perspectives, done either as quick drafts, working drawings, or explanatory renderings; more or less accurate (more or less free) copies of works of art from the past, including annotated surveys or studies of such works; the landscape study; the figure, portrait or nude; and finally the still-life. Photography, itself organized according to the last three genres, forms a separate category. For the fundamental study of Le Corbusier's early drawings, see Patricia May Sekler, *The Early Drawings of Charles-Edouard Jeanneret (Le Corbusier) 1902-1908* (New York and London: Garland, 1977). See also Stanislaus von Moos, "Charles Edouard-Jeanneret and the Visual Arts," in *Le Corbusier. Painter and Architect*, exhib. cat. (Aalborg: Nordjyllands Kunstmuseum, 1995): 59–82.
23. See *Le Corbusier: Le Passé à réaction poétique*, Hôtel de Sully (Paris: Caisse nationale des Monuments historiques et des Sites and Ministère de la Culture et de la Communication, 1988). For a brief general discussion of copying in the context of design reform around 1900 see Stanislaus von Moos, *Industrieästhetik*, vol. 11 (Disentis: Desertina Verlag, 1991): 215–36.
24. An example are the studies of the niches of Orsanmichele, in Florence. Whereas Jeanneret concentrates on the decorative treatment of the architectural envelope, giving the sculpture itself that stands in the niche as a mere cloud, Perrin directly focuses on the character of Donatello's figure (Fondation Perrin); see Gresleri, *Viaggio in Toscana* (1987): pl. 15.
25. Jeanneret's praise of Santa Croce is one of the rare instances in which his view emphatically differs from that expressed by Ruskin, who denounces the interior for its lack of vaulting, writing that it has "the roof of a farmhouse barn" (*Mornings in Florence* [New York: John W. Lovell [n.d.]: 14). See also Brooks, *Formative Years* (1997): 101.
26. For even more impressive examples from Pisa and Florence see Gresleri, *Viaggio in Toscana* (1987): 51, pl. 3.
27. Brooks gives a somewhat "naturalistic" reading of Jeanneret's work as he describes the "strange, luminous after-effects of a violent, early evening thunderstorm" that is rendered here as "his most moving experience in Siena" (*Formative Years* [1997]: 107). What may have made these after-effects so interesting to Jeanneret is that they were exploitable in terms of his evolving "Nabi"-taste.
28. [La couleur, elle aussi, n'est pas de description mais d'évocation; symbolique toujours. Elle est but et non moyen.], CEJ, "En Orient. Quelques impressions," in *Feuille d'Avis de La Chaux-de-Fonds*, 25 July 1911; quoted in *Le Corbusier. Peintre avant le Purisme*, exhib. cat., (La Chaux-de-Fonds: Musée des Beaux-Arts, 1987): 12. For short excerpts (translated into Italian) from the correspondence relating to the visit to Tuscany (1907) and for a selection of letters (also translated into Italian) written during the "Voyage d'Orient" (1911), see Gresleri, *Viaggio in Toscana* (1987).
29. [Ne me critiquez pas trop cette impression de la place du Pallio [*sic*] à Sienne. Vous savez que Sienne est la ville de la couleur, et que pour peu qu'un orage soit survenu, et qu'après avoir allumé tous les tons, telle une aquarelle fraîche, il s'en soit allé égrenant quelques gros nuages noirs dans un ciel de couchant vert cru, et que la terre apaisée ait exhalé sa béatitude en de merveilleuses nuées roses, venant lécher les murs tapissés de châles de Perse du formidable palais communal, vous comprendrez que devant pareille symphonie on se soit laissé emballer et pénétrer de ces sonores harmonies... mais peut-être, au fait, ne comprendrez-vous pas du tout, qu'un gosse comme moi ait cru bon d'objectiver ses impressions, en une croûte fausse de dessin, de perspective et de valeurs. / Quand je repense à ce soir-là, je m'enthousiasme car vraiment c'était prenant . . .], CEJ to Charles L'Eplattenier, n.d. [1908], quoted in: Sekler, *Early Drawings* (1977): 454.
30. Cuno Amiet (1868–1958) is a likely reference. Amiet, a Swiss painter and one time admirer of Paul Gauguin, had spent some time in Pont-Aven and became associated around 1906–7 with the "Brücke" group in Dresden. Jeanneret was fairly familiar with his work, if not an admirer; see also n. 39, below.
31. [Le Dôme à 6 heures du soir est une féerie de couleur, c'est la quintessence des jaunes de toute qualité, valeur, du blanc d'ivoire et des patines noires, cela sur un outre-mer d'une valeur extraordinaire; à force de le regarder on le voit noir. La partie sur laquelle le baptistère projète son ombre est une douce vibration des jaunes cossus, des marbres rouges incrustés qui se réveillent, des marbres bleus qui bleuissent; c'est la revanche des surfaces planes qui vibrent et parlent doucement. - 7 heures [de] soir, ce dôme est encore plus beau que jamais, quels tons! C'est je ne sais, quel brun, ni quel bleu, c'est d'un calme! Derrière moi le ciel est orange et mauve, le vert des portes est mort, des marbres jaunes se révelent, ils sont sienne naturel, tandis que les colonnes sont d'un rose *blanc* comme un pétale d'églantine. Sous les petits arcs des voûtes on dirait les fresques d'ici à côté, les belles fresques or et rouges; l'ombre portée diffusée des colonnettes est vert émeraude et le marbre noir gris comme certaines gorges d'oiseaux. Dans cet andante éclatent les 3 mosaiques, dans l'or desquelles miroite le plus beau couchant; doucement vibre la robe verte de la vierge. Les carmin ont disparu - des bambinos jouent sur le devant, un petit en robe rouge écarlate devant une des portes de bronze vert. - A quoi donc nous servent les peintres? L'émotion des pierres! Voyez-vous, j'étais tellement emballé que je me disais: Flûte des peintres, flûte de leurs croutes, un coin du Dôme vaut mieux que tous les barbouilleurs du monde.], CEJ to Charles L'Eplattenier, quoted from Gresleri, *Viaggio in Toscana* (1987): 8.
32. Works such as *Après l'orage* make it difficult, in my view, to follow Brooks entirely when he states that Jeanneret's "taste was not characteristic of the early twentieth century but rather that of the 1860s and the Gothic Revival," and that "he was inevitably *retardataire* rather than avant-garde" (Brooks, *Formative Years* [1997]: 96 and 96, n.3).
33. CEJ to William Ritter, Neubabelsberg, 1 March 1911; see Gresleri, *Viaggio in Oriente* (1984): 392. The painting Jeanneret had seen in Munich is probably *La Corne d'or: Les Minarets* (1907; private collection); see Françoise Cachin, *Paul Signac: Catalogue raisonné de l'œuvre peint* (Paris: Gallimard, 2000): pl. p. 69; cat. no. 454.
34. Jeanneret continues: "One thing remains plausible: that Signac had been here very early in the morning." CEJ to L'Eplattenier, 18 July 1911, FLC; quoted from the Italian translation in Gresleri, *Viaggio in Oriente* (1984). The "Signac effect" is also discussed at length in a letter to Karl Ernst Osthaus, Hagen, 28 July 1911, reprinted in: *Le Corbusier: Le Passé* (1988): 162. The case has more recently been discussed in Hidalgo Hermosilla, "La Arquitectura del Croquis" (2000).
35. Adolphe Appia comes to mind with his Symbolist stage-designs that show temple areas surrounded by a sea of open space. It is not quite clear, however, whether Jeanneret was familiar with Appia's stage-designs at the Bildungsanstalt Jacques Dalcroze in Hellerau at the time of his visit to the Acropolis. In a letter to his parents of 28 October 1910 Jeanneret refers to a friend called "Appia" whom he had met in Paris, but it is not certin that this is Adolphe Appia (see, however, Gresleri, *Viaggio in Oriente* (1984): 32f.; 371).
36. LC, *Voyage d'orient* (1966): 78.
37. LC-Saugnier, *Vers une architecture* (Paris: Crès, 1923: 22.The phrase appears for the first time, if elliptically, in CEJ to L'Eplattenier, 16 January 1911, FLC: "volumes qui jouent sous la lumière en rythmes à base géométrique, joie de la forme enfin retrouvée pour le régal des yeux" (volumes playing under the light in rhythms of geometrical order, joy of form found again at last for the feast of the eyes).
38. CEJ to L'Eplattenier, 16 January 1911, FLC.
39. Jeanneret had been critical of Amiet's paintings in the Kunstmuseum in Berne describing Amiet as "crazy about colours, a man of fixed ideas, a mason deep in his soul, otherwise without any soul," CEJ to L'Eplattenier, 19 September 1907.
40. See Pierre Vaisse, "De l'architecture considérée comme un des beaux-arts," in: *Les passions Le Corbusier*, ed. Thierry Paquot (Paris: Editions de La Villette, 1989): 117–28.
41. Ibid. For Le Corbusier's changing attitude to the German cultural legacy see Stanislaus von Moos, "Der Fall Le Corbusier: Kreuzbestäubungen, Allergien, Infektionen," in *Moderne Architektur in Deutschland 1900-1950. Expressionismus und Neue Sachlichkeit*, ed. Vittorio Magnago Lampugnani and Romana Schneider, exhib. cat., Deutsches Architektur-Museum, Frankfurt (Stuttgart: Hatje, 1994): 161–84.
42. This section is partly taken from an earlier study; see Stanislaus von Moos, *Fernand Léger: 'La ville'. Zeitdruck, Grossstadt, Wahrnehmung* (Frankfurt: Fischer, 1999): 56–66.
43. For *Prose du Transsibérien et de la Petite Jehanne de France* see Anne-Marie Jaton, *Blaise Cendrars* (Geneva: Editions de l'Unicorne, n.d.): 39–46; for a complete biography see Miriam Cendrars, *Blaise Cendrars* (Paris: Editions Balland): 1993. For archetypal Cendrars attempts to "synthesize" poetry and film see Blaise Cendrars, *La fin du monde filmée par l'Ange Notre-Dame* (Paris: Editions de la Sirene, 1919); this book illustrated by Fernand Léger and designed to resemble a filmscript.
44. See Sekler, *Early Drawings* (1977): 385f. and 500f. Sekler offers no explanation for this curious stylistic device.
45. [Le ciné peut être Gargantua comme il peut être Ali Baba. Mais il peut bien d'avantage. Après avoir employé les hommes, les paysages, l'air, la mer, il peut, par le dessin animé, montrer les généses les plus inattendues; il peut, par des constructions géométriques successives, régler des virtualités impressionnantes, jusqu'ici inconcevables.], De Fayet [pseud.], "Toepffer précurseur du cinéma" (1921): 1337. The origins and logic of Le Corbusier's fascination with cinema demand to be studied in depth. He himself collaborated on a film on his early villas in 1931, and in the Philips pavilion at the Brussels World Fair in 1958, the audio-visual spectacle shown included both photography and film.
46. For the most recent and insightful discussion of *L'Esprit nouveau*, see Beatriz Colomina, *Privacy and Publicity: Modern Architecture as Mass Media* (Cambridge, Mass. and London: MIT Press, 1994), esp. pp. 76–200 (graphic design). Colomina rightly stresses the influence of advertising in the graphic design of the magazine, especially Le Corbusier's method of producing messages by cropping photographs or juxtaposing images and words in unusual ways (see ibid., pp. 124ff. and passim). She also discusses Marcel Duchamp at some length in this context (pp. 170–80), but pays less attention to more immediate allies of *L'Esprit nouveau* as Blaise Cendrars, Fernand Léger, and Robert Delaunay.
47. [Nous n'oublierons pas la démonstration que nous donna un jour de pluie un bourriquot fortement chargé. Nous étions à la fenêtre d'un immeuble fermant le haut d'une rue montante à peine [*sic*] continue. La pluie tombée à l'instant avait fait de la chaussée un tapis bien uni sur lequel les roues du char trainées par le baudet marquaient deux traits luisants. Au bas de la rue les sillons partirent parallèles aux trottoirs; mais tôt après, ils se rapprochèrent de l'un des bords, puis ensuite de l'autre, puis de nouveau du premier et ainsi de suite pendant quelque cent mètres. Puis la ligne sinueuse se détendit; les inflexions devenant moins accusées, elle retrouva le parallèle des trottoirs. Alors le baudet s'arrêta; mais comme on lui administrait le fouet, il reprit une course très sinueuse qui s'accusa de plus en plus, jusqu'à ce que arrivé au haut de la rue l'attelage disparut. . . . La leçon de l'âne est à retenir.], *Charles-Edouard Jeanneret, La Construction des villes. Genèse et devenir d'un ouvrage écrit de 1910 à 1915 et laissé inachevé par Charles-Edouard Jeanneret-Gris dit Le Corbusier*, ed. Marc E. Albert Emery (Paris and Héricourt: Editions L'Age d'Homme, 1992): 94. For the origin of the manuscript see Brooks, *Formative Years* (1997): 200–208.
48. Camillo Sitte, *Der Städtebau nach seinen künstlerischen Grundsätzen* (Vienna: Graeser, 1889). Jeanneret owned Camille Martin's French translation of Sitte's text (1902), which was slightly enlarged, with a new chapter on "streets"; the French edition played up Sitte's interest in the medieval while downplaying his interest in the Baroque, effectively putting the text through a strong "Gallic filter"; see George R. Collins and Christiane Crasemann Collins, *Camillo Sitte and the Birth of Modern City Planning* (London: Phaidon, 1965): 63–67.
49. [L'homme marche droit parce qu'il a un but; il sait où il va. ...L'âne zigzague, muse un peu, cervelle brûlée et distrait, zigzague pour éviter les gros cailloux, pour esquiver la pente,

pour rechercher l'ombre; il s'en donne le moins possible." LC, *Urbanisme* (1925): 5.

50. LC, *Quand les cathédrales étaient blanches: Voyage au pays des timides* (1937; reprint, Paris: Denoël, 1965): 58.
51. Finding "self-portraits" among Le Corbusier's enigmatic statements and figurative formulas is almost a sport. If Krustrup is correct, Le Corbusier the painter has variously used a pentagon, window, camel, eye, crystal, door, man running along a beach, and a pair of glasses as self-portrait; see Krustrup, *Porte Email* (1991): 29; 36; 45; 47; 49, and passim.
52. Like Duchamp and Picabia, Jeanneret was interested in geometry and machinery, which correspond with gendered codes, as well as decorative arts around 1914–18; see Molly Nesbit, *Their Common Sense* (**city?:** Black Dog Publishing, 2000), passim. Le Corbusier himself was not exactly afraid of playing out gender connotations in the discussion of his work.
53. [Je dessine un fleuve. Le but est précis: aller d'un point à un autre: fleuve ou idée. Surgit un incident infime, - les incidences de l'esprit: de suite, un petit coude de rien du tout, à peine sensible. L'eau est rejetée à gauche, elle entame la rive; de là, par incidence, elle est rejetée à droite. Alors, la droite n'est plus. A gauche, à droite, toujours plus profond, l'eau ronge, creuse, entame; - toujours plus élargie, l'idée bat la campagne. La droite est devenue sinueuse; l'idée s'est garnie d'incidences. La sinuosité devient caractérisée, le méandre se dessine; l'idée s'est ramifiée. . . .] [Les boucles du méandre ont fait comme des huit, et c'est imbécile. Subitement, au moment le plus désespérant, les voilà qui se touchent au point le plus gonflé des courbes! Miracle! Le fleuve coule droit! Ainsi l'idée pure a jailli, la solution est apparue. Une nouvelle étape commence. . .], LC, *Précisions* (1930): 142–43.
54. [Cette seconde maison sera donc un peu comme une *promenade architecturale*. On entre: le spectacle architectural s'offre de suite au regard; on suit un itinéraire et les perspectives se développent avec une grande variété.], *Le Corbusier et Pierre Jeanneret: Oeuvre complète,* vol. 1, *1910–1929*, ed. Willy Boesiger and Oscar Stonorov (Zürich: Girsberger, 1937): 60.
55. [Les architectures se classent en mortes ou en vivantes selon que la règle du *cheminement* n'a pas été observée, ou qu'au contraire la voilà exploitée brillammant.], LC, *Entretien avec les étudiants des écoles d'architecture* (Paris: Denoël, 1943): n.p.
56. Richard A. Etlin, *Frank Lloyd Wright and Le Corbusier: The Romantic Legacy* (Manchester and New York: Manchester University Press, 1994): 77. See also, in this context, Elisabeth Blum, *Le Corbusier's Wege: Wie das Zauberwerk in Gang gesetzt wird*, Braunschweig / Wiesbaden: Vieweg, 1988). While Etlin locates the roots of Le Corbusier's concept of the "promenade" in Romantic theory as well as in Choisy and Sitte, Blum stresses the importance of such sources as Edouard Schuré, *Les grands initiés* (Paris, 1907), in which the "path" appears linked to the concept of biological evolution as well as spiritual initiation.
57. [ACROPOLE D'ATHÉNES. Coup d'oeil sur le Parthénon, l'Erechthéion, l'Athéna Parthenos depuis les Propylées. Il ne faut pas oublier que le sol de l'Acropole est très mouvementé, avec des différences de niveaux considérables qui ont été employées pour constituer des socles imposants aux édifices. Les fausses équerres ont fourni des vues riches et d'un effet subtil; les masses asymétriques des édifices créent un rhythme intense. Le spectacle est massif, elastique, nerveux, écrasant d'acuité, dominateur.], LC-Saugnier, *Vers une architecture* (1923): 31.
58. As the phrase "sensorial rhythm" suggests, Le Corbusier's view of architecture as being defined by its unfolding in time may owe something to his profound interest in music; but unfortunately the question cannot be pursued here. See Christopher Pearson, "Le Corbusier and the Acoustical Trope: An Investigation of Its Origins," in *Journal of the Society of Architectural Historians* 56, no. 2 (1997): 168–83; and Peter Bienz, *Le Corbusier und die Musik* (Braunschweig / Wiesbaden: Vieweg, 1999).
59. This is perhaps why the project offered the pretext, as we have seen, for launching the concept of the *promenade architecturale*. It comes as no surprise that the villa serves as a witness for both Etlin's and Blum's discussions of the *promenade*; see Etlin, *Frank Lloyd Wright and Le Corbusier* (1994); and Blum, *Le Corbusier's Wege* (1988). For the design of the Villa La Roche see Tim Benton, *Les Villas de Le Corbusier et Pierre Jeanneret, 1920–1930* (Paris: Philippe Sers, 1984): 45–75; and, more recently, idem, "'Villa La Rocca'. Die Planungs- und Baugeschichte der Villa La Roche," in *Ein Haus für den Kubismus. Die Sammlung Raoul La Roche*, ed. Katharina Schmidt and Hartwig Fischer, exhib. cat., Kunstmuseum, Basel (Ostfildern-Ruit: Hatje, 1998): 227–43. See also Arthur Rüegg, ed., *Polychromie architecturale. Le Corbusier's Farbenklaviaturen von 1931 und 1959 / Le Corbusier's .Color .Keyboards from 1931 and 1959/Les .Claviers de couleurs de Le Corbusier de 1931 et de 1959* (Basel, Boston, and Berlin: Birkhäuser, 1997).
60. Kurt W. Forster, "Antiquity and Modernity in the La Roche-Jeanneret Houses of 1923," *Oppositions* 15/16 (1979): 131–53.
61. See Stanislaus von Moos, ed., *Le Corbusier: Album La Roche*, facsimile edition (Milan: Electa, 1996). Töpffer, *Voyages en zigzag* (1846 / 1998): 281-448.
62. For van Doesburg and van Eesteren as references for the final design of the hall see Bruno Reichlin, "Le Corbusier vs. De Stijl," in *De Stijl et l'architecture en France*, ed. Y.-A. Bois and B.Reichlin (Paris: Mardaga, 1985): 91–108. For more recent discussions of the hall as a stylistic enigma see Beatriz Colomina, "Where Are We?", in *Architecture and Cubism*, ed. Nancy Troy and Eve Blau (Cambridge, Mass., and London: MIT Press, 1997): 141–66, Yve-Alain Bois, "Cubistic, Cubic, and Cubist," in ibid., pp. 187–94; and Bruno Reichlin, "Jeanneret-Le Corbusier, Painter-Architect," in ibid., pp. 195–218.
63. [Blaise Cendrars et Mme Delaunay-Terck [*sic*] ont fait une PREMIÈRE TENTATIVE DE SIMULTANÉITÉ ÉCRITE où des contrastes de couleurs habituaient l'oeil à lire d'un seul regard l'ensemble d'un poème, comme un chef d'orchestre lit D'UN SEUL COUP les notes superposées dans la partition, comme on voit d'un seul coup, d'oeil les éléments plastiques imprimés d'une affiche.], quoted in Anne-Marie Jaton, *Blaise Cendrars* (n.d.):41
64. Willy Boesiger and Oscar Storonov, ed., *Le Corbusier: Oeuvre complète* (Zurich: Girsberger, 1936):189.
65. [très généreux / on affirme à l'exterieur une volonté architecturale, on satisfait à l'intérieur à tous les besoins fonctionnels (insolation, contiguités, circulation).], ibid.
66. [L'architecture arabe nous donne un enseignement précieux. Elle s'apprécie *à la marche*, avec le pied; c'est en marchant, en se déplacant que l'on voit se développer les ordonnances de l'architecture.], *Le Corbusier et Pierre Jeanneret: Oeuvre complète,* vol. 2, *1929-1934*, ed. Willy Boesiger (Zürich: Girsberger, 1935): 24.

CHAPTER 2
LE CORBUSIER AND THE GOTHIC
Pierre Vaisse

1. Henry-Russell Hitchcock and Philip Johnson, *The International Style: Architecture Since 1922* (1932; reprint, New York: W.W. Norton & Company, 1966): 24. The authors' interpretation of the International Style had been developed by Hitchcock in his earlier book, *Modern Architecture: Romanticism and Reintegration* (1929; reprint, New York: AMS Press, 1972).
2. See Luciano Patetta, "Il gotico dei goticisti come laboratorio e cantiere d'avanguardia," in *Il neogotico nel XIX e XX secolo*, ed. Rossana Bossaglia (Milan: Mazzota, 1989), 1: 309–22; and Maija Bismanis, "Medievalism and Modernism: An Architectural Link," in *L'Art et les révolutions*, Acts of the twenty-seventh International Congress of the History of Art, section 6, Survivances et réveils de l'architecture gothique (Strasbourg: Société alsacienne pour le Développement de l'Histoire de l'Art, 1992): 77–84.
3. Bruno Zevi, *Architettura e storiografia* (Turin: Piccola Biblioteca Einaudi, 1974). Zevi wrote on the indebtedness of modern architecture to the styles of the past.
4. For Le Corbusier's relationship to the art and architecture of the past, see *Le Corbusier: Le Passé à réaction poétique*, exhib. cat. (Paris: Caisse national des Monuments historiques et des Sites, 1987–88). This work contains abundant documentation, though unfortunately presented in a fragmentary and uncritical fashion.
5. The project was published in 1914 in the review *L'Education en Suisse*. See also H. Allen Brooks, "Formation," in *Le Corbusier: une encyclopédie*, ed. Jacques Lucan (Paris: Centre Georges Pompidou, 1987): 159. Brooks judges it to be in the Art Nouveau style, but of course the extent to which Art Nouveau could be inspired by Gothic is well known.
6. Viollet-le-Duc, *Dictionnaire raisonné de l'architecture française du XIe au XVIe siècle* (Paris: Bance, then Morel, 1854–68). According to Maurice Besset, who claimed to have gotten the information from Le Corbusier himself, the *Dictionnaire* was the first purchase Le Corbusier made with the money he earned working for the architect Auguste Perret in Paris in 1908–9.
7. [Et j'allai à Notre-Dame et je suivis la fin du cours gothique de Magne—aux Beaux-Arts . . . et je compris. . . . Boennelwald a repris un cours d'architecture romane-gothique et là éclate ce qu'est l'architecture], CEJ to Charles L'Eplattenier, ca. 22–25 November 1908, reproduced in LC, *Vers une architecture* (1923; reprint, ed. Eugène Claudius-Petit, Paris: Éditions Arthaud, 1977): 247–53. "Boennelwald" is obviously an erroneous rendering of "Boeswillwald" (Paul-Louis Boeswillwald), who was professor at the École des beaux-arts from 1863 on.
8. [J'eus la ferveur de la "construction". Je passais des après-midi entières sur Notre-Dame de Paris, muni du trousseau énorme des clefs du Ministère des Beaux-Arts. Je connus les moindres recoins de la cathédrale jusqu'à l'extrémité des tours, des pinacles et des arcs-boutants. Ce fut pour moi l'épopée gothique], LC, "Confession," in *L'Art décoratif d'aujourd'hui* (1925; reprint, Paris: Vincent, Fréal, 1959): 207–8.
9. [Mais les admirations que j'eusse volontiers vouées à la forme et à la poésie gothiques s'étaient repliées sur la structure. Aujourd'hui je suis frappé de saisissement devant la beauté première d'un plan de cathédrale, et de stupéfaction devant la pauvreté plastique première de l'œuvre elle-même. Le plan et la coupe gothique sont magnifiques, étincelantes d'ingéniosité. Mais leur vérification n'est apportée par la contrôle des yeux. Etonnante apogée d'ingénieur, défaite plastique], Ibid., pp. 208–9.
10. [L'architecture gothique n'est pas, dans son fondement, à base de sphères, cônes et cylindres. La nef seule exprime une forme simple, mais d'une géométrie complexe de second ordre (croisée d'ogives). C'est pour cela qu'une cathédrale n'est pas très belle et que nous y cherchons des compensations d'un ordre subjectif, hors de la plastique. Une cathédrale nous intéresse comme l'ingénieuse solution d'un problème difficile, mais dont les données ont été mal posées parce qu'elles ne procèdent pas des grandes formes primaires. *La cathédrale n'est pas une oeuvre plastique; c'est un drame: la lutte contre la pesanteur, sensation d'ordre sentimental*], LC, *Vers une architecture* (1923/1977): 19; idem, *Towards a New Architecture*, trans. Frederick Etchells (New York: Payson & Clarke, 1927): 30.
11. Anatole de Baudot, *L'Architecture, le passé, le présent* (Paris: Renouard et H. Laurens, 1916).
12. Paul V. Turner, *The Education of Le Corbusier* (New York and London: Garland Publishing, 1977): 47.
13. For Viollet-le-Duc's influence abroad, see the *Actes du Colloque International Viollet-le-Duc, 1980* (Paris: Nouvelles Editions Latines, 1982); for Viollet-le-Duc and Switzerland, see Viollet-le-Duc: *Centenaire de la mort à Lausanne*, exhib. cat. (Lausanne: Musée historique de l'Ancien Evêché, 1979). Viollet-le-Duc died in Lausanne, where he had been called to restore the cathedral steeple, and where he had built himself a villa.
14. For the importance of Ruskin to Jeanneret, see Turner, *Education* (1977): passim.
15. Giuliano Gresleri, "Antiquité. Vers une architecture classique," in *Le Corbusier: une encyclopédie* (1987): 41; William Curtis, *Le Corbusier: Ideas and Forms* (Oxford: Phaidon, 1986):18; see also Mary P. M. Sekler, "Le Corbusier, Ruskin, the Tree and the Open Hand," in *The Open Hand: Essays on Le Corbusier*, ed. Russell Walden (Cambridge, Mass., and London: MIT Press, 1977): 42–95. According to William Curtis, the diffusion in La Chaux-de-Fonds of the ideas of the Arts and Crafts movement was helped by the presence at Neuchâtel of the Englishman Clement Heaton, designer of several designs for stained-glass windows. Heaton and L'Eplattenier may have made a voyage to England together (Mary P. M. Sekler, "The Early Drawings of Charles-Edouard Jeanneret [Le Corbusier], 1902–1908," Ph.D. diss., Harvard University, 1973). Nicole Quellet-Soguel, who has studied the life and work of Heaton, stated that she knew of no document attesting to any relationship between the two artists; see Nicole Quellet-Soguel, "L'idéal esthétique de Clement Heaton," in *Clement Heaton, 1861–1940*, exhib. cat., Musée d'art et d'histoire de Neuchâtel (London, Neuchâtel, New York, Hauterive: Editions Gilles Attinger, 1996): 199, n. 6. Still, the two towns are too close for L'Eplattenier and Jeanneret not to have been aware of Heaton.
16. LC, *Quand les cathédrales étaient blanches* (1937; reprint Paris: Denoël/Gonthier, 1977): 21–22.
17. *Le Corbusier: Le Passé* (1987–88): 89–90. The sketches of Chartres Cathedral (and other travel scenes) are in Carnet 10, FLC.
18. LC, *Vers une architecture* (1923/1977): 59 ; idem, *Towards a New Architecture* (1927): 77.
19. Auguste Choisy, *Histoire de l'architecture* ([1899]; reprint, Paris: Vincent, Fréal, 1964), 2: 316 (where he shows an interior elevation of Notre-Dame, not the facade). For the date of Le Corbusier's acquisition of the book, see Turner, *Education* (1977): 234.
20. For Le Corbusier's lecture of 12 June 1924 at the Sorbonne, see "L'Esprit nouveau en architecture," *Almanach d'architecture* (1925): 37. Le Corbusier returned to the theme of Choisy's book and its importance to him in *Le Modulor* (1951; reprint, Paris: Denoël/Gonthier, 1977): 23. On Choisy's ideas, see Reyner Banham, *Theory and Design in the First Machine Age*

(Cambridge, Mass.: MIT Press, 1960): 23–34. It seems somewhat surprising that Le Corbusier did not refer to the article "Proportion" from Viollet-le-Duc's *Dictionnaire raisonné*.
21. Turner, *Education* (1977): 119.
22. Choisy, *Histoire de l'architecture* ([1899]/ 1964), 1: 114; Marcel Dieulafoy, *L'Art antique de la Perse* (Paris, 1885); LC, *Vers une architecture* (1923/1977): 58; idem, *Towards a New Architecture* (1927):76. For Dieulafoy and Le Corbusier, see Turner, *Education* (1977): 189; and Pierre Saddy, "Tracés," in *Le Corbusier: Le Passé* (1987–88): 60–61.
23. LC, *Le Modulor* (1951/1977): 23.
24. This connection was established in Jacques Paul, *Einige Vorfahren zu Le Corbusiers Proportionstheorie*, Renaissance Lecture 1 (Nuremberg: Museen der Stadt, n.d.). See also Heinrich Wölfflin, "Zur Lehre von den Proportionen" (1889), in *Kleine Schriften* (Basel: Benno Schwabe, 1946): 48–50; August Thiersch, *Handbuch der Architektur*, pt. 4, first half-vol., *Die architektonische Composition* (1883; reprint, Darmstadt, 1893). For the rapprochement with Thiersch, see Winfried Nerdinger, "Standard und Typ: Le Corbusier und Deutschland, 1920–1927," in *L'Esprit nouveau: Le Corbusier und die Industrie, 1920–1925*, exhib. cat. (Zürich and Berlin: Museum für Gestaltung and Wilhelm Ernst and Sohn, 1987): 45. According to Nerdinger, Theodor Fischer introduced Le Corbusier to Thiersch's book in Munich in the spring of 1910.
25. Werner Oechslin, "Allemagne. Influences, confluences et reniements," in *Le Corbusier: une encyclopédie* (1987): 33; and idem, "Le Corbusier und die Schweiz: eine schwierige Beziehung," in *Le Corbusier und die Schweiz: Dokumente einer schwierigen Beziehung* (Zürich: Institut für Geschichte und Theorie der Architektur der E.T.H., 1987): 8 ff. For Le Corbusier's attack on German architecture, see Paul Boulard [pseud.], "Allemagne," *L'Esprit nouveau*, no. 27 (November 1924), n.p.
26. [Et la cathédrale est là, en formes aiguës, en silhouette déchiquetée, avec un désir d'ordre évident, mais totalement dépourvue du calme et de l'équilibre qui témoignent des civilisations abouties (cathédrale de Rouen)], LC, *Urbanisme* (1925; reprint, Paris: Vincent, Fréal, 1966): 36.
27. [. . . une esthétique toute différente], LC, "L'Esprit nouveau" (1925): 23.
28. Ibid., p. 22: ". . . des hommes arrivés de tous côtés, de nouveaux peuples, achevaient leur mélange avec d'anciens peuples; il en résultait un chaos général" (. . . men arrived from every side, new peoples, and completed their mixing with the older peoples; the result was a general chaos).
29. Hermann Drüe, "Die psychologische Ästhetik im Deutschen Kaiserreich," in *Ideengeschichte und Kunstwissenschaft im Kaiserreich*, ed. E. Mai, St. Waetzoldt, and G. Wolandt (Berlin: Gebr. Mann Verlag, 1983): 71–98.
30. Heinrich Wölfflin, "Prolegomena zu einer Psychologie der Architektur" (1886), in *Kleine Schriften* (1946): 13–47.
31. LC, "L'Esprit nouveau" (1925): 33; and idem, "Architecture d'époque machiniste," *Journal de Psychologie normale et pathologique*, 23rd Annual (1926): 343–44.
32. Another possible influence has sometimes been cited: Victor Basch, "L'Esthétique nouvelle et la science de l'art," letter to the editor, *L'Esprit nouveau*, no. 1 (15 October 1920): 5–12. This only begs the question of why the editors chose this for the first issue of the journal in the first place; Basch was a professor of aesthetics at the Sorbonne.
33. [Man könnte fast sagen, der Gegensatz von südlichem und nördlichem Lebensgefühl sei ausgedrückt in dem Gegensatz der liegenden und stehenden Proportionen], Wölfflin, "Prolegomena" (1886/1946): 33.
34. [. . . le style gothique découvert par le génie créateur de formes gallo-romaines se libéra peu à peu de la mentalité gothique qui lui était étrangère, se développa dans l'esprit de sa race, c'est-à-dire devint roman et horizontal], Wilhelm Uhde, *Picasso et la tradition française: Notes sur la peinture actuelle* (Paris: Editions des Quatre Chemins, 1928): 48.
35. [L'emploi systématique de la verticale, en Allemagne, est un mysticisme, un mysticisme dans les choses de la physique, le poison de l'architecture allemande], Le Corbusier-Saugnier [pseud.], "Curiosité' Non: anomalie," *L'Esprit nouveau*, no. 9 (June 1920): 1017.
36. LC, "Descartes est-il américain?" (1931), in *La Ville radieuse* (Boulogne, Seine: Éditions de l'architecture d'aujourd'hui, 1935): 127–34.
37. [Deux esprits s'opposent: la tradition de France, Notre-Dame, plan "Voisin" (les gratte-ciel "horizontaux") et la ligne américaine (tumulte, hérissement, premier état explosif d'un nouveau moyen âge], Ibid., p. 71. The drawings of skyscrapers were studies by Hugh Ferriss for his book, *The Metropolis of Tomorrow* (New York: I. Washburn, 1929).
38. [. . . la mesure la plus humainement perceptible de l'univers], LC, *Le Voyage d'orient* (Paris: Les Editions Forces Vives, 1966): 125; see also ibid., pp.126, 128, 132.
39. LC, "Un standard meurt. Un standart naît," *Almanach d'Architecture Moderne* (Paris: G. Crès, 1925): 83–90.
40. [. . . seule horizontale sur le ciel, qui soit comme les confins de la mer sur le ciel] [sans ce couronnement horizontal sur le fronton il n'y aurait plus pour nos yeux de pays breton], Ibid., p. 87.
41. See *Le Corbusier et la Méditerranée*, exhib. cat. (Marseille: Centre de la Vieille Charité and Editions Parenthèses, 1987).
42. A. Cingria-Vaneyre, *Les Entretiens de la villa du Rouet: Essais dialogués sur les arts plastiques en Suisse romande* (Genève: A. Jullien, 1908).
43. Turner, *Education* (1977): 83–91.
44. [. . . terminaison horizontale ou du moins surbaissée des toitures et des faites], Cingria-Vaneyre, *Les Entretiens* (1908): 308–10.
45. See Turner, *Education* (1977): 86.
46. This hypothesis has been made by Nerdinger, "Standard und Typ" (1987): 44. For other influences that might have weighed on Le Courbusier at this time, see Geoffrey Baker, "The Early Villas in La Chaux-de-Fonds by Charles-Edouard Jeanneret-Gris," in *Le Corbusier: Early Works by Charles-Edouard Jeanneret-Gris*, ed. Geoffrey Baker and Jacques Gubler (London: Academy Editions, and New York: St. Martin's Press, 1987): 16, n. 18.
47. [. . . la fausse direction de notre vie nationale] [. . . reprendre la cause latine aux frontière de l'empire et redonner à la Suisse romande le droit de vivre come culture et comme nation parmi les peuples de l'Europe], Cingria-Vaneyre, *Les Entretiens* (1908): vii, viii. For an even more explicit declaration, see ibid., p. 308: "Le fond de notre désir, c'est de nous affirmer fortement méditerranéens et de rompre, par conséquent, tout ce qui nous relie avec les civilisations celto-germaniques" (Our ultimate desire is to affirm ourselves as thoroughly Mediterranean, and consequently to sever all ties that bind us to Celto-Germanic civilizations).
48. [. . . une sorte de maladie de notre esprit européen] [les toitures de toute couleurs . . . les vieux bourgs suisses, . . . leur silhouette germanique affirmera qu'au XXme siècle l'Helvétie conquit définitivement de coin de terre classique et belle], Ibid., pp. 7, 22–23.
49. LC, *Carnets* (Paris: Herscher/Dessain et Tolra, 1981), 1: 138 (Carnet A2), note of 21 June 1916: "Je suis invité par Cingria" (I was invited by Cingria).
50. Turner, *Education* (1977): 91.
51. Adolf Max Vogt, "Le Corbusier: Der zornerfüllte Abschied von La Chaux-de-Fonds 1917," *Nos Monuments d'Art et d'Histoire* 43, no. 4 (1992): 539–47.
52. LC, "Mes rapports avec la Suisse," in *Le Corbusier und die Schweiz: Dokumente einer schwierigen Beziehung* (Zürich: Institut für Geschichte und Theorie der Architektur der E.T.H., 1987): 42–50.
53. Regarding the change in Le Corbusier's architecture, see Peter Serenyi, "Le Corbusier's Changing Attitude Toward Form," *Journal of the Society of Architectural Historians* 24, no. 1 (March 1965): 15–23.
54. LC, *Sur les quatres routes* (1941; reprint, Paris: Denoël/Gonthier, 1970): 27–29.
55. [. . . un acte d'optimisme, un geste de courage, un signe de fierté, une preuve de maitrise] [noir de suie et rongé par l'usure], LC, *Quand les cathédrales* (1937/1977):12.
56. LC, *Sur les quatres routes* (1941/1970): 174.
57. LC, *Manière de penser l'urbanisme* (1946; reprint, Paris: Denoël/Gonthier, 1970): 64.

CHAPTER 3
JEANNERET, THE CITY, AND PHOTOGRAPHY
Leo Schubert

1. [Je me suis acheté la petite camera Kodak que Kodak vendait six francs pour pouvoir vendre de la pellicule à tous les idiots qui emploient ça, et j'étais du nombre, et je me suis aperçu qu'en confiant mes émotions à un objectif j'oubliais à les faire passer par moi, ce qui était grave, alors j'ai laissé tomber la Kodak et j'ai pris mon crayon et depuis, j'ai toujours dessiné tout et n'importe où], statement by Le Corbusier, in *Le Corbusier: un Film de Jacques Barsac*, part 1 (1887–1929), prod. Christian Archambeaud and Jacques Barsac, Ciné Service Technique, Paris, 1987.
2. Of the approximately 340 negatives and glass plates made during the Voyage d'Orient, 300 have been printed and published by Giuliano Gresleri, *Le Corbusier, Viaggio in Oriente: Charles Edouard Jeanneret, fotografo e scrittore*, 3rd ed. (Venice: Marsilio, 1995). All subsequent citations are to this edition. From previous visits to Italy, Vienna, and France around thirty negatives survive. The remaining negative material, now archived in the Bibliothèque de la Ville de La Chaux-de-Fonds, stems from the years 1910–19; it includes around twenty photographs of townscapes and architecture from France, together with some twenty-five from Switzerland, including landscapes. The rest are photographs of family and friends. Still untraced are the photographs of La Chaux-de-Fonds mentioned in "La Construction des villes"; see Marc E. Albert Emery, ed., *Charles-Edouard Jeanneret, la construction des villes: genèse et devenir d'un ouvrage écrit de 1910 à 1915 et laissé inachevé par Charles-Edouard Jeanneret-Gris dit Le Corbusier* (Paris and Héricourt: Editions L'Age d'Homme, 1992): 49. There are more than ninety extant negatives by Jeanneret of Villa Jeanneret-Perret, and eight negatives of Villa Favre-Jacot. The remaining, high-quality images of Villa Favre-Jacot now at the Fondation Le Corbusier in Paris were taken with the equipment of a professional photographer (FLC, L3-18-53, 54, 59, 60, 62–64). For some photographs taken by Le Corbusier after 1920, see cat. nos. oo, in this volume. For Le Corbusier and photography, in general, see Italo Zannier, "Nota a margine su Le Corbusier fotografo," in Gresleri, *Viaggio* (1995): 479–82, and Beatriz Colomina, "Le Corbusier und die Fotografie," in *L'Esprit nouveau: Le Corbusier und die Industrie, 1920–1925*, ed., Stanislaus von Moos, exhib. cat., Museum für Gestaltung Zürich and Bauhaus-Archiv, Museum für Gestaltung Berlin (Berlin: Ernst und Sohn, 1987): 32–43; see also idem, *Privacy and Publicity: Modern Architecture as Mass Media* (Cambridge, Mass., and London: MIT Press, 1994): 128–39.
3. Beginning in 1890, George Eastman marketed comparatively inexpensive and easy-to-operate cameras under the trade name Kodak, using celluloid roll films, which paved the way for modern amateur photography. See, e.g., Italo Zannier, *Storia e tecnica della fotografia* (Bari: Laterza, 1982): 211–13.
4. The camera is in the collection of the Fondation Le Corbusier. For the date of purchase (presumably April 1911), see CEJ to L'Eplattenier, 18 July 1911, and CEJ to August Klipstein, 10 March 1911, reprinted in Italian in Gresleri, *Viaggio* (1995): 409, 467. For the Cupido 80, see Zannier, "Nota a margine su Le Corbusier Fotografo," in ibid., p. 481.
5. Jeanneret's use of photography has been known since at least 1984, when Giuliano Gresleri published the first edition of his monograph on the Voyage d'Orient in 1984; see above, n. 2.
6. [Ô le miracle de la photographie! Brave objectif: quel œil surnuméraire précieux. Je me suis offert un fameux appareil. C'est toute une histoire que de travailler avec. Mais les résultats sont parfaits et depuis avril, je n'ai pas raté une plaque], CEJ to L'Eplattenier, 18 July 1911, FLC E2-12-92–93; see also Gresleri, *Viaggio* (1995): 409).
7. CEJ to L'Eplattenier, 26 February 1908, FLC E2-12-23–25.
8. [Désillusion d'autant plus flagrante que nous avions sous les yeux les épatantes reproductions reçues de vous, des intérieurs de Hoffmann], ibid.; see also Colomina, "Le Corbusier und die Fotografie" (1987): 36f.
9. Camillo Sitte, *L'art de bâtir les villes: Notes et réflexions d'un architecte,* trans. Camille Martin (Paris: Libraire Renouard, H. Laurens, 1902).
10. On "La Construction des villes," see H. Allen Brooks, *Le Corbusier's Formative Years: Charles-Edouard Jeanneret at La Chaux-de-Fonds* (Chicago and London: University of Chicago Press, 1997): 200–208. Marc E. Albert Emery has attempted a transcription of the manuscript; see Emery, *La Construction* (1992). The photographs are reproduced in Gresleri, *Viaggio* (1995): 145–64. For a small selection of the postcards archived at the BV, see Rosario De Simone, *Ch. E. Jeanneret-Le Corbusier: Viaggio in Germania, 1910–1911* (Rome: Officina, 1989): figs. 56–75; and H. Allen Brooks, "Jeanneret e Sitte: le prime idee di Le Corbusier sulla costruzione della città," *Casabella*, no. 514 (1985): 41.
11. [Vous pensez combien cette perte me serait désastreuse. Car le voyage fait dans onze villes d'Allemagne l'été passé, n'était que pour prendre des clichés destinés à mon livre], undated fragment of letter, probably to L'Eplattenier, FLC E2-12-3–4.
12. [Je trouve que la photo n'illustre pas bien ce que nous pensons souligner], CEJ to L'Eplattenier, n.d., FLC E2-12-72–73; the context suggests a dating of April–May 1910. See also De

Simone, *Viaggio in Germania* (1989): 59; and Gresleri, *Viaggio* (1995): 392f.

13. Stanislaus von Moos, *Le Corbusier: Elemente einer Synthese* (Frauenfeld and Stuttgart: Huber, 1968): 190–91; Maurice Besset, *Qui était Le Corbusier* (Geneva: Skira, 1968): 151, 174.
14. In April and May of 1910, Jeanneret asked L'Eplattenier several times to forward the French translation to him, as it was not available in Germany; see Gresleri, *Viaggio* (1995): 392, 394. Other books consulted by him include works by Werner Hegemann, Karl Henrici, Théodor Goecke, and Siegfried Sitte, as well as the periodical *Der Städtebau*; see Brooks, "Jeanneret e Sitte" (1985): 44f.
15. Paul Schultze-Naumburg, *Kulturarbeiten*, 9 vols. (Munich: Callwey, 1901–17. The volume titles are: vol. 1, *Hausbau* (1901); vol. 2, *Gärten* (1902) and supplement to vol. 2 (1904); vol. 3, *Dörfer und Kolonien* (1905); vol. 4, *Städtebau* (1906); vol. 5, *Das Kleinbürgerhaus* (1907); vol. 6, *Das Schloss* (1910); vols. 7–9, *Die Gestaltung der Landschaft durch den Menschen* (1916–17). See also below, n. 18.
16. Schultze-Naumburg, *Kulturarbeiten* (1901), 1: foreword.
17. See Emery, *La Construction* (1992): 43f.
18. [Schulze-Naumburg, lui, a tout à fait capitulé et copie textuellement Louis XVI jusque dans ses moindres détails. Son influence est énorme], CEJ to L'Eplattenier, 16 January 1911, FLC E-2-12 54 – 59). The "um 1800" (circa 1800) movement derived its name from Paul Mebes, ed., *Um 1800: Architektur und Handwerk im letzten Jahrhundert ihrer traditionellen Entwicklung* (Munich: Bruckmann, 1908). Although Hermann Muthesius sarcastically dubbed the movement "Heilserum 1830" (i.e., the Biedermeier Serum), he later went on to prophesy that Schultze-Naumburg's *Kulturarbeiten* would perform "mehr Wunder . . . als 20 Jahrgänge unserer besten Fachzeitschriften" (more miracles than twenty years of our best professional journals); see Norbert Borrmann, *Paul Schultze-Naumburg, 1869–1949: Maler, Publizist, Architekt. Vom Kulturreformer der Jahrhundertwende zum Kulturpolitiker im Dritten Reich* (Essen: Bacht, 1989): 59. As is well known, the architects who drew inspiration from the Biedermeier at that time included not only Emanuel von Seidl, Bruno Paul, Heinrich Tessenow, Paul Mebes, and Richard Riemerschmid, but also Mies van der Rohe, Walter Gropius, Hans Scharoun, and Bruno Taut.
19. FLC B 2-20-327 in Emery, *La construction* (1992): 204, fig. 8; and FLC B-2-20-301 in ibid., p. 207, fig. 15. For the grid street plan see Schultze-Naumburg, *Kulturarbeiten* (1906), 4:65, fig. 26; for regulation of streets, see ibid., 4:187, figs. 108–10, and 163, fig. 94; for planning development on sloping ground, see ibid., 4:194, fig. 114f.
20. [Geschickte Ausnutzung des vorhandenen Terrains zu Strassenanlagen mit Terrassen.] [Gegenbeispiel: Strassen und Hanganlage ohne Ausnutzung des Terrains], Schultze-Naumburg, *Kulturarbeiten* (1906), 4:194, fig. 114f. Schultze-Naumburg showed flights of steps in Erfurt, Prague, and Pirna, ibid., 4: 182, 184f. Elsewhere, Jeanneret traced Schultze-Naumburg's typical page layout, which combines a photograph with a schematic location plan and a brief explanatory text concerning a bridge over a street at Mühlheim an der Ruhr (FLC B2-20-302); the source is Schultze-Naumburg, *Kulturarbeiten* (1906), 4:197, fig. 117.
21. Photograph in Gresleri, *Viaggio* (1995): 152.; sketch in Giuliano Gresleri, ed., *Ch.-E. Jeanneret – Le Corbusier: Les Voyages d'Allemagne, Carnets* (Milan: Electa, 1994), Carnet 2:159.
22. [Beispiel guter Strassenführung mit abschliessendem Prospekt . . . seitlich gelagerter Platz der eine stille Insel im Verkehr bildet], Schultze-Naumburg, *Kulturarbeiten* (1906), 4:51, 56, 96.
23. Gresleri, *Viaggio* (1995): 154; [vorgelegte Terrasse an der Ecke], Schultze-Naumburg, *Kulturarbeiten* (1906), 4:269.
24. Gresleri, *Viaggio* (1995): 152; [Beispiel eines Verbindungsweges zur Erleichterung des Verkehrs und zur Entlastung der Hauptstrassen], Schultze-Naumburg, *Kulturarbeiten* (1906), 4:108. The relevant sketch plan is reproduced in Gresleri, ed., *Les Voyages d'Allemagne* (1994), Carnet 2: 161.
25. Gresleri, *Viaggio* (1995): 152, 191; [Hausflucht, mit Mauer vorgesetzt], Schultze-Naumburg, *Kulturarbeiten* (1906), 4:392.
26. [Die Mauer bringt diese Stimmungswerte nicht bloss für die Innenseite des Grundstücks, sondern auch für den Anblick von aussen . . . sie ist die edelste und schönste Art der Umwehrung überhaupt. . . . Die Gefühle, die eine Mauer in uns erweckt, sind so ausserordentlich mannigfaltige, dass es nur mit der äussersten Verrohung unseres Augenempfindens zu erklären ist, wie dieser Massenkampf gegen die Mauer aufkommen konnte], Schultze-Naumburg, *Kulturarbeiten* (1906), 4:393.
27. [Un mur est beau, non seulement de sa beauté plastique, mais aussi des impressions qu'il peut éveiller. Il parle de confort, il parle de délicatesse; il parle de puissance et de brutalité; il est rébarbatif ou il est accueillant; il détient le mystère parfois. Un mur est évocateur de sentiments], Emery, *La Construction* (1992): 137; see also Brooks, "Jeanneret e Sitte" (1985): 46.
28. [. . . les vues publiées de La Chaux-de-Fonds correspondent à la réalité, et c'est précisément cette réalité qui est fautive et non l'objectif de notre Kodak], Emery, *La construction* (1992): 49.
29. Gresleri, *Viaggio* (1995): 184; Schultze-Naumburg, *Kulturarbeiten* (1906), 4:390.
30. [C'est pas tout facile d'aimer Constantinople. Il faut bougrement travailler], CEJ to L'Eplattenier, 18 July 1911, FLC E2-12-92–93.
31. Gresleri, *Viaggio* (1995): 301–04; see also cat. no. 00
32. Ibid., pp. 271, 273.
33. For more on *promenade architecturale*, see von Moos, chapter 1.
34. The reference is to the column of the sundial on the Forum, which Jeanneret sketched several times; it was the only object on his sketch plan of the Forum that he marked with an arrow. See Giuliano Gresleri, ed., *Ch.-E. Jeanneret-Le Corbusier: Voyage d'Orient* (Milan: Electa, 1994), Carnet 4:30f, 35; and Gresleri, *Viaggio* (1995): 361; for photographs of gladiatorial barracks and Via dei Sepolcri, see ibid., 361f.
35. [. . . et au fond l'éclat du jardin], Gresleri, ed., *Voyage d'Orient*, (1994), Carnet 4:126 and sketches. The text that accompanies the sketch plan of the Casa delle Nozze d'Argento (not "del Noce," as Jeanneret erroneously called it), shows how consistently Jeanneret studied recurrent architectural solutions, and how he set up his own "principles." He wrote: "La variation des grandeurs de porte joue un rôle énorme . . . Et comme à Brousse, il y a des masses [claires, deleted] lumineuses et des volumes obscurs" (The variation in the door sizes plays an enormous part . . . And, as at Bursa, there are [light, deleted] luminous masses and very dark volumes"), ibid., Carnet 4:127.
36. Gresleri, ed., *Voyage d'Orient* (1994): 364.
37. Sketches and photograph in ibid., p. 360.
38. On the Forum at Pompeii, Martin writes: "Les monuments ne sont pas situés en son centre, mais sur ses côtés. En un mot, le forum joue dans les villes le rôle de l'atrium dans la maison" (The monuments are not located in the center but along the sides. In a word, the forum plays the same role in the cities that the atrium plays in a house); see Camille Martin, *L'Art de bâtir les villes* (Geneva: Ch. Eggiman, 1902): 11–12. For Jeanneret at Pompeii, see Giuliano Gresleri, "Il silenzio delle pietre, le parole dei numeri, la solitudine, il 'deflagrante ricordo,'" in *Le Corbusier e l'antico: Viaggi nel Mediterraneo*, ed. Benedetto Gravagnuolo, exhib. cat., Palazzo Reale, Naples, (Milan: Electa, 1997): 71–83, and Claude Malecot, "Pompéi," in *Le Corbusier: Le Passé à réaction poétique*, exhib. cat., Hôtel de Sully (Paris: Caisse nationale des Monuments historiques et des Sites – Ministère de la Culture et de la Communication, 1988): 64–69.
39. See Le Corbusier-Saugnier [pseud.], "Architecture II, L'Illusion des plans," *L'Esprit nouveau*, no. 15 (February 1922): 1767–80; LC, *Vers une architecture*, 2d ed. (Paris: Cres, 1924): 141–60. For the genesis of Le Corbusier's *promenade architecturale*, see Richard A. Etlin, *Frank Lloyd Wright and Le Corbusier: The Romantic Legacy* (Manchester and New York: Manchester University Press, 1994): 106–18.
40. In the BV, there are fifty-three negatives of Villa Jeanneret-Perret, without people, thirty-seven with people, and six of the construction site. A selection of prints from these is archived in an album at the FLC.
41. Schultze-Naumburg, *Kulturarbeiten* (1906), 4:374; Gresleri, *Viaggio* (1995): 281.
42. For Le Lac, at Corseaux, near Vevey, see Willy Boesiger and Oscar Stonorov, eds., *Le Corbusier et Pierre Jeanneret: Oeuvre complète*,. vol. 1, *1910–1929* (Zürich: Girsberger, 1937): 74–75; see also Bruno Reichlin, "La 'petite maison' à Corseaux. Une analyse structurale," in Isabelle Charollais and André Ducret, eds., *Le Corbusier à Genève, 1922–1932: projets et réalisations*, exhib. cat., Immeuble Clarté and Galerie Bonnier, Geneva (Lausanne: Payot, 1987): 119–34 (also as offprint); and Stanislaus von Moos, *Album La Roche* (Milan: Electa, 1996): 63–78.
43. LC, *Une petite maison* (Zürich: Girsberger, 1954): 28.
44. Le Corbusier recorded that the photographs were taken by "Mademoiselle Peter, professeur de photographie à Vevey" (ibid., p. 59).
45. The carefully composed photographs of his buildings taken for print advertisements are an extreme instance (an example is the view from inside the front door of Villa La Roche in an advertisement for the reinforced-concrete construction company G. Summer); see LC, *Almanach d'architecture moderne* (Paris: Crès, 1926).

CHAPTER 4
ARCHITECTURE: PROPORTION, CLASSICISM AND OTHER ISSUES
Francesco Passanti

AUTHOR'S NOTE: The principal publication of Le Corbusier's work is his *Oeuvre complète*, 7 vols. (Zurich: Girsberger, 1930–1971), with slight variations of author, editors, and title from volume to volume; the exact citation for the first volume, which interests us here, is *Le Corbusier and Pierre Jeanneret, Oeuvre complète, 1910–1929*, ed. Willy Boesiger and Oscar Stonorov (1937; reprint, Zurich: Girsberger, 1964), originally published as *Ihr Gesamtes Werk von 1910–1929*, ed. Boesiger and Stonorov (Zurich, 1930). Le Corbusier's best-known theoretical book is *Vers une architecture* (Paris: Crés, 1923), in English as *Towards a New Architecture*, trans. Frederick Etchells (New York: Payson and Clarke, and London: Rodker, 1927). Le Corbusier's architectural drawings are kept at the FLC, each designated by an "FLC number," and can be consulted in H. Allen Brooks, ed., *The Le Corbusier Archive*, 32 vols. (New York: Garland, and Paris: FLC, 1982–84). Le Corbusier's correspondence is located in various archives: that with his family and with August Klipstein is at the BV; that with L'Eplattenier is at the FLC; that with William Ritter is at the Schweizerische Landesbibliothek in Bern, with copies at the BV; that with Auguste Perret is at the Institut Français d'Architecture, fonds Perret. In quoting Le Corbusier's own notes and letters, I have left his grammatical errors uncorrected, without pointing to them each time. All translations are mine, unless otherwise indicated.—FP

1. The most recent and comprehensive work on early Le Corbusier is H. Allen Brooks, *Le Corbusier's Formative Years* (Chicago and London: University of Chicago Press, 1997), to which I will frequently refer in this essay.
2. The fullest documentation of the villa is now found in Brooks, *Formative Years* (1997): 329–41. About the client and the watchmaking milieu see Jacques Gubler, "In Time with the Swiss Watchmakers," in Geoffrey Baker and Jacques Gubler, *Le Corbusier: Early Works by Charles-Edouard Jeanneret-Gris* (London: Academy, and New York: St. Martin's, 1987), 121–27, especially 125–26.
3. On Le Corbusier's studies abroad see Brooks, *Formative Years* (1997): 93–303. In addition, for the French stay and later contacts see Giovanni Fanelli and Roberto Gargiani, *Perret e Le Corbusier, Confronti* (Rome and Bari: Laterza, 1990). For the German stay see Giuliano Gresleri, ed., *Le Corbusier (Ch.-E. Jeanneret), Les Voyages d'Allemagne, Carnets* (Milan: Electa, and Paris: FLC, 1994), hereafter cited as *Allemagne Carnets*, and an abundant literature predating the publication of the *carnets*: Winfried Nerdinger, "Standard und Typ: Le Corbusier und Deutschland, 1920–27," in *L'Esprit nouveau, Le Corbusier und die Industrie 1920–1925*, ed. Stanislaus von Moos, (Berlin: Ernst und Sohn, 1987): 44–53; Werner Oechslin, "Allemagne," in *Le Corbusier: une encyclopédie* (Paris: Centre Georges Pompidou, 1987), 33–39; Rosario de Simone, *Ch.-E. Jeanneret - Le Corbusier, Viaggio in Germania, 1910–1911* (Rome: Officina, 1989); Stanislaus von Moos, "Der Fall Le Corbusier: Kreuzbestäubungen, Allergien, Infektionen," in *Moderne Architektur in Deutschland, 1900 bis 1950: Expressionismus und Neue Sachlichkeit*, ed. Vittorio Magnago Lampugnani and Romana Schneider (Stuttgart: Hatje, 1994): 161–83. For the Voyage d'Orient see LC, *Le Voyage d'orient* (Paris: Forces Vives, 1966); in English as *Journey to the East*, trans. Ivan Zaknic (Cambridge: MIT Press, 1987); Giuliano Gresleri, *Le Corbusier, viaggio in Oriente* (Venice: Marsilio, 1984); Giuliano Gresleri, ed., *Le Corbusier (Ch.-E. Jeanneret), Voyage d'Orient, Carnets* (Milan: Electa, and Paris: FLC, 1987), hereafter cited as *VDO Carnets*. In general, there is a much richer record of Le Corbusier's German stay and his Voyage d'Orient than of his earlier stay in Paris (for the reasons see Brooks, *Formative Years* [1997]: 156, n. 7), and this certainly accounts for the asymmetry in the literature.
4. The best compendium of this architecture is a book that Le Corbusier certainly knew: Paul Mebes, *Um 1800: Architektur und Handwerk im letzten Jahrhundert ihrer traditionellen Entwicklung* (Munich: Bruckmann, 1908). Stylistic similarity to Behrens has been suggested by Stanislaus von Moos, *Le Corbusier: Elemente einer Synthese* (Frauenfeld: Huber, 1968); in English as *Le Corbusier: Elements of a Synthesis* (Cambridge: MIT Press, 1979): 29 and others. The relationship to Schinkel and Behrens will be discussed in more detail later.

5. See especially Stanford Anderson, "The Legacy of German Neo-Classicism and Biedermeier: Behrens, Loos, Mies, and Tessenow," *Assemblage* 15 (October 1991): 62–87.
6. The similarity is particularly visible if one compares the plan of the Erechtheion with a "purified" plan of the Villa Favre-Jacot, obtained by removing the L-shaped circulation system that converges onto the kitchen: this circulation was not part of the initial concept of the villa, which is shown in a bird's-eye sketch by Le Corbusier (FLC 30277, also shown in Brooks, *Formative Years* [1997]: 330, fig. 253).
7. *VDO Carnets*, 4:87. Le Corbusier's observations from the visit were then elaborated in the essay, "Architecture II: L'Illusion des plans," *L'Esprit nouveau* 15 (February 1922): 1767–80, later included in *Vers une architecture*.
8. In fact, to emphasize the separation, Le Corbusier provided the wall with its own frame, a square molding that he also used on the entry facade to articulate its proportions.

Besides Schinkel and the neoclassical architecture of *um 1800*, another precedent for the network of moldings and the flat orders, especially on the entry facade, is the sixteenth-century Villa Lante on the Gianiculum in Rome, by Giulio Romano; Le Corbusier had photographed and drawn it, and he noted that the network of moldings on its walls "affirms the unity of the block by covering its four faces with lines" (affirmation du cube homogène en le couvrant de linéaments sur les 4 faces), *VDO Carnets*, 5:18–19.
9. In this respect, another relevant work by Behrens is the Wiegand house of 1910–12. Behrens laid out a symmetrical master block (its axis marked by a square portico toward the street and by two symmetrically projecting wings toward the garden) and then obliterated part of the street facade by inserting a service block to the left. The result, seen from the street, is tense and enigmatic; one sees an asymmetrical composition, yet one senses an axis at work. For the Wiegand house see Wolfram Hoepfner, Fritz Neumeyer, et al., *Das Haus Wiegand von Peter Behrens in Berlin-Dahlem*, Deutsche Archäologische Institut, Geschichte und Dokumente, vol. 6 (Mainz: Philipp von Zabern, 1979).

H. Allen Brooks has pointed out that the Wiegand house was being designed while Le Corbusier worked in the office and that he was sufficiently interested to keep two sketches of it (*Formative Years* [1997]: 242–43). For the purposes of this discussion, however, note that the tension between symmetry and asymmetry was not present in the sketches that Le Corbusier kept; it is not known whether it was developed during the period of his employment with Behrens, or only later.

Soon after leaving Behrens, Le Corbusier interpreted the House of the Tragic Poet in Pompeii in similar terms of axis/asymmetry and then echoed that precedent in the plan of the Villa Favre-Jacot. In the 1920s, the same attitude surfaced in the villas La Roche–Jeanneret. After being forced by circumstances to abandon a symmetrical termination of the dead-end-street, Le Corbusier left La Roche's gallery like a curved billboard centered on the axis and used it to anchor the asymmetry of the rest of the house. The same tension will reappear in Le Corbusier's Villa Stein and in the competition entry for the League of Nations, to mention just a few other works.
10. In the interest of brevity, in the following discussion I will simply state what the proportions are, without documenting the accuracy of my assertions and without justifying the compatibility of the various proportional figures with each other. For much fuller discussion see my forthcoming book on Le Corbusier, from which the composite diagrams in this essay are taken. Indeed, it can be shown that the various figures are compatible with each other, and that they can be derived by rigorous geometric steps from one initial figure. I thank H. Allen Brooks for his encouragement of my work on this topic and for kindly lending good photographs of plan and elevations.
11. A recent book has shown how pervasively Le Corbusier used the golden section throughout his career; see Klaus-Peter Gast, *Le Corbusier, Paris-Chandigarh*, with foreword by Arthur Rüegg (Basel-Berlin-Boston: Birkhäuser, 2000). Gast focuses on Le Corbusier's plans, from the Villa Schwob to Chandigarh. A central contribution of this book is to show that the proportional system is applied *systematically* to the whole plan. This is important because it proves that the proportional order of the plan was intentional and consciously achieved. My own discussion of Le Corbusier's use of proportions, in this essay, was developed independently from Gast and confirms his conclusions, extending them back in time to earlier designs by Le Corbusier.
12. The square is an inherent component of golden rectangles not only in terms of *perception* but also in terms of *generation*. We have just seen how this is so in terms of perception: faced with a golden rectangle, it is easy to mentally subtract a square from it, and notice the similarity of the remaining rectangle with the initial one. In terms of generation, a standard geometric construction goes as follows. Start from a square ABCD (counterclockwise from the bottom left); on the base AB, take the middle point M, draw the diagonal MC connecting that middle point to the top right corner; pivot that diagonal clockwise around M and project it onto the base, thus identifying the point F; the rectangle with base AF and height AD will be a golden rectangle. This construction, while appealing to the mind, is not important for the legibility and combinatory potential of golden rectangles.
13. This extension of the main block by adding an L-shaped circulation system is not just a conceptual step in my reading of the plan, but was also an actual phase of the design process, as noted above in n. 6.
14. Note that, for the elevation of the entry facade, a discussion of the proportions is complicated by several factors. First, there are three separate layers: the flat symmetrical facade centered on the door and partly "hidden" behind the projecting wings, its flat extension sliding out on the right, and the wings in front of the flat facades. Second, the flat facade is articulated by several kinds of architectural members: corner piers and entablature, thin moldings, and, around the central square window, an abstracted architectural order acting as ornamental frame. Third, the proportional figures ordering the facade (golden rectangles and squares) concern the *lines* on the facade, and not properly its architectural *members*: thus, at the center of the whole facade is a system of two squares, one inside the other, but the outer square does not correspond to any coherent architectural member—its bottom side is the molding capping the baldaquin, its top side is the cornice line of the building, its vertical sides are the edges of moldings and actually run through the entablature to meet the cornice. Le Corbusier's proportional systems are conceptualized on the elevation, as an ordering of flat figures, and do not take account of the projection of the wings.
15. In the above discussion, we have considered the facade up to the *top* edge of the entablature, where the cornice draws its line of shadow. A whole other set of very clear proportional relationships based on the square arises if we consider the *bottom* edge of the entablature. It is not possible to develop this distinction further in this short essay, but it should be noted that, at first glance, a visitor does not draw a clear distinction between figures determined by the top or bottom edges of the entablature, and small visual adjustments are always possible given the thickness of the various moldings on the facade. Thus, in practice one experiences the two systems of proportional figures as overlapping.
16. Le Corbusier, *Le Modulor* (Boulognes, Seine: Editions de l'Architecture d'Aujourd'hui, 1950), chap. 2. According to Le Corbusier's version, the discovery was occasioned by the study of nature, by the chance visit of a house built by the Dutch architect Lauweriks in Hagen, and by play with a postcard of the Campidoglio; only after that, said Le Corbusier, did he study proportions in Choisy.
17. For example, Reyner Banham calls Le Corbusier's interest in proportions "academic"; see Banham, *Theory and Design in the First Machine Age* (London: Architectural Press, and New York: Praeger, 1960): 223. Arthur Rüegg contrasts Le Corbusier's reliance on history (including proportions) with his functionalism and sees proportions as essentially classical: Rüegg, in Gast, *Le Corbusier* (2000): 9. Gast constrasts Le Corbusier's rational, universal, and transcendent side (achieved through proportions) with his irrational and subjective one: ibid, pp. 186–88. Both Rüegg and Gast find the essence of Le Corbusier's architecture in the tension between opposite poles, with proportions representing the timeless pole, and functionalism or subjectivity representing the modern one.
18. Perret and Behrens will be discussed further below. For Berlage see Manfred Bock, *Anfänge einer neuen Architektur: Berlages Beitrag zur Architektonischen Kultur der Niederlande im ausgehenden 19. Jahrhundert* (The Hague: Staatsuitgeverij, and Wiesbaden: Steiner, 1983): 63–70; and Iain Boyd Whyte, introduction to *Hendrik Petrus Berlage: Thoughts on Style, 1886–1909*, by Hendrik Petrus Berlage (Santa Monica: Getty, 1996): 14–15, 32. For Fischer see Winfried Nerdinger, *Theodor Fischer: Architekt und Städtebauer, 1862–1938* (Berlin: Ernst und Sohn, 1988): 96–102. For Lutyens see John Rollo, "Metiendo Vivendum: 'By Measure We Must Live'," *arq* 3/2 (1999): 147–63.

For a general history of proportions in architecture see Peter H. Scholfield, *The Theory of Proportion in Architecture* (Cambridge: Cambridge University Press, 1958). Twentieth-century architects seem to have treated proportions like a professional secret. Thus, Perret and Behrens rarely spoke about the issue, yet used proportions pervasively in their work. Berlage is a notable exception. Le Corbusier himself wrote repeatedly about the topic and published some elevations of his work with proportional diagonal lines drawn on them, but these diagrams are mostly intended to remind the reader that proportions are at work, not to explain how the proportions actually operate in the elevation. In fact, some of these diagrams are intentionally misleading. Because of all this, the only reliable sources of information, in studying most architects, are the designs themselves, not the architects' writings, nor their published diagrams.
19. Arthur Rüegg points to a set of instructional lithographs, meant for primary schools and showing those constructions, which was produced in La Chaux-de-Fonds in 1894, the year when Le Corbusier entered school: *Cours de dessin pour les écoles primaires*, litographs by A. Chateau (La Chaux-de-Fonds: Chateau, 1894), discussed by Rüegg in his foreword to Gast, *Le Corbusier* (2000): 9–10. Exposure to geometry had begun even earlier in kindergarten, at the Froebel school: see Marc Solitaire, "Le Corbusier et l'urbain: la rectification du damier froebelien," in *La Ville et l'urbanisme après Le Corbusier, actes du colloque* (La Chaux-de-Fonds: Editions d'en Haut, 1993): 93–117, also cited by Rüegg.
20. In the complex non-axial plan of Villa Fallet, the diagonals of the enveloping rectangle determine a center, marked by the fireplace and by the principal transversal wall, while they also serve to align the corners of the living-dining suite and those of the terrace (hence, the front and side wings of the terrace have different widths). This flexible scheme, which could have any proportion and size, is then fixed by using round numbers for some of the measurements: the specific slope of the diagonals is determined by the internal size of the living-dining suite (8 x 4.5 meters), and the external overall dimensions are determined by the total length of the building (14 meters).

In the elevation, the height of an equilateral triangle, with its base overlapping the full width of the terrace floor, sets the top of the roof, as in Viollet-le-Duc's discussion of of Saint-Sernin: Emmanuel Viollet-le-Duc, entry on "Proportion" in the *Dictionnaire raisonné de l'architecture française du XIe au XVIe siècle*, vol. 7 (Paris: Morel, 1864): 540. And, starting from that top, another triangle, practically identical to those formed by the diagonals in the plan, sets the incline of the roof slopes, hence the profile of the sgraffito facade and the level of the bedroom floor.
21. Charles Blanc, *Grammaire des arts du dessin* (Paris: Laurens, 1867): 98–101 (1880 edition). Le Corbusier used the book in the winter 1907–8 in Vienna, having requested it in a letter to his parents of 1 November 1907, but he may have read Blanc earlier too, since a copy was in the library of the Ecole d'Art in La Chaux-de-Fonds.
22. At this stage, however, Le Corbusier's receptivity to this view was probably limited by his opposition to classicism.
23. For Perret's use of proportions, see Roberto Gargiani, *Auguste Perret, 1874–1954* (Milan: Electa, 1993): 172–83, which documents the use of proportional systems in several key designs, including some from the time when Perret was a student at the École des Beaux-Arts. My own research confirms the pervasiveness of this use, even beyond the examples discussed by Gargiani. The fact that Perret had used such systems since his school years suggests not only that Le Corbusier would have encountered the issue repeatedly in the office, but also that it would have been treated as a routine aspect of design, the sort of thing that one learns in school.

While in Perret's office, Le Corbusier drew the facade of an apartment building whose proportions are based on the square and on the Egyptian triangle (a right-angled triangle with sides in the ratio of 3:4:5), combined in a construction proposed by Auguste Choisy. He kept a blueprint of the facade, which is now at the FLC: it is reproduced in Brooks, *Formative Years* (1997): 160. On Choisy, see n. 24 below.
24. The diagram was first proposed by Choisy in his study of the Arsenal at Pyraeus, included in Auguste Choisy, *Etudes épigraphiques sur l'architecture grecque* (Paris: Libraire de la Société Anonyme de publications périodiques, 1883–84). Choisy claimed that the lost facade of the Arsenal was based on a combination of squares and of so-called Egyptian triangles. The figure of the facade, with the generating geometric construction, was then included in Choisy's *Histoire de l'architecture* (Paris: Gauthier-Villars, 1899), 1:389. Le Corbusier used the figure from the *Histoire* in his own essay on regulating lines, mentioned below. Perret used mostly squares and Choisy's diagram; occasionally he used the $\sqrt{2}$ ratio. Before 1909 only one design by Perret, the facade of the Garage Ponthieu (1906–7), con-

tains golden proportions, and it is not clear whether they were intended or simply the by-product of a geometric construction chosen for other reasons.

25. Le Corbusier-Saugnier [pseud.], "Les tracés régulateurs," *L'Esprit nouveau* 5 (February 1921): 563–72; later incorporated in *Vers une architecture*.

26. On this discourse see Harry F. Mallgrave, introduction to *Empathy, Form, and Space: Problems in German Aesthetics, 1873–1893*, ed. Harry F. Mallgrave and Eleftherios Ikonomou (Santa Monica: Getty, 1994): 1–85.

27. August Thiersch, "Proportionen in der Architektur," in *Handbuch der Architektur*, vol. 4, no. 1 (Darmstadt, 1883).

To the Thierschian notion of "similar *parallel* rectangles," Heinrich Wölfflin soon added the notion of "similar *perpendicular* rectangles," proposing that the eye picks up not only the similarity of rectangles oriented parallel to each other, but also that of rectangles oriented at 90° to each other: for example, at the Farnesina, the vertical rectangle of one wing is similar to the horizontal one composed by the center block and the other wing. Heinrich Wölfflin, "Zur Lehre von den Proportionen," *Deutsche Bauzeitung* 23, no. 46 (8 June 1889): 264–72, reprinted in *Kleine Schriften* (Basel: Schwabe, 1946): 48–50. Both Thiersch and Wölfflin were then extensively quoted in Jacob Burckhardt, *Geschichte der Renaissance in Italien*, 3rd ed. (Stuttgart, 1891), and from then on their contributions were received together as one package.

28. For the first proposal of a connection between Thiersch, Wölfflin, and Le Corbusier, see Jacques Paul, "Neo-Classicism and the Modern Movement," *Architectural Review* 152, no. 907 (September 1972): 176–80.

29. [Die Proportionen haben nicht an sich, sondern nur in Bezug auf ihre Wirkung ästhetische Bedeutung], Fritz Hoeber, *Orientierende Vorstudien zur Systematik der Architekturproportionen auf historischer Grundlage* (Frankfurt: Kunz & Gabel, 1906). This was originally his doctoral dissertaion at the university of Strassburg. Hoeber lists ten "Thesen" or concluding points: the fifth is the one quoted here.

30. Fritz Hoeber, *Peter Behrens* (Munich: Müller & Rentsch, 1913). As Behrens wrote, he was interested in "für das Auge sinnfällige Wirkung" (effect obvious to the eye); see Behrens, "Kunst und Technik," *Elektrotechnische Zeitschrift* 31, no. 22 (2 June 1910): 552–55, most recently reprinted in Tillmann Buddensieg and Henning Rogge, eds., *Industriekultur: Peter Behrens und die AEG, 1907–1914* (Berlin: Mann, 1979): D278–85, quote from D283. On Behrens in general see Stanford Anderson, *Peter Behrens and a New Architecture for the Twentieth Century* (Cambridge: MIT Press, 2000).

Note that Behrens's focus on *Wirkung*, the effect on the viewer, does not imply that viewers should be able to make out the proportions, to know which precise proportions are affecting them. What mattered to Behrens was that viewers be affected by the proportions and their tensions in a way that he, Behrens, had controlled. And the effect on the viewers may be more intense if they are not rationally conscious of what is acting on them.

Behrens's use of proportions has attracted little attention, and has been discussed with regard to two buildings only. For the Oldenburg pavilion of 1905, see Hoeber, *Behrens* (1913): 35. Hoeber showed that the building's elevation is governed by a grid of diagonals of the kind used by Berlage in his Bourse. His analysis is confirmed in Kurt Asche, *Peter Behrens und die Oldenburger Ausstellung 1905* (Berlin: Mann, 1992). For the Wiegand house of 1911–12, see Fritz Neumeyer, "Zwischen Monumentalkunst und Moderne—Architekturgeschichte eines Wohnhauses", in Hoepfner and Neumeyer, *Wiegand*. Neumeyer saw the proportional system of the Wiegand house as a combination of squares in plan and diagonal grid in elevation (as in Oldenburg), while also placing Behrens's use of proportions within a broader aesthetic strategy of setting up tensions.

On the basis of this limited *corpus* it would seem that Behrens's use of proportions was limited to squares in plan and diagonal grid in elevation, and that he was a direct heir of the Dutch architects J. L. M. Lauweriks and H. P. Berlage, who were well known to Behrens, and who had, in turn, systematized some aspects of Viollet-le-Duc's theory. An extensive analysis of Behrens's work, however, leads me to think that Behrens's proportional systems were far more varied and incorporated many sources, and that his aesthetic outlook, focused on form and the psychology of visual perception, was radically different from that of Berlage and especially Lauweriks.

31. Note that August Thiersch's son had worked for Behrens three years earlier, when his office was still in Düsseldorf; see Brooks, *Formative Years* (1997): 447.

32. In particular, it is probably in Behrens's office that Le Corbusier learned to use golden rectangles singly and paired by their long side, as seen in the Villa Favre-Jacot: translated in mathematical terms, this means using two series of dimensions .... 1/Ø 1 Ø Ø^2.... and .... 2/Ø 2 2Ø 2Ø^2.... which can be intercalated to provide a more gradual composite scale .... 1 2/Ø Ø 2 Ø^2 2Ø ...., as Le Corbusier will later do in his Modulor system.

33. Neumeyer, "Zwischen Monumentalkunst und Moderne" (1979): passim, esp. 24.

34. Note that one should really speak of near-squares. Behrens was singlemindedly concerned with *Wirkung*: in this perspective, a square is a square as long as its sides are apprehended as equal. Thus, in the Obenauer plan, several of the squares are not exactly so in plan: but the house is experienced by walking around it, one side at a time, and the difference does not matter.

35. As we have seen, if one starts from a golden rectangle and subtracts a square from it, the remaining rectangle is a golden rectangle at 90° to the first; within that rectangle one can perform the same operation, leaving a smaller golden rectangle; and so on. The process produces a spiralling pattern of ever smaller golden rectangles. If one starts from 5 x 3 squares, the ratio of length to width is 5/3 = 1.666..., i.e. the overall rectangle is "too long": by slightly shortening the longitudinal direction of the squares, the overall length is shortened, hence the ratio is brought closer to Ø = 1.618... A similar tension between modular and non-modular systems underlies the proportioning of the Wiegand house.

36. This is how proportions (including the golden section) had been seen, together with lines and color, by the neo-Impressionist painter Georges Seurat, influenced by the scientific aesthetics of Charles Henry, who was in turn building upon Helmholtz and others: see Robert Herbert, "Parade de Cirque et l'esthétique scientifique de Charles Henry," *Revue de l'art* (1980); English trans., in Herbert, *Seurat's Drawings and Paintings* (New Haven and London: Yale Unversity Press, 2001): 137–53. Seurat and Henry will have a big place in Le Corbusier's and Ozenfant's journal *L'Esprit nouveau*. But in 1910–11 it was from Behrens that Le Corbusier learned this view.

37. [L'oeuvre . . . se ramasse sur elle-même, se concentre, s'unifie, exprime dans toute sa masse la même loi, devient massive], LC, "Tracés régulateurs" (1921): 570–71; included in *Vers une architecture* (1923): 59–60.

38. For further examples see Gast, *Le Corbusier* (2000). Note that Le Corbusier gives careful proportions to all his designs, from expensive villas (Favre-Jacot; Schwob, Stein, Savoye) to standardized house types (Dom-ino, Saint-Gobain, Citrohan) to slaughterhouses (Challuy, see the catalogue entry) to a whole city (*Ville contemporaine*).

39. This can be easily demonstrated mathematically. The twenty-four skyscrapers occupy 6 × 4 square city blocks. Let's first consider two extreme situations. If the skyscrapers filled each block completely, the composite parallelepiped of skyscrapers downtown would have an overall proportion of 6:4 = 1.5. If, on the other hand, the skyscrapers were reduced to their vertical axis, like so many thin sticks, they would outline a composite parallelepiped of 5 × 3 axis-to-axis intervals, with an overall proportion of 5:3 = 1,666... The real situation falls between these two extremes, because the skyscrapers do not take up the full width of each square, hence they are separated by wide gaps: they are like thick posts, and the parallepiped that they collectively outline has an overall proportion intermediate between 1.5 and 1.666...., which is very close to the golden ratio Ø = 1.618...

40. Le Corbusier was quite conscious of current trends and had a formidable understanding of them. For example, in a letter to L'Eplattenier of 16 January 1911, he wrote: "le mouvement sécessioniste a fini de vivre en Allemagne. On me l'a repèté suffisamment à Münich...Max Läuger s'affirme péremptoirement classique...Schulze-Naumburg, lui, a tout-à-fait capitulé et compie *textuellement* Louis XVI...Messel a tiré Behrens, son successeur, des folies pénibles de Darmstadt. Messel copiait textuellement le Petit Trianon et le Parthénon. Behrens ne s'inspire que de dorique et d'empire...Bruno Paul enfin s'est, en ces 3 dernières années, – (comme Behrens et Schultze Naumburg) – affirmé en cette profession de foi...Quant à Bruno Schmitz sa fastueuse et quelque peu tapageuse grandeur allie à la forme apprise de la Grèce, les influences opposées d'un sentimentaliste d'antique mythologie germaine" (the Secessionist movement in Germany has died. That was told to me enough times in Munich... Max Lauger has peremptorily declared himself a classicist... Schulze-Naumburg had capitulated entirely and copies Louis XVI word for word... Messel drew Behrens, his successor, from his pathetic stupidities at Darmstadt. Messel copied the Petit Trianon and the Parthenon word for word. Behrens now draws his inspiration uniquely from the Doric and the Empire... Finally, during these last three years Bruno Paul (like Behrens and Schultze Naumburg) had declared himself an adherent of this particular faith... As for Bruno Schmitz, his celebratory and a little bit boisterous grandeur joins forms learned from Greece to the opposed influences of someone sentimental about ancient German mythology.)

41. The entry and exit by boat were choices on Le Corbusier's part, since in both cases there were more direct rail connections available. Entering Italy, Le Corbusier used the Gotthard line and stopped in Lugano to see some frescoes. But then, instead of continuing by train via Como to Milan, he took a boat down the long lake of Lugano, to Porto Ceresio on the Italian shore, where the Italian railroad had a terminal station. This emerges from a letter to L'Eplattenier of 19 September 1907: "A Porto-Ceresio le bal a commencé." The regular steamer service from Lugano to Porto Ceresio and the railroad from there to Milan are both mentioned in a contemporary Baedeker: Karl Baedeker, *Northern Italy* (Leipzig: Baedeker, 1906): 183–87. Goethe had used instead the Brenner pass and the lake of Garda in 1786; see Johann Wolfgang Goethe, *Italienische Reise*, ed. Christoph Michel (Frankfurt: Insel, 1976), 1: 39–52. Le Corbusier's exit from Venice, by boat, is mentioned in a card to his parents, 7 November 1907, where he also comments that "on ne quitte pas une terre pareille sans de grands regrets" (one does not leave such land without much regret), using the mythical term "terre" (land) instead of the more prosaic "pays" (country). Lake Garda, the lake of Virgil, is described as "ce séjour des dieux" (CEJ to L'Eplattenier, 1 November 1907).

The delicate lemon trees, mentioned by Goethe, grow in the open air during the good season but are sheltered during the winter in characteristic wooden shelters (*limonaie* in Italian, *citronniers* in French).

Le Corbusier's father had a strong love for the South, and Le Corbusier's letters during the trip often associated the father with Italy. The mythical overtones of the trip were partly a sign of his identification with him.

42. [par la negation...j'apprends ce qu'est l'architecture," and "là éclate ce qu'est l'architecture], CEJ to L'Eplattenier, 22 November 1908.

43. Brooks, *Formative Years* (1997): 153–55.

44. [alors rayonna la clarté classique], CEJ to L'Eplattenier, 16 January 1911.

45. On Le Corbusier's appreciation of Fischer and Moser see Brooks, *Formative Years* (1997): 211–13; and especially de Simone, *Viaggio* (1989): 54–57, with full documentation. Le Corbusier's manuscript on urban planning has been published as Charles-Edouard Jeanneret, *La Construction des villes*, ed. Marc E. Albert Emery (Lausanne: L'Age de l'Homme, 1992). For this work by Le Corbusier see Brooks, *Formative Years* (1997): 200 ff; and de Simone, *Viaggio* (1998): 58 ff.

When assessing Le Corbusier's architectural taste upon arrival in Germany in April 1910, a big unresolved question is the status of his design for the Ateliers d'Art Réunis, of which he published two drawings in his *Oeuvre complète, 1910–1929* (p. 22) with a date of 24 January 1910, between his French and German stays. Oechslin and Brooks have seen this design as classicist, its symmetry inspired by Behrens's Oldenburg pavilion; see Oechslin, "Allemagne" (1987): 38–39; Brooks, *Formative Years* (1997): pp. 197–200. Fanelli and Gargiani attribute the centrality to the program, which called for a central teaching hall, and the symmetry to the influence of the Ecole des Beaux-Arts: Fanelli and Gargiani, *Perret e Le Corbusier* (1990): 29–30. I would add three observations. First, the pyramid was probably meant as a skylight over the central court, fully or partially made up of glass. At a time when such skylights were common in banks and post offices, the pyramid had a utilitarian rather than monumental connotation, and an understanding of it along the lines of today's Louvre pyramid by I. M. Pei was unlikely. Second, a specific source of this design was clearly Bernhard Pankok's 1906 Atelier building for the Verein Württenberger Kunstfreunde in Stuttgart, a utilitarian building from which Le Corbusier took the pyramidal glass skylight and the curved transition between wall and cornice. It had been recently published in *Deutsche Kunst und Dekoration*, 20 (June 1907): 117–63, which Le Corbusier certainly consulted at the library of the school in La Chaux-de-Fonds. Third, the centrality of Le Corbusier's plan can be explained in terms of program, both the teaching program which called for a central hall (as Fanelli and Gargiani noted), and the construction program which called for successive building campaigns as needs arose (the concentric rings of the design). Altogether, I see this design as an intentionally diagrammatic embodiment of a functional concept, not as a classicist monumental statement.

46. *Allemagne Carnets*, 2:131–37; CEJ to Ritter, 20 June 1910; CEJ to his parents, 21 June 1910; CEJ to L'Eplattenier, 27 June 1910.
47. [la vie moderne ne peut plus s'en accomoder], *Allemagne Carnets*, 2:164.
48. *Construction des villes* (1992): 98–99.
49. CEJ to August Klipstein, 30 September 1910, quoted in Brooks, *Formative Years* (1997): p. 230.
50. [Et voici que maintenant j'ai tous mes enthousiasmes pour la Grèce pour l'Italie et seulement un intérêt éclectique pour ces arts qui me donnent le malaise, gothiques du nord, barbaries russes, tourments germains], CEJ to L'Eplattenier, 16 January 1911.
51. [Pour moi, l'impression d'admiration absolue pour les ingénieurs et administrateurs géniaux de cette colossale affaire, trouve 1 équilibrante de navrement, de souffrance, à la vue de ces milliers d'hommes et de femmes subordonnées aux machines et moins habiles qu'elles. Bientôt le bras humain sera tout à fait inutile. J'ai vu plusieurs machines surveillées par 1 seul homme. Les opérations plus variées s'effectuent automatiquement], *Allemagne Carnets*, 1:44.
52. [Il y a là de quoi ébranler sérieusement nos principes sur le faux et le véritable. Quoi qu'il en soit, les matériaux ainsi produits sont très beaux], *Allemagne Carnets*, 2:100.
53. This confrontation with the facts of industrial modernity, and surrender to them, was not a simple matter of intellectual categories or Ruskinian aesthetics. For Le Corbusier, son of an artisan in watchmaking, it was a matter of personal experience, and it was painful. Once a home industry, watchmaking in La Chaux-de-Fonds had first become specialized and then moved from the home to the factory, and semi-independent artisans like Le Corbusier's father had been forced into tedious repetitive tasks that Le Corbusier considered "nauseating and humiliating," as he would write to his friend Ritter on 9 May 1913. In Le Corbusier's formative years there were two such painful confrontations and surrenders. We have just discussed the first in 1910, at the AEG. The second confrontation, with Taylorism, the "horrible et inéluctable vie de demain" (horrible and unstoppable life of tomorrow), would take place at the end of 1917, in the course of designing the "Taylorized" slaughterhouse of Challuy (CEJ to Ritter, 29 December 1917). In both cases, Le Corbusier chose not to fight these developments that he abhorred, but to conceptualize architecture in a way that would attribute a higher meaning to them, thus following the line of Behrens and the German Werkbund.
54. [Ah mais, moi aussi je leur dois une chandelle à ces Stauffifer de m'avoir arraché à ma gangue moyen-âgeuse en me revèlant ces styles admirables...Versailles ... la clarté classique. Ce fut long tout de même jusqu'à ce que je puisse me défaire de tant de petites mesquineries qui me faisaient voir l'art très petit], CEJ to L'Eplattenier, 16 January 1911.
55. Albert E. Brinckmann, *Platz und Monument* (Berlin: Wasmuth, 1908). Le Corbusier's knowledge of Brinckmann emerges in "La Construction des villes," in the chapter devoted to urban squares, where many specific analyses repeat points made by Brinckmann: for example, the discussion of Donatello's monument to Gattamelata in Padua and the discussion of the Place des Vosges and Place des Victoires in Paris.
56. I am not aware of any comprehensive treatment of this issue in the secondary literature. A synthetic approach to the issue is proposed in Anderson, "Legacy of German Neo-Classicism" (1991). The primary literature is too extensive to list here.
57. As if to underline the normative and nonindividualistic intent of this kind of classicism, in Behrens's office Le Corbusier was encouraged to *copy* the architectural orders from Schinkel and from standard printed compendia (CEJ to L'Eplattenier, 16 January 1911).
58. [pour aider au cube], CEJ to Ritter, 10 February 1913.
59. LC, *Construction des villes* (1992): "Les éléments plastiques indispensables à la beauté d'une place dérivent tous d'une condition primordiale: *la corporalité*" (The visual elements necessary to the beauty of a square derive, all of them, from a basic condition: *corporeality*), p. 104; "Dans la place publique, le monument est donc un *ornement*. Mais qu'est-ce que cette chose qu'autrefois on nommait et dont depuis un siècle on a perdu la signification? *Elle est une chose objective*, indépendante de toute idée subjective, quelle qu'elle soit; ne ressortant que des trois domaines de la couleur, de la ligne et du volume. Un ornement est une chose *qui fait bien*, avant que d'esprimer quoi que ce soit, ce qui implique donc des idées d'équilibre—mais non forcément de symétrie—et de rythme; exaltation des couleurs, ou formes jouant en de beaux volumes sous les caresses de la lumière ... [emphasis by Le Corbusier]" (In public squares, then, the monument is an *ornament*. But what is this thing that one used to call by its name, and whose meaning was lost a century ago? *It is something objective*, independent from any subjective idea, whatever it may be; it is something arising exclusively from the three domains of color, line, and volume. An ornament is something *that feels good*, before expressing anything, and this implies a notion of balance—but not necessarily symmetry—and of rhythm; triumph of colors, or forms playing in beautiful volumes caressed by the light), p. 121. The chapter on urban squares was probably begun before the visit in Berlin of June 1910, but it was certainly finished after the visit, since its mention of some Berlin monuments (on p. 131) implies a personal acquaintance with them.
60. Le Corbusier's statement that squares must have "le caractère de volume, de chambre" goes back, of course, to Camillo Sitte's book *Der Städtebau*, which Le Corbusier was also reading at the time. On the first page of chapter 3, Sitte compares squares to "Zimmer" (rooms), and talks of "Geschlossenheit des Raumes" (enclosure of the space): Sitte, *Der Städtebau nach seinen künstlerischen Grundsätzen*, 4th ed. (Vienna: Graeser, 1909): 38. Also from Sitte comes the notion that a monument is an ornament to the square: on the first page of chapter 1, Sitte talks of monuments, fountains, and important buildings resulting in "kostbar geschmückten Plätze" (richly ornamented squares; ibid., p. 13).
61. On Blanc's eclectic sources, see Misook Song, *Art Theories of Charles Blanc, 1813–1882* (Ann Arbor: UMI, 1984). A couple of years after reading Blanc, in May 1910 in Munich, Le Corbusier read the principal source of Blanc, the philosopher Victor Cousin who had imported German aesthetic philosophy into France after 1818; Victor Cousin, *Du vrai, du beau et du bien* (Paris: Didier, 1853). Le Corbusier read the 1904 edition and mentioned it in a letter to L'Eplattenier, 19 May 1910. Also, shortly before reading Blanc, Le Corbusier had read Henry Provensal, *L'Art de demain* (Paris: Perrin, 1904), another eclectic work, heavily based on Hegel.
62. Hegel's observation is mentioned in Blanc, *Grammaire* (1880 edition): 62. [combinaison de lignes et de surfaces, de pleins et de vides], ibid., p. 67. [combinaison rationnelle de ces volumes] and [drâme plastique...sous l'activité bienfaisante de la lumière], Provensal, *Art de demain* (1904): 162 and 312.
63. For this section I rely on Mallgrave's excellent synthetic introduction to *Empathy, Form, and Space* (1994). The concept of purposiveness was formulated by Kant in his *Kritik der Urtheilskraft* (1790).
64. Behrens, "Kunst u. Technik" in *Industriekultur*, ed. Buddensieg and Rogge (1979): D280, D282. Brinckmann and Behrens are in turn feeding upon Wölfflin, whose famous dissertation was built around the concept that "our own bodily organization is the form through which we apprehend everything physical" (Unsre leibliche Organisation ist die Form, unter der wir alles Körperliche auffassen). Heinrich Wölfflin, *Prolegomena zu einer Psychologie der Architektur* (Munich: Wolf und Sohn, 1886); English trans. in *Empathy, Form, and Space* by Mallgrave and Ikonomou (1994): 149–185; quote from 157–58.
65. Le Corbusier met Klipstein in late June 1910, immediately upon returning from his first visit to Berlin.
66. The word *corporalité* does not exist in the French dictionary and was clearly translated from the German "Körperlichkeit." The comment about Hamlet, written in September 1910 in Munich, is found in *Allemagne Carnets*, 3:5–6.
67. The Symbolist label had been applied to the circle of *poets* around Mallarmé since 1886. The *painters* around Gauguin and van Gogh had been called, instead, Synthetist and neo-Traditionist: they only acquired the Symbolist label in 1891, thanks to their close association with the poets.
68. [un tableau avant d'être une représentation de quoi que ce soit, c'est une surface plane recouverte de couleurs en un certain ordre assemblées, et pour le plaisir des yeux;] Gauguin and his followers [ont cru qu'il existait à toute émotion, à toute pensée humaine, un équivalent plastique, décoratif.], Maurice Denis, "Préface à la IXe exposition des peintres impressionnistes et symbolistes" (1895), in *Théories, 1890–1910: Du Symbolisme et de Gauguin vers un nouvel ordre classique* (Paris: Occident, 1912): 25–29. Denis had been saying this, in virtually the same words, since 1890.
69. In a famous juxtaposition of symbol and allegory, Goethe had said that, in a work of art using a symbolic approach, objects "appear to exist for themselves alone and are nevertheless significant at the deepest level." Goethe, "Über die Gegenstände der bildenden Kunst" (1797), in *Jubiläumsausgabe*, vol. 33, 94; note that Goethe articulated many different versions of the same definition over the following decades. For the crystallization of the concept of "Symbol" around the time of Goethe see Tzvetan Todorov, *Theories of the Symbol* (Oxford: Blackwell, 1982): 199–209. Todorov points out that, today, we might use the term "motivated sign."

    That Denis had the concept of "symbol" in mind, when writing of "équivalent plastique, décoratif," is confirmed in a later essay, which Le Corbusier certainly read, in which Denis wrote that Gauguin and his friends operated through "la théorie de l'équivalence ou du symbole." Denis, "De Gauguin et de Van Gogh au classicisme" (1909), in *Théories* (1912): 262–78.

    Denis was well aware of current German culture, like most young French intellectuals at that time; in his case, two specific links were his friendship with André Gide, who had spent time in Munich and was deeply influenced by Goethe, and since 1894–95 his acquaintance with the German critic Julius Meier-Graefe.

    In Paris other critics besides Denis were attempting to set up a critical framework that would account for the painting of Gauguin and van Gogh. While Denis stressed form, albeit symbolic, Denis's chief competitor Aubert Aurier stressed content (temperament, idea, and so on). His essays were gathered in Albert Aurier, *Textes critiques, 1889–1892: De l'Impressionnisme au symbolisme* (1893; reprint, Paris: École Nationale des Beaux-Arts, 1995).
70. Denis's turn to classicism was formalized in his article, "Les Arts à Rome ou la méthode classique" (1898), in *Théories* (1912): 45–56.
71. "Au point de vue objectif, la composition décorative, esthétique et rationnelle . . . devenait la *contre-partie, le correctif nécessaire* de la théorie des équivalents. Celle-ci autorisait en vue de l'expression toutes les transpositions même caricaturales, tous les excès de caractère; la déformation objective obligeait à son tour l'artiste à tout transposer en Beauté. En résumé, la synthèse expressive, le symbole d'une sensation devait en être une transcription éloquente, et *en même temps* un objet composé pour le plaisir des yeux" (From an objective point of view, the decorative or aesthetic or rational composition . . . became *the counterpoint, the needed correction* to the theory of equivalents [i.e., to the theory of symbolism]. For the sake of expression, this theory authorized any transposition, even ridiculous ones, any exaggeration of character; objective deformation, in turn, forced the artist to translate everything into Beauty. Summing up: the expressive synthesis, the symbol had to be an eloquent translation of a sensation, and *at the same time* it had to be an object composed for the pleasure of the eye), Denis, "De Gauguin et de Van Gogh au classicisme," in ibid., p. 268.
72. Denis's criticism was written in French, which made it more accessible to Le Corbusier. Denis had launched the career of sculptor Aristide Maillol, who was highly successful in Germany at the time of Le Corbusier's stay there (including with Behrens), and several articles were translated into German, all of which facilitated dialogue for Le Corbusier while in Munich and Berlin. Also, through Geneva and the movement "La Voile Latine," Denis was well known to Le Corbusier's friend in Munich, William Ritter; and finally, again through Geneva, Denis was an important influence in the rythmic dance movement of Jacques Dalcroze. Not only did Le Corbusier's brother Albert belong to this group, but the group was located in Dresden-Hellerau while Le Corbusier was in Berlin.
73. Note that the notion of "symbolic form" used by Denis was fully understood by Le Corbusier. Thus, in Munich in September 1910, he critized Fritz Erler's sets for a performance of Hamlet: "Banalité, aucune transposition, du naturalisme... il faut sortir d'1 cadre naturel, et hardiment prendre la ligne, le volume, et la couleur symboliques. Il faut que les costumes soient des ornements et que les groupements soi[en]t absolument descriptifs en eux-même" (Banality, no transposition, just naturalism . . . one must get out of a naturalist frame of mind, and boldly use symbolic lines, volumes and colors. Costumes must be ornaments, and any arrangement must absolutely speak for itself), *Allemagne Carnets*, 3:5–6; this is the same passage in which Le Corbusier uses the word *wirktaient* mentioned earlier.
74. CEJ to L'Eplattenier, 16 January 1911. Le Corbusier is speaking here of "la nouvelle tendance d'aujourd'hui" (the new trend of today), and he repeatedly refers by the letter "X" to a sculptor whose name he has forgotten: but it is clear from the context that he is thinking of Maillol, who was much admired at that time in Behrens's office.
75. Le Corbusier-Saugnier [pseud.], "Trois rappels à MM. les architectes. Premier rappel: le volume," *L'Esprit nouveau* 1 (October 1920): 92, later incorporated in *Vers une architecture*, p. 16.
76. [du volume à la façon d'1 Stuck ou d'un Behrens], *Allemagne*

Carnets, 4:37; [le bloc n'y est pas], ibid, p. 47. Le Corbusier had visited Stuttgart and Darmstadt on 20 and 22–23 April 1911.

77. See, for example, the exquisite sketches made in April and May 1911, after leaving Behrens: for Munich, House in Gabelsbergerstrasse, see reproduction in Gresleri, *Viaggio* (1984): 21; for Munich, Theatinerkerk and Odeonsplatz, see de Simone *Viaggio* (1989): figs. 187–88; for Prague, see Brooks, *Formative Years* (1997): 260. See also the catalogue section in this volume.

78. [Ce sont les cubes qui agissent], *VDO Carnets*, 2:116–17; [entente des volumes admirable], ibid., 3:32. The notes were made around 1 and 16–18 August 1911, respectively.

79. [Mais Rome a les vieux Romains de la brique cuite, et le bon Dieu a permis que tous les revêtements de marbre aient été volés. Alors c'est magnifique, unique, subjugant. Ça c'est du musée pour architecte!], CEJ to Klipstein, ca. 27 October 1911.

80. See the long tirade written in Naples, soon after his arrival from Athens, in Le Corbusier's notebook: "Je suis très affecté par toutes ces choses d'Italie. J'avais vécu ces 4 mois de magistrale simplicité: la mer, des monts tous de pierre et tous de même profil. La Turquie av. les mosquées et les maisons de bois et les cimetières, la Grece avec l'athos et l'église byzantine, le Temple et la cahute. Le Temple c'est toujours des colonnes et un entablement....C'était le principe unitaire à outrance. —De Brindisi j'ai vu tous les styles et toutes les sortes de maisons, et toutes sortes d'arbres et de fleurs, de l'herbe. Les monts ont une ~~personnalité~~ [crossed out by LC] figure. Mais surtout les styles se compliquent. C'est des complexes souvent laids, affreux, degoutants...Les gens dans les rues crient et manquent de tact. Tout porte à distinguer les Turcs. Ils étaient polis, graves; ils avaient le *respect* des choses. Leur oeuvre est immense et belle, grandiose. Quelle unité! Quelle immuabilité, quelle sagesse. Hélas pourquoi ça s'écroule-t-il? Cà s'écroule partout. Toute honnêteté tombe...il ne reste plus rien qui soit *Original*. Pourquoi notre progrès est-il laid. Pourquoi ceux qui ont encore un sang vierge aiment-ils prendre de nous le plus mauvais..." [emphasis by LC] (I am deeply affected by all these Italian things. I had lived these 4 months in magisterial simplicity: the sea, the mountains, all of stone and all with the same profile. Turkey w/the mosques and the wood houses and the cemeteries, Greece with the athos and the Byzantine church, the Temple and the hut. The Temple is always columns and an entablature... It was the unitary principle, all the way. Since Brindisi I have seen every style and type of house, and all sorts of trees and flowers and grasses. The mountains have a ~~personality~~ figure. But above all the styles get complicated. Complexes that are often ugly, horrible, disgusting... The people in the streets are loud and often lack tact. Everything makes one single out the Turks. They were polite, serious; they had a *respect* for things. Their work is immense and beautiful, grandiose. What unity! What immutability, what wisdom. Alas, why is it all collapsing? Its falling to pieces all over. All honesty collapses.... nothing remains that is *Original*. Why is our progress ugly. Why do those who still possess a virgin blood love to take the worst things from us...) *VDO Carnets*, 4:67–69. With some modifications, this text was used in the chapter titled "En Occident," in *Voyage d'orient* (1966).

81. CEJ, "La Maison Suisse," *Les Etrennes helvétiques* (1914): 33–39, written in September 1913 (CEJ to William Ritter, 25 September 1913), submitted in December 1913 and published the following year. The original passage, from p. 33, reads: "Vers les pays de l'Est où tout se résout en une simplification extrême, nous avions pu limpidement discuter d'architecture grecque, turque, tschèque ou serbe; c'était le règne fort et serein d'un *type*, symbole d'une race unitaire, d'institutions unitaires, d'une nature égale." This passage is based on the remarks transcribed above, in n. 80. After this passage, the article asked whether such unity of type is possible in Switzerland and concluded that Switzerland's ethnic and topographical fragmentation militated against it. Note that the article was written before Le Corbusier read Adolf Loos (later in that fall) and before he witnessed the debate on type at the Cologne meeting of the Werkbund (in the following summer).

82. The attitude is particularly obvious in Le Corbusier's early essays about the Balkan vernacular (houses, pottery, music) written during the first part of the Voyage d'Orient. Some were published in a local newspaper in La Chaux-de-Fonds and were later included in *Le Voyage d'orient* (1966). We know that Le Corbusier read Schultze-Naumburg because he copied several figures from one of his books, Paul Schultze-Naumburg, *Kulturarbeiten*, vol. 4, *Städtebau* 3rd ed. (Munich: Callwey, 1909). For Ritter and the sources and implications of Le Corbusier's interest for the vernacular see Francesco Passanti, "The Vernacular, Modernism, and Le Corbusier," *Journal of the Society of Architectural Historians* 56, no. 4 (December 1997): 438–51, esp. 444–45.

83. We have already seen, in discussing the issue of architectural volume, that Le Corbusier was familiar with the notion of "symbol," used by Maurice Denis and ultimately derived from Goethe; and this familiarity predated the Voyage d'Orient. Here we are interested in the intersection of "symbol" and "type," which emerges only during the Voyage d'Orient.

84. [J'avais vécu...un entablement], *VDO Carnets*, 4:67–69. For full quotation see above, n. 80.

85. Ibid., 4:138–41, 178–81. Le Corbusier's interest in distilling visual symbols down to their essentials is pervasive in this period, and by no means limited to architecture. He was also making notes about the stock characters of the Commedia dell'Arte (Harlequin, Pulcinella, etc.); see ibid., pp. 156–59. And he was seeking shorthand depictions of the human body. Shortly before sketching the visual logos of Belvedere and so on, he had noted about a Roman statue, a standing male nude, that its back was "une grosse vague, tandis que devant c'est 1 planche" (a big wave, while the front is like a board), ibid., p. 59; and shortly afterward, at the Uffizi in Florence, he commented about Titian's Venus of Urbino that "1 femme c'est toujours *une* ligne au dos, et une vague devant—au contraire de l'homme [emphasis by LC]" (a woman is always *one* line behind, and a wave in front—unlike a man), *VDO Carnet*, 5:110.

86. [Je crois que l'horizontalité du toujours même horizon et surtout, en plein midi, l'uniformité imposante des matériaux perçus, installent en chacun la mesure la plus humainement perceptible de l'absolu. Dans l'irradiation de l'après-midi, voici qu'apparut la pyramide d'Athos!...Des pélerins...maintiennent en leur foule un silence radieux ou anxieux qui, au moment où les hélices suspendent leur action, confère aux brefs ordres partis de la passerelle haute, la solennité d'un arrêt. Le grincement des chaines, les ancres immergées, l'immobilité...L'obsession du symbole est au fond de moi d'une expression-type du langage, circonscrite à la valeur de quelques mots. La vocation en est cause: le régime des pierres et des charpentes, des volumes, des pleins et des vides, m'a valu une compréhension peut-être trop générale de la verticale et de l'horizontale, du sens de la longueur, de la profondeur, de la hauteur. Et de considérer ces éléments, ces mots même, comme détenteurs de significations infinies, inutiles à diluer puisque le mot en soi, dans son absolue et forte unité, les exprime toutes...Je laisserai s'étioler ma culture, scrupuleuse du détail, qu'un maître m'inculqua. La considération du Parthénon, bloc, colonnes et architraves, suffira à mes désirs comme la mer en soi et rien que pour ce mot...Tout l'Orient m'a paru forgé à grands coups de symboles...Et j'aimerais les rapports géométriques, le carré, le cercle, et les proportions d'un rapport simple et caractérisé], LC, *Voyage d'orient* (1966): 125–27.

This text was written during the spring of 1914 for the chapter on Mount Athos; the manuscript ends with the inscription, "ce 24 juin 1914" (BV, LC MA 84). For dating of the whole chapter see also Brooks, *Formative Years* (1997): 257–58.

87. [L'élément puriste est comme un mot plastique dûment formé, complet, à réactions précises et universelles], Amédée Ozenfant and CEJ, "Le Purisme," *L'Esprit nouveau*, no. 4 (January 1921): 369–86, quote from p. 377.

88. Referring to this quality of Le Corbusier's interior spaces, von Moos writes aptly of his "spatial sequences, with their 'open' grouping and mainly lateral connections" ('offen' gruppierten, meist seitlich miteinander verknüpften Raumfolgen); see Stanislaus von Moos, "Le Corbusier und Loos," in *L'Esprit nouveau: Le Corbusier und die Industrie* (1987): 132.

Adolf Loos's *Raumplan* and the halls of English houses have been proposed as sources of this quality in Le Corbusier's architecture; see ibid.; and Max Risselada, ed., *Raumplan versus Plan Libre: Adolf Loos and Le Corbusier, 1919–1930* (New York: Rizzoli, 1988). To these sources I would add ancient Roman houses, of which Le Corbusier had had a more direct and emotional experience during the Voyage d'Orient (they are discussed below, in the section devoted to the Villa Schwob). What matters here, in our discussion of Le Corbusier's concept of visual "words," is that this concept informs his *interpretation* of those precedents and accounts for the specifically Corbusian quality of his interiors.

89. For example, commenting on current painting, the critic Téodore de Wyzewa wrote: "Voici désormais ces couleurs, et ces contours, et ces expressions, liés dans notre âme à ces émotions; et les voici devenus non plus seulement les signes des sensations visuelles, mais les signes aussi de nos émotions ... comme les syllabes de la poésie, comme les notes de la musique, des *signes émotionnels* [emphasis by Wyzewa]" (Here from now on these colors, and these contours, and these expressions are linked in our soul to these emotions; and now they have become not only signs of visual sensations, but signs also of our emotions... like the syllables of poetry, like the notes of music, *emotional signs*), Téodore de Wyzewa, "L'Art Wagnérien; la peinture" (1886), quoted in Robert Herbert, "Les théories de Seurat et le Néo-Impressionnisme," in Jean Sutter, *Les Néo-impressionnistes* (Lausanne, 1970): 36–37.

Le Corbusier compared the visual arts to verbal language frequently in this period. A few months before composing the essay on Mount Athos he had written to Perret that, once architects will have gotten rid of their superfluities, one will find in architecture the kind of emotive power that one finds in poetry: "Alors la partie *art* de l'architecture, d'instant éclatera; je veux dire qu'en certains lieux ou points de la demeure on trouvera une note émotive *en plastique* aussi intense et pure que toutes celles que si modernement, nous *aimons* savoir enfouies sous les deux pages de garde uniformément jaunes de nos bouquins à 3.50 f. [emphasis by LC]" (Then the *art* part of architecture will burst forth at once; I mean that in certain places or points of the residence there will be an emotive *plastic* note as intense and pure as all those that, in such modern fashion, we *love* to experience buried between the two uniformly yellow covers of our 3.50 f. books), CEJ to Perret, 27 November 1913. And while writing the essay on Mount Athos, Le Corbusier referred to architecture, as "s'épanouissant au dehors en la *parole* de grands et amples volumes [emphasis added]" (blossoming outside in the *language* of large and ample volumes), CEJ to Ritter, 24 March 1914.

90. Le Corbusier had been familiar with Mallarmé at least since his return from the Voyage d'Orient, if not during the trip already. Le Corbusier first mentions reading Mallarmé in a letter to Ritter of 15 December 1911 (postmarked 18 December), but he may well have known Mallarmé's poetry before that, through Perret in Paris during 1908–9, through his friend Ritter in Munich during 1910–11, or through contacts with the French-speaking group around Jacques Dalcroze, with whom Le Corbusier visited in Dresden several times, from Berlin, in the winter of 1910–11. Also, Le Corbusier talked about recent French poetry with Perret when they met by chance in Istanbul during the Voyage d'Orient in the summer of 1911, as we know from Le Corbusier's correspondence. It is quite possible that he started reading Mallarmé during the second part of the Voyage d'Orient. Eventually, in 1914 Le Corbusier bought Mallarmé's *Vers et prose* (Paris: Perrin, 1912), which was first published in 1893, and kept reading the book later in life, as testified by a stub from Air France left among its pages. I thank Mardges Bacon for checking the book for me at the FLC.

91. [Un désir indéniable à mon temps est de séparer comme en vue d'attributions différentes le double état de la parole, brut ou immédiat ici, là essentiel...A quoi bon la merveille de transposer un fait de nature en sa presque disparition vibratoire selon le jeu de la parole, cependant; si ce n'est pour qu'en émane, sans la gêne d'un proche ou concret appel, la notion pure. Je dis: une fleur! et, hors de l'oubli où ma voix relègue aucun contour, en tant que quelque chose d'autre que les calices sus, musicalement se lève, idée même et suave, l'absente de tous bouquets], Mallarmé, "Crise de vers," (1886) in *Oeuvres complètes*, Bibliothèque de la Pléiade (Paris: Gallimard, 1945): 368; English translation from Mallarmé, *Selected Prose Poems, Essays & Letters*, trans. Bradford Cook (Baltimore: Johns Hopkins, 1956): 42. This passage appeared first in Mallarmé's preface to René Ghil, *Traité du Verbe* (Paris, 1886). It was then included in the essay "Divagation première: relativement au vers," in Mallarmé's *Vers et prose* (Paris, 1893), which Le Corbusier owned; a slightly modified version of this essay subsequently appeared as "Crise de vers," in Mallarmé's *Divagations* (Paris, 1897).

The influence of Mallarmé is felt not only in the content of Le Corbusier's passage, but also in its literary style, which is rich in Mallarméan mannerisms, for example in the sentence, "L'obsession du symbole est au fond de moi d'une expression-type du langage . . . " (cited in full in n. 86 above).

92. The foundational article of Purism, in which the call for Phileban solids occurs, is Amédée Ozenfant and CEJ, "Sur la Plastique," *L'Esprit nouveau*, no. 1 (October 1920): 38–48, esp. p. 43. The use of Phileban solids is justified, there, by the positivist statement that certain simple forms provoke controllable and repeatable sensations. But the Platonic overtones are undeniable and consonant with the postwar politics of "retour à l'ordre."

In the same issue Le Corbusier published his article "Trois rappels...le volume," and came back to the same solids. This article was later included in *Vers une architecture*.

The figures of Phileban solids from the article "Sur la Plastique" were later shown in the article "Architecture: I, La leçon de Rome," *L'Esprit nouveau*, no. 14 (January 1922), and also in *Vers une architecture*.

Rayner Banham called attention to the Platonic overtone of these solids: see Banham, *Theory and Design* (1960): 205, 225. Banham was correct in considering the call for Phileban solids a concession to the academic approach and to the general mood of *retour à l'ordre* in postwar France. What the prewar essay by Le Corbusier shows, however, is that his initial impulse had been a Symbolist search for intensified meaning, and that after the war, with Ozenfant, he created a mixed Platonic-Positivist justification for what he sought.

93. The concept of *Sachlichkeit* has already been briefly mentioned at the end of the discussion of classicism. It had arisen since the 1890s within a broad pursuit of cultural unity, in reaction to the perceived disaggregation of society that industrialization had brought. Hence, opposition to individualism (nouveau-riche extravagance, artistic originality) and appreciation of the normal and normative. Within this broad cultural pursuit, advocates of *Sachlichkeit* in Germany and Austria felt that the "facts" of daily life might act as unifying factors, both because they are widely shared and understood and because they are inherently characteristic of modern society. First, Loos, Muthesius, and and Heinrich Tessenow focused on the humble facts of domestic use and practicality; then Scheffler, Behrens (and later Gropius and Muthesius) focused on the monumental facts of urban life, factories, and department stores; and finally, Friedrich Naumann and Muthesius focused on standardized consumer products. The association Deutsche Werkbund acted as clearing house and pressure group.

For a broader discussion of the concept of *Sachlichkeit*, with bibliography, see Passanti, "Vernacular" (1997): 442–43 and nn.

94. Walter Gropius, "Die Entwicklung moderner Industriebaukunst," in *Jahrbuch des Deutschen Werkbundes 1913* (Jena: Diederichs, 1913): 17–22; illustrations before p. 17. Le Corbusier owned this *Jahrbuch* and took from it the idea of using images of grain silos and factories (and he also took three specific photographs) for his own essays "Trois rappels...le volume" and "Trois rappels...la surface," in *Vers une Architecture*. He had probably acquired the *Jahrbuch* at the stand of the Deutsche Werkbund, when he visited the International Baufachausstellung in Leipzig, in June 1913. In any case, he owned this *Jahrbuch* by 1915, when he offered to lend it to Perret (CEJ to Perret, 30 June 1915).

95. [scheint sich bei ihren Erbauern der natürliche Sinn für grosse, knapp gebundene Form, selbständig, gesund und rein erhalten zu haben], Gropius, "Entwicklung" (1913): 22. The praise for the engineer was reinforced by another article on a similar topic in the same volume; see Hermann Muthesius, "Das Form-Problem im Ingenieurbau," in *Jahrbuch*... (1913): 23–32. It is quite likely that Le Corbusier read this one as well. Like Gropius, Muthesius praised the aesthetic sense of the engineers and the boldness and visibility of their work. But while Gropius admired the *unselfconscious* work of the engineers, Muthesius advocated a *conscious* pursuit of beauty on their part; and while Gropius was impressed by the massive closed form of factories and silos, Muthesius admired open structures such as bridges just as well.

96. [Je cherche à partir pour l'Amérique...J'ai besoin de grand travail], CEJ to Karl Ernst Osthaus, 7 August 1913. Le Corbusier's thought of moving to America was prompted by a sharp economic downturn in La Chaux-de-Fonds, which had left him without work and encouraged the rethinking of his role in society as an architect. By this time, Le Corbusier probably owned the *Jahrbuch* and had read Gropius's article. He had probably also read H. P. Berlage's "Neuere amerikanische Architektur," *Schweizerische Bauzeitung* 60 (14 September 1912): 148–50; ibid. (21 September 1912): 165–67; ibid. (28 September 1912): 178, with good illustrations of work by Louis Sullivan and Frank Lloyd Wright. In a letter to H. T. Wijdeveld of 5 August 1923, and in the introduction to *Oeuvre complète, 1910–1929* (1937/1964): 10, Le Corbusier acknowledged having seen this publication in 1913 or 1914–15 and expressed his admiration for both architects. However, it is not known exactly when he saw this publication. What matters, in any case, is that economic and ideal considerations coalesced to sharpen Le Corbusier's receptivity to the *sachlich* argument and to America at this time. It was at this point that America, land of the modern "noble savage" and a new monumentality, and big jobs, first acquired its lure for Le Corbusier.

97. Perret lent the essays to Le Corbusier, probably during a trip to Paris in October 1913. Le Corbusier comments in a letter of 27 November 1913.

The essay "Architektur" had first appeared in Berlin, when Le Corbusier was there, in *Der Sturm* 42 (15 December 1910), but Le Corbusier was not aware of it. It was then published in French as "L'architecture et le style moderne," *Les Cahiers d'aujourd'hui* 2 (December 1912): 829 ff., and eventually it was included in Adolf Loos, *Trotzdem* (Innsbruck: Brenner, 1931).

The essay "Architektur und Verbrechen" was probably written in late 1908, was known to insiders by 1909, and read to a group in Vienna in 1910. It was first published in French as "Ornement et crime," *Les Cahiers d'aujourd'hui* 5 (June 1913): 247 ff. The first documented German printing was in 1929. Eventually it was included in Loos's *Trotzdem*. For the history of publication see Burkhardt Ruckschio and Roland Schachel, *Adolf Loos* (Vienna: Residenz, 1982): 118, 121, 147, 182, 352, 367.

98. For example the art critic Octave Mirbeau, feeding on the rationalist position, wrote in *Figaro* (1890): "Pendant que l'art... piétine sur place, embarassée et timide, le regard encore tourné vers le passé, l'industrie marche de l'avant, explore l'inconnu, conquiert des formes" (While art marks time, confused and timid, still looking back to the past, industry moves ahead, explores the unknown, conquers new forms), quoted in Paul Chemetov and Bernard Marrey, *Architectures, Paris, 1848–1914* (Paris: Dunod, 1980): 77.

99. Rousseau's notion of "noble savage" had had a special place in Le Corbusier's education since childhood. See Adolf Max Vogt, *Le Corbusier, der edle Wilde* (Braunschweig: Vieweg, 1996); English transl., *Le Corbusier, The Noble Savage* (Cambridge: MIT Press, 1998).

100. [le rythme, la cadence des volumes, l'engendrement des masses, la proportion], CEJ, "Le Renouveau dans l'architecture," *L'Oeuvre, revue mensuelle* (Bern) 2 (June 1914): 33–37. Le Corbusier wrote the article in the second half of January 1914. Aimed at the Swiss audience, the essay begins by ridiculing those who fear the aesthetic dissonance of old and new in cities and by arguing that change and progress are inevitable, and it ends by affirming that a willfully regionalist architecture is impossible. Note that most illustrations in the article, devoted to the new Zurich university by Curjel and Moser, are unrelated to Le Corbusier's article and in fact rather contradict his argument. They belong with the article following that of Le Corbusier in the same issue. The debt to Loos is particularly palpable in this article; several passages are lifted directly from Loos's articles already mentioned. On this, see von Moos, "Le Corbusier und Loos" (1987): 122–33, esp. 128.

101. [lorsque l'architecte aura mis dans la maison l'honnête expression du constructeur de paquebot...la partie *art* de l'architecture d'instant éclatera...on trouvera une note émotive *en plastique*] (emphasis by LC), CEJ to Perret, 27 November 1913.

102. Le Corbusier was in Cologne 1–5 July 1914 as a correspondent for *L'Art de France*; the congress of the Werkbund took place on 3–4 July. For chronology see Brooks, *Formative Years* (1997): 369–72.

103. For a more extended discussion of Muthesius's intervention, and for bibliography, see Passanti, "Vernacular" (1997): 442–43.

104. Le Corbusier understood quite well this central *sachlich* concept: that types—vernacular and industrial alike—gain their formal and functional quality, as well as their representativeness, precisely from the anonymity of the process by which they are slowly refined. He was explicit in 1923 when, in a critique of the Bauhaus program, he insisted that the perfection of type ("le standart") arises from below, and cannot be imposed from above: "Pédagogie," *L'Esprit nouveau* 19 (December 1923), n.p. On this, see von Moos, "Le Corbusier und Loos" (1987): 124–25, and Nerdinger, "Standard und Typ," 48–49.

105. It is also possible that Le Corbusier picked up the meaning "industrial brand" which the root word "*Typ*" has in German—though his German may not have been good enough for it. If he did, that would have reinforced a penchant for slogans that he had learned from Perret. For example, a house type that Le Corbusier drew under Perret's instructions was called "Maison Bouteille" because Perret had stated that "une maison, c'est une bouteille," i.e. a container. Whether spurred by Perret or by the German debate, Le Corbusier often used brand names for his housing schemes (Dom-ino, Citrohan, Monol, etc.), names that signify and enhance the typicality of the housing types.

106. Note that, for the sake of concision, this essay jumps from the villas Jeanneret and Favre-Jacot in 1912 to the Villa Schwob in 1916 without mentioning any designs between these two moments. This should not leave the impression that Le Corbusier devoted himself to pure theoretical speculation during those years. In fact, he produced numerous architectural designs that remained unbuilt: a Schinkelesque remodeling of an old farm known as the Maison du Diable in 1912; a classicizing commercial building for the watchmaking firm of Paul Ditisheim in 1913; a classicizing competition design for the Banque Cantonale de Neuchâtel in early 1914; a house for August Klipstein's brother Felix in late 1914, inspired by memories of the Voyage d'Orient; the Pont Butin in early 1915, inspired by ancient Roman viaducts; the Dom-ino housing system in 1914–16; the remodeling of a farmhouse for Fritz Zbinden in early 1915; an apartment house for La Chaux-de-Fonds in 1916 with Parisian overtones; a seaside villa, maybe for Paul Poiret, in 1916; and others. Also, he produced numerous interiors. And finally, he designed and built the classicizing cinema La Scala at the same time as Villa Schwob. Brooks, *Formative Years* (1997) contains good discussions and illustrations for most of them. For the purposes of this essay, however, it is more productive to focus on a built work of architecture; and of the two that were built—Villa Schwob and the cinema La Scala—it is the first that best reflects his current preoccupations.

107. Le Corbusier was quite conscious of these shifts. Just a few days after settling on the design, he wrote: "Vous vous souvenez des études de la `maison bouteille' en 1909. Ce sera un peu le principe du *plan*, mais les façades avec terrasses et `à la française'...mais beton armé...Je crois que vous m'approuverez en partie, et que vous mesurerez que Auguste Perret a laissé en moi davantage que Peter Behrens" (You remember the studies for the "bottle house" in 1909. That would be more or less the principle of the *plan*, but the facades with terraces and "à la française"... but in reinforced concrete... I think that you will partly approve of what I am doing, and that you will see that Auguste Perret left more in me than Peter Behrens), CEJ to Perret, 21 July 1916. This admits the influence of Perret on his present work and that of Behrens on his earlier one. Note that the shift of emphasis from Germany to France had started at the end of 1912, when Le Corbusier began regular trips to Paris, partly occasioned by his growing activity as interior decorator in La Chaux-de-Fonds. Since then, contacts with Perret and his milieu had become increasingly close. The start of World War I had sharpened the connection, and Le Corbusier moved to Paris in early 1917.

108. On the Villa Schwob see Brooks, *Formative Years* (1997): 424–63; and Gast, *Le Corbusier* (2000): 16–25, esp. 16–20, for a good formal analysis.

In 1917 Le Corbusier built a small water tower in Podensac near Bordeaux, clearly inspired by early nineteenth-century classicism, and a few unexecuted designs of 1917 also have a clear classicist character. But these were all small jobs where he had little at stake. See Brooks, *Formative Years* (1997): 474–77.

109. The original inspiration from the Maison Bouteille is acknowledged by Le Corbusier himself in a letter to Perret of 21 July 1916, and in *L'Esprit Noveau*, no. 6 (March 1921): 704, at the end of an article presenting Villa Schwob. For all evidence and an excellent discussion about the Maison Bouteille, see Brooks, *Formative Years* (1997): 165–66, illus. pp. 166–69 and 431.

110. As Brooks shows, in designing the master block of Villa Schwob, Le Corbusier inflected the Maison Bouteille through two other precedents. One was the villa of Le Corbusier's parents, with a T-shaped arrangement of main rooms and two smaller square rooms filling the corners. This house had been liked by an aunt of Anatole Schwob and was naturally in mind when Le Corbusier developed the new villa (Brooks, *Formative Years* (1997): 425–26). The other precedent was the studio of the painter Théodore van Rysselberghe on the French coast, a very tall rectangular space with a large, floor-to-ceiling window at one end, visited by Le Corbusier in the previous year, and sketched by him in a recent letter to Perret (ibid., p. 459).

111. Brooks, *Formative Years* (1997): 433, fig. 360.

112. In the interest of brevity, there is no discussion of the proportions in Villa Schwob here. Requiring detailed geometric analysis, such a discussion would be long and in the end would add little to the general discussion of proportions earlier in this essay. An extensive analysis is found in Gast, *Le Corbusier* (2000): 20–25. The proportional system used at Villa Schwob is based on the golden section, and Le Corbusier was sufficiently pleased with the result to publish several diagrams of the elevations. See Julien Caron [pseud.], "Une villa de Le Corbusier 1916," *L'Esprit nouveau*, no. 6 (March 1921): 679–704. Julien Caron was a pseudonym for Amédée Ozenfant, who produced the journal together with Le Corbusier; the article was probably written by Le Corbusier himself, and certainly inspired by him. As Gast shows, the proportions are even more pervasive than Le Corbusier acknowledges, and they affect the plan as well as the elevations, much as in the Villa Favre-Jacot.

113. Hoepfner and Neumeyer, *Wiegand* (1979): passim.

114. The blind panel has been explained by Colin Rowe as a modern equivalent of Mannerist unease, by Fanelli and Gargiani as an echo of Perret's Théatre des Champs Elysées, and by Brooks as

the logical outcome of incorporating the Maison Bouteille scheme, which calls for a stairhall at that location; Brooks also clearly established that the panel was intended to contain some kind of ornament. Colin Rowe, "Mannerism and Modern Architecture" (1950), in *The Mathematics of the Ideal Villa and Other Essays* (Cambridge: MIT Press, 1976), 30–57; Fanelli and Gargiani, *Perret e Le Corbusier* (1990): 56; Brooks, *Formative Years* (1997): 432, 459–61.

115. Note that this tension was probably part of the design concept from the beginning, even before a service addition was interposed between master block and street. The initial master block based on the Maison Bouteille was itself directional, open to the garden and closed to the street; see Brooks, *Formative Years* (1997): 432. And the initial master block was not isolated but backed up against the street, with its street facade continuous with the property wall, as two early sketches show; see ibid., p. 430, fig. 356 and 436, fig. 363, right.

116. For Le Corbusier's notes and sketches from his visit see *VDO Carnets*, 4:116–21. For a contemporary reconstruction of the Villa of Diomedes see August Mau, *Pompeji in Leben und Kunst*, 2d ed. (Leipzig: Engelmann, 1908), 376–81: Le Corbusier probably knew this book too.

Whereas I focus on the tension between closed street and open garden side and interpret it in Pompeian terms, and Brooks sees it as the automatic result of using the Maison Bouteille scheme, Gast focuses on the "directionality" of the plan and sees in it a recurring aesthetic preference by Le Corbusier, beginning with his early houses Stotzer and Jaquemet of 1907–8; see Gast, *Le Corbusier* (2000): 16–17.

117. Note that the lower garden appears in early schemes for the house (Brooks, *Formative Years* [1997]: 430), then is eliminated in intermediate schemes (ibid., p. 432), and reappears again in the executed version. Note also a detail that makes the parallel between the Villa of Diomedes and the Villa Schwob even more precise: in the Villa of Diomedes, the rounded master bedroom was housed in an absidal wing that stuck out of the otherwise straight boundary of the villa.

118. This Pompeian association also throws light on the undeniably polemical "strangeness" of the villa in La Chaux-de-Fonds. In 1916 Le Corbusier was angry, isolated, and trying to leave town; a comment about the Villa Schwob and its flat roof, in a letter, shows him projecting these feelings on his architecture: "En l'occasion, de toit il n'y en aura point; enfin! Des bains de soleil sur le toit et des fleurs; en hiver, de la neige, hélas oui. J'ai beau faire, la clef de l'architecture de ce pays ne se révèle pas. Je suis bien trop volontaire et orgueilleux; mais baiser la savate aux sapins ne me dit rien, tant que les aloé ou autres cactus ne m'auront pas flanqué leur pied quelqu'part" (In this case, there will be no roof: so there! Sunbaths on the roof and flowers; in winter, snow, alas yes. No matter what I do, the key to the architecture of this place escapes me. True, I am too stubborn and proud. But I don't care to kiss the boots of our pine trees, and I would rather have aloe and cactus, at least until I get fed up with them), CEJ to Ritter, 17 September 1916. In the last sentence, the idiomatic expression ("baiser . . . quelqu'part") represents a gesture of nostalgic defiance; Le Corbusier uses the Mediterranean to jab at La Chaux-de-Fonds.

119. For an earlier, similar "Roman" reading of the entry hall at the Villa La Roche, see Kurt Forster, "Antiquity and Modernity in the La Roche-Jeanneret Houses of 1923," *Oppositions* 15, no. 16 (winter/spring 1979): 130–53. The importance of the Maison Bouteille, as a souce of the hierarchical space arrangements in Le Corbusier's later work, has been pointed out in H. Allen Brooks, "L'évolution de la conception de l'espace au cours des années d'apprentissage de Charles Edouard Jeanneret à La Chaux-de-Fonds," in *La ville et l'urbanisme après Le Corbusier: Actes du colloque* (La Chaux-de-Fonds: Editions d'en Haut, 1993): 13–31.

120. [Il faut retenir ça que ds toute salle romaine il y a toujours 3 murs pleins. L'autre mur s'ouvre largement et fait participer la salle à l'ensemble], *VDO Carnets*, 5:83. This association was certainly reinforced by Le Corbusier's memory of the Rysselberghe studio, which was on his mind while designing the Villa Schwob. See n. 110, above.

121. Note that the qualities of spatial play and typicality, which had only just surfaced in the villas Jeanneret and Favre-Jacot, remain timid in the Villa Schwob, where the axial diagram dominates and distracts from the character of the individual spaces and from their interplay. Only in Le Corbusier's later work will these qualities emerge strongly and nurture his continued interest for the type. Even so, the Villa Schwob clearly played a central role in the crystallization, from Maison Bouteille to Maison Citrohan, of a spatial type.

122. Initially intended as a flower planter, as all drawings show, the Schwob cornice was eventually built as a simple surface flaring out.

123. On Dom-ino, see Brooks, *Formative Years* (1997): 384–91, with further references.

124. The multiplicity and range of precedents testifies to the homework that Le Corbusier invested in the development of this critical component of the Dom-ino design. Sources for the idea of a planter-parapet were two recent buildings that Le Corbusier noted in Paris—Henri Sauvage's stepped building in Rue Vavin, and a more conventional apartment house with several stepped penthouses near the Eiffel Tower—both with obvious references to Babylonian hanging gardens. These buildings are seen in the drawing FLC 19135, which includes numerous sketches; the house near the Eiffel Tower is identified by a sketchbook note: see *Le Corbusier Sketchbooks*, vol. 1 (New York: Architectural History Foundation and Cambridge: MIT Press, 1981), A2:126–27.

The key formal source is Louis Sullivan's bank at Owatonna, which Le Corbusier had recently seen and admired in Berlage, "Neuere amerikanische Architektur" (1912) pl. 33. The effect of Sullivan's bank is clearly visible in the drawing FLC 19135, where one of the many sketches shows a cubic building with the characteristic cornice and corner frames of Owatonna. Sullivan, in turn, had been inspired by archaeological publications, like those by Charles Chipiez, which Le Corbusier also consulted: see David van Zanten, "Sullivan to 1890," in *Louis Sullivan: The Function of Ornament*, ed. Wim de Wit (New York: Norton, 1986): 13–63.

A further source is Assyrian architecture; its various reconstructions rely, for their cornice, on a bas-relief discovered by Paul-Emile Botta in the mid-nineteenth-century at Khorsabad, showing a hunting pavilion and reproduced by everybody else. Le Corbusier could have seen this pavilion in many archaeological treatises at the Bibliothèque Nationale, among them Georges Perrot and Charles Chipiez, *Histoire de l'art dans l'antiquité*, vol. 1 (Paris: Hatchette, 1882) and Choisy, *Histoire* (1899), 1: 92. I thank Irene Winter, Harvard University, for discussing the archaeological background with me. Whereas Sullivan's cornice is striated, made up of stepped layers of brick, the Khorsabad cornice is smooth, and many of the Dom-ino schemes sketched by Le Corbusier use a smooth cornice. In looking at such archaeological sources, Le Corbusier was probably following the advice of Perret, who used such cornices often during the 1920s. Egyptian and Assyrian cornices, looking more like ceremonial crowns than tectonic support and implying a flat roof, may have been deemed more expressive of the new slab construction.

Still another source is found in Ottoman architecture, where cornices have a nontectonic role as explicitly formal frames for the cubic mass of the building (and often, for the surface of individual walls, in which case the frame entails both vertical and horizontal portions). Le Corbusier had sketched many of these framing cornices, and would reproduce some of his sketches in *Oeuvre complète, 1910–1929* (1937/1964): 18.

The striations of the Schwob cornice may have been borrowed from Josef Hoffmann, for example, from his Austrian pavilion at the International Art Exhibition, Rome 1911, and his Autrian pavilion at the German Werkbund Exhibition, Cologne 1914, both of which Le Corbusier had visited. Other more vernacular sources are suggested in Brooks, *Formative Years* (1997): 462–63.

125. On this, see the excellent work by Réjean Legault, "*L'Appareil de l'architecture moderne*: New Materials and Architectural Modernity in France (1889–1934)," Ph. D. diss., Massachusetts Institute of Technology, 1997.

126. Le Corbusier had come across (and admired) Wright's buildings in the same article in which he had found Sullivan's work; see Berlage, "Neuere amerikanische Architektur" (1912).

Wright's influence on Le Corbusier has been discussed since the 1920s, and more recently by Turner, who finds it extensive, and Brooks, who minimizes it: Paul Venable Turner, "Frank Lloyd Wright and the Young Le Corbusier," *JSAH* 42 (December 1983): 350–59; and Brooks, *Formative Years* (1997): 312–13, 323, 458. The discussion has focused on the ribbon window and the openness of plan and internal spaces. Here, I am interested in narrower stylistic aspects that helped Le Corbusier in crystallizing the architectural language of Villa Schwob.

Le Corbusier's admiration, acknowledged ten years later in a letter to the Dutch architect H. T. Wijdeveld, focused on two aspects, order and reinforced concrete: "ses façades faisaient état du ciment armé" (his facades adknowledged the construction in reinforced concrete); see CEJ to Wijdeveld, 5 August 1925, cited in Turner, "Frank Lloyd Wright and the Young Le Corbusier" (1983): 359. This idea, that Wright was an architect of reinforced concrete, was a misunderstanding, but it helps explain why Le Corbusier would think of Wright while designing the Villa Schwob. Three buildings by Wright, illustrated in the Berlage article, left a mark in Le Corbusier's villa. First, the Larkin building (pl. 37), with its unbroken brick skin which also, like Le Corbusier's, "turns the corner." Second, the smaller Martin house (pl. 35), also in brick, whose tripartite window probably inspired those of the bedroom floor in Villa Schwob: a large rectangular opening flanked by two narrow vertical slits, all three cut directly and without frame in the smooth brick skin and resting on one uninterrupted windowsill in stone or concrete. Above the window, however, Wright keeps the bricks horizontal, thus emphasizing their uniformity, while Le Corbusier lays them vertically, hence techtonically, evoking a flat arch. Third, Unity Temple (pl. 40), whose thin roof slabs jutting in several orthogonal directions may have inspired those that cap the penthouse of Villa Schwob. Le Corbusier was probably familiar, as well, with at least one of the Wasmuth publications of Wright's work, and procured a copy for Perret ("J'ai fait venir pour vous les maisons américaines de Lloyd Wright dont je vous avais parlé" [I procured for you the American houses by Lloyd Wright that I had talked about], CEJ to Perret, 30 June 1915).

127. [Le cube de marbre du portique penètre arbitrairement d(an)s le cylindre de la nef], *VDO Carnets*, 5:13.

128. Bruno Reichlin, "Jeanneret-Le Corbusier, Painter-Architect," in *Architecture and Cubism*, eds. Eve Blau and Nancy Troy (Montreal: Canadian Centre for Architecture, and Cambridge: MIT Press, 1997): 195–218.

129. Ibid.; see also Bruno Reichlin, "Le Corbusier vs De Stijl," in *De Stijl et l'architecture en France*, eds. Yve-Alain Bois and Bruno Reichlin (Liège and Bruxelles: Mardaga, 1985): 91–108; Yve-Alain, Bois, "Cubistic, Cubic, and Cubist," in *Architecture and Cubism*, (1997): 186–94, based on Bois's earlier writings about cubism, esp. "Kahnweiler's Lesson" (1987), in *Painting as Model* by Bois (Cambridge: MIT Press, 1990): 65–97.

130. Reichlin, "Jeanneret-Le Corbusier, Painter-Architect" (1997): 207.

131. Pierre Reverdy, "L'Emotion," *Nord-Sud* 8 (October 1917); and idem, "L'Image," *Nord-Sud* 13 (March 1918): both essays are reprinted in Reverdy, *Oeuvres complètes*: *Nord-Sud, Self defence et autres écrits sur l'art et la poésie (1917–1926)* (Paris: Flammarion, 1975): 52–60 and 73–75. In the first essay, Reverdy argued that a work of art is constructed through elements taken from life. In the second, he argued that the poetic image is born "from the bringing together of two more or less remote realities" (du rapprochement de deux réalités plus ou moins éloignées). Christopher Green has already pointed out the importance of Reverdy for the painting of Juan Gris in the late teens, and for that of Le Corbusier in the late thirties: see Green, *Cubism and Its Enemies* (London and New Haven: Yale University Press, 1987), passim; idem, "The Architect as Artist," in, *Le Corbusier, Architect of the Century*, exhib.cat. (London: Arts Council, 1987): 117.

In the essay "Crise de vers," Mallarmé states that the goal of poetry is to "instituer une relation entre les images, exacte, et que s'en détache un tiers aspect fusible et clair" (to set up a sharp relationship between two images, such that a third element will rise, clear and fusible), and that "Le vers . . . de plusieurs vocables refait un mot total, neuf, étranger à la langue et comme incantatoire" (Out of several words, poetry makes a single new word, total, foreign to the language, a kind of incantation), Mallarmé, *Oeuvres complètes* [1945]: 365, 368. Le Corbusier had taken the concept of visual "words" from that essay, either directly or from conversations with friends, but he seems to have missed the idea of a new reality arising from the tension between "words."

Le Corbusier betrays his knowledge of Reverdy, who contributed to *L'Esprit nouveau*, in the caption under the photograph of an airplane cockpit, in "Des yeux qui ne voient pas. . . Les autos," *L'Esprit nouveau* no. 10 (summer 1921): 1147, later included in *Vers une architecture*. The caption reads: "La poésie n'est que dans le verbe. Plus forte est la poésie des faits. Des objets qui signifient quelque chose et qui sont disposés avec tact et talent créent un fait poétique" (Poetry is not just in the word. Stronger is the poetry of facts. Objects that mean something, arranged with tact and talent, create a poetic fact).

132. The "play" of the Jeanneret volumes is made even more explicit by the fact that one of them (with the tall studio window), appears shifted in plan toward the street, generating the projecting bay window on the facade and leaving behind a corresponding gap through which one enters. Able to slide autonomously from the rest, the shifted volume thus affirms

both its autonomous identity as a spatial "word," and its participation in a "play" with other volumes.

The first design by Le Corbusier in which internal volumes clearly show such "play" is the Villa Berque, designed in the fall of 1921, around the time Le Corbusier wrote the caption mentioned in n. 131 above.

133. [Vous êtes dans un grand espace blanc de marbre, inondé de lumière. Au delà se présente un second espace semblable et de mêmes dimensions, plein de pénombre et surélevé de quelques marches (répétition en mineur); de chaque côté, deux espaces de pénombre encore plus petits; vous vous retournez, deux espaces d'ombre tout petits. De la pleine lumière à l'ombre, un rythme. Des portes minuscules et des baies très vastes. Vous êtes pris, vous avez perdu le sens de l'échelle commune. Vous êtes assujetti par un rythme sensoriel (la lumière et le volume) et par des mesures habiles, à un monde en soi qui vous dit ce qu'il a tenu à vous dire], Le Corbusier-Saugnier, "Architecture...l'illusion des plans," *L'Esprit nouveau*, no. 15 (February 1922): 1769–70, later included in *Vers une architecture*.

CHAPTER 5
THE CHALLENGE OF THE "GRAND SIÈCLE"
Antonio Brucculeri

1. For the various catalogues that have appeared to date, see Phillippe Duboy, "Architecture de la ville, culture et triomphe de l'urbanisme: Ch.-E Jeanneret, 'La Construction des villes,' Bibliothèque Nationale de Paris, 1915," prepared with the Ministère de l'Urbanisme, du Logement et Transport. Paris, 1985; and idem, "Ch.-E. Jeanneret à la Bibliothèque Nationale, Paris, 1915," *AMC. Architecture, mouvement, continuité* 49 (1979): 9–12.
2. According to Bibliothèque Nationale (BN) call slips, Jeanneret consulted two volumes by Charles-Antoine Jombert: *Les Délices de Paris et de ses environs* (Paris: Jombert, 1753); and *Les Délices de Versailles* (Paris: Jombert, 1766); for the call slips, see B2-20-431 and B2-20-391, Fondation Le Corbusier (FLC). Probably as a result of these early readings, he consulted the complete works of Pérelle's engravings, especially vols. 2 and 3, Cabinet des Estampes, BN, Ed.76.b and Ed.76.c. See Pierre Patte, *Monumens érigés en France à la gloire de Louis XV* (Paris, by the author, 1765). Jeanneret consulted yet another work by Patte, *Essai sur l'architecture théâtrale relativement à l'optique et l'acoustique, avec plans des principaux théâtres d'Europe* (Paris: Chez Moutard, 1782). See the call slip, FLC B2-20-408.
3. See Henry Lemonnier, *Procès-verbaux de l'Académie royale d'architecture (1671–1793)*, 10 vols. (Paris: Colin, 1911–29). For Jeanneret's BN call slip, see B2-20-204, FLC. Lemonnier wrote essays on French art and architecture of the seventeenth and eighteenth centuries. See also Henry Lemonnier, *L'Art français à l'époque de Richelieu et Mazarin* (Paris: Hachette, 1893); and idem, *L'Art français au temps de Louis XIV (1661–1691)* (Paris: Hachette, 1911). On Lemonnier, see Lyne Therrien, *L'Histoire de l'art en France: Genèse d'une discipline universitaire* (Paris: Editions du C.T.H.S., 1998): 314–32.
4. See CEJ to Charles L'Eplattenier, Berlin, 16 January 1911, FLC E2-12-54-59, quoted in Rosario De Simone, *Ch.E. Jeanneret-Le Corbusier: Viaggio in Germania, 1910–1911* (Rome: Officina, 1989): 120–26. Jeanneret refers to some sixty images of the interiors of Versailles, Compiègne, and Fontainebleau that he had collected. These are now at the Fondation Le Corbusier: L5-7-287-293, 303-312 and 318-320; L5-5-162-146 and 191. The group includes twenty-six postcards: seven of the interiors of the palace of Versailles dating to the First Empire; ten of the Grand [Trianon]; three of the Petit Trianon; five of the castles in Compiègne; and one of Fontainebleau.
5. Hautecoeur had already expressed his criticism in his doctoral dissertation, which was published as *Rome et la Renaissance de l'antiquité à la fin du XVIIIe siècle* (Paris: Fontemoing, 1912). In 1914 he published an essay and bibliographical account on the topic. See Louis Hautecoeur, "Les origines de l'art Empire," *Revue des études napoléoniennes* 3 (March–April 1914): 145–61; and idem, "Etudes sur l'art du Premier Empire," ibid., (July-August 1914): 122–37. See also François Benoît, *L'art français sous la Révolution et l'Empire: Les doctrines, les idées, les genres* (Paris: L.-H. May, 1897).
6. See Pierre de Nolhac, *La Création de Versailles, d'après les sources inédites: Étude sur les origines et les premières transformations du château et des jardins* (Versailles: L.Bernard, 1901): and idem, *Le Château de Versailles sous Louis XV: recherches sur l'histoire de la cour et sur les travaux des bâtiments du roi* (Paris: Champion, 1898). De Nolhac presented a course in the art of Versailles at the École du Louvre during the academic year 1910–11.
7. See especially Marcel Poëte, *L'Enfance de Paris: Formation et croissance de la ville des origines jusqu'à Philippe-Auguste* (Paris: Colin, 1908); and idem, *La transformation de Paris sous le Second Empire* (Paris: P. Dupont, 1910). For the call slips for these texts, see FLC B2-20-390 and B2-20-414. In the interim Poëte had published a popular text that synthesized the history of the city. See Philippe Duboy, "Bibliothèque Nationale: Paris, 1915," in *Le Corbusier: une encyclopédie* ed. Jacques Lucan (Paris: Centre Georges Pompidou, 1987): 75. For information about Poëte, see Donatella Calabi, *Parigi anni venti: Marcel Poëte e le origini della storia urbana* (Venice: Marsilio, 1997), translated as *Marcel Poëte et le Paris des années vingt: Aux origines de "l'histoire des villes,"* trans. Pierre Savy (Paris: L'Harmattan, 1998).
8. Poëte thanked Le Corbusier for the invitation to the conference on the *Ville contemporaine pour trois millions d'habitants*. Later he wrote to thank him again for sending a copy of his texts *Urbanisme* and *L'Art décoratif d'aujourd'hui*. See Poëte to LC, 20 December 1922, 1 July 1925, and 27 October 1925, FLC A2-11-20, F2-14-275, and 276.
9. See Marcel Poëte, *Paris durant la grande Epoque Classique* (Paris: Dupont, 1911). See also idem, *Promenades et jardins (depuis le XVe siècle jusqu'à 1830)*, exhib. cat. (Paris: Dupont, 1913). This source concentrated on the Jardins des Plantes of the Luxembourg and the Royal Palace during the seventeenth century, using the former as the primary model; two years later Jeanneret focused on four Parisian engravings by Pérelle, one of which also represented the Jardin des Plantes.
10. See Kevin L. Justus, "Louis XV and Versailles: Selective Patrimony in the French Third Republic, Pierre de Nolhac and the Formation of a Scholarly Tradition," Ph.D. diss., University of Arizona, 1991, pp. 39–88.
11. See Antonio Brucculeri, "Dal rigore scientifico all'impegno culturale: Louis Hautecoeur e le mostre di storia dell'architettura francese a Strasburgo e Parigi, 1922–1923," *Annali della Scuola Normale Superiore di Pisa*, ser. 4, no. 2 (1999): 595–613.
12. The ironic appellation, *cité future*, rather than *ville contemporaine*, comes from Vaillat himself. See Léandre Vaillat, "Au Salon d'Automne," *Bâtiment et Travaux Publics* 18, no. 45 (7 December 1922), in newspaper clipping file, FLC X1-2-81.
13. [au train dont va le monde, songeons que tel qui se dit moderne, maintenant, avec orgueil, sera plus rapidement ridicule et démodé que ces maîtres de jadis], idem, "L'Architecture française aux XVIIe et XVIIIe siècles," *Bâtiment et Travaux Publics* 19, no. 8 (28 January 1923).
14. For more on the deterioration of relations between Perret and Le Corbusier, see Giovanni Fanelli and Roberto Gargiani, *Perret e Le Corbusier: Confronti* (Bari-Rome: Laterza, 1990): 137–60.
15. See Bruno Reichlin, "Für und wider das Langfenster: Die Kontroverse Perret-Le Corbusier," *Daidalos* 13 (1984): 65–77.
16. See LC, "Perret par Le Corbusier," *L'Architecture d'aujourd'hui* 3, no. 7 (1932): 8.
17. Perret's opinions are contemporary with those of Le Corbusier. See Auguste Perret,"Architecture et poésie," *La Construction Moderne* 48, no. 2 (12 October 1932): 2–3, quoted in Joseph Abram, *Perret et l'Ecole du classicisme structurel* (Villers-lès-Nancy: CEMPA, 1985), 2: 32–34.
18. See CEJ, "Le Renouveau dans l'architecture," *L'Oeuvre* 1, no. 2 (1914): 33–37, quoted in *Charles-Edouard Jeanneret, La Construction des villes: Genèse et devenir d'un ouvrage écrit de 1910 à 1915 et laissé inachevé par Charles-Edouard Jeanneret-Gris dit Le Corbusier*, ed. Marc E. Albert Emery (Paris-Héricourt: Editions L'Age d'Homme, 1992): 186–89.
19. It was Hautecoeur, editor in chief of the journal, who contacted Le Corbusier on the subject. See Hautecoeur to LC,15 November 1922, FLC A2-11-25. See also Paul Lafollye to LC, 9 March 1923, FLC A2-11-60. Lafollye was originally commissioned by the editorial board to write the article about plans for the *Ville contemporaine*; he asked Le Corbusier himself to suggest someone competent to write the article.
20. [sans doute objectera-t-on la monotonie de ces avenues rectilignes. Nos perspectives rectilignes n'attirent-elles pas cependant les étrangers et ne forcent-elles pas l'admiration: rue de Rivoli, les Champs-Elysées, la place Vendôme, la place des Vosges, la rue Royale], Raymond Cogniat, "Une conception nouvelle de l'urbanisme," *L'Architecture* 36, no. 15 (1923): 229. Cogniat had already responded favorably to Le Corbusier's plans. See "En Attendant," a newspaper clipping dated December 1922, FLC X1-2-96.
21. For a summary of the discussion begun by Teige, see Alena Kubova, "Le Mundaneum, erreur architecturale?" in *Le Corbusier: Le Passé à reaction poétique*, exhib. cat., Hôtel de Sully (Paris: Caisse nationale des Monuments historiques et des Sites – Ministère de la Culture et de la Communication, 1988): 48–53.
22. He consulted the Pérelle collection, "Places, portes, fontaines, églises et maisons de PARIS," Cabinet des Estampes, BN, Ve 15, in-fol., but there are no traces of graphic or written notations taken from this work. For the call slip, see FLC B2-20-441. Jeanneret consulted another work by Pérelle, "Vues de France et d'Italie," Cabinet des Estampes, BN, Ve 16, in-fol. For the call slip, see FLC B2-20-442.
23. Jeanneret named each element, one by one, built along the bridge's axis, pointing them out in a series of letters. For the sketch, see FLC B2-20-248; for the engraving by Pérelle, see Cabinet des Estampes, BN, Ed.76.c: 56.
24. [admirable image de bosquets taillés avec bassins profonds, palissades, allées etc. *(très plastique)*], See drawing by Jeanneret, FLC B2-20-256.
25. [gravures représentant les jardins de Lenôtre [*sic*], prises à vol d'oiseau] [pénètre-t-on dans la maison, voilà les volumes qui agissent, qui se rythment, qui s'éclairent ou s'obscurent, qui se colorent intensément, violemment ou délicatement. Ainsi quand on pénètre dans les jardins de Lenôtre], handwritten note by Jeanneret, FLC B2-20-47.
26. In drawing up a balance sheet of the development of the garden in France, Jeanneret observed: "le parallelisme d[an]s la conception de l'architecte et d[an]s celle du jardinier" (the parallels between the concept of architect and that of gardener) that emerged during the period of Claude Mollet, emphasizing the "mise en valeur des terrains par des multiples aménagements qui attirent l'oeil sans le fatiguer" (value of the landscapes conveyed through multiple layouts that tirelessly attract the eye); see Jeanneret's handwritten notations, FLC B2-20-370.
27. Jeanneret carefully studied the plates included in the chapter on *bosquets* in the text by D'Argenville; see especially the drawings FLC B2-20-258 and B2-20-259, in which several of the figures in plates 6C and 7C, 8C and 9C, respectively, in D'Argenville are reexamined. In FLC B2-20-259 Jeanneret depicted a detail of the *palisades percées en arcades*; D'Argenville had made a three-dimensional drawing of the map of a *cloître en galerie* (plate 9C, fig. 4); see also Claude Malécot, "Les Jardins," in *Le Corbusier: Le Passé* (1988): 110–18, Malécot reproduces a few of these drawings and only transcribes these annotations.
28. [qui joue av[ec] les parterres unis], FLC 2180, published in Malécot, "Les Jardins" (1988): 118, fig. 242.
29. See the folio of drawings by Jeanneret, FLC B2-20-255. Of particular interest is the small drawing on the lower right of the fountain of Latone, in which the groups of *bosquets* acquire still stronger chiaroscuro tones.
30. [le prestige de Louis XIV est grand à cause de Versailles d'aujourd'huy [*sic*] et non à cause d'une disparue merveille dont les récits coloriés pourraient bien nous paraître sauces de courtisans], ibid.
31. [Les grandes allées – aujourd'hui, nefs de cathédrales grandioses, sont d'innombrables petites bandes de marronniers au bout d'un baton – [...] à Clagny, à Sceaux comme à Versailles on a vu grand et pour l'avenir], ibid.
32. These drawings are FLC B2-20-256 and B2-20-242.
33. [un homme n'a que deux yeux à 1 m. 70 du sol, et qui ne fixent qu'un point à la fois. Les bras des étoiles ne sont visibles que l'un après l'autre et c'est une droite sous une frondaison. Une droite n'est pas une étoile; les étoiles s'effondrent. Et tout ainsi de suite; le grand bassin, les parterres de broderies qui sont hors d'une vision d'ensemble, les bâtiments qu'on ne voit que par fragments et en se déplaçant. C'est le leurre, l'illusion. Louis XIV s'est trompé sous sa propre instigation. Il a transgressé les vérités de l'architecture car il n'a pas procédé avec les éléments objectifs de l'architecture], LC, *Vers une architecture* (1923; reprint, Paris: Flammarion, 1995): 158–59.
34. Ibid., 46. For the first appearance of the drawing of the *rue à redents,* see Le Corbusier–Saugnier [pseud.], "Trois rappels à MM. les architects. 3e article," *L'Esprit nouveau* 4 (1921): 469.
35. For Geneva, see FLC 23318; and Patrick Devanthéry and Inès Lamunière, "S.D.N. Un Palais moderne?", in *Le Corbusier à Genève, 1922–1932: Projets et realisations*, ed. Isabelle Charollais and André Ducret, exhib. cat., Immeuble Clarté et Galerie Bonnier, Geneva (Lausanne: Payot, 1987): 17–34. The allusion to the Palais de Versailles for this project seems to extend and reinforce a prominent reference by Le Corbusier to the culture of French classicism beyond World War I, with its implications concerning the defeat of Germany.
36. [A voir les estampes de Pérelle on trouve un Paris si peu

ordonné, si pittoresque, si sale, qu'on s'imagine le désir de nettoyer, et aussi la quasi impuissance de réaliser un ensemble car tout sera à refaire, quais, maisons, etc. Palais, clochetons, pignons, flèches, lanternes etc. On comprend que Louis XIV ait fichu le camp à Versailles Ville neuve], Jeanneret's notation on FLC B2-20-84. In discussing *Le Bernin en France, les travaux du Louvre et les statues de Louis XIV* by L. Mirot (Nogent-le-Rotrou: Impr. de Daupeley-Gouverneur, 1904), Jeanneret invoked Bernini's disdain for Parisian architecture in support of his personal views about the city in the late seventeenth century: "J'ai l'impression que Paris est plus beau aujourd'hui qu'avant. Pas étonnant, quand on voit d[an]s les grav[ures] de Pérelle le Paris chaotique, morcelé," (I have the impression that Paris is more beautiful today than before, which is not surprising when one sees Pérelle's engravings of a chaotic, divided Paris), Jeanneret's notation on FLC B2-20-45.

37. It is significant that the series of drawings after Pérelle's engravings showing Paris as their subject ends with a landscape drawn in perspective of the courtyard of the Palais de Versailles; see FLC B2-20-242. Jeanneret speaks of *courage* and *hardiesse*, underscoring the completion of these urban episodes "en pleine campagne ou banlieue" (in the open countryside or suburbs) —including Versailles. See the handwritten note on drawing FLC B2-20-504.
38. Jacques-François Blondel, *Discours sur la nécessité de l'étude de l'architecture* (Paris, 1754); and idem, *Discours sur la manière d'étudier l'architecture et les arts qui sont relatifs à celui de bastir* (Paris, 1747). See Jeanneret's handwritten list of works consulted, FLC B2-20-53. With respect to the *Architecture françoise*, Jeanneret emphasized the concern for understanding the history of the monuments of Paris, but not for his own studies into the city (see FLC B2-20-2 and 3). Blondel's influence on certain aspects of Le Corbusier's private architecture has been investigated; see Monique Eleb-Vidal, "Hôtel particulier," in *Le Corbusier: une encyclopédie* (1987): 174–76. Jeanneret was also interested, however, in the more eccentric aspects of the architectural culture of the period, such as the work of Meissonnier, d'Oppenord and, above all, Antoine Le Pautre. See the handwritten list cited above and Duboy, "Ch.-E. Jeanneret à la Bibliothèque Nationale" (1979): 11.
39. See H. Allen Brooks, "Jeanneret and Sitte: Le Corbusier's Earliest Ideas on Urban Design," in *In Search of Modern Architecture: A Tribute to Henry-Russell Hitchcock*, ed. Helen Searing (Cambridge, Mass., and London: MIT Press, 1982): 278–97. See also the transcription of Jeanneret's manuscript in Emery, *La Construction* (1992). For a succinct account of this work by Jeanneret, see idem, "Urbanisme: Premières réflexions: le manuscrit inédit de 'La Construction des villes,'" in *Le Corbusier: une encyclopédie* (1987): 432–35.
40. See Werner Oechslin, "Allemagne. Influences, confluences et reniements," in *Le Corbusier: une encyclopédie* (1987): 33–39. In 1915 Jeanneret continued to make explicit reference to Brinckmann's work in his drawing of a circular system for a Place Louis XV; see FLC B2-20-328.
41. For a preliminary presentation that assesses several of Jeanneret's drawings and Patte's engraved plates, see Philippe Duboy, "L.C.B.N. 1.9.1.5.," *Casabella* 51, nos. 531/532 (1987): 94–103. Jeanneret disregarded the historical interpretation of Patte's work, defining it as an "ouvrage de courtisan d[an]s son avant-propos" (work by a courtesan in the introduction), FLC B2-20-62. Interest immediately turned to the projects that were presented; see Jeanneret's handwritten notation on FLC B2-20-111. This did not deflect from his interest in the history of that period, especially with regard to Paris. See C. Piton, *Paris sous Louis XV. Rapports des inspecteurs de police au Roi*, 5 vols. (Paris: Mercure de France, 1910–14); see also FLC B2-20-46.
42. Jeanneret studied the map of Valenciennes and noted the irregularities of access, eventually reinterpreting the general view in Patte's plates, in a drawing that reflected the thinking about modularity and repetition of the elements. See Patte, *Monumens érigés en France* (1765): pls. 18 and 19; see also drawing FLC B2-20-241.
43. [enchaînement d'édifices remarquables, dont la Place du Roi pouvoit passer pour le centre], Jeanneret's notation on drawing FLC B2-20-251; see also Patte, *Monumens érigés en France* (1765): 178.
44. [bâtiments décorés uniformément aux dépenses du Roy] [*sic*] Notation on drawing reworked by Jeanneret, FLC B2-20-229; after Patte, *Monumens érigés en France* (1765): pl. 24.
45. [Rien n'est si beau et rien s'annonce avec plus de majesté que cet edifice. Le rez-de-chausée est ouvert et conduit à un jardin public], ibid.
46. See drawing FLC B2-20-281, after an engraving by Jacques Caillot in 1624, and the later drawing of a map drawn by Jenneret, FLC B2-20-335, reproduced in H. Allen Brooks, *Le Corbusier's Formative Years: Charles-Edouard Jeanneret at La Chaux-De-Fonds* (Chicago: University of Chicago Press, 1997): 406, fig. 334.
47. See FLC B2-20-250, and Patte, *Monumens érigés en France* (1765): pl. 2.
48. See Marcel Poëte, *La Promenade à Paris au XVIIe siècle, L'art de se promener, Les lieux de promenade dans la ville et aux environs* (Paris: Colin, 1913): 3.
49. See drawing B2-20-250, FLC. Jeanneret addressed the reading of the elements in detail—the "guérites très décorées" (well-decorated sentry boxes), but also the "4 pavillons (cours de la reine et l'autre, pour fontainiers, gardes et portiers)" (4 pavilions [the queen's path and the other, for fountain attendants, guards and doormen])—from the drawings in Patte's work which he reworked in later drawings. See Patte, *Monumens érigés en France* (1765): pls.7 and 8; and Jeanneret's drawing FLC B2-20-247.
50. See Patte, *Monumens érigés en France* (1765): 71, and Jeanneret's drawing FLC B2-20-228, reproduced in Brooks, *Formative Years* (1997): 407, fig. 335.
51. [Le sentiment du volume si puissant aux époques antérieures a disparu au XIXe siècle. Le "classicisme" de cette période n'a voulu retenir du passé que les lignes qu'il avait employées pour s'exprimer; il en a perdu l'esprit. Hypnotysés par les souvenirs majestueux du Louis XIV et du Louis XV, nos édiles ont constellé les villes de places en étoile ou en carré avec monument au milieu géométrique, sous prétexte que les formes splendides transmises par le XVIIe et le XVIIIe siècle n'étaient point autres. Appliquant la formule sèche et aride, ils oublient l'art, c'est-à-dire, qu'ils ne se soucièrent ni de volume, ni de contrastes, ni "d'échelle humaine"; en un mot, ils ignorèrent la *corporalité*], Quoted in Emery, *La Construction* (1992): 126–27.
52. See Jeanneret's drawing FLC B2-20-249, and the map from which it was taken in Patte, *Monumens érigés en France* (1765): pl. 39.
53. [. . . nouvelle cathédrale à la place dauphine, colossale] [g[ran]d escalier tout direct sur pont neuf], Jeanneret's drawing FLC B2-20-249.
54. [Thèse intéressante: dans Louis XV, on voit ce qu'on sait prévoir (Patte). Tout s'ouvrait, respirait, prenait de l'ampleur. Mais aujourd'hui cela serait d'un mode inutilisable puisque pour vivre, ces places doivent avoir d'étroits embouchements de rues etc. Aujourd'hui il en faut d'énormes, il faut quantité d'autres facteurs: créons donc en rapport, avec autant de hardiesse!], handwritten notation by Jeanneret on drawing FLC B2-20-162.

CHAPTER 6
MARCEL LEVAILLANT AND "LA QUESTION DU MOBILIER"
Arthur Rüegg

1. These pieces were produced and first exhibited in Zurich; see *Le Corbusier 1929: Sitzmöbel sièges chairs*, exhib. cat. (Zürich: Heidi Weber Gallery /"mezzanin" meubles & arts, 1959); and Arthur Rüegg, "Fauteuil grand confort 1928, Reedition Heidi Weber 1959," in *Swiss Furniture and Interiors, 1900–2000*, ed. Arthur Rüegg (Basel, Boston, and Berlin: Birkhäuser, 2002). The chairs have been produced since 1965 by Figli di Amedeo Cassina, Meda (Milano), Italy.
2. See Charlotte Perriand, *Une vie de création* (Paris: Editions Odile Jacob, 1998); and Charlotte Perriand. *Un art de vivre*, exhib. cat. (Paris: Musée des Arts Décoratifs / Flammarion, 1985).
3. This applies above all to the apartment at 20 rue Jacob in Paris (1917–34), and to the studio space at 24 rue Nungesser-et-Coli; there, the objects in the living area were arranged with care. See Arthur Rüegg, ed., *Le Corbusier, Photographs by René Burri/Magnum: Moments in the Life of a Great Architect* (Basel, Berlin, and Boston: Birkhäuser, 1999), including special chapters devoted to Le Corbusier's office and apartment.
4. The reference here is to the transfer of the cantilever principle, central to all modernist architecture, to a new seat type, the "Freischwinger," with no back legs. See Werner Möller and Otakar Ma_el, *Ein Stuhl macht Geschichte* (Munich: Prestel, 1992).
5. Raoul La Roche to Pierre Jeanneret, 18 November 1930, FLC. On 20 March 1925, Maple and Co. had invoiced 2,225 francs for a "Franklin" club chair and 1,975 francs for a "Newstead" model (FLC).
6. For Jeanneret's early undertakings connected with the École d'Art, see especially H. Allen Brooks, *Le Corbusier's Formative Years: Charles-Edouard Jeanneret at La Chaux-de-Fonds* (Chicago and London: The University of Chicago Press, 1997). For the interiors after 1912, see also Arthur Rüegg, "Charles-Edouard Jeanneret, architecte-conseil pour toutes les questions de décoration intérieure . . . ," *Archithèse* 13, no. 2 (1983): 39–43.
7. The author, in conjunction with the Fondation Le Corbusier, is compiling an inventory of Corbusier's furniture designs; a comprehensive publication on his furniture and interiors is in preparation. See also George H. Marcus, *Le Corbusier: Inside the Machine for Living* (New York: The Monacelli Press, 2000); this study is based on archival and published sources and concentrates on the period after 1925.
8. Since 1979, the author has researched and archived the correspondence, designs, and artifacts in the estate of Marcel Levaillant. The documents—as originals or copies—are now held by the Fondation Le Corbusier in a number of different files. Furniture and a number of original drawings and letters are in private hands. The author has an archive of copies of most of the documents, made while the originals were in the possession of the heirs or subsequent purchasers; these therefore bear no archive numbers but are cited here by the present locations of the originals (where known). Thanks are due to Madeleine and Marianne Schwob, Jacqueline Jeanneret, and Jean-Pierre Jornod, among others.
9. For further detail, see Jacques Gubler, "A l'heure des horlogers jurassiens," *Revue neuchâteloise* 23, no. 91 *Le Corbusier pourquoi* (1980): 7–37.
10. See Jacques Gubler, "La Chaux-de-Fonds," in *Inventar der neueren Schweizer Architektur*, 1850–1920 [INSA], vol. 3 (Bern: Gesellschaft für Schweizerische Kunstgeschichte, 1982): 127–217.
11. See Brooks, *Formative Years* (1997); and *Un mouvement d'art à La Chaux-de-Fonds: A propos de la Nouvelle section* (La Chaux-de-Fonds: Imprimerie Georges Dubois, 1914).
12. Yvonne Schwob's salon even found a place in a novel that also gives a sympathetic portrait of Charles-Edouard Jeanneret: see Jean-Paul Zimmermann, *Le Concert sans orchestre* (Paris and Neuchâtel: Editions Victor Attinger, 1937); and see also Maurice Favre, "Au pays du prophète," *Revue neuchâteloise* 23, no. 91 Le Corbusier pourquoi (1980): 39-44.
13. For a time, Charles Humbert had been a student of Charles L'Eplattenier and was a friend of Jeanneret's; see *Charles Humbert, 1891–1958*, exhib. cat., (La Chaux-de-Fonds: Musée des Beaux-Arts, 2001). Humbert, too, was principally supported by the Jewish elite of the city. After the death of his wife, the painter Madeleine Woog, in 1929, he idolized Yvonne Schwob.
14. See Claude Garino, *Le Corbusier. De la Villa turque à L'Esprit Nouveau* (La Chaux-de-Fonds: Idéa Editions, 1995). The Villa Schwob was also known as the Villa Turque.
15. Here I would like to acknowledge the help of Madeleine Schwob (1901–2000), who told me her own story in 1980, and of the painter Lucien Schwob (1895–1985), the second husband of Camille Schwob-Levaillant, with whom I was in contact in the years 1981–84. My thanks are also due to Marianne and Francis Schwob for much information and assistance.
16. Jeanneret's price quotation dates from 18 February 1914, and his final account from 9 May 1914, FLC.
17. This complex, consisting of factory and dwelling, was built for the watch and clock manufacturer C. Eberhard by Léon Boillot in 1906. The dome on the corner of rue Léopold-Robert is crowned with an eagle, Eberhard's trademark; see Gubler, "La Chaux-de-Fonds" (1982): 205.
18. See Jeanneret's note of fees dated 17 July 1914, in which the dates of visits to Paris are marked and their purpose given as "choix de meubles et lustrerie" (selection of furniture and lighting), Bibliothèque de la Ville de la Chaux-de-Fonds (cited hereafter as BV).
19. Whereabouts unknown; a color photograph of the piece survives, as does Jeanneret's design for it (LC ms 139, undated, BV,).
20. See Hans Hoffmann, *Schloss Charlottenhof und die Römischen Bäder* (Potsdam-Sanssouci: Generaldirektion der Staatlichen Schlösser und Pärke, 1991). Jeanneret examined these pieces of furniture very closely; for his comments on another writing desk at Charlottenhof, that of the Crown Prince, see Giuliano Gresleri, ed., *Ch.-E. Jeanneret – Le Corbusier: Voyage d'Orient, Carnets, Reisetagebücher, 1910/11* (Milano and Munich: Electa and Bangert, 1987), 1:34.
21. See, e.g., *Peinture encadrée*, sketch dated 20 September 1959, FLC 24185; and a bar fixture with a watercolor by Le

Corbusier inserted, which was exhibited at Galerie Arteba, Zürich, in 2001.

22. CEJ, *Etude sur le mouvement d'art décoratif en Allemagne* (1912; reprint, New York: Da Capo Press, 1968); see also Werner Oechslin, "Influences, confluences et reniements," in *Le Corbusier: une encyclopédie*, ed. Jacques Lucan (Paris: Centre Georges Pompidou, 1987): 33–39.

23. See the notes in the *Carnet Bleu* of December 1912, FLC T 71, and postcards, FLC L5-7, e.g., 288–309. On this, see also Brooks, *Formative Years* (1997): 344–46.

24. See above, n. 18; see also Brooks, *Formative Years* (1997): 351.

25. See Pierre Monnier and Louis Vuille, *Les Meubles d'Yverdon* (Yverdon: Editions du Faubourg de la Croix-Blanche, 1979).

26. Eva-Maria Preiswerk-Lösl, *Kunsthandwerk* (Disentis: Desertina Verlag, 1991), 8: 126–28.

27. Jeanneret is the author of the twenty-six pages of handwritten minutes of the founding meeting of L'Oeuvre at Yverdon on 9 November 1913 (L'Oeuvre archive, Archives du Canton de Vaud, Lausanne). In this connection, it is worth mentioning Jeanneret's admiration of Alexandre Cingria-Vaneyre, the author of *Les entretiens de la villa du Rouet: Essais dialogués sur les arts plastiques en Suisse romande* (Geneva: A. Jullien, 1908), with its celebration of the uniqueness of the Greco-Roman–oriented culture of Romandie (French-speaking Switzerland). Jeanneret became personally acquainted with Cingria-Vaneyre in the summer of 1916; see Brooks, *Formative Years* (1997): 237–38, 411.

28. Jeanneret's first furniture designs had been made in connection with École d'Art projects for the music room of Albert Matthey-Doret and for the villa of Louis Fallet. See Brooks, *Formative Years* (1997): 76-87.

29. In her masterly analysis of the French decorative art of the period, Nancy Troy sets up two opposing categories: the Constructeurs, who worked in the tradition of French furniture making and of Art Nouveau; and the Coloristes, who practiced a more additive style inspired by neoclassicism. However, in this context her proof of influces by identifying a sketch from Jeanneret's *Carnet Bleu* as an elevation drawing of a chair by the Coloriste André Groult does not carry conviction; in my view, this is a Directoire chair with a carved plat. See Nancy Troy, *Modernism and the Decorative Arts in France: Art Nouveau to Le Corbusier* (New Haven and London: Yale University Press, 1991): 146–47.

30. Quoted in Maurice Favre, "Le Corbusier in an Unpublished Dossier and a Little-Known Novel," in *The Open Hand: Essays on Le Corbusier*, ed. Russell Walden, (Cambridge, Mass., and London: MIT Press, 1977): 96–113.

31. Ibid.

32. Ibid.

33. Ibid.

34. CEJ to William Ritter, 18 December 1915, Nachlass Ritter, Schweizerische Landesbibliothek Bern.

35. This term derives from the products of a factory set up at Jouy, near Versailles, in the eighteenth century to make decorative fabrics (later also wallpapers) with often exotic patterns. According to surviving invoices, Jeanneret used monochrome printed fabrics in red and blue.

36. As early as October 1910, he made a note of a fabric shade, attached loose to the ceiling, with four light bulbs recessed into the ceiling: "a stunning light fitment . . . made with nothing" (lustre épatant . . . fait avec rien"). See Giuliano Gresleri, ed., *Ch.-E. Jeanneret – Le Corbusier: Les voyages d'Allemagne, Carnets* (Milan: Electa, 1994); 3:49.

37. Jeanneret's invoice, 9 March 1914, FLC.

38. See "Mémoire," 9 March 1914, FLC: "Les décors de Monsieur Humbert seront aussi rétribués directement, le panneau peint n'ayant pas été prévu lors de la lettre du 18 février, car la bibliothèque était alors projetée et le pupitre était de beaucoup plus simple" (The decorations by Monsieur Humbert will also be paid for directly, the painted panel not having been envisaged at the time of the letter of 18 February, since the bookcase was then projected and the desk was very much simpler). The price quotation dates from 18 February 1914, estimating a cost of 120 francs; the invoice dates from 9 May 1914, mentioning the sum of 150 Swiss francs (FLC).

39. [Je vous répète que je m'intéresse à cette installation afin d'en faire réclame. Mais je vous prierais de ne pas communiquer le prix à qui que ce soit. Ce prix ne pourrait pas être maintenu pour une seconde entreprise], see Jeanneret's price quotation, 18 February 1914, FLC.

40. Confirmation from Jeanneret's office to Levaillant, 29 September 1917. For the reproduction of a sketch of the object, see *Le Corbusier Sketchbooks*, vol. 1, *1914–1948*, with

commentary by Françoise de Franclieu (London: Thames and Hudson, 1981), sheet A1-26. A description exists in Jeanneret's letter to Fritz Ernst Jeker, who purchased Villa Jeanneret-Perret, 11 September 1919, FLC; see also p. 238 in this volume. In 1916, the touring exhibition of L'Oeuvre was to be seen in Geneva, Lausanne, and (in August) La Chaux-de-Fonds.

41. See the catalogue of the auction of Yvonne Schwob's estate by Pierre-Yves Gabus, Geneva, October 28–30, 1982, lot 367 ("Drawing-room [furniture] comprising one daybed, two bergères, and two upright chairs, wood painted claret and black . . . daybed with stamp of Jacob Frères" ("Salon comprenant un lit de repos, deux bergères, et deux chaises, bois peint bordeaux et noir. . . . Lit de repos estampillé Jacob Frères"); and ibid., lot 368 ("Important sofa in the manner of Jacob, Directoire period" ("Important sofa. . . . dans le goût de Jacob, Epoque Directoire"). In the library designed by Jeanneret there were two unsigned Directoire armchairs with gray and black painted woodwork.

42. This is supported by parallels between Jeanneret's and Jacob's designs, such as in the motifs in the backs of the chairs Jeanneret designed for Anatole Schwob. This view is shared by Brooks, *Formative Years* (1997): 397.

43. Not one drawing for seat furniture of this period has survived. There is much to suggest that—as in later periods—Jeanneret sometimes ordered furniture with slight modifications from the catalogues of suppliers such as Perrenoud of Cernier (furniture for Marguerite Hauser-Jeanneret). Drawings intended for L'Artisan SA, of Geneva are known to have existed (furniture for Ernest-Albert Ditisheim). The pieces made by the master ébéniste Jean Egger, in particular, bear the unmistakable mark of Jeanneret's hand, alongside Egger's technical sophistication.

44. See Arthur Rüegg, "Der Pavillon de l'Esprit Nouveau als Musée Imaginaire," in *L'Esprit nouveau: Le Corbusier und die Industrie, 1920–1925*, ed. Stanislaus von Moos, exhib. cat., Museum für Gestaltung Zürich and Bauhaus-Archiv, Museum für Gestaltung Berlin (Berlin: Ernst und Sohn, 1987): 134–51.

45. See Leza Dosch, "1900–1925," in *Swiss Furniture* (2002).

46. [Un tout mû dans une seule direction], CEJ to Salomon Schwob, 7 December 1913, BV.

47. The inquiry of 2 February 1922, is lost, but Le Corbusier's answer, dated 7 February 1922, is extant, FLC. It is not clear whether the letter was by Madeleine or her mother, Hélène Floersheim-Levaillant.

48. The designs are in a private collection, Switzerland.

49. Handwritten note added by Le Corbusier to the letter 1 December 1923, and Levaillant's answer of 4 December 1923, concerning Madeleine Schwob, FLC. The old debt in question was owed to the photographer J. Groepler for pictures taken at Villa Schwob in 1917; Jeanneret asked Levaillant to dispose of the matter by offering the creditor 200 francs.

50. Levaillant's inquiries of 3 and 8 November 1922 are lost, but Le Corbusier's affirmative reply of 10 November 1922, is extant, FLC: "Je veux bien m'en occuper en souvenir de notre amitié de ce que tu demandes bien que mon temps soit véritablement pris par ailleurs" (I certainly will take care of what you ask, for friendship's sake, although the truth is that my time is fully taken up elsewhere).

51. Le Corbusier's note of fees due, 1 December 1923, FLC, with detailed list of all designs and all visits to suppliers.

52. "Nous avons chargé Egger, qui passe pour le meilleur ébéniste de la ville (ébéniste d'art, même!) ayant travaillé des années au Fb St Antoine, et faisant des meubles sur commande" (We have given the work to Egger, who is regarded as the best cabinetmaker in town (an art cabinetmaker, even!), having worked for years in the Faubourg Saint-Antoine [in Paris] and making furniture to order), CEJ to Jules Ditisheim, April 1914, BV. Egger retired to Pully in 1943.

53. The sketch plan with dimensions noted by Le Corbusier, FLC 23092, and two perspective sketches of the bedroom and library (private collection), show not only the desk but also the piano and seating area in different positions. Most of the final designs for the furniture and the perspective drawing of the library are now in private hands.

54. At Villa Berque (see cat. no. xxx), the wardrobe was planned for the dressing room between the two large bedrooms on the second floor (FLC 9329/23104/9330/9349/9331). For the self-contained area of Villa Montmorency in which the Villa Berque lies, see *Hameaux, villas et cités de Paris*, Collection Paris et son Patrimoine, ed. Béatrice de Andia (Paris: Action artistique de la Ville de Paris, 1998): 137–43; and Tim Benton,

Les villas de Le Corbusier, 1920–1930 (Paris: Philippe Sers, 1984): 18–21.

55. This yellow strip of paper (private collection), approximately 21 by 5 cm, is annotated, "armoire ch. à coucher / intérieur jaune clair / un peu plus vif que ce papier" (bedroom wardrobe / inside light yellow / a bit brighter than this paper).

56. See Brooks, *Formative Years* (1997): 347–49.

57. See Rüegg, "Pavillon de l'Esprit Nouveau" (1987); and idem, "Du casier à la ville, de la ville au casier," in *La Chaux-de-Fonds et Jeanneret avant Le Corbusier*, exhib. cat. (La Chaux-de-Fonds: Musée des Beaux-Arts, 1987): 11–16.

58. [Le programme: nier l'Art Décoratif . . . un nouveau terme remplace le terme de mobilier . . . Le mot nouveau c'est l'équipement de la maison. L'équipement c'est, par l'analyse du problème, classer les divers éléments nécessaires à l'exploitation domestique. Les casiers . . ., les sièges seuls demeurent, et les tables], quoted from *Le Corbusier et Pierre Jeanneret: Oeuvre complète*, vol. 1, *1910–1929*, ed. Willy Boesiger and Oscar Stonorov (Zürich: Girsberger, 1937): 100.

59. CEJ to Levaillant, 9 February 1923, FLC. For the description of the types of wood, see Jean Egger's invoice of 13 July 1923 (private collection).

60. The term meubles paysans (farm furniture) was used, for instance, in connection with similar stick chairs from the château de Compiègne, with splats decorated with motifs carved in alder wood. See Egon and Waldemar Hessling, eds., *Möbel im Directoirestil* (Paris, Berlin, and London: Egon and Waldemar Hessling, 1914), plate 9.

61. See. *Le Corbusier Sketchbooks* (1981), 1: A1-13–24.

62. FLC 19097.

63. Troy, *Modernism and the Decorative Arts* (1991): 145. She discusses the term production normale in connection with Adolf Loos and with two reports by Jeanneret, both dating from 1914, on a drawing competition held by L'Oeuvre and on the teaching of drawing in the context of the Schweizerische Landesausstellung in Bern.

64. "J'ai commandé deux fauteuils chez Maple en marocain [sic] . . . Ces deux fauteuils ont la même forme, mais le Bernard est plus profond et sera très agréable pour les personnes à longues jambes (pour moi, par exemple!)" (I have ordered two "maroquin" armchairs from Maple's. Both are the same shape, but the Bernard is deeper and will be very agreeable for long-legged individuals [such as myself]!), LC to Levaillant, 22 March 1923, FLC.

65. [Il existe les chaises de paille des églises à 5 francs, les fauteuils Maple à 1'000 francs et les morris-chairs à inclinaison graduée avec tablette mobile pour le livre en lecture, tablette pour la tasse de café, rallonge pour étendre ses pieds, dossier basculant avec manivelle pour prendre les positions les plus parfaites depuis la sieste jusqu'au travail, hygiéniquement, confortablement, correctement. Vos bergères, vos causeuses en Louis XVI avec Aubusson ou Salon d'Automne à potirons, sont-elles des machines à s'asseoir?] Le Corbusier-Saugnier [pseud.], "Des Yeux qui ne voient pas . . . Les Avions," *L'Esprit nouveau*, no. 9 (1921): 980.

66. See Arthur Rüegg, "Equipement," in *Le Corbusier: une encyclopédie* (1987): 128.

67. Raoul La Roche possessed one "Franklin" and one "Newstead," and these, too, are still extant. See also the invoice from Maple and Company, Paris, dated 20 March 1925, FLC.

68. LC, *L'Art décoratif d'aujourd'hui* (Paris: Crès, 1925): 76.

69. [. . . d'une lisibilité parfaite et reconnus sans effort, ils évitent la dispersion, la déviation de l'attention qui serait perturbée dans sa contemplation par des singularités, l'inconnu, le mal connu], Amédée Ozenfant and CEJ, *La Peinture moderne* (Paris: Crès, 1925): 168.

70. These featured an almost exclusive use of chrome- or nickel-plated bent steel tubes. Welded joints were avoided as much as possible.

71. Villa Besnus has been remodeled, but the balcony railing is still visible on the facade.

72. Evidently, Jeanneret had built the Scala for a flat fee. During construction, the client was arrested in a foreign country, and the tradesmen remained partly unpaid. In October and November of 1925, the Sébastien Brunschwyler central heating company tried to extract its money from the architect. See LC to Levaillant, 1, 13, 19 November 1925 and 10 December 1925, FLC.

73. There still exists a letter of introduction written by Le Corbusier for Levaillant, addressed to Raoul La Roche, 5 January 1926, FLC.

74. Private collection. One of the prints is reproduced in Rüegg, "Pavillon de l'Esprit Nouveau" (1987): 149.
75. Postcard, LC to Levaillant, 12 June 1926 (FLC?): "Mon cher. J'ai vu à l'emballage le petit meuble casier. Il est affreux, mal vernis, mal fini, travail de grande série. Il faudra dire à Egger de le nettoyer, polir et revernir et d'entailler les faces des tiroirs de façon à en alléger l'aspect (je t'enverrai un croquis)" (My dear. I saw the little cabinet piece being packed. It is hideous, badly varnished, badly finished, a mass-production job. Egger will have to be told to clean it up, polish and revarnish it, and bevel the edges of the drawers to lighten the look of it [I'll send you a sketch]). Egger lightened the outside of the chest (now in a private collection) and the drawer fronts and probably added the cutouts in the drawer fronts that are typical of Innovation chest furniture.
76. [jusqu'au 25 janvier, j'étais invisible bouclé dans un travail de forçat avec une douzaine de dessinateurs pour le concours du Palais des Nations], postcard, LC to Levaillant, 26 February 1927, private collection.
77. [Un saut dans la peinture moderne . . . c'est peut-être dur] Le Corbusier dispatched the four volumes on 18 February 1926, as a way of thanking Levaillant for help with the "affaire Brunschwyler" (see above, n. 72). After Levaillant's death, they were sold separately by an antiquarian dealer in Zürich and are now in private collections.
78. On the relevance of this theme to cubism, see Jeffrey Weiss, "Picasso, Collage, and the Music Hall," in *Modern Art and Popular Culture: Readings in High and Low*, ed. Kirk Varnedoe and Adam Gopnik (New York: Harry N. Abrams, 1990): 82–115.
79. [Je n'ai pas camelotté; je ne veux pas que mon nom soit sous des saletés], LC to Levaillant, 5 November 1926, FLC. [On m'a dit que j'étais un criminel de les vendre. Ceci te flattera, heureux propriétaire. – Je joins à la liasse un mode d'emploi. Pas de blague! Il ne s'agit pas d'encadrer ces navets. Ca ne vaut que vu rapidement, en cinéma. Je compte sur toi . .], ibid., 19 September 1927. The directions for use: [Faire vite, passer vite, regarder vite. Ça suffit. Le music-hall est une chose passagère rapide; il en naît un certain éblouissement provenant de la cacophonie et des cuisses des dames], ibid. After Levaillant's death, the fifty watercolors were exhibited at Galerie Cour Saint-Pierre in Geneva (23 November through 12 December 1972) and offered for sale piecemeal.
80. See, e.g., Romy Golan, *Modernity and Nostalgia: Art and Politics in France Between the Wars* (New Haven and London: Yale University Press, 1995): 62–63, 72ff.
81. On the sketchbooks, see cat. nos. 9, 10, by Giuliano Gresleri, in this volume. The objects that made up the collection particulière are still for the most part held by the FLC; a number are on exhibit at the Paris apartment on rue Nungesser-et-Coli and others at Villa Le Lac, Corseaux.
82. [Une question vous préoccupe à juste titre: c'est celle des menus objets, vases, tableaux, dessins, estampes, bibelots, etc.... Ne vous inquiétez pas à ce sujet. Sutout ne vous pressez pas d'acheter: vous ne trouverez rien chez vous tandisqu'ici, je puis vous comprendre dans la liste de certains de mes amis et de mes clients qui m'ont donné mandat de leur acheter diverses choses, mandat qui m'est très facile remplir dans une ville comme PARIS où tout se trouve pour qui sait chercher en bonne place et à des conditions et des prix étonnants. (...) A ce sujet, je vous prierais seulement, si cela pouvait vous agréer, de m'alouer un crédit dont je vous donnerais la justification au fur et à mesure des achats], CEJ to Fritz Ernst Jeker, 11 September 1919, FLC.
83. The invoice from the Atelier des moulages at the Louvre is dated 14 May 1923, private collection. Two undated drawings (FLC H3–7) show, respectively, the placing of the pieces in the apartment and the positioning of the "tête turban" (turban head).
84. [Pas trouvé de vase grec; il n'y en a plus. Par contre pour 10'000 f., pour 4'000 ou pour 3'000 on peut avoir chez Paul Guillaume de magnifiques bois nègres (têtes) comme dans l'EN no. (sculptures nègres], LC to Levaillant, 18 February 1926, FLC.
85. [les bois nègres sont très bien et font bel effet sur la bibliothèque. Contre toute attente ils ont beaucoup d'admirateurs. Humbert est venu l'autre soir et les a pelotés dans tout les sens], Levaillant to LC, 12 June 1926, FLC. Le Corbusier had previously written: "As-tu reçu tes 2 nègres et quelle impression?" (Did you get your 2 Negroes? What's your impression?), postcard, LC to Levaillant, 10 June 1926, FLC?.
86. [. . . d'aspect rappelant le Picasso que tu m'avais montré], LC to Levaillant, 2 September 1926, FLC. Le Corbusier later reported that the Braque had been auctioned for a "prix fabuleux" (fabulous price), ibid., 5 November 1926.
87. On this, see Katharina Schmidt, "Raoul La Roche," in *Ein Haus für den Kubismus: Die Sammlung Raoul La Roche*, ed. Katharina Schmidt and Hartwig Fischer, exhib. cat., Kunstmuseum Basel (Ostfildern-Ruit: Hatje, 1998): 14.
88. See Rüegg, "Pavillon de l'Esprit Nouveau" (1987) 141.
89. See Francesco Passanti, "The Vernacular, Modernism, and Le Corbusier," *Journal of the Society of Architectural Historians* 56 (1997): 438–50.
90. [Reconnaître les 'séries', créer à travers temps et espace, des 'unités', rendre palpitante la vue des choses où l'homme a inscrit sa presence . .], *Le Corbusier et Pierre Jeanneret: Oeuvre complète*, vol. 3, *1934–1938*, ed. Max Bill (Zürich: Girsberger, 1939): 157. This was prompted by *Les Arts dits primitifs dans la maison d'aujourd'hui*, an exhibition held at the apartments of Louis Carré and Le Corbusier, 3–13 July 1935.
91. [Befriedigung der gleichen Bedürfnisse mit gleichen Mitteln], Hannes Meyer, "Die neue Welt," *Das Werk* 13, no. 7 (1926): 223.
92. See Rüegg, "Pavillon de l'Esprit Nouveau" (1987): 138–39.
93. [Tête de nègre]; [cachou]; [gris foncé noirâtre]; [J'insiste tout particulièrement sur cette question qui joue un rôle capital: en effet, un ton de fond sonnant mal compromettrait tout l'ensemble], CEJ to Fritz Ernst Jeker, 11 September 1919, FLC.
94. [Couleur dain plus pâle que tête de nègre, très jolie]; [ces tapis sont une véritable occasion et donneront un cachet tout spécial à ton installation], LC to Levaillant, 6 March 1923, FLC.
95. [Je suis certain que l'harmonie des couleurs choisies sera tout à fait heureuse et très ferme], ibid.
96. "A l'intérieur, premiers essais de polychromie, basés sur les réactions spécifiques des couleurs, permettant le 'camouflage architectural', c'est-à-dire l'affirmation de certains volumes, ou, au contraire, leur effacement" (Inside, first attempts at polychromy, based on the specific reactions of colors, leading to 'architectural camouflage': i.e., the emphasizing—or, conversely, the obscuring—of certain volumes), *Oeuvre complète 1910–1929* (1937), 1: 60.
97. See Arthur Rüegg, "Colour Concepts and Colour Scales in Modernism," *Daidalos*, no. 51 (1994): 66–77.
98. [Voici mon 7eme voyage à l'étranger depuis Noël. A l'un de mes passages à Paris, j'ai trouvé ta lettre. Voici ce que tu peux faire: demande à ton marchand de papiers peints la collection 'Salubra Le Corbusier'. Il y a là en unis tout ce qu'il faut pour agir avec sécurité], LC to Levaillant, 26 February 1933 (letterhead of Hôtel d'Angleterre), FLC.
99. Le Corbusier, *Claviers de couleurs Salubra* (Basel: Salubra, 1931); Arthur Rüegg, ed., *Polychromie architecturale: Le Corbusier's Farbenklaviaturen von 1931 und 1959 / Le Corbusier's Color Keyboards from 1931 and 1959 / Les claviers de couleurs de Le Corbusier de 1931 et de 1959* (Basel, Boston, and Berlin: Birkhäuser, 1997).
100. [L'essentiel de ma lettre est pour te dire que si tu veux être dans une ambiance colorée admissible, tu ne peux et ne dois employer que les couleurs Matroil des Etablissements "Peintures Berger" . . . Il n'y a pas d'autre couleur à opposer à celle-là et si ton peintre fait des objections, fous-le à la porte], LC to Levaillant, 7 June 1956, FLC. The letter was accompanied by a plan (now in a private collection) of the apartment, on Chemin Krieg in Geneva, with notes by Le Corbusier and six color samples of Matroil paints. Le Corbusier later asked for documentation of the color scheme, together with color samples and a 24 by 36 mm color transparency, 28 April 1958, FLC.
101. Le Corbusier, *Claviers de couleurs Salubra*, vol. 2 (Basel: Salubra, 1959); Rüegg, ed., *Polychromie architecturale* (1997).
102. " . . . une table pour moi, qui remplacerait celle tant désirée (le tronc d'arbre) que tu n'as pu obtenir" (a table for me, in place of the one I wanted so much [the tree trunk], which you were unable to get), Levaillant to LC, 27 June 1954, FLC.
103. [Table tronc d'arbre], ibid.
104. LC to Levaillant, 17 July 1954. The drawing was auctioned, together with the table itself, at Galerie Koller, Zürich, in October 1975.
105. On this synthesis, see also Andreas Vowinckel and Thomas Kesseler, eds., *Le Corbusier: Synthèse des Arts, Aspekte des Spätwerks, 1945–1965*, exhib. cat., Badischer Kunstverein Karlsruhe (Berlin: Ernst und Sohn, 1986).
106. Comparable pieces are the two benches faced with enamel plaques for the Pavillon Suisse at the Cité Universitaire in Paris (1957) and the painted liturgical items (tabernacle, crosses) for the church at Ronchamp (also made in 1957).
107. Levaillant also possessed an armchair with an adjustable back (fauteuil à dossier basculant), probably one from the first postwar batch made in 1959, and two wooden colonial armchairs, which presented an interesting didactic contrast.
108. [Mon cher Marcel, tu es le meilleur des types! Tes chocolats, eux-mêmes, l'affirment. Je suis très sensible à ton amitié demeurée valable depuis si longtemps. Car, de La Chaux, tu fus, (avec Georges Aubert expatrié) le seul à être gentil. . .], LC to Levaillant, 27 January 1959, FLC. This handwritten letter contains a caricature of Le Corbusier in full figure, with dress sword, as a member of the Institut (the organization of French Academies) and the annotation: "Tu me vois, armé comme Bayard!" (You see me armed like Bayard!)

CHAPTER 7
FROM ART NOUVEAU TO PURISM: LE CORBUSIER AND PAINTING
Françoise Ducros

1. These watercolors were exhibited at the Salon d'Automne in Paris, at the fourth Exposition neuchâteloise de la société des peintres, sculpteurs et architectes suisses at Neuchâtel in 1912, and at the Kunsthaus in Zürich in 1913.
2. See Susan Nasgaard, "Jeanneret's Development as a Painter, 1912 to 1918," Ph.D. diss., University of Toronto, 1976; H. Allen Brooks, *Le Corbusier's Formative Years: Charles-Edouard Jeanneret at La Chaux-de-Fonds* (Chicago and London: The University of Chicago Press, 1997); Stanislaus von Moos, "Charles Edouard Jeanneret og billedkunsten / Charles Edouard Jeanneret and the Visual Arts," in: *Le Corbusier. Maler og arkitekt / Le Corbusier. Painter and Architect*, exhib. cat. (Aalborg, Nordjyllands Kunstmuseum, 1995): 59–82.
3. Le Corbusier does not seem to have known the German Expressionist painters directly, but it is possible that he knew of them through Swiss painters, and in particular Cunot Amiet, who belonged to Die Brücke.
4. See Jacques Lucan, "Acropole. Tout a commencé là . . .", in: *Le Corbusier: une encyclopédie*, ed. Jacques Lucan (Paris: Centre Georges Pompidou, 1987): 20–25.
5. [Je balbutie de la géométrie élémentaire avec l'avidité de savoir et de pouvoir un jour. Dans leur course folle, le bleu et le jaune sont devenus blanc. Je suis fou de couleur blanche, du cube, de la sphère, du cylindre et de la pyramide et du disque tout uni et d'une grande étendue vide. Les prismes se dressent, s'équilibrent, se rythment, se mettent en marche], ibid., pp. 22–23.
6. See Françoise Ducros, *Amédée Ozenfant* (Paris: Cercle d'Art, 2002).
7. See Nasgaard, *Jeanneret's development* (1976): 19ff. Ozenfant helped Jeanneret recognize the plastic values in Picasso's painting.
8. For his part, Ozenfant recorded the richness of the intellectual exchanges surrounding the composition of their first joint text, *Après le Cubisme*, which more or less coincided with the Armistice: "le soir, tantôt chez lui tantôt chez moi, nous nous réunission pour rédiger après le Cubisme, en organisant mes notes de Paimboeuf et d'Andernos augmentées du résultat de nos discussions à la recherche des moyens de réaiguiller l'art sur l'époque: lui l'architecture, moi la peinture. Jeanneret apportait ses justes révoltes contre la décadence de son art. nous tirions des leçons des belles choses de la technique industrielle chère à son maître Auguste Perret et à moi-même, surtout depuis ma familiarité avec les machines de vitesse. il s'épanchait en diatribes contre l'art décoratif tombé à un degré surprenant de niaiserie; il me fit lire les articles précurseurs écrits au début du siècle par le viennois Loos" (in the evening, either at his place or at mine, we would get together to work on après le cubisme, organizing my notes on Paimboeuf and d'Andernos, augmented with the fruits of our discussions concerning our quest for ways to realign art with the times: architecture for him, and for me painting. Jeanneret brought his own revolts against the decadence of his art. we drew lessons from the beautiful things of industrial technique dear to his master Auguste Perret and to myself, above all since I had become familiar with high-speed machines. He vented in diatribes against a decorative art that had fallen to such a surprising degree of ridiculousness; he made me read precursor articles written at the start of the century by the Viennese Loos); see Amédée Ozenfant, *Mémoires, 1886–1962* (Paris: Seghers, 1968): 104.
   On Purism in painting, see Carol S. Eliel, ed., *L'Esprit Nouveau: Purism in Paris, 1918–1925*, exhib. cat. (Los Angeles: Los Angeles County Museum of Art, 2001); and idem, *L'Esprit Nouveau: Le purisme à Paris, 1918–1925*, exhib. cat., Musée de Grenoble (Paris: Réunion des Musées Nationaux, 2001).
9. See *L'Elan*, no. 9 (March 1916): 14; and Ozenfant, *Mémoires* (1968): 93.

10. Idem, "Notes sur le Cubisme," *L'Elan,* no. 10 (December 1916).
11. Le Corbusier was sensitive to the smooth and polished character of Ozenfant's painting, a characteristic trait of his classical method and of his correlation with the industrial aesthetic. See Ducros, *Amédée Ozenfant*, (2002).
12. Brooks, *Formative Years* (1997): 500ff.
13. See Guy de Tervarent, *Attributs et symboles dans l'art profane* (Geneva: Droz, 1997): 170–71.
14. Stanislaus von Moos, "Le Corbusier und der Kubismus. Stilleben, Architektur und Ornament", in *Ein Haus für den Kubismus. Die Sammlung Raoul La Roche: Picasso, Braque, Léger, Gris – Le Corbusier und Ozenfant*, ed. Katharina Schmidt and Hartwig Fischer, exhib. cat., Kunstmuseum Basel (Ostfildern-Ruit: Hatje, 1998): 193 and fig. 7.
15. Ozenfant and Jeanneret, "Sur la plastique: 1. Examen des conditions primordiales," *L'Esprit nouveau*, no. 1 (October 1920): 34–48; "Le purisme," *L'Esprit nouveau*, no. 4 (January 1921): 369–86.
16. See Ozenfant, *Mémoires* (1968): 104 n. 3 (unnumbered), and chap. 5. The note reads: "Kahnweiller nous raconte que lors de sa visite à l'atelier d'Ozenfant que celui-ci partageait à cette époque avec Jeanneret, il a constaté que leur peinture ressemblait à leurs personnalités et à leur vie presque ascétique. 'Samir Rafi' (Kahnweiler told us that at the time of his visit to Ozenfant's studio, the one that he shared with Jeanneret during this period, he reported that their painting resembled their personalities and their almost ascetic life. "Samir Rafi").
17. [Il me restait à faire une dernière visite, à la revue L'Esprit Nouveau dirigée par Amédée Ozenfant et Jeanneret, deux peintres, les maîtres et d'ailleurs les seuls représentants de l'école puriste. Jeanneret commençait déjà à être plus connu comme rénovateur de l'architecture sous le nom de Le Corbusier. Leur purisme pictural était une sorte de Cubisme austère, tiré au cordeau, sur un plan de projection unique. Les révérents frères puristes, comme on les appelait parfois, pareillement graves et tout de noir vêtus, dans leur bureau où l'on voyait que chaque chaise, chaque planche, chaque feuille de papier avaient leur utilisation strictement déterminé, m'intimidèrent fort], Jean Epstein, *Ecrits sur le cinéma, 1921–1953*, vol. 1 (Paris: Cinéma Club / Seghers, 1974/75): 42.
18. See, e.g., Louis Delluc, "Cinéma," *L'Esprit nouveau,* no. 3 (December 1920): 349–51; idem, "Cinéma," ibid., no. 4 (January 1920): 480–82; idem, "Photogénie," ibid., no. 5 (February 1921): 589–90; idem, "Pro Cinéma," ibid., no. 14 (January 1922): 1666–68); Jean Epstein, "Cinéma," ibid., no. 14 (January 1922): 1669–70; Elie Faure, "Charlot," ibid., no. 6 (March 1921): 657–66); De Fayet [pseud.], "Toeppfer précurseur du cinéma." ibid., no. 11/12 (March 1921): 1336–43; Fernand Léger, "Ballet mécanique," ibid., no. 28, (January 1925): 2336–37; B. Tokine, "L'Esthétique du cinéma," ibid., no.1 (October 1920): 84–89.
19. [Perspective veut dire création d'espace virtuel. Le purisme admet comme un moyen constructif de premier ordre la sensation de profondeur qui est génératrice de la sensation d'espace sans lequel le volume est un vain mot], Amédée Ozenfant and Charles-Edouard Jeanneret, "Intégrer," *Création*, no. 2 (November 1921): 9–10.
20. [Dans ce système, une seule image mouvementée et animée comme l'édifice lui-même, tient lieu de la figuration abstraite, par plan, coupe et élévation. Le lecteur a sous les yeux, à la fois, le plan, l'extérieur de l'édifice, sa coupe et ses dispositions intérieures], Auguste Choisy, *Histoire de l'architecture* (1899; reprint, Paris: Vincent, Fréal, 1964), 1:7.

NOTES TO THE CATALOGUE

In each of the four parts, the full reference is given on first citation and a short form, including the date of publication, is used in subsequent citations. For oft-cited sources, the following short forms have been used, occasionally with different publication dates when authors cited editions other than those listed in the key below. For more information on the Jeanneret/Le Corbusier correspondence in archives, see the Bibliography.

Brooks, *Formative Years* (1997)
H. Allen Brooks. *Le Corbusier's Formative Years: Charles-Edouard Jeanneret at La Chaux-de-Fonds.* Chicago and London: University of Chicago Press, 1997.

***Carnets* (1987)**
Giuliano Gresleri, ed. *Ch.-E.Jeanneret – Le Corbusier: Voyage d'Orient, Carnets.* Milan: Electa, 1987.

***Le Corbusier: Le Passé* (1988)**
Le Corbusier: Le Passé à réaction poétique, exhib. cat., Hôtel de Sully (Paris: Caisse nationale des Monuments historiques et des Sites, Ministère de la Culture et de la Communication, 1988.

Oeuvre complète 1910–1929
Willy Boesiger and Oscar Stonorov, eds. *Le Corbusier et Pierre Jeanneret. Oeuvre complète.* Vol. 1, *1910–1929.* Zurich: Girsberger, 1937.

Oeuvre complète 1929–1934
Willy Boesiger, ed. *Le Corbusier et Pierre Jeanneret: Oeuvre complète.* Vol. 2, *1929–1934.* Zürich: Girsberger, 1935

Sketchbooks 1914–1948
Le Corbusier Sketchbooks. Vol. 1, *1914-1948.* New York and Cambridge, Mass.: The Architectural History Foundation / MIT Press, 1981.

***Urbanisme* (1925)**
Le Corbusier. *Urbanisme.* Paris: Crès, 1925.

***Vers une architecture* (1923)**
Le Corbusier-Saugnier. *Vers une architecture.* Paris: Crès, 1923.

***Viaggio in oriente* (1984)**
Giuliano Gresleri, ed. *Le Corbusier, Viaggio in oriente: Gli inediti di Charles Edouard Jeanneret, fotografo e scrittore.* Venice: Marsilio, 1984.

***Viaggio in Toscana* (1987)**
Giuliano Gresleri, ed. *Le Corbusier: Il viaggio in Toscana (1907).* Exhib. cat., Palazzo Pitti, Firenze. Venice: Marsilio, 1987.

***Voyage d'orient* (1966)**
Le Corbusier. *Le Voyage d'orient.* Edited by Jean Petit. Paris: Forces Vives, 1966.

Abbreviations:

CEJ	Charles Edouard Jeanneret
LC	Le Corbusier
BN	Bibliothèque Nationale, Paris
BV	Bibliothèque de la Ville, La Chaux-de-Fonds
FLC	Fondation Le Corbusier, Paris

Part 1: Itinerant Education

Cat. no. 1. Florence and Siena

1. See Giuliano Gresleri, "Camere con vista e disattesi itinerari: 'Le voyage d'Italie' di Ch.E.Jeanneret, 1907," in *Viaggio in Toscana* (1987): 2–26, and, more recently: Brooks, *Formative Years* (1997): 95–116.
2. [Mur uni; entrée tout à coté dans l'axe de l'avant-dernière fenêtre, symétriquement en avant de la porte à chaque côté deux statues très laides, Adam et Eve. En avant encore et sur des grands socles cubiques statues colossales, le vainqueur très laid et le David de Michel-Ange (actuellement le David a été enlevé de son socle...)], CEJ, notation on drawing FLC 2173.
3. CEJ to Charles L'Eplattenier, 19 September 1907, BV, quoted in Patricia May Sekler, *The Early Drawings of Charles-Edouard Jeanneret (Le Corbusier) 1902–1908* (New York and London: Garland, 1977): 437ff.
4. [...comme la voyaient les étrangers du moyen-age lorsqu'ils arrivaient au sommet d'une colline et que tout à coup surgissait dans la brume blueue du matin, ce monstre de pierre, colline plus grande que celles d'alentour parce qu'ordonnée], CEJ to Charles L'Eplattenier, 1 November 1907, BV.
5. Brooks, *Formative Years* (1997): 104; the source for this information is a letter to his parents dated 8 October ; see also *Viaggio in Toscana* (1987): 17. For Ruskin's comments on the wall-tombs, see *Mornings in Florence* (New York: John W. Lovell Company, n.d.): 77. Ruskin mentions that he purchased a drawing of these tombs, probably by Thomas Mattheus (1842–1942); reproduced in Jeanne Clegg and Paul Tucker, *Ruskin and Tuscany*, exhib. cat., (London: Accademia Italiana, 1993).
6. Brooks, *Formative Years* (1997): 97.
7. For illustrations see *Viaggio in Toscana* (1987): figs. 33, 34, 35. Perrin also made a drawing of Cellini's *Perseus*.

Cat. no. 2. Venice

8. Brooks, *Formative Years* (1997): 114f.; see also *Viaggio in Toscana* (1987): 24f. CEJ to Ch. L'Eplattenier, 1 November 1907, BV. The full quotation reads: "Cette ville ne me plairait pas pour un séjour prolongé. Trop de moments d'oisiveté forcée, ces éternels bateaux, qui vous donnent le gout de la grande fleme. Les crayons ne s'usent plus et le papier reste blanc" (I would not like to have a prolonged sojourn in this city. Too many moments of forced laziness, those eternal boats, which sap your will. The pencils are no longer used, and the paper remains white).
9. [la noble et fine harmonie des amples surfaces du palais des Doges, ou la chaude cadence des voûtes et des clochetons de St.Marc], CEJ to Albert Jeanneret, 2 February 1908, BV.
10. CEJ to his parents, 2 February 1908, BV.
11. Stanislaus von Moos, "La lezione di Venezia," in *Le Corbusier: Album La Roche* (Milan: Electa, 1996): 24-40; idem, "Le Corbusier und Palladio: vor Ort, 1922," in *Ein Haus für den Kubismus, Die Sammlung Raoul La Roche: Picasso, Braque, Léger, Gris — Le Corbusier und Ozenfant*, ed. Katharina Schmidt and Hartwig Fischer, exhib. cat., Kunstmuseum Basel (Ostfildern-Ruit: Hatje, 1998): 215–26.
12. See *Urbanisme* (1925): 52 (Procurazie vecchie); LC, *La Ville radieuse* (Boulogne-sur-Seine: Editions de L'Architecture d'aujourd'hui, 1935): 268f. (separation of traffic lines and the quality of "anonymous" architecture); LC, *Propos d'urbanisme* (Paris: Bourrelier, 1946): 47 ff. ("harmony"). For the vernacular (as opposed to monumental) heritage of Venice, see also LC, *Quand les cathédrales étaient blanches* (Paris: Plon, 1937): 8ff. The first critic to underscore the importance of this passage was Manfredo Tafuri, *Teoria e storia dell'architettura* (Bari: Laterza, 1968): 57ff.

Cat. no. 3. Paris and Rouen

13. For Jeanneret's readings and the intellectual turmoils that resulted from them see Paul V. Turner, *The Education of Le Corbusier* (New York and London: Garland, 1977); and Brooks, *Formative Years* (1997): 172–75. If Brooks is correct, the impact made by Ernest Renan's *Vie de Jésus* (1863) on Jeanneret's view of his own role as a prophet was even greater than Nietzsche's *Thus Spake Zarathustra.*
14. Private collection, La Chaux-de-Fonds; see Anne Prache, "Le Corbusiers Begegnung mit Notre-Dame in Paris," in *Bau- und Bildkunst im Spiegel internationaler Forschung. Festschrift zum 80. Geburtstag von Prof. Dr. Edgar Lehmann,* ed. Institut für Denkmalpflege der Deutschen Demokratischen Republik (Berlin [DDR]: Verlag für Bauwesen, 1989): 276–79.
15. Brooks, *Formative Years* (1997): 171–73 (and for the quote from the letter to L'Eplattenier). See also chap. 2, by Pierre Vaisse, in this volume.
16. For a good selection of Chartres-related statements and sketches see *Le Corbusier: Le Passé* (1988): 89f.
17. See Brooks, *Formative Years* (1997): 178f.
18. Jeanneret also took a picture showing the tracery of the one of the towers flanking the transept (FLC L4-19-46). A pencil drawing by Perrin shows the same detail (Musée Perrin, Môtiers). The similarity in vantage point confirms that the two companions were once again standing side by side — this time on the roof of the south transept of Rouen cathedral.
19. *Le Corbusier: Le Passé* (1988): 91–93.
20. [formes aigües, en silhouette déchiquetée, avec un désir d'ordre évident, mais totalement dépourvu du calme et de l'équilibre qui témoignent des civilisations abouties], *Urbanisme* (1925): 5, 32; this passage is echoed, with greater detail, in: LC, *Manière de penser l'urbanisme* (1946; reprint, Geneva: Gonthier, 1963): 49–56.
21. Ibid.; see also chap. 2, by Pierre Vaisse, in this volume.

Cat. no. 4. Paris: Museum Studies

22. [Les musées m'ont fourni les certitudes sans trous, sans embûches. Les oeuvres sont là comme des entiers, et la conversation est sans fard, le tête-à-tête est à merci de celui qui questionne; l'oeuvre répond toujours aux questions qu'on lui pose. . . . je n'ai questionné que ce qu'on n'appelle pas le Grand Art. J'allais bien le dimanche voir les Cimabue, les Breughel, les Raphael, les Tintoret, etc.. Mais pour travailler, pour dessiner, pour comprendre la richesse suffisante qu'il faut donner à son travail, le degré de concentration, de transposition, d'invention, de re-création, je m'arrêtais là où de ce temps personne ne plantait son chevalet, - bien loin de la "Grande Galerie". J'étais toujours seul...avec les gardiens], LC, *L'Art décoratif d'aujourd'hui*

(Paris: Crès, 1925): 201–2.
23. For a selection of those sketches, see ibid., pp. 201–4. For the best survey of these museum studies and their significance, see *Le Corbusier: Le Passé* (1988): 85ff and 135–43; but see also the notes below for further references.
24. Note also the beautiful study of a Hindu column from the same collection (FLC 1927).
25. *Le Corbusier: Le Passé* (1988): 85. For a selection of Jeanneret's studies after works in the Musée de Sculpture Comparée, see ibid., pp. 86f.
26. Here too, Jeanneret has made many drawings; see, e.g., *Le Corbusier: Le Passé* (1988): 135–43.
27. Some of these plaster casts have since been reinstalled for permanent display at the Abbaye de St. Riquier, Département Somme.
28. As of this writing, it has been closed and is scheduled to reopen in 2003 as part of the Cité de l'Architecture.
29. See *Viaggio in Toscana* (1987): 22f. Wilhelm Worringer included similar studies in *Abstraktion und Einfühlung* (1909), but it was not until 1911 that Jeanneret was introduced to Worringer's ideas (by August Klipstein; see cat. nos. 8, 11).
30. The building itself had been designed by L'Eplattenier in collaboration with René Chapallaz. See *Schweizerische Bauzeitung* 82 (1923): 210; 291; and Jacques Gubler, "La Chaux-de-Fonds," in *INSA. Inventar der neueren Schweizer Architektur 1850–1920*, ed. Gesellschaft für Schweizerische Kunstgeschichte, vol. 3, *Städte* (Bern, 1982): 127–217; for the Musée des Beaux-Arts see ibid., p. 129. This volume covers Biel, La Chaux-de-Fonds, Chur, Davos.
31. For L'Eplattenier see Maurice Jeanneret, *Charles L'Eplattenier* (Neuchâtel: La Baconnière, 1933). These studies have not been catalogued, and we cannot be sure that the example shown here predates comparable studies by Jeanneret.
32. For reproductions including the transcriptions of such notes see *Le Corbusier: Le Passé* (1988): 141–43.
33. For further examples see ibid., p. 139f.

Cat. no. 5. Versailles

34. [Ce n'est pas, pour moi, *l'architecture*, loin de là, mais c'est un exquis chapitre sur la proportion, le charme et l'échelle humaine], LC, "Perret par Le Corbusier," *L'Architecture d'aujourd'hui* 3, no. 7 (1932): 8. The chronology of the early visits to Versailles in 1909 is described in Brooks, *Formative Years* (1997), especially pp. 155 and 181–82.
35. FLC L4-19-48, 50, 51, 57, 58, 59.
36. [je chois dans les parterres du château de la Belle au Bois Dormant; et je me trouve nez-à-nez avec l'Orangerie, au pied de l'Escalier des Cent-Marches], LC, "Perret par Le Corbusier" (1932): 8.
37. Of these photographs, see especially FLC L4-19-54 and 55. Three watercolors were executed from the same viewpoint; see FLC 1919, 2467, 4087. In 1935 Le Corbusier returned to the image of the Staircase of the Hundred Steps, which he defined—alongside other photographic images (Parthenon, Coliseum, Baptistery of Pisa, Saint Peter's)—as "the flowers of the human spirit . . . , the lofty places of thought . . . the essential food." See LC, *Ville radieuse* (1935): 139.
38. See *Vers une architecture* (1923): 61.
39. For the pavilion, see Bruno Reichlin, "L'Ancien et le nouveau: Le Corbusier, le Pavillon de la Villa Church," *AMC—Architecture, mouvement, continuité* 1 (1983): 100–111.
40. CEJ to L'Eplattenier, 16 January 1911, FLC.
41. Postcard, CEJ to Ritter, 2 January 1913, FLC. Jeanneret stayed at Versailles at least twice in 1909, and once in 1912, but repeated visits through 1913 also seem likely.
42. [Ariane endormie des jardins de Versailles . . . déshabillée . . . peinte comme une grande fraise opulente, sur un fond de vert intense], CEJ to Ritter, 6 April 1913, FLC. Jeanneret acquired a postcard depicting the sculpture (FLC L5-7-283), which is the subject of two drawings probably completed between 1912 and 1913 (FLC T71, fols. 97 and 99).

Cat. no. 6. Switzerland I

43. Brooks, *Formative Years* (1997): 201.
44. H. Allen Brooks, "Jeanneret and Sitte: Le Corbusier's Earliest Ideas on Urban Design," in *In Search of Modern Architecture: A Tribute to Henry-Russell Hitchcock*, ed. Helen Searing (Cambridge, Mass., and London: MIT Press, 1982): 278–97; idem, *Formative Years* (1997): 200–208 (the quote is from p. 201). Charles L'Eplattenier,"L'Esthétique des villes," in *Compte-Rendu des Délibérations de l'Assemblée Génerale des Délégués de l'Union des Villes Suisses* (Zurich, 1910): 24–31.
45. CEJ to his parents, 29 June 1910, BV; quoted in Brooks, *Formative Years* (1997): 201.
46. See Rosario De Simone, *Ch. E. Jeanneret–Le Corbusier: Viaggio in Germania, 1910–1911* (Roma: Officina, 1989): 54ff.
47. See Sekler, *Early Drawings* (1977): 425.
48. [Tout le peuple qui s'en va vers la Mort riant toujours dans quelque coin, fait penser aux fleurs d'orchis les plus extravagantes, aux insectes des Amériques et à ces oiseaux coloriés et querelleurs que l'on apporte des îles], Alexandre Cingria-Vaneyre, *Les Entretiens de la villa du Rouet: Essais dialogués sur les arts plastiques en suisse romande* (Geneva: A. Jullien, 1908): 57.
49. Gubler, "La Chaux-de-Fonds"(1982): 183. Note that Jeanneret interrupted his journey through Germany in the summer of 1910 to attend the inauguration of L'Eplattenier's monument (Brooks, *Formative Years* [1997]: 208).
50. Marc E. Albert Emery, ed., *Charles-Edouard Jeanneret, La Construction des villes: Genèse et devenir d'un ouvrage écrit de 1910 à 1915 et laissé inachevé par Charles-Edouard Jeanneret-Gris dit Le Corbusier* (Paris and Héricourt: Editions L'Age d'Homme, 1992): 48.

Cat. no. 7. Munich

51. For Jeanneret's time in Munich, see De Simone, *Viaggio in Germania* (1989): passim, esp. chaps. 2–6; Brooks, *Formative Years* (1997): 209ff.; and, especially, Karen Michels, "Augen, die sehen: Le Corbusiers Beobachtungen in München," *Jahrbuch des Zentralinstituts für Kunstgeschichte* 5–6 (1989–90): 471–98.
52. Jeanneret's sketch is reproduced by Brooks, "Jeanneret and Sitte"(1982): 283.
53. See De Simone, *Viaggio in Germania* (1989), fig. 186.
54. Michels, "Augen, die sehen" (1989–90): 482–83.
55. At another church, Saint Peter, Jeanneret once more chose to draw the outside of the choir, on the Viktualienmarkt side. For the main facade, in its urban context, he used a photograph.

Cat. no. 8. Prague

56. The dating follows that given by Brooks, *Formative Years* (1997): 249–50, n. 57.
57. [Praha: nemusím hovorit o staré Praze, verte, ze se mi líbí velmi uprímne. Nikoliv Svaty Vít, ale staré domy krásnych proporcí, civilní stavby, trebas skromné, mají tu vznesenost a noblesu; je to architektura jizního ducha], Karel Teige, "Le Corbusier v Praze," *Rozpravy Aventina* 4 (1928–29): 31; quoted in Teige, "Le Corbusier in Prague," in Miroslav Masák, Rostislav Švácha, and Jindřich Vybíral, *The Trade Fair Palace in Prague* (Prague: National Gallery, 1995): 40.
58. [Baroque: Prague la plus formidable des villes européennes], *Carnets* (1987), 2:23 [21].
59. The original negatives/plates and the four watercolors are at the Bibliothèque de la Ville de La Chaux-de-Fonds, LC ms 125-1 – LC ms 125-4. For illustrations, see *Viaggio in oriente* (1984): 129–40; Giuliano Gresleri, ed., *Le Corbusier: Il linguaggio delle pietre,* exhib. cat., Crema, Centro culturale S.Agostino (Venice: Marsilio, 1988), figs. 11–14.
60. Paul Schultze-Naumburg, *Kulturarbeiten*, vol. 4, *Städtebau* (Munich: Callwey, 1906).
61. Ibid., p. 184.
62. For instance, he did not use any examples from Prague in his planned study "La Construction des villes."
63. See Vladimír Šlapeta, "Die Wirkung in der Ferne—Le Corbusier und die tschechische Architektur," *Arch+,* nos. 90–91 (1987): 87–92.

Cat. no. 9. The Balkans

64. The literature concerning Le Corbusier's Voyage d'Orient is vast. Essays, articles, and extensive quotations from his writings have appeared in the last several years without significantly affecting the results of my own research that has appeared continuously since 1974. Listed here (in full citation) are only those works that are essential to understanding this exceptional moment in Le Corbusier's development. —G.G.

Giuliano Gresleri, *Le Corbusier, Viaggio in Oriente: Gli inediti di Charles Edouard Jeanneret fotografo e scrittore*, 2d ed. (Venice: Marsilio, 1985) and 3rd ed., 1995 with the title *Viaggio in Oriente. Le Corbusier, Charles Edouard Jeanneret, fotografo e scrittore* (1995).
——, "Partir et revenir: Le voyage d'Italie," in *Le Corbusier et la Méditerannée*, exhib. cat., Vieille Charité (Marseille: Editions Parenthèses, 1985): 23–35.
——, ed., *Ch.-E.Jeanneret – Le Corbusier: Voyage d'Orient, Carnets* (Milan: Electa, 1987).
——, "Ch. E. Jeanneret: From Prague to the Parthenon, The 'drift' and the 'perfect ecstasy'," *Architektonika temata / Architecture in Greece*, no. 21 (1987): 22–103.
——, "Viaggio e scoperta, descrizione e trascrizione," *Casabella* 51, no. 531/532 (1987): 8–10.
——, ed., *Le Corbusier: Il viaggio in Toscana (1907),* exhib. cat, Palazzo Pitti, Firenze, (Venice: Marsilio, 1987).
——, ed., *Le Corbusier: Il linguaggio delle pietre*, exhib. cat., Crema, Centro culturale S.Agostino (Venice: Marsilio, 1988).
——, ed., *Ch.-E. Jeanneret – Le Corbusier: Les voyages d'Allemagne, Carnets,* (Milan: Electa, 1994).
——, "Il silenzio delle pietre, le parole dei numeri, la solitudine, il 'deflagrante ricordo'," in *Le Corbusier e l'Antico: Viaggi nel Mediterraneo*, ed. Benedetto Gravagnuolo, exhib. cat., Palazzo Reale (Naples: Electa, 1997): 71–83.2.
Le Corbusier, *L'Art décoratif d'aujourd'hui* (Paris: Crès, 1925): esp. 197–218.
——, *Le Voyage d'orient,* ed. Jean Petit (Paris: Forces Vives, 1966). This work is a collage of several of Le Corbusier's writings that were added to the original manuscript of 1911 with notes and variations made by the author on his earlier writings during the journey.
Paul V. Turner, "The Beginnings of Le Corbusier's Education," *The Art Bulletin* 53, no. 2 (1971): 214–24.
Stanislaus von Moos, *Le Corbusier: Elemente einer Synthese* (Frauenfeld-Stuttgart: Huber, 1968); in English as *Le Corbusier: Elements of a Synthesis* (Cambridge, Mass: MIT Press, 1979): esp. chap.1.

65. [. . . quelques ponts de fer jetés hardiment sur l'eau. C'est chaque foi le même type: une longue poutre rigide et tout ajourée, chef d'oeuvre de legéreté et de technique], *Voyage d'orient* (1966): 38.
66. [L'un de ces ponts est l'oeuvre d'Eiffel], ibid., p. 44
67. See *Vers une architecture* (1923): 1; and LC, *Une Maison, un palais* (Paris: Crés, 1928): 20.
68. [Justement, la veille, au matin, nous avions vu au bord du fleuve, vingtsix tours carrés flanquant un grand mur sévère], *Voyage d'orient* (1966): 43.
69. *Adalberto Libera: Opera completa* (Milan: Electa, 1989): 19.

Cat. no. 10. Istanbul

70. *Oeuvre complète 1910–1929*, p. 37.
71. The work was discovered on the occasion of the exhibition *Le Corbusier: Il linguaggio delle pietre* (Crema, 1988) and published in the accompanying catalogue. See *Linguaggio delle pietre* (1988).
72. See *Voyage d'orient* (1966): 107ff; and especially *Viaggio in Oriente* (1984): 247ff.
73. The other sketches known to date are FLC 6127 (int.) and FLC 6098. For a drawing (now lost) of the *avlu* fountain, see LC, *Almanach d'architecture moderne* (Paris: Crès, 1926): 57. When I began research for the first edition of *Viaggio*, virtually none of Le Corbusier's drawings bore any annotations useful for identifying the subjects; identification could only be made by comparing the sketch with actual locations.—G.G.
74. LC, *Almanach* (1926): 55ff.
75. Ibid., p. 59.
76. *Viaggio in Oriente* (1984): 286.
77. See *Voyage d'orient* (1966): 76ff, and LC, *Almanach* (1926): 55ff.
78. *Oeuvre complete 1910–1929*, p. 29 ("Troyes").
79. Both drawings are at the FLC.
80. Jeanneret seemed very interested in this theme because it allowed him to compare Pierre Loti's descriptions of the Turkish interiors with his own observations. For comments on the Eyüp house, see Loti, *Phantôme d'Orient* (Paris: Calman Levy, 1892): 214ff. Jeanneret had visited an important exhibition of Muslim art in Munich the year before (mentioned in *Étude sur le mouvement d'art décoratif en Allemagne*) at which he would have seen examples of domestic Turkish furnishings; for his sketches of these, see *Linguaggio delle pietre* (1988), nos. 55, 56, 57.
81. Pierre Loti is considered the creator of the "Orientalist" literary genre; Claude Farrère, whose writings contain several stylistic similarities to Jeanneret's, was one of Loti's followers. Jeanneret came into contact with the works of both novelists in his visits to Ritter's library in Munich. He commented in his notebook that he read Loti's *Aziyadè* during his stay in Pera.

Cat. no. 11. Athens

82. Adolf Max Vogt, "Die 'verkehrte' Grand Tour des Charles Edouard Jeanneret," *Bauwelt*, no. 38/39, 78 (1987): 1430–39. For a useful survey of the drawings and photographs relating to Athens, see Françoise Véry, "Athènes," in *Le Corbusier: Le Passé*: 54–59. For detailed accounts of the visit to Athens, see *Carnets* (1987); Gresleri, "Itinera Architectonica. Gli antichi, miei soli maestri," in *Viaggio in Oriente* (1984): 21–110; and Brooks, *Formative Years* (1997): 279–89.
83. Worringer's book *Abstraktion und Einfühlung* (Abstraction and empathy; 1909) was in Klipstein's luggage; see Vogt, "Die 'verkehrte' Grand Tour" (1987): 1432; Brooks, *Formative Years* (1997): 256.
84. Jeanneret wrote a long letter to William Ritter shortly before his arrival in Athens, during the quarantine period.
85. [L'impression que me fit Athènes est de beaucoup la plus forte que j'aie jamais ressentie. Il y a un lieu où la perfection existe; il n'y a pas deux: . . . Je n'avais rien imaginé de pareil. C'était

l'idéal cristallisé en marbre penthélique qui se montrait à moi], Ernest Renan, *Prière sur l'Acropole* (Athens: Eleftheroudakis & Darth, n.d.): 1; see idem, *Oeuvres complètes* (Paris: Calmann-Lévy, 1948): 753.

86. [Je ne sais trop pourquoi cette colline recèle l'essence de la pensée artistique. . . . J'ai longtemps accepté que ce soit ici comme le dépôt de l'étalon sacré, base de toute mensuration d'art . . . Mais pourquoi . . . dois-je le désigner comme le Maître incontestable le Parthénon, lorsqu'il surgit de son assiette de pierre, et m'incliner, même avec colère, devant sa suprématie?], *Voyage d'orient* (1966): 158f.
87. Especially if we agree with H. Allen Brooks that the three fine watercolors from *Langage des pierres* were painted only later, probably in 1914 (*Formative Years* [1997]: 284).
88. *Carnets* (1987), 3:98–130.
89. Above all, from Maxime Collignon and Frédéric Boissonas, *Le Parthénon: L'Histoire, l'architecture et la sculpture* (Geneva: Librairie Centrale d'Art et d'Architecture, 1914). Only a few of Jeanneret's own sketches are interspersed among the photographs. For Boissonas, see *L'Esprit nouveau*, no. 15 (May 1922); and Nicolas Bouvier, *Boissonas: Une Dynastie de photographes, 1864–1963* (Lausanne: Payot, 1983): 128 and passim.
90. S. B. M. [Bruno Maurer], "Akropolis," in *L'Esprit nouveau: Le Corbusier und die Industrie* (1987): 174–77. For Le Corbusier and the "myth of Greece," see "Le Corbusier's 'Hellas'. Fünf Metamorphosen einer Konstruktion," *Kunst + Architecture in der Schweiz* 50, no. 1 (1999): 20–30. See also Josep M. Rovira, "El valor de la antigüedad. Le Corbusier y la Acrópolis," in *Las casas del alma. Maquetas de la antigüedad*, exhib. cat. (Barcelona: Centre de Cultura Contemporània de Barcelona, 1996–97): 139–44.

Cat. no. 12. Pompeii

91. See *Pompéi: Travaux et envois des architectes francais au XIXe siècle* (Paris and Rome: École nationale supérieure des Beaux-Arts / École française de Rome, 1980).
92. For an excellent survey of Jeanneret's studies, see Claude Malécot, "Pompéi," in: *Le Corbusier: Le Passé* (1988): 64–69; see also Giuliano Gresleri, "Il silenzio delle pietre, le parole dei numeri, la solitudine, il deflagrante ricordo," in *Le Corbusier e l'Antico: Viaggi nel Mediterraneo,* ed. Benedetto Gravagnuolo, exhib. cat., Palazzo Reale, Naples (Naples: Electa, 1997): 71–83; and Maria Salerno, "Mare e memoria: la casa mediterranea nell'opera di Le Corbusier," in ibid., pp. 106–113.
93. On the verso of the same drawing, plans, elevations and an axonometry illustrate the macellum situated next door.
94. FLC 2859; see Gresleri, "Silenzio delle pietre" (1997): 74 and Malécot, "Pompéi" (1988): 64. A first version of the view from Jupiter's temple onto the forum was drawn in his sketchbook; see *Carnets* (1987), 4:103.
95. *Carnets* (1987), 5:83.
96. For earlier roots of Le Corbusier's hierarchical spatial arrangements, see H. Allen Brooks, "L'évolution de la conception de l'espace au cours des années d'apprentissage de Charles-Edouard Jeanneret à La Chaux-de-Fonds," in *La Ville et l'urbanisme après Le Corbusier: Actes du colloque* (La Chaux-de-Fonds: Etions d'en Haut, 1993): 13–31.
97. For the impact of the analysis of Pompeian atrium and impluvium on the language of Le Corbusier's house designs in the 1920s and 1930s, see Malécot, "Pompéi" (1988); and Kurt W. Forster, "Antiquity and Modernity in the La Roche–Jeanneret Houses of 1923," *Oppositions* 15/16 (1979): 131–53. The key reference among Le Corbusier's own writings is *Vers une architecture* (1923): 141–60.

Cat. no. 13. Rome

98. CEJ to August Klipstein, 30 September 1910, quoted in Brooks, *Formative Years* (1997): 230. CEJ to his parents, 2 December 1910, BV.
99. The second nature of the villa as a "cube" is made explicit in Jeanneret's sketchbooks, in which there are two preliminary studies of the watercolor; see *Carnets* (1987), 5:17–19.
100. CEJ to William Ritter, 30 July 1921, BV. The chronology of this second trip to Rome can only be reconstructed indirectly, via the correspondence with Ritter, Ozenfant, and Le Corbusier's wife, Yvonne. Ozenfant appears to have interrupted his stay in Rome, after some kind of dispute (CEJ to Ozenfant, Rome, [1921] and Châbles, 7 September 1921, FLC).
101. E.g., Bramante's Cortile S. Damaso served as a "Rappel à MM les architectes: la surface" in *L'Esprit nouveau*, no. 2; later included in *Vers une architecture* (1923): 21.
102. LC-Saugnier [pseud.], "Architecture 1: La leçon de Rome," *L'Esprit nouveau*, no. 14 (January 1922): 1591–1607; De Fayet [pseud.], "La Sixtine de Michel-Ange," ibid., pp. 1609–22; LC-Saugnier [pseud.], "Architecture 2: L'illusion des plans," ibid., no. 15 (February 1922): 1767–80. The first and third were reprinted in *Vers une architecture.* Although "De Fayet" was often used as a pseudonym by Ozenfant, the manuscript on the Sistine Chapel is clearly by Le Corbusier (FLC). The other two articles under the by-line "Le Corbusier-Saugnier" appear to have been written jointly.
103. [cette toute petite église de Sainte-Marie, église des gens misérables, proclame, dans Rome bruyamment luxueuse, le faste insigne de la mathématique, la puissance imbattable de la proportion, l'éloquence souveraine des rapports], LC-Saugnier [pseud.], "Architecture I. La leçon de Rome," in *L'Esprit nouveau*, no. 14 (January 1922): 1591–1607.
104. [Michel-Ange est l'homme de nos derniers mille ans comme Phidias fut celui du dernier millénaire], ibid., p. 1597.
105. [L'oeuvre de Michel-Ange est une *création*, non une renaissance, création, qui domine les époques classées. . . . Colisée a été vu par lui et ses heureuses mesures retenues . . .], ibid., p. 1601. See also *Le Corbusier: Le Passé* (1988): 108f.

Cat. no. 14. Pisa

106. See *Viaggio in Toscana* (1987): 18f.; pls. 1–7. It is symptomatic that at that moment the wall decorations in the camposanto were given more attention than the architecture.
107. *Oeuvre complète 1929–1934*, p. 132.
108. Note in particular the similarity between the general views of the Duomo and baptistery in the two most frequently published drawings (FLC 2491 and FLC 2506), which are neither signed nor dated, and his photographs; or between his sketches of the interior of the baptistery (*Carnets* [1987], 5:25, 6:27) and the postcards he purchased in Pisa.

Cat. no. 15. Switzerland II

109. Alexandre Cingria-Vaneyre, *Les Entretiens de la villa du Rouet: Essais dialogués sur les arts plastiques en Suissse romande* (Geneva: A. Jullien, 1908).
110. "La Maison Suisse," in *Les Etrennes helvétiques: Almanach illustré* (Dijon, La Chaux-de-Fonds, and Paris: n.p., 1914): 33–39.
111. Note, however, that for Cingria-Vaneyre the "Village suisse" had been synonymous with the "literary malady" of Swiss architecture around 1900 (*Les Entretiens* [1908]: 13); Jeanneret would probably have agreed. For issues of cultural politics see Jacques Gubler, *Nationalisme et internationalisme dans l'architecture moderne de la Suisse* (Lausanne: L'Age d'Homme, 1975); for more recent discussions, see Armand Brulhart, "Les chalets dans la ville," in *Le chalet dans tous ses états: La Construction de l'imaginaire helvétique*, ed. Valentina Anker, Jacques Gubler, et al. (Chêne-Bourg and Genève: Editions Chênoises, 1999): 123–72.
112. See von Moos, "Le Corbusier's 'Hellas'" (1999): 20–30. A postcard shows the exact location of the site: "C'est mon pays vu de notre Jura. . . . Dans l'axe même de ce port que vous voyez au bas de cette carte, s'élèvera la banque cantonale, édifice imposant . . . " (This is my country as seen from our Jura. . . . In the center of the harbor which you can see at the bottom of this card, the Banque Cantonale will be built, an impressive building. . . .), CEJ to Perret, 15 March 1914, FLC.
113. He praises the beauty of the cathedral of Solothurn: "C'est si merveilleusement adapté aux lignes du pays à sa topographie, que Soleure, ville terne et petite cité devient peut-être le plus beau fleuron de la Suisse. Preuve que ceci est encore une question d'esprit. . . . Et de nouveau, le sens de la patrie nous apparût . . . " (It is so marvelously adapted to the lines of the countryside, to its topography, that Solothurn, a dull and small town will perhaps become the most beautiful flower of Switzerland. Proof that this too is a question of spirit . . . . And once again, the sense of home appeared to us. . . .), CEJ to Auguste Perret, 26 January 1916, FLC.
114. [J'ai fait un problème admirable: le concours pour un pont gigantesque de 800m de long au dessus d'une gorge profonde, dans un paysage digne du sujet. La pierre était imposée, et ça devenait romain tout naturellement. . .], CEJ to Auguste Perret, (1915), FLC.
115. For more details see Brooks, *Formative Years* (1997): 382ff.; for a particularly beautiful sketch see "Le Landeron" Carnet, 1916, FLC W1-1/53.
116. "Landeron 1914" (Sketchbook A1, dated 1914) in *Sketchbooks 1914–1918*.

Cat. no. 16. Parisian Urbanism

117. See Philippe Duboy, "Architecture de la ville: culture et triomphe de l'urbanisme: Ch.-E. Jeanneret, 'La Construction des villes,' Bibliothèque Nationale de Paris, 1915," Ph.D. diss., Paris, (1985); idem, "L.C.B.N. 1.9.1.5.," *Casabella* 51, nos. 531/532 (1987): 94–103. For Jeanneret's researches while preparing "La Construction des villes," see Brooks, "Jeanneret and Sitte"(1982): 278–97; Emery, *Construction des villes* (1992).
118. CEJ, notation on drawing FLC B2-20-272; see also FLC B2-20-276. The latter sketch was published ten years later in *Urbanisme* (1925).
119. CEJ, notations on drawing FLC B2-20-278.
120. [Existaient alors Places des Vosges, Place Vendôme, des Victoires. Le résultat fut: place Louis XV (Concorde)], FLC B2-20-172.
121. For Le Corbusier's comments on the *Plan Voisin*, see LC, *Précisions sur un état present de l'architecture et de l'urbanisme* (Paris: Crès, 1930): 194–96.
122. [J'admire ici l'intention des architects de Louis XV qui tracèrent des plans d'embellissement de Paris. Les iconoclasts ne sont pas d'aujourd'hui], LC, *Propos d'urbanisme* (Paris: Bourrelier, 1946): 30.
123. [volumes sous la lumière (en bosse)], Ibid., 26. For the Île de la Cité, see sketches FLC B2-20-249 and B2-20-161, which were reworked in *Urbanisme* (1925): 253–54, and *Propos d'urbanisme* (1946): 30–31.
124. [Le rêve que nous faisons aujourd'hui de supprimer la boue des banlieues, de voir les blés, les prairies et les vergers buter tout contre la ville. . . un roy [sic] déjà l'a vécu. Alors pourquoi, amix, désespérer à l'heure où le monde possède toutes les puissances?], LC, *Propos d'urbanisme* (1946): 32. Accompanying the text on this page, Le Corbusier published sketch FLC B2-20-228, portraying the Jardin des Tuileries; it was also reproduced in *Urbanisme* (1925).

Part 2: Architecture

Cat. no. 17. Early Houses

1. [il [L'Eplattenier] voulut faire de moi un architect. J'avais horreur de l'architecture et des architectes [mais] j'acceptais le verdict et j'obéis; je m'engageais dans l'architecture], quoted in Jean Petit, *Le Corbusier lui-même* (Genève: Edition Rousseau, 1970): 25, 28.
2. Louis Fallet, the client, designed and fabricated jewelry and watches. He also served on the Board of the École d'Art.

Cat. no. 18. Inhabiting the Vernacular

3. The significance of the *chambre du tué* for Le Corbusier's future architectural career was initially pointed out in H. Allen Brooks, ed., *The Le Corbusier Archive*, vol. 1, *Early Buildings and Projects, 1912–23* (New York, London, and Paris: Garland Publishing, 1982): xxi, fig. 1–4. The chapter was later republished in idem, ed., *Le Corbusier* (Princeton, N.J.: Princeton University Press, 1987): 27–45.

Cat. no. 19. Villa Jeanneret-Perret

4. The Villa Jeanneret-Perret was sold in 1919. In 2000 it was purchased by the Association Maison Blanche; there are plans to restore and open the building to the public.
5. Asbestos cement products were made in Switzerland under the trademark Eternit from 1903 onward. Jeanneret used this "new" material for door panels (for rooms as well as furniture), and in 1918 he took out a number of patents for the use of the French-made Everite asbestos cement to make concrete formwork, sewer pipes, doors, furnishings, and so on. See Jean Petit, ed., *Le Corbusier: BSGDG (Breveté sans garantie du gouvernement)* (Zürich and Lugano: Hans Grieshaber and Fidia Edizioni d'Arte, 1996). In the planned restoration of the Villa Jeanneret-Perret, Eternit tiles are being tested as a roof covering to replace the present clay tiles.
6. See Brooks, *Formative Years* (1997): 310–29. Brooks points out that in this project Jeanneret enjoyed complete creative freedom.
7. [. . . à un moment où rentré d'un long voyage en GRÈCE, en ASIE, en TURQUIE et en ITALIE j'étais encore plein de grande architecture claire et formelle des pays méditerranéens, les seuls architectures que je reconnaisse], CEJ to Fritz Ernst Jeker, 11 September 1919, BV; written after the sale of the house.
8. [Votre type d'appartement, mais c'est juste la maison de mon père, qui plaît tant ici], CEJ to Auguste Perret, 20 June 1916, Institut français d'architecture, Fonds Perret (535 AP 318). Jeanneret consulted his former teacher, Perret, both on "Projet F" and on the project for La Scala cinema. A ground plan for an apartment, apparently sent by Perret, caused Jeanneret to think immediately of the plan of the Villa Jeanneret-Perret.
9. [Chez nous . . . tous les bâtiments ont toujours le rectangle parfait et jour sur quatre façades], ibid. These words immediately precede the passage cited in n. 8. Perret must have suggested a ground plan that was not rectangular in overall shape.
10. The linoleum in the living and dining area still survives. The floor of the *petit salon* is marked off from the main room by a darker color scheme but has a light border and frieze and, in the center, a square motif made up of strips of lighter linoleum.

Cat. no. 21. Maison Dom-ino

11. Jeanneret/Le Corbusier refers to the scheme as "domino" and "jeu de cartes" in his sketchbooks of 1915; as "Domino" in the article "Maisons en série" of December 1921; and as "Dom-

ino" in his *Oeuvre complète 1910–1929*. For Dom-ino see Eleanor Gregh, "The Dom-ino Idea," *Oppositions*, 15/16 (winter/spring 1979): 61–87, and Brooks, *Formative Years* (1997): 384–91.

12. Le Corbusier defined architecture as "le jeu savant, correct et magnifique des volumes assemblés sous la lumière" (the masterly, correct and magnificent play of volumes arranged under the light), *Vers une architecture* (1923): 16 (translation F.P.).
13. Karl Scheffler, "Ein Weg zum Stil," *Berliner Architekturwelt* 5, no. 9 (1902): 291–95; Walter Curt Behrendt, *Die einheitliche Blockfront als Raumelement im Stadtbau. Ein Beitrag zur Stadtbaukunst der Gegenwart* (Berlin: Cassirer, 1911).
14. The best-known statement of this position was Hermann Muthesius's call for "Typisierung" at the meeting of the Deutsche Werkbund in Cologne, July 1914, at which Jeanneret was present. For discussion and bibliography see Francesco Passanti, "The Vernacular, Modernism, and Le Corbusier," *Journal of the Society of Architectural Historians* 56, no. 4 (December 1997): 442–43.
15. [d'elles même, mes rues s'érigeraient en un rythme de palais, d'une tranquillité pompéienne], CEJ to Perret, 30 March 1915, Institut français d'architecture, Paris.
16. [L'intuition agit par éclairs inattendus. Voici en 1914 la conception pure et tótale de tout une système de consturire envisageant tous les problèmes qui vont naître a la suite de la guerre], *Oeuvre complète 1910–1929*, p. 23 (translation F.P.).
17. [La nouvelle forme, ça pouvait n'être qu'ingénieur. Vous avez fait de l'architecture], CEJ to Auguste Perret, 26 January 1916, Institut français d'architecture, Paris.

Cat. no. 22. "Projet F"

18. The plans and sketches were first identified by Brooks, *Formative Years* (1997): 411–14. Brooks based his identification on the records of the Schwob/Jeanneret lawsuit of July 1918.
19. [L'un des futurs locataires, directeur d'une de nos grosses fabriques de montres, s'est laissé entortiller et c'est un petit hôtel que je vais lui construire. . . . L'immeuble locatif a donné lieu à un plan bizarre mais qui se tient: un éventail et toutes les pièces absolument et entièrement régulières, propres], CEJ to Auguste Perret, 21 July 1916, Institut français d'architecture, Fonds Perret (535 AP 318). Jeanneret's letter of 20 June 1916 also seems to be a reaction to a suggestion from Perret concerning "Projet F"(see. cat. no. 19 and nn. 8, 9). This apparently involved a ground plan similar to that of the Villa Jeanneret-Perret of 1912: "Votre type d'appartement, mais c'est juste la maison de mon père qui plaît tant ici, et que je n'avais pas l'idée de transporter dans la locative [sic]" (Your apartment type, why, this is just exactly my father's house, which is so well liked here, and which it never occurred to me to transpose into the rental sector).
20. Brooks, *Formative Years* (1997): 412 and fig. 341.
21. See Giovanni Fanelli and Roberto Gargiani, *Perret e Le Corbusier: Confronti* (Rome and Bari: Laterza, 1990): 16ff. The FLC holds a number of blueprint copies of such studies, annotated in Jeanneret's hand (FLC F2-13.182–185).

Cat. no. 23. Villa Schwob

22. The standard reference on this design is now Brooks, *Formative Years* (1997): 424–63.
23. This paragraph and the next are derived from chap. 4, by Francesco Passanti, in this volume. Detailed references are found in the footnotes to that essay and are not repeated here.
24. [je me consacre à des oeuvres sérieuses, même savantes, c.- à dire, à des peintures qui soient au moins le prolongement de ma villa Schwob. . . . mon attention est fixée sur le Parthénon et sur Michel Ange. . . . Un art sans défaillance. Et le tempérament jugulé: mobile encore une fois: le Parthénon, ce drame], CEJ to William Ritter, 19 June 1920, BV, after receiving the photographs of the villa.
25. Colin Rowe, "Mannerism and Modern Architecture" (1950), in *The Mathematics of the Ideal Villa and Other Essays* (Cambridge, Mass., and London: MIT Press, 1976): 29–57. Rowe later published a collection of essays under the title, *As I Was Saying* (Cambridge, Mass., and London: MIT Press, 1996).

Cat. no. 24. Challuy Slaughterhouse

26. Brooks, *Formative Years* (1997): 485–88.
27. [la réellement bonne ordonnance de [Challuy], sa hardiesse, sa grandeur, son modernisme harmonieux . . . c'est . . . vivant . . . j'ai l'impression d'avoir fait oeuvre d'architecte. C'est certainement ma première oeuvre d'envergure.] [Challuy . . . etait vraiment une bannière], Le Corbusier's journal, part of his correspondence with William Ritter, 29 December 1917 and 31 January 1918, BV.
28. The standard textbook was F. W. Wilder, *The Modern Packing House*, Chicago: Nickerson and Collins, 1905), probably consulted by Le Corbusier.
29. [ce travail me laisse tout triste et réticent] [le taylorisme, l'horrible et inéluctable vie de demain], Le Corbusier's journal, 18 November and 29 December 1917, BV.

Cat. no. 25. "Everite"

30. Patricia Sekler, "Le Corbusier, Jeanneret, Patented Ideas and the Urban Cell," in *La Ville et l'urbanisme après Le Corbusier: Actes du colloque* (La Chaux-de-Fonds: Etions d'en Haut, 1993): 122–38, from a colloquium held in 1987; Dario Matteoni, "The 16 Patents of Le Corbusier 1918–1961," *Rassegna*, no. 46 (June 1991): 70–79; Brooks, *Formative Years* (1997): 490.

Cat. no. 26. Villa Berque

31. Historical information supplied by Gilles Plum, "Villa Montmorency," in *Hameaux, villas et cités de Paris* (Paris: Action artistique de la Ville de Paris, Collection Paris et son patrimoine, 1998): 137–43.
32. The term *picturesque* applies to Le Corbusier's famous sequence of sketches of the "4 compositions," in which Villa La Roche-Jeanneret appears as an instance of the "genre plutôt facile, pittoresque, mouvementé" (rather easy, picturesque, lively type). See *Oeuvre complète 1910–1929*, p. 189.
33. See Arthur Rüegg, ed., *Le Corbusier: Polychromie architecturale* (Basel, Boston, and Berlin: Birkhäuser, 1997): 18–19.
34. For the most complete account to date see Tim Benton, *The Villas of Le Corbusier, 1920–1930* (New Haven and London: Yale University Press, 1987): 18–21.

Part 3: Toward "L'Equipement de la Maison"

Cat. no. 27. Armchairs

1. [Architecte-conseil . . . c'est-à-dire le représentant de vos intérêts vis à vis des fournisseurs devant collaborer à l'installation de votre villa]; all documents on Jeanneret's work for Ernest-Albert and Hermann Ditisheim are now at the BV.
2. These contemporaries were the Coloristes, a group of artists who practiced a relatively additive style considerably indebted to neoclassicism. See Nancy Troy, *Modernism and the Decorative Arts in France: Art Nouveau to Le Corbusier* (New Haven and London: Yale University Press, 1991): esp. 67–70.

Cat. no. 28. Sideboard and Bookcase

3. [Meuble av. placage d'acajou superbe de galbe. et tant de logique.], unsigned, undated, FLC 2238; Brooks gives the date as December 1912; see Brooks, *Formative Years* (1997): 347.
4. In fact, the type of "commode à battants d'encoignures" built under Louis XVI by Riesener, Schumann, and other is the closest relative to this sideboard; see Nicole de Reyniès, *Le Mobilier domestique: Vocabulaire typologique*, vol. 1 (Paris: Imprimerie Nationale, 1992): 503.

Cat. no. 29. Cabinet

5. Giulano Gresleri, ed., *Charles-Edouard Jeanneret - Le Corbusier: Les Voyages d'Allemagne, Carnets* (Milan: Electa, 1994), 1:84–85.

Cat. no. 31. Lumière

6. [Mes clients savent très bien que je suis dessinateur de 'Lumière' . . . patte de sculpteurs sur bois de profession . . . lampe Descoeudres.], CEJ to Léon Perrin, n.d. [1914–15], BV.
7. *Sketchbooks 1914–1918*, A1, sheets 25 and 26.
8. I owe this information to H. Allen Brooks, who discovered the lamp with blue decorations when Léon Perrin was still alive. The attributions were made by Perrin at that time. I thank H. Allen Brooks for making his original color slide available to us for publication.
9. In Munich, in October 1910, Jeanneret noted a loose fabric shade, fastened to the ceiling, with four light bulbs housed in a recess. See chap. 6, n. 36, in this volume.
10. [. . . trépied portant une vasque de jade remplie d'eau avec poissons vivants; le dessus de la vasque étant éclairé par une ampoule noyé dans un vase contenant des roses. La lumière éclairait, d'une part, les roses qui apparaissaient en transparence, et, d'autre part, la vasque dans laquelle les poissons scintillaient donnant une impression véritablement très rare.] CEJ to Fritz Ernst Jeker, 11 September 1919, FLC.

Cat. no. 32. Divan Bed

11. Paul Mebes, *Um 1800: Architektur und Handwerk im letzten Jahrhundert ihrer traditionellen Entwicklung* (Munich: Bruckmann, 1908). This was one of the most influential works published in the German speaking countries in connection with the *retour à l'ordre*.

Cat.no. 33. Wall-Covering

12. [Jardin des tentations]; see LC, "Polychromie architecturale: Etude faite par un architecte (mêlée, d'ailleurs, à l'aventure de la peinture contemporaine) pour des architectes," in Arthur Rüegg, ed., *Polychromie architecturale: Le Corbusier's Farbenklaviaturen von 1931 und 1959 / Le Corbusier's Color Keyboards from 1931 and 1959 / Les claviers de couleurs de Le Corbusier de 1931 et de 1959* (Berlin, Boston, and Basel: Birkhäuser, 1997): 138.
13. The Jouy wallpaper used for the boudoir of Villa Schwob (figs. 391, 395) was "Chasse de Diane" (Nantes, ca. 1785). The motif was originally used for toile de Jouy, a product that is still available (in blue, coral, red, and brown).
14. [J'apporterai aussi alors les miennes peintes . . . sur papier ou sur toile, par d'autres plus malins que moi, les Süe, les Drésa, les Carlègle. Et nous verrons ce qui conviendra aux entre-colonnements de votre salle à manger. Et en fin de compte, voici l'amorce pour vous faire "stopper" ici: mes liasses si lourdes et nombreuses de merveilleuses tissus et de papiers anciens et modernes. Ce sera une réédition différente des imageries d'Epinal], CEJ to Théophile Robert, 1 April 1915, Théophile Robert Archive. I owe the quotation to Corinne Charles, Geneva, who is preparing a monograph on Paul-Théophile Robert for an exhibition scheduled at the Musée d'Art et d'Histoire, Neuchâtel, in 2004. "Epinal" prints were famous broadsides of popular subjects and stories—precursors of the comic strip—made and sold in Epinal, France.

Cat. no. 34. Floor Lamp

15. Reprinted in *Vers une architecture* (1923): 141–60.
16. See chap. 6, n. 54, in this volume.
17. [. . . de petites appliqués qu'on peut acquérir ici dans les bazars de Paris à très bon marché et qui sont semblables au croquis que je vous adresse par courrier. Ces appliques sont très jolies bien que faites avec une simplicité extrême et ne coûtent presque rien. On peut les équiper très joliment avec des bougies et un abat-jour], CEJ to Mme Schwob, 3 May 1922, FLC.
18. [Cet appareil . . . serait muni d'un phare d'auto dans le fond et jetterait sa lumière violemment au plafond, éclairant ainsi toute la pièce], ibid. The correspondence and invoice for this floor lamp are in the FLC.

Cat. no. 36. *Casiers Standard*

19. See Arthur Rüegg, "Der Pavillon de l'Esprit Nouveau als Musée imaginaire," in *L'Esprit Nouveau: Le Corbusier und die Industrie, 1920–1925*, ed. Stanislaus von Moos, exhib. cat., Museum für Gestaltung Zürich and Bauhaus-Archiv, Museum für Gestaltung Berlin (Berlin: Ernst und Sohn, 1987): 140–51.

Cat. no. 37. Vases

20. For this part of his collection, see the photographs in *Le Corbusier, Photographs by René Burri/Magnum: Moments in the Life of a Great Architect*, ed. Arthur Rüegg (Basel, Berlin, and Boston: Birkhäuser, 1999): 147–79.
21. *Carnets* (1987): 1(V):s.124–29.
22. [Je viens pour te parler de vases, de vases paysans, de poterie populaire . . . Tu connais ces joies: palper la bedaine généreuse d'un vase et caresser son col gracile, et puis explorer les subtilités de son galbe. Les mains remises au profond des poches et les yeux mis-clos, se laisser doucement griser de la féerie des émaux, l'éclat des jaunes, le velouté des bleus; s'attacher à la lutte mouvementée des masses noires brutales et, des éléments blancs victorieux . . . cet art populaire comme une immuable caresse chaude, enveloppe la terre entière, la couvrant des mêmes fleurs unissant ou confondant les races, les climats et les lieux . . . Nous retrouvions au long du Danube, et puis, plus tard à Adrinople, exactement ces formes que couvraient d'arabesques noires les peintres mycéniens . . .], *Voyage d'orient* (1966): 13–15.
23. [Sache bien que nous nous sommes assurés depuis Budapest, un arsenal des panses et de goulots . . . Pour les dénicher nous avions passé en revue tout le triste bric-à-brac sans patrie et sans famille qui inonde l'Europe entière.], ibid.

Cat. no. 38. *Bergères à paille*

24. [Une confusion de mon père lui a fait écrire dans la liste des meubles vendus la table ovale de ma chambre. Je tiens à cette table que j'ai toujours eue; elle ne vaut du reste pas cher et si sa forme vous plaisait, EGGER, l'ébéniste pourrait vous en refaire une à très bon compte. Vous ne m'en voudrez pas de cette réclamation posthume], CEJ to Fritz Ernst Jeker, 11 September 1919, FLC.
25. [. . . qui sont toujours d'un goût parfait, très confortables et faciles à manier], ibid. See also *Sketchbooks 1914–1918*, A1:13–14.
26. [Chaises de paille des églises à 5 francs], Le Corbusier-Saugnier [pseud.], "Des Yeux qui ne voient pas . . . Les Avions," *L'Esprit nouveau*, no. 9 (1921): 980; for more of this quotation, see n. 65, chap. 6, in this volume.

Cat. no. 39. Bentwood Chairs

27. See Alexander von Vegesack, ed., *Das Thonet Buch* (Munich: Bangert,1987).
28. [Vos chaises dites de Vienne], CEJ to Marcel Levaillant, 19 February 1914, FLC.
29. Amédée Ozenfant, *Mémoires* (Paris: Seghers, 1968): 103.
30. [Six demi-fauteuils accoudoirs sans dossiers tel que j'en ai exécuté un chez Hermann Ditisheim pour son bureau de travail; ces sièges sont extrémement confortables et donneront beau-

coup de grandeur et d'espace à la piéce . .], CEJ to Fritz Ernst Jeker, 11 September 1919, FLC.

31. This was confirmed on 27 June 2001 in an interview with Markus Landolt, president of the Board of Horgen-Glarus, whose company archives contain, among other things, a catalogue sheet from the firm of Robert Mey entitled "Manufacture de meubles en bois courbé (Marque "Glaris" déposé)," with a note that reads: "Aucune de mes marchandises n'est d'origine austro-allemande" (None of my merchandise is of German or Austrian origin).

Cat. no. 40. Gras Lamps

32. For discussion of his early, intense interest in the production of imaginative lighting, see p. 238 and for the design of a "torche" in 1922/23 see p. 244.

33. These are the "Rampes Chalier": lighting tubes mounted end to end in a series. See brochures from the firm of Marc Chalier, Paris, in the Dossier "Pavillon de l'Esprit Nouveau," FLC.

34. Correspondence with L. Malabert and Company, summer 1926, FLC; the sketch annotated with Le Corbusier's suggestion to have a pyramid-shaped base rather than the stepped one is undated.

35. Roger Ginsburger, "Kunstgewerbe und Industrie in Frankreich," in *Franzssische Ausstellung*, exhib. cat. (Zurich: Kunstewerbemuseum, 1931): 15. See Arthur Rüegg, "Giedion in der Industrie: Programmierung und Entwurf," in *Sigfried Giedion, 1888–1968: Der Entwurf einer neuen Tradition*, exhib. cat., Museum für Gestaltung (Zurich: Ammann, 1989): 166. For an early publication of the "Gras" lamps see V. Rubor, "Une Lampe électrique orientable à volonté," *La Science et la Vie*, no. 62 (May 1922): 553.

Part 4: Paintings, Drawings, Sketches, Watercolors
Cat. no. 41. Masters: Grasset and L'Eplattenier

1. [Jusqu'en 1907, dans ma ville natale, j'ai eu le bonheur d'avoir un maître, L'Eplattenier, qui fut un pédagogue captivant; c'est lui qui m'a ouvert les portes de l'art. Nous avons étudié avec lui les chefs d'oeuvre de tous les temps et de tous les pays. Je me souviens de cette modeste bibliothèque, installée dans une simple armoire de notre salle de dessin et dans laquelle notre maître avait réuni tout ce qu'il considérait nécessaire à notre nourriture spirituelle"], *Oeuvre complète 1910–1929*: 8.

2. Eugène Grasset, *Méthode de composition ornementale*, 2 vols. (Paris: Librairie Centrale des Beaux-Arts, 1905).

3. Located in the 6th Arrondissement, this institution, also known as the École normale d'enseignement du dessin, was founded in 1881 by the architect Alphonse-Théodore Guérin. It was among the most celebrated private preparatory schools in Paris for the artistic professions. Despite its reputation and its first-rate roster of artists and architects, as well as subsidies from the city and government, the school had to close in 1903 for financial reasons.

4. [Où les Parisiens mettent une feuille modelée d'après nature et les Allemands un carré poli comme un miroir, eh bien, nous mettrons un triangle avec des pives], CEJ to Charles L'Eplattenier, 26 February 1908, FLC E 2-12-25.

5. [notre sapin doit être réduit à une forme géométrique.] CEJ to Léon Perrin, 28 April 1910, FLC E 2-18-243.

6. LC, *L'Art décoratif d'aujourd'hui* (Paris: Crès, 1925): 134.

7. [Il fallut avec lui [Grasset] admirer jusque dans le secret de leur structure toutes les fleurs], ibid., pp. 134–35.

8. [il m'a causé avec la prudence d'un prophète], Albert Jeanneret to his parents, April 1908, FLC.

9. [La France ne sut comprendre ni soutenir l'effort d'un Grasset], CEJ, "Etude sur le mouvement décoratif en Allemagne: Le Renouveau," *Tendances nouvelles*, no. 62 (May 1914): 1541.

10. [Il est dans la vie des hommes bienfaisants; et lorsque les circonstances vous ont fourni l'extrême bonheur de rencontrer des hommes comme L'Eplattenier d'abord, comme par un hasard miraculeux et bienfaisant, des prêtres comme Grasset, . . . de ces génies solides, de ces bergers robustes, . . . ces rencontres là vous donnent le feu dans la poitrine], CEJ to his parents, 2 June 1908, FLC.

42. The Mentor: William Ritter

11. Introduction to *Oeuvre complète 1910–1929*, p. 12.

12. For a comprehensive overview (as well as further reading and archive information on Ritter) see Philippe Kaenel, "William Ritter (1867–1955): Un critique cosmopolite, böcklinien et antihodlérien," *Schweizerische Zeitschrift für Geschichte* 48, no. 1 (1998): 73–98. See also "William Ritter (1867–1955): Au temps d'une autre Europe," *Nouvelle revue neuchâteloise* 16, no. 61, special issue (1999). For more on Ritter's graphic output see Josef Tcherv, *William Ritter, 1867–1955* (Bellinzona: Casagrande, 1971).

13. For more on Ritter's contacts with Slavic cultural circles see Joseph M. Rydlo, "Helvetus Peregrinus: William Ritter et la Slovaquie," *Hispo*, no. 10 (1989): 7–20.

14. William Ritter, *Aegyptiacque* (Paris: Albert Savine, 1891); idem, *Études d'art d' étranger* (Paris: Mercure de France, 1906).

15. For more on the relationship between Jeanneret and Ritter see Giuliano Gresleri, "Ritter (William)," in *Le Corbusier: Une encyclopédie*, Jacques Lucan ed. (Paris: Centre Georges Pompidou, 1987): 349–50; Maria Bonaiti, *Ch. E. Jeanneret: Oltre il regionalismo: Germania 1910–1911* (Venice: Istituto universitario di architettura, 1990): 63–145; Brooks, *Formative Years* (1997): 216–18. The correspondence between Jeanneret and Ritter is held in the Schweizerische Landesbibliothek in Bern, the Bibliothéque de la Ville de La Chaux-de-Fonds, and the Fondation Le Corbusier in Paris.

16. William Ritter, *L'Entêtement slovaque* (Paris: Bibliothèque de l'Occident, 1910). Just one year later a Czech translation was published: *Poličtost slovenská* (Moravská Ostrava: Vyd. Družstva Moravsko-Slezské Revue, 1911). See also idem, *Fillette slovaque* (Paris: Mercure de France, 1903).

Cat. no. 43. Landscapes

17. This painting might be compared to his *Vue intérieure sur cour avec arbres* (Interior view onto the court with trees) of 1917, FLC 4507.

Cat. no. 44. Still Lifes and Genre Scenes

18. [la dernière oeuvre en chantier de Rupert Carabin. Un coffret précieux la contiendra], notation on drawing, FLC 5112.

19. See *Rupert Carabin*, exhib. cat. (Strasbourg: Musées de la Ville, 1994).

20. See Brooks, *Formative Years* (1997): 479; Charles Jencks, *Le Corbusier and the Continual Revolution in Architecture* (New York: Monacelli Press, 2000): 85.

21. See Ch.-E. Jeanneret and Amédée Ozenfant, *La peinture moderne* (Paris: Crès, 1925): 83–86, esp. ill. p. 84. In the cited still life, *Nu couché* is depicted on a table.

Cat. no. 45. A Friend: P.-Théophile Robert

22. This information is from the artist's oldest son, Jean-Paul Robert, who died in June 2001. The article is dedicated to him, with regret that he did not live to see the exhibition devoted to his father, and the accompanying monograph, scheduled for 2004 at the Musée d'Art et d'Histoire in Neuchâtel. — C.C.

23. [un peintre qui est à corps perdu dans les affaires comme moi et qui peint…de son bureau à la lampe le soir, des choses d'une force remarquable et d'un modernisme fort], CEJ to Théophile Robert, 20 March 1918, Archives Théophile Robert, Neuchâtel (private collection).

24. The Galerie Thomas in Paris had planned to edit several volumes of "commentàires." Jeanneret and Ozenfant were the authors of the first volume in the series, *Aprés le cubisme*.

25. CEJ to Théophile Robert, 9 November 1918, Archives Théophile Robert, Neuchâtel (private collection).

26. [J'aurais voulu vous envoyer des photos de mes derniers tableaux. Je préfère vous les apporter; je crois que vous serez surpris des changements survenus dans mes travaux ou plutôt du développement auquel mes recherches de ces dernières années ont abouti], Théophile Robert to CEJ, 27 November 1918, FLC E2-20

27. [attendre le moment de se mettre enfin à travailler 'avec la machine sous haute pression], ibid.

28. [Nous aurons le plaisir, dans une quinzaine, à vous convier à venir voir chez THOMAS quelques oeuvres de Robert qui s'est rallié au groupe puriste], Amédée Ozenfant to Louis Vauxelles, FLC B2-13.

29. [statique, clair, lucide, organique, général, grave, contrôlé, concentré, clairement conçu et clairement exécuté], promotional brochure for *Aprés le cubisme*, 15 October 1918.

Cat. no. 46. Purism

30. Auguste Choisy, *L'Histoire de l'Architecture*, vol. 1 (Paris: Gauthier-Villars, 1899): 358–59.

31. *Bulletin Thomas*, reprinted in *Aprés le cubisme* (Paris: Editions des Comentaires, 1918): appendix. Other drawings by Jeanneret were also reproduced in this publication: *Nature morte avec verre* (Still life with glass) and *Portrait d'Ozenfant* (Portrait of Ozenfant).

32. Amédée Ozenfant, Ch.-E. Jeanneret, "Le Purisme," *L'Esprit nouveau*, no. 4 (January 1921): 369–86.

33. Alfred H. Barr, *Cubism and Abstract Art*, exhib. cat. (New York: Museum of Modern Art, 1936): 164–65.

Cat. no. 47. Le Siphon

34. This is confirmed by the La Roche Album (1921) and linked to his Venice trip; see Stanislaus von Moos, ed., *Ch.-E. Jeanneret – Le Corbusier: Album La Roche* (Milan: Electa, 1996).

Works are listed under the following alphabetically arranged headings:

APPLIED ARTS

    FURNITURE

    MISCELLANEOUS

ARCHITECTURAL MODELS

MISCELLANEOUS

PAINTINGS

PHOTOGRAPHY

POSTCARDS

SCULPTURE

WORKS ON PAPER

    BY CHARLES-EDOUARD JEANNERET

    ARCHITECTURAL DRAWINGS

    DRAWINGS FOR FURNITURE

    PURIST STUDIES

    STUDIES AFTER ENGRAVINGS

    BY OTHER ARTISTS

Under each heading works by Jeanneret / Le Corbusier are listed first, followed by works by other artists, and finally anonymous works, in chronological order within each subsection. figure numbers at the end of each entry refer to illustrations in the catalogue. At the Bard Graduate Center the exhibition is arranged thematically.

SYMBOLS AND ABBREVIATIONS

*   works exhibited at Museum Langmatt, Baden, only

†   works exhibited at the Bard Graduate Center, New York, only

All other works are exhibited at both venues

BV   Bibliothèque de la Ville de La Chaux-de-Fonds – Fonds Le Corbusier

FLC   Fondation Le Corbusier, Paris

MBA   Musée des Beaux-Arts, La Chaux-de-Fonds

APPLIED ARTS
FURNITURE

1. Charles-Edouard Jeanneret 1887–1965
Sofa from the smoking room in Hermann Ditisheim's Apartment, La Chaux-de-Fonds, 1915
    Mahogany, original upholstery
    39 ⅛ × 94 ½ × 31 ½ in. (99.5 × 240 × 80 cm)
    MBA 917.01

2. Charles-Edouard Jeanneret
Armchair with footrest from the smoking room in Hermann Ditisheim's Apartment, La Chaux-de-Fonds, 1915
    Mahogany, new upholstery
    42 ⅞ × 28 × 31 ½ in. (109 × 71 × 80 cm),
    footrest: 15 × 19 ⅝ × 14 ¼ in. (38 × 50 × 36 cm)
    MBA 917.05; fig. 368

3. Charles-Edouard Jeanneret
Salon table from the smoking room in Hermann Ditisheim's Apartment, La Chaux-de-Fonds, 1915
    Mahogany
    H: 29 ¾ × 27 ½ Ø in. (75.5 cm, Ø: 70 cm)
    MBA 917.10

4. Charles-Edouard Jeanneret
Commode from the smoking room in Hermann Ditisheim's Apartment, La Chaux-de-Fonds, 1915
    Mahogany
    39 × 55 ½ × 19 ½ in. (99 × 141 × 49.5 cm)
    MBA; fig. 370

5.† Charles-Edouard Jeanneret
Library from the smoking room in Hermann Ditisheim's Apartment, La Chaux-de-Fonds, 1915
    Mahogany and glass
    63 ¾ × 74 × 18 ⅞ in. (162 × 187.8 × 48 cm)
    MBA 917.02; fig. 372

6.† Charles-Edouard Jeanneret
Desk chair from the smoking room in Hermann Ditisheim's Apartment, La Chaux-de-Fonds, 1915
    Mahogany, original upholstery
    29 ⅝ × 24 ½ × 22 ⅛ in. (75 × 62 × 56 cm)
    MBA 917.12; fig. 418

7.† Charles-Edouard Jeanneret
Work table from the smoking room in Hermann

Ditisheim's Apartment, La Chaux-de-Fonds, 1915
    Mahogany and glass
    29 ⅜ × 51 ¾ × 31 ½ in. (74.5 × 131.5 × 80 cm)
    MBA 917.04

8.† Charles-Edouard Jeanneret
Armchair from the smoking room in Hermann Ditisheim's Apartment, La Chaux-de-Fonds, 1915
    Mahogany, original covering
    39 ⅜ × 25 ⅞ × 23 ⅝ in. (100 × 65.5 × 60 cm)
    MBA 917.07

9.† Charles-Edouard Jeanneret
Toy chest from Ernest-Albert Ditisheim's Apartment, La Chaux-de-Fonds, 1915
    Painted wood, painted Eternit-panels, linoleum (renewed 2002)
    36 ¾ × 89 ½ × 19 ½ in. (93.5 × 227.5 × 49.5 cm)
    MBA 1853

10. Charles-Edouard Jeanneret
Desk for Charlotte-Amélie Jeanneret-Perret, 1915–16
    Walnut
    41 ⅛ × 56 ⅞ × 23 in. (102 × 144.5 × 58.5 cm)
    FLC; fig. 378

11.† Charles-Edouard Jeanneret
"Grand fauteuil" (armchair) for the Veranda of Moïse Schwob's Apartment, La Chaux-de-Fonds, 1916
    Natural wood, original covering
    34 ⅞ × 32 ¾ × 27 ⅜ in. (88.5 × 83 × 69.5 cm)
    MBA 1963.01; fig. 133

12. Charles-Edouard Jeanneret
Divan for Marcel Levaillant's Apartment, La Chaux-de-Fonds, 1917
    Painted wood and fabric (probably original 1923)
    32 ¼ × 100 × 64 ⅛ in. (82 × 254 × 163 cm)
    MBA 1713; fig. 387, 390

13. Le Corbusier
Bookcase with desk and storage for engravings from Madeleine Schwob's Library, La Chaux-de-Fonds, 1922
    Wild cherry wood and grey marble

55 ½ × 12 × 34 in. (140 × 86 × 29 cm) (plan chest), 55 ½ × 44 × 31 ½ in. (140 × 79.5 × 107 cm) (desk), 55 ½ × 12 × 95 in. (140 × 241 × 29.5 cm) (bookshelf), 55 ½ × 12 × 37 ⅜ in. (140 × 95 × 30 cm) (radiator cover)
MBA 1960; fig. 135, 400

14. Le Corbusier
Floorlamp from Madeleine Schwob's Library, La Chaux-de-Fonds, 1922–23
Wrought iron, profiled iron and frosted glass
60 ⅝ × 17 ⅜ dia. in. (H = 154 cm, Ø = 44 cm)
FLC; fig. 396, 397, 399

15.† Le Corbusier
Casier Standard (Standard Cabinet), 1925
Painted wood, mahogany veneer
59 × 29 ¾ × 14 ⅝ in. (150 × 75.5 × 37 cm)
Nationalmuseum, Stockholm NMK 65/1969; fig. 405

16.† Charles Humbert (1891-1958, Swiss)
Armchair from Georges Schwob's Apartment, La Chaux-de-Fonds, 1922
Wood and original velvet covering
36 × 26 ¼ × 23 ⅝ in. (91.5 × 66.5 × 60 cm)
MBA 1962

17. Charles Humbert (1891-1958, Swiss)
Floorlamp from Georges Schwob's Apartment, La Chaux-de-Fonds, 1922
Wood, lampshade drawings by Madeleine Woog
69 ⅜ × 23 ⅝ × 23 ⅝ in. (176 × 60 × 60 cm)
MBA 1961; fig. 383

18.† "Bergère à paille", bought by Charles-Edouard Jeanneret for the Villa Jeanneret-Perret c. 1915–16
Early 19th century
FLC (at Villa Le Lac, Corseaux); fig. 412

19.† "Bergère à paille", bought by Charles-Edouard Jeanneret for the Villa Jeanneret-Perret c. 1915–16
Early 19th century
FLC (at Villa Le Lac, Corseaux); fig. 415

20.† "Bergère à paille", bought by Charles-Edouard Jeanneret for the Villa Jeanneret-Perret c. 1915–16
Early 19th century
FLC (at Villa Le Lac, Corseaux); fig. 415

21. Club chair called "Franklin"
Maple & Co., London and Paris, 1923
Marocco leather
29 ½ × 30 ¾ × 37 ⅜ in. (75 × 78 × 95 cm)
Private collection; fig. 146

22. Bentwood chair, Model 1224, c. 1925
Manufactured by the Möbelfabrik Horgen-Glarus (Switzerland)
Painted bentwood, stamped "GLARIS"
32 ¼ × 20 ⅞ × 20 ⅞ in. (82 × 53 × 53 cm)
FLC

23.† Garden chair, 1920s
Painted iron
Private collection

24.† Floorlamp "modèle Gras, type dessinateur," 1920
Nickeled iron and cast-iron, brass, and aluminium
FLC; fig. 421

APPLIED ARTS
MISCELLANEOUS

25. Charles-Edouard Jeanneret
Watchcase belonging to Jeanneret's father, Edouard Jeanneret-Gris, 1906
Steel case with chased gold, silver, and copper ornament, and diamonds
FLC; fig. 309

26. Wall clock
Bern Pendule style, c. 1800
Gilded wood case
25 ½ × 13 ¾ × 4 ¾ in. (65 × 35 × 12 cm)
Museum Langmatt, Baden

27. Vase, purchased in 1911 by Charles-Edouard Jeanneret during his Voyage d'Orient between Budapest and Istanbul
Ceramic
13 ¾ × 9 ⅞ dia. in. (H = 35 cm, Ø = 25 cm)
FLC 34; fig. 406

28. Vase, purchased in 1911 by Charles-Edouard Jeanneret during his Voyage d'Orient between Budapest and Istanbul
Ceramic
15 × 8 ⅝ in. (H = 38 cm, Ø = 22 cm)
FLC 36; fig. 407

29. Vase, purchased in 1911 by Charles-Edouard Jeanneret during his Voyage d'Orient between Budapest and Istanbul
Ceramic
14 ½ × 9 dia. in. (H = 37 cm, Ø = 23 cm)
FLC 37; fig. 408

30. Vase, purchased in 1911 by Charles-Edouard Jeanneret during his Voyage d'Orient between Budapest and Istanbul
Ceramic
15 ⅜ × 8 ¼ dia. in. (H = 39 cm, Ø = 21 cm)
FLC 38; fig. 411

31. Wallpaper sample "for the Hall-Salon"
Ditisheim (?), La Chaux-de-Fonds, c. 1915
Print, yellow/green, with a hand-written note by Jeanneret
28 ¼ × 22 ⅜ in. (66.9 × 49.7 cm)
BV LCms 129

32. Striped wallpaper sample from the large bedroom of Villa Schwob, La Chaux-de-Fonds, 1916–17 (found 1987)
Print, blue/beige
13 ¾ × 9 in. (35 × 23 cm)
Private collection; fig. 395

33. Flower wallpaper sample from the small bedroom of Villa Schwob, La Chaux-de-Fonds, 1916–17 (found 1987)
Print, red, blue, black, green on yellowish paper
11 ⅞ × 9 in. (30 × 23 cm)
Private Collection

34. Jouy wallpaper sample "Diana the Huntress" c. 1785, from the Boudoir of Villa Schwob, La Chaux-de-Fonds, 1916–17 (found 1987)
Red on beige paper
47 × 9 in. (119.5 × 23 cm)
Private Collection

35. Jouy wallpaper sample from Le Corbusier's apartment in Paris, 20 rue Jacob, c. 1917–18
Red on beige paper, with hand written note by Jeanneret
6 ¾ × 15 ½ in. (17.3 × 39.3 cm)
BV LCms 129; fig. 391

36.† "Objets types" table and glass ware
Private Collection

ARCHITECTURAL MODELS

37. Villa Fallet, La Chaux-de-Fonds, 1906–07
Model 1:50, 1987
Painted wood
13 ½ × 18 ⅜ × 23 ¾ in. (34.3 × 47 × 60.4 cm)
Archives de la construction moderne – EPFL

38. Villa Jeanneret-Perret, La Chaux-de-Fonds, 1912
Model 1:50, 2002
MDF
18 ½ × 45 × 31 ½ in. (47 × 115 × 80 cm)
Faculty of Architecture, TU Delft/Max Risselada, Chairman

39. Villa Jeanneret-Perret, La Chaux-de-Fonds, 1912
Computer visualisation by Johannes Herold, 2002

40. Villa Schwob, La Chaux-de-Fonds, 1916–17
Model 1:50, 1987
Painted wood
10 × 29 ¾ × 19 ¾ in. (30 × 76 × 50 cm)
Archives de la construction moderne – EPFL

41. DOM-INO MODULE
Model 1:5, 2002
Painted wood and plywood
13 ¾ × 20 ½ × 12 ¼ in. (35 × 52 × 31 cm)
Faculty of Architecture, TU Delft/Max Risselada, Chairman

MISCELLANEOUS

42. Invoice for a floorlamp in Marcel Levaillant's Apartment, La Chaux-de-Fonds, December 1916
10 ⅝ × 8 ¼ in. (27 × 21 cm)
Private collection; fig. 384

43. † Invoice for the installation of the Head of Prince Gudea and other pieces in Marcel Levaillant's Apartment, Villa Les Eglantines, La Chaux-de-Fonds, 1923
10 ⅝ × 8 ¼ in. (27 × 21 cm)
Private collection

44. Model airplane
Nieuport 29 V, 1920 (model: 1984)
Tin, brass
10 ¼ × 23 ⅝ × 24 ⅜ in. (26 × 60 × 62 cm)
Musée de l'air et de l'espace, Paris–Le Bourget

PAINTINGS

45. Charles-Edouard Jeanneret
Femme et coquillage [1915–16]
(Woman and Shells)
Oil on canvas
16 × 12 ¼ in. (40.5 × 32.5 cm)
FLC 202; fig. 446

46. Charles-Edouard Jeanneret
Fleurs et livres [1916]
Oil on canvas
27 × 35 cm
Not signed, not dated
FLC 204; fig. 165

47. Charles-Edouard Jeanneret
Vue sur les toits de Paris [1917]
(The Roofs of Paris)
Oil on canvas
18 ⅛ × 15 in. (46 × 38 cm)
FLC 203; fig. 164

48. Charles-Edouard Jeanneret
La cheminée, 1918
(The Mantlepiece)
Oil on canvas
23 ⅝ × 29 ½ in. (60 × 75 cm)
Signed and dated
FLC 134; figs. 168, 454

49. Charles-Edouard Jeanneret
Nature morte à l'œuf, 1919
(Still Life with an Egg)
Oil on canvas
33 ⅜ × 31 ⅞ in. (100 × 81 cm)
Signed and dated
FLC 136; fig. 456

50. † Charles-Edouard Jeanneret
Nature morte à la pile d'assiettes et au livre, 1920
(Still Life with a Pile of Plates and a Book)
Oil on canvas
31 ⅞ × 39 ¼ in. (81 × 99.7 cm)
Museum of Modern Art, New York; figs. 161, 458

51. † Charles-Edouard Jeanneret/Le Corbusier
Nature morte au siphon, 1921
(Still Life with a Siphon)
Oil on canvas
28 ¾ × 23 ⅝ in. (73 × 60 cm)
Signed and dated
FLC 139; fig. 462

52. † Charles-Edouard Jeanneret/Le Corbusier
Nature morte pâle à la lanterne, 1922
(Pale Still Life with a Lantern)
Oil on canvas
31 ⅞ × 32 ⅜ in. (81 × 100 cm)
Signed and dated
FLC 209

53. † Charles-Edouard Jeanneret/Le Corbusier
Nature morte au verre, 1922
(Still Life with a Glass)
Oil on canvas
15 × 18 ⅛ in. (38 × 46 cm)
Signed and dated
Private Collection

54.* Charles-Edouard Jeanneret/Le Corbusier
Verres, pipe et bouteilles sur fond clair [1922]
(Glasses, Pipe and Bottles against a Light Background)
Oil on canvas
23 ⅝ × 28 ¾ in. (60 × 73 cm)
Signed
Öffentliche Kunstsammlung Basel, Kunstmuseum, Bequest of Raoul La Roche
G 1963.7

55. Victor Darjou (1804-1877, French)
Portrait of Monsieur Le Corbézier (Charles-Edouard Jeanneret's maternal godfather) [1841]
Oil on canvas
29 ⅛ × 23 ⅝ in. (74 × 60 cm)
Signed, not dated
MBA 214

56.* Juan Gris (1887–1927, born Madrid, resided France)
Verre et carafe, 1917
(Glass and Carafe)
Oil on canvas
14 ¾ × 24 in. (37.5 × 61 cm)
Signed and dated
Kunstmuseum Winterthur 1178, Bequest of Clara and Emil Friedrich-Jezler, 1973

57.* Charles Humbert (1891–1958, Swiss)
Portrait of Lucien Schwob, 1916
Oil on canvas
24 × 18 ⅛ in/ (61 × 46 cm)
Signed and dated
MBA 928

58. Charles L'Eplattenier (1874–1946, Swiss)
Au sommet, 1904
(At the Summit)
Oil on canvas
29 ⅛ × 68 ½ in. (74 × 174 cm)
Signed and dated
MBA 26

59.† Fernand Léger (1881–1955, French)
Le Balustre, 1925
(The Baluster)
Oil on canvas
51 × 38 ¼ in. (129.9 × 97.2 cm)
Museum of Modern Art, New York

60.† Amédée Ozenfant (1886–1966, French)
Verre et pipe, 1919
(Glass and Pipe)
Oil on canvas
13 ¾ × 10 ⅝ in. (35 × 27 cm)
Signed and dated
Philadelphia Museum of Arts, Philadelphia, Collection A. E. Gallatin

61.* Amédée Ozenfant (1886-1966, French)
Verre, vase et bouteille, c. 1926
(Glass, Vase and Bottle)
Oil on canvas
39 ⅜ × 31 ⅞ in. (100 × 81 cm)
Signed
Kunstmuseum Winterthur 1201, Bequest of Clara and Emil Friedrich-Jezler, 1973

62.† Paul-Théophile Robert (1879-1954, Swiss)
Nature morte aux livres et au pot de tabac
(Still Life with Books and a Tobacco Jar)
1917
Oil on canvas
15 × 18 ⅛ in. (38 × 46 cm)
Private Collection

63.* Paul-Théophile Robert (1879-1954, Swiss)
Nature morte à la cafetière et au journal [1919]
(Still Life with a Coffee Pot and newspaper)
Oil on canvas
27 ¼ × 23 ⅝ in. (69 × 60 cm)
Signed
Private Collection; fig. 450

PHOTOGRAPHY

64. Charles-Edouard Jeanneret
Villa Fallet, La Chaux-de-Fonds, 1906–07
1907 (?), old print
3 ¾ × 2 ⅞ in. (9.6 × 7.4 cm)
BV LC/108/734-3; fig. 311

65.* Charles-Edouard Jeanneret
Gabrovo, Bulgaria. Square with tower and fountain
June 1911, new print
FLC L4(20)128; fig. 244

66. Charles-Edouard Jeanneret
Istanbul. The Terrace of Rüstem Paša Mosque in the Egyptian Bazaar
Photograph by Jeanneret, July 1911, new print
FLC L5(1)94; fig. 250

67. Charles-Edouard Jeanneret
Istanbul. Selimiye Mosque
July 1911, new print
BV LC/108/393

68. Charles-Edouard Jeanneret
Istanbul. The great fire, July 23, 1911
new print
BV LC/108/13; fig. 247

69. Charles-Edouard Jeanneret
Istanbul. Wooden houses
July 1911, new print
FLC L5(1)88; fig. 255

70. Charles-Edouard Jeanneret
Istanbul, Hagia Sophia. South facade with Main entrance
1911, new print
BV LC/108/14

71.† Charles-Edouard Jeanneret
Athens. North side of the Erechtheum
September 1911, new print
FLC L4(19)79; fig. 263

72.† Charles-Edouard Jeanneret
Athens, Acropolis Museum. Kouros
September 1911, new print
FLC L4(19)85

73.† Charles-Edouard Jeanneret
Athens, Acropolis Museum, Hecatompedon. Three-bodied Nereos
September 1911, new print
FLC L4(19)86

74. Charles-Edouard Jeanneret
Pompeii. The Forum as seen from Jupiter's Temple
October 1911, new print
FLC L4(19)114; fig. 268

75. Charles-Edouard Jeanneret
Pompeii. Via dei Sepolcri
October 1911, new print
BV LC/108/501; fig. 49

76. Charles-Edouard Jeanneret
Pompeii. Via dei Sepolcri
October 1911, new print
FLC L4(19)120; fig. 270

77. Charles-Edouard Jeanneret
Pompeii. Archway, Via dei Sepolcri
October 1911, new print
FLC L4(19)108; fig. 271

78. Charles-Edouard Jeanneret

Pompeii. Via dell'Abbondanza
October 1911, new print
FLC L4(19)107; fig. 269

79. Charles-Edouard Jeanneret
Pompeii (?)
October 1911, new print
FLC L4(19)113; fig. 273

80. Charles-Edouard Jeanneret
Rome, the Forum. Basilica of Maxentius, as seen
from the Temple of the Dioscures
October 1911, new print
FLC L4(19)152; fig. 276

81. Charles-Edouard Jeanneret
Rome, Baths of Caracalla
October 1911, new print
BV LC/108/452; fig. 278

82. Charles-Edouard Jeanneret
Rome, View of St. Peter's Square from the Steps
of St. Peter's
October 1911, new print
BV LC/108/506

83. Charles-Edouard Jeanneret
Rome, Piazza del Campidoglio
October 1911, new print
3 1/4 × 4 1/2 in. (8.1 × 11.4 cm)
FLC L4(20)216; fig. 280

84. Charles-Edouard Jeanneret
Rome, Gardens of Villa Medici
October 1911, new print
2 1/2 × 3 1/4 in. (6 × 8.4 cm)
FLC L4(19)128; fig. 279

85. Charles-Edouard Jeanneret
Rome, View from the Palatine Hill
October 1911, new print
2 1/4 × 3 1/4 in. (5.8 × 8.4 cm)
FLC L4(19)133

86. Charles-Edouard Jeanneret
Villa Jeanneret-Perret, La Chaux-de-Fonds, 1912
View from West
1912 (?), new print
4 1/8 × 5 7/8 in. (10.4 × 14.8 cm)
BV LC/108/201; fig. 323

87. Charles-Edouard Jeanneret
Villa Jeanneret-Perret, La Chaux-de-Fonds, 1912
View of the West facade
1912 (?), new print
BV LC/108/178; fig. 73

88. Charles-Edouard Jeanneret
Villa Jeanneret-Perret, La Chaux-de-Fonds, 1912
View from Southwest
1912 (?), new print
BV LC/108/284

89. Charles-Edouard Jeanneret
Villa Jeanneret-Perret, La Chaux-de-Fonds, 1912
Living room
1912 (?), new print
BV LC/108/274

90. Charles-Edouard Jeanneret
Villa Favre-Jacot, Le Locle, 1912
View along promenade and terrace; on the terrace
Albert Jeanneret (1886–1973)
1912 (?), new print
BV LC/108/49

91. Charles-Edouard Jeanneret
Villa Favre-Jacot, Le Locle, 1912
View of the garden facade
1912 (?), new print
BV LC/108/56

92.* Charles-Edouard Jeanneret
Murten/Morat, Switzerland. Town Hall and walls
1916, old print
FLC L4(20)178; fig. 27, 305

93.* Charles-Edouard Jeanneret
Customs-house at Faoug, Lake Murten,
Switzerland
1916, old print
FLC L4(19)179; fig. 304

94.* Charles-Edouard Jeanneret
Payerne, Switzerland, Monastery church. View
through the tracery of the bell chamber
1916, old print
FLC L5(1)38

95. Charles-Edouard Jeanneret
Desk for Charlotte-Amélie Jeanneret-Perret in the
Villa Jeanneret-Perret, 1915–16
c. 1916–19, new print
FLC L3(16)36-33; fig. 379

96. Charles-Edouard Jeanneret or Amédée
Ozenfant (?)
Rome. On the roof of St. Peter's
1921, old print
1 7/8 × 2 3/4 in. (4.6 × 6.9 cm)
FLC L4(19)151; fig. 285

97. Charles-Edouard Jeanneret or Amédée
Ozenfant (?)
Rome. Drum of St. Peter's
1921, old print
1 7/8 × 2 5/8 in. (4.6 × 6.8 cm)
FLC L4(19)129; fig. 286

98. Charles-Edouard Jeanneret or Amédée
Ozenfant (?)
Rome. Drum of St. Peter's
1921, old print
1 3/4 × 2 3/4 in. (4.5 × 6.9 cm)
FLC L4(19)130

99. Charles-Edouard Jeanneret or Amédée
Ozenfant (?)
Rome. Choir of St. Peter's
1921, new print
BV LC/108/441

100. Charles-Edouard Jeanneret or Amédée
Ozenfant (?)
Rome. Cancelleria
1921, old print
1 3/4 × 2 3/4 in. (4.5 × 7 cm)
FLC L4(19)140

101. Charles-Edouard Jeanneret or Amédée
Ozenfant (?)
Rome. Entrance to the Cancelleria
1921, old print
2 5/8 × 1 7/8 in. (6.8 × 4.6 cm)
FLC L4(20)42

102. Charles-Edouard Jeanneret or Amédée
Ozenfant (?)
Rome. View of St. Peter's
1921, old print

1 3/4 × 2 3/4 in. (4.5 × 6.9 cm)
FLC L4(20)40; fig. 287

103. Charles-Edouard Jeanneret or Amédée
Ozenfant (?)
Rome. View of the Apse of St. Peter's
1921, old print
1 7/8 × 2 5/8 in. (4.6 × 6.8 cm)
FLC L4(20)59; fig. 288

104. Charles-Edouard Jeanneret or Amédée
Ozenfant (?)
Rome. View of the Belvedere Courtyard
1921, old print
1 3/4 × 2 3/4 in. (4.5 × 6.9 cm)
FLC L4(20)47

105. Charles-Edouard Jeanneret or Amédée
Ozenfant (?)
Rome. S. Ivo della Sapienza
1921, old print
2 5/8 × 1 3/4 in. (6.7 × .3 cm)
FLC L4(20)45; fig. 290

106. Charles-Edouard Jeanneret
Le Corbusier's brother Albert, and their parents in
their Chalet at Blonay, Lake Geneva
September 1922 (?), new print
BV LC/108/307

107. Charles-Edouard Jeanneret
Le Corbusier's parents, his brother Albert and, in
the background, Amédée Ozenfant (?) in the
Chalet at Blonay, Lake Geneva
September 1922 (?), new print
BV LC/108/318

108. Albert Jeanneret (1886-1973, Swiss)
Le Corbusier and his parents in their Chalet at
Blonay, Lake Geneva
September 1922 (?), new print
BV LC/108/308

109. Amédée Ozenfant (?) (1886–1966, French)
Rome. Le Corbusier on the roof top of St. Peter's
1921, old print
1 7/8 × 2 3/4 in. (4.6 × 7 cm)
FLC L4(19)124; fig. 289

110.† Istanbul. Charles-Edouard Jeanneret (right)
and August Klipstein, acting a harem scene in their
room in Pera
1911, new print
4 1/2 × 5 7/8 in. (10.4 × 14.8 cm)
BV LC/108/8

111.† Athens. Jeanneret next to a column of the
Parthenon
September 1911, new print
FLC L4(19)66; fig. 257

112. Villa Jeanneret-Perret, La Chaux-de-Fonds,
1912
Patio with pergola (Jeanneret's parents, in the background Charles-Edouard and his brother Albert)
c. 1915–16, new print
BV LC/108/186; fig. 71

113. Villa Jeanneret-Perret, La Chaux-de-Fonds,
1912, Pergola (in the background Charles-Edouard,
his parents and his brother Albert)
c. 1915–16, new print
BV LC/108/280

114. Amédée Ozenfant, Albert and Charles-

Edouard Jeanneret in Jeanneret's Studio in the Villa
Jeanneret-Perret
August 1919, new print
BV LC/108/278; page 13, fig. 409

POSTCARDS

115.† Château de Versailles
c. 1900
FLC L5(7)271

116.† Château de Versailles. Salon of Marie-
Antoinette
c. 1900
FLC L5(7)289

117.† Château de Versailles. Hall of the Grand
Trianon
c. 1900
FLC L5(7)303

118.† Château de Versailles. Family Hall in the
Grand Trianon
c. 1900
FLC L5(7)309

119.† Château de Versailles. The "Salle des
Princes" in the Grand Trianon
c. 1900
FLC L5(7)304

120.† Château de Versailles. Boudoir in the "Petit
appartment" of Marie-Antoinette
c. 1900
FLC L5(7)290

121.† Château de Versailles. The library of Marie-
Antoinette
c. 1900
FLC L5(7)288; fig. 131

122.† Rouen, Cathedral. The Portail de la Calende
c. 1910
FLC L5(7)132

123.† Rouen, Cathedral. Main facade with "Tour de
beurre" on the right
c. 1910
FLC L5(7)130; fig. 209

124.† Rouen, Cathedral. Main facade
c. 1910
FLC L5(7)131

125.† Paris, Notre-Dame. Group of gargoyles
c. 1910
FLC L5(6)117; fig. 38

126. Pompeii. Via dell'Abbondanza
c. 1910
FLC L5(8)165

127. Rome. Sistine Chapel
c. 1910
FLC L5(8)239

128. Rome. Pyramid of Caius Cestius
c. 1910
FLC L5(8)208

129. Rome, Forum. Basilica of Maxentius
c. 1910
FLC L5(8)211

130. Rome. Baths of Caracalla
c. 1910
FLC L5(8)212

131. Rome. Pantheon
c. 1910
FLC L5(8)186

132.† Pisa. Interior of the Bapistery
c. 1910
FLC L5(8)143

133.† Pisa. The Duomo and Campanile
c. 1910
FLC L5(8)135

134.† Pisa. Night view of the Piazza del Duomo
c. 1910
FLC L5(8)141

135.† Pisa. Night view of the Baptistery
c. 1910
FLC L5(8)142

SCULPTURE

136.* Léon Perrin
Relief for Villa Schwob
Model
Musée Léon Perrin, Môtiers

137.* Fragment of an antique statue (Head), probably purchased by Jeanneret during the *Voyage
d'Orient* 1911, Period of Marcus Aurelius (?)
Stone
28 × 16 cm
FLC 4

138. Head of the Chaldean Prince Gudea, Lagash,
2130 B.C., found 1881, Louvre Museum, Paris.
Modern plaster cast mounted on wooden base
16 ½ × 9 ⅞ × 11 in. (42 × 25 × 28 cm) (Head)
Private collection; fig. 157

WORKS ON PAPER
BY CHARLES-EDOUARD JEANNERET

139.† Charles-Edouard Jeanneret
Lotus leaf and papyrus (after Owen Jones, *The
Grammar of Ornament. Illustrated by examples from vari-
ous styles of ornament*, London, 1856, pl. iv
[1901–02(?)]
Gouache on paper
12 ¾ × 10 in. (32.5 × 25.5 cm)
FLC 1777; fig. 313

140.* Charles-Edouard Jeanneret
Jura Landscape, c. 1905
Gouache on paper
3 ⅜ × 5 ⅛ in. (8.5 × 13 cm)
FLC 2204; fig. 434

141.† Charles-Edouard Jeanneret
*Landscape study with pine trees, various close-up studies
and ornamental derivations* [c. 1905–06]
Pencil and watercolor on paper
8 ⅜ × 10 ¾ in. (21.2 × 27.4 cm)
FLC 5817; fig. 316

142.† Charles-Edouard Jeanneret
Study of pine trees [c. 1905–06]
Black gouache and pencil on paper
6 ⅛ × 6 ¾ in (15.5 × 17.3 cm)
FLC 2520; fig. 315

143.* Charles-Edouard Jeanneret
Fribourg. Study of the Town hall [June 1907]
Pencil on paper

7 ⅛ × 4 ¾ in. (17.9 × 12 cm)
FLC 2076

144.* Charles-Edouard Jeanneret
Fribourg. The Spire of St. Nicolas's Cathedral [June
1907]
Pencil on paper
7 ¼ × 4 ¾ in. (18.1 × 12.1 cm)
FLC 2073

145.* Charles-Edouard Jeanneret
*Florence, Museo Archeologico. Etruscan Mural with a
Banquet Scene*, September 1907
Pencil and watercolor on paper
6 ⅛ × 6 ⅞ in. (15.5 × 17.5 cm)
Dated
FLC 1929

146.* Charles-Edouard Jeanneret
Florence. View of the Palazzo Vecchio (from
Jeanneret's room in the Via dei Calzaioli)
[September 1907]
Pencil, black and blue ink on grey paper
14 ¼ × 9 ⅞ in. (36 × 25 cm)
FLC 2173; fig. 172

147.* Charles-Edouard Jeanneret
Pisa. General view and detail study of the Baptistery
[September 1907]
Pencil on paper
9 ⅝ × 12 ¾ in. (24.5 × 32.5 cm)
FLC 2169

148.* Charles-Edouard Jeanneret
*Florence. Study of the Cantoria in the Old Sacristy of S.
Lorenzo* (School of Donatello) [September 1907]
Pencil and charcoal on paper
13 ⅝ × 10 in. (34.5 × 25.5 cm)
FLC 1978; fig. 184

149.* Charles-Edouard Jeanneret
Florence. Study of the Baptistery Pavement, September
1907
Pencil and watercolor on paper, pasted on
cardboard
6 ¼ × 6 ⅝ in. (16 × 16.7 cm)
Signed and dated
FLC 2164; fig. 174

150.* Charles-Edouard Jeanneret
Florence. Interior of S. Croce [September/October
1907]
Pencil and watercolor on paper
9 ⅝ × 12 ¾ in. (24.5 × 32.3 cm)
FLC 2175; fig. 11

151.* Charles-Edouard Jeanneret
*Florence. Study of the Tabernacle (by Andrea Orcagna) in
Or San Michele* [September/October 1907]
Pencil and watercolor on paper
4 ¾ × 5 ⅝ in. (12 × 14.4 cm)
FLC 1938

152.† Charles-Edouard Jeanneret
*Florence. Study of St. Mark (by Donatello) on the facade of
Or San Michele* [October 1907]
Pencil and watercolor on ivory paper
12 ¼ × 6 ⅛ in. (31 × 15.5 cm)
Signed and dated
FLC 1938

153* Charles-Edouard Jeanneret
Siena. View of S. Domenico (from Jeanneret's room in

the pension "La Scala", or after a postcard from
the pension) [September/October 1907]
    Pencil and watercolor on paper
    5 ⁷⁄₈ × 4 ⅛ in. (15 × 10.3 cm)
    FLC 1917; fig. 152

154.† Charles-Edouard Jeanneret
Siena. Facade and Detail Studies of the Baptistry
September/October 1907
    Pencil, ink and watercolor on paper
    9 ¾ × 12 ¾ in. (24.6 × 32.4 cm)
    Dated
    FLC 1791; fig. 14, 189

155.† Charles-Edouard Jeanneret
*Siena. Study of the Palazzo Pubblico, with the Torre del
Mangia* September/October 1907
    Pencil and watercolor on paper
    7 ¼ × 6 ¼ in. (18.5 × 15.8 cm)
    Signed and dated
    FLC 2852; fig. 13

156.* Charles-Edouard Jeanneret
Siena. Study of the facade of Palazzo Grottanelli,
October 1907
    India ink and tempera on paper
    9 ¾ × 4 ⅜ in. (24.8 × 11.2 cm)
    Dated
    FLC 2125; fig. 41

157.† Charles-Edouard Jeanneret
*Siena, Palazzo Pubblico. Study of the Allegory of Good
Government (by Ambrogio Lorenzetti),* October 1907
    Gouache and pencil on paper
    9 × 6 ¼ in. (23 × 16 cm)
    Signed and dated
    FLC 5842; fig. 186

158.* Charles-Edouard Jeanneret
*Florence. Ideal view of the Duomo and the Palazzo
Vecchio* [October 1907]
    Watercolor and indian ink on paper
    5 ⅜ × 7 in. (13.7 × 17.7 cm)
    FLC 1979; fig. 173

159.* Charles-Edouard Jeanneret
*Florence. Study of the wall-tombs on the exterior of S.
Maria Novella,* October 1907
    Pencil, watercolor, gouache and indian ink on
    paper
    8 ⅝ × 7 ½ in. (22 × 19 cm)
    Signed and dated
    FLC 5845; fig. 176

160.† Charles-Edouard Jeanneret
*Paris, Musée de Sculpture comparée (?).Study of a cast of
the choir-stalls of Amiens Cathedral,* 1908
    Pencil on two pages of sketch book, pasted
    together
    6 ⅞ × 8 ½ in. (17.5 × 21.5 cm)
    Signed and dated
    FLC 5830

161.† Charles-Edouard Jeanneret
*Paris. Study of the roofs of Paris with Notre-Dame from
Jeanneret's studio,* 1908
    Pencil and watercolor on paper
    8 × 7 ⅛ in. (20,5 × 18 cm)
    Dated
    FLC 1920

162.† Charles-Edouard Jeanneret
Paris. View of Notre-Dame [1908–09]

Pencil and watercolor on paper
9 ½ × 6 ¾ in. (24.2 × 17 cm)
FLC 1923; fig. 205

163.† Charles-Edouard Jeanneret
*Paris. Study of the roofs of Paris with Notre-Dame from
Jeanneret's studio* [1908–09]
    Pencil and gouache on thick paper
    11 ⅛ × 8 ⅛ in. (28.2 × 20.7 cm)
    FLC 2197

164.* Charles-Edouard Jeanneret
Paris, Musée du Trocadéro (?). Study of a Hindu column
[1908–09]
    Pencil and gouache on paper
    14 ¾ × 10 ⅜ in. (37.5 × 26.5 cm)
    FLC 1927

165.* Charles-Edouard Jeanneret
Paris, Musée du Louvre. Study of a terracotta relief
[1908–09]
    Pencil and chalk on paper
    4 ¼ × 7 in. (10.8 × 17.6 cm)
    FLC 2241; fig. 216

166.† Charles-Edouard Jeanneret
Paris, Musée du Louvre (?). Studies of Egyptian furniture
[1908–09]
    Pencil on grey paper
    14 ¼ × 9 ¾ in. (36.2 × 25 cm)
    FLC 3785

167.† Charles-Edouard Jeanneret
Paris, Musée du Trocadéro. Study of Peruvian vases, July
1909
    Pencil, ink and watercolor on yellowish paper
    10 ⅛ × 14 ¼ in. (25.7 × 36 cm)
    Dated
    FLC 1984; fig. 218

168.* Charles-Edouard Jeanneret
Paris, Musée du Trocadéro. Study of Peruvian vases, July
1909
    Pencil and gouache on paper
    9 ⅞ × 14 ¼ in. (25 × 36.4 cm)
    Signed and dated
    FLC 5858; fig. 219

169.* Charles-Edouard Jeanneret
Paris, Musée du Trocadéro. Study of Peruvian vases
[1909]
    Pencil and gouache on yellow paper
    14 ¼ × 10 in. (36.5 × 25.3 cm)
    FLC 6337

170.* Charles-Edouard Jeanneret
*Paris, 25 bis, rue Franklin (A. & G. Perret, 1903–04).
Sketch of the Rooftop Terrace, in the background Place de
la Concorde and Sacré-Cœur,* 1909 (?)
    Pencil and indian ink on paper
    8 ¼ × 5 ⅞ in. (21 × 15 cm)
    FLC 5587

171.† Charles-Edouard Jeanneret
Mittenwald. View of Chapel, July 24, 1910
    Pencil and watercolor on paper
    10 ⅝ × 7 ¾ in. (27 × 19.8 cm)
    Signed and dated
    FLC 1759

172.† Charles-Edouard Jeanneret
Potsdam. View of the Orangerie at Schloss Sanssouci,
Nov. 5, 1910

Pencil and watercolor on paper, pasted on
cardboard
11 ⅜ × 8 ⅝ in. (29 × 22 cm)
Signed and dated
FLC 2857; fig. 15

173.† Charles-Edouard Jeanneret
*Nürnberg. Study of the Markt, with Schöner Brunnen and
Marienkirche beyond* [1910]
    Pencil on paper
    11 ⅝ × 12 ½ in. (29.8 × 31.6 cm)
    FLC 2212; fig. 45

174.* Charles-Edouard Jeanneret
*Munich. View from Theatinerstrasse along Feldherrnhalle
(right) towards Odeonsplatz* [1910–11]
    Pencil on paper
    5 × 7 ⅞ in. (12.6 × 20 cm)
    FLC 2030; fig. 231

175.† Charles-Edouard Jeanneret
*Munich. Study of Nymphenburg Palace, Kronprinzen
Trakt* [1910–11]
    Pencil and gouache on paper
    6 ⅞ × 9 ¾ in. (17.4 × 24.8 cm)
    FLC 2053

176.* Charles-Edouard Jeanneret
Munich. Study of Theatinerkirche St. Kajetan [April
1911]
    Pencil on paper
    10 × 7 in. (25.5 × 17.8 cm)
    FLC 2036; fig. 233

177.† Charles-Edouard Jeanneret
*Prague. View of stairs between Nerudova and Loretánská
Street, as seen from Ke Hradu Street* [May 1911]
    Pencil and watercolor on tracing paper
    10 ⅜ × 8 ⅜ in. (26.4 × 21.2 cm)
    BV LCms 125-2; fig. 239

178.† Charles-Edouard Jeanneret
Prague. View of the Main Entrance to Prague Castle
[May 1911]
    Pencil and watercolor on tracing paper
    8 ⅜ × 10 ⅜ in. (21.4 × 26.3 cm)
    BV LCms 125-1; fig. 237

179.* Charles-Edouard Jeanneret
Budapest area. View of a farmhouse, June 1911
    Pencil and yellow pencil on paper
    7 ⅞ × 4 ⅞ in. (19.9 × 12.3 cm)
    Signed and dated on the reverse
    FLC 6102

180.* Charles-Edouard Jeanneret
Gabrovo, Bulgaria. Church exterior, 1911
    Pencil and watercolor on paper
    12 ⅛ × 15 ½ in. (30.7 × 39.5 cm)
    Signed and dated
    FLC 2853; fig. 245

181.† Charles-Edouard Jeanneret
Edirne. View into the Caravanserai, with plan and
notes [July 1911]
    Pencil on paper
    9 ¼ × 6 ¾ in. (23.7 × 17 cm)
    Signed (on the reverse)
    FLC 6107; fig. 249

182.* Charles-Edouard Jeanneret
*Istanbul. View of the north facade of the Süleymaniye
Mosque* [July 1911]

Pencil on paper
4 ¾ × 8 in. (12.4 × 20.2 cm)
FLC 2384; fig. 252

183.* Charles-Edouard Jeanneret
Istanbul. Süleymaniye Mosque [July 1911]
    Black pencil on paper
    5 × 8 in. (12.5 × 20.2 cm)
    Signed and incorrectly dated 1910
    FLC 5876; fig. 251

184.* Charles-Edouard Jeanneret
Istanbul. Street with garden walls, verandas and trees [July 1911]
    Pencil on paper
    4 ⅞ × 7 ⅞ in. (12.3 × 20.1 cm)
    FLC 2457

185.* Charles-Edouard Jeanneret
Istanbul. View on Pera (probably from Taxim) towards the Golden Horn and the Süleymaniye Mosque [July 1911]
    Watercolor on paper
    12 ⅜ × 7 ⅞ in. (31.3 × 20 cm)
    FLC 1938; fig. 248

186.* Charles-Edouard Jeanneret
Istanbul. View of Eyüp cemetery enclosure wall, July 1911
    Pencil on paper
    4 ⅞ × 8 in. (12. × 20.4 cm)
    Signed and dated on the reverse
    FLC 6105; fig. 256

187.* Charles-Edouard Jeanneret
Istanbul. Eyüp cemetery with tombstones and cypresses, 1911
    Pencil and watercolor on paper
    11 ⅜ × 12 ⅜ in. (29 × 31.5 cm)
    Signed and dated on the reverse
    FLC 2854

188.† Charles-Edouard Jeanneret
Istanbul (?). Study of a Marble Fountain [July 1911]
    Pencil on paper
    8 × 4 ⅝ in. (20.2 × 12.4 cm)
    FLC 2392

189.† Charles-Edouard Jeanneret
Istanbul. View of Mosque wall with Wooden Houses [July 1911]
    Watercolor, pen and pencil on paper
    4 ⅝ × 7 ⅞ in. (12.5 × 20 cm)
    FLC 2455; fig. 253

190.† Charles-Edouard Jeanneret
Istanbul. Study of the Süleymaniye Mosque [July 1911]
    Pencil on paper
    4 ⅞ × 8 in. (12.5 × 20.2 cm)
    Signed and incorrectly dated 1910
    FLC 5883

191.† Charles-Edouard Jeanneret
Istanbul. Study of a building in Eyüp (?), detail of Cornice and Cupola [July 1911]
    Pencil on paper
    7 ⅞ × 4 ⅞ in. (20 × 12.5 cm)
    FLC 5869

192.† Charles-Edouard Jeanneret
Istanbul. Study of a Column from the Platea near the Hippodrome [July 1911]
    Pencil on paper
    5 ⅛ × 7 ¼ in. (18,4 × 13 cm)

Signed (posterior), not dated
FLC 6079

193.† Charles-Edouard Jeanneret
Istanbul. Sketch of the Aqueduct of Valens [July 1911]
    Pencil on paper
    4 ⅞ × 6 ½ in. (12.5 × 16.6 cm)
    Signed
    FLC 6115

194.* Charles-Edouard Jeanneret
Panorama of Istanbul, the Golden Horn and the sea of Marmara beyond [July 1911]
    Watercolor on paper
    3 ½ × 11 ⅝ in. (9 × 29.5 cm)
    FLC 1794; fig. 246

195.* Charles-Edouard Jeanneret
Istanbul. View of the Seraglio from the Bosporus with ships and sails [1911]
    Watercolor on paper
    9 ⅛ × 11 ⅜ in. (23.2 × 29 cm)
    FLC 1939; fig. 18

196.† Charles-Edouard Jeanneret
Istanbul. View of the Seraglio from the Bosporus with ships and sails, 1911
    Pencil, pen and watercolor on paper, pasted on cardboard
    9 ⅞ × 12 ½ in. (25 × 32 cm)
    Signed and dated
    FLC 2858

197.* Charles-Edouard Jeanneret
Athens, Acropolis. View from the Parthenon towards Piraeus [September 1911]
    Watercolor on paper
    5 ⅛ × 8 ¼ in. (13 × 21 cm)
    FLC 1782

198.† Charles-Edouard Jeanneret
Athens, Acropolis. View from the Parthenon, 1911
    Watercolor on paper
    5 ⅛ × 8 ½ in. (13 × 21.5 cm)
    Signed and dated
    FLC 2850; fig. 19, 260

199.† Charles-Edouard Jeanneret
Athens, Acropolis. View of the Propyleae, 1911
    Watercolor on paper
    6 ¾ × 10 ¼ in. (17 × 26.3 cm), pasted on cardboard 17 ¾ × 17 ¾ in. (45 × 45 cm)
    Signed and dated
    FLC 2849; fig. 264

200.† Charles-Edouard Jeanneret
Athens. View of the Acropolis with the Parthenon, after an illustration in Baedecker travel guide, July 1911
    Pencil on paper
    10 ⅝ × 8 ⅜ in. (27 × 21.2 cm)
    Signed (on the reverse?)
    FLC 2454; fig. 264

201.* Charles-Edouard Jeanneret
Athens, National Museum. Study after Greek Vase (Two Lions killing a bull) [September 1911]
    Gouache on paper
    8 ¾ × 11 ⅜ in. (22.3 × 29 cm)
    FLC 2249

202.* Charles-Edouard Jeanneret
Pompeii. Temple of Jupiter on the Forum in current (top) *and reconstructed condition* (below) [1911]

Pencil on paper
9 ⅝ × 11 ⅝ in. (24.5 × 29.6 cm)
FLC 1937; fig. 227

203.* Charles-Edouard Jeanneret
Pompeii. View of the Forum in presumed original condition, as seen from the Temple of Jupiter through reconstructed columns, 1911
    Watercolor on paper, pasted on board
    9 ¼ × 12 in. (23.5 × 30.5 cm)
    Signed and dated
    FLC 2859

204.† Charles-Edouard Jeanneret
Rome. View of the Villa Lante (by Giulio Romano) [1911]
    Black pencil and green pastel on paper
    7 ⅛ × 5 ⅛ in. (13 × 18 cm)
    FLC 6110; fig. 282

205.* Charles-Edouard Jeanneret
Pisa. Sketch of the Baptistery with the Duomo (left) *and Camposanto* (right) [October 1911]
    Indian ink and pencil on sketch paper
    5 ⅛ × 8 ¼ in. (13 × 21 cm)
    FLC 2506; fig. 296

206.* Charles-Edouard Jeanneret
Pisa. Sketch of the Leaning Tower and the Duomo [October 1911]
    Pencil on sketch paper
    5 ⅛ × 8 ¼ in. (13 × 21 cm)
    FLC 2510

207.* Charles-Edouard Jeanneret
Paris, Musée des Arts Décoratifs. Study of a Louis XV Commode [December 1912]
    Pencil and watercolor on notepaper
    10 ¾ × 14 ¾ in. (26.5 × 37.3 cm)
    FLC 2238; fig. 369

208.† Charles-Edouard Jeanneret
Un Versailles du Grand Turc, 1913
    Pencil and gouache on board
    12 ⅛ × 12 ¾ in. (30.8 × 32.4 cm)
    Dated
    FLC 4097; fig. 221

209.* Charles-Edouard Jeanneret
Solothurn. View of St. Ursen's Cathedral, 1915
    Pencil and watercolor on paper
    11 ½ × 16 ⅛ in. (29.2 × 41 cm)
    Dated
    FLC 4077; fig. 300

210.† Charles-Edouard Jeanneret
Vue romantique de Paris (Romantic View of Paris), 1917
    Pencil and watercolor on paper
    18 ¾ × 24 ¾ in. (47.8 × 63 cm)
    Dated
    FLC 4074; fig. 432

211.† Charles-Edouard Jeanneret
Chartres Cathedral, c. 1917
    Original gelatine print
    24 × 19 ⅝ in. (61 × 50 cm)
    Institut für Geschichte und Theorie der Architektur, ETH Zürich

212.† Charles-Edouard Jeanneret
Chartres Cathedral, c. 1917
    Original gelatine print

24 × 19 ⅝ in. (61 × 50 cm)
Institut für Geschichte und Theorie der
Architektur, ETH Zürich

213.† Charles-Edouard Jeanneret
Cube Drawing
FLC 2304

214.† Charles-Edouard Jeanneret
Landscape study [1921]
Pencil on paper [?], [SIZE]
FLC [?]

WORKS ON PAPER
ARCHITECTURAL DRAWINGS
215.* Charles-Edouard Jeanneret and René
Chapallaz
Jaquemet House, La Chaux-de-Fonds, 1907–08
Facade studies, 1908
Pencil and charcoal on tracing paper
15 × 36 in. (38 × 91.3 cm)
BV

216. Charles-Edouard Jeanneret
Villa Jeanneret-Perret, La Chaux-de-Fonds, 1912
South facade
Blueprint
19 × 21 ¼ in. (48.2 × 54 cm)
BV LCms 123

217. Charles-Edouard Jeanneret
Villa Jeanneret-Perret, La Chaux-de-Fonds, 1912
East facade
Blueprint
19 × 21 ¼ in. (48.2 × 54 cm)
BV LCms 123; fig. 325

218. Charles-Edouard Jeanneret
Villa Jeanneret-Perret, La Chaux-de-Fonds, 1912
North facade
Blueprint
19 × 21 ¼ in. (48.2 × 54 cm)
BV LCms 123; fig. 326

219. Charles-Edouard Jeanneret
Villa Jeanneret-Perret, La Chaux-de-Fonds, 1912
Plan of the basement
Blueprint
19 × 21 ¼ in. (48.2 × 54 cm)
BV LCms 123

220. Charles-Edouard Jeanneret
Villa Jeanneret-Perret, La Chaux-de-Fonds, 1912
Plan of the ground floor
Blueprint
19 × 21 ¼ in. (48.2 × 54 cm)
BV LCms 123; fig. 328

221. Charles-Edouard Jeanneret
Villa Jeanneret-Perret, La Chaux-de-Fonds, 1912
Plan of the upper floor
Blueprint
19 × 21 ¼ in. (48.2 × 54 cm)
BV LCms 123

222. Charles-Edouard Jeanneret
Villa Favre-Jacot, Le Locle, 1912
Perspective view, March 1912
Pencil on paper
8 ⅝ × 28 in. (22 × 71 cm)
Signed and dated
FLC 30277

223. Charles-Edouard Jeanneret
Project for a Department store for Paul Ditisheim,
La Chaux-de-Fonds, 1913
Charcoal on tracing paper
18 ½ × 26 ¾ in. (47 × 68 cm)
FLC 30270; fig. 142

224. Charles-Edouard Jeanneret
Competition design for the Pont Butin, Geneva,
1915
Perspective view, February 1915
Charcoal on paper
25 ¼ × 48 in. (64 × 122 cm)
Dated
FLC 30279; fig. 301

225.† Charles-Edouard Jeanneret
Project for Maison Dom-ino
Perspective of a Dom-ino module [1915]
India ink, black and colored pencil on paper
18 ½ × 22 ½ in. (47 × 57 cm)
FLC 19209; fig. 334

226.† Charles-Edouard Jeanneret
Project for Maison Dom-ino
Floor slab, view and section [1915]
India and colored ink and black pencil on
tracing paper
20 ½ × 28 in. (52 × 71 cm)
FLC 19202; fig. 337

227.† Charles-Edouard Jeanneret
Project for Maison Dom-ino
Ground floor with proposed layout for Type
B [1915]
Gelatine print
15 × 22 ½ in. (38 × 57 cm)
FLC 19211; fig. 336

228.† Charles-Edouard Jeanneret
Water Tank, Podensac, France, 1915–16
Interior view of the look-out platform below the
tank
Black pencil and ink on sketch paper
13 ¾ × 21 ⅝ in. (35 × 55 cm)
FLC 22407

229.† Charles-Edouard Jeanneret
Villa Schwob, La Chaux-de-Fonds, 1916–17
Views of the villa and interior perspective of the
daughter's room, July 24, 1916
Heliograph on drawing paper
35 × 17 ¼ in. (89 × 44 cm)
Signed and dated
FLC 30083

230.† Charles-Edouard Jeanneret
Villa Schwob, La Chaux-de-Fonds, 1916–17
Interior perspective of the boudoir, July 24, 1916
Heliograph on drawing paper
39 ¼ × 18 ½ in. (100 × 47 cm)
Signed and dated
FLC 30082; fig. 393

231.† Charles-Edouard Jeanneret
Villa Schwob, La Chaux-de-Fonds, 1916–17
Interior perspective of the bathroom, July 24, 1916
India ink on tracing paper
9 ½ × 12 ¼ in. (24 × 31 cm)
Signed and dated
FLC 32105; fig. 352

232.† Charles-Edouard Jeanneret

Villa Schwob, La Chaux-de-Fonds, 1916–17
Interior perspective of the hall gallery, July 24,
1916
India ink on tracing paper
8 ¾ × 11 ½ in. (22 × 29 cm)
Signed and dated
FLC 32106

233.† Charles-Edouard Jeanneret
Villa Schwob, La Chaux-de-Fonds, 1916–17
Plan of the ground floor 1:50, September 8, 1916
Heliograph on drawing paper
27 ½ × 32 ¼ in. (70 × 82 cm)
Signed and dated
FLC 32107

234. Charles-Edouard Jeanneret
Villa Schwob, La Chaux-de-Fonds, 1916–17
Perspective view of kitchen forecourt, March 3,
1917
India ink on tracing paper
9 × 12 ⅝ in. (23 × 32 cm)
Signed and dated
FLC 32107; fig. 349

235.† Charles-Edouard Jeanneret
Villa Schwob, La Chaux-de-Fonds, 1916–17
View of villa and garden from the south
India ink on tracing paper
5 ½ × 9 in. (14 × 23 cm)
Signed
FLC 32104; fig. 348

236.† Charles-Edouard Jeanneret
Project for Workers' Settlement at Saint-Nicolas
d'Aliermont, 1917
Perspective view
Black pencil and ink on office stationery
8 ¼ × 10 ⅝ in. (21 × 27 cm)
FLC 19328

237.† Charles-Edouard Jeanneret
Project for Challuy Slaughterhouse, 1917
Bird's Eye View, December 25, 1917
India ink on tracing paper
21 ⅝ × 23 ⅜ in. (55 × 72 cm)
Signed and dated
FLC 22360; fig. 354

238.† Charles-Edouard Jeanneret
Project for Maison Monol
Perspective view of a group of houses [1919]
Heliograph
11 × 29 ⅛ in. (28 × 74 cm)
FLC 19123; fig. 360

239.† Charles-Edouard Jeanneret
Everite formwork for the construction of concrete
columns
Study relating to a patent application [October
1918]
India ink and black pencil on tracing paper
8 ⅝ × 28 ¾ in. (22 × 73 cm)
FLC 22368; fig. 358

240.† Charles-Edouard Jeanneret
Everite formwork for the construction of concrete
columns
Study relating to a patent application [October 1918]
India ink and black pencil on tracing paper
8 ⅝ × 28 ¾ in. (22 × 73 cm)
FLC 22367; fig. 359

241.† Charles-Edouard Jeanneret
Everite formwork for construction in concrete
Study relating to a patent application [October 1918]
    India ink and black pencil on tracing paper
    10 ⅝ × 8 ¼ in. (27 × 21 cm)
    FLC 22366; fig. 357

242.* Le Corbusier
Project for the "Ville contemporaine pour 3 mil-
lions d'habitants" applied to the topography of
Paris, perspective view [1922]
    Black pencil on tracing paper
    26 ¾ × 55 ⅛ in. (68 × 140 cm)
    FLC 31003

WORKS ON PAPER
DRAWINGS FOR FURNITURE

243. Charles-Edouard Jeanneret
Study for the Desk for Charlotte-Amélie Jeanneret-
Perret, 1915–16
    Pencil on yellow paper, pasted on board
    10 × 12 in. (25.5 × 30.6 cm)
    BV LCms 135-1; fig. 380

244. Charles-Edouard Jeanneret
Divan for Marcel Levaillant's Apartment, La
Chaux-de-Fonds, 1917
    Plans, 1:10
    Pencil on paper
    11 ⅝ × 20 in. (29.5 × 51 cm)
    Private collection; fig. 389

245.† Charles-Edouard Jeanneret
Divan for Marcel Levaillant's Apartment, La
Chaux-de-Fonds, 1917
    Working drawing of balustrade
    Pencil and coloured pencil on paper
    23 ¼ × 11 ⅝ in. (59 × 29.5 cm)
    FLC 30524; fig. 388

246. Le Corbusier
Library for Madeleine Schwob, La Chaux-de-
Fonds, 1922
    Plan 1:20, March 1922
    India ink on yellow tracing paper
    12 ½ × 8 ½ in. (32 × 47 cm)
    Private collection; fig. 401

247.† Le Corbusier
Library for Madeleine Schwob, La Chaux-de-
Fonds, 1922
    Perspective view, March 3, 1922
    Heliograph on paper, watercolor
    16 ¾ × 25 ½ in. (42.5 × 65 cm)
    FLC 30526; fig. 134

248.* Le Corbusier
Library for Madeleine Schwob, La Chaux-de-
Fonds, 1922
    Perspective view, March 3, 1922
    Black pencil on tracing paper
    13 × 18 ⅞ in. (33 × 48 cm)
    FLC 30525

249.† Le Corbusier
Library for Madeleine Schwob, La Chaux-de-
Fonds, 1922
    Working drawing, March 30, 1922
    Black and colored pencil on paper
    46 ½ × 58 ¼ in. (118 × 148 cm)
    FLC 30127; fig. 402

250. Le Corbusier
Library for Madeleine Schwob, La Chaux-de-
Fonds, 1922
    Drawing of the storage for engravings, plan of the
library, sections and details with dimensions, March
30, 1922
    India ink and colored pencil on drawing
    paper
    37 ⅜ × 59 ⅛ in. (95 × 150 cm)
    FLC 23047

251.† Le Corbusier
Library for Madeleine Schwob, La Chaux-de-
Fonds, 1922
    Working drawing with dimensions, notes and cap-
tion, March 30, 1922
    India ink and colored pencil on drawing
    paper
    39 × 56 ¾ in. (99 × 144 cm)
    FLC 23045

252. Le Corbusier
Marcel Levaillant's Apartment, Villa Les
Eglantines, La Chaux-de-Fonds, 1923
    Studies and plans
    Pencil on paper
    28 ⅞ × 39 ⅜ in. (53 × 100 cm)
    FLC 23092v

253. Le Corbusier
Marcel Levaillant's Apartment, Villa Les
Eglantines, La Chaux-de-Fonds, 1923
    Sketch of the bedroom
    Blue ink on paper
    10 ⅝ × 8 ¼ in. (10 ⅝ × 8 ¼ in. (27 × 21 cm))
    Private collection

254. Le Corbusier
Marcel Levaillant's Apartment, Villa Les
Eglantines, La Chaux-de-Fonds, 1923
    Sketch of the library
    Blue ink on paper
    10 ⅝ × 8 ¼ in. (27 × 21 cm)
    Private collection

255. Le Corbusier
Marcel Levaillant's Apartment, Villa Les
Eglantines, La Chaux-de-Fonds, 1923
    Sketches of two Maple's armchairs
    Blue ink on paper
    10 ⅝ × 8 ¼ in. (27 × 21 cm)
    Private collection; fig. 148

256. Le Corbusier
Marcel Levaillant's Apartment, Villa Les
Eglantines, La Chaux-de-Fonds, 1923
    Note by Le Corbusier, March 12, 1923
    Blue ink on paper
    10 ⅝ × 8 ¼ in. (27 × 21 cm)
    Private collection

257. Le Corbusier
Drawing postioning a cast of the head of Prince
Gudea in Marcel Levaillant's Apartment, Villa Les
Eglantines, La Chaux-de-Fonds, 1923
    Ink on paper
    10 ⅝ × 8 ¼ in. (27 × 21 cm)
    FLC H3-7-268

258. Le Corbusier
Drawing postioning various casts from the Louvre
Museum, Marcel Levaillant's Apartment, Villa Les
Eglantines, La Chaux-de-Fonds, 1923
    Ink on paper
    10 ⅝ × 8 ¼ in. (27 × 21 cm)
    FLC H3-7-269; fig. 156

WORKS ON PAPER
PURIST STUDIES

259.* Charles-Edouard Jeanneret
Nature morte avec vase aux anémones (Still Life with
Vase of Anemones) 1917
    Pencil and gouache on drawing paper
    24 ⅞ × 18 ⅝ in. (63 × 47.5 cm)
    Dated (on the reverse)
    FLC 4502; fig. 446

260.* Charles-Edouard Jeanneret
Nature morte au livre ouvert et boîte de pastels (Still Life
with an open book and a box of pastels, 1918
    Gouache on paper, pasted on board
    18 ⅝ × 21 ¼ in. (47.5 × 54 cm)
    Signed, dated
    FLC 4059

261.† Charles-Edouard Jeanneret
Study for "La cheminée" (The Mantelpiece), 1918
    Pencil on paper
    22 ⅝ × 28 in. (57.5 × 71 cm)
    Signed, dated
    FLC 2304

262.* Charles-Edouard Jeanneret
Etude puriste (Purist Study), c. 1921
    Pencil on paper
    9 ⅞ × 14 ¾ in. (25 × 37.5 cm)
    FLC 2483

263.† Charles-Edouard Jeanneret (Le Corbusier)
Nature morte avec verre, théière, pipe et bilboquet (Still life
with glass, teapot and toy, c. 1921
    Pastel on tracing paper
    10 ⅛ × 13 ⅝ in. (25.8 × 34.5 cm)
    FLC 1635; fig. 460

264.* Le Corbusier
*Three drawings with small pitcher, glass, pipe and playing
cards on a program "Fête de nuit à Montparnasse"* [1922]
    Pencil on paper
    8 ¼ × 10 ⅝ in. (21 × 27 cm)
    FLC 1636; fig. 459

WORKS ON PAPER
STUDIES AFTER ENGRAVINGS

265.† Charles-Edouard Jeanneret
The Observatoire, the Invalides, the Jardin des
Plantes, the Tuileries, the Château at Versailles:
Sketches after engravings in the Bibliothèque
Nationale, Paris by Gabriel Pérelle [1915]
    Ink and pencil on tracing paper
    9 ⅞ × 17 ¾ in. (25 × 45 cm)
    FLC B2-20-242; fig. 117

266.† Charles-Edouard Jeanneret
Bassin de Flore, Gardens of Versailles: Sketches
after engravings in the Bibliothèque Nationale,
Paris by Gabriel Pérelle [1915]
    Purple pencil on transparent paper
    10 ⅝ × 20 ¼ in. (27 × 51.5 cm)
    FLC B2-20-256; fig. 11

267.† Charles-Edouard Jeanneret
Squares of Paris: Sketches after engravings in the Bibliothèque Nationale, Paris by Gabriel Pérelle [1915]
> Ink on paper
> 10 ⁵⁄₈ × 8 ½ in. (27 × 21.5 cm)
> FLC B2-20-657; fig. 307

268.† Charles-Edouard Jeanneret
The Tuileries gardens: Sketches after engravings in the Bibliothèque Nationale, Paris by Gabriel Pérelle [1915]
> Ink on tracing paper
> 6 ⁷⁄₈ × 9 ⁷⁄₈ in. (17.5 × 25 cm)
> FLC B2-20-228

269.† Charles-Edouard Jeanneret
The Tuileries, Rue Royale, Place Louis XV: Sketches after engravings in the Bibliothèque Nationale, Paris by Gabriel Pérelle [1915]
> Ink on paper
> 9 ⁷⁄₈ × 22 ¾ in. (25 × 57.6 cm)
> FLC B2-20-250; fig. 119

270.† Charles-Edouard Jeanneret
Rouen Cathedral: Sketches after engravings in the Bibliothèque Nationale [1915]
> Ink on paper
> 8 ³⁄₈ × 10 ⅛ in. (21.3 × 25.6 cm)
> FLC B2-20-260

271.† Charles-Edouard Jeanneret
The Portail de la Calende, Rouen Cathedral, studies after engravings in the Bibliothèque Nationale, Paris [1915]
> Brown ink on yellow paper
> 8 ³⁄₈ × 10 ⅛ in. (21.2 × 25.8 cm)
> FLC B2-20-262

272.† Charles-Edouard Jeanneret
The Markt, Nürnberg, studies after engravings in the Bibliothèque Nationale, Paris [1915]
> Ink on paper
> 8 ½ × 10 in. (21.5 × 25.6 cm)
> FLC B2-20-214

273.† Charles-Edouard Jeanneret
Famous Buildings of Ancient Rome and other places, studies after engravings in the Bibliothèque Nationale, Paris [1915]
> Ink on paper
> 9 ⁷⁄₈ × 16 in. (25 × 40.6 cm)
> FLC B2-20-203; fig. 275

274.† Charles-Edouard Jeanneret
Buildings in Rome, after engravings in the Bibliothèque Nationale, Paris by Piranesi [1915]
> Ink on tracing paper
> 9 ⁷⁄₈ × 15 ¾ in. (25 × 40 cm)
> FLC B2-20-345

275.† Charles-Edouard Jeanneret
The Basilica of Maxentius, the Pantheon, the Pyramid of Cestius and the Forum, sketches after engravings in the Bibliothèque Nationale, Paris [1915]
> Ink on paper
> 8 ⅛ × 11 ⅝ in. (20.5 × 29.5)
> FLC B2-20-204

WORKS ON PAPER BY OTHER ARTISTS

276. Adolphe Appia (1862–1928, Swiss)
Espace rythmique. Dépendance [1909–10]
> Pencil and charcoal on paper
> 18 ⅛ × 25 ⅝ in. (46 × 65 cm)
> Schweizerische Theatersammlung, Bern F 7c; fig. 20

277.* Charles L'Eplattenier (1874–1946, Swiss)
Study for "Le temps de mars" [1907]
> Pastel on paper
> 19 ¼ × 30 ⅛ in. (49 × 76.5 cm)
> Signed
> MBA 1956

278.* Charles L'Eplattenier
"Vue des Alpes," Lake Neuchâtel and the Swiss Midlands
> Pencil and watercolor on paper
> 5 ⅝ × 15 ⅜ in. (14.4 × 39.2 cm)
> BV

279.* Charles L'Eplattenier
Sculpture Studies from various Museums
> Pencil and indian ink on 9 sheets of notepaper, pasted on wrapping paper
> 15 ⅞ × 21 ½ in. (40.4 × 54.5 cm)
> Signed
> BV; figs. 9, 217

280.* Charles L'Eplattenier
Studies of fountain sculptures from Bern, Fribourg, and Le Landeron
> Pencil and indian ink on 9 sheets of notepaper, pasted on wrapping paper
> 14 ⅞ × 19 ¾ in. (37.7 × 50.2 cm)
> BV; fig. 224

281.* Amédée Ozenfant (?) (1886–1966, French)
Etude, serviette pliée, (Study of a folded serviette) c. 1919
> Pencil on paper
> 11 × 8 ⅞ in. (28 × 22.5 cm)
> FLC 1729

282.* Léon Perrin (1886–1978, Swiss)
Fribourg. View of St. Nicolas's Cathedral
> Pencil on paper
> 7 ⅛ × 4 ¾ in. (18.1 × 12.1 cm)
> Signed
> Musée Léon Perrin, Môtiers

283.* Léon Perrin
Florence. Interior study of S. Croce [September/October 1907]
> Pencil on paper
> 7 × 4 ¾ in. (17.9 × 12.1 cm)
> Signed on the reverse
> Musée Léon Perrin, Môtiers; fig. 10

284.* Léon Perrin
Florence, S. Maria Novella. Study of the base moulding profile [1907]
> Pencil on paper
> 7 ⅛ × 4 ⅛ in. (18.2 × 10.4 cm) (pasted into Carnet G2)
> Musée Léon Perrin, Môtiers; fig. 178

285.* Léon Perrin
Florence. Study of the Cantoria in the Old Sacristy of S. Lorenzo (School of Donatello), 1907
> Pencil and colored pencil on paper
> 9 × 6 ½ in. (22.9 × 16.6 cm)
> Signed and dated (on the reverse?)
> Musée Léon Perrin, Môtiers E VI 217; fig. 179

286.* Léon Perrin
Venice, Doges' Palace. Studies of capitals [1907]
> Pencil on paper
> 4 × 7 ¼ in. (10 × 18.5 cm)
> Signed
> Musée Léon Perrin, Môtiers E VI 210

287. William Ritter (1867–1955, Swiss)
View of Lake Neuchâtel, 1886
> Watercolor on paper
> 9 ½ × 6 in. (24 × 15.2 cm)
> Signed and dated
> BV; fig. 430

288. William Ritter
Myjava, Slovakia. View of a traditional farmhouse, 1906
> Watercolor on paper
> 10 ⅞ × 14 ⅝ in. (27.8 × 37.3 cm)
> Signed and dated
> BV; fig. 433

289. William Ritter
Munich. View of the Hofgarten, Bazar-Gebäude, Theatinerkirche and the twin towers of the Frauenkirche in the background, April 1908
> Watercolor on paper
> 10 ½ × 12 in. (26.7 × 30.5 cm)
> Signed and dated
> BV; fig. 230

LIST OF SOURCES CITED

ARCHIVES

Bibliothéque de la Ville, La Chaux-de-Fonds (BV)
    includes correspondence with his family and with August Klipstein; and documents
    relating to projects for Ernest-Albert and Hermann Ditisheim
Fondation Le Corbusier in Paris (FLC)
    includes correspondence with Charles L'Eplattenier
Schweizerische Landesbibliothek, Bern
    includes correspondence with William Ritter
Institut Français d'Architecture, Fonds Perret
    includes correspondence with Auguste Perret
Many of the original letters in the BV and FLC have been transcribed and are available on
computer at the FLC.

PUBLICATIONS BY LE CORBUSIER

Selected titles, in chronological order

Jeanneret, Charles-Edouard. *Etude sur le mouvement d'art décoratif en Allemagne.* La Chaux-de-
    Fonds: Editions Haefeli, 1912. Reprint, New York: Da Capo Press, 1968.
——. "La Maison Suisse." In *Etrennes Helvétiques: Almanach Illustré.* Paris, Dijon, La Chaux-
    de-Fonds: n.p., 1914, pp. 31–39.
——. "Le Renouveau dans l'architecture." *L'Oeuvre, revue mensuelle* (Bern) 2 (June 1914):
    33–37.
Jeanneret, Charles-Edouard, and Amédée Ozenfant. *Après le cubisme.* (Paris: Edition des
    commentaires, 1918.
——. "Intégrer." *Création,* no. 2 (November 1921): 9–10.
Le Corbusier-Saugnier. *Vers une architecture.* Paris: Crès, 1923. Translated by Frederick
    Etchells under the title *Towards a New Architecture* (New York: Payson and Clarke;
    London: Rodker, 1927).
Jeanneret, Charles-Edouard, and Amédée Ozenfant. *La Peinture moderne.* Paris: Crès, 1925.
Le Corbusier. *Urbanisme.* Paris: Crès, 1925.
——. *L'Art décoratif d'aujourd'hui.* Paris: Crès, 1925. Translated under the title *The Decorative
    Art of Today* (London: The Architectural Press, 1987).
——. *Almanach d'architecture moderne.* Paris: Crès, 1926.
——. "Architecture d'époque machiniste." *Journal de Psychologie normale et pathologique* 23
    (1926): 343–44.
——. *Une maison, un palais.* Paris: Crès, 1928.
——. *Oeuvre complète.* 7 vols. Zurich: Girsberger, 1930–71. Author and editors vary slightly
    from volume to volume; of greatest interest here is vol. 1, *1910–1929,* edited by Willy
    Boesiger and Oscar Stonorov (1937).
——. *Précisions sur un état présent de l'architecture et de l'urbanisme.* Paris: Crès, 1930.
——. *Clavier de couleur Salubra.* Basel: Salubra, 1931. 2d ed., 1959.
——. "Descartes est-il américain?" 1931. In *Les plans de Paris, 1922–1956.* Paris: Les Editions
    de Minuit, 1956, pp. 65–73.
——. "Perret par Le Corbusier." *L'Architecture d'aujourd'hui* 3, no. 7 (1932): 8.
——. *Quand les cathédrales étaient blanches.* Paris: Plon, 1937. Translated by Francis E. Hyslop
    under the title *When the Cathedrals Were White: A Journey to the Country of the Timid People*
    (New York: Reynal and Hitchcock, 1947).
——. *La ville radieuse.* Boulogne-sur-Seine: Editions de L'Architecture d'aujourd'hui, 1935.
    Translated under the title *The Radiant City* (London: Faber, 1967).
——. *Sur les quatre routes.* Paris: Gallimard, 1941. Translated under the title *The Four Routes*
    (London: D. Dobson, 1947).
——. *Entretien avec les étudiants des écoles d'architecture.* Paris: Denoël, 1943.
——. *Manière de penser l'urbanisme.* Boulogne-sur-Seine: Editions de L'Architecture d'aujour-
    d'hui, 1946. 2d ed., Geneva, Gonthier, 1963.
——. *Propos d'urbanisme.* Paris: Bourrelier, 1946.
——. *Le Modulor: essai sur une mesure harmonique a l'échelle humaine applicable universellement à l'ar-
    chitecture et à la mécanique.* Boulogne: Editions de l'architecture d'Aujourd'hui, 1950.
    Translated by Peter de Francia and Anna Bostock under the title *The Modular: A
    Harmonious Measure to the Human Scale, Universally Applicable to Architecture and Mechanics*
    (Cambridge, Mass.: MIT Press, 1954).
——. *Une petite maison.* Zurich: Girsberger, 1954.
——. *Textes et planches.* Paris: Vincent & Fréal, 1960. German edition under the title Mein
    Werk (Stuttgart: Hatje, 1960).
——. *Le Voyage d'orient.* Paris: Forces Vives, 1966. Translated by Ivan Zaknic under the title
    Journey to the East (Cambridge, Mass.: MIT Press, 1987).
*Charles-Edouard Jeanneret, La construction des villes: Genèse et devenir d'un ouvrage écrit de 1910 à 1915
    et laissé inachevé par Charles-Edouard Jeanneret-Gris dit Le Corbusier.* Edited by Marc E.
    Albert Emery. Paris and Héricourt: Editions L'Age d'Homme, 1992.

PUBLISHED COLLECTIONS OF ARCHIVAL MATERIALS

Ch.-E. Jeanneret - Le Corbusier: Album La Roche. Edited by Stanislaus von Moos. Milan:
    Electa, 1996. In English and French under the same title (Paris: Gallimard, 1996).
The Le Corbusier Archive. Edited by H. Allen Brooks. 32 vols. New York, London, and Paris,
    1982–84).
Le Corbusier (Ch.-E. Jeanneret), Les Voyages d'Allemagne, Carnets. Edited by Gresleri, Giuliano.
    Milan and Paris: Electa, in association with Fondation Le Corbusier, 1994.
Le Corbusier (Ch.-E. Jeanneret): Voyage d'Orient, Carnets. Edited by Giuliano Gresleri. Milan
    and Paris: Electa, in association with Fondation Le Corbusier, 1987.
Le Corbusier Sketchbooks. Edited by Maurice Besset. 4 vols. New York: Architectural History
    Foundation, and Cambridge, Mass.: MIT Press, 1981. French edition, *Le Corbusier
    Carnets* (Paris: Herscher/Dessain et Tolra, 1981).
Le Corbusier, Viaggio in Oriente: Gli inediti di Charles Edouard Jeanneret fotografo e scrittore. Edited
    by Gresleri, Giuliano. Venice: Marsilio, 1984. 2d ed., 1985. 3rd ed. under the title *Viaggio
    in Oriente. Le Corbusier, Charles Edouard Jeanneret, fotografo e scrittore,* 1995.

OTHER SOURCES

*Includes most sources consulted by the authors of this catalogue; many publications that were influential to
    Le Corbusier during the period; and selected exhibition catalogues.*

Anderson, Stanford. "The Legacy of German Neo-Classicism and Biedermeier: Behrens,
    Loos, Mies, and Tessenow." *Assemblage* 15 (October 1991): 62–87.
——. *Peter Behrens and a New Architecture for the Twentieth Century.* Cambridge, Mass.: MIT
    Press, 2000.
"L'Art nouveau à La Chaux-de-Fonds." *Revue historique neuchâteloise* (1998), no. 2, special
    issue.

Asche, Kurt. *Peter Behrens und die Oldenburger Ausstellung 1905*. Berlin: Mann Verlag, 1992.

Aurier, Albert. *Textes critiques, 1889–1892: De l'Impressionnisme au symbolisme*. 1893. Reprint, Paris: Ecole Nationale des Beaux Arts, 1995.

Bacon, Mardges. *Le Corbusier in America. Travels in the land of the timid*. Cambridge, Mass.: MIT Press, 2001.

Baedeker, Karl. *Northern Italy*. Leipzig: K. Baedeker, 1906.

Baker, Geoffrey H. *Le Corbusier – The Creative Search: The Formative Years of Charles-Edouard Jeanneret*. London: Chapman & Hall, 1996.

Baker, Geoffrey, and Jacques Gubler. *Le Corbusier: Early Works by Charles-Edouard Jeanneret-Gris*. Architectural Monographs, no. 12. London and New York: Academy Editions and St. Martin's Press, 1987.

Banham, Reyner. *Theory and Design in the First Machine Age*. London and New York: Architectural Press and Praeger, 1960.

Barr, Alfred H. *Cubism and Abstract Art*. Exhib. cat. New York: Museum of Modern Art, 1936.

Baudot, Anatole de. *L'Architecture, le passé, le présent*. Paris: Renouard et H. Laurens, 1916.

Behrendt, Walter Curt. *Die einheitliche Blockfront als Raumelement im Stadtbau: Ein Beitrag zur Stadtbaukunst der Gegenwart*. Berlin: Cassirer, 1911.

Behrens, Peter. "Kunst und Technik." *Elektrotechnische Zeitschrift* 31/22 (2 June 1910): 552–55.

——— "Kunst und Technik." In *Industriekultur: Peter Behrens und die AEG, 1907-1914*, edited by Tilmann Buddensieg and Henning Rogge. Berlin: Mann, 1979, pp. D278–85.

Benoît, François. *L'Art français sous la Révolution et l'Empire: Les doctrines, les idées, les genres*. Paris: L. H. May, 1897.

Benton, Tim. *Les Villas de Le Corbusier et Pierre Jeanneret, 1920–1930*. Paris: P. Sers, 1984. In English under the title *The Villas of Le Corbusier, 1920–1930*. New Haven and London: Yale University Press, 1987.

Berlage, Hendrik Petrus. "Neuere amerikanische Architektur." Parts 1–3. *Schweizerische Bauzeitung* 60 (14 September 1912): 148–50; (21 September 1912): 165–67; (28 September 1912): 178.

Besset, Maurice. *Qui était Le Corbusier?* Geneva: Skira, 1968.

Bienz, Peter. *Le Corbusier und die Musik*. Braunschweig and Wiesbaden: Vieweg, 1999.

Blau, Eve, and Nancy Troy, eds. *Architecture and Cubism*. Montreal and Cambridge, Mass: Canadian Centre for Architecture and MIT Press, 1997.

Blondel, Jacques-François. *Discours sur la manière d'étudier l'architecture et les arts qui sont relatifs à celui de bastir*. Paris: P. J. Mariette, 1747.

———. *Discours sur la nécessité de l'étude de l'architecture, dans lequel on essaye de prouver, combien il est important pour le progrès des arts, que les hommes en place en acquièrent les connoissances élémentaires: que les artistes en approfondissent la théorie, & que les artisans s'appliquent aux développemens du ressort de leur profession*. Paris: C. A. Jombert, 1754.

Blum, Elisabeth. *Le Corbusier's Wege: Wie das Zauberwerk in Gang gesetzt wird*. Braunschweig and Wiesbaden: Vieweg, 1988.

Bock, Manfred. *Anfänge einer neuen Architektur. Berlages Beitrag zur Architektonischen Kultur der Niederlande im augehenden 19. Jahrhundert*. The Hague and Wiesbaden: Staatsuitsverij and Steiner, 1983.

Bois, Yve-Alain, and Bruno Reichlin, eds. *De Stijl et l'architecture en France*. Liège and Bruxelles: Mardaga, 1985.

Bonaiti, Maria. *Ch. E. Jeanneret: Oltre il regionalismo: Germania 1910–1911*. Venice: Istituto universitario di architettura, 1990.

Borrmann, Norbert. *Paul Schultze-Naumburg, 1869–1949: Maler, Publizist-Architekt. Vom Kulturreformer der Jahrhundertwende zum Kulturpolitiker im Dritten Reich*. Essen: Bacht, 1989.

Brinckmann, Albert E. *Platz und Monument: Untersuchungen zur Geschichte und Ästhetik der Stadtbaukunst in neuerer Zeit*. Berlin: Ernst Wasmuth A.-G., 1908.

Brooks, H. Allen. "Jeanneret and Sitte: Le Corbusier's Earliest Ideas on Urban Design." In *In Search of Modern Architecture: A Tribute to Henry-Russell Hitchcock*. Edited by Helen Searing. Cambridge, Mass., and London: The MIT Press, 1982, pp. 278–97. In Italian under the title "Jeanneret e Sitte: le prime idee di Le Corbusier sulla costruzione della città." *Casabella* 48, no. 514 (1984): 41.

———. *Le Corbusier's Formative Years. Charles-Edouard Jeanneret at La Chaux-de-Fonds*. Chicago and London: University of Chicago Press, 1997.

Brooks, H. Allen, ed. *Le Corbusier*. Princeton, N.J.: Princeton University Press, 1987.

Calabi, Donatella. *Parigi anni venti: Marcel Poëte e le origini della storia urbana*. Venice: Marsilio, 1997. In French, translated by Pierre Savy under the title *Marcel Poëte et le Paris des années vingt: Aux origines de "l'histoire des villes."* Paris and Montreal: L'Harmattan, 1998.

Celik, Zeynep. "Le Corbusier, Orientalism, Colonialism." *Assemblage* 17 (1992): 61–77.

Cendrars, Blaise. *La fin du monde filmée par l'Ange Notre-Dame*. Illustrated by Fernand Léger. Paris: Editions de la Sirene, 1919.

Charollais, Isabelle, and André Ducret, eds. *Le Corbusier à Genève, 1922–1932: Projets et réalisations*. Exhib. cat. Geneva and Lausanne: Immeuble Clarté and Galerie Bonnier / Payot, 1987.

Chemetov, Paul, and Bernard Marrey. *Architectures, Paris, 1848-1914*. Paris: Dunod, 1980.

Choisy, Auguste. *Histoire de l'architecture*. Paris: Gauthier-Villars, 1899.

Cingria-Vaneyre, A. *Les Entretiens de la villa du Rouet: Essais dialogués sur les arts plastiques en Suisse romande*. Genève: A. Jullien, 1908.

Cohen, Jean-Louis. *Le Corbusier et la mystique de l'URSS. Théories et projets pour Moscou, 1928-1936*, Liège: Mardaga, 1987. Translated under the title *Le Corbusier and the mystique of the USSR. Theories and projects for Moscow 1928-1936* (Princeton, New Jersey: Princeton University Press, 1992).

Collins, George R., and Christiane Crasemann Collins. *Camillo Sitte and the Birth of Modern City Planning*. London: Phaidon, 1965.

Colomina, Beatriz. *Privacy and Publicity: Modern Architecture as Mass Media*. Cambridge, Mass. and London: MIT Press, 1994.

Colquhoun, Alan. *Essays in Architectural Criticism: Modern Architecture and Historical Change*. Cambridge, Mass., MIT Press, 1981.

———. *Modernity and the Classical Tradition: Architectural Essays, 1980–1987*. Cambridge, Mass.: MIT Press, 1989.

Cours de dessin pour les écoles primaires. Lithographs by A. Chateau. La Chaux-de-Fonds: Chateau, 1894.

Curtis, William. *Le Corbusier: Ideas and Forms*. Oxford: Phaidon, 1986.

De Simone, Rosario. *Ch. E. Jeanneret-Le Corbusier: Viaggio in Germania, 1910–1911*. Rome: Officina, 1989.

"Les débuts de L'Ecole d'art à La Chaux-de-Fonds." *Nouvelle revue neuchâteloise 9*, no. 34 (1992), special issue.

Denis, Maurice. *Théories, 1890–1910. Du Symbolisme et de Gauguin vers un nouvel ordre classique*. Paris: Occident, 1912.

Dieulafoy, Marcel. *L'Art antique de la Perse*. 5 parts in 2 vols. Paris: Librairie Centrale d'Architecture, 1884–89.

Duboy, Philippe, "Ch.-E. Jeanneret à la Bibliothèque Nationale, Paris, 1915." *AMC — Architecture, mouvement, continuité* 49 (1979): 9–12.

———. "Architecture de la ville, culture et triomphe de l'urbanisme: Ch.-E Jeanneret, 'La Construction des villes,' Bibliothèque Nationale de Paris, 1915." Ph.D. diss. Prepared with the Ministère de l'Urbanisme, du Logement et Transport. Paris, 1985.

———. "L.C.B.N. 1.9.1.5." *Casabella* 51, nos. 531/532 (1987): 94–103.

Ducros, Françoise. *Amédée Ozenfant*. Paris: Cercle d'Art, 2002.

Eliel, Carol S. *L'Esprit Nouveau: Purism in Paris, 1918–1925*. Exhib. cat. Los Angeles and New York: Los Angeles County Museum of Art and Harry N. Abrams, 2000. In French under the title *L'Esprit Nouveau: Le purisme à Parism, 1918–1925* (Paris: Réunion des Musées Nationaux and Musée de Grenoble, 2001).

Epstein, Jean. *Ecrits sur le cinéma, 1921–1953*. Vol. 1. Paris: Cinéma Club / Seghers, 1974–75.

L'Esprit Nouveau, no. 1 (1920)–no. 28 (1925). Facsimile-Reprint: New York: Da Capo Press, 1968/69.

Etlin, Richard A. *Frank Lloyd Wright and Le Corbusier: The Romantic Legacy*. Manchester and New York: Manchester University Press, 1994.

Fanelli, Giovanni, and Roberto Gargiani. *Perret e Le Corbusier, Confronti*. Rome and Bari: Laterza, 1990.

Favre, Maurice. "Au pays du prophète." *Revue neuchâteloise* 23, no. 91, Le Corbusier pourquoi (1980): 39–44.

Ferriss, Hugh. *The Metropolis of Tomorrow*. New York: I. Washburn, 1929.

Forster, Kurt W. "Antiquity and Modernity in the La Roche-Jeanneret Houses of 1923." *Oppositions* 15/16 (winter/spring 1979): 130–53.

Frampton, Kenneth, ed. "Le Corbusier, 1905–1933." *Oppositions* 15/16 (winter/spring 1979), special issue.

———. *Le Corbusier*. London: Thames & Hudson, 2001. First published in French (Paris: Hazan, 1997).

Gargiani, Roberto. *Auguste Perret, 1874–1954*. Milan: Electa, 1993.

Garino, Claude. *Le Corbusier: De la Villa turque à L'Esprit Nouveau*. La Chaux-de-Fonds: Idéa Editions, 1995.

Gast, Klaus-Peter. *Le Corbusier, Paris-Chandigarh*. With a foreword by Arthur Rüegg. Basel-Berlin-Boston: Birkhäuser, 2000.

Ghil, René. *Traité du verbe*. Paris: Giraud, 1886.

Goethe, Johann Wolfgang von. *Italienische Reise*. Edited by Christoph Michel. Frankfurt: Insel, 1976.

Golan, Romy. *Modernity and Nostalgia: Art and Politics in France Between the Wars*. New Haven and London: Yale University Press, 1995.

Grasset, Eugène. *Méthode de composition ornementale*. 2 vols. Paris: Librairie Centrale des Beaux-Arts, 1905.

Gravagnuolo, Benedetto, ed. *Le Corbusier e l'Antico: Viaggi nel Mediterraneo*. Exhib. cat. Naples: Palazzo Reale and Electa, 1997.

Green, Christopher. *Cubism and Its Enemies*. London and New Haven: Yale University Press, 1987.

Gregh, Eleanor. "The Dom-ino Idea." *Oppositions*, 15/16 (winter/spring 1979): 61–87.

Gresleri, Giuliano, ed. *Le Corbusier: Il viaggio in Toscana (1907)*. Exhib. cat. Florence: Palazzo Pitti, and Venice: Marsilio, 1987.

——. *Le Corbusier: Il linguaggio delle pietre*. Exhib. cat. Crema and Venice: Centro culturale S.Agostino and Marsilio, 1988.

Gropius, Walter. "Die Entwicklung moderner Industriebaukunst." In *Kunst in Industrie und Handel*. Jahrbuch des Deutschen Werkbundes. Jena: E. Diederichs, 1913, pp. 17–22.

Gubler, Jacques. *Nationalisme et internationalisme dans l'architecture moderne de la Suisse*. Lausanne: L'Age d'Homme, 1975.

——. "A l'heure des horlogers jurassiens." *Revue neuchâteloise* 23, no. 91, Le Corbusier pourquoi (1980): 7–37.

——. "La Chaux-de-Fonds." In *Inventar der neueren Schweizer Architektur, 1850–1920* [INSA]. Vol. 3, *Städte (Biel, La Chaux-de-Fonds, Chur, Davos)*. Bern: Gesellschaft für Schweizerische Kunstgeschichte, 1982, pp. 127–217.

Hautecoeur, Louis. *Rome et la Renaissance de l'antiquité à la fin du XVIIIe siècle*. Paris: Fontemoing et cie, 1912.

Hessling, Egon, and Waldemar Hessling, eds. *Möbel im Directoirestil*. Paris, Berlin, and London: Egon and Waldemar Hessling, 1914.

Hidalgo Hermosilla, German. "La Arquitectura del Croquis. Dibujos de Ch.E.Jeanneret en Italia, 1907, y en Oriente 1911: un estudio de sus antecedentes." Ph.D. diss. Escuela Tecnica Superior, Barcelona, 2000.

Hitchcock, Henry-Russell. *Modern Architecture: Romanticism and Reintegration*. 1929.

Hitchcock, Henry Russell and Philip Johnson. *The International Style: Architecture Since 1922*. 1932.

Hoeber, Fritz. *Orientierende Vorstudien zur Systematik der Architekturproportionen auf historischer Grundlage*. Frankfurt: Kunst and Gabel, 1906.

——. *Peter Behrens*. Munich: Müeller and Reutsch, 1913.

Hoepfner, Wolfram, and Fritz Neumeyer. *Das Haus Wiegand von Peter Behrens in Berlin-Dahlem*. Deutsche Archäologische Institut, Geschichte und Dokumente, vol. 6. Mainz: Philipp von Zabern, 1979.

Jeanneret, Maurice. *Charles L'Eplattenier*. Neuchâtel: La Baconnière, 1933.

Jencks, Charles. *Le Corbusier and the Continual Revolution in Architecture*. New York: Monacelli Press, 2000.

Jenger, Jean. *Le Corbusier. L'Architecture pour émouvoir*. Paris: Gallimard, 1993.

Jombert, Charles-Antoine. *Les Délices de Paris et de ses environs*. Paris: Jombert, 1753.

——. *Les Délices de Versailles*. Paris: Jombert, 1766.

Jordy, William. "The Symbolic Essence of Modern Architecture. . . ." *Journal of the Society of Architectural Historians* 22, no. 3 (October 1963): 177–87.

Kaenel, Philippe. "William Ritter (1867–1955): Un Critique cosmopolite, böcklinien et anti-hodlérien." *Schweizerische Zeitschrift für Geschichte* 48, no. 1 (1998): 73–98.

Krustrup, Mogens. *Porte Email / Emaljeporten / la porte emaillée / the enamel door: Le Corbusier, Palais de l'Assemblée de Chandigarh*. Copenhagen: Arkitektens Forlag and Kunstakademiets Forlag, 1991.

Kunzle, David. *The History of the Comic Strip: The 19th Century*. Berkeley, Los Angeles, and Oxford: University of California Press, 1990.

"La Chaux-de-Fonds und/et Jeanneret (Le Corbusier)." *Archithese* 13, no. 2 (March/April 1983), special issue.

La Chaux-de-Fonds et Jeanneret avant Le Corbusier. Exhib. cat. La Chaux-de-Fonds: Musée des Beaux-Arts, 1987.

La Ville et l'urbanisme après Le Corbusier: Actes du colloque. La Chaux-de-Fonds: Editions d'en Haut, 1993.

Le Corbusier: Architect of the Century. Exhib. cat. London: Hayward Gallery and Arts Council, 1987.

Le Corbusier et la Méditerranée. Exhib. cat. Marseille: Centre de la Vieille Charité and Editions Parenthèses, 1987.

Le Corbusier: Le Passé à réaction poétique. Edited by Pierre Saddy. Exhib. cat. Paris: Hôtel de Sully, Caisse nationale des Monuments historiques et des Sites, and Ministère de la Culture et de la Communication, 1988.

Le Corbusier: Maler og arkitekt / Le Corbusier: Painter and Architect. Exhib. cat. Aalborg: Nordjyllands Kunstmuseum, 1995

Le Corbusier 1929: Sitzmöbel sièges chairs. Exhib. cat. Zurich: Heidi Weber Gallery, 1959.

Le Corbusier: Peintre avant le Purisme. Exhib. cat. La Chaux-de-Fonds: Musée des Beaux-Arts, 1987.

Le Corbusier: Pittore e scultore. Exhib. cat. Venice: Museo Correr, and Milan: Mondadori, 1986.

Le Corbusier und Raoul La Roche: Architekt und Maler — Bauherr und Sammler. Exhib. cat. Basel: Architekturmuseum, 1987.

Le Corbusier: Un Film de Jacques Barsac. Part 1 (1887–1929). Produced by Christian Archambeaud and Jacques Barsac. Paris: Ciné Service Technique, 1987.

L'Eplattenier, Charles. "L'Esthétique des villes." In *Compte-Rendu des Délibérations de l'Assemblée Génerale des Délégués de l'Union des Villes Suisses*. Zurich, n.p., 1910, pp. 24–31.

Loti, Pierre. *Phantôme d'Orient*. Paris: Calman Levy, 1892.

Lucan, Jacques, ed. *Le Corbusier: Une encyclopédie*. Paris: Centre Georges Pompidou, 1987.

Legault, Réjean. "L'Appareil de l'architecture moderne: New Materials and Architectural Modernity in France (1889–1934)." Ph.D. diss. Massachusetts Institute of Technology, Cambridge, 1997.

Loos, Adolf. *Ins Leere gesprochen, 1897–1900*. Paris: Crès, 1921.

——. *Trotzdem, 1900–1930*. Innsbruck: Brenner-Verlag, 1931.

Mallarmé, Stéphane. *Divagations*. Paris: Fasquelle, 1897.

——. *Oeuvres complètes*. Bibliothèque de la Pléiade, vol. 65. Paris: Gallimard, 1945.

Marcus, George H. *Le Corbusier: Im Inneren der Wohnmaschine*. Munich: Schirmer/Mosel, 2000.

Martin, Camille. *L'Art de bâtir les villes*. Geneva: Ch. Eggiman, 1902.

Matteoni, Dario. "The 16 Patents of Le Corbusier 1918–1961." *Rassegna*, no. 46 (June 1991): 70–79.

Mebes, Paul. *Um 1800: Architektur und Handwerk im letzten Jahrhundert ihrer traditionellen Entwicklung*. Munich: Bruckmann, 1908.

Meyer, Hannes. "Die neue Welt." *Das Werk* 13, no. 7 (1926): 223.

Michels, Karen. "Augen, die sehen. Le Corbusiers Beobachtungen in München." *Jahrbuch des Zentralinstituts für Kunstgeschichte* 5/6 (1989/90): 471–98.

Monnier, Gérard. *Le Corbusier: Essai*. Tournai: La Renaissance du Livre, 1999.

Moos, Stanislaus von. *Le Corbusier: Elemente einer Synthese*. Frauenfeld: Huber, 1968. Translated under the title *Le Corbusier: Elements of a Synthesis* (Cambridge: MIT Press, 1979).

——. "Le Corbusier as Painter." *Oppositions*, no. 19–20 (1980): 87–107.

——. "Der Fall Le Corbusier: Kreuzbestäubungen, Allergien, Infektionen." In *Moderne Architektur in Deutschland 1900 bis 1950, Expressionismus und Neue Sachlichkeit*. Edited by Vittorio Magnago Lampugnani and Romana Schneider. Exhib. cat. Frankfurt: and Stuttgart: Deutsches Architektur-Museum and Hatje, 1994, pp. 161–83.

——. "Le Corbusiers 'Hellas': Fünf Metamorphosen einer Konstruktion." *Kunst + Architektur in der Schweiz* 50, no. 2 (1999): 20–30.

Moos, Stanislaus von, ed. *L'Esprit nouveau: Le Corbusier und die Industrie, 1920–1925*. Exhib. cat. Zurich and Berlin: Museum für Gestaltung and Bauhaus-Archiv, Museum für Gestaltung, with Ernst & Sohn, 1987.

Nasgaard, Susan. "Jeanneret's Development as a Painter, 1912 to 1918." Ph.D. diss., University of Toronto, 1976.

Nerdinger, Winfried. "Le Corbusier und Deutschland: Genesis und Wirkungsgeschichte eines Konflikts, 1910–1933." *Arch+*, no. 90–91 (1987): 80–86, 97.

——. *Theodor Fischer, Architekt und Städtebauer, 1862–1938*. Berlin: Ernst & Sohn, 1988.

Oechslin, Werner. "Le Corbusier und die Schweiz: eine schwierige Beziehung." In *Le Corbusier und die Schweiz: Dokumente einer schwierigen Beziehung*. Edited by Jos Bosman. Zurich: Institut für Geschichte und Theorie der Architektur and Ammann, 1987, pp. 8–16.

——. "Allemagne. Influences, confluences et reniements." In Lucan, Jacques, ed. *Le Corbusier: Une encyclopédie*. Paris: Centre Georges Pompidou, 1987, pp. 33–39. German ed. under the title "Le Corbusier und Deutschland: 1910/1911." In Oswald, Franz, and Werner Oechslin, ed. *Le Corbusier im Brennpunkt. Vorträge an der Abteilung für Architektur ETHZ*. Zurich: Verlag der Fachvereine an den schweizerischen Hochschulen und Techniken, 1988, pp. 28–47.

Oelek, Sambal. *Jünglingserwachen: Die ersten 38% aus Le Corbusiers Leben*. Glattbrugg, 1990.

Ozenfant, Amédée. *Mémoires, 1886-1962*. Paris: Seghers, 1968.

Paquot, Thierry. *Les Passions Le Corbusier*. Paris: Editions de La Villette, 1989.

Passanti, Francesco. "The Vernacular, Modernism, and Le Corbusier." *Journal of the Society of Architectural Historians* 56, no. 4 (December 1997): 438–51.

Patte, Pierre. *Monumens érigés en France à la gloire de Louis XV*. Paris: n.p., 1765.

Paul, Jacques. "Neo-Classicism and the Modern Movement." *Architectural Review*, 152/907 (September 1972): 176–80.

Pearson, Christopher. "Le Corbusier and the Acoustical Trope: An Investigation of Its Origins." *Journal of the Society of Architectural Historians* 56, no. 2 (1997): 168–83

Perret, Auguste. "Architecture et poésie." *La Construction Moderne* 48, no. 2 (12 October 1932): 2–3, Reprint, in *Perret et l'Ecole du classicisme structurel (1910–1960)* by Joseph Abram, Nancy: CEMPA, 1985, 2:32–34.

Perriand, Charlotte. *Un art de vivre*. Exhib. cat. Paris: Musée des Arts Décoratifs and Flammarion, 1985.

——. *Une vie de création*. Paris: Editions Odile Jacob, 1998.

Perrot, Georges, and Charles Chipiez. *Histoire de l'art dans l'antiquité*. 10 vols. Paris: Hachette, 1882–1914.

Petit, Jean. *Le Corbusier lui-même*. Geneva: Editions Rousseau, 1970.

Petit, Jean, ed. *Le Corbusier: BSGDG (Breveté sans garantie du gouvernement)*. Zurich and Lugano: Hans Grieshaber and Fidia Edizioni d'Arte, 1996.

Pinkwart, Ralf-Peter. *Paul Schultze-Naumburg: Ein konservativer Architekt des frühen 20. Jh. Das Bauliche Werk*. Halle, 1991.

Poëte, Marcel. *L'Enfance de Paris: Formation et croissance de la ville des origines jusqu'à Philippe-Auguste*. Paris: Colin, 1908.

——. *La transformation de Paris sous le Second Empire*. Paris: P. Dupont, 1910.

——. *Paris durant la grande Epoque Classique*. Paris: Dupont, 1911.

——. *La promenade à Paris au XVIIe siècle, L'art de se promener, Les lieux de promenade dans la ville et aux environs*. Paris: Colin, 1913.

——. *Promenades et jardins de Paris (depuis le XVe siècle jusqu'en 1830)*. Exhib. cat. Paris: Imp. P. Dupont, 1913.

Prache, Anne. "Le Corbusiers Begegnung mit Notre-Dame in Paris." In *Bau- und Bildkunst im Spiegel internationaler Forschung. Festschrift zum 80. Geburtstag von Prof. Dr. Edgar Lehmann*, ed. Institut für Denkmalpflege der Deutschen Demokratischen Republik. Berlin (DDR): Verlag für Bauwesen, 1989, pp. 276–79.

Preiswerk-Lösee, Eva-Maria. *Kunsthandwerk*. Disentis: Desertina Verlag, 1991. (Ars Helvetica, vol. VIII).

Prélorenzo, Claude, ed. *Le Corbusier: Ecritures*. Paris: Fondation Le Corbusier, 1993.

Provensal, Henry. *Vers l'harmonie intégrale: L'Art de demain*. Paris: Perrin, 1904.

Ragot, Gilles, and Mathilde Dion. *Le Corbusier en France. Projets et réalisations*. Milan and Paris: Electa France, 1987.

Reichlin, Bruno. "L'Ancien et le nouveau: Le Corbusier, le Pavillon de la Villa Church." *AMC—Architecture, mouvement, continuité* 1 (1983): 100–111.

——. "Für und wider das Langfenster: Die Kontroverse Perret-Le Corbusier." *Daidalos* 13 (1984): 65–77.

Renan, Ernest. *Prière sur l'Acropole*. Athens: Eleftheroudakis & Darth, n.d.

Reverdy, Pierre. *Oeuvres complètes: Nord-Sud, Self defence et autres écrits sur l'art et la poésie (1917–1926)*. Paris: Flammarion, 1975.

Risselada, Max, ed., *Raumplan versus Plan Libre: Adolf Loos and Le Corbusier, 1919–1930*. New York: Rizzoli, 1988.

"William Ritter (1867–1955): Au temps d'une autre Europe." *Nouvelle revue neuchâteloise* 16, no. 61 (1999), special issue.

Rovira, Josep M. "El valor de la antigüedad. Le Corbusier y la Acrópolis." In *Las casas del alma: Maquetas de la antigüedad*. Exhib. cat. Barcelona: Centre de Cultura Contemporània de Barcelona, 1996–97.

Rowe, Colin. "Neoclassicism and Modern Architecture." *Oppositions* 1 (September 1973): 1–26.

——. *The Mathematics of the Ideal Villa and Other Essays*. Cambridge, Mass.: MIT Press, 1976.

Rüegg, Arthur. "Charles-Edouard Jeanneret, architecte-conseil pour toutes les questions de décoration intérieure. . . ." *Archithese* 13, no. 2 (March/April 1983): 39–43.

——. "Du casier à la ville, de la ville au casier." In *La Chaux-de-Fonds et Jeanneret avant Le Corbusier*. Exhib. cat. La Chaux-de-Fonds: Musée des Beaux-Arts, 1987, pp. 11–16.

——. "Colour Concepts and Colour Scales in Modernism." *Daidalos*, no. 51 (1994): 66–77.

——. ed. *Le Corbusier — Photographs by René Burri/Magnum: Moments in the Life of a Great Architect*. Basel, Berlin, and Boston: Birkhäuser, 1999.

——. *Polychromie architecturale: Le Corbusier's Farbenklaviaturen von 1931 und 1959 / Le Corbusier's Color Keyboards from 1931 and 1959 / Les claviers de couleurs de Le Corbusier de 1931 et de 1959*. Basel, Boston, and Berlin: Birkhäuser, 1997.

——. *Swiss Furniture and Interiors, 1900–2000*. Basel, Boston, and Berlin: Birkhäuser, forthcoming.

Rukschcio, Burkhardt, and Roland L. Schachel. *Adolf Loos, Leben und Werk*. Salzburg and Vienna: Residenz Verlag, 1982.

Rupert Carabin. Exhib. cat. Strasbourg: Musées de la Ville, 1994.

Ruskin, John. *Mornings in Florence*. New York: John W. Lovell, n.d.

——. *The Seven Lamps of Architecture*. London, 1849.

——. *The Stones of Venice*. London, 1851–53.

Schmidt, Katharina, and Hartwig Fischer, eds. *Ein Haus für den Kubismus — Die Sammlung Raoul La Roche: Picasso, Braque, Léger, Gris – Le Corbusier und Ozenfant*. Exhib. cat. Basel and Ostfildern-Ruit: Kunstmuseum Basel and Hatje, 1998.

Scholfield, Peter H. *The Theory of Proportion in Architecture*. Cambridge: Cambridge University Press, 1958.

Schultze-Naumburg, Paul. *Kulturarbeiten*. 9 vols. Munich: Callwey, 1901–17.

Sekler, Patricia May. *The Early Drawings of Charles-Edouard Jeanneret (Le Corbusier) 1902–1908*. New York and London: Garland, 1977.

Serenyi, Peter. "Le Corbusiers's Changing Attitude Toward Form." *Journal of the Society of Architectural Historians* 24, no. 1 (March 1965): 15–23.

——. "Le Corbusier, Fourier, and the Monastery of Ema." *Art Bulletin* 49, no. 4 (December 1967): 277–86.

Sitte, Camillo. *L'Art de bâtir les villes: Notes et réflexions d'un architecte*. In French, translated by Camille Martin. Paris: Libraire Renouard, H. Laurens, 1902.

——. *Der Städte-Bau nach seinen künstlerischen Grundsätzen*. 4th ed. Vienna: C. Graeser, 1909.

Slapeta, Vladimír. "Die Wirkung in der Ferne—Le Corbusier und die tschechische Architektur." *Arch+*, nos. 90–91 (1987): 87–92.

Song, Misook. *Art Theories of Charles Blanc, 1813–1882*. Ann Arbor, Mich.: UMI Research Press, 1984.

Taylor, Brian Brace. *Le Corbusier at Pessac*. Exhib. cat., 2 vols. in 1 (vol. 2 under the title *Le Corbusier et Pessac*). Cambridge, Mass., and Paris: Carpenter Center for the Visual Arts, Harvard University and Fondation Le Corbusier in association with Spadem, 1972.

Töpffer, Rodolphe. *Voyages en zigzag: Ou excursions d'un pensionnat en vacances dans les cantons suisses et sur le revers italien des Alpes*. 1846. Reprint, Geneva: Slatkine, 1998.

Troy, Nancy. *Modernism and the Decorative Arts in France: Art Nouveau to Le Corbusier*. New Haven and London: Yale University Press, 1991.

Tsiomis, Y., ed. *Le Corbusier: Rio de Janeiro, 1929 / 1936*. Rio de Janeiro: Secretaria Municipal de Urbanismo / Centro de Arquitetura e Urbanismo de Rio de Janeiro, 1998. In French and Portuguese.

Turner, Paul V. "The Beginnings of Le Corbusier's Education." *The Art Bulletin* 53, no. 2 (1971): 214–24.

——. *The Education of Le Corbusier*. New York and London: Garland Publishing, 1977.

——. "Frank Lloyd Wright and the Young Le Corbusier." *Journal of the Society of Architectural Historians* 42 (December 1983): 350–59

Uhde, Wilhelm. *Picasso et la tradition française: Notes sur la peinture actuelle*. Paris: Editions des Quatre Chemins, 1928.

Vaillat, Léandre. "Au Salon d'Automne." *Bâtiment et Travaux Publics* 18, no. 4 (7 December 1922).

——. "L'Architecture française aux XVIIe et XVIIIe siècles." *Bâtiment et Travaux Publics* 19, no. 8 (28 January 1923).

Vaisse, Pierre. "Le Corbusier et le gothique." *Revue de l'art*, 118, no. 4 (1997): 17–27.

Viollet-le-Duc, Eugène-Emmanuel. *Dictionnaire raisonné de l'architecture française du XIe au XVIe siècle*. 10 vols. (Paris: B. Bance (vols. 1-6), A. Morel (vols. 7-10), 1854–68.

Vogt, Adolf Max. "Die 'verkehrte' Grand Tour des Charles Edouard Jeanneret." *Bauwelt* 38/39, no. 78 (1987): 1430–39.

——. "Le Corbusier: Der zornerfüllte Abschied von La Chaux-de-Fonds, 1917." *Unsere Kunstdenkmäler* 43, no. 4 (1992): 539–47.

——. *Le Corbusier, der edle Wilde: zur Archäologie der Moderne*. Wiesbaden: Vieweg, 1996. Translated by Radka Donnell under the title *Le Corbusier: The Noble Savage*. (Cambridge: MIT Press, 1998).

Les voix, no. 1 (1919)—no. 12 (1920).

Vowinckel, Andreas, and Thomas Kesseler, eds. *Le Corbusier, Synthèse des Arts: Aspekte des Spätwerks, 1945–1965*. Exhib. cat. Karlsruhe and Berlin: Badischer Kunstverein and Ernst & Sohn, 1986.

Walden, Russell, ed. *The Open Hand: Essays on Le Corbusier*. Cambridge, Mass., and London: MIT Press, 1977.

Wölfflin, Heinrich. *Prolegomena zu einer Psychologie der Architektur*. 1886. Reprint, in *Kleine Schriften*, edited by Heinrich Wölfflin and Joseph Gantner, Basel: Benno Schwabe, 1946, pp. 13–47.

Zevi, Bruno. *Architettura e storiografia*. Turin: Piccola Biblioteca Einaudi, 1974.

PHOTOGRAPHIC CREDITS

11. FLC 217512. FLC 2263
13. FLC 2852
14 . FLC 1791
15. FLC 2857
19. FLC 2850
20. Schweizerische
Theatersammlung, Bern F 7p
21. FLC 4079
38. FLC L5(7)117
39. FLC L5(6)113
40. © H. Allen Brooks
41. FLC 2125
42. FLC 5117
45. FLC 2212
46. BV LCi 623
47. FLC B2-20-214
49. BV LC/108/498
50. BV LC/108/254
53. FLC B2-20-307
55. BV LC/108/298
58. BV LC/108/339
61. BV LC/108/337
62 . BV LC/108/165,
64 . BV LC/108/349,
65. BV LC/108/459,
66. BV LC/108/472,
67. BV LC/108/453
68. FLC 5887
69. FLC 5887
70. BV LC/108/279
71. FLC L3(16)36-26
72. BV LC/108/441
73. BV LC/108/178,
75. photo Willy Boesiger
76. photo Francesco Passanti 1983
77. photo Francesco Passanti 1984
78. from: Fritz Hoeber, *Peter Behrens*, Munich, 1913
79. photo by Francesco Passanti, 1983
80. © H. Allen Brooks
81. photo by H. Allen Brooks, 1983
82. from: David Joseph, *Geschichte der Baukunst vom Altertum bis zur Neuzeit*, Berlin and New York, 1902
84. from: Karl Friedrich Schinkel, *Sammlung architektonischer Entwürfe*, Berlin 1866
87, 87. plans © H. Allen Brooks, diagrams by Francesco Passanti
89, 90. from: Fritz Hoeber, *Peter Behrens*, Munich, 1913, digram by Francesco Passanti
93. BV LCi 621
98 . photo Francesco Passanti, 1983
100. BV LC/108/750
102. from: Fritz Hoeber, *Peter Behrens*, Munich, 1913
107. FLC B2 20 255
108. BN Est., Ed.76.b
109. FLC B2 20 248
110. BN Est., Ed.76.c
111. BN Est., Ed.76.b

112. FLC B2 20 256
113–15. FLC B2 20 259
117. FLC B2 20 242
118. FLC B2 20 251
119. FLC B2 20 250
122. FLC B2 20 249
124. FLC 6459
126. Photo © Luftbild Schweiz, Regensdorf-Watt
131. FLC L5(7)288
133. © Franz Xaver Jaggy, MfGZ
134. FLC 30526
135. © Franz Xaver Jaggy, MfGZ
138. FLC 23092
142. FLC 30270
143. © Franz Xaver Jaggy, MfGZ
146, 147, 149. © Arthur Rüegg
154. FLC H3 7 269
155. FLC H3 7 268
161. The Museum of Modern Art, New York. Van Gogh Purchase Fund, photo © 2001
163. FLC 205
166. FLC 2483
168. FLC 134
172. FLC 2173
173. FLC 1979
174. FLC 2164
175. FLC L5(8)30
176. FLC 5845
177. FLC L4(19)95
178. Musée Léon Perrin, Môtiers, carnet G2
179. Musée Léon Perrin, Môtiers, E VI 217
180. FLC G ITA 61
182. FLC G ITA 60
184. FLC 1978
185. FLC L5(8)268
186. FLC 5842
187. FLC L5(8)263
188. FLC 1917
189. FLC 1791
190. FLC L5(8)262
191. FLC 2176
192. Musée Léon Perrin, Môtiers, E VI 216
193. BV LC/108/474
194. FLC L4(19)157
195. FLC L4(19)155
196. FLC L4(19)161
197. FLC B2-20-263
202. photo © H. Allen Brooks
203. FLC L4(19)30
204. BV LC/108/593
205. FLC 1923
206. FLC L5(6)113
207. FLC B2-20-260
208. FLC L4(19)37
209. FLC L5(7)130
210. Musée Léon Perrin, Môtiers, 150
211. FLC 1975
212. FLC L4(19)15
213. FLC L4(19)20
214. FLC L4(19)33
215. FLC L4(19)24

216. FLC 2241
218. FLC 1984
219. FLC 5858
220. FLC 6488
221. FLC L4(19)55
222. FLC L4(19)51
225. BV LC/108/296
226. FLC L5(1)150
227. FLC L4(19)182
228. FLC L5(1)127
229. FLC L5(1)130
231. FLC 2030
233. FLC 2036
235. ETH Zürich, 40-IKB-3
236. BV LC/108/108
237. BV LCms 125-3
239. BV LCms 125-2
241. FLC L4(20)164
242. FLC L5(1)124
243. FLC L4(20)128
244. BV LC/108/13
246. FLC 1794
247. BV LC/108/13
248. FLC 1938
249. FLC 6107
250. FLC L5(1)94
251. FLC 5876
252. FLC 2384
253. FLC 2455
254. FLC 6100
255. FLC L5(1)88
256. FLC 6105
257. FLC L4(19)66
258. FLC B1(19)42
259. FLC 2850
260. FLC L4(19)165
262. FLC L4(19)63
263. FLC L4(19)79
264. FLC 2849
267. FLC L4(19)114
268. FLC L4(19)107
269. FLC L4(19)108
270. FLC L4(19)120
271. FLC L4(19)106
272. FLC L4(19)113
273. FLC 1937
274. FLC L4(19)139
275. FLC B2-20-203
276. FLC L4(19)152
277. FLC L4(19)126
278. FLC L4(20)124
279. FLC L4(19)131
281. FLC L4(19)128
282. FLC L4(20)216
283. FLC L4(19)143
284. FLC 6110
285. FLC L4(19)124
286. FLC L4(19)129
287. FLC L4(20)40
288. FLC L4(20)59
289. FLC L4(19)151
290. FLC L4(20)45
293. FLC L5(8)132
294. FLC L4(19)99
295. FLC 2510
296. FLC 2506
297. FLC E1(11)98

298. FLC L5(9)112
299. ETH Zürich, 44-022-2
300. FLC 4077
301. FLC 30279
302. L5(9)44
304. FLC L4(19)179
305. FLC L4(20)178
307. FLC B2 20 657
312. FLC 1777
313. BV LC/108/734-3
314. BV LC/108/733-2
315. FLC 2520
316. FLC 5817
317. FLC L3(16)1
318. photo © H. Allen Brooks
319. FLC #FP Dossier C [FP 54]
320. BV LC/108/38
321. BV LC/108/40
323. BV LC/108/201
324. BV LC/108/280
325. FLC 33138
326. FLC 33140
327. FLC L3(16)36-24
328. FLC 33135
329. FLC L3(16)27
333. FLC 6449
334. FLC 19209
335. FLC 19204
336. FLC 19202
337. FLC 19211
341. FLC 30084
342. FLC 30276
344. BV LCms 131-6
345. FLC L3(16)68
346. FLC L3(16)55
347. FLC 32104
348. FLC 32107
349. FLC L3(16)40
350. FLC L3(16)46
351. FLC 32105
352. FLC 22357
353. FLC 22360
354. FLC 22352
356. FLC 22366
357. FLC 22368
358. FLC 22367
359. FLC 19123
360. FLC 9325
361. FLC 9340
362. FLC 9315
364. photo © Arthur Rüegg
365. FLC L2(1)8 2
368. MBA, photo © Franz Xaver Jaggy, MfGZ
369. FLC 2238
370, 372. MBA, photo © Franz Xaver Jaggy, MfGZ
374. photo © Arthur Rüegg
375, 378. MBA, photo © Franz Xaver Jaggy, MfGZ
379. FLC L3(16)36 33
380. BV LCms 135 1
383. MBA, photo © Franz Xaver Jaggy, MfGZ
388. FLC 30524
390. MBA, photo © Franz Xaver Jaggy, MfGZ

391. BV LCms 129
393. FLC 30082
395. photo © Arthur Rüegg
398. FLC H3-7-289
400. MBA, photo © Franz Xaver Jaggy, MfGZ
402. FLC 23047
403. MBA, photo © Franz Xaver Jaggy, MfGZ
405. photo © Nationalmuseum Stockholm, 1980
406. FLC 38
407. FLC 36
408. FLC 46
409. FLC L3(16)36-25
410. FLC 4500
411. FLC 37
412. photo © Franz Xaver Jaggy, MfGZ
414. FLC L3(16)36 12
415. photo © Franz Xaver Jaggy, MfGZ
416. FLC L2(12)119
417. FLC A2-14-132
418, 419, 420. MBA, photo © Franz Xaver Jaggy, MfGZ
422. FLC H1 3 297
424. Musée d'Orsay, ARO 1993-3.439
426. FLC 2520
427. FLC 1764
429. FLC 4079
430. FLC 5129
431. FLC 5116
432. FLC 4074
433. FLC 5119
434. FLC 5145
435. FLC 5112
436. FLC 4502
437. FLC 1735
438. FLC 4070
439. FLC 5155
440. FLC 5151
441. FLC 4100
443. FLC 4097
444. FLC 5154
445. FLC 4508
446. FLC 202
448. FLC 4069
450. FLC 5705
451. FLC 4069
452. FLC 134
453. FLC 2368
454. FLC 135
455. FLC 136
457. © The Museum of Modern Art, New York 2001
458. FLC 1635
459. FLC 139
460. FLC 1636